Modern Classics on Leadership

The International Library of Leadership

Editors: J. Thomas Wren
Associate Professor of Leadership Studies
Jepson School of Leadership Studies, University of Richmond, USA

Douglas A. Hicks
Associate Professor of Leadership Studies and Religion
Jepson School of Leadership Studies, University of Richmond, USA

Terry L. Price
Associate Professor of Leadership Studies
Jepson School of Leadership Studies, University of Richmond, USA

1 Traditional Classics on Leadership

2 Modern Classics on Leadership

3 New Perspectives on Leadership

For a list of all Edward Elgar published titles visit our site on the World Wide Web at
www.e-elgar.com

Contents

Acknowledgements

The editors and publishers wish to thank the authors and the following publishers who have kindly given permission for the use of copyright material.

Administrative Science Quarterly, Johnson Graduate School of Management, Cornell University for article: David G. Bowers and Stanley E. Seashore (1966), 'Predicting Organizational Effectiveness with a Four-Factor Theory of Leadership', *Administrative Science Quarterly*, **11** (2), September, 238–63.

American Psychological Association for articles: Charles N. Greene (1975), 'The Reciprocal Nature of Influence Between Leader and Subordinate', *Journal of Applied Psychology*, **60** (2), 187–93; Gary Yukl and Cecilia M. Falbe (1990), 'Influence Tactics and Objectives in Upward, Downward, and Lateral Influence Attempts', *Journal of Applied Psychology*, **75** (2), 132–40; Alice H. Eagly and Blair T. Johnson (1990), 'Gender and Leadership Style: A Meta-Analysis', *Psychological Bulletin*, **108** (2), September, 233–56.

Elsevier for articles: Fred E. Fiedler (1972), 'How Do You Make Leaders More Effective? New Answers to an Old Puzzle', *Organizational Dynamics*, **1** (2), Autumn, 3–18; Victor H. Vroom (1973), 'A New Look at Managerial Decision Making', *Organizational Dynamics*, Managerial Decision Making (Revised Edition), 1–15; Steven Kerr and John M. Jermier (1978), 'Substitutes for Leadership: Their Meaning and Measurement', *Organizational Behavior and Human Performance*, **22** (3), December, 375–403; Edgar H. Schein (1983), 'The Role of the Founder in Creating Organizational Culture', *Organizational Dynamics*, **12** (1), Summer, 13–28; Bernard M. Bass (1985), 'Leadership: Good, Better, Best', *Organizational Dynamics*, **13** (3), Winter, 26–40.

Free Press, an imprint of Simon and Schuster Adult Publishing Group, for excerpts: Max Weber (1947/1964), 'Charismatic Authority', in Talcott Parsons (ed.), *The Theory of Social and Economic Organization*, Chapter III, Section IV, Translated by A.M. Henderson and Talcott Parsons, 358–63; Bernard M. Bass (1990), 'Concepts of Leadership', in *Bass and Stogdill's Handbook of Leadership: Theory, Research, and Managerial Applications*, Third Edition, Chapter 1, 3–20, references.

Grid International, Inc. for excerpt: Robert R. Blake and Jane Srygley Mouton (1964/1971), 'The Managerial Dilemma', in *The Managerial Grid: Key Orientations for Achieving Production Through People*, Chapter Two, 5–17.

Heldref Publications for articles: Kurt Lewin, Ronald Lippitt and Ralph K. White (1939), 'Patterns of Aggressive Behavior in Experimentally Created "Social Climates"', *Journal of*

Social Psychology, **10** (2), May, 271–99; Ralph M. Stogdill (1948), 'Personal Factors Associated with Leadership: A Survey of the Literature', *Journal of Psychology*, **25**, January, 35–71.

James G. Hunt for excerpt: George Graen and James F. Cashman (1975), 'A Role-Making Model of Leadership in Formal Organizations: A Developmental Approach', in James G. Hunt and Lars L. Larson (eds), *Leadership Frontiers*, Section III, 143–65.

Journal of Contemporary Business for articles: Edwin P. Hollander (1974), 'Processes of Leadership Emergence', *Journal of Contemporary Business*, **3** (4), Autumn, 19–33; Robert J. House and Terence R. Mitchell (1974), 'Path-Goal Theory of Leadership', *Journal of Contemporary Business*, **3** (4), Autumn, 81–97.

Research Center for Group Dynamics, Institute for Social Research, University of Michigan for excerpt: John R.P. French, Jr. and Bertram Raven (1959), 'The Bases of Social Power', in Dorwin Cartwright (ed.), *Studies in Social Power*, Chapter 9, 150–67.

Sage Publications, Inc., for article: Linda Smircich and Gareth Morgan (1982), 'Leadership: The Management of Meaning', *Journal of Applied Behavioral Science*, **18** (3), 257–73.

Southern Illinois University Press for excerpt: Robert J. House (1977), 'A 1976 Theory of Charismatic Leadership', in James G. Hunt and Lars L. Larson (eds), *Leadership: The Cutting Edge: A Symposium held at Southern Illinois University Carbondale, October 27–28, 1976*, Chapter 12, 189–207, re-set, references.

Barry M. Staw for excerpt: Bobby J. Calder (1977), 'An Attribution Theory of Leadership', in Barry M. Staw and Gerald R. Salancik (eds), *New Directions in Organizational Behavior*, Chapter Five, 179–204.

In addition the publishers wish to thank the Library of the University of Warwick and the Library of Indiana University at Bloomington, USA for their assistance in obtaining these articles.

Authors' Acknowledgements

Completing a collection of this sort requires many hands and minds, and the editors are deeply grateful to a number of people who made it possible. Noreen Cullen and Nancy Vick in the interlibrary loan office at Boatwright Memorial Library at the University of Richmond processed literally hundreds of requests with unfailing good humor. Eric Wilson, Christopher Griffin, John Armstrong, Jonathan Wight, Dean Simpson, and Juliette Landphair provided guidance by suggesting readings for the collection, helping with translations, and offering interpretations of selections that bettered those of the editors. Gill Hickman, Richard Couto, and Elizabeth Faier, faculty colleagues at the Jepson School of Leadership Studies at the University of Richmond, were constant sources of ideas and inspiration. Fred Jablin as Acting Dean of the Jepson School provided considerable institutional support and personal encouragement. Joanne Ciulla, another faculty colleague, and Bruce Avolio read all or parts of the results of our efforts and offered useful advice and criticism along the way.

In the actual production of the work we were fortunate to enjoy superb editorial and administrative assistance. Nicola Mills at Edward Elgar Publishing spearheaded this project from the beginning, and graciously accommodated the whims of her sometimes cranky editors. Edward Elgar himself never failed to respond quickly and creatively to our occasionally unorthodox requests. We also thank Caroline McLin and Clare Arnold at Edward Elgar for their fine work in the production phase. At the University of Richmond, Kathy Bradley, Judy Mable, Sue Murphy, Jackie Duresky, Melissa Foster, Michael Frankston, Emily Latshaw, and Kristina Lam provided helpful administrative and technological support.

Our research assistant, Cassie King, deserves special mention and appreciation. She devoted untold hours to this project. Not only did she do the bulk of the legwork, but it is safe to say that nary a word or a comma in this entire collection has escaped her meticulous attention. This work is as much hers as it is our own.

Of course, our families contributed to this endeavor in the way that the families of academics always contribute: in the missed opportunities for shared time together, and in their toleration of distracted spouses and fathers. For that we thank, with love, Catherine, Lori, Noah, Harper, Suzanne, and Jack.

Preface

J. Thomas Wren, Douglas A. Hicks and Terry L. Price

This book is one of a three-volume set devoted to bringing together in one place the most significant writings and scholarship on leadership. When Edward Elgar Publishing first contacted the editors about creating a reference collection pertaining to leadership, an opportunity presented itself to reshape the traditional formulation of leadership studies and to suggest a deeper and more fundamental understanding of the phenomenon. In scholarly circles, the term *leadership studies* has often been used to connote a rather narrow corpus of social science analyses, chiefly from the fields of social psychology and management science. Such studies have contributed mightily to our understanding of leadership, yet they are limited in scope and purpose. On the other hand, the recent popularity of 'leadership' has spurred an outpouring of publications in the trade press. These popular treatments are almost invariably simplistic and shallow.

The premise underlying this collection is that the phenomenon of leadership is too important and too complex to leave the field to these champions alone. Our view of leadership is that it is a universal component of the human condition. It is the process by which and through which groups, organizations, and societies seek to achieve their perceived needs and objectives. As such, leadership has occupied center stage throughout human history. It embraces far more than the mere running of modern formal organizations, and it is much too complex to summarize neatly in a short paperback. Fortunately, because leadership has played such a central role in the human endeavor, it has not lacked for study and analysis. Indeed, the greatest minds in history have considered its implications, probed its dilemmas, and prescribed solutions for its problems.

The goal of this collection is to make readily available to the serious student of leadership a compilation of sources the editors think are representative of the best insights into this important phenomenon. The selections contained in these volumes, it should be noted, come solely from Western traditions. Many works from other cultural traditions are obviously relevant, but constraints of space would limit our inclusion of them to anecdotal status. Such works deserve fuller treatment, perhaps in a future Edward Elgar collection.

Volume I, *Traditional Classics on Leadership*, contains our version of the most insightful and important writings on leadership from ancient times to the dawn of the twentieth century. Moreover, the selections are arranged according to what we believe have been the key leadership issues in the preindustrial age. The volume begins with the central question of the moral purpose of leadership. The selections in this section – from Plato, Aristotle, Rousseau, Kant, Madison, and Nietzsche – suggest the sort of intellectual capital that has been brought to bear upon our topics. Other issues that the volume addresses include: What is the nature of ideal leadership? What constitutes legitimate authority? What is the role of followers? How might one go about challenging authority? We have taken care to include voices that have traditionally been out of the mainstream: women such as Christine de Pizan, Mary Wollstonecraft, Elizabeth Cady Stanton, and Virginia Woolf, and men of color such as David Walker and W.E.B. Du Bois. Taken together, the selections in this volume provide a rich and textured reference collection for an initial understanding of some of the central issues of leadership.

Volume II we have labeled *Modern Classics on Leadership*. It is here that we collect for the reader the seminal articles and chapters that have shaped what is commonly known as the modern field of leadership studies. With the rise of the modern business corporation (and other precedent-shattering developments such as modern warfare), there was an increasing perception that the role of leadership needed closer study. Concurrent with this was the rise of professional academic disciplines in the social sciences. Thus began a fortuitous pairing of leadership with serious academic scholarship that has spawned enormous insights. This volume seeks to bring together the best of that work. Beginning with the paradigm-shaping work of Frederick Winslow Taylor early in the twentieth century, this volume traces the field of leadership studies as it evolved throughout the twentieth century and became a sophisticated scholarship of considerable influence. We place at the reader's disposal the path-breaking studies that led to trait theory, behavior theory, contingency theories of leadership, transformational leadership, charismatic leadership, cognitive approaches to leadership, and studies of power. We also trace the insights that social scientists have brought to the study of followers, organizational culture, and such specific leadership issues as the role of gender. Thus, this volume provides in one place the 'giants' of modern social science leadership literature.

Volume III we call *New Perspectives on Leadership*. Here we seek to demonstrate how the insights of many intellectual approaches contribute to an understanding of current leadership issues. In this volume you will find writings by contemporary philosophers, management scientists, political scientists, social and political activists, and others. We have sought to organize these writings around the questions and themes that we believe most pertain to the study of leadership in the postmodern age. The questions include how leadership should be conceptualized; the role of power and authority; and questions of values, morality, and ethics. The themes that this volume explores reflect what we believe are the most important for our contemporary society: leadership and service, social change, democratic leadership and inclusion, and international leadership. Volume III of the Edward Elgar collection, then, should provide an important intellectual foundation for anyone interested in the current challenges of leadership.

If one were to take a step back and look at the Edward Elgar *International Library of Leadership* collection as a whole, it is our hope that the view thus gained would be one of coherence. It has been our goal in this editing project to do more than just collate good writings on leadership. Our aim has been one of integration. The challenges of our modern world make an understanding of leadership too important to leave to happenstance or haphazard experience. We have sought to make it possible for those serious about leadership to have easy access to the best thinking of the great minds of past and present. Moreover, we have arranged these selections around what we believe are the central issues that modern leaders continue to confront. Many of the selections in these volumes are not an easy read. But they represent what the editors believe to be the most important collection of sources on leadership now available. The 'unity' we have sought is the unity of a common subject matter that has, through the ages, occupied the attention of the brightest luminaries. We hope that this collection may serve as the steppingstone toward a better understanding of the subject of leadership and, in the process, a better world.

Introduction

J. Thomas Wren, Douglas A. Hicks and Terry L. Price

In Volume I of this Edward Elgar *International Library of Leadership* collection, entitled *Traditional Classics on Leadership*, the editors created a reference work containing some of the most important writings on leadership from ancient times through to the early years of the twentieth century. Those collected classics address profound questions related to the phenomenon of leadership: its ends, its means, and the manner in which the participants in the leadership process should pursue desired ends. All of the selections in that volume deal with leadership in the public realm. The current volume seemingly is a departure from that approach, but perhaps less so than it might at first appear. The selections contained in this volume represent the best of academic scholarship on leadership in the twentieth century, are uniformly grounded in the social sciences, and are generally focused upon leadership in formal organizations. While the academic studies contained in this second volume clearly have a different flavor from the selections in the first volume, the astute reader will notice how these studies continue to explore similar themes of the ideal leader and the roles of leaders and followers. In the introductory annotation below, we will attempt to make those larger leadership issues apparent.

Beginning approximately at the start of the twentieth century, the study of leadership took a dramatic new turn. Although important studies of leadership in the public realm continued, the field of 'leadership studies' came to be more narrowly defined both in scope and method. There were reasons for this. As the nineteenth century drew to a close, there was a fortuitous coincidence of two important developments. First, there was the rising importance of the modern business corporation and other large bureaucratic organizations. As these entities came to dominate the social and economic landscape, the intellectual world of the university was similarly changed by the emergence of professional academic disciplines, primarily in the social sciences. What followed could not have made more sense: the scholars in these emerging disciplines applied their sophisticated research techniques to learn more about these new and important societal entities, to include the study of leadership. Indeed, the field of leadership studies in the twentieth century has been characterized by its focus (formal organizations) and its approach (social science methodology, chiefly from the disciplines of social psychology and management science). Although this characterization is somewhat simplistic, the basic generalization holds. This is not to say, of course, that important work on leadership did not take place in other contexts and by other methods. It did, of course, and those contributions will be a part of Volume III. Here we present the best of 'leadership studies' in the twentieth century.

The corpus of scholarship on leadership is huge and growing exponentially. In this reference work, designed for those with a serious interest in leadership, the editors have chosen to include only those studies that have proved to be seminal to the field. Our choice of the term *seminal* to depict the contents of this volume is purposeful. A popular dictionary defines it as 'highly original and influencing the development of future events.' These articles certainly qualify. The editors have taken some care to choose for inclusion only those scholarly efforts that, with their publication, marked a new departure for the field of leadership studies and have been cited by subsequent scholars and researchers as the starting point for further inquiry regarding the chosen topic. We have arranged the selections in such a way as to provide the reader with a sense of the development of the field of leadership studies in the twentieth century. That is to say, the selections as presented trace out the increasing sophistication of the field over the course of the century and provide some sense of the maturing field of leadership studies.

The following introductory essay attempts to place the contents of this volume within a narrative of the development of the field of leadership studies.

The Nature of Leadership

It is useful to place the course of leadership scholarship within a framework of the subject itself. The initial selection in this volume comes from Bernard Bass's magisterial *Handbook of Leadership*. In it, Bass provides an introduction to the concept of leadership from its earliest times. He then turns to 'leadership as a subject of inquiry,' and, drawing from his extensive review of the extant social science literature, offers an organizing typology of approaches to the study of leadership. Bass suggests that leadership has been studied as: a focus of group process, a personality attribute, the art of inducing compliance, the exercise of influence, a particular act or behavior, a form of persuasion, a power relation, an instrument of goal achievement, the effect of interaction, a differentiated role, the initiation of structure, or some combination of the above elements. The very scope of Bass's typology suggests the richness of the field of leadership studies. In the remaining sections of the volume will be found the studies that gave rise to many of Bass's categories of analysis.

Early Approaches

Engineer-turned-manager Frederick Winslow Taylor published a truly ground-breaking work in 1911. Taylor was among the first to study the workplace systematically, and, in particular, the relations of managers and workers. His observations led to a dramatic new method of leadership that he called *scientific management*. Seeking to create a new and productive relationship between workers and employers, Taylor attempted to structure work according to 'scientific laws' of efficiency. Then managers, carefully supervising workers, could ensure maximum productivity. The result would be higher profits for the owner and higher wages for the workman. Analysts criticized Taylor's time-and-motion studies, arguing that his model treats workers as rational machines. The significance of this study for the field of leadership is that it suggests how the careful use of the 'scientific' approach (although Taylor was not particularly scientific) could yield important insights into leadership. Soon true social scientists would contribute many revelations.

Trait Theory

The earliest scholarship that addressed leadership *per se* was an enormous volume of work that has come to be known as *trait theory*. Grounded in the 'Great Man' approach to leadership, these studies sought to identify the specific traits and personality characteristics that yielded individuals who were good leaders. Such studies, after a fashion, echoed the classical attempts to portray the ideal leader found in Volume I of this series. In 1948, leadership scholar Ralph M. Stogdill conducted an extensive review of this literature, and the resulting article has become one of the most respected – and most cited – in the field. Stogdill attempts to identify and summarize from the literature the personal factors associated with leadership. He finds that these can be grouped under the general headings of capacity, achievement, responsibility, participation, and status. More important is what Stogdill does *not* find. He does not find that the possession of traits, standing alone, sufficiently explains good leadership. 'A person does not become a leader by virtue of the possession of some combination of traits,' Stogdill says, 'but the pattern of personal characteristics must bear some relevant relationship to the characteristics, activities, and goals of the followers.' Moreover, 'the evidence suggests that leadership is a relation that exists between persons in a social situation, and that persons who are leaders in one situation may not necessarily be leaders in other situations.' Thus, while Stogdill finds a certain constellation of traits related to good leadership, trait theory in and of itself is insufficient to explain the phenomenon.

Behavior Theory

The inability to find a specific set of *traits* that explains good leadership caused a number of scholars to consider whether there might not be certain leader *behaviors* that account for effective leadership. This spawned an important literature that continues to shape the study of leadership to this day. The selections in this section represent the core studies in this area.

A path-breaking study in the 1930s helped to define the course of what would become known as the *behavior theory* of leadership. In it, Kurt Lewin, Ronald Lippitt, and Ralph K. White analyze the impact of differing leadership 'styles' upon the behavior of pre-adolescent boys. The chosen leadership styles are those of 'autocratic,' 'democratic,' and 'laissez-faire' leaders. Results indicate that the democratic style has somewhat more beneficial results on group processes than the other styles. The importance of the study is less in its results, which focus upon aggression and hostility among the subjects, than in its definition of leadership in terms of behavioral style. Moreover, the choice of specific styles – autocratic and directive versus participative – had a profound impact upon later research and theory. Thus began a course of research into leadership that continues to influence the field profoundly.

Beginning in 1945, a group of researchers under the direction of Ralph M. Stogdill at Ohio State University began an extensive and systematic study directed toward the identification of leader behaviors that were associated with effective group leadership. This group devised an instrument called the Leader Behavior Description Questionnaire (LBDQ), and several studies subsequently used that instrument to explore leadership in a variety of organizational settings. In the next selection Andrew W. Halpin and B. James Winer apply the LBDQ to Air Force bomber crews and their commanders. Using factor analysis, Halpin and Winer are able to identify two leader behaviors that are linked to effectiveness and follower satisfaction. They label these two styles 'Consideration' (roughly equivalent to relationship behavior) and 'Initiating Structure' (similar to task-oriented behavior). Halpin and Winer find Initiating Structure more closely related to effectiveness, while Consideration is more related to crew satisfaction. Studies such as this eventually resulted in an almost exclusive focus upon these two specific leader behavior styles (sometimes known as the Ohio State dimensions of leadership) in subsequent literature.

The next selection represents an equally famous series of studies of leader behavior conducted at the University of Michigan. Building upon the research of Rensis Likert and others at that institution, David G. Bowers and Stanley E. Seashore draw upon four basic dimensions of leadership in their analysis: support, interactive facilitation, goal emphasis, and work facilitation. Applying these in a study of leaders in life insurance companies, Bowers and Seashore suggest that these leader behaviors form 'the basic structure of what one may term "leadership".' Interestingly, while they find that such behaviors are necessary to group effectiveness, it is not required that the formal leader provide these behaviors; anyone in the group may serve this role.

The final selection in this section is from *The Managerial Grid*, authored by Robert R. Blake and Jane S. Mouton. This conceptualization of leader behavior, more recently re-labeled *The Leadership Grid*, has become one of the most influential interpretations of leadership. Blake and Mouton modify (and simplify) the earlier scholarly studies of leader behavior and reduce them to a dyadic set of issues: concern for production (task) and concern for people (relationship). Blake and Mouton plot all possible combinations of these concerns, with 'concern for production' along the x-axis and 'concern for people' along the y-axis, thereby creating the 'Managerial Grid.' The authors proceed to depict the various approaches to leadership created by a leader's attention to one or the other of these concerns. Blake and Mouton end up championing what has come to be called 'high–high' leadership, wherein the leader has high concern for both production and people.

Each of the studies in this section has become a classic in its own right but, taken together, they represent an important advance in the attempt by social scientists to understand leadership. The focus, as is the case with trait theory, is still upon the leader, but the impact of behavior theory upon our current conceptualizations of leadership has been profound. Although, as we shall see in the next section, weaknesses persist in behavior theory, its identification of specific leadership 'styles' continues to frame the manner in which leadership studies scholars seek to understand the phenomenon.

Contingency Theories

Although behavioral approaches to leadership appeared to offer more insight than had the earlier trait theory, the problem remained that the behaviorists could not identify a specific leader behavior or set of behaviors that invariably proved effective. Nor could they demonstrate why certain behaviors appeared to work well in some situations but not in others. Recalling the insights of Ralph Stogdill in his overview of trait research, some scholars began to look to the role of situational factors that, in conjunction with certain leader behaviors, might predict effectiveness. These attempts by social scientists to integrate the role of followers and the situation are roughly analogous to the classical writings of the first volume which explore the nature of followers and when and how their activity might prove useful. The social science approaches to leadership included in this section, variously called *situational* or *contingency theories*, are considerably more sophisticated than the earlier twentieth-century theories that had gone before them. This section presents the most prominent of these theories.

One of the most famous of these theories is Fred Fiedler's *contingency theory* of leadership. Fiedler's work represents one of the most well known, most researched, and most commented-upon theories in the entire field of leadership studies. Fiedler rejects the premise that leaders can readily move from one style of leadership to another. Instead, each leader has a dominant and persisting approach to leadership – either task or relationship oriented. An individual leader's style of leadership can be identified by means of an instrument that measures the leader's attitude towards a 'least-preferred co-worker' (LPC). A high LPC score indicates a relationship-oriented style, a low one a task-oriented approach. Moreover, Fiedler argues that there are certain aspects of the environment that determine which style of leadership will be most effective. These situational factors, in descending order of importance, are leader–member relations, task structure, and position power. There are eight possible combinations of these weighted factors, which Fiedler calls 'octants.' Fiedler projects that a specific leadership style is appropriate for each octant. The contingency theory marked a new departure in terms of the sophistication of social science approaches to the understanding of leadership. It spawned, in turn, other attempts at developing models of leadership that would take into account the complexities of the surrounding context.

One of the most important of these attempts is the *path-goal theory* of leadership. In the selection included here, Robert J. House and Terence R. Mitchell provide a sophisticated model of the leadership process. The path-goal theory represents an advance in complexity at several levels. The model suggests that there are four possible leader behaviors, rather than the two of earlier theories (and, indeed, leaves open the possibility of adding more). These four leader behaviors are directive, supportive, participative, and achievement oriented. Moreover, the theory attempts to account for many more factors in the environment, to include subordinate characteristics (such as the need for affiliation, preferences for structure, desires for control, and self-perceived levels of task ability) as well as task characteristics (such as task design, the formal authority system, and the nature of the primary work group). Beyond seeking to incorporate more situational factors, path-goal theory attempts to explain how and why certain leader behaviors result in the desired outcomes. House and Mitchell draw upon the *expectancy theory* of motivation to link a subordinate's needs to his/her performance. Finally, path-goal theory provides guidance for leader behavior. A leader should make rewards for followers available and attractive and ensure that the path to these payoffs is easy in order to achieve desired goals. The path-goal theory thus suggests the level of complexity that the social science approach to leadership can achieve.

The final selection in this section devoted to contingency theories of leadership is more focused upon one particular aspect of the leadership process. Here, Victor H. Vroom presents a model that addresses the use of participative decision making in an organizational context. Specifically, Vroom creates a 'decision tree' by means of a series of questions about the nature of the followers and the problem to be resolved. By following the respective branches of that tree, a leader can determine what sort of leadership style should be used, ranging from autocratic to participative. Vroom's work became a classic example of applied theory grounded in a contingency approach to leadership.

If the contingency theories of leadership suggest the increasing complexity of leadership studies in the twentieth century, they represent only a small portion of the insights that the rapidly expanding social science literature on leadership has come to provide. The following sections tap the best of those studies and seek to organize them within a coherent thematic framework.

Transactional Approaches

One class of studies can be loosely termed *transactional* approaches to leadership. Sometimes called *social exchange theories*, these approaches depict the nature and operation of interactions between leaders and followers. Edwin P. Hollander's 'Processes of Leadership Emergence' represents an early and path-breaking study of this kind. In this, our initial selection, Hollander explicitly maintains that leadership is 'a transactional process.' There is a 'social exchange' in which the leader fulfills expectations, provides rewards, and helps attain group goals. The followers reciprocate by offering the leader status, esteem, and heightened influence. Hollander's model also accounts for dynamism and change within the organization via a concept known as 'idiosyncrasy credit.' An individual gains such credits by demonstrating competence and commitment to the group. This enables him/her to become a leader, and, more, provides that leader the latitude to make innovations. Hollander's work thus provides an early insight into the dynamics of the leader–follower relation.

The work of George Graen and his associates shows that the nature of the exchange processes between leaders and followers can have important effects upon group performance and morale. In the selection included here, Graen and James F. Cashman depict the nature of relationships between a leader and individual followers, an approach sometimes referred to as *vertical dyad linkage theory* or, later, *leader–member exchange theory*. Graen and Cashman demonstrate that a leader develops a specific and unique exchange with each of his or her subordinates. These linkages or relationships are of two general types. One type is based upon the defined roles of the formal employment contract. The other leader–follower relationship is based upon expanded and negotiated roles and responsibilities. Followers who enjoy the more expanded roles become a part of the 'in-group,' while those in the more formalized relationship become a part of the 'out-group.' 'In-group' members display more loyalty and trust and are more productive.

If the transactional approaches to leadership provided new insights into the nature of leader– follower relationships, the related conception of transformational leadership has become a dominant trend in the field.

Transformational Leadership

The notion of leadership as *transformational* first came to prominence with the politically oriented work of James MacGregor Burns. Burns's work is treated in some depth in Volume III of this series. Here, our attention focuses upon the work of social scientist Bernard M. Bass, whose application of the concept to organizational life has had a formative impact upon leadership studies. Bass contrasts transformational leadership with transactional leadership. While transactional leadership is merely an exchange that leads to desired outcomes, transformational leadership 'motivates us to do more than we originally expected to do.' This can be achieved, says Bass, by 'raising our level of consciousness about the importance and value of designated outcomes and ways of reaching these outcomes ..., [by] getting us to transcend our own self-interests for the sake of the ... organization ....,' and by raising need levels of followers. The transformational leader draws upon inspirational leadership (charisma), individualized consideration, and intellectual stimulation to 'induce followers to [attain] ...

much higher levels of productivity.' Bass's work has spawned an entire industry touting transformational leadership techniques, but his initial formulation remains the touchstone of the field.

Charismatic Leadership

In his discussion of transformational leadership, Bass includes the concept of *charismatic* leadership, but does not explore the notion in great detail. Charismatic leadership, however, has received more detailed attention from other scholars. In this section, the reader becomes acquainted with the two most influential treatments of charisma in leadership. The first is by the famous sociologist Max Weber. Weber applies the term *charisma* to 'a certain quality of an individual personality by virtue of which he is set apart ... as endowed with ... superhuman, or at least ... exceptional powers and qualities.' Charismatic leaders generate extremely intense loyalty, passion, and devotion on the part of followers, who often give blind obedience to the leader. The potential consequences of such a leader–follower relationship are obviously significant.

Robert J. House strives to subject charismatic leadership to more rigorous scholarly scrutiny and to explore its application in an organizational setting. His 'A 1976 Theory of Charismatic Leadership' has proven to be a ground-breaking piece of leadership literature. In it, House seeks to identify the traits of charismatic leaders (dominance, self-confidence, need for influence, and moral conviction), their behaviors (role modeling, image building, goal articulation, and demonstration of high expectations and confidence in followers), and their impact upon followers (in terms of self-esteem, goal acceptance, and feelings of empowerment). House goes on to posit that charismatic leadership is most likely to arise in certain stressful situations. House's careful social scientific approach to charismatic leadership set the standard for all subsequent treatments of the topic.

Power Approaches

As scholars explored further the nature of the interactions between leaders and followers, they began to pay more attention to the role of power in leadership. Two of the most influential studies along these lines appear in this section. The first is an enduring classic by John R.P. French and Bertram Raven. In this study, French and Raven seek to plumb the basis of social power. Defining 'power' as the ability to induce change in one's environment, the two scholars identify five types of power: reward, coercive, legitimate, referent, and expert. This typology of power became the standard in subsequent studies.

In the second selection, Gary Yukl and Cecilia M. Falbe identify eight influence tactics that stem from the bases of power: consultation, rational persuasion, inspirational appeals, ingratiating tactics, coalition tactics, pressure tactics, personal appeals, and exchange tactics. These tactics vary in their efficacy according to their 'direction'; that is, according to whether they are directed upward, downward, or laterally in an organization. Knowledge of how such tactics can yield results represents an important new insight into the processes of leadership.

Cognitive Approaches

Yet another departure in the study of leadership occurred when certain scholars began to explore the cognitive aspects of the phenomenon. In our first selection of this section, Linda Smircich and Gareth Morgan define the phenomenon of leadership from the perspective of cognition. Specifically, leaders, according to Smircich and Morgan, provide meaning to events for others. Some individuals emerge as leaders because they frame 'experience in a way that provides a viable basis for action.' Thus leaders help to 'construct reality' for followers, and leadership should be viewed as 'the management of meaning.' Viewing leadership from such a psychological vantage point opens up new possibilities for our understanding of leadership.

Another important contribution in this vein is Bobby J. Calder's *attribution theory of leadership*. Calder argues that leadership processes and effects exist primarily as perceptual processes in the minds of followers and observers. These perceptions are filtered through the biases the perceiver brings to the situation. Specifically, each individual holds an 'implicit theory' of leadership, which serves as a cognitive filter to determine what the observer will perceive as leadership. Viewing leadership in such a light fundamentally changes the focus from the leader to the followers.

Role of Followers

The role that followers might play in the leadership relation is the subject of an early study by William Haythorn and his associates. These scholars explore the impact of various combinations of leaders and followers with authoritarian and egalitarian attitudes. The Haythorn studies find that there is a significant amount of mutual influence. For example, the authoritarian or egalitarian attitudes of followers determine their reactions to a leader's style. Such findings suggest the extent to which the behavior of individuals in groups is dependent upon the personalities of group members and, in particular, the importance of understanding the nature of this interaction between leaders and followers.

Similarly, Charles N. Greene's study, 'The Reciprocal Nature of Influence Between Leader and Subordinate,' finds that follower performance may shape the amount of task and relationship behavior exhibited by the leader and that leader behavior affects subordinates. More specifically, Greene suggests that the broad Ohio State categories of Initiating Structure and Consideration appear to be linked in a feedback loop involving followers. If followers perform well, the leader displays more consideration behavior. If not, the leader displays more structuring behavior. Thus, leadership scholars have begun to examine the leadership process from multiple perspectives and to integrate these perspectives.

Leader Substitutes

The recognition of the importance of factors beyond the leader was a continuing trend in the history of leadership studies in the twentieth century. The focus upon leader traits and behaviors gave way to contingency theories, which were supplemented by transactional views of leader–follower relations. Cognitive leader theories, when coupled with the follower-centered theories discussed above, shifted the focus toward followers. Perhaps the studies that reach the farthest along this continuum are those of 'leader substitutes.' In this section, we present the foundational article in this tradition. Steven Kerr and John M. Jermier question the one assumption of most leadership theories: that is, that in each and every situation some form of leadership will be effective. Instead, Kerr and Jermier suggest that certain individual, task, and organizational variables can act as 'substitutes' for leadership. Thus, the ability of the subordinate, his/her need for independence, or his/her professional orientation might take the place of the leader's role. Similarly, routine and unambiguous tasks, or tasks with intrinsic feedback, could obviate the role of a leader. So, too, such situational factors as cohesive work groups could have the same impact. The work of Kerr and Jermier demonstrates the wide scope of the field of leadership studies in the modern era.

Organizational Culture

Our volume ends with two examples of important, specific areas of scholarly attention that have helped to shape the field. The first is the impact of leadership upon organizational culture. The most prominent scholar in this field is Edgar H. Schein. In the selection included, Schein states that 'groups and organizations do not form accidentally or spontaneously. They are usually created because someone takes a leadership role in seeing how the concerted action of a number of people could accomplish something that would be impossible through individual action alone. ...The process of culture formation in the organization begins with the founding of the group.' Only by understanding how leaders can help establish and maintain the appropriate organizational culture are group goals likely to be achieved.

Gender and Leadership

Our final selection draws upon the best of leadership scholarship related to gender. In it, Alice H. Eagly and Blair T. Johnson conduct a meta-analysis of a large number of studies pertaining to this topic. They find that in leadership studies of formal organizations, men and women do not significantly differ in their task and relationship styles of leadership. In other studies, there is more of a difference along the lines predictable by stereotypes; that is, women are more relationship oriented. Eagly and Johnson hypothesize that in formal organizations, role expectations override any gender differences in style. Across all types of studies, women were found to be more democratic and participative in their style than were men, but only slightly so. Such studies help us to gain insight into one of our more important leadership issues.

This volume contains many of the key social science studies of leadership published in the twentieth century. Such studies suggest the insights that the social sciences can bring to the study of leadership. This volume, then, fits nicely into the overall Edward Elgar leadership collection. Volume I of this series provides the classic underpinnings for our understanding of leadership, while this volume assembles the path-breaking studies of the twentieth century. Volume III presents the best and latest scholarship concerning our subject.

Part I
The Nature of Leadership

[1]

Concepts of Leadership

Leadership is one of the world's oldest preoccupations. The understanding of leadership has figured strongly in the quest for knowledge. Purposeful stories have been told through the generations about leaders' competencies, ambitions, and shortcomings; leaders' rights and privileges; and the leaders' duties and obligations.

The Beginnings

Leaders as prophets, priests, chiefs, and kings served as symbols, representatives, and models for their people in the Old and New Testaments, in the Upanishads, in the Greek and Latin classics, and in the Icelandic sagas. In the *Iliad*, higher, transcendental goals are emphasized: "He serves me most, who serves his country best" (Book X, line 201). The *Odyssey* advises leaders to maintain their social distance: "The leader, mingling with the vulgar host, is in the common mass of matter lost" (Book III, line 297). The subject of leadership was not limited to the classics of Western literature. It was of as much interest to Asoka and Confucius as to Plato and Aristotle.

Myths and legends about great leaders were important in the development of civilized societies. Stories about the exploits of individual heroes (and occasionally heroines) are central to the Babylonian *Gilgamesh*, *Beowolf*, the *Chanson de Roland*, the Icelandic sagas, and the Ramayana (now they would be called cases). All societies have created myths to provide plausible and acceptable explanations for the dominance of their leaders and the submission of their subordinates (Paige, 1977). The greater the socioeconomic injustice in the society, the more distorted the realities of leadership—its powers, morality and effectiveness—in the mythology.

The study of leadership rivals in age the emergence of civilization, which shaped its leaders as much as it was shaped by them. From its infancy, the study of history has been the study of leaders—what they did and why they did it. Over the centuries, the effort to formulate principles of leadership spread from the study of history and the philosophy associated with it to all the developing social sciences. In modern psychohistory, there is still a search for generalizations about leadership, built on the in-depth analysis of the development, motivation, and competencies of world leaders, living and dead.

Written philosophical principles emerged early. As can be seen in Figure 1.1, the Egyptian hieroglyphics for leadership (*seshemet*), leader (*seshemu*) and the follower (*shemsu*) were being written 5,000 years ago.

In 2300 B.C. in the Instruction of Ptahhotep, three qualities were attributed to the Pharoah. "Authoritative utterness is in thy mouth, perception is in thy heart, and thy tongue is the shrine of justice" (Lichtheim, 1973). The Chinese classics, written as early as the sixth century B.C., are filled with hortatory advice to the country's leaders about their responsibilities to the people. Confucius urged leaders to set a moral example and to manipulate rewards and punishments for teaching what was right and good. Taoism emphasized the need for the leader to work himself out of his job by making the people believe that successes were due to their efforts.

Greek concepts of leadership were exemplified by the hereos in Homer's *Iliad*. Ajax symbolized inspirational leadership and law and order. Other qualities that the Greeks admired and thought were needed (and sometimes wanting) in heroic leaders were (1) justice and judgment (Agamemnon), (2) wisdom and counsel (Nestor), (3) shrewdness and cunning (Odysseus), and (4) valor and activism (Achilles) (see Sarachek, 1968). (Shrewdness and cunning are not regarded as highly in contemporary society as they once were.)

Figure 1.1. Egyptian Hieroglyphics for Leadership, Leader, and Follower

Seshemet-Leadership

Seshemu-Leader

Shemsu-Follower

Later, Greek philosophers, such as Plato in the *Republic*, looked at the requirements for the ideal leader of the ideal state (the philosopher king). The leader was to be the most important element of good government, educated to rule with order and reason. In *Politics*, Aristotle was disturbed by the lack of virtue among those who wanted to be leaders. He pointed to the need to educate youths for such leadership. Plutarch, although he was involved with prosocial ideals about leadership, compared the traits and behavior of actual Greek and Roman leaders to support his point of view in *The Parallel Lives* (Kellerman, 1987).

A scholarly highlight of the Renaissance was Machiavelli's (1513/1962) *The Prince*. Machiavelli's thesis that "there is nothing more difficult to take in hand, more perilous to conduct, or more uncertain in its success, than to take the lead in the introduction of a new order of things" is still a germane description of the risks of leadership and the resistance to it. Machiavelli was the ultimate pragmatist. He believed that leaders needed steadiness, firmness, and concern for the maintenance of authority, power, and order in government. It was best if these objectives could be accomplished by gaining the esteem of the populace, but if they could not, then craft, deceit, threat, treachery, and violence were required (Kellerman, 1987). Machiavelli is still widely quoted as a guide to an effective leadership of sorts,

which was the basis for a modern line of investigation with the Mach scale (Christie & Geis, 1970). A 1987 survey of 117 college presidents reported that they still found *The Prince* highly relevant.

In the same way, a fundamental principle at West Point today can be traced back to Hegel's (1830/1971) *Philosophy of Mind* which argued that by first serving as a follower, a leader subsequently can best understand his followers. Hegel thought that this understanding is a paramount requirement for effective leadership.

Universality

Leadership is a universal phenomenon in humans and in many species of animals.

Animal Origins. Leadership predates the emergence of humankind. Allee (1945, 1949, 1951) maintained that all vertebrates that live in groups exhibit social organization and leadership. High-ranking males feed more freely than do other members of the group and tend to have more ready access to females. In some cases, high status involves guard duty and protection of the herd.

Pecking Order. Individual animals dominate or submit their local spaces to others in the well-known pecking order. In one of the early experiments on animal social relations, Murchison (1935) placed roosters at opposite ends of a narrow runway and measured the distance that each advanced toward the other. As a result of successive pairings, he was able to determine a strict hierarchy of dominance. Rooster A invariably dominated all the remaining subjects. At the bottom of the hierarchy was the rooster who yielded to all the others.

Douglis (1948) removed hens from their home flocks and placed them in other flocks for short periods. The hens' pecking order in each flock was observed. It was found that a hen can become an assimilated member in at least five different flocks and have a different status in each. The hen can recognize and react to the status or esteem of as many as 27 individuals. Highly dominant hens become assimilated within three days, but hens that were not dominant required three to six weeks to become assimilated. Once established, a hierarchy tended to maintain itself.

Dominance Effects in Primates. Miller and Murphy (1956) and Warren and Maroney (1969) tested pairs of monkeys who were competing for food in an area and observed strict dominance hierarchies. Subordinate animals were more successful in obtaining low-preference, rather than middle- or high-preference, foods. Bernstein (1964) noted that when the dominant male was removed from a group of monkeys, the activities of other males increased. After the dominant male returned, he resumed his dominant status and the activities of other males decreased.

Carpenter (1963) studied societies of monkeys and apes. His general findings suggested that the leader tended to control the group's movement in its search for food and shelter, regulate intragroup status, defend the group, and maintain its integrity in its contacts with other organized groupings. When the dominant male was removed from the group, the territory covered by the group was markedly reduced. Thus, the leader enlarged the freedom of the group's movement. But the dominant male tended to be avoided by low-ranking males. In some bands, the one or two males that were next in rank stood by the leader to ward off intruders and were permitted to groom him on occasion.

Again, Mason (1964) reported that leaders among groups of monkeys and apes appeared to have the primary function of initiating progressions and determining the line of march. The dominant males quelled intragroup fights, protected the females and young, were attractive to all members, were sought out by females, and influenced the size of the group's territorial range.

Zajonc (1969) interpreted the fact that fighting disappears almost entirely in primate groups after a hierarchy of dominance has been established as evidence that such groups develop norms. The norms are learned by group members, are stable but can be changed, and are complied with by the majority of members. Koford (1963) observed that the relative dominance of two bands of monkeys that meet at an eating place is usually determined by the relative dominance of the leaders of the bands. Once the dominance of a band has been established, it is observed by the other group, even in the absence of the other leader. Experimentation and observation in natural settings suggest that groups of animals develop strongly differentiated status hierarchies that their members recognize and observe. In primate groups, leaders obtain privileges that tend to bolster their dominance. Their presence is an advantage to the group in gaining possession of a desired territory and in expanding the area of free movement for the group. However, whether these findings and similar results reported for packs of wolves and hyenas, elephant matriarchies, bands of gorillas, and pods of whales are relevant to understanding the human condition remains controversial.

Humans. Parenthood, a condition that unarguably cuts across cultural lines, makes for ready-made patterns of leadership. Nevertheless, the patterns of behavior that are regarded as acceptable in leaders differ from time to time and from one culture to another. Citing various anthropological reports on primitive groups in Australia, Fiji, New Guinea, the Congo, and elsewhere, H. L. Smith and Krueger (1933) concluded that leadership occurs among all people, regardless of culture, be they isolated Indian villagers, nomads of the Eurasian steppes, or Polynesian fisherfolk. Lewis (1974) concluded, from a more recent anthropological review, that even when a society does not have institutionalized chiefs, rulers, or elected officials, there are always leaders who initiate action and play central roles in the group's decision making. No societies are known that do not have leadership in some aspects of their social life, although many may lack a single overall leader to make and enforce decisions.

Leaders, such as Abraham, Moses, David, Solomon, and the Macabees, were singled out in the Old Testament for a detailed exposition of their behavior and relations with God and their people. God was the supreme leader of his Chosen People who clarified, instructed, and directed what was to be done through the words of his Prophets and arranged for rewards for compliance and punishment for disobedience to the laws and rules He had handed down to Moses. In Islam, the ideal caliphate leadership was based on religious law (Rabi, 1967).

In *The Parallel Lives,* Plutarch (1932), in about A.D. 100, tried to show the similarities between 50 Greek and Roman leaders. Latin authors, such as Caesar, Cicero, and Seneca to name just a few, wrote extensively on the subject of leadership and administration. Their influence was considerable on the medieval and Renaissance periods, which looked back to the classics for guidance. Their influence on Thomas Jefferson and James Madison has an impact on the design of the U.S. government as we know it, as did such Renaissance scholars as Montesquieu in his *The Spirit of Laws* (1748).

Military writings about leadership stretch from the Chinese classics to the present. Napoleon listed 115 qualities that are essentials for a military leader. Meyer (1980) called for a renaissance in the concern for military leadership, in contrast to the focus on the "over-management" of logistics. Resources must be managed by the military leader but are no substitute for effective leadership.

Theory versus Problem Orientation

The earliest social science literature on leadership was concerned predominately with theoretical issues. Theorists sought to identify different types of leadership and to relate them to the functional demands of society. In addition, they sought to account for the emergence of leadership either by examining the qualities of the leader or the elements of the situation.

Earlier theorists can be differentiated from more recent ones in that they did not consider the interaction between individual and situational variables. Also, they tended to develop more comprehensive theories than do their more recent counterparts. Between 1945 and 1960, students of leadership devoted more of their efforts to empirical research and, as a consequence, ignored various issues that the theorists regarded as important. But research on leadership became theory driven again from the 1970s onward, although these theories tended to focus on a few phenomena and were less ambitious than those of the past.

Research on leadership in some segments of the population (students, military personnel, and business managers) was heavy but sparse on other segments (such as leaders of volunteer agencies, police officers, and health administrators). Because of the growing employment in the health, social service, and protection fields, there has been an upsurge in studies of leadership among nurses, social workers, and the police. In

the same way, the increase and upgrading of minorities in the U.S. labor force has resulted in an examination of leadership among women and minorities. Cross-cultural studies of leadership have burgeoned as well.

The emerging propositions about leadership maintain their validity over time in strong cultures. Nonetheless, they also are subject to change because of cultural changes. Thus, over 50 percent of over 1,000 students from 8 U.S. universities who were surveyed about their attraction to the television series, "MASH," indicated that watching the program had modified their attitudes or behavior about organizational life. All but 5 percent considered "MASH" to be a realistic portrayal of organizational values and processes. The respondents felt an increased desire to work with superiors who treat subordinates with understanding and respect (Dyer & Dyer, 1984).

The Importance of Leaders and Leadership

Napoleon expressed his feelings about the importance of leadership in his quip that he would rather have an army of rabbits led by a lion than an army of lions led by a rabbit. Surveys of job satisfaction from the 1920s onward illustrated the importance of leadership.[1] They uniformly reported that employees' favorable attitudes toward their supervisors contributed to the employees' satisfaction. In turn, employees' favorable attitudes toward their supervisors were usually found to be related to the productivity of the work group (see, for example, Lawshe & Nagle, 1953). Since then, countless surveys can be cited to support the contention that leaders make a difference in their subordinates' satisfaction and performance. Leaders also can make the difference in whether their organizations succeed or fail.

The usual efforts to estimate the number of leaders in the United States use census data on proprietors and officials. But Gardner (1986c) noted that although owners, managers, and officials are in the position to do so, they do not necessarily act as leaders. Cleveland (1985) estimated the number of opinion leaders in the United States and how they grew in number between 1955

[1]Bergen (1939), Houser (1927), Kornhauser and Sharp (1932), and Viteles (1953).

and 1985. In 1955, he estimated that there were 555,000 opinion leaders, whereas in 1971, he guessed that at least 1 million Americans could be classified as opinion leaders. He considered seven out of ten public executives to be opinion leaders—policymakers in public, philanthropic, voluntary, and large-scale "private" enterprises—in 1971. By 1985 he estimated the number to have multiplied to 1 out of every 200 Americans.

As Cleveland (1985, p. 4) stated: There are some 83,000 government units in the United States, and about 175,000 corporations each doing more than $1 million worth of business a year. The galloping rate of growth of complexity means that a growth curve of the requirement for leaders (if anyone were clever enough to construct such an index) would show a steeper climb than any other growth rate in our political economy.

Is Leadership a Figment of the Imagination? Some critics argue that all the effects of leadership are in the eyes of their beholders. Followers attribute effects that are due to historical, economic, or social forces to leadership, as in romantic fiction (Meindl & Ehrlich, 1987; Meindl, Ehrlich, & Dukerich, 1985). Other critics, such as Pandey (1976), regard leadership as a useless concept for understanding social influence. For Calder (1977), the objective contributions of the "leader" to outcomes may be more interesting than true. The extreme position taken by some attribution theorists is that organizational outcomes are determined primarily by other factors, but leaders are credited with what happened after the fact.

Organizational leaders who are perceived to be exerting leadership on organizational performance are merely the subjects of misperceptions, some critics contend. That is, organizational outcomes are objectively determined by environmental and organizational factors in which leadership, at best, can play only a minor role. For instance, M. C. Brown (1982, p. 1) concluded that "once other factors influencing effectiveness are accounted for, it is likely that leadership will have little bearing on organizational performance."

Pfeffer (1977) took a similar but not as extreme position: Leadership is a sense-making heuristic to account for organizational performance and is important primarily for its symbolic role in organizations. Leaders are selected or self-selected to fulfil the fate of the organization and are highly constrained by organizational and external factors. Therefore, they can have only a limited impact on organizational outcomes compared to external factors. Leaders are able only to react to contingencies, to facilitate the adjustment of the organization in its context, and to alter that environment to some limited extent. Also they have no control over many factors that affect organizational performance and they typically have unilateral control over few resources.

Despite these constraints, management and leadership seem to have a substantial effect on some organizational outcomes. Thus, when Lieberson and O'Connor (1972) examined the effects of top management on the success of 167 firms over a 20-year period, they found that the effects depended on which outcomes were considered. Managers had the greatest effect on profit margins but the least effect on sales; they also were of less consequence in capital-intensive industries. In the same way, Salancik and Pfeffer (1977) showed that the mayors of 30 U.S. cities had considerable influence only on those budgetary issues, such as libraries and parks, that were not in the domain of important special-interest groups, such as the police, fire fighters, and highway maintenance personnel. In all, Pfeffer concluded that since people want to achieve the feeling that they are in control of their environment, they find it useful to attribute outcomes of their group and organizational performance to leaders, rather than to the complex internal and external environmental forces that actually are most important. Meindl and Ehrlich (1987) showed that if performance outcomes of firms were attributed to the leadership of the top management, rather than to the employees, market conditions, or the government, the judges gave better evaluations of the outcomes. Meindl and Ehrlich attributed this finding to the judges' assumption that leaders have a reliable and potent impact on outcomes.

Even when the true causes of outcomes were logically not determinable, Meindl, Ehrlich, and Dukerich (1985) showed that there was a tendency to view leadership as the likely cause of the outcomes. This study and the one by Meindl and Ehrich (1987) were thought to demonstrate that leadership is more of a romantic notion than a phenomenon that truly affects group and organizational outcomes.

Then there is evidence that would-be followers, subordinates, and groups of employees are so constrained by technology, rules, job requirements, and organizational policies that there is little discretionary room for a superior or leader to make much of a difference in how things get done (Katz & Kahn, 1966). Furthermore, subordinates may have much more effect on the behavior of their superiors than vice versa (Goodstadt & Kipnis, 1970).

Miner (1975, p. 200) was ready to abandon the concept of leadership, stating that "the concept of leadership itself has outlived its usefulness. Hence, I suggest that we abandon leadership in favor of some other, more fruitful way of cutting up the theoretical pie." In 1982a, Miner recanted this statement but still maintained that the concept has limited usefulness because so much of the empirical research has been on emergent leadership in small groups, rather than within more complex organizations. For Miner, the fragile, distressed, leadership that arises in the small, temporary group to develop, maintain, and enforce the norms of the group may have little relevance for leadership in the impersonal "task system" of the traditional organization.

Leaders Do Make a Difference. Despite the skepticism about the reality and importance of leadership, all social and political movements require leaders to begin them. As Tucker (1981, p. 87) put it, "in the beginning is the leadership act. A 'leaderless movement' is naturally out of the question." This does not mean that formal, institutionalized leadership is required. In fact, no leader in an institutional form appeared in the numerous peasant revolts from the sixteenth to nineteenth centuries in Southern Germany. The same was true for journeymen's strikes during the eighteenth century. Leadership remained informal and egalitarian. Only in the middle of the nineteenth century did definite leaders, such as Ferdinand Lasalle, emerge. Lasalle placed himself at the head of the German workers' movement and worked out its explicit ideology, along with the myth that he founded the movement (Groh, 1986). This behavior is consistent with most cases of

institutional development: Leaders determine the direction they will take. The historical records of the early British Royal Society of the seventeenth century illustrate that its secretaries were responsible for who joined the society and what kinds of science were sponsored (Mulligan & Mulligan, 1981).

Indeed, leadership is often regarded as the single most critical factor in the success or failure of institutions. For instance, T. H. Allen (1981) argued that the school principal's leadership is the most important factor in determining a school's climate and the students' success. Sylvia and Hutchison (1985) concluded that the motivation of 167 Oklahoma teachers depended considerably on their perceptions of the quality of their relationships with their superiors. And Smith, Carson, and Alexander (1984) found that among the 50 Methodist ministers they studied, some were more effective leaders than were others. The effectiveness of these ministers was evidenced by the differential impact that their ministries had on church attendance, membership, property values, and contributions to the church.

In the business and industrial sector, Maccoby (1979, p. 313) concluded, from his observations of the manager as a game-playing politician, that the need of firms to survive and prosper in a world of increasing competition, of technological advances, of changing governmental regulations, of changing worker attitudes, requires "a higher level of leadership than ever before." When an organization must be changed to reflect changes in technology, the environment, and the completion of programs, its leadership is critical in orchestrating the process (Burke, Richley, & DeAngelis, 1985). Mintzberg and Waters (1982) examined the evolution of a retail firm over a 60-year-period and found that a senior executive could successfully reorient the firm by intervening to change previous strategies and organizational structures. In the same way, Day and Lord (1986) noted that when confounding errors are controlled in studies of the effects of executive succession, differences in executive leaders can explain as much as 45 percent of their organizations' performance. Agreeing with Chandler (1962), they stated that historical analyses of changes of leadership over significant periods have shown that leadership has a profound influence on an organization. Concurrent correlational analyses of a sample of executives and their organizations at the same point in time reach similar conclusions, although the effects are not as strong.

In a review of experiments in the United States on the productivity of workers between 1971 and 1981, Katzell and Guzzo (1983) concluded that supervisory methods seemed particularly effective in increasing output. In Sweden, Westerlund (1952a) observed that the high-quality performance of supervisors improved that attitudes and performance of telephone operators. Also in Sweden, Ekvall and Arvonen (1984) found that leadership styles accounted for 65 percent of the variance in organizational climate in the 25 units they studied. Virany and Tushman (1986) stated that the senior managers of better-performing minicomputer firms were systematically different from those of firms that performed poorly. The senior management in the better firms had had previous experience in the electronic industry and was more likely to include the founder of the firm who still served as chief executive officer. Although most attention has been paid to industrial leaders as developers and builders, Hansen (1974) pointed out that the success with which a firm, such as the Ford Motor Company, closed a plant without much human dislocation depended on effective leadership.

Leadership has been considered a critical factor in military successes since records have been kept; that is, better-led forces repeatedly have been victorious over poorly led forces. Thus, not unexpectedly, morale and cohesion among Israeli and U.S. enlisted soldiers correlated with measures of the soldiers' confidence in their company, division, and battalion commanders (Gal & Manning, 1984).

Personnel of the Mississippi Cooperative Extension reported that they felt less job stress if they saw their supervisors displaying more leadership in structuring the work to be done and showing concern for the subordinates' needs (Graham, 1982). In a study of 204 innovations in state programs, Cheek (1987) found that the governors came up with 55 percent of the innovations and the agencies with only 36 percent.

Studies by Tucker (1981), Hargrove and Nelson (1984), and Hargrove (1987) concluded that the style and performance of a U.S. president makes a big difference in what happens to legislation, policy, and programs. Successful presidents are more sensitive to the inherent politics of policy-making. They define and publicize the policy dilemmas facing the country and earn widespread public and Congressional support for their positions. They construct their policy agendas with the felt needs of the country in mind and create political support for their agendas; they also realize that timing is important (Tucker, 1981). But like Jimmy Carter, they can fail if they push for what they deem to be right but what is not politically feasible and if they favor comprehensive integrated solutions, rather than incremental steps (Hargrove, 1987). Presidents can make decisions that are not implemented because they or their assistants do not follow them up. For example, as part of the agreement to resolve the Cuban missile crisis, President Kennedy ordered the removal of U.S. missiles from Turkey on the border of the Soviet Union. Six months later, he was astonished to learn that the missiles were still in place (Manchester, 1988). Although presidents spend relatively little time trying to make major reorientations in policy, they have an important impact on the smaller substantive decisions that affect the larger overall strategies (Neustadt, 1980). History may be drastically altered by a sudden change in presidents. Before leaving Washington, D.C., for his fateful trip to Texas in November 1963, Kennedy signed the first order for a phased withdrawal from Vietnam. On assuming office after Kennedy's assassination, Lyndon Johnson rescinded the order. The war continued for another decade.

According to Richard Nixon's "Silent Majority" speech in 1969, presidents may have to take an unpopular stand, but when they do, they can strengthen acceptance by explaining their reasons, soliciting support, and winning approval (Safire, 1975). Presidents also provide symbolic support for the development of norms, values, and beliefs that contribute to subsequent national and organizational development (Sayles, 1979). As Gardner (1988a) noted, for a society to function, its people must share beliefs and values regarding the standards of acceptable behavior. Leaders can revitalize those shared beliefs and help keep the values fresh. "They have a role in creating the state of mind that is the society" (Gardner, 1988a, p. 18). They conceive and articulate goals that move people from their own interests to unite for higher ends.

Often, the effects of leadership are indirect. For example, Katzell (1987) showed through a path analysis that although supervisors' direct influence on their subordinates was modest, they exerted indirect influence and increased the employees' morale by providing rewards, relating rewards to performance, and treating employees equitably; the increased morale, in turn, improved the employees' performance.

Jongbloed and Frost (1985) modified Pfeffer's (1977) reasoning to argue that leaders still have an important general role to play. What leaders really manage in organizations are the employees' interpretations or understanding of what goes on in the organizations. The leaders manage meanings and, therefore, exert a strong impact on organizational outcomes. Jongbloed and Frost showed how the laboratory director in one Canadian hospital, compared to another in a second hospital with the same formal assignments and the same absence of control of issues, successfully lobbied for the importance of pathology and convinced the hospital administrators to allocate more funds for operations and budget than were allocated in the second hospital.

The importance of leadership is attested by academic and lay interest in leadership as a subject for development, training, and education (Campbell, 1977).[2] Although U.S. college presidents believe that our educational institutions are reluctant to incorporate leadership education into their curricula (Cronin, 1984), the college landscape is not bleak. Gregory's (1986) survey of all known U.S. degree-granting institutions of higher learning uncovered 53 that offered an academic course on leadership, 70 that made it possible to major or concentrate in the subject, 181 that incorporated the study of leadership in an academic course or a student-affairs

program, and 81 that offered the subject in continuing education or professional programs.[3]

Leadership as a Subject of Inquiry

The importance of leadership is also demonstrated by its place in social science research. According to Mitchell (1979) and DeMeuse (1986), leadership has been one of the frequent subjects of empirical research, concentrating on the antecedents of leaders' behavior and the factors that contribute to its effectiveness. Leadership is a featured topic in almost every textbook on organizational behavior (McFillen, 1984–87). The scholarly books on leadership number in the hundreds, and articles, reports, and essays number in the thousands.

Several different schools of thought have prevailed simultaneously since leadership first was studied. The early sociological theorists tended to explain leadership in terms of either the person or the environment. Later researchers tended to view leadership as an aspect of role differentiation or as an outgrowth of social interaction processes. Recently, the naïve theories of leadership we hold have been considered most important in explaining what is going on. But this is as it should be. Theory and empirical research should move forward together, each stimulating, supporting, and modifying the other. Neither can stand alone. An elegant theory without prospects of elegant data gathering makes for a sketchy theory. Early in a line of investigation, crude data and theory may be useful. Later, as understanding develops and practice improves, more stringent standards are required (Bass, 1974).

Assumptions

The research discussed in the following chapters is based on a wide variety of theoretical assumptions. Despite differences in the philosophies that guide them and the research methods used, there is remarkable convergence of findings on many problems. This convergence, when it occurs, can be regarded as strong evidence of the validity of the findings.

An almost insurmountable problem is the question of the extent to which we pour old wine into new bot-

[2]Recognition of the importance to the nation of leadership and its development for all types of organizations is witnessed by the Alliance for Leadership Development, which includes the following members: American Leadership Forum of Houston; Association of American Colleges of Washington, D.C.; Association of Governing Boards of Universities and Colleges; Center for Creative Leadership of Greensboro, N.C.; Coro Foundation of St. Louis; International Leadership Center of Dallas; National Association of Secondary School Principals of Reston, Va.; and the National Executive Service Corps of New York. The Alliance's programs include the promotion of research on and teaching of leadership, related conferences and publications, a clearinghouse of information on leadership programs at universities and secondary schools, leadership development programs in the community, and development programs for corporate executives.

[3]Details about these can be found in Clark, Freeman, and Britt (1987).

tles when proposing "new" theories. For instance, Julius Caesar's descriptions of his leadership style in the Gallic Wars in the first century B.C. are clear, succinct endorsements of the need for what Blake and Mouton (1964) conceived as "9-9" style—a style that Fleishman (1953a) described in terms of high initiation and consideration and that in the year 2500 some new theorist will give a new name. When does a field advance? Are we beyond Caesar's understanding of how to lead infantry shock troops?

My hope in this book is to catalog what is known about leadership and to suggest some of the things that we do not know and should try to find out. Although I agree with Burns (1978, p. 2) that "leadership is one of the most observed . . . phenomena on earth," I disagree with Burns that "it is one of the least understood."

The Meaning of Leadership

The word leadership is a sophisticated, modern concept. In earlier times, words meaning "head of state," "military commander," "princeps," "proconsul," "chief," or "king" were common in most societies; these words differentiated the ruler from other members of society. A preoccupation with leadership, as opposed to headship based on inheritance, usurpation, or appointment, occurred predominantly in countries with an Anglo-Saxon heritage. Although the *Oxford English Dictionary* (1933) noted the appearance of the word "leader" in the English language as early as the year 1300, the word "leadership" did not appear until the first half of the nineteenth century in writings about the political influence and control of British Parliament. And the word did not appear in the most other modern languages until recent times.

Defining Leadership

There are almost as many different definitions of leadership as there are persons who have attempted to define the concept.[4] Moreover, as Pfeffer (1977) noted,

[4]Different definitions and conceptions of leadership have been reviewed briefly by Morris and Seeman (1950), Shartle (1951a, 1951b, 1956), L. F. Carter (1953), C. A. Gibb (1954, 1969a), Bass (1960), Stogdill (1975), and Schriesheim and Kerr (1977b).

many of the definitions are ambiguous. Furthermore, the distinction between leadership and other social-influence processes is often blurred (Bavelas, 1960; Hollander & Julian, 1969). The many dimensions into which leadership has been cast and their overlapping meanings have added to the confusion. Therefore, the meaning of leadership may depend on the kind of institution in which it is found (Spitzberg, 1986). Nevertheless, there is sufficient similarity among definitions to permit a rough scheme of classification. Leadership has been conceived as the focus of group processes, as a matter of personality, as a matter of inducing compliance, as the exercise of influence, as particular behaviors, as a form of persuasion, as a power relation, as an instrument to achieve goals, as an effect of interaction, as a differentiated role, as initiation of structure, and as many combinations of these definitions.

Leadership as a Focus of Group Processes

Early on, definitions of the leader tended to view the leader as a focus of group change, activity, and process. Cooley (1902) maintained that the leader is always the nucleus of a tendency, and (that) all social movements, closely examined, will be found to consist of tendencies having such nuclei. Mumford (1906–07) observed that "leadership is the preeminence of one or a few individuals in a group in the process of control of societal phenomena." Blackmar (1911) saw leadership as the "centralization of effort in one person as an expression of the power of all." Chapin (1924b) viewed leadership as "a point of polarization for group cooperation." According to L. L. Bernard (1927), leaders are influenced by the needs and wishes of the group members; in turn, they focus the attention and release the energies of group members in a desired direction. Regarding the dominance of the leader's personality M. Smith (1934) commented that "the social group that express its unity in connected activity is always composed of but two essential portions: the center of focal activity, and the individuals who act with regard to the center." For Redl (1942), the leader is a central or focal person who integrates the group.

As a nation develops, it needs a centralized locus for its operation which can only be achieved by a single leader (Babikan, 1981). All important decisions and their implementation center on the cult of the leader even when, as in parliamentary democracies, actual decision making is diffuse. The leader embodies the collective will. This single leader sorts out the essential problems, offers possible solutions, establishes priorities, and launches developmental operations.

J. F. Brown (1936) maintained that "the leader may not be separated from the group, buy may be treated as a position of high potential in the field." Following in the same tradition, Krech and Crutchfield (1948) observed that "by virtue of his special position in the group he serves as a primary agent for the determination of group structure, group atmosphere, group goals, group ideology, and group activities." For Knickerbocker (1948), "when conceived in terms of the dynamics of human social behavior, leadership is a function of needs existing within a given situation, and consists of a relationship between an individual and a group."

This emphasis on the leader as the center, or focus, of group activity directed attention to group structure and group processes in studying leadership. On the one hand, some of the earliest theorists, such as Cooley and Mumford, were sophisticated in their concept of leadership. On the other hand, several of the definitions placed the leader in a particularly fortuitous, if not helpless, position, given the inexorable progress of the group. Leaders were thought to have to stay one pace ahead of the group to avoid being run over. Centrality of location in the group can permit a person to control communications, and hence is likely to place him or her in a position of leadership, but centrality, in itself, is not leadership.

Leadership as Personality and Its Effects

The concept of personality appealed to several early theorists, who sought to explain why some persons are better able than are others to exercise leadership. A. O. Bowden (1926) equated leadership with strength of personality: "Indeed, the amount of personality attributed to an individual may not be unfairly estimated by the degree of influence he can exert upon others." Bingham (1927) defined a leader as a person who possesses the greatest number of desirable traits of personality and character. According to L. L. Bernard (1926), "Any person who is more than ordinarily efficient in carrying psychosocial stimuli to others and is thus effective in conditioning collective responses may be called a leader"; the leader must possess prestige and "must know what stimuli will condition adequate responses for his purposes and develop a technique for presenting these stimuli." Tead (1929) regarded leadership as a combination of traits that enables an individual to induce others to accomplish a given task.

The personality theorists tended to regard leadership as a one-way effect: Leaders possess qualities that differentiate them from followers. But these theorists did not acknowledge the extent to which leaders and followers have interactive effects by determining which qualities of followers are of consequence in a situation. What theorists now see is that the personal qualities of a would-be leader determine his or her *esteem* in the eyes of potential followers. Some personality traits, such as ascendancy or social boldness, more often than not go hand in hand with being esteemed and attaining leadership, but social boldness is not leadership. At the extreme, in times of crisis, followers *endow* a highly dominant figure who is empathic to their critical needs with charisma. The hero's personality then makes it possible for him or her to perform enormous feats of leadership (Stark, 1970).

Leadership as the Art of Inducing Compliance

Munson (1921) defined leadership as "the ability to handle men so as to achieve the most with the least friction and the greatest cooperation. . . . Leadership is the creative and directive force of morale." According to F. H. Allport (1924), "leadership . . . is personal social control." B. V. Moore (1927) reported the results of a conference at which leadership was defined as "the ability to impress the will of the leader on those led and induce obedience, respect, loyalty, and cooperation." Similarly, Bundel (1930) regarded leadership as "the art of inducing others to do what one wants them to do." According to T. R. Phillips (1939), "leadership is the imposition, maintenance, and direction of moral unity to our ends." Warriner (1955) suggested that "leadership as a form of relationship between persons requires that one or several persons act in conformance with the request of another." For Bennis (1959), "leadership can be defined as the process by which an agent induces a subordinate to behave in a desired manner."

The compliance-induction theorists, perhaps even more than the personality theorists, tended to regard leadership as a unidirectional exertion of influence and as an instrument for molding the group to the leader's will. They expressed little recognition of the rights, desires, and necessities of the group members or of the group's traditions and norms. This disregard for the followers and the group was rejected by various other theorists, who sought to remove, by definition, any possibility of legitimating an authoritarian concept of leadership. Yet, regardless of the sentiments of some behavioral scientists, one cannot ignore that much leadership is authoritarian, directive, and even coercive. Its effects are seen in public compliance but not necessarily in private acceptance.

Leadership as the Exercise of Influence

Use of the concept of influence marked a step in the direction of generality and abstraction in defining leadership. J. B. Nash (1929) suggested that "leadership implies influencing change in the conduct of people." Tead (1935) defined it as "the activity of influencing people to cooperate toward some goal which they come to find desirable." Stogdill (1950) termed it "the process of influencing the activities of an organized group in its efforts toward goal setting and goal achievement."

Shartle (1951a, 1951b) proposed that the leader be considered an individual "who exercises positive influence acts upon others" or "who exercises more important influence acts than any other members of the group or organization." Similarly, Tannenbaum, Weschler, and Massarik (1961) defined leadership as "interpersonal influence, exercised in a situation and directed, through the communication process, toward the attainment of a specified goal or goals." This definition was expanded by Ferris and Rowland (1981), who conceived of the leadership-influence process as a contextual influence that has an impact on subordinates' attitudes and performance through effects on the subordinates' perceptions of their job characteristics.

The interactive aspect became apparent as leadership was linked by definition to influence processes. Haiman (1951) suggested that "direct leadership is an interaction process in which an individual, usually through the medium of speech, influences the behavior of others toward a particular end." According to Gerth and Mills (1953), "leadership . . . is a relation between leader and led in which the leader influences more than he is influenced: because of the leader, those who are led act or feel differently than they otherwise would." For Cartwright (1965), leadership was equated with the "domain of influence." Katz and Kahn (1966) considered "the essence of organizational leadership to be the influential increment over and above mechanical compliance with routine directions of the organization." They observed that although all supervisors at the same level of organization have equal power, they do not use it with equal effectiveness to influence individuals and the organization. In the same way, Hollander and Julian (1969) suggested that "leadership in the broadest sense implies the presence of a particular influence relationship between two or more persons."

According to Hemphill (1949a) and Bass (1960), an individual's effort to change the behavior of others is attempted leadership. When the other members actually change, this creation of change in others is successful leadership. If the others are reinforced or rewarded for changing their behavior, this evoked achievement is effective leadership. The distinctions between attempted, successful, and effective leadership are important because the dynamics of each are quite different.

The concept of influence recognizes the fact that individuals differ in the extent to which their behaviors affect the activities of a group. It implies a reciprocal relationship between the leader and the followers, but one that is not necessarily characterized by domination, control, or induction of compliance by the leader. It merely states that leadership exercises a determining effect on the behaviors of group members and on activities of the group. The definition of influence also recognizes that leaders can influence group members by their own example. The Israeli lieutenant leads with the call, "Follow me." Leaders serve as models for the followers. As Gandhi suggested: "clean examples have a curious method of multiplying themselves" (quoted in Paige, 1977, p. 65).

Defining effective leadership as successful influence by the leader that results in the attainment of goals by the influenced followers, that is, defining leadership in terms of goal attainment (to be discussed later in the chapter) is particularly useful, for it permits the use of reinforcement theory to understand leader-follower behavior.

Limited to Discretionary Influence. Numerous theorists wanted to limit leadership to only that influence which is not mandated by the leader's role. As noted before, Katz and Kahn (1966) defined leadership as an influential increment over and above compliance with the routine directives of the organization. J. A. Miller (1973a) saw leaders exerting influence "at the margin" to compensate for what was missing in the specified process and structure. Jacobs and Jaques (1987) conceived and viewed leadership in complex organizations as "discretionary action directed toward dealing with unanticipated events that otherwise would influence outcomes of critical tasks at the actor's level" (as did Osborn, Hunt, & Jauch, 1980). It is influence over and above what is typically invested in the role—influence beyond what is due to formal procedures, rules, and regulations. Thus, managers are leaders only when they take the opportunity to exert influence over activities beyond what has been prescribed as their role requirements.

Leadership as an Act or Behavior

One school of theorists preferred to define leadership in terms of acts or behaviors. For L. F. Carter (1953), "leadership behaviors are any behaviors the experimenter wishes to so designate or, more generally, any behaviors which experts in this area wish to consider as leadership behaviors." Shartle (1956) defined a leadership act as "one which results in others acting or responding in a shared direction."

Hemphill (1949a) suggested that "leadership may be defined as the behavior of an individual while he is in-

volved in directing group activities." Fiedler (1967a) proposed a somewhat similar definition:

> By leadership behavior we generally mean the particular acts in which a leader engages in the course of directing and coordinating the work of his group members. This may involve such acts as structuring the work relations, praising or criticizing group members, and showing consideration for their welfare and feelings.

Leadership as a Form of Persuasion

Both Presidents Eisenhower and Truman emphasized the persuasive aspect of leadership. According to Eisenhower, "leadership is the ability to decide what is to be done, and then to get others to want to do it" (quoted in Larson, 1968, p. 21). According to Truman (1958, p. 139), "a leader is a man who has the ability to get other people to do what they don't want to do, and like it." And for Lippmann (1922), such persuasiveness is long lasting: "The final test of a leader is that he leaves behind him in other men the conviction and the will to carry on." Several theorists defined leadership as successful persuasion without coercion; followers are convinced by the merits of the argument, not by the coercive power of the arguer. Neustadt (1960) concluded, from his study of U.S. presidents, that presidential leadership stems from the power to persuade. Schenk (1928) suggested that "leadership is the management of men by persuasion and inspiration rather than by the direct or implied threat of coercion." Merton (1969) regarded leadership as "an interpersonal relation in which others comply because they want to, not because they have to." According to Cleeton and Mason (1934), "leadership indicates the ability to influence men and secure results through emotional appeals rather than through the exercise of authority." Copeland (1942) maintained that

> leadership is the art of dealing with human nature. . . . It is the art of influencing a body of people by persuasion or example to follow a line of action. It must never be confused with drivership . . . which is the art of compelling a body of people by intimidation or force to follow a line of action.

Odier (1948) differentiated between the value and the valence of a leader. Valence is the power of a person to act on the feeling or value of another person or group of persons, of modifying (strengthening or weakening) it in one fashion or another. Thus, valence is defined not by the value of the leader's personality but by the quality of the influences he or she exerts on the members of a group. Koontz and O'Donnell (1955) regarded leadership as "the activity of persuading people to cooperate in the achievement of a common objective."

Persuasion is a powerful instrument for shaping expectations and beliefs—particularly in political, social, and religious affairs. The definition of leadership as a form of persuasion tended to be favored by students of politics and social movements and by military and industrial theorists who were opposed to authoritarian concepts. It was also the province of rhetoricians and communications theorists. Research on persuasion, persuasibility, and communications has paralleled research on leadership (W. Weiss, 1958). Persuasion can be seen as one form of leadership. Much of what has been learned from studies of persuasion can be incorporated into an understanding of leadership.

Leadership as a Power Relation

Most political theorists, from Machiavelli through Marx to the academic political scientists of the twentieth century, have seen power as the basis of political leadership. Social psychologists J. R. P. French (1956) and Raven and French (1958a, 1958b) defined leadership in terms of differential power relationships among members of a group. For the latter, interpersonal power—referent, expert, reward based, coercive, or legitimate—is conceived "as a resultant of the maximum force which A can induce on B minus the maximum resisting force which B can mobilize in the opposite direction." Similarly, Janda (1960) defined "leadership as a particular type of power relationship characterized by a group member's perception that another group member has the right to prescribe behavior patterns for the former regarding his activity as a member of a particular group."

M. Smith (1948) equated leadership with control of the interaction process. Thus, "the initiator of an interaction, A, gives a stimulus to the second participant,

B. A asserts his control by interfering with B's original course of action."

Power is regarded as a form of influence relationship. It can be observed that some leaders tend to transform any leadership opportunity into an overt power relationship. In fact, the very frequency of this observation, combined with the often undesirable consequences for individuals and societies, has induced many theorists to reject the notion of authoritarian leadership. Nevertheless, many of those who were most committed at one time to trust building, openness, and participatory approaches, like Bennis (1970), have faced the world as it is, not as they would like it to be, and have come to acknowledge the importance of power relations in understanding leadership.

The power relationship may be subtle or obscure. "As a power relation, leadership may be known to both leader and led, or unknown to either or both" (Gerth & Mills, 1953). For instance, myths and symbols about the master-slave relationship may unconsciously influence superior-subordinate relationships in modern organizations (Denhardt, 1987).

Leadership as an Instrument of Goal Achievement

Numerous theorists have included the idea of goal achievement in their definitions. Several have defined leadership in terms of its instrumental value for accomplishing a group's goals and satisfying its needs. According to Cowley (1928), "a leader is a person who has a program and is moving toward an objective with his group in a definite manner." Bellows (1959) defined leadership as "the process of arranging a situation so that various members of a group, including the leader, can achieve common goals with maximum economy and a minimum of time and work." For Knickerbocker (1948), "the functional relation which is leadership exists when a leader is perceived by a group as controlling means for the satisfaction of their needs."

The classical organizational theorists defined leadership in terms of achieving a group's objectives. R. C. Davis (1942) referred to leadership as "the principal dynamic force that motivates and coordinates the organization in the accomplishment of its objectives." Similarly, Urwick (1953) stated that the leader is "the personal representation of the personification of common purpose not only to all who work on the undertaking, but to everyone outside it." K. Davis (1962) defined leadership as "the human factor which binds a group together and motivates it toward goals."

For Jacobs and Jaques (1987), leaders give purpose to others to expend and mobilize energy to try to compete. Cattell (1951) took the extreme position that leadership is whatever or whoever contributes to the group's performance; it is the group's *syntality*, resulting from its members and the relations among them. To measure each member's leadership, Cattell noted, remove him or her from the group, one at a time, and observe what happens to the group's performance. In a similar vein, as noted earlier, both Calder (1977) and Pfeffer (1977) stated that leadership is mainly influence and is even attributed to participants after the fact. The attributions may be based on implicit theories of leadership (Rush, Thomas, & Lord, 1977). Outcomes are attributed more readily to the leader, thus, when things to wrong, the leader is likely to be blamed and even removed (Hollander, 1986).

For Burns (1978), Bennis (1983), Bass (1985a), and Tichy and Devanna (1986), leadership transforms followers, creates visions of the goals that may be attained, and articulates for the followers the ways to attain those goals. As Luiz Muñoz Marín, former governor of Puerto Rico, said: "A political leader is a person with the ability to imagine non-existing states of affairs combined with the ability to influence other people to bring them about" (quoted in Paige, 1977, p. 65).

Envisioning the goals involves intuition, fantasy, and dreaming, not just analytical, systematic, conscious thought processes. For Jack Sparks, the chief executive officer who transformed the Whirlpool Corporation,

> . . . the vision came after years of mulling over the kind of organization that Whirlpool could be, and after his constant interaction with people in other organizations and academics. The vision was his; and the strategic planning process became the vehicle for implementing that vision, not its source. (Tichy & Devanna, 1985, p. 138)

Tucker (1981) observed that most current politicians must focus the attention of their constituents on short-term goals and programs. More statesmanlike opinion leaders are necessary to arouse and direct a democracy toward achieving longer-term goals, such as stabilization of the population, improvement of the environment, and arms control.

Leadership as an Emerging Effect of Interaction

Several theorists have viewed leadership not as a cause or control of group action but as an effect of it. Bogardus (1929) stated that "as a social process, leadership is that social interstimulation which causes a number of people to set out toward an old goal with new zest or a new goal with hopeful courage—with different persons keeping different places." For Pigors (1935), "leadership is a process of mutual stimulation which, by the successful interplay of individual differences, controls human energy in the pursuit of a common cause." For H. H. Anderson (1940), "a true leader in the psychological sense is one who can make the most of individual differences, who can bring out the most differences in the group and therefore reveal to the group a sounder base for defining common purposes."

This group of theorists was important because they called attention to the fact that emergent leadership grows out of the interaction process itself. It can be observed that leadership truly exists only when it is acknowledged and conferred by other members of the group. Although the authors probably did not mean to imply it, their definitions suggest that this quality amounts to little more than passive acceptance of the importance of one's status. An individual often emerges as leader as a consequence of interactions within the group that arouse expectations that he or she, rather than someone else, can serve the group most usefully by helping it to attain its objectives.

Leadership as a Differentiated Role

According to role theory, each member of a society occupies a position in the community, as well as in various groups, organizations, and institutions. In each position, the individual is expected to play a more or less well-defined role. Different members occupying different positions play different roles. Birth and class may force the differentiation of roles. According to the leader of Ponape, Heinrich Iriarte, some Micronesians are born to rule while others are born to serve (Paige, 1977, p. 65).

Leadership may be regarded as an aspect of role differentiation. H. H. Jennings (1944) observed that "leadership . . . appears as a manner of interaction involving behavior by and toward the individual 'lifted' to a leadership role by other individuals." Similarly, C. A. Gibb (1954) regarded group leadership as a *position* emerging from the interaction process itself. For T. Gordon (1955), leadership was an interaction between a person and a group or, more accurately, between a person and the group members. Each participant in this interaction played a role. These roles differed from each other; the basis for their difference was a matter of influence—that is, one person, the leader, influenced, and the other persons responded.

Sherif and Sherif (1956) suggested that leadership is a role within the scheme of relations and is defined by reciprocal expectations between the leader and other members. The leadership role is defined, as are other roles, by stabilized expectations (norms) that, in most matters and situations of consequence to the group, are more exacting and require greater obligations from the leader than do those for other members of the group.

Newcomb, Turner, and Converse (1965) observed that members of a group make different contributions to the achievement of goals. Insofar as any member's contributions are particularly indispensable, they may be regarded as leaderlike; and insofar as any member is recognized by others as a dependable source of such contributions, he or she is leaderlike. To be so recognized is equivalent to having a role relationship to other members.

Much of the research on the emergence and differentiation of roles pertains equally well to leadership. As Sherif and Sherif (1956) indicated, roles are defined in terms of the expectations that group members develop in regard to themselves and other members. Thus, the theory and research pertaining to the reinforcement, confirmation, and structuring of expectations applies also to the leadership problem. Of all the available definitions, the role conception of leadership is most firmly buttressed by research findings.

The recognition of leadership as an instrument of goal attainment, as a product of interaction processes, and as a differentiated role adds to the development of a coherent theory that fits much of the facts available to date. Leadership as a differentiated role is required to integrate the various other roles of the group and to maintain unity of action in the group's effort to achieve its goals.

Leadership as the Initiation of Structure

Several commentators viewed leadership not as the passive occupancy of a position or as acquisition of a role but as a process of originating and maintaining the role *structure*—the pattern of role relationships. M. Smith (1935a) equated leadership with the management of social differentials through the process of giving stimuli that other people respond to integratively. Lapiere and Farnsworth (1936) observed that situations may be distinguished from one another by the extent to which they are organized by one member of the group. Such organization is usually spoken of as leadership, with its nature and degree varying in different social situations.

Gouldner (1950) suggested that there is a difference in effect between a stimulus from a follower and one from a leader. The difference is in the probability that the stimulus will structure the group's behavior. The stimulus from a leader has a higher probability of structuring a group's behavior because of the group-endowed belief that the leader is a legitimate source of such stimuli. Gouldner disagreed with C. A. Gibb (1947) regarding the notion that once the group's activity is dominated by an established and accepted organization, leadership tends to disappear. Thus, Bavelas (1960) defined organizational leadership as the function of "maintaining the operational effectiveness of decision-making systems which comprise the management of the organization."

Homans (1950) identified the leader of a group as a member who "originates interaction." For Hemphill (1954), "to lead is to engage in an act that initiates a structure in the interaction as part of the process of solving a mutual problem." And Stogdill (1959) defined leadership as "the initiation and maintenance of structure in expectation and interaction."

This group of theorists attempted to define leadership in terms of the variables that give rise to the differentiation and maintenance of role structures in groups. Such a definition has greater theoretical utility than do those that are more concrete and descriptive to a lay person: It leads to a consideration of the basic processes involved in the emergence of the leadership role.

Again, what must be kept in mind is that leadership is more than just the initiation of structure. As Gouldner (1950) noted, we need room for acts of leadership in the completely structured group. Stogdill's (1959) inclusion of maintenance of structure is important. Furthermore, if structure is the consistent pattern of differentiated role relationships within a group, we must be sure also to consider the persons, resources, and tasks within the differentiated roles.

Leadership as a Combination of Elements

Naturally, some scholars combine several definitions of leadership to cover a larger set of meanings. Bogardus (1934) defined leadership as "personality in action under group conditions . . . not only is leadership both a personality and a group phenomenon, it is also a social process involving a number of persons in mental contact in which one person assumes dominance over the others." Previously, Bogardus (1928) described leadership as the creation and setting forth of exceptional behavioral patterns in such a way that other persons respond to them. For Jago (1982), leadership is the exercise of noncoercive influence to coordinate the members of an organized group to accomplishing the group's objectives. Leadership is also a set of properties attributed to those who are perceived to use such influences successfully. Other definitions, such as Barrow's (1977), combine interpersonal influence and collective efforts to achieve goals into the definition of leadership. Dupuy and Dupuy (1959) add to this combination of definitions that leadership also involves obedience, confidence, respect, and loyal cooperation from followers. Still others prefer to discuss leadership as a collection of roles that emerge from an interactional process. For Tichy and Devanna (1986), the combination of power with personality defines the transformational leader as a skilled, knowledgeable change agent with power, legitimacy, and energy. Such a leader is courageous, considerate, value driven, and able to deal with ambiguity and complexity.

The search for the one and only proper and true definition of leadership seems to be fruitless, since the appropriate choice of definition should depend on the methodological and substantive aspects of leadership in which one is interested. For instance, if one is to make extensive use of observation, then it would seem important to define leadership in terms of acts, behavior, or roles played; its centrality to group process; and compliance with the observed performance, rather than in terms of personality traits, perceived power relations, or perceived influence. Contrarily, if extensive examination of the impact of the leadership was the focus of attention, then it would seem more important to define leadership in terms of perceived influence and power relations.

Leadership and Headship

The concepts of leadership and headship can be completely differentiated. Holloman (1968, 1986) conceived headship as being imposed on the group but leadership as being accorded by the group. In similar fashion, C. A. Gibb (1969a, p. 213) distinguished leadership from headship as follows:

1. Headship is maintained through an organized system and not by fellow group members' spontaneous recognition of the individual's contribution to group progress.

2. The group goal is chosen by head persons in line with their interests and is not internally determined by the group itself.

3. In headship, there is little or no sense of shared feeling or joint action in pursuit of the given goal.

4. In headship, there is a wide social gap between the group members and the head, who strives to maintain this social distance as an aid in the coercion of the group.

5. The leader's authority is spontaneously accorded by fellow group members and particularly by followers. The authority of the head derives from some extra-group power which he or she has over the members of the group, who cannot meaningfully be called followers. They accept domination

for fear of punishment, rather than follow in anticipation of rewards.

Kochan, Schmidt, and de Cotiis (1975) agreed with Gibb because they saw that managers, executives, an agency officers must be both leaders and heads.

In its conception, leadership can include headship. Defined more broadly, leadership includes the many ways it is exerted by leaders and heads and the various sources of power that make it work (Bass, 1960). With the broader definition, *heads* lead as a consequence of their status—the power of the position they occupy. Without such status, *leaders* can still gain a commitment to goals and can pursue arbitrary coercive paths with their power if their esteem—their accorded value to the group—is high. Both status and esteem are not all-or-none quantities. In any group, members will vary in both. Therefore, leadership will be distributed among them in similar fashion.[5] Although there is usually one head of a group, one cannot ordinarily attribute all leadership that occurs in a group to just one of its members. Until an "academy of leadership" establishes a standard definition, we must continue to live with both broad and narrow definitions, making sure to understand which kind is being used in any particular analysis.

An Evolving, Expanding Conceptualization

Definitions can be used to serve a variety of purposes. Bass (1960) noted that the definition used in a particular study of leadership depends on the purposes of the study. Consistent with this, Yukl (1981, p. 5) concluded that "leadership research should be designed to provide information relevant to the entire range of definitions, so that over time it will be possible to compare the utility of different conceptualizations and arrive at some consensus on the matter."

Either by explicit statement or by implication, various investigators have developed definitions to serve the following different purposes: (1) to identify the object to be observed, (2) to identify a form of practice, (3) to satisfy a particular value orientation, (4) to avoid

[5]See Chapter 11.

a particular orientation or implication for a practice, and (5) to provide a basis for the development of theory. (The hope is that the definitions will provide critical new insights into the nature of leadership.)

The definitions indicate a progression of thought, although historically, many trends overlapped. The earlier definitions identified leadership as a focus of group process and movement, personality in action. The next type considered it as the art of inducing compliance. The more recent definitions conceive of leadership in terms of influence relationships, power differentials, persuasion, influence on goal achievement, role differentiation, reinforcement, initiation of structure, and perceived attributions of behavior that are consistent with what the perceivers believe leadership to be. Leadership may involve all these things.

Applicability

Leadership research faces a dilemma. A definition that identifies something for the factory manager or agency head is not necessarily the most useful one for the development of a broad theory. Thus, a definition that enables the research to identify a group leader—the person whose behavior exercises a determining effect on the behavior of other group members—may not provide much insight into the processes and structures involved in the emergence and maintenance of leadership. But if the research results are to be applied by the factory manager or agency head, then the definitions must be couched as closely as possible to their ways of "wording the world" (Van de Vall & Bolas, 1980).

A definition should do more than identify leaders and indicate the means by which they acquire their positions. It should also account for the maintenance and continuation of leadership. Thus, few groups engage in interaction merely for the purpose of creating leaders and dropping them as soon as they emerge. For the purposes of this handbook, leadership must be defined broadly.

The Handbook Definition. Leadership is an interaction between two or more members of a group that often involves a structuring or restructuring of the situation and the perceptions and expectations of the members. Leaders are agents of change—persons whose acts affect other people more than other people's acts affect them. Leadership occurs when one group member modifies the motivation or competencies of others in the group. Research in the 1970s and 1980s often expressed this idea as the directing of attention of other members to goals and the paths to achieve them. It should be clear that with this broad definition, any member of the group can exhibit some amount of leadership, and the members will vary in the extent to which they do so.

The introduction of the concepts of goal attainment and the solution of problems in certain definitions recognizes the fact that leadership serves a continuing function in a group. But these concepts do not account for the continuation of leadership. The concepts of role, position, reinforcement of behavior, and structuring expectation serve better to account for the persistence of leadership. For the purposes of theory development, it would seem reasonable to include variables in the definition of leadership that account for the differentiation and maintenance of group roles. Finally, room is needed for a conception of leadership as an attribution that is consistent with the implicit theories about it that are held by the individuals and groups who are led.

Summary and Conclusions

The study of leaders and leadership is coterminous with the rise of civilization. It is a universal phenomenon. It is not a figment of the imagination, although there are conditions in which the success or failure of

groups and organizations will be incorrectly attributed to the leaders, rather than to environmental and organizational forces over which the leaders have no control. In industrial, educational, and in military settings and in social movements, leadership plays a critical, if not the most critical role, and as such, is an important subject for study and research.

How to define leadership can be a long-drawn-out discussion that dominates the early portion of deliberations of a scholarly meeting on the subject of leadership. In this chapter, we have seen the rich variety of possibilities, which leads to our conclusion that the definition of leadership should depend on the purposes to be served by the definition. Leadership has been seen as the focus of group processes, as a personality attribute, as the art of inducing compliance, as an exercise of influence, as a particular kind of act, as a form of persuasion, as a power relation, as an instrument in the attainment of goals, as an effect of interaction, as a differentiated role, and as the initiation of structure. Definitions can be broad and include many of these aspects or they can be narrow. A distinction may be made between headship and leadership. One complex definition that has evolved, particularly to help understand a wide variety of research findings, delineates effective leadership as the interaction among members of a group that initiates and maintains improved expectations and the competence of the group to solve problems or to attain goals. Types of leaders can be differentiated according to some of these definitions, more often on the basis of role, functional, or institutional differences.

References

Allee, W. C. (1945). Social biology of subhuman groups. *Sociometry, 8*, 21–29.

Allee, W. C. (1951). *Cooperation among animals, with human implications.* New York: Schuman.

Allee, W. C., Emerson, A. E., Park, O., Park, T., & Schmidt, K. P. (1949). *Principles of animal ecology.* Philadelphia: Saunders.

Allen, T. H. (1981). Situational management roles: A conceptual model. *Dissertation Abstracts International, 42* (2A) 465.

Allport, F. H. (1924). *Social psychology.* Boston: Houghton Mifflin.

Anderson, H. H. (1940). An examination of the concepts of domination and integration in relation to dominance and ascendance. *Psychological Review, 47*, 21–37.

Babikan, K. (1981). The leader-entrepreneur in the public sector. In F. I. Khuri (Ed.), *Leadership and Development in Arab Society.* Beirut: American University of Beirut, Center for Arab and Middle East Studies.

Barrow, J. C. (1977). The variables of leadership: A review and conceptual framework. *Academy of Management Review, 2*, 231–251.

Bass, B. M. (1960). *Leadership, psychology, and organizational behavior.* New York: Harper.

Bass, B. M. (1974). The substance and the shadow. *American Psychologist, 29*, 870–886.

Bass, B. M. (1985a). *Leadership and performance beyond expectations.* New York: Free Press.

Bavelas, A. (1960). Leadership: Man and function. *Administrative Science Quarterly, 4*, 491–498.

Bellows, R. M. (1959). *Creative leadership.* Englewood Cliffs, NJ: Prentice-Hall.

Bennis, W. G. (1959). Leadership theory and administrative behavior: The problems of authority. *Administrative Science Quarterly, 4*, 259–301.

Bennis, W. G. (1970). *American bureaucracy.* Chicago: Aldine.

Bennis, W. G. (1983, April). Transformative leadership. *Harvard University Newsletter.*

Bergen, H. B. (1939, April). Finding out what employees are thinking. *Conference Board Management Record*, 53–58.

Bernard, L. L. (1926). *An introduction to social psychology.* New York: Holt.

Bernard, L. L. (1927). Leadership and propaganda. In J. Davis & H. E. Barnes, *An introduction to sociology.* New York: Heath.

Bernstein, I. S. (1964). Group social patterns as influenced by removal and later reintroduction of the dominant male Rhesus. *Psychological Reports, 14*, 3–10.

Bingham, W. V. (1927). Leadership. In H. C. Metcalf, *The psychological foundations of management.* New York: Shaw.

Blackmar, F. W. (1911). Leadership in reform. *American Journal of Sociology, 16*, 626–644.

Blake, R. R., & Mouton, J. S. (1964). *The managerial grid.* Houston, TX: Gulf.

Bogardus, E. S. (1928). World leadership types. *Sociology and Social Research, 12*, 573–599.

Bogardus, E. S. (1929). Leadership and attitudes. *Sociology and Social Research, 13*, 377–387.

Bogardus, E. S. (1934). *Leaders and leadership.* New York: Appleton-Century.

Bowden, A. O. (1926). A study of the personality of student leaders in the United States. *Journal of Abnormal and Social Psychology, 21*, 149–160.

Brown, J. F. (1936). Psychology and the social order. New York: McGraw-Hill.

Brown, M. C. (1982). Administrative succession and organizational performance: The succession effect. *Administrative Science Quarterly, 27*, 1–16.

Bundel, C. M. (1930). Is leadership losing its importance? *Infantry Journal, 36*, 339–349.

Burke, W., Richley, E. A., & DeAngelis, L. (1985). Changing leadership and planning processes at the Lewis Research Center, National Aeronautics and Space Administration. *Human Resource Management, 24*(1), 81–90.

Burns, J. M. (1978). *Leadership.* New York: Harper & Row.

Calder, B. J. (1977). An attribution theory of leadership. In B. M. Staw and G. R. Salancik (Eds.), *New directions in organizational behavior.* Chicago: St. Clair.

Campbell, J. P. (1977). The cutting edge of leadership. An overview. In J. G. Hunt and L. L. Larson (Eds.), *Leadership: The cutting edge.* Carbondale: Southern Illinois University Press.

Carpenter, C. R. (1963). Societies of monkeys and apes. In C. H. Southwick (Ed.), *Primate social behavior.* Princeton, NJ: Van Nostrand.

Carter, L. F. (1953). Leadership and small group behavior. In M. Sherif & M. O. Wilson (Eds.), *Group relations at the crossroads.* New York: Harper.

Cartwright, D. (1965). Influence, leadership, control. In J. G. March (Ed.), *Handbook of organizations.* Chicago: Rand McNally.

Cattell, R. B. (1951). New concepts for measuring leadership in terms of group syntality. *Human Relations, 4*, 161–184.

Chandler, A. D., Jr. (1962). *Strategy and structure: Chapters in the history of the industrial enterprises.* Cambridge, MA: M.I.T. Press.

Chapin, F. S. (1942b). Leadership and group activity. *Journal of Applied Sociology, 8*, 141–145.

Cheek, S. K. (1987). *Recent state initiatives: The governor as policy leader: The governor as chief administrator.* Paper, Academy of Management, New Orleans.

Christie, R., & Geis, F. L. (1970). *Studies in Michiavellianism.* New York: Academic Press.

Clark, M. B., Freeman, F. H., & Britt, S. K. (1987). *Leadership education '87: A source book.* Grensboro, NC: Center for Creative Leadership.

Cleeton, G. U., & Mason, C. W. (1934). *Executive ability—its discovery and development.* Yellow Springs, OH: Antioch Press.

Cleveland, H. (1985). *The knowledge executive: Leadership*

in an information society. New York: Dutton.

Cooley, C. H. (1902). *Human nature and the social order*. New York: Scribners.

Copeland, N. (1942). *Psychology and the soldier*. Harrisburg, PA: Military Service Publishing.

Cowley, W. H. (1928). Three distinctions in the study of leaders. *Journal of Abnormal and Social Psychology, 23*, 144–157.

Cronin, T. E. (1984). Thinking and learning about leadership. *Presidential Studies Quarterly, 14*(1), 22–34.

Davis, K. (1962). *Human relations at work*. New York: McGraw-Hill.

Davis, R. C. (1942). *The fundamentals of top management*. New York: Harper.

Day, D. V., & Lord, R. G. (1986). *Executive leadership and organizational performance: Suggestions for a new theory and methodology*. Paper, Academy of Management, Chicago. Also: (1988). *Journal of Management, 14*, 453–464.

DeMeuse, K. P. (1986). A compendium of frequently used measures in industrial/organizational psychology. *The Industrial-Organizational Psychologist, 23*(2), 53–59.

Denhardt, R. B. (1987). Images of death and slavery in organizational life. *Journal of Management, 13*, 543–556.

Douglis, M. B. (1948). Social factors influencing the hierarchies of small flocks of the domestic hen; Interactions betwen resident and part-time members of organized flocks. *Physiological Zoology, 21*, 147–182.

Dupuy, R. E., & Dupuy, T. N. (1959). *Brave men and great captains*. New York: Harper & Row.

Dyer, W. G., & Dyer, J. H. (1984). The M*A*S*H generation: Implications for future organizational values. *Organizational Dynamics, 13*(1), 66–79.

Ekvall, G., & Arvonen, J. (1984). *Leadership styles and organizational climate for creativity: Some findings in one company* (Report 1). Stockholm: Faradet.

Ferris, G. R., & Rowland, K. M. (1981). Leadership, job perceptions, and influence: A conceptual integration. *Human Relations, 34*, 1069–1077.

Fielder, F. E. (1967a). *A theory of leadership effectiveness*. New York: McGraw-Hill.

Fleishman, E. A. (1953a). The measurement of leadership attitudes in industry. *Journal of Applied Psychology. 37*, 153–158.

French, J. R. P. (1956). A formal theory of social power. *Psychological Review, 63*, 181–194.

Gardner, J. W. (1988a). *The task of motivating* (Leadership paper No. 9). Washington, DC: Independent Sector.

Gerth, H., & Mills, C. W. (1953). *Character and social structure*. New York: Harcourt, Brace.

Gibb, C. A. (1947). The principles and traits of leadership. *Journal of Abnormal and Social Psychology, 42*, 267–284.

Gibb, C. A. (1954). Leadership. In G. Lindzey (Ed.), *Handbook of social psychology*. Cambridge, MA: Addison-Wesley.

Gibb, C. A. (1969a). Leadership. In G. Lindzey & E. Aronson (Eds.), *The handbook of social psychology*, 2nd ed., Vol. 4. Reading, MA: Addison-Wesley.

Goodstadt, B. E., & Kipnis, D. (1970). Situational influences

on the use of power. *Journal of Applied Psychology, 54*, 201–207.

Gordon, T. (1955). *Group-centered leadership—a way of releasing the creative power of groups*. Boston: Houghton Mifflin.

Gouldner, A. W. (1950). Studies in leadership. New York: Harper.

Graham, F. C. (1982). Job stress in Mississippi cooperative extension service county personnel as related to age, gender, district, tenure, position and perceived leadership behavior of immediate supervisors. *Dissertation Abstracts International, 43*(7A), 2180.

Gregory, R. A. (1986). *Leadership education in institutions of higher education: An assessment*. Greensboro, NC: Center for Creative Leadership.

Groh, D. (1986). The dilemma of unwanted leadership in social movements: The German example before 1914. The G. F. Graupman & S. Moscovici (Eds.), *Changing conception of leadership*. New York: Springer-Verlag.

Haiman, F. S. (1951). *Group leadership and democratic action*. Boston: Houghton-Mifflin.

Hansen, P. (1974). *Sex differences in supervision*. Paper, American Psychological Association, New Orleans.

Hargrove, E. C. (1987). *Jimmy Carter as President*. Paper, Conference on the Presidency, Princeton University, Princeton, NJ.

Hargrove, E. C., & Nelson, M. (1984). *Presidents, politics, and policy*. Baltimore: Johns Hopkins University Press.

Hegel, G. F. (1830/1971). Philosophy of mind. (Trans. W. Wallace.) *Encyclopedia of the philosophical sciences*. Oxford: Clarendon Press.

Hemphill, J. K. (1949a). The leader and his group. *Journal of Educational Research, 28*, 225–229, 245–246.

Hemphill, J. K. (1954). *A proposed theory of leadership in small groups* (Tech. Rep.). Columbus: Ohio State University, Personnel Research Board.

Hollander, E. P. (1986). On the central role of leadership processes. *International Review of Applied Psychology, 35*, 39–52.

Hollander, E. P., & Julian, J. W. (1969). Contemporary trends in the analysis of leadership processes. *Psychological Bulletin, 71*, 387–397.

Holloman, C. R. (1968). Leadership and headship. There is a difference. *Personnel Administration, 31*(4), 38–44.

Holloman, C. R. (1986). "Headship" vs. leadership. *Business and Economic Review, 32*(2), 35–37.

Homans, G. C. (1950). *The human group*. New York: Harcourt, Brace.

Houser, J. D. (1927). *What the employer thinks*. Cambridge, MA: Harvard University Press.

Jacobs, T. O., & Jaques, E. (1987). Leadership in complex systems. In J. Zeidner (Ed.), *Human productivity enhancement*. New York: Praeger.

Jago, A. G. (1982). Leadership: Perspectives in theory and research. *Management Science, 28*, 315–336.

Janda, K. F. (1960). Towards the explication of the concept of leadership in terms of the concept of power. *Human Relations, 13*, 345–363.

Jennings, H. H. (1944). Leadership—a dynamic re-definition.

Journal of Educational Sociology, 17, 431–433.

Jongbloed, L., & Frost, P. J. (1985). Pfeffer's model of management: An expansion and modification. *Journal of Management, 11,* 97–110.

Katz, D., & Kahn, R. L. (1966, 1978). *The social psychology of organizations.* New York: Wiley.

Katzell, R. (1987). *How leadership works.* Paper, Conference on Military Leadership: Traditions and Future Trends, United States Naval Academy, Annapolis, MD.

Katzell, R. A., & Guzzo, R. A. (1983). Psychological approaches to productivity improvement. *American Psychologist, 38,* 468–472.

Kellerman, B. (1987). *The politics of leadership in America: Implications for higher education in the late 20th century.* Paper, Invitational Interdisciplinary Colloquium on Leadership in Higher Education, National Center for Postsecondary Governance and Finance, Teachers College, Columbia University, New York.

Knickerbocker, I. (1948). Leadership: A conception and some implications. *Journal of Social Issues, 4,* 23–40.

Kochan, T. A., Schmidt, S. M., & de Cotiis, T. A. (1975). Superior-subordinate relations: Leadership and headship. *Human Relations, 28,* 279–294.

Koford, C. B. (1963). Group relations in an island colony of Rhesus monkeys. In C. H. Southwick (Ed.), *Primate social behavior.* Princeton, NJ: Van Nostrand.

Koontz, H., & O'Donnell, C. (1955). *Principles of management.* New York: McGraw-Hill.

Kornhauser, A. W., & Sharp, A. A. (1932). Employee attitudes. *Personnel Journal, 10,* 393–404.

Krech, D., & Crutchfield, R. S. (1948). *Theory and problems of social psychology.* New York: McGraw-Hill.

Lapiere, R. T., & Farnsworth, P. R. (1936). *Social psychology.* New York: McGraw-Hill.

Larson, A. (1968). *Eisenhower: The president nobody knew.* New York: Popular Library.

Lawshe, C. H., & Nagle, B. F. (1953). Productivity and attitude toward supervisor. *Journal of Applied Psychology, 37,* 159–162.

Lewis, H. S. (1974). Leaders and followers: Some anthropological perspectives. *Addison-Wesley Module in Anthropology No. 50.* Reading, MA: Addison-Wesley.

Lichtheim, M. (1973). *Ancient Egyptian literature. Vol. 1: The old and middle kingdoms.* Los Angeles: University of California Press.

Lieberson, S., & O'Connor, J. F. (1972). Leadership and organizational performance: A study of large corporations. *American Sociological Review, 37*(2), 117–130.

Lippmann, W. (1922). *Public opinion.* New York: Harcourt, Brace.

Maccoby, M. (1979). Leadership needs of the 1980's. *Current Issues in Higher Education, 2,* 17–23.

Machiavelli, N. (1513/1962). *The prince.* New York: Mentor Press.

Manchester, W. (1988). Manchester on leadership. *Modern Maturity, 31*(5), 40–46, 108–111.

Mason, W. A. (1964). Sociability and social organization in monkeys and apes. In L. Berkowitz (Ed.), *Advances in experimental social psychology.* New York: Academic

Press.

Meindl, J. R., & Ehrlich, S. B. (1987). The romance of leadership and the evaluation of organizational performance. *Academy of Management Journal, 30,* 90–109.

Meindl, J. R., Ehrlich, S. B., & Dukerich, J. M. (1985). The romance of leadership. *Administrative Science Quarterly, 30,* 78–102.

Merton, R. K. (1969). The social nature of leadership. *American Journal of Nursing,* 69, 2614–2618.

Meyer, E. C. (1980). Leadership: A return to the basics. *Military Review, 60*(7), 4–9.

Miller, J. A. (1973a). *Structuring destructuring: Leadership in open systems.* (Tech. Rep. No. 64). Rochester, NY: University of Rochester, Management Research Center.

Miller, R. E., & Murphy, J. V. (1956). Social interactions of Rhesus monkeys: I. Food-getting dominance as a dependent variable. *Journal of Social Psychology, 44,* 249–255.

Miner, J. B. (1975). The uncertain future of the leadership concept: An overview. In J. G. Hunt & L. L. Larson (Eds.), *Leadership frontiers.* Kent, OH: Kent State University Press.

Miner, J. B. (1982a). The uncertain future of the leadership concept: Revisions and clarifications. *Journal of Applied Behavioral Science, 18,* 293–307.

Mintzberg, H., & Waters, J. A. (1982). Tracking strategy in an entrepreneurial firm. *Academy of Management Journal, 25,* 465–499.

Mitchell, T. R. (1979). Organizational behavior. *Annual Review of Psychology, 30,* 243–281.

Moore, B. V. (1927). The May conference on leadership. *Personnel Journal, 6,* 124–128.

Morris, R. T., & Seeman, M. (1950). The problem of leadership: An interdisciplinary approach. *American Journal of Sociology, 56,* 149–155.

Mulligan, L., & Mulligan, G. (1981). Reconstructing restoration science: Styles of leadership and social composition of the early royal society. *Social Studies of Science, 11,* 327–364.

Mumford, E. (1906/1907). Origins of leadership. *American Journal of Sociology, 12,* 216–240, 367–397, 500–531.

Munson, E. L. (1921). *The management of men.* New York: Holt.

Murchison, C. (1935). The experimental measurement of a social hierarchy in Gallus Domesticus. *Journal of General Psychology, 12,* 3–39.

Nash, J. B. (1929). Leadership. *Phi Delta Kappan, 12,* 24–25.

Neustadt, R. (1960). *Presidential power.* New York: Wiley.

Neustadt, R. E. (1980). *Presidential power: The politics of leadership from FDR to Carter.* New York: Wiley.

Newcomb, T. M., Turner, R. H., & Converse, P. E. (1965). *Social psychology.* New York: Holt, Rinehart & Winston.

Odier, C. (1948). Valeur et valence du chef. *Schweizerisches Archiv für Neurologisches Psychiatrie, 61,* 408–410.

Osborn, R. N., Hunt, J. G., & Jauch, L. R. (1980). *Organization theory: An integrated approach.* New York: Wiley.

Oxford English Dictionary. (1933). London: Oxford University Press.

Paige, G. D. (1977). *The scientific study of political leadership*. New York: Free Press.

Pandey, J. (1976). Effects of leadership style, personality characteristics and methods of leader selection on members' leaders' behavior. *European Journal of Social Psychology*, 6, 475–489.

Pfeffer, J. (1977). The ambiguity of leadership. *Academy of Management Review*, 2, 104–112.

Phillips, T. R. (1939). Leader and led. *Journal of the Coast Artillery*, 82, 45–58.

Pigors, P. (1935). *Leadership or domination*. Boston: Houghton Mifflin.

Plutarch. (1932). *Lives of the noble Grecians and Romans*. New York: Modern Library.

Rabi, M. M. (1967). *The political theory of Ibn Khaldun*, Leiden: Brill.

Raven, B. H., & French, J. R. P. (1958a). Group support, legitimate power, and social influence. *Journal of Personality*, 26, 400–409.

Raven, B. H., & French, J. R. P. (1958b). Legitimate power, coercive power, and observability in social influence. *Sociometry*, 21, 83–97.

Redl, F. (1942). Group emotion and leadership. *Psychiatric*, 5, 573–596.

Rush, M. C., Thomas, J. C., & Lord, R. G. (1977). Implicit leadership theory: A potential threat to the internal validity of leader behavior questionnaires. *Organizational Behavior and Human Performance*, 20, 93–110.

Safire, W. (1975). *Before the fall: An inside view of the pre-Watergate White House*. New York: Doubleday.

Salancik, G. R., & Pfeffer, J. (1977). Constraints on administrator discretion: The limited influence of mayors on city budgets. *Urban Affairs Quarterly*, 12, 475–498.

Sarachek, B. (1968). Greek concepts of leadership. *Academy of Management Journal*, 11, 39–48.

Sayles, L. (1979). *Leadership: What effective managers really do . . . and how they do it*. New York: McGraw-Hill.

Schenk, C. (1928). Leadership. *Infantry Journal*, 33, 111–122.

Schriesheim, C. A., & Kerr, S. (1977b). Theories and measures of leadership: A critical appraisal of present and future directions. In J. G. Hunt & L. L. Larson (Eds.), *Leadership: The cutting edge*. Carbondale: Southern Illinois University Press.

Shartle, C. L. (1951a). Leader behavior in jobs. *Occupations*, 30, 164–166.

Shartle, C. L. (1951b). Studies in naval leadership. In H. Guetzkow (Ed.), *Groups, leadership, and men*. Pittsburgh, PA: Carnegie Press.

Shartle, C. L. (1956). *Executive performance and leadership*. Englewood Cliffs, NJ: Prentice-Hall.

Sherif, M., & Sherif, C. W. (1956). *An outline of social psychology*. New York: Harper.

Smith, H. L., & Krueger, L. M. (1933). *A brief summary of literature on leadership*. Bloomington: Indiana University, School of Education Bulletin.

Smith, J. E., Carson, K. P., & Alexander, R. A. (1984). Leadership: It can make a difference. *Academy of Management Journal*, 27, 765–776.

Smith, M. (1934). Personality dominance and leadership.

Sociology and Social Research, 19, 18–25.

Smith, M. (1935a). Leadership: The management of social differentials. *Journal of Abnormal and Social Psychology*, 30, 348–358.

Smith, M. (1948). Control interaction. *Journal of Social Psychology*, 28, 263–273.

Spitzberg, I. J., Jr. (1986). *Questioning leadership*. Unpublished manuscript.

Stark, S. (1970). Toward a psychology of charisma: III. Intuitional empathy, Vorbilder, Fuehrers, transcendence-striving, and inner creation. *Psychological Reports*, 26, 683–696.

Stogdill, R. M. (1950). Leadership, membership and organization. *Psychological Bulletin*, 47, 1–14.

Stogdill, R. M. (1959). *Individual behavior and group achievement*. New York: Oxford University Press.

Stogdill, R. M. (1975). The evolution of leadership theory. *Proceedings, Academy of Management*, New Orleans, LA, 4–6.

Sylvia, D., & Hutchison, T. (1985). What makes Ms. Johnson teach? A study of teacher motivation. *Human Relations*, 38, 841–856.

Tannenbaum, R., Weschler, I. R., & Massarik, F. (1961). *Leadership and organization*. New York: McGraw-Hill.

Tead, O. (1929). The technique of creative leadership. In *human nature and management*. New York: McGraw-Hill.

Tead, O. (1935). *The art of leadership*. New York: McGraw-Hill.

Tichy, N., & Devanna, M. (1986). *Transformational leadership*. New York: Wiley.

Truman, H. S. (1958). *Memoirs*. New York: Doubleday.

Tucker, R. C. (1981). *Politics as leadership*. Columbia: University of Missouri Press.

Urwick, L. F. (1953). *Leadership and morale*. Columbus: Ohio State University, College of Commerce and Administration.

Van de Vall, M., & Bolas, C. (1980). Applied social discipline research or social policy research: The emergence of a professional paradigm in sociological research. *American Sociology*, 15, 128–137.

Virany, B., & Tushman, M. L. (1986). *Executive succession: The changing characteristics of top management teams*. Paper, Academy of Management, Chicago.

Viteles, M. S. (1953). *Motivation and morale in industry*. New York: W. W. Norton.

Warren, J. M., & Maroney, R. J. (1969). Competitive social interaction between monkeys. In R. B. Zajonc (Ed.), *Animal social psychology*. New York: Wiley.

Warriner, C. K. (1955). Leadership in the small group. *American Journal of Sociology*, 60, 361–369.

Weiss, W. (1958). The relationship between judgments of communicator's position and extent of opinion change. *Journal of Abnormal and Social Psychology*, 56, 380–384.

Westerlund, G. (1952a). *Behavior in a work situation with functional supervision and with group leaders*. Stockholm: Nordisk Rotogravyr.

Yukl, G. A. (1981, 1989). *Leadership in organizations*. Englewood Cliffs, NJ: Prentice-Hall.

Zajonc, R. B. (1969). *Animal social psychology: A reader of experimental studies*. New York: Wiley.

Part II
Early Approaches

[2]
The Principles of
Scientific Management

CHAPTER I

FUNDAMENTALS OF SCIENTIFIC MANAGEMENT

THE principal object of management should be
to secure the maximum prosperity for the employer, coupled with the maximum prosperity for
each employé.

The words "maximum prosperity" are used, in
their broad sense, to mean not only large dividends
for the company or owner, but the development of
every branch of the business to its highest state of
excellence, so that the prosperity may be permanent.

In the same way maximum prosperity for each
employé means not only higher wages than are
usually received by men of his class, but, of more importance still, it also means the development of each
man to his state of maximum efficiency, so that he
may be able to do, generally speaking, the highest
grade of work for which his natural abilities fit him,
and it further means giving him, when possible,
this class of work to do.

It would seem to be so self-evident that maxi-

10 THE PRINCIPLES OF SCIENTIFIC MANAGEMENT

mum prosperity for the employer, coupled with maximum prosperity for the employé, ought to be the two leading objects of management, that even to state this fact should be unnecessary. And yet there is no question that, throughout the industrial world, a large part of the organization of employers, as well as employés, is for war rather than for peace, and that perhaps the majority on either side do not believe that it is possible so to arrange their mutual relations that their interests become identical.

The majority of these men believe that the fundamental interests of employés and employers are necessarily antagonistic. Scientific management, on the contrary, has for its very foundation the firm conviction that the true interests of the two are one and the same; that prosperity for the employer cannot exist through a long term of years unless it is accompanied by prosperity for the employé, and *vice versa;* and that it is possible to give the workman what he most wants — high wages — and the employer what he wants — a low labor cost — for his manufactures.

It is hoped that some at least of those who do not sympathize with each of these objects may be led to modify their views; that some employers, whose attitude toward their workmen has been that of trying to get the largest amount of work out of them for the smallest possible wages, may be led to see that a more liberal policy toward their men will pay them better; and that some of those workmen who begrudge a fair and even a large profit to their

FUNDAMENTALS OF SCIENTIFIC MANAGEMENT   11

employers, and who feel that all of the fruits of their labor should belong to them, and that those for whom they work and the capital invested in the business are entitled to little or nothing, may be led to modify these views.

No one can be found who will deny that in the case of any single individual the greatest prosperity can exist only when that individual has reached his highest state of efficiency; that is, when he is turning out his largest daily output.

The truth of this fact is also perfectly clear in the case of two men working together. To illustrate: if you and your workman have become so skilful that you and he together are making two pairs of shoes in a day, while your competitor and his workman are making only one pair, it is clear that after selling your two pairs of shoes you can pay your workman much higher wages than your competitor who produces only one pair of shoes is able to pay his man, and that there will still be enough money left over for you to have a larger profit than your competitor.

In the case of a more complicated manufacturing establishment, it should also be perfectly clear that the greatest permanent prosperity for the workman, coupled with the greatest prosperity for the employer, can be brought about only when the work of the establishment is done with the smallest combined expenditure of human effort, plus nature's resources, plus the cost for the use of capital in the shape of machines, buildings, etc. Or, to state the same

12   THE PRINCIPLES OF SCIENTIFIC MANAGEMENT

thing in a different way: that the greatest prosperity can exist only as the result of the greatest
possible productivity of the men and machines of the
establishment — that is, when each man and each
machine are turning out the largest possible output;
because unless your men and your machines are
daily turning out more work than others around
you, it is clear that competition will prevent your
paying higher wages to your workmen than are paid
to those of your competitor.   And what is true as to
the possibility of paying high wages in the case of
two companies competing close beside one another
is also true as to whole districts of the country and
even as to nations which are in competition.   In a
word, that maximum prosperity can exist only as
the result of maximum productivity.   Later in this
paper illustrations will be given of several companies
which are earning large dividends and at the same
time paying from 30 per cent. to 100 per cent.
higher wages to their men than are paid to similar
men immediately around them, and with whose
employers they are in competition.   These illustrations will cover different types of work, from the
most elementary to the most complicated.

If the above reasoning is correct, it follows that
the most important object of both the workmen
and the management should be the training and
development of each individual in the establishment,
so that he can do (at his fastest pace and with the
maximum of efficiency) the highest class of work for
which his natural abilities fit him.

FUNDAMENTALS OF SCIENTIFIC MANAGEMENT   13

These principles appear to be so self-evident that many men may think it almost childish to state them. Let us, however, turn to the facts, as they actually exist in this country and in England. The English and American peoples are the greatest sportsmen in the world. Whenever an American workman plays baseball, or an English workman plays cricket, it is safe to say that he strains every nerve to secure victory for his side. He does his very best to make the largest possible number of runs. The universal sentiment is so strong that any man who fails to give out all there is in him in sport is branded as a "quitter," and treated with contempt by those who are around him.

When the same workman returns to work on the following day, instead of using every effort to turn out the largest possible amount of work, in a majority of the cases this man deliberately plans to do as little as he safely can — to turn out far less work than he is well able to do — in many instances to do not more than one-third to one-half of a proper day's work. And in fact if he were to do his best to turn out his largest possible day's work, he would be abused by his fellow-workers for so doing, even more than if he had proved himself a "quitter" in sport. Underworking, that is, deliberately working slowly so as to avoid doing a full day's work, "soldiering," as it is called in this country, "hanging it out," as it is called in England, "ca canae," as it is called in Scotland, is almost universal in industrial establishments, and prevails also to a

14   THE PRINCIPLES OF SCIENTIFIC MANAGEMENT

large extent in the building trades; and the writer asserts without fear of contradiction that this constitutes the greatest evil with which the working-people of both England and America are now afflicted.

It will be shown later in this paper that doing away with slow working and "soldiering" in all its forms and so arranging the relations between employer and employé that each workman will work to his very best advantage and at his best speed, accompanied by the intimate cooperation with the management and the help (which the workman should receive) from the management, would result on the average in nearly doubling the output of each man and each machine. What other reforms, among those which are being discussed by these two nations, could do as much toward promoting prosperity, toward the diminution of poverty, and the alleviation of suffering? America and England have been recently agitated over such subjects as the tariff, the control of the large corporations on the one hand, and of hereditary power on the other hand, and over various more or less socialistic proposals for taxation, etc. On these subjects both peoples have been profoundly stirred, and yet hardly a voice has been raised to call attention to this vastly greater and more important subject of "soldiering," which directly and powerfully affects the wages, the prosperity, and the life of almost every working-man, and also quite as much the prosperity of every industrial establishment in the nation.

The elimination of "soldiering" and of the several causes of slow working would so lower the cost of production that both our home and foreign markets would be greatly enlarged, and we could compete on more than even terms with our rivals. It would remove one of the fundamental causes for dull times, for lack of employment, and for poverty, and therefore would have a more permanent and far-reaching effect upon these misfortunes than any of the curative remedies that are now being used to soften their consequences. It would insure higher wages and make shorter working hours and better working and home conditions possible.

Why is it, then, in the face of the self-evident fact that maximum prosperity can exist only as the result of the determined effort of each workman to turn out each day his largest possible day's work, that the great majority of our men are deliberately doing just the opposite, and that even when the men have the best of intentions their work is in most cases far from efficient?

There are three causes for this condition, which may be briefly summarized as:

First. The fallacy, which has from time immemorial been almost universal among workmen, that a material increase in the output of each man or each machine in the trade would result in the end in throwing a large number of men out of work.

Second. The defective systems of management which are in common use, and which make it necessary for each workman to soldier, or work slowly,

16   THE PRINCIPLES OF SCIENTIFIC MANAGEMENT

in order that he may protect his own best interests.

Third. The inefficient rule-of-thumb methods,
which are still almost universal in all trades, and in
practising which our workmen waste a large part
of their effort.

This paper will attempt to show the enormous
gains which would result from the substitution by
our workmen of scientific for rule-of-thumb methods.

To explain a little more fully these three causes:

First. The great majority of workmen still believe
that if they were to work at their best speed they
would be doing a great injustice to the whole trade
by throwing a lot of men out of work, and yet the
history of the development of each trade shows that
each improvement, whether it be the invention of a
new machine or the introduction of a better method,
which results in increasing the productive capacity
of the men in the trade and cheapening the costs,
instead of throwing men out of work make in the
end work for more men.

The cheapening of any article in common use
almost immediately results in a largely increased
demand for that article. Take the case of shoes,
for instance. The introduction of machinery for
doing every element of the work which was formerly
done by hand has resulted in making shoes at a
fraction of their former labor cost, and in selling
them so cheap that now almost every man, woman,
and child in the working-classes buys one or two
pairs of shoes per year, and wears shoes all the time,

FUNDAMENTALS OF SCIENTIFIC MANAGEMENT   **17**

whereas formerly each workman bought perhaps one pair of shoes every five years, and went barefoot most of the time, wearing shoes only as a luxury or as a matter of the sternest necessity. In spite of the enormously increased output of shoes per workman, which has come with shoe machinery, the demand for shoes has so increased that there are relatively more men working in the shoe industry now than ever before.

The workmen in almost every trade have before them an object lesson of this kind, and yet, because they are ignorant of the history of their own trade even, they still firmly believe, as their fathers did before them, that it is against their best interests for each man to turn out each day as much work as possible.

Under this fallacious idea a large proportion of the workmen of both countries each day deliberately work slowly so as to curtail the output. Almost every labor union has made, or is contemplating making, rules which have for their object curtailing the output of their members, and those men who have the greatest influence with the working-people, the labor leaders as well as many people with philanthropic feelings who are helping them, are daily spreading this fallacy and at the same time telling them that they are overworked.

A great deal has been and is being constantly said about "sweat-shop" work and conditions. The writer has great sympathy with those who are overworked, but on the whole a greater sympathy for

18   THE PRINCIPLES OF SCIENTIFIC MANAGEMENT

those who are *under paid*. For every individual, however, who is overworked, there are a hundred who intentionally underwork — greatly underwork — every day of their lives, and who for this reason deliberately aid in establishing those conditions which in the end inevitably result in low wages. And yet hardly a single voice is being raised in an endeavor to correct this evil.

As engineers and managers, we are more intimately acquainted with these facts than any other class in the community, and are therefore best fitted to lead in a movement to combat this fallacious idea by educating not only the workmen but the whole of the country as to the true facts. And yet we are practically doing nothing in this direction, and are leaving this field entirely in the hands of the labor agitators (many of whom are misinformed and misguided), and of sentimentalists who are ignorant as to actual working conditions.

Second. As to the second cause for soldiering — the relations which exist between employers and employés under almost all of the systems of management which are in common use — it is impossible in a few words to make it clear to one not familiar with this problem why it is that the *ignorance of employers* as to the proper time in which work of various kinds should be done makes it for the interest of the workman to "soldier."

The writer therefore quotes herewith from a paper read before The American Society of Mechanical Engineers, in June, 1903, entitled "Shop Man-

FUNDAMENTALS OF SCIENTIFIC MANAGEMENT　19

agement," which it is hoped will explain fully this cause for soldiering:

"This loafing or soldiering proceeds from two causes. First, from the natural instinct and tendency of men to take it easy, which may be called natural soldiering. Second, from more intricate second thought and reasoning caused by their relations with other men, which may be called systematic soldiering.

"There is no question that the tendency of the average man (in all walks of life) is toward working at a slow, easy gait, and that it is only after a good deal of thought and observation on his part or as a result of example, conscience, or external pressure that he takes a more rapid pace.

"There are, of course, men of unusual energy, vitality, and ambition who naturally choose the fastest gait, who set up their own standards, and who work hard, even though it may be against their best interests. But these few uncommon men only serve by forming a contrast to emphasize the tendency of the average.

"This common tendency to 'take it easy' is greatly increased by bringing a number of men together on similar work and at a uniform standard rate of pay by the day.

"Under this plan the better men gradually but surely slow down their gait to that of the poorest and least efficient. When a naturally energetic man works for a few days beside a lazy one, the logic of the situation is unanswerable.

'Why should I work hard when that lazy fellow gets the same pay that I do and does only half as much work?'

"A careful time study of men working under these conditions will disclose facts which are ludicrous as well as pitiable.

"To illustrate: The writer has timed a naturally energetic workman who, while going and coming from work, would walk at a speed of from three to four miles per hour, and not infrequently trot home after a day's work. On arriving at his work he would immediately slow down to a speed of about one mile an hour. When, for example, wheeling a loaded wheelbarrow, he would go at a good fast pace even up hill in order to be as short a time as possible under load, and immediately on the return walk slow down to a mile an hour, improving every opportunity for delay short of actually sitting down. In order to be sure not to do more than his lazy neighbor, he would actually tire himself in his effort to go slow.

"These men were working under a foreman of good reputation and highly thought of by his employer, who, when his attention was called to this state of things, answered: 'Well, I can keep them from sitting down, but the devil can't make them get a move on while they are at work.'

"The natural laziness of men is serious, but by far the greatest evil from which both workmen and employers are suffering is the *systematic soldiering* which is almost universal under all of the ordinary

FUNDAMENTALS OF SCIENTIFIC MANAGEMENT   **21**

schemes of management and which results from a
careful study on the part of the workmen of what
will promote their best interests.

"The writer was much interested recently in hearing
one small but experienced golf caddy boy of twelve
explaining to a green caddy, who had shown special
energy and interest, the necessity of going slow and
lagging behind his man when he came up to the ball,
showing him that since they were paid by the hour,
the faster they went the less money they got, and
finally telling him that if he went too fast the other
boys would give him a licking.

"This represents a type of *systematic soldiering*
which is not, however, very serious, since it is done
with the knowledge of the employer, who can quite
easily break it up if he wishes.

"The greater part of the *systematic soldiering*,
however, is done by the men with the deliberate
object of keeping their employers ignorant of how
fast work can be done.

"So universal is soldiering for this purpose that
hardly a competent workman can be found in a
large establishment, whether he works by the day
or on piece work, contract work, or under any of
the ordinary systems, who does not devote a considerable part of his time to studying just how slow
he can work and still convince his employer that he
is going at a good pace.

"The causes for this are, briefly, that practically
all employers determine upon a maximum sum
which they feel it is right for each of their classes

22   THE PRINCIPLES OF SCIENTIFIC MANAGEMENT

of employees to earn per day, whether their men
work by the day or piece.

"Each workman soon finds out about what this
figure is for his particular case, and he also realizes
that when his employer is convinced that a man is
capable of doing more work than he has done, he
will find sooner or later some way of compelling him
to do it with little or no increase of pay.

"Employers derive their knowledge of how much
of a given class of work can be done in a day from
either their own experience, which has frequently
grown hazy with age, from casual and unsystematic
observation of their men, or at best from records
which are kept, showing the quickest time in which
each job has been done.   In many cases the employer
will feel almost certain that a given job can be done
faster than it has been, but he rarely cares to take
the drastic measures necessary to force men to do it
in the quickest time, unless he has an actual record
proving conclusively how fast the work can be done.

"It evidently becomes for each man's interest,
then, to see that no job is done faster than it has
been in the past.   The younger and less experienced
men are taught this by their elders, and all possible
persuasion and social pressure is brought to bear
upon the greedy and selfish men to keep them from
making new records which result in temporarily
increasing their wages, while all those who come
after them are made to work harder for the same
old pay.

"Under the best day work of the ordinary type,

FUNDAMENTALS OF SCIENTIFIC MANAGEMENT   23

when accurate records are kept of the amount of
work done by each man and of his efficiency, and
when each man's wages are raised as he improves,
and those who fail to rise to a certain standard are
discharged and a fresh supply of carefully selected
men are given work in their places, both the natural
loafing and systematic soldiering can be largely
broken up. This can only be done, however, when
the men are thoroughly convinced that there is no
intention of establishing piece work even in the
remote future, and it is next to impossible to make
men believe this when the work is of such a nature
that they believe piece work to be practicable. In
most cases their fear of making a record which will
be used as a basis for piece work will cause them to
soldier as much as they dare.

"It is, however, under piece work that the art
of systematic soldiering is thoroughly developed;
after a workman has had the price per piece of the
work he is doing lowered two or three times as a
result of his having worked harder and increased
his output, he is likely entirely to lose sight of his
employer's side of the case and become imbued with
a grim determination to have no more cuts if soldiering can prevent it. Unfortunately for the character
of the workman, soldiering involves a deliberate
attempt to mislead and deceive his employer, and
thus upright and straightforward workmen are com-
pelled to become more or less hypocritical. The
employer is soon looked upon as an antagonist, if
not an enemy, and the mutual confidence which

24   THE PRINCIPLES OF SCIENTIFIC MANAGEMENT

should exist between a leader and his men, the enthusiasm, the feeling that they are all working for the same end and will share in the results is entirely lacking.

"The feeling of antagonism under the ordinary piece-work system becomes in many cases so marked on the part of the men that any proposition made by their employers, however reasonable, is looked upon with suspicion, and soldiering becomes such a fixed habit that men will frequently take pains to restrict the product of machines which they are running when even a large increase in output would involve no more work on their part."

Third. As to the third cause for slow work, considerable space will later in this paper be devoted to illustrating the great gain, both to employers and employés, which results from the substitution of scientific for rule-of-thumb methods in even the smallest details of the work of every trade. The enormous saving of time and therefore increase in the output which it is possible to effect through eliminating unnecessary motions and substituting fast for slow and inefficient motions for the men working in any of our trades can be fully realized only after one has personally seen the improvement which results from a thorough motion and time study, made by a competent man.

To explain briefly: owing to the fact that the workmen in all of our trades have been taught the details of their work by observation of those immediately around them, there are many different ways in common use for doing the same thing, perhaps forty, fifty, or a hundred ways of doing each act in each trade, and for the same reason there is a great variety in the implements used for each class of work. Now, among the various methods and implements used in each element of each trade there is always one method and one implement which is quicker and better than any of the rest. And this one best method and best implement can only be discovered or developed through a scientific study and analysis of all of the methods and implements in use, together with accurate, minute, motion and time study. This involves the gradual substitution of science for rule of thumb throughout the mechanic arts.

This paper will show that the underlying philosophy of all of the old systems of management in common use makes it imperative that each workman shall be left with the final responsibility for doing his job practically as he thinks best, with comparatively little help and advice from the management. And it will also show that because of this isolation of workmen, it is in most cases impossible for the men working under these systems to do their work in accordance with the rules and laws of a science or art, even where one exists.

The writer asserts as a general principle (and he proposes to give illustrations tending to prove the fact later in this paper) that in almost all of the mechanic arts the science which underlies each act of each workman is so great and amounts to so much that the workman who is best suited to actually doing the work is incapable of fully understanding this science, without the guidance and help of those who are working with him or over him, either through lack of education or through insufficient mental capacity.   In order that the work may be done in accordance with scientific laws, it is necessary that there shall be a far more equal division of the responsibility between the management and the workmen than exists under any of the ordinary types of management.   Those in the management whose duty it is to develop this science should also guide and help the workman in working under it, and should assume a much larger share of the responsibility for results than under usual conditions is assumed by the management.

The body of this paper will make it clear that, to work according to scientific laws, the management must take over and perform much of the work which is now left to the men; almost every act of the workman should be preceded by one or more preparatory acts of the management which enable him to do his work better and quicker than he otherwise could. And each man should daily be taught by and receive the most friendly help from those who are over him, instead of being, at the one extreme, driven or coerced by his bosses, and at the other left to his own unaided devices.

This close, intimate, personal cooperation between the management and the men is of the essence of modern scientific or task management.

FUNDAMENTALS OF SCIENTIFIC MANAGEMENT 27

It will be shown by a series of practical illustrations that, through this friendly cooperation, namely, through sharing equally in every day's burden, all of the great obstacles (above described) to obtaining the maximum output for each man and each machine in the establishment are swept away. The 30 per cent. to 100 per cent. increase in wages which the workmen are able to earn beyond what they receive under the old type of management, coupled with the daily intimate shoulder to shoulder contact with the management, entirely removes all cause for soldiering. And in a few years, under this system, the workmen have before them the object lesson of seeing that a great increase in the output per man results in giving employment to more men, instead of throwing men out of work, thus completely eradicating the fallacy that a larger output for each man will throw other men out of work.

It is the writer's judgment, then, that while much can be done and should be done by writing and talking toward educating not only workmen, but all classes in the community, as to the importance of obtaining the maximum output of each man and each machine, it is only through the adoption of modern scientific management that this great problem can be finally solved. Probably most of the readers of this paper will say that all of this is mere theory. On the contrary, the theory, or philosophy, of scientific management is just beginning to be understood, whereas the management itself has been a gradual evolution, extending over a period

28   THE PRINCIPLES OF SCIENTIFIC MANAGEMENT

of nearly thirty years. And during this time the employés of one company after another, including a large range and diversity of industries, have gradually changed from the ordinary to the scientific type of management. At least 50,000 workmen in the United States are now employed under this system; and they are receiving from 30 per cent. to 100 per cent. higher wages daily than are paid to men of similar caliber with whom they are surrounded, while the companies employing them are more prosperous than ever before. In these companies the output, per man and per machine, has on an average been doubled. During all these years there has never been a single strike among the men working under this system. In place of the suspicious watchfulness and the more or less open warfare which characterizes the ordinary types of management, there is universally friendly cooperation between the management and the men.

Several papers have been written, describing the expedients which have been adopted and the details which have been developed under scientific management and the steps to be taken in changing from the ordinary to the scientific type. But unfortunately most of the readers of these papers have mistaken the mechanism for the true essence. Scientific management fundamentally consists of certain broad general principles, a certain philosophy, which can be applied in many ways, and a description of what any one man or men may believe to be the best mechanism for applying these general principles should in no way be confused with the principles themselves.

It is not here claimed that any single panacea exists for all of the troubles of the working-people or of employers. As long as some people are born lazy or inefficient, and others are born greedy and brutal, as long as vice and crime are with us, just so long will a certain amount of poverty, misery, and unhappiness be with us also. No system of management, no single expedient within the control of any man or any set of men can insure continuous prosperity to either workmen or employers. Prosperity depends upon so many factors entirely beyond the control of any one set of men, any state, or even any one country, that certain periods will inevitably come when both sides must suffer, more or less. It is claimed, however, that under scientific management the intermediate periods will be far more prosperous, far happier, and more free from discord and dissension. And also, that the periods will be fewer, shorter and the suffering less. And this will be particularly true in any one town, any one section of the country, or any one state which first substitutes the principles of scientific management for the rule of thumb.

That these principles are certain to come into general use practically throughout the civilized world, sooner or later, the writer is profoundly convinced, and the sooner they come the better for all the people.

Part III
Trait Theory

[3]

Published as a separate and in *The Journal of Psychology*, 1948, **25**, 35-71.

PERSONAL FACTORS ASSOCIATED WITH LEADERSHIP: A SURVEY OF THE LITERATURE*[1]

Research Foundation, Ohio State University

Ralph M. Stogdill

Smith and Krueger (100) have surveyed the literature on leadership to 1933. Recent developments in leadership methodology, as related especially to military situations, were reviewed in 1947 by Jenkins (54). The present survey is concerned only with those studies in which some attempt has been made to determine the traits and characteristics of leaders. In many of the studies surveyed leadership was not defined. In others the methods used in the investigation appeared to have little relationship to the problem as stated. An attempt has been made to include all studies bearing on the problem of traits and personal factors associated with leadership. In all except four cases the original book or article has been read and abstracted in detail. The data from one American and three German publications have been derived from competent abstracts.

The present survey lists only those factors which were studied by three or more investigators. Evidence reported by fewer investigators has not been regarded as providing a satisfactory basis for evaluation. It is realized that the number of investigations in which a factor was studied is not necessarily indicative of the importance of the factor. However, the frequency with which a factor was found to be significant appears to be the most satisfactory single criterion for evaluating the data accumulated in this survey, but other criteria, such as the competency of the experimental methods employed and the adequacy of the statistical treatment of data have also been regarded in evaluating the results of a particular study.

In analyzing data obtained from various groups and by various methods the question arises as to the extent to which results may be influenced by differences in social composition of the groups, differences in methodology,

---

*Received in the Editorial Office on September 1, 1947, and published immediately at Provincetown, Massachusetts. Copyright by The Journal Press.

[1]A coöperative contribution of the U. S. Navy, Office of Naval Research, and the Ohio State University Research Foundation. This study represents one aspect of a program of research on leadership being conducted by the Personnel Research Board of the Ohio State University, under the direction of Dr. C. L. Shartle. The opinions expressed herein are not to be regarded as representing the opinion of, or having the endorsement of, the Navy Department.

and differences in leadership criteria. There is no assurance, for example, that the investigator who analyzes the biographies of great men is studying the same kind of leadership behavior that is revealed through observation of children's leadership activities in group situations. It is of interest, however, that some of the studies employing the the two different methods yield remarkably similar results. On the other hand, there are some factors that appear only in certain age and social groups or only when certain methods are employed.

A. METHODS

The primary methods which have been employed for the identification and study of the personal characteristics of leaders have been the following: (*a*) observation of behavior in group situations, (*b*) choice of associates (voting), (*c*) nomination or rating by qualified observers, (*d*) selection (and rating or testing) of persons occupying positions of leadership, and (*e*) analysis of biographical and case history data. The various studies employing these methods are listed, and the salient details of the methods are briefly described below.

1. *Observation and Time Sampling of Behavior in Group Situations* (21, 22, 40, 47, 49, 50, 55, 63, 73, 78, 81, 89, 112, 115, 118)

In these studies the behavior of two or more individuals is observed in situations which permit the emergence of leadership activities. The situation may be highly structured in advance, as in the studies of children's groups by Henning (49), Luithlen (63), Miller and Dollard (73), and Terman (112); or the situation may be natural and uncontrolled, as in some of the boys' gangs studied by Thrasher (115). The periods of observation may range from five-second periods at definitely spaced intervals to an hour or more of continuous observation. The relative merits of the various time sampling methods have been evaluated by Arrington (2). Chapple and Donald (21) have devised a method for recording the frequency and duration of observed social contacts by executives on a polygraph.

The observational studies which have yielded the most relevant data on leadership are those of Chevaleva-Ianovskaia (22) and the pioneering investigation of Terman (112). Henning (49) has devised a number of ingenious experimental situations for the study of leadership in pairs of children, but the investigations in which these methods are employed have proved disappointingly unproductive.

2. *Choice of Associates (Voting, Naming, Ranking, Sociometrics)* (4, 7, 10, 15, 16, 31, 32, 33, 34, 35, 39, 52, 53, 55, 60, 66, 68, 74, 77, 78, 79, 82, 86, 101, 106, 108, 117, 124)

The usual procedure in these studies, most of which use children or students as subjects, is to ask the members of a group to name the persons whom they would prefer as leaders, and, in some cases, to describe the characteristics of each nominee which make him desirable as a leader. Sociometrics is an extension of this method which involves the construction of a "sociogram" or chart showing graphically the preference relationship of each member to every other member of the group. The outstanding investigation of this group is that of Jennings (55), who has combined observational with sociometric methods to produce a study of unusual human insight. Another study which is characterized by insight into human behavior is that of Buttgereit (15). Other studies which are outstanding as to methodology and statistical treatment of data are those of Dunkerley (33), Partridge (82) and Tryon (117).

3. *Nomination by Qualified Observer* (3, 14, 23, 25, 26, 57, 80, 88, 95, 96, 102)

In these studies, leaders are named by teachers, club leaders, or other adult observers who are regarded as being in a position to identify the leaders in the groups selected for study. The leaders are compared with the members of control groups. None of the studies employing this method are in any way outstanding.

4. *Selection of Persons Occupying Positions of Leadership* (5, 8, 11, 12, 17, 18, 20, 24, 37, 38, 41, 42, 44, 45, 46, 51, 61, 67, 72, 75, 76, 85, 90, 91, 92, 93, 94, 99, 109, 111, 116, 120, 121)

Leadership in these studies is regarded as synonymous with holding office or some position of responsibility. The majority of the studies use high school or college subjects, and define leadership as holding some office such as president of student body, president of a fraternity or sorority, captain of athletic or debating team, chairman of a club, and the like. However, a number of the studies deal with adults in rural communities and small cities. The study of Carlson and Harrell (18) is concerned with congressmen. Thurstone (116) studied government administrators. The most competent of the studies from the point of view of methodology and treatment of data are those of Bellingrath (5), Caldwell and Wellman (17), Flemming (38), Sward (109) and Thurstone (116).

5. *Analysis of Biographical and Case History Data* (1, 6, 13, 27, 30, 58, 59, 69, 70, 71, 83, 104, 105, 114, 122, 123)

Ackerson (1) and Brown (13) base their studies on the analysis of case histories of delinquent children. The remaining studies are based on the analysis of biographical data. The works of Merriam (69, 70), and Michels (71) might be classified with this group. Outstanding contributions based on these methods are those of Ackerson (1) and Cox (27).

6. *The Listing of Traits Considered Essential to Leadership* (29, 41, 48, 56, 107, 110)

In all of these studies except that of Jones (56) the authors have asked different groups of persons, usually business executives and members of the professions, to list the traits which they believe to be essential to leadership. Little uniformity is found among the items contained in such lists. Only intelligence, initiative, and responsibility are mentioned twice each among the top five items in the lists reported by Gowin (41), Heath and Gregory (48), Jones (56) and Starch (107).

7. *Supplementary Aspects of Methodology*

Various supplementary measures have been employed in an effort to determine the traits associated with leadership. The most frequently used are tests of intelligence and personality; but questionnaires, rating scales, and interviews have been utilized in some cases. For purposes of reference, the various studies employing these methods are listed below.

　　a. Standardized tests.

　　　　(1). Intelligence tests (1, 8, 12, 28, 37, 50, 66, 67, 68, 78, 82, 88, 90, 91, 118).

　　　　(2). Personality tests (7, 14, 25, 26, 45, 46, 62, 75, 92, 93, 94).

　　　　(3). Intelligence and personality tests (9, 17, 33, 34, 52, 53, 65, 98, 109, 116).

　　b. Questionnaires (5, 11, 23, 24, 29, 41, 42, 48, 60, 102, 111).

　　c. Rating scales (3, 4, 27, 32, 34, 35, 36, 38, 40, 42, 57, 72, 80, 82, 91, 95, 97, 113, 117, 119, 120, 124).

　　d. Interviews (11, 13, 20, 51, 76, 78, 88, 96, 106, 109).

　　e. Factor analysis (9, 18, 26, 33, 38, 43, 116, 117).

8. *Age Groups Studied*

For purposes of reference and evaluation tl. various investigations are classified below according to age groups studied.

a. Preschool age (40, 47, 81).

b. Elementary school age (1, 7, 15, 50, 61, 64, 66, 68, 73, 78, 79, 82, 85, 89, 112, 117, 118).

c. High school age (1, 3, 5, 11, 12, 13, 15, 16, 17, 23, 24, 34, 35, 37, 38, 39, 55, 61, 64, 78, 82, 85, 86, 88, 90, 91, 94, 95, 96, 101, 102, 108, 117, 120).

d. College students (4, 8, 14, 32, 33, 36, 44, 45, 48, 52, 53, 57, 65, 67, 72, 74, 75, 77, 80, 92, 97, 98, 106, 109, 119, 124).

e. Adults (6, 18, 20, 21, 25, 26, 29, 30, 41, 42, 46, 51, 52, 58, 59, 69, 70, 71, 76, 83, 93, 99, 103, 104, 105, 107, 110, 111, 114, 116, 122, 123).

B. Results

The results of this survey are presented in the form of discussions of the evidence accumulated on those factors which were studied by three or more investigators. When contradictory evidence is presented, the bibliographic references are listed to show separately those studied presenting positive, negative, and neutral data respectively.

1. *Chronological Age*

a. Leaders found to be younger (3, 5, 37, 39, 53, 90).

b. Leaders found to be older (5, 15, 40, 41, 75, 78, 79, 81, 82, 124).

c. No differences found (1, 11).

d. Differs with situation (17).

The evidence as to the relation of age to leadership is quite contradictory. Pigors (84) observes that leadership does not appear in children before the age of two or three years, and even then usually takes the form of overt domination. Active leadership of a group seldom appears before the age of nine or ten, at which age the formation of groups and gangs may become a noticeable feature in the social development of children. According to Pigors the four following stages are necessary for the appearance of leadership in children, (*a*) development of determination and self control, (*b*) grasp of abstractions and social ideals, (*c*) awareness of personalities, and (*d*) sufficient memory span to pursue remote goals rather than immediate objectives. Arrington (2), however, finds no evidence from a survey of time sampling experiments to support the proposition that leadership increases with age in preschool children.

Baldwin (3), Finch and Carroll (37), Garrison (39), Hunter and Jordan (53) and Remmelin (90) find leaders to be younger than their followers. In the latter two studies these differences are statistically reliable.

Bellingrath (5) finds girl leaders to be younger than non-leaders, but boy leaders to be older. Leaders are found to be older than followers by Buttgereit (15), Goodenough (40), Gowin (41), Moore (75), Newstetter (78), Nutting (79), Parten (81), Partridge (82), and Zeleny (124). Gowin found outstanding executives to be 12.2 years older on the average than the average of lesser executives. Ackerson (1) and Brown (11)

TABLE 1
CORRELATION OF VARIABLES WITH LEADERSHIP

Author	IQ	Grades	Age	Height	Weight
Ackerson (boys)	.18		—.01		
(girls)	.32		—.11		
Bellingrath (boys)	—.139*	.05*	.27	.17	.25
(girls)			—.32	.44	.42
Drake	.47				
Eichler	.0614	.1155	.2067		
Flemming	.44				
Garrison (School 1)		.30	—.12	—.02	—.02
(School 2)		.36	—.25	—.13	—.04
Goodenough	.10		.71	.71	.52
Howell	.08	.39			
Levi (Elem.)	.259	—.274			
(Jr. H. S.)	.255	—.0005			
Newstetter	.17		.45		
Nutting	.90	.11	.20		
Parten	.34		.67	.67	
Partridge	.54		.55	.43	.46
Reynolds	.22	.27			
Sheldon	.060	.190		.049	.024
Zeleny	.44		.487	.346	.204

*Total scores of boys and girls combined.

do not find leaders and followers to be differentiated on the basis of age. The correlation coefficients reported by a number of these authors are shown in Table 1. These correlation coefficients range from —.32 to .71, with the average coefficient being approximately .21.

According to Caldwell and Wellman (17), the relationship of age to leadership differs in various situations. Leaders in athletics are found to be close to the class average in age, while boy editors and student council members are younger than average, as are girl club leaders and student council and citizenship representatives. In view of these various findings, chronological age cannot be regarded as a factor which is correlated with leadership in any uniform direction or degree.

2. *Height*

a. Leaders found to be taller (5, 34, 40, 41, 75, 81, 82, 97, 124).

b. Leaders found to be shorter (39, 53).

c. No differences found (3, 91).

d. Depends upon situation (17).

Inspection of Table 1 reveals correlations between height and leadership ranging from —.13 to .71. The general trend of these studies is to indicate a low positive relationship between height and leadership, the average correlation being about .30. Hunter and Jordan (53) and Garrison (39) find student leaders to be somewhat shorter than non-leaders, and Baldwin (3) and Reynolds (91) find no relation between height and leadership in students.

3. *Weight*

a. Leaders found to be heavier (3, 5, 40, 41, 82, 97, 124).

b. Leaders found to be lighter (53, 75).

c. No differences found (39, 97).

The correlation coefficients shown in Table 1 suggest a low positive relationship between weight and leadership. The average correlation coefficient is about 23. Hunter and Jordan (53) find leaders to be significantly lighter than non-leaders. Garrison (39) and Moore (75) also report leaders to be somewhat lighter than followers, although the differences are not significant.

4. *Physique, Energy, Health*

a. Physique (6, 57, 79, 97, 119).

b. Athletic ability, physical prowess (15, 38, 82, 87, 106, 115, 119).

c. Energy (5, 13, 27, 108, 120).

d. Health (3, 5, 88, 108).

e. Health and physical condition not a factor (1, 3, 8, 53).

Bernard (6), Kohs and Irle (57), Nutting (79), Sheldon (97), and Webb (119) report that superior physique is a characteristic of leaders. However, the correlation coefficients of .28, .18, .114, and .23 reported by Kohs and Irle (57), Nutting (79), Sheldon (97), and Webb (119) respectively suggest that this relationship is very slight. Bowden (8) concludes from the results of his study of college students that leadership is not the result of a dominating physique. Baldwin (3) finds that high school leaders do not differ from followers in freedom from physical defects.

Leaders, according to Baldwin (3), Bellingrath (5), Reals (88), and Stray (108) appear to have some advantage over non-leaders in possessing better health, although Ackerson (1) and Hunter and Jordan (53) do not find health to be a differentiating factor.

Athletic ability and physical prowess do appear to be associated with leadership status in boys' gangs and groups. Evidence to this effect is presented by Buttgereit (15), Flemming (38), Partridge (82), Puffer (87), Spaulding (106), Thrasher (115), and Webb (119). Coefficients of correlation of .38, .62, and .40 between athletic ability and leadership are reported by Flemming, Partridge, and Webb respectively.

According to Bellingrath (5), Brown (13), Cox (27), Stray (108), and Wetzel (120), leaders are also characterized by a high rate of energy output. Cox (27) finds various groups of great leaders to differ markedly in physique, energy output, and athletic prowess, with only the military leaders being outstanding in these traits.

5. *Appearance*

a. Leaders present a better appearance (3, 4, 6, 11, 33, 38, 80, 82, 88, 112, 117).

b. Leaders are better dressed (33, 112).

c. No relationship found (124).

d. Appearance negatively correlated with leadership (1, 40).

The evidence presented in these studies suggests a possible relationship between appearance and leadership. Dunkerley (33) found that students chosen as leaders in social activities differed significantly from non-leaders in appearance and dress, but students chosen as leaders in intellectual and religious activities did not differ markedly from non-leaders in these respects. Partridge (82) found a correlation of .81 between appearance ratings and leadership status. A correlation of .21 between attractive appearance and leadership is reported by Flemming (38), but the correlation between beautiful and leadership is .05. Tryon's (117) study suggests that appearance is more closely associated with leadership in boys than in girls. She reports correlation coefficients of .49 and .06 respectively for 15-year-old boys and girls, while the correlation coefficients for 12-year-old boys and girls are .31 and .08 respectively. In Goodenough's (40) study, beauty was found to be negatively correlated with leadership in pre-school children, the correlation coefficient being —.20. Ackerson (1) reports correlation coefficients of .12 and —.06 between slovenly and leadership for boys and girls respectively, while slovenly and leading others into misconduct are correlated .32 and .31 for delinquent boys and girls.

6. *Fluency of Speech* (6, 14, 22, 40, 45, 60, 65, 70, 98, 112, 116, 117, 124)

Baldwin (3) reports a definite trend for leaders to be rated by their teachers as confident in tone of voice, while non-leaders tend to be rated as lacking in confidence as to tone of voice. A factor analysis (38) of teachers' ratings of high school leaders reveals "pleasant voice" as one of the four factors found to be associated with leadership. Flemming (38) reports a correlation of .28 between "pleasing voice" and leadership in high school students. Partridge (82) reports that boy leaders can be reliably distinguished from non-leaders when taken into the presence of strange boys, but hidden from view so that judgments must be made on speech alone. However, Fay and Middleton (36), in repeating this experiment under somewhat similar conditions, found a correlation of only .08 between leadership ratings and degree of leadership as estimated by voice alone. Eichler (34) also reports a correlation of —.112 between voice and leadership.

Talkativeness and leadership are reported by Tryon (117) to be correlated to the extent of .41 and .31 for 12-year-old boys and girls respectively, while the correlation coefficients for 15-year-old boys and girls are .15 and .44 respectively. In Goodenough's (40) study a correlation of .61 between talkativeness and leadership is found. Thurstone (116) did not find highly paid administrators to surpass their lesser well paid associates in word fluency test scores but he did find a significant difference in linguistic ability test scores. Simpson (98) also reports verbal ability to be correlated with capacity to influence others. The correlation coefficient is .45.

Chevaleva-Ianovskaia (22) finds that child leaders are characterized by longer duration of verbal excitation. Terman (112) reports that leaders are more fluent of speech, and Leib (60) finds leaders to excel in speaking ability. The same skills are reported in adult leaders by Bernard (6) and Merriam (70). Zeleny (124) reports a correlation of .59 between leadership ratings and total remarks made in class. Interesting conversation and leadership are correlated .28 in Flemming's (38) study. Further evidence is found in the studies of Burks (14) and Malloy (65), who report that vividness and originality of expression and facility of conversation are associated with successful social relationships. Considering the size of the experimental groups, the competence of the experimental methods employed, and the positive nature of the evidence presented, it would appear that fluency of speech, if not tone of voice, is a factor to be considered in the study of leadership. It has long been recognized that effective leadership cannot be maintained in an organization without an adequate system of intercommunication. Thus it does not seem surprising that some of the most searching studies of leadership should reveal the capacity for ready communication as one of the skills associated with leadership status.

7. *Intelligence*

   a. Leaders brighter (1, 11, 12, 27, 33, 38, 40, 50, 53, 57, 67, 78, 79, 81, 82, 91, 97, 101, 109, 112, 113, 119, 124).
   b. No difference (5, 11, 34, 52, 98).
   c. Too great differences militate against leadership (37, 50, 64, 67, 118).

All except four of these studies present evidence which indicates that the average child or student leader surpasses the average member of his group in intelligence. Statistically reliable differences are reported by Hunter and Jordan (53), Remmelin (90), and Sward (109). In most of these studies there is considerable overlapping of intelligence test scores, indicating that superior intelligence is not an absolute requirement for leadership. Nevertheless, the general trend of the findings indicate that leadership status is more often than not associated with superiority in intelligence. The correlation coefficients shown in Table 1 reveal a consistently positive relationship. The average of these coefficients is approximately .28.

Recent factorial studies reveal a number of points which may be of considerable significance for the future study of leadership. Cattell (19), for example, reports that the intelligence factor is heavily weighted with such character elements as wise, emotionally mature, persevering, mentally alert, vigorous, conscientious, etc. These items correspond fairly closely to the factors which are found in the present survey to be supported by an excess of positive over negative evidence. Thorndike (114) reports a correlation of .60 between intellectual ability and estimability of character in 305 male members of European royal families. Thus it appears that high intelligence may be associated with other characteristics which contribute toward a person's value as a leader.

One of the most significant findings concerning the relation of intelligence to leadership is that extreme discrepancies between the intelligence of potential leaders and their followers militate against the exercise of leadership. Hollingworth (50) found that "among children with a mean *IQ* of 100, the *IQ* of the leader is likely to fall between 115 and 130 *IQ*. That is, the leader is likely to be more intelligent, but *not too much more* intelligent than the average of the group led." Observation further showed that a child of 160 *IQ* has very little chance of being a popular leader in a group of children of average intelligence but may become a leader in a group of children with a mean *IQ* of 130. One of the difficulties in this connection seems to be concerned with communication. The average child cannot comprehend a large part of the vocabulary employed by a child of unusually superior intelligence to express exact meanings in relation to his more mature and complicated interests. Differences in interests, goals, and activity patterns also act as barriers to joint participation, which is a necessary condition for group leadership. Hollingworth's findings are confirmed by a number of investigations. Finch and Carroll (37), studying groups of 66 gifted, 66 superior, and 66 average children, arrive at the conclusions that "given a superior group of children to lead, the leading will tend to be done by the gifted children," even though the leaders as a group tend to be younger than the group led. In an early study of the formation of boys' gangs, Warner (118) found that leaders and followers differ much more in chronological age than in mental age. She observed that older boys with mentalities below normal tend to group with younger boys who have a mental age near their own and slightly higher, and that when groups of retarded delinquent boys contact groups of brighter delinquents the contacts are "so short and non-social that no noticeable event takes place." Maller (64), studying coöperation and competition among children, found that homogeneity of intelligence rather than level of intelligence is important in coöperative behavior. McCuen (67) studied leadership in 58 college student organizations. He found that "there is a tendency to select leaders with scores slightly above the average of their respective groups." He concludes that "the crowd seems to desire to be led by the average person. Evidently in a democratic society the leader must not be too far detached from the group."

Two studies by Lehman (58, 59) are of interest in this connection. In the earlier study he determined the age intervals at which outstanding men in various professions made their best contributions. In the second study he determined the optimal age intervals for eminent leadership. Chemists, for example, were found to make their best contributions during the age intervals 28-32 years, while the optimal ages for eminent leadership in chemistry are 45-49 years. Thus it appears that even in science, a man's contributions and communications must be understood by, and in accord with the thinking of, his contemporaries in order for him to rise to a position of leadership in his profession.

8. *Scholarship*

a. Leaders make better scholastic records (1, 3, 5, 15, 17, 28, 33, 39, 52, 53, 75, 80, 90, 91, 97, 98, 109, 112, 119, 120, 121, 123).

b. Leaders make poorer scholastic records (79).

c. No differences found (5, 24, 34, 57).

Leaders are found, with a high degree of uniformity, to make better average scholastic grades than do non-leaders. These results are not surprising in light of the fact that leaders are found to be more intelligent on the average than their followers. The findings by such investigators as Buttgereit (15), Caldwell (17) and others suggest that superior scholarship may not be a mere byproduct of superior intelligence, but may possess direct value for leadership status when it comprises one aspect of a general ability to get things done. There is also a suggestion that superior accomplishment along lines that are valued by the group carries prestige value which may also contribute toward leadership status. But there is an abundance of evidence which indicates that a position of leadership is ordinarily not founded upon superior intelligence and accomplishment alone since these two factors may be present to a high degree in many persons who do not occupy positions of leadership. The magnitude of the correlation coefficients shown in Table 1 suggest that intelligence and scholarship account for only a fraction of the total complex of factors associated with leadership status.

9. *Knowledge* (10, 14, 15, 16, 31, 38, 71, 79, 89, 108, 124)

The results of these studies suggest that persons chosen as leaders tend to be those who know how to get things done. Of particular interest is Caldwell's (16) experiment in which he asked 282 high school pupils to nominate boy and girl leaders for three different situations: (*a*) a trip to the wharf, (*b*) the production and presentation of a program before a neighboring school and, (*c*) the reorganization of a program for administering athletics in the school. There was revealed "a clear judgment on the part of these pupils as to the members of the group best fitted to lead them." The most important abilities ascribed to these leaders were intelligence and practical knowledge relative to the situations for which they were chosen as leaders. In this connection it seems worth while to consider the findings of Baldwin (3) and Burks (14) relative to the association between leadership and the ability to make constructive and creative suggestions. Burks, for example, finds that ability to present constructive ideas relative to difficult situations is closely associated with successful social relationships. Also in this connection should be considered the studies of Cox (27), Drake (32), Flemming (38), Stray (108), and Thrasher (115), who find that originality and constructive imagination are characteristics of leaders. Additional evidence relative to the ability to get things done is presented by Bellingrath (5) and Dunkerley (33). Cox (27) and Peck (83) report that great leaders are characterized, and differentiated from the average by greater intensity of application and industry. In summarizing the results of these various studies, it appears that specialized knowledge and ability to get things done are factors which contribute toward leadership status.

10. *Judgment and Decision*

a.   Soundness and finality of judgment (5, 32, 33, 38, 119).
b.   Speed and accuracy of thought and decision (26, 33, 45, 119).

In view of the positive correlations found between intelligence and leadership, it is not surprising to find a similar relationship between judgment and leadership. Bellingrath (5), Drake (32), and Webb (119) report correlations ranging from .34 to .69 between common sense and leadership, while Bellingrath (5), Drake (32), Flemming (38), and Webb (119) report correlations of .60, .34, .28, and .69 respectively between judgment and leadership. Farsightedness and leadership are found to be correlated to the extent of .55, .25, and .33 in the studies of Bellingrath, Drake and Webb. Two of the factor analysis studies, those of Cowley (26) and Dunkerley (33), reveal soundness and finality of judgment as a factor common to leaders. In addition to the judgment factor, Cowley (26) also found three factors which appeared to represent speed of decision. In spite of the small number of studies bearing on judgment and decision, the general competence of the methods employed lends confidence to the results obtained. Hanawalt, Richardson, and Hamilton (45) find that leaders use the "?", or "undecided," response on the Bernreuter test significantly less frequently than non-leaders, and this tendency is especially noticeable on the most differentiating items.

11. *Insight*

a.   Keenly alive to environment, alert (13, 15, 17, 27, 33, 35).
b.   Ability to evaluate situations (8, 15, 22, 70, 116).
c.   Social insight (8, 47, 55, 84, 124).
d.   Self insight (27, 77).
e.   Sympathetic understanding (10, 14, 38, 47, 55, 74, 119).

Traditionally, insight has been regarded as one aspect of general intelligence. However, the discussion of Jennings (55) and others suggests that insight may be socially conditioned to a high degree. Some of the most competent investigators of the leadership problem have contributed evidence which suggests that insight and awareness are factors associated with leadership ability. Brown (13), Buttgereit (15), Caldwell and Wellman (17), ·Cox (27), Dunkerley (33), and Fauquier and Gilchrist (35) find that leaders are characterized by alertness and keen awareness of environment. Ability to evaluate situations is found to be a factor in the studies of Bowden (8), Buttgereit (15), Chevaleva-Ianovskaia (22), Merriam and Gosnell (70), and Thurstone (116). Less clearly defined, is social insight, reported to be a factor associated with leadership in the studies of Bowden (8), Hanfmann (47), Jennings (55), Pigors (84), and Zeleny (124). "Studies the motives of others," is an item found by Brogden (9) and Guilford (43) to measure Guilford's T factor, which is described as intellectual leadership or thinking introversion. The results of these various studies suggest that alertness to the surrounding environment and understanding of situations are intimately associated with leadership ability, yet very little is understood regarding the nature of these processes. No worker who is responsible for improving the social effectiveness of individuals can fail to be impressed by the persistent blindness of maladapted individuals to the social situations in which they are attempting to adjust. From the point of view of understanding personal qualifications for leadership, it would appear that one question which is in need of thorough investigation is that concerning the fundamental nature of awareness and social insight.

12. *Originality* (5, 14, 27, 32, 38, 108, 119)

Although the number of studies containing data on this trait is rather small, the magnitude of the correlations found suggests that the relationship between originality and leadership is worthy of further investigation. The correlation coefficients reported by Bellingrath (5), Drake (32), Flemming (38), and Webb (119) range from .38 to .70, and are higher on the average than those for any other trait except popularity. Cox (27) finds great leaders to rate unusually high in originality.

13. *Adaptability* (8, 14, 17, 21, 22, 34, 38, 47, 70, 85)

These studies suggest that ready adaptability to changing situations is a factor which may be associated with leadership capacity, although the correlation coefficients of .13 and .21 reported by Eichler (34) and Flemming (38) are not impressive. Ability to adjust to situations has also been regarded traditionally as an aspect of general intelligence but, as described in the references considered here, this factor appears to contain a large social component. This fact has long been recognized by clinical observers, who have repeatedly pointed out that persons of high intelligence may be rendered ineffectual in their vocational, social, and other adjustments through extreme self-preoccuptaion and inhibition to action, the latter of which is found to be negatively correlated with leadership.

14. *Introversion-Extroversion*

a. Leaders found to be more extroverted (17, 40, 75, 92, 109).
b. Leaders found to be more introverted (27, 72).
c. No differences found (5, 32, 53, 90).

The only studies which report a marked relationship between extroversion and leadership are those of Goodenough (40) and Sward (104). Goodenough reports a correlation of .46 between extroversion and leadership in children. Sward finds that leaders rate reliably higher than non-leaders in extroversion as rated on the Heidbreder scale. Richardson and Hanawalt (92) find that college leaders rate reliably lower in introversion than the Bernreuter norms and also lower than non-leaders, although the difference between leaders and non-leaders is not significant. Hunter and Jordan (53) and Remmelin (90), also report that Bernreuter introversion scores do not differentiate leaders from non-leaders. Middleton (72) finds leaders rating low in extroversion, while Bellingrath (5) and Drake (32) find no significant correlations between introversion-extroversion scores and leadership.

All the groups of great leaders except soldier-statesmen in Cox's (27) study are rated as introverted, with soldier-fighters rating very high in introversion. Thurstone's (116) study of Washington administrators revealed successful administrators as rating higher than less successful administrators in Guilford's (43) *T* factor, which is measured by such items as, "introspective, analyzes himself," "often in a meditative state," "analyzes the motives of others," and "not more interested in athletics than in intellectual pursuits." Brogden and Thomas (9) add to this last such items as ,"he does not want anyone to be with him when he receives bad news," "he does not try to find someone to cheer him up when in low spirits," "prefers to make hurried decisions alone." These items are of interest when considered in relation to the findings on mood control. In view of the diversity of findings it appears very doubtful that leaders can be described with any degree of uniformity in terms of introversion-extroversion.

Much the same situation exists in regard to self-sufficiency. Hunter and Jordan (53) and Richardson and Hanawalt (93) find that leaders make high self-sufficiency scores on the Bernreuter test, but Dunkerley (33), Remmelin (90), and Richardson and Hanawalt (92) find no significant differences.

15. *Dominance*

a. Leaders found to be more dominant, ascendant (1, 8, 21, 27, 32, 53, 75, 90, 92, 93, 117).

b. Bossy, domineering persons rejected as leaders (10, 16, 47, 55).

c. No differences found (34, 119).

The evidence concerning the relationship of dominance to leadership is contradictory. Cox (27) and Drake (32) find "desire to impose will" to be associated with leadership, but Webb (119) reports a zero order correlation between those two factors. Ackerson (1) reports a correlation of approximately .20 between bossiness and leadership in problem children. Leadership and bossiness are related to some extent in the children studied by Tryon (117), who reports correlations of .28 and .29 between these two factors for 15-year-old boys and girls respectively. Chapple and Donald (21), Richardson and Hanawalt (92, 93), and Hunter and Jordan (53) find leaders to be significantly more dominant than non-leaders. Small but positive differences in ascendance are reported by Bowden (8) and Moore (75). Eichler (34), however, finds that leaders and non-leaders do not differ in dominance. Still stronger contradictory evidence is presented by Broich (10), Jennings (55), and Hanfmann (47) who find that bossy, domineering persons are rejected as leaders. Caldwell (16) reports that high school pupils express preference for leaders who can keep order without being bossy. These findings indicate that leadership cannot be defined in terms of personal dominance.

16. *Initiative, Persistence, Ambition*

a. Initiative and willingness to assume responsibility (1, 5, 14, 15, 18, 32, 33, 45, 74, 97, 108, 120).

b. Persistence in the face of obstacles (5, 15, 27, 32, 71, 72, 74, 84, 85, 97, 119, 124).

c. Ambition, desire to excel (3, 5, 6, 27, 32, 44, 119).

d. Application and industry (5, 18, 27, 33, 38, 83).

All except one of the studies in which initiative was found to be a trait ascribed to leaders were investigations in which student leaders were nominated by their associates and the traits which were thought to make them desirable as leaders were described. The study of Carlson and Harrell (18) represents some departure from this method, in that 53 Washington correspondents were asked to name the 10 ablest senators and 10 ablest representatives in rank order, and to rate them from 1 to 10 on integrity, intelligence, industry, and influence. A factor analysis of these ratings revealed Factor I to be heavily loaded with industry and influence, and might be called push or aggressiveness. Industry and leadership are correlated .55 and .16 in the studies of Bellingrath (5) and Flemming (38). Dunkerley's (33) factor analysis also reveals a trait cluster identified as initiative which is descriptive of intellectual and social leaders, but not religious leaders. Drake (32) and Sheldon (97) report correlations of .56 and .52 between aggressiveness and leadership.

Cox (27) finds that great face to face leaders are characterized to an outstanding degree by "persistence in the face of obstacles," "capacity to work with distant objects in view," "degree of strength of will or perseverence," and "tendency not to abandon tasks from mere changeabiility." Pigors (84) finds that the development of determination, and sufficient memory span to pursue remote goals rather than immediate objectives are necessary conditions for the appearance of leadership in children. The remainder of the studies which present evidence on this point represent a variety of points of view. Pinard (85), in an experimental study of perseveration in 194 "difficult" children, ages 8 to 15, found that of 24 leaders, 17 belonging to the moderate non-perseverator group were rated as more reliable, self controlled and persistent, and as the most constructive leaders. Drake (32) and Webb (119) find correlations of .23 and .59 between leadership and strength of will. Webb (119) reports a correlation of .70 between leadership and "persistence in overcoming obstacles," and of .53 between leadership and persistence. In Bellingrath's (5) study of high school students, persistence is found to be correlated with leadership to the extent of .68, while Eichler (34) and Sheldon (97) report correlations of .23 and .339 between leadership and persistence. An interesting sidelight is presented in Ackerson's (1) study of problem children, among whom stubbornness was correlated with leadership to the extent of .15 for boys and .12 for girls.

Cox (27) also presents evidence which indicates that great face to face leaders, such as soldiers, religious leaders, and statesmen, are characterized to an outstanding degree by "desire to excel at performances." Hanawalt and Hamilton (44), in a study of 20 college leaders and 20 non-leaders, found that level of aspiration of leaders is significantly higher than that of non-leaders. Coefficients of correlation of .47, .29, and .64 between leadership and desire to excel are reported by Webb (119), Drake (32), and Bellingrath (5) respectively.

That leadership is related to work, rather than to passive status or position, is suggested by the fact that a number of investigators have found leaders to rate high in application and industry. Cox (27) finds great leaders to rank unusually high in this respect. The correlation coefficients reported by Bellingrath (5), Flemming (38), and Webb (119) range from .16 to .55.

17. *Responsibility* (1, 3, 5, 14, 16, 27, 32, 33, 38, 55, 74, 79, 82, 85, 108, 119, 120)

Student leaders are found to rate somewhat higher than followers in dependability, trustworthiness, and reliability in carrying out responsibilities in the studies of Baldwin (3), Bellingrath (5), Burks (14), Caldwell (16), Dunkerley (33), Moore (74), Nutting (79), Pinard (85), and Wetzel (120). Trustworthiness and leadership are correlated .64 in Webb's (119) study, .37 in Drake's (32) study, and .10 in Flemming's (38) study. Correlations of .42, .21, and .53 between conscientiousness and leadership are reported by Webb (119), Drake (32), and Bellingrath (5) respectively. Partridge (82) reports a correlation of .87 between dependability and leadership. Jennings (55) finds that the girls chosen as leaders tend to be those who inspire confidence. Cox (27) finds all groups of great face to face leaders rating high in trustworthiness and conscientiousness, with religious leaders rating outstandingly high in these traits.

18. *Integrity and Conviction*

a. Integrity, fortitude (6, 18, 27, 70, 72, 83).
b. Strength of convictions (17, 20, 27, 71, 74, 98, 119).

Intellectual fortitude and integrity of character represent traits which are apparently associated with eminent leadership in maturity. All the studies which contribute evidence on this point are concerned with outstanding adult leaders, except that of Middleton (72), who found that "character" is one of the traits associated with leadership in college students.

Michels (71) reports that strength of convictions is also a characteristic of successful political leaders. Cox (27) finds that the great face to face leader is characterized to an outstanding degree by "absence of readiness to accept the sentiments of his associates." This trait is especially conspicuous in revolutionary statesmen. Webb (119) reports a correlation of —.32 between leadership and acceptance of sentiments of others. Caldwell and Wellman (17) find that one of the characteristics of high school leaders is insistence upon acceptance of their ideas and plans.

Adult leaders, in a community studied by Chapin (20), appeared to hold opinions similar in general to those of the group but they "expressed the trends of opinion of the rank and file more sharply, more decisively, and more consistently." Simpson (98), in a study of those who influence and those who are influenced in discussion, found that influence score correlated —.41 with influenceability score. It appears that persons in various types of groups may be valued as leaders because they know what they want to accomplish and are not likely to be swayed from their convictions.

The evidence on liberalism-conservatism suggests that the attitudes which will be regarded as acceptable in leaders are largely determined by the nature of the situation. Hunter and Jordan (53) found college student leaders to be somewhat more liberal than non-leaders in attitudes toward social questions. Newcomb (77) reports that in a college where liberalism is a tradition and ideal those women students having the most prestige are regarded as most liberal. Middleton (72), on the other hand, reports campus leaders to be rated low in radicalism. In Thurstone's (116) study of Washington administrators the Allport-Vernon Social Values scale was found to be the most effective of a battery of 75 tests in differentiating higher salaried from lower salaried administrators. Successful administrators rated significantly higher in social and theoretically values and significantly lower in economic and religious values. Drake (32) and Webb (119) have found low positive correlations between leadership and interest in religion.

19. *Self Confidence*

   a. Self assurance (5, 15, 26, 27, 32, 74, 92, 93, 117, 119, 124).
   b. Absence of modesty (1, 27, 38, 72, 117, 119).

The authors reporting data on the relationship of self confidence to leadership are uniform in the positive direction of their findings. The following correlation coefficients are reported: .58 by Bellingrath (5), .59 by Drake (32), and .12 by Webb (119). Cowley (26) found self confidence to be one of six factors possessed in common by three widely different types of leaders. Cox (27) finds great leaders to be characterized to an unusual degree by such traits as self confidence, esteem of own special talents, and tendency to rate them correctly. Buttgereit (15), Moore (74), and Zeleny (124) also report leaders to rate high in self confidence. Richardson and Hanawalt (92, 93) find college and adult leaders to make higher self confidence scores on the Bernreuter test than non-leaders. Hunter and Jordan (53) and Remmelin (90) do not find Bernreuter self confidence scores to differentiate between leaders and non-leaders. Tryon (117) describes leaders as assured in class and as assured with adults.

Sward (109) finds that inferiority scores on the Heidbreder rating scale do not differentiate leaders from non-leaders, although women leaders rate themselves higher in inferiority attitudes than do their associates. Ackerson (1) reports correlations of —.02 and .08 between inferiority feelings and leadership in boys and girls.

The following findings suggest that leaders tend to be persons who are not handicapped by an excessive degree of modesty. Cox (27) reports that great military leaders and statesmen are characterized to a greater than average degree by eagerness for the admiration of the crowd, and desire for the limelight, although they exhibit offensive manifestations of self esteem to a lesser degree than average. Middleton (72) also finds leaders to rate low in modesty. A correlation of —.09 between leadership and modesty is reported by Flemming (38). Eagerness for admiration is correlated —.16 with leadership in Webb's (119) study, while Drake (32) reports a correlation of —.11 between conceit and leadership. Both Ackerson (1) and Tryon (117) report positive correlations between leadership and attention-getting or show-off tendencies. These correlation coefficients range from .15 to .30. The general trend of these findings suggests that leaders rate higher than their followers in self confidence and self esteem.

20. *Mood Control, Mood Optimism*

a. Controlled in mood, seldom gloomy (17, 55, 65, 119).
b. Moods not controlled (1, 27).
c. Happy, cheerful disposition (32, 40, 117, 119).
d. Happiness not a factor (1, 3).
e. Sense of humor (14, 32, 38, 108, 117, 119).

Jennings (55) states that one of the characteristics of girl leaders in an institution is the ability to control their own moods so as not to impose their negative feelings, depressions, and anxieties on others. Caldwell and Wellman (17) and Malloy (65) also find leaders to be characterized by constancy of mood. Webb (119) reports a correlation of —.45 between depression and leadership. Ackerson (1) and Cox (27), however, report some association between leadership and moods of depression, although not to a significant degree, and the extent differs with different groups.

Drake (32), Tryon (117), and Webb (119) find that a cheerful, happy disposition is associated with leadership. These authors report correlation coefficients ranging from .29 to .60 between leadership and cheerfulness. Ackerson (1) and Baldwin (3) do not find cheerfulness to be a distinguishing factor in leadership. Ackerson (1) finds that "unhappy" and "leadership" are correlated —.03 for boys and .06 for girls. Drake (32), Flemming (38), Tryon (117), and Webb (119) report correlation coefficients ranging from .34 to .64 between leadership and sense of humor. Stray (108) also finds leaders to be characterized by a sense of humor. Goodenough's (40) finding of a correlation of .53 between leadership and laughter is also relevant to this subject.

The scarcity of evidence concerning the relation of mood control to leadership cannot be regarded as confirmation of its unimportance. The evidence available suggests that mood control may be significantly related to leadership effectiveness. The question appears to warrant thorough investigation.

21. *Emotional Control*

a. Leaders found to be more stable and emotionally controlled (3, 5, 8, 17, 32, 34, 72, 84, 112, 119, 120).

b. Leaders found to be less well controlled (1, 27, 35, 97, 117).

c. No differences found (32, 38, 124).

A number of manuals which outline the practical techniques for gaining friends and becoming a leader regard self-control as a very important prerequisite for attaining these goals. The evidence relating to this contention is divided. Eichler (34) reports a correlation of .18 between leadership and self-control. Baldwin (3), Pigors (84), and Wetzel (120) also find self-control to be a factor related to leadership. Bellingrath (5) and Drake (32) report correlation coefficients of .70 and .38 respectively between leadership and stability. Leaders are found by Middleton (72) and Terman (112) to rate low in emotionality, while Bowden (8) and Caldwell and Wellman (17) find leaders to be well balanced and self composed in comparison with their followers. Webb (119) reports correlations of —.25 between irritability and leadership, and —.36 between readiness for anger and leadership.

Cox (27), however, finds great face to face leaders to rate high in degree of excitability. This trait is present to an unusual degree in revolutionary statesmen. Ackerson (1) reports correlation coefficients of .12 for boys and .36 for girls between irritability and leadership in problem children. A correlation of .158 between leadership and excitability was found by Sheldon.

Fauquier and Gilchrist (35) also report leaders to be more excitable than non-leaders. Zeleny (124) finds no difference between leaders and non-leaders in degree of emotional control. Drake (32) and Flemming (38) report zero order coefficients of correlation between leadership and excitability.

The data relating to anger and fighting throw further light on this subject. Cox (27) finds great face to face leaders, except statesmen, to be characterized by a tendency toward liability to anger, and "a tendency to flare up on slight provocation." Ackerson (1) reports that "temper tantrums" and "leader" are positively correlated, while "temper tantrums" and "follower" are negatively correlated. Webb (119), however, finds a correlation of —.12 between leadership and occasional extreme anger. Tryon (117) reports correlation coefficients of .59, .48, .25, and .40 between fighting and leadership for 12-year-old boys, 15-year-old boys, 12-year-old girls, and 15-year-old girls respectively. Ackerson (1) finds fighting and leadership to be correlated .13 for boys and —.17 for girls, but fighting and leading others into bad conduct are correlated .20 for boys and .36 for girls. Incorrigibility and defiance are also positively correlated with leadership, and to a still higher degree with leadership in misconduct, while these traits are correlated negatively with "followers."

These studies do not lend convincing support to the view that leaders are necessarily persons who are characterized by a high degree of self control or by lack of capacity for emotional expression.

22. *Social and Economic Status*

a. Leaders come from higher socio-economic background (5, 11, 12, 20, 30, 39, 51, 53, 88, 90, 99, 104, 109, 111, 123).

b. No difference (3, 40).

Evidence presented in studies representing a wide variety of leadership situations indicates that leaders tend to come from a socio-economic background superior to that of the average of their followers. Only two investigators, Baldwin (3) and Goodenough (40), report negligible differences. On the other hand the differences in social and economic status between leaders and non-leaders are usually not extreme. Only Remmelin (90) finds differences which are statistically reliable.

23. *Social Activity and Mobility*

a. Leaders participate in more group activities (1, 3, 5, 11, 12, 20, 24, 45, 53, 62, 70, 77, 88, 90, 91, 92, 94, 102, 103, 124).

b. Leaders exhibit a higher rate of social mobility (104, 105, 115, 118, 123).

Baldwin (3), Brown (11), Chapin (20), Courtenay (24), Richardson and Hanawalt (92), Roslow (94), Link (62), Merriam (70), Reals (88), Smith and Nystrom (102), Sorokin (103), and Zeleny (124) find that leaders surpass followers in the number, extent, and variety of group activities in which they participate. Zeleny (124) reports correlations ranging from .17 to .682 between leadership and participation in extra curricular activities. Leadership has been defined by a number of authors as "occupying one or more positions of responsibility in group activities."

Physical and social mobility is found by Sorokin (103), Sorokin and Zimmerman (105), and Winston (122) to be a factor associated with adult leadership. Sorokin and Zimmerman report that farmer leaders are characterized to a high degree by a tendency to shift from place to place, and from one occupational or economic position to another. The same tendency in inventors is observed by Winston (123). Social mobility, or perhaps more properly, social detachment, appears to be a factor in the formation of boys' gangs studied by Thrasher (115) and Warner (118).

24. *Bio-Social Activity*

a. Active in games (10, 13, 15, 31, 89, 117).
b. Lively, active, restless (1, 13, 21, 22, 38, 60, 65, 74, 117).
c. Daring, adventurous (112, 115, 117).

This list of traits is difficult to classify, since in few cases is the behavior clearly defined. The majority of investigators appear to emphasize the social aspects of these behaviors, although in some cases emphasis seems to be placed on an underlying physical component of energy or vitality. This is merely one example of the difficulty, and perhaps futility, mentioned by a number of investigators, of attempting to analyze human behavior into distinct and separate traits.

Broich (10), Brown (13), Buttgereit (15), and Reininger (89), find that child leaders are more active in games than non-leaders. In Tryon's (117) study leadership and "active in games" are correlated .52 to .74 for groups of 12- and 15-year-old boys and girls. Terman (112), Thrasher (115), and Tryon (117) find leaders to be more daring and adventurous than followers. Correlations of .57 to .78 between daring and leadership are reported by Tryon (117). Cowley (26) finds motor impulsion to be a factor common to different types of leaders. According to Chevaleva-Ianovskaia

(22), leaders are characterized by a predominance of excitation over inhibition. Liveliness is reported by Leib (60) and Brown (13) to characterize leaders. Flemming (38) finds a correlation of .47 between leadership and liveliness, while Goodenough (40) reports a correlation of .29 between physical activity and leadership. Ackerson (1) and Tryon (117) report correlation coefficients of the order of approximately .20 between "restlessness" and leadership. These findings suggest that physical activity and mobility are factors associated with leadership.

25. *Social Skills*

a. Sociability (1, 7, 14, 34, 38, 40, 55, 65, 72, 74, 77, 86, 97, 117).
b. Diplomacy, tact (6, 32, 38, 47, 81, 108, 119, 120).

Fairly high positive correlations between sociability and leadership are reported by Bonney (7), Drake (32), Flemming (38), Eichler (34), Goodenough (40), Sheldon (97), Tryon (117), and Webb (119). These correlation coefficients are shown in Table 2.

TABLE 2
CORRELATION BETWEEN SOCIAL TRAITS AND LEADERSHIP

Investigator	Variable	Correlation with leadership
Bonney	Social skills	.53
Drake	Sociability	.52
Flemming	Sociability	.33
Eichler	Social intelligence	.098
Goodenough	Sociability	.98
Sheldon	Sociability	.471
Tryon	Friendly	.44 to .74
Webb	Sociability	.39

Burks (14), Malloy (65), Middleton (72), and Prosh (86) also find student leaders to rate higher than non-leaders in sociability. Ackerson (1) finds that belonging to a gang is correlated .26 with leader and .21 with follower. Leader and intimate circle are correlated .39 in Webb's (119) study. Moore (74) and Newcomb (77) report friendliness and social skills respectively as factors which distinguish leaders from followers. Cox (27) also finds great leaders to rate above average, but not to an outstanding degree in fondness for companionship and social gatherings.

Courtesy, tact, and diplomacy are found by Bernard (6), Wetzel (120), Drake (32), Flemming (38), Hanfmann (47), Parten (81), Stray (108), and Webb (119) to be traits which distinguish leaders from non-leaders. Drake, Flemming, and Webb report correlations of .08, .27, and .73 respectively between tact and leadership. Flemming (38), however, finds a correlation of —.03 between courtesy and leadership. Ackerson reports correlations of .10 and .07 between rudeness and leadership for boys and girls respectively, while the correlations between rudeness and leading others into bad conduct are .24 and .40 for boys and girls respectively. Ackerson also finds that both bashfulness and seclusiveness are negatively correlated with leadership.

Ackerson (1), Goodenough (40), and Webb (119) find correlations ranging from —.29 to .21 between offensive manifestations and leadership. Ackerson's (1) findings suggest that misconduct is not necessarily a bar to leadership. Stealing, for example, is correlated .12 and .21 with leadership, while stealing and leading others into misconduct are correlated .46 and .16 for boys and girls respectively.

26. *Popularity, Prestige* (1, 5, 18, 27, 39, 71, 73, 79, 117, 124)

Evidence from a diversity of studies indicates that leaders are persons who tend to rate higher than average in popularity. The correlation coefficients shown in Table 3 reveal a fairly high relationship between popularity and leadership. Nutting (79) points out, however, that popularity cannot

TABLE 3
CORRELATION BETWEEN POPULARITY AND LEADERSHIP

Investigator	Variable	Correlation with leadership
Ackerson (boys)	Popularity	.32
(girls)		.40
Bellingrath	Popularity	.80
Garrison (School 1)	Admiration	.82
(School 2)		.58
Nutting	Popularity	.60
Tryon (boys, age 12)	Popularity	.47
(boys, age 15)		.64
(girls, age 12)		.23
(girls, age 15)		.68

be regarded as synonymous with leadership. The evidence presented by Ackerson (1), Bellingrath (5), Carlson and Harrell (18), Cox (27), Garrison (39), Michels (71), Miller and Dollard (73), Nutting (79), Tryon (117), and Zeleny (124) indicate that popularity and prestige are rather closely associated with leadership status.

27. Coöperation

a. Coöperativeness (3, 10, 16, 32, 33, 35, 47, 65, 77, 119, 120).

b. Work for the group, corporate responsibility (10, 15, 27, 55, 60, 79, 84, 119).

c. Ability to enlist coöperation (3, 16, 47, 55, 69, 70, 79).

Leaders are found by Baldwin (3), Dunkerley (33), Fauquier and Gilchrist (35), Newcomb (77), and Wetzel (120) to rate higher in coöperativeness than followers. Drake (32) and Webb (119) report correlations of .44 and .69 between coöperativeness and leadership. Ability to enlist coöperation and to control others in a group enterprise are found by Baldwin (3), Caldwell (16), Hanfmann (47), Merriam (69, 70), and Nutting (79) to be characteristics associated with leadership ability. Broich (10), Jennings (55), Leib (60), Nutting (79), and Pigors (84) find that leaders tend to be persons who are able to work for the group welfare. A sense of social responsibility is found by Buttgereit (15) to be a characteristic of leaders. Webb (119) reports a correlation of .69 between leadership and corporate spirit. Cox (27) also reports that great leaders rate outstandingly high in sense of corporate spirit.

28. *Patterns of Leadership Traits Differ with the Situation* (1, 5, 17, 23, 25, 27, 29, 33, 45, 46, 55, 76, 77, 82, 95, 96, 109, 112, 116)

There is a preponderance of evidence from a wide variety of studies which indicates that patterns of leadership traits differ with the situation. Ackerson's study (1) reveals marked differences in the conduct and personality patterns of children who are regarded as leaders in general and children who are regarded as leaders in misconduct. Boys and girls in these two groups also differ somewhat. Bellingrath (5) finds marked differences in the extent to which leaders in athletics, student government, publications, and clubs participate in extra-curricular activities and are chosen as leaders under varying circumstances. The investigation of Caldwell and Wellman (17) reveals athletic leaders to be tallest among the leaders and to excel in physical achievements, while editors are younger, and shorter than average, but rank higher in scholarship than other groups of leaders studied. Cowley's (25) studies reveal marked differences in the traits of criminal leaders, Army leaders, and student leaders. The profiles of average trait ratings of groups of great leaders studied by Cox (27) differ markedly from one group to another, especially in physical and emotional traits, but much less so in traits which might be classified as intellectual, self regard, and persistence.

Dunkerley's (33) factor analysis of the intercorrelations of 15 variables representing trait ratings of 167 women college students, reveals a factor identified as social leadership, and two factors identified as religious leadership.

Hanfmann (47) observes three types of leadership among preschool children: (a) the objective leader who engages in constructive play and gets what he wants by saying why he needs it, (b) the social leader whose goal is play with another rather than play in itself, and (c) the gangster who gets his way by force and complete disregard for others. Schuler (95) concludes that as age increases, dominant-submissive behavior in adolescent boys may be ascertained with increasing reliability by teachers in one situation, such as the school, but at the same time it becomes less possible to predict those tendencies in another environment, such as the home.

Superior socio-economic status as well as higher intelligence and scholastic attainment are found by Sward (109) to differentiate 125 campus leaders from 125 followers. However a classification of the leaders into subgroups reveals the following distinguishing differences: (a) bright, relatively unmotivated, unsocial, self confident campus editors, (b) rather insecure, intellectualistic and very intelligent debaters, (c) strongly socialized and intellectually mediocre campus politicians, and (d) extroverted women leaders.

Terman (112) finds that children who are leaders in one experimental situation may not be leaders when matched against different children in other situations. Children who are "automatons," or non-leaders, in most situations, may achieve leadership in some situations. Those children who are leaders in most situations are said by their teachers to be characterized by intelligence, congeniality, liveliness, and goodness.

In Tryon's study (117), the trait clusters found to characterize boys and girls at 12 years of age differ from those found at 15 years of age. This is especially true for girls, who appear to mature somewhat more rapidly in social interests than do boys. The leadership cluster for 12-year-old boys is composed of the items: daring, leader, active in games, friendly; while that for 15-year-old boys contains the items: daring, leader, active in games, fights. The leadership trait cluster for 12-year-old girls contains the items: daring, leader, humor about jokes; while for 15-year-old girls the following items appear: popular, friendly, enthusiastic, happy, humor about jokes, daring, leader.

The total weight of evidence presented in this group of studies suggests that if there are general traits which characterize leaders, the patterns of such traits are likely to vary with the leadership requirements of different situations.

29. *Transferability and Persistence of Leadership* (23, 24, 57, 61, 80, 96)

Follow up studies, although yielding somewhat variable results, suggest a certain degree of persistence or transferability of leadership. Levi (61) studied 230 leaders in elementary and junior high school, 206 of whom were studied again in senior high school. The correlation between leadership in elementary school and leadership in senior high school is .188, while the correlation between junior high school leadership and leadership in senior high school is .515. There is a low negative correlation between athletic leadership in elementary school and in high school, but a correlation of .442 was found between athletic leadership in the junior and senior high school situations.

Kohs and Irle (57) made a follow up study of the military careers of 116 college students. Three faculty members rated these students on various traits. Correlations between army rank and various ratings ranged from .108 to .39. The best criteria for predicting military success were found to be judges' estimates of potential value to the service and judges' estimates of intelligence. Judges' estimates of leadership were correlated .108 with Army rank. Scholarship was not predictive of Army rank. Page (80), studying cadets at West Point, found first year leadership rank to be correlated .667 with fourth year leadership rank. Rank in bearing and appearance was most highly correlated with rank in leadership; while rank in athletic activities, tactics, and academic standing were correlated with leadership rank in progressively lesser degrees.

Clem and Dodge (23) made a comparative study of the post school success of 27 leaders, 36 high ranking scholars, and 38 random pupils from six successive high school graduating classes. Leaders rank highest in outstanding achievements, number of honors received, and quantity of publications. The random group ranks highest in community leadership and amount of money accumulated. In general, the leaders tended to be more successful than scholars and the random group, although the differences are not impressive. Courtenay (24) studied 100 women leaders and 100 non-leaders from 13 successive high school graduating classes. The two groups were matched as to socio-economic background, ethnic heritage, scholarship, and age at graduation. It was found that 72 leaders went to college, while only 29 non-leaders went to college. Twice as many leaders as non-leaders were engaged in professional work. The average salary of leaders exceeded that of non-leaders. The leaders were more active in community work. Shannon (96) compared leaders, scholars (honor roll members), and a random group from five high school graduating classes. It was found that graduates who were on the honor roll were but little more successful than the random group. It was concluded that "whatever is required to excel in the extra-curricular life of the high school, seems to be the same thing that contributes most to success later."

These findings suggest rather strongly that high scholarship alone may not be predictive of success after graduation from high school. Leadership in school activities is somewhat more predictive of later success, but the extent to which leadership persists and transfers is not clearly determined.

C. Summary

1. The following conclusions are supported by uniformly positive evidence from 15 or more of the studies surveyed:

a. The average person who occupies a position of leadership exceeds the average member of his group in the following respects: (1) intelligence, (2) scholarship, (3) dependability in exercising responsibilities, (4) activity and social participation, and (5) socio-economic status.

b. The qualities, characteristics, and skills required in a leader are determined to a large extent by the demands of the situation in which he is to function as a leader.

2. The following conclusions are supported by uniformly positive evidence from 10 or more of the studies surveyed:

a. The average person who occupies a position of leadership exceeds the average member of his group to some degree in the following respects: (1) sociability, (2) initiative, (3) persistence, (4) knowing how to get things done, (5) self confidence, (6) alertness to, and insight into, situations, (7) coöperativeness, (8) popularity, (9) adaptability, and (10) verbal facility.

3. In addition to the above, a number of factors have been found which are specific to well defined groups. For example, athletic ability and physical prowess have been found to be characteristics of leaders in boys' gangs and play groups. Intellectual fortitude and integrity are traits found to be associated with eminent leadership in maturity.

4. The items with the highest overall correlation with leadership are originality, popularity, sociability, judgment, aggressiveness, desire to excel, humor, coöperativeness, liveliness, and athletic ability, in approximate order of magnitude of average correlation coefficient.

5. In spite of considerable negative evidence, the general trend of results suggests a low positive correlation between leadership and such variables as chronological age, height, weight, physique, energy, appearance, dominance,

and mood control. The evidence is about evenly divided concerning the relation to leadership of such traits as introversion-extroversion, self sufficiency, and emotional control.

6. The evidence available suggests that leadership exhibited in various school situations may persist into college and into later vocational and community life. However, knowledge of the facts relating to the transferability of leadership is very meager and obscure.

7. The most fruitful studies, from the point of view of understanding leadership, have been those in which leadership behavior was described and analyzed on the basis of direct observation or analysis of biographical and case history data.

D. DISCUSSION

The factors which have been found to be associated with leadership could probably all be classified under the general headings of *capacity, achievement, responsibility, participation,* and *status:*

1. *Capacity* (intelligence, alertness, verbal facility, originality, judgment).

2. *Achievement* (scholarship, knowledge, athletic accomplishments).

3. *Responsibility* (dependability, initiative, persistence, aggressiveness, self confidence, desire to excel).

4. *Participation* (activity, sociability, coöperation, adaptability, humor).

5. *Status* (socio-economic position, popularity).

These findings are not surprising. It is primarily by virtue of participating in group activities and demonstrating his capacity for expediting the work of the group that a person becomes endowed with leadership status. A number of investigators have been careful to distinguish between the leader and the figure-head, and to point out that leadership is always associated with the attainment of group objectives. Leadership implies activity, movement, getting work done. The leader is a person who occupies a position of responsibility in coördinating the activities of the members of the group in their task of attaining a common goal. This leads to consideration of another significant factor.

6. *Situation* (mental level, status, skills, needs and interests of followers, objectives to be achieved, etc.).

A person does not become a leader by virtue of the possession of some combination of traits, but the pattern of personal characteristics of the leader must bear some relevant relationship to the characteristics, activities, and goals of the followers. Thus, leadership must be conceived in terms of the interaction of variables which are in constant flux and change. The factor of change is especially characteristic of the situation, which may be radically altered by the addition or loss of members, changes in interpersonal relationships, changes in goals, competition of extra-group influences, and the like. The personal characteristics of leader and of the followers are, in comparison, highly stable. The persistence of individual patterns of human behavior in the face of constant situational change appears to be a primary obstacle encountered not only in the practice of leadership, but in the selection and placement of leaders. It is not especially difficult to find persons who are leaders. It is quite another matter to place these persons in different situations where they will be able to function as leaders. It becomes clear that an adequate analysis of leadership involves not only a study of leaders, but also of situations.

The evidence suggests that leadership is a relation that exists between persons in a social situation, and that persons who are leaders in one situation may not necessarily be leaders in other situations. Must it then be assumed that leadership is entirely incidental, haphazard, and unpredictable? Not at all. The very studies which provide the strongest arguments for the situational nature of leadership also supply the strongest evidence indicating that leadership patterns as well as non-leadership patterns of behavior are persistent and relatively stable. Jennings (55) observes that "the individual's choice behavior, in contrast to his social expansiveness, appears as an expression of needs which are, so to speak, so 'central' to his personality that he must strive to fulfill them whether or not the possibility of fulfilling them is at hand." A somewhat similar observation is made by Newstetter, Feldstein, and Newcomb (78), who report that:

> Being accepted or rejected is not determined by the cordiality or antagonism of the individual's treatment of his fellows, nor evidently, is the individual's treatment of his fellows much affected by the degree to which he is already being accepted or rejected by them. Their treatment of him is related to their acceptance or rejection of him. Their treatment of him is, of course, a reaction to some or all of his behaviors, but we have been completely unsuccessful in attempting to measure what these behaviors are.

The authors conclude that these findings provide "devastating evidence" against the concept of the operation of measurable traits in determining social interactions. The findings of Newstetter and his associates do not appear to provide direct evidence either for or against a theory of traits, but they do indicate that the complex of factors that determines an individual's status in a group is most difficult to isolate and evaluate.

The findings of Jennings and Newstetter suggest that the problem of selecting leaders should be much less difficult than that of training non-leaders to become leaders. The clinician or group worker who has observed the fruitless efforts of socially isolated individuals to gain group acceptance or leadership status is aware of the real nature of the phenomena described by Jennings and Newstetter. Some individuals are isolates in almost any group in which they find themselves, while others are readily accepted in most of their social contacts.

A most pertinent observation on this point is made by Ackerson (1), who reports that "the correlation for 'leaders' and 'follower' are not of opposite sign and similar magnitude as would be expected of traits supposed to be antithetical." These may not be the opposite poles of a single underlying trait. "It may be that the true antithesis of 'leader' is not 'follower,' but 'indifference,' i.e., the incapacity or unwillingness either to lead or to follow. Thus it may be that some individuals who under one situation are leaders may under other conditions take the rôle of follower, while the true 'opposite' is represented by the child who neither leads nor follows."

The findings suggest that leadership is not a matter of passive status, or of the mere possession of some combination of traits. It appears rather to be a working relationship among members of a group, in which the leader acquires status through active participation and demonstration of his capacity for carrying coöperative tasks through to completion. Significant aspects of this capacity for organizing and expediting coöperative effort appear to be intelligence, alertness to the needs and motives of others, and insight into situations, further reinforced by such habits as responsibility, initiative, persistence, and self confidence. The studies surveyed offer little information as to the basic nature of these personal qualifications. Cattell's (19) studies suggest that they may be founded to some degree on basic intelligence, but Cattell and others also suggest that they are socially conditioned to a high degree. Problems which appear to be in need of thorough investigation are those relating to factors which condition social participation, insight into situations, mood control, responsibility, and transferability of leadership from one situation to another. Answers to these questions seem basic not only to any adequate understanding of the personal qualifications of leaders, but also to any effective training for leadership.

RALPH M. STOGDILL   67

References

1. ACKERSON. L. Children's Behavior Problems: Relative Importance and Inter-correlation among Traits. Chicago: Univ. Chicago Press, 1942.

2. ARRINGTION, R. E. Time sampling in studies of social behavior: A critical review of techniques and results with research suggestions. *Psychol. Bull.,* 1943, **40**, 81-124.

3. BALDWIN, L. E. A study of factors usually associated with high school male leadership. Unpublished Master's thesis, Ohio State Univ., 1932.

4. BARKER, R. G. The social interrelations of strangers and acquaintances. *Sociometry,* 1942, **5**, 169-179.

5. BELLINGRATH, G. C. Qualities associated with leadership in extra-curricular activities of the high school. *Teach. Coll. Contr. Educ.,* 1930, No. 399.

6. BERNARD, J. Political leadership among North American Indians. *Amer. J. Sociol.,* 1928, **34**, 296-315.

7. BONNEY, M. E. The constancy of sociometric scores and their relationship to teacher judgments of social success and to personality self-ratings. *Sociometry,* 1943, **6**, 409-424.

8. BOWDEN, A. O. A study of the personality of student leaders in colleges in the United States. *J. Abn. & Soc. Psychol.,* 1926, **21**, 149-160.

9. BROGDEN, H. E., & THOMAS, W. F. The primary traits in personality items purporting to measure sociability. *J. of Psychol.,* 1943, **16**, 85-97.

10. BROICH, K. Führeranforderungen in der Kindergruppe. *Z. angew. Psychol.,* 1929, **32**, 164-212.

11. BROWN, M. Leadership among high school pupils. *Teach. Coll. Contr. Educ.,* 1933, No. 559.

12. ———. Leadership among high school pupils. *Teach. Coll. Rec.,* 1934, **35**, 324-326.

13. BROWN, S. C. Some case studies of delinquent girls described as leaders. *Brit. J. Educ. Psychol.,* 1931, **1**, 162-179.

14. BURKS, F. W. Some factors related to social success in college. *J. Soc. Psychol.,* 1938, **9**, 125-140.

15. BUTTGEREIT, H. Führergestalten in der Schulklass. *Z. angew. Psychol.,* 1932, **43**, 369-413.

16. CALDWELL, O. W. Some factors in training for leadership. *Nat. Ass. Sec. Sch. Prin., Fourth Yearb.,* 1920, 2-13.

17. CALDWELL, O. W., & WELLMAN, B. Characteristics of school leaders. *J. Educ. Res.,* 1926, **14**, 1-15.

18. CARLSON, H. B., & HARRELL, W. An analysis of Life's "Ablest Congressman" poll. *J. Soc. Psychol.,* 1942, **15**, 153-158.

19. CATTELL, R. B. Description and Measurement of Personality. New York: World Book, 1946.

20. CHAPIN, F. S. Community Leadership and Opinion in Red Wing. Minneapolis: Univ. Minnesota Press, 1945.

21. CHAPPLE, E. D., & DONALD, G., JR. A method of evaluating supervisory personnel. *Harvard Bus. Rev.,* 1946, **24**, 197-214.

22. CHEVALEVA-IANOVSKAIA, E., & SYLLA, D. Essai d'une étude sur les enfants meneurs. *J. de Psychol.,* 1929, **26**, 604-612.

23. CLEM,, O. M., & DODGE, S. B. The relation of high school leadership and scholarship to post-school success. *Peabody J. Educ.* 1933, **10**, 321-329.

24. COURTENAY, M. E. Persistence of leadership. *Sch. Rev.,* 1938, **46**, 97-107.

25. COWLEY, W. H. Three distinctions in the study of leaders. *J. Abn. & Soc. Psychol.*, 1928, **23**, 144-157.

26. ————. Traits of face-to-face leaders. *J. Abn. & Soc. Psychol.*, 1931, **26**, 304-313.

27. COX, C. M. The Early Mental Traits of Three Hundred Geniuses. Stanford University: Stanford Univ. Press, 1926.

28. CRAWFORD, A. B. Extra-curriculum activities and academic work. *Person, J.*, 1928, **7**, 121-129.

29. DASHIELL, J. F. Personality traits and the different professions. *J. Appl. Psychol.*, 1930, **14**, 197-201.

30. DAVIS, J. A study of one hundred sixty-three outstanding communist leaders. *Publ. Amer. Sociol. Soc.*, 1930, **24**, 42-55.

31. DETROIT TEACHERS COLLEGE. How Children Choose Friends. Detroit: Detroit Teachers College, 1929.

32. DRAKE, R. M. A study of leadership. *Charac. & Pers.*, 1944, **12**, 285-289.

33. DUNKERLEY, M. D. A statistical study of leadership among college women. *Stud. Psychol. & Psychiat.*, 1940, **4**, 1-65.

34. EICHLER, G. A. Studies in student leadership. *Penn. St. Coll. Stud. Educ.*, 1934, No. 10.

35. FAUQUIER, W., & GILCHRIST, T. Some aspects of leadership in an institution. *Child Devel.*, 1942, **13**, 55-64.

36. FAY, P. J., & MIDDLETON, W. C. Judgment of leadership from the transmitted voice. *J. Soc. Psychol.*, 1943, **17**, 99-102.

37. FINCH, F. H., & CARROLL, H. A. Gifted children as high school leaders. *J. Genet. Psychol.*, 1932, **41**, 476-481.

38. FLEMMING, E. G. A factor analysis of the personality of high school leaders. *J. Appl. Psychol.*, 1935, **19**, 596-605.

39. GARRISON, K. C. A study of some factors related to leadership in high school. *Peabody J. Educ.*, 1935, **11**, 11-17.

40 GOODENOUGH, F. L. Inter-relationships in the behavior of young children. *Child Devel.*, 1930, **1**, 29-48.

41. GOWIN, E. B. The Executive and His Control of Men. New York: Macmillan, 1915.

42. ————. The Selection and Training of the Business Executive. New York: Macmillan, 1918.

43. GUILFORD, J. P., & GUILFORD, R. B. Personality factors, *D, R, T,* and *A*. *J. Abn. & Soc. Psychol.*, 1939, **34**, 21-36.

44. HANAWALT, N. G., HAMILTON, C. E., & MORRIS, M. L. Level of aspiration in college leaders and non-leaders. *J. Abn. & Soc. Psychol.*, 1934, **38**, 545-548.

45. HANAWALT, N. G., RICHARDSON, H. M., & HAMILTON, R. J. Leadership as related to Bernreuter personality measures: II. An item analysis of responses of college leaders and non-leaders. *J. Soc. Psychol.*, 1943, **17**, 251-267.

46. HANAWALT, N. G., & RICHARDSON, H. M. Leadership as related to the Bernreuter personality measures: IV. An item analysis of responses of adult leaders and non-leaders. *J. Appl. Psychol.*, 1944, **28**, 397-411.

47. HANFMANN, E. Social structure of a group of kindergarten children. *Amer. J. Orthopsychiat.*, 1935, **5**, 407-410.

48. HEATH, C. W., & GREGORY, L. W. What it takes to be an officer. *Infantry J.*, 1946, **58**, 44-45.

49. HENNING, H. Ziele und Möglichkeiten der experimentellen charakterprüfung *Jarbuch d. Charakterol.*, 1929, **6**, 213-273.

50. HOLLINGWORTH, L. S. Gifted Children. New York: Macmillan, 1926.

51. HOOKER, E. R. Leaders in village communities. *Soc. For.*, 1928, **6**, 605-614.

52. HOWELL, C. E. Measurement of leadership. *Sociometry*, 1942, **5**, 163-168.

53. HUNTER, E. C., & JORDAN, A. M. An analysis of qualities associated with leadership among college students. *J. Educ. Psychol.*, 1939, **30**, 497-509.

54. JENKINS, W. O. A review of leadership studies with particular reference to military problems. *Psychol. Bull.*, 1947, **44**, 54-79.

55. JENNINGS, H. H. Leadership and Isolation. New York: Longmans Green, 1943.

56. JONES, A. J. The Education of Youth for Leadership. New York: McGraw-Hill, 1938.

57. KOHS, S. C., & IRLE, K. W. Prophesying Army promotion. *J. Appl. Psychol.*, 1920, **4**, 73-87.

58. LEHMAN, H. C. The creative years in science and literature. *Sci. Mon.*, 1937, **45**, 65-75.

59. ———. Optimum ages for eminent leadership. *Sci. Mon.*, 1942, **54**, 162-175.

60. LEIB, A. Vorstellungen und Urteile von Schülern über Fuhrer in der Schulklasse. *Z. angew, Psychol.*, 1928, **30**, 241-346.

61. LEVI, I. J. Student leadership in elementary and junior high school, and its transfer into senior high school. *J. Educ. Res.*, 1930, **22**, 135-139.

62. LINK, H. C. The definition of social effectiveness and leadership through measurement. *Educ. & Psychol. Meas.*, 1944, **4**, 57-67.

63. LUITHLEN, W. F. Zur Psychologie der Initiative und der Führereigenschaften. *Z. angew. Psychol.*, 1931, **39**, 56-122.

64. MALLER, J. B. Coöperation and competition: An experimental study in motivation. *Teach. Coll. Contr. Educ.*, 1925, No. 384.

65. MALLOY, H. Study of some of the factors underlying the establishment of successful social contacts at the college level. *J. Soc. Psychol.*, 1936, **7**, 205-228.

66. McCANDLESS, B. R. Changing relationships between dominance and social acceptability during group democratization. *Amer. J. Orthopsychiat.*, 1942, **12**, 529-535.

67. McCUEN, T. L. Leadership and intelligence. *Education*, 1929, **50**, 89-95.

68. McGAHAN, F. E. Factors associated with leadership ability. *Texas Outlook*, 1941, **25**, 37-38.

69. MERRIAM, C. E. Four American Party Leaders. New York: Macmillan, 1926.

70. MERRIAM, C. E., & GOSNELL, H. E. The American Party System. New York: Macmillan, 1929.

71. MICHELS, R. Political Parties. New York: Macmillan, 1915.

72. MIDDLETON, W. C. Personality qualities predominant in campus leaders. *J. Soc. Psychol.*, 1941, **13**, 199-201.

73. MILLER, N. E., & DOLLARD, J. Social Learning and Imitation. New Haven: Yale Univ. Press, 1941.

74. MOORE, L. H. Leadership traits of college women. *Sociol. & Soc. Res.*, 1932, **17**, 44-54.

75. ———. Leadership traits of college women. *Sociol. & Soc. Res.*, 1935, **20**, 136-139.

76. NAFE, R. W. A psychological description of leadership. *J. Soc. Psychol.*, 1930, **1**, 248-266.

77. NEWCOMB, T. M. Personality and Social Change. New York: Dryden Press, 1943.

78. NEWSTETTER, W. I., FELDSTEIN, M. J., & NEWCOMB, T. M. Group Adjustment: A Study in Experimental Sociology. Cleveland: Western Reserve Univ., 1938.

79. NUTTING, R. L. Some characteristics of leadership. *Sch. & Soc.*, 1923, **18**, 387-390.

80. PAGE, D. P. Measurement and prediction of leadership. *Amer. J. Sociol.*, 1935, **41**, 31-43.

81. PARTEN, M. B. Leadership among preschool children. *J. Abn. & Soc. Psychol.*, 1933, **27**, 430-440.

82. PARTRIDGE, E. D. Leadership among adolescent boys. *Teach. Coll. Contr. Educ.*, 1934, No. 608

83. PECK, E. M. A study of the personalities of five eminent men. *J. Abn. & Soc. Psychol.*, 1931, **26**, 37-57.

84. PIGORS, P. Leadership and domination among children. *Sociologus*, 1933, **9**, 140-157.

85. PINARD, J. W. Tests of perseveration. *Brit. J. Psychol.*, 1932, **32**, 5-19.

86. PROSH, F. The basis on which students choose their leaders. *Amer. Phys. Educ. Rev.*, 1928, **33**, 265-267.

87. PUFFER, J. A. Boys gangs. *Ped. Sem.*, 1905, **12**, 175-213.

88. REALS, W. H. Leadership in the high school. *Sch. Rev.*, 1938, **46**, 523-531.

89. REININGER, K. Das soziale Verhalten von Schulneulingen. *Wien Arb. pädag. Psychol.*, 1927, **7**, 14.

90. REMMELIN, M. K. Analysis of leaders among high school seniors. *J. Exp. Educ.*, 1938, **6**, 413-422.

91. REYNOLDS, F. J. Factors of leadership among seniors of Central High School, Tulsa, ·Oklahoma. *J. Educ. Res.*, 1944, **37**, 356-361.

92. RICHARDSON, H. M., & HANAWALT, N. G. Leadership as related to Bernreuter personality measures: I. College leadership in extra-curricular activities. *J. Soc. Psychol.*, 1943, **17**, 237-249.

93 ———. Leadership as related to the Bernreuter personality measures: III. Leadership among adult men in vocational and social activities. *J. Appl. Psychol.*, 1944, **28**, 308-317.

94. ROSLOW, S. Nation-wide and local validation of the *PQ* or Personality Quotient test. *J. Appl. Psychol.*, 1940, **24**, 529-539.

95. SCHULER, E. A. A study of the consistency of dominant and submissive behavior in adolescent boys. *J. Genet. Psychol.*, 1935, **46**, 403-432.

96. SHANNON, J. R. The post-school careers of high school leaders and high school scholars. *Sch. Rev.*, 1929, **37**, 656-665.

97. SHELDON, W. H. Social traits and morphologic type. *Person. J.*, 1927, **6**, 47-55.

98. SIMPSON, R. H. A study of those who influence and of those who are influenced in discussion. *Teach. Coll. Contr. Educ.*, 1938, No. 748.

99. SMITH, C. Social selection in community leadership. *Soc. For.*, 1937, **15**, 530-545.

100. SMITH, H. L., & KRUEGER, L. M. A brief summary of literature on leadership. *Bull. Sch. Educ., Indiana Univ.*, 1933, **9**, No. 4.

101. SMITH, M. Comparative study of Indian student leaders and followers. *Soc. For.*, 1935, **13**, 418-426.

102. SMITH, M., & NYSTROM, W. C. A study of social participation and of leisure time of leaders and non-leaders. *J. Appl. Psychol.*, 1937, **21**, 251-259.

103. SOROKIN, P. A. Social Mobility. New York: Harper, 1927.

104. ————. Leaders of labor and radical movements in the United States and foreign countries. *Amer. J. Sociol.*, 1927, **33**, 382-411.

105. SOROKIN, P. A., & ZIMMERMAN, C. C. Farmer leaders in the United States. *Soc. For.*, 1928, **7**, 33-46.

106. SPAULDING, C. B. Types of junior college leaders. *Sociol. & Soc. Res.*, 1934, **18**, 164-168.

107. STARCH, D. How to Develop Your Executive Ability. New York: Harper, 1943.

108. STRAY, H. F. Leadership traits of girls in girls' camps. *Sociol. & Soc. Res.*, 1934, **18**, 241-250.

109. SWARD, K. Temperament and direction of achievement. *J. Soc. Psychol.*, 1933, **4**, 406-429.

110. SWIGART, J. S. A study of the qualities of leadership and administrative qualifications of thirty-eight women executives. Master's thesis, Ohio State Univ., 1936.

111. TAUSSIG, F. W., & JOSLYN, C. S. American Business Leaders. New York: Macmillan, 1932.

112. TERMAN, L. M. A preliminary study in the psychology and pedagogy of leadership. *Ped. Sem.*, 1904, **11**, 413-451.

113. TERMAN, L. M., *et al.* Genetic Studies of genius: I. Mental and Physical Traits of a Thousand Gifted Children. Stanford: Stanford Univ. Press, 1925.

114. THORNDIKE, E. L. The relation between intellect and morality in rulers. *Amer. J. Sociol.*, 1936, **42**, 321-334.

115. THRASHER, F. The Gang: A Study of 1,313 Gangs in Chicago. Chicago: Univ. Chicago Press, 1927.

116. THURSTONE, L. L. A Factorial Study of Perception. Chicago: Univ. Chicago Press, 1944.

117. TRYON, C. M. Evaluations of adolescent personality by adolescents. *Monog. Soc. Res. Child Devel.*, 1939, **4**, No. 4.

118. WARNER, M. L. Influence of mental level in the formation of boys' gangs. *J. Appl. Psychol.*, 1923, **7**, 224-236.

119. WEBB, U. Character and intelligence. *Brit. J. Psychol. Monog.*, 1915, No. 20.

120. WETZEL, W. A. Characteristics of pupil leaders. *Sch. Rev.*, 1932, **40**, 532-534.

121. WILKINS, E. H. On the distribution of extra-curricular activities. *Sch. & Soc.*, 1940, **51**, 651-656.

122. WINSTON, S. Studies in negro leadership: Age and occupational distribution of 1,608 negro leaders. *Amer. J. Sociol.*, 1932, **37**, 595-602.

123. WINSTON, S. Bio-social characteristics of American inventors. *Amer. Soc. Rev.*, 1937, **2**, 837-849.

124. ZELENY, L. Characteristics of group leaders. *Sociol. & Soc. Res.*, 1939, **24**, 140-149.

Personnel Research Board
Ohio State University
19 Derby Hall
Columbus 10, Ohio

Part IV
Behavior Theory

[4]

The Journal of Social Psychology, S. P. S. S. I. Bulletin, 1939, 10, 271-299.

PATTERNS OF AGGRESSIVE BEHAVIOR IN EXPERI-MENTALLY CREATED "SOCIAL CLIMATES"

Child Welfare Research Station, State University of Iowa

KURT LEWIN, RONALD LIPPITT, AND RALPH K. WHITE

A. PROBLEMS AND METHODS

The present report is a preliminary summary on one phase of a series of experimental studies of group life which has as its aim a scientific approach to such questions as the following: What underlies such differing patterns of group behavior as rebellion against authority, persecution of a scapegoat, apathetic submissiveness to authoritarian domination, or attack upon an outgroup? How many differences in subgroup structure, group stratification, and potency of ego-centered and group-centered goals be utilized as criteria for predicting the social resultants of different group atmospheres? Is not democratic group life more pleasant, but authoritarianism more efficient? These are the sorts of questions to which "opinionated" answers are many and varied today, and to which scientific answers, are, on that account, all the more necessary. An experimental approach to the phenomena of group life obviously raises many difficulties of creation and scientific control, but the fruitfulness of the method seems to compensate for the added experimental problems.

In the first experiment Lippitt organized two clubs of 10-year-old children, who engaged in the activity of theatrical mask-making for a period of three months. The same adult leader, changing his philosophy of leadership, led one club in an authoritarian manner and the other club in accordance with democratic techniques, while detailed observations were made by four observers. This study, reported in detail elsewhere (6), suggested more hypotheses than answers and led to a second and more extensive series of experiments by White and Lippitt. Four new clubs of 10-year-old boys were organized, on a voluntary basis as before, the variety of club activities was extended, while four different adult leaders participated. To the variables of authoritarian and democratic procedure was added a third, *"laissez-faire"* or group life without adult participation. Also the behavior of each club was studied in different "social cli-

271

272　　　　　JOURNAL OF SOCIAL PSYCHOLOGY

mates." Every six weeks each group had a new leader with a different technique of leadership, each club having three leaders during the course of the five months of the experimental series. The data on aggressive behavior summarized in this paper are drawn from both series of experiments.

Some of the techniques used for the equating of groups have been described previously (4), but will be summarized here with the improvements in method of the second experiment. Before the clubs were organized the schoolroom group as a whole was studied. Using the sociometric technique developed by Moreno (8) the interpersonal relations of the children, in terms of rejections, friendships, and leadership, were ascertained. Teacher ratings on relevant items of social behavior (e.g., teasing, showing off, obedience, physical energy) were secured, and observations were made on the playground and in the schoolroom by the investigators. The school records supplied information on intellectual status, physical status, and socio-economic background. From the larger number of eager volunteers in each room it was then possible to select from each schoolroom two five-member clubs, which were carefully equated on patterns of interpersonal relationships, intellectual, physical, and socio-economic status, in addition to personality characteristics. The attempt was not to equate the boys within a particular club, but to ensure the same pattern in each group as a whole.

In spite of the methods described above to control by selection some of the more elusive social variables, it was essential to use a number of experimental controls which would help to make the results more clear-cut. First of all, to check on the "individuality" of the club as a whole, each group was studied in different social atmospheres so that it could be compared with itself. A second question raised by the first experiment was that concerning the personality of the leader as a factor in the creating of social atmospheres. The second experiment, with four leaders, makes possible a comparison of the authoritarianism and democracy of four different leaders, and the *"laissez-faire"* method of two different leaders. In two cases it is also possbile to compare the same atmosphere, created by two different leaders with the same club.

One other type of control seemed very important, the nature of the club activity, and the physical setting. Using the same clubrooms (two clubs met at the same time in adjacent but distinctly

KURT LEWIN, RONALD LIPPITT, AND RALPH K. WHITE　273

separate areas of the same large room) seemed to answer the latter problem, but the question of activity was more complex. The following technique was developed: a list of activities which were of interest to all the children was assembled (e.g., mask-making,

TABLE 1

Authoritarian	Democratic	*Laissez-faire*
1. All determination of policy by the leader.	1. All policies a matter of group discussion and decision, encouraged and assisted by the leader.	1. Complete freedom for group or individual decision, without any leader participation.
2. Techniques and activity steps dictated by the authority, one at a time, so that future steps were always uncertain to a large degree.	2. Activity perspective gained during first discussion period. General steps to group goal sketched, and where technical advice was needed the leader suggested two or three alternative procedures from which choice could be made.	2. Various materials supplied by the leader, who made it clear that he would supply information when asked. He took no other part in work discussions.
3. The leader usually dictated the particular work task and work companions of each member.	3. The members were free to work with whomever they chose, and the division of tasks was left up to the group.	3. Complete nonparticipation by leader.
4. The dominator was "personal" in his praise and criticism of the work of each member, but remained aloof from active group participation except when demonstrating. He was friendly or impersonal rather than openly hostile.	4. The leader was "objective" or "fact-minded" in his praise and criticism, and tried to be a regular group member in spirit without doing too much of the work.	4. Very infrequent comments on member activities unless questioned, and no attempt to participate or interfere with the course of events.

mural painting, soap carving, model airplane construction, etc.). Meeting first, in chronological time, the democratic groups used these possibilities as the basis for discussion and voted upon their club activity. The authoritarian leaders were then ready, as their clubs met, to launch the same activity without choice by the members. The *"laissez-faire"* groups were acquainted with the variety of materials which were available, but they were not otherwise influenced in their choice of activity; in their case, consequently, the activity factor could not be completely controlled.

The contrasting methods of the leaders in creating the three types of group atmosphere may be briefly summarized as in Table 1.

It should be clear that due to the voluntary nature of the group participation, and the coöperation of the parents and school systems, no radically autocratic methods (e.g., use of threats, instilling fear, etc.) were used. Fairly congenial extra-club relationships were maintained with each member by the leader.

The kinds of data collected during the course of the experiments may be classed roughly as: (*a*) pre-club data, described above in relation to the problem of equating the groups; (*b*) observations of behavior in the experimental situation; and (*c*) extra-club information.

Observations of club behavior consisted of:

(*a*). A quantitative running account of the social interactions of the five children and the leader, in terms of symbols for directive, compliant, and objective (fact-minded) approaches and responses, including a category of purposeful refusal to respond to a social approach.

(*b*). A minute by minute group structure analysis giving a record of: activity subgroupings, the activity goal of each subgroup was initiated by the leader or spontaneously formed by the children, and ratings on degree of unity of each subgrouping.

(*c*). An interpretive running account of significant member actions, and changes in dynamics of the group as a whole.

(*d*). Continuous stenographic records of all conversation.

(*e*). An interpretive running account of inter-club relationships.

(*f*). An "impressionistic" write-up by the leader as to what he saw and felt from within the group atmosphere during each meeting.

(*g*). Comments by guest observers.

(*h*). Movie records of several segments of club life.

All of these observations (except *f, g,* and *h*) were synchronized at minute intervals so that side by side they furnish a rather complete cross sectional picture of the ongoing life of the group. The major purpose of this experiment in methodology of observation was to record as fully and with as much insight as possible the total behavior of the group, a distinct break away from the usual procedure of recording only certain pre-determined symptoms of behavior. The second aim was to ascertain whether data collected by this method could be fruitfully analyzed from both a sociological and psychological point of view (5).

Extra-club information is of the following types:

(*a*). Interviews with each child by a friendly "non-club" person during each transition period (from one kind of group atmosphere and leader to another) and at the end of the experiment, concerning such items as comparison of present club leader with previous ones, with the teacher, and with parents; opinions on club activities; how the club could be run better; who were the best and poorest club members; what an ideal club leader would be like, etc.

(*b*). Interviews with the parents by the investigators, concentrating on kinds of discipline used in the home, status of the child in the family group (relations with siblings, etc.), personality ratings on the same scale used by the teachers, discussion of child's attitude toward the club, school, and other group activities.

(*c*). Talks with the teachers concerning the transfer to the schoolroom, of behavior patterns acquired in the club.

(*d*). Administration of a Rorschach test to each club member.

(*e*). Conversations with the children during two summer hikes arranged after the experiment was over.

These data were gathered with a view to correlating the individual pattern of behavior in the club situation with the types of group membership which existed outside the experiment, and with the more or less stable individual personality structure. The individual differences in "social plasticity" seem to be rather striking.

Two other points of experimental technique seem of interest. The first concerns the introduction of observers into the club situation. In Lippitt's first experiment it was found that four observers grouped around a table in a physically separated part of the club room attracted virtually no attention if it was explained at the first meeting that "those are some people interested in learning how a mask-making club goes; they have plenty to do so they won't bother us and we won't bother them." In the second experiment the arrangement was even more advantageous and seemed to make for equally unselfconscious behavior on the part of the clubs. In this set-up the lighting arrangement was such that the observers were grouped behind a low burlap wall in a darkly shaded area, and seemed "not to exist at all" as far as the children and leaders were concerned.

The second point of interest is the development of a number of "group test" situations, which aided greatly in getting at the actual social dynamics of a given group atmosphere. One test used systematically was for the leader to leave the room on business during the course of the club meeting, so that the "social pressure" factor could be analyzed more realistically. Another practice was for the leader to arrive a few minutes late so that the observers could record the individual and "atmospheric" differences in spontaneous work initiation and work perspective. A third fruitful technique was that of having a stranger (a graduate student who played the rôle of a janitor or electrician) enter the club situation and criticize the group's work efforts. A rather dramatic picture of the results of this type of situation may be seen in Figures 5 and 6. Further variations of such experimental manipulations are being utilized in a research now in progress.

B. RESULTS

The analysis of the results from the second experiment is now proceeding in various directions, following two main trends: (*a*) interpretation of sociological or "group-centered" data; (*b*) interpretation of psychological or "individual-centered" data. The sociological approach includes such analyses as differences in volume of social interaction related to social atmosphere, nature of club activity, outgroup relationship, differences in pattern of interaction related to outgroup and ingroup orientation, atmosphere differences in leadergroup relationship, effect upon group structure pattern of social atmosphere and types of activity, group differences in language behavior, etc. The psychological approach includes such analyses as relation of home background to pattern of club behavior, range of variation of member behavior in different types of social atmos-

KURT LEWIN, RONALD LIPPITT, AND RALPH K. WHITE   277

phere, patterns of individual reaction to atmosphere transitions in relation to case history data, correlation between position in group stratification and pattern of social action, etc. In this paper will be presented only certain data from the partially completed general analysis which are relevant to the dynamics of individual and group aggression.

We might first recall one or two of the most striking results of the first experiment (6). As the club meetings progressed the authoritarian club members developed a pattern of aggressive domination toward one another, and their relation to the leader was one of submission or of persistent demands for attention. The interactions in the democratic club were more spontaneous, more fact-minded, and friendly. Relations to the leader were free and on an "equality basis." Comparing the two groups on the one item of overt hostility the authoritarian group was surprisingly more aggressive, the ratio being 40 to 1. Comparing a constellation of "ego-involved" types of language behavior (e.g., hostile, resistant, demands for attention, hostile criticism, expression of competition) with a group of objective or "nonemotive" behaviors, it was found that in the authoritarian group 73 per cent of the analyzed language

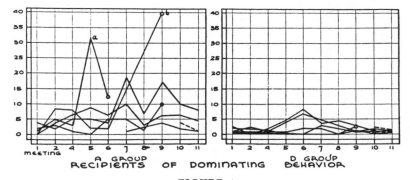

FIGURE 1

THE EMERGENCE OF SCAPEGOATS IN AN AUTOCRATIC ATMOSPHERE
(LIPPITT, 1937)

The curves (which indicate the amount of aggression directed against each individual) show a much lower general level of dominating behavior in the democratic (*D*) than in the autocratic (*A*) group. Twice during the meetings of the authoritarian club the aggression of four members was focused upon the fifth (*a* and *b*). In both cases the scapegoat dropped out of the group immediately or soon afterwards.

behavior was of the "ego-involved" type as compared to 31 per cent in the democratic club. Into the objective category went 69 per cent of the behavior of the democratic group as compared to 37 per cent of the language activities of the authoritarian group.

A second type of data related to the dynamics of aggression as it existed in the first experiment may be seen in Figure 1. Twice during the course of the meetings of the authoritarian club the situation shifted from one of mutual aggression between all members to one of concentrated aggression toward one member by the other four. In both cases the lowered status of a scapegoat position was so acutely unpleasant that the member left the group, rationalizing his break from the club by such remarks as, "The doctor says my eyes are so bad I'll have to play outdoors in the sunshine instead of coming to club meetings." Interestingly enough the two members who were singled out for persecution had been rated by the teachers as the two leaders in the group, one of them scoring second in popularity by the sociometric technique, as well as being physically the strongest. After the emergence of both scapegoats, there was a rather brief rise in friendly coöperative behavior between the other members of the group.

In the second experiment (see previous discussion, p. 4) there were five democratic, five autocratic, and two *"laissez-faire"* atmospheres. The fact that the leaders were successful in modifying their behavior to correspond to these three philosophies of leadership is clear on the basis of several quantitative indices. For instance, the ratio of "directive" to "compliant" behavior on the part of the autocratic leaders was 63 to 1; on the part of the democratic leaders it was 1.1 to 1. The total amount of leader participation was less than half as great in *"laissez-faire"* as in either autocracy or democracy.

The data on aggression averages in these three atmospheres are summarized in Figures 2, 3, and 4. All of them indicate average amounts of aggression per 50-minute, five-member club meeting. They represent behavior records, as recorded by the interaction observer, and include all social actions, both verbal and physical, which he designated as "hostile" or "joking hostile." Figure 2 shows especially the bimodal character of the aggression averages in autocracy; four of the five autocracies had an extremely low level of aggression, and the fifth had an extremely high one. For com-

KURT LEWIN, RONALD LIPPITT, AND RALPH K. WHITE   279

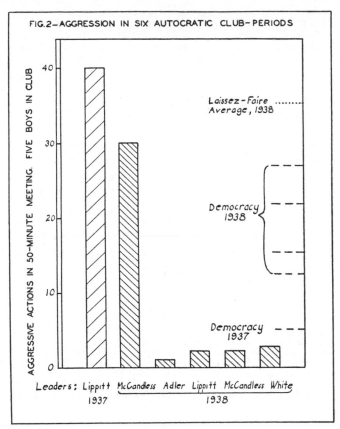

FIGURE 2

AGGRESSION IN AUTOCRACY

The amount of aggression is either very great or very small compared with aggression in democracy.

parison, a sixth bar has been added to represent aggression in Lippitt's 1937 experiment, computed on the same basis. It is obviously comparable with the single case of exceptionally aggressive behavior in the 1938 experiment. For comparison, also, four lines have been added which indicate the aggression level in the two *laissez-faire* groups, in the four 1938 democracies, and in Lippitt's 1937 democra-

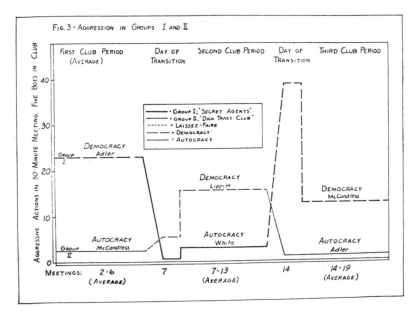

FIGURE 3

THE SAME GROUP IN DIFFERENT ATMOSPHERES

In each group, aggression was at a medium level in democracy and at a very low level in autocracy. Note that the leaders in the third period were the same as in the first, but reversed. Note also the sharp rise of aggression in one group on the day of transition to democracy. Group I shows "release of tension" on the first day of freedom (14) after apathetic autocracy. The name of the leader is indicated below that of the atmosphere.

cy. It can be seen that two of the six autocracies are above the entire range of democracies, and are in this respect comparable with the two *laissez-faire* groups. The other four autocracies are at the opposite extreme, below the entire range of the democracies.

Figures 3 and 4 show especially the character of the experimental controls. Together, they show how each of four groups was carried through three different periods with three different adult leaders. The relative importance of the deliberately created social atmosphere, as compared with either the personality make-up of the group or the personality of the adult leader, can be estimated from the character of these curves. It is clear that the same group usually changes markedly, and sometimes to an extreme degree, when it is changed to a new atmosphere under a different leader.   In such transitions the factor of group personnel is held relatively constant, while the factors of leader personality and social atmosphere are varied.   In addition, the factor of leader personality was systematically varied, as can be seen if the four curves are compared with each other.   Each of the four leaders played the rôle of a democratic leader at least once; also each played the rôle of an autocrat at least once; two of them (Adler and White) played in addition the rôle of bystander in a *"laissez-faire"* group.   One leader (Lippitt) was democratic with two different groups; and one (Mc-Candless) was autocratic with two different groups.   Through this systematic variation of both club personnel and leader's personality, the effects of the deliberately created social atmosphere (autocracy, democracy, *laissez-faire*) stand out more clearly and more reliably than would otherwise be possible.

In Figure 3, for instance, the two curves both tell the same story: a moderate amount of aggression in democracy and an abnormally small amount in autocracy, regardless of the personality of the leader (note that the rôles of Lippitt and McCandless were reversed, with each playing once the rôle of autocrat and once the rôle of democratic leader), and regardless of the personnel of the group itself (note that the curves cross once when the atmospheres are reversed, and cross back again when the atmospheres return to what they were at the beginning).   In Figure 4, the two *laissez-faire* atmospheres give very high levels of aggression although different groups and different leaders are involved.   The most extreme change of behavior recorded in any group occurred when Group IV was changed from autocracy (in which it had shown the apathetic reaction) to *laissez-faire*.   One of the autocratic groups (Figure 4) reacted apathetically, the other very aggressively.   The aggressiveness of Group III may be due to the personalities of the boys, or to the fact that they had just previously "run wild" in *laissez-faire*.

The average number of aggressve actions per meeting in the different atmospheres was as follows:

Laissez-faire	38
Autocracy (aggressive reaction)	30
Democracy	20
Autocracy (apathetic reaction)	2

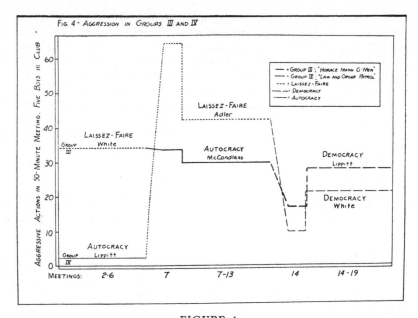

FIGURE 4

THE SAME GROUP IN DIFFERENT ATMOSPHERES

Group IV shows changes to the levels typical for each atmosphere. It shows also the "release of tension" on the first day of freedom (7) after apathetic autocracy. Group III seemed resistant to change; it was relatively aggressive even in democracy.

Critical ratios for these comparisons have not yet been computed. The data are comparable, however, with Lippitt's 1937 data, in which the critical ratios for the more important indices ranged between 4.5 and 7.5.

In the interpretation of these data it is natural to ask: Why are the results for autocracy paradoxical? Why is the reaction to autocracy sometimes very aggressive, with much rebellion or persecution of scapegoats, and sometimes very nonaggressive? Are the underlying dynamics in these two cases as different as the surface behavior? The high level of aggression in some autocracies has often been interpreted mainly in terms of tension, which presumably results from frustration of individual goals. Is it, then, an indication of non-frustration when the aggression level in some other autocracies is found to be extremely low?

Four lines of evidence in our experiments indicate that this is not the case, and that the low level of aggression in the apathetic autocracies is not due to lack of frustration.

First of all, there are the sudden outbursts of aggression which occurred on the days of transition from a repressed autocratic atmosphere to the much freer atmosphere of democracy or *laissez-faire*. Two of these are well illustrated in Figure 4. The boys behaved just as if they had previously been in a state of bottled-up tension, which could not show itself overtly as long as the repressive influence of the autocrat was felt, but which burst out unmistakably when that pressure was removed.

A second and very similar type of evidence can be obtained from the records on the days when the leader left the room for 10 or 15 minutes. In the three other atmospheres (*laissez-faire*, aggressive autocracy, and democracy) the aggression level did not rise when the leader left the room. In the apathetic autocracies, however, the level of aggression rises very rapidly to 10 times its former level. These data should not be overstressed, because aggression even then does not rise to a level significantly above that of the other atmospheres. It is so extremely low in the apathetic atmosphere that even multiplication by 10 does not produce what could be called a high level of aggression. (The effect of the leader's absence is shown more significantly in a deterioration of work than in an outburst of aggression.) Nevertheless, the rapid disappearance of apathy when the leader goes out shows clearly that it was due to the repressive influence of the leader rather than to any particular absence of frustration. In this connection it should be added that the autocratic leader never forbade aggression. His "repressive influence" was not a prohibition created by explicit command but a sort of generalized inhibition or restraining force.

In the third place, there are the judgments of observers who found themselves using such terms as "dull," "lifeless," "submissive," "repressed," and "apathetic" in describing the nonaggressive reaction to autocracy. There was little smiling, joking, freedom of movement, freedom of initiating new projects, etc.; talk was largely confined to the immediate activity in progress, and bodily tension was often manifested. Moving pictures tell the same story. The impression created was not one of acute discontent, by any means, and the activities themselves were apparently enjoyable enough so that the net result for most of the boys was more pleasant than unpleasant. Nevertheless, they could not be described as genuinely contented.

The fourth and perhaps the most convincing indication of the existence of frustration in these atmospheres is the testimony of the boys themselves. They were individually interviewed, just before each day of transition to a new atmosphere, and again at the end of the whole experiment. The interviewing was done by an adult who had not served as a leader in the boy's own group. On the whole good rapport was achieved, and the boys talked rather freely, comparing the three leaders under whom their club had been conducted. (For them it was a question of comparing leaders they liked or did not like, as they were unaware of the deliberate change in the behavior of the same leader from one atmosphere to another or of the nature of the experiment.) With surprising unanimity the boys agreed in a relative dislike for their autocratic leader regardless of his individual personality. Nineteen of the 20 boys liked their leader in democracy better than their leader in autocracy. The twentieth boy, as it happened, was the son of an army officer (the only one in the group), and consciously put a high value upon strict discipline. As he expressed it, the autocratic leader *"was the strictest, and I like that a lot."* The other two leaders *"let us go ahead and fight, and that isn't good."* For the other 19, strictness was not necessarily a virtue, their description of the autocrat being that he was *"too strict."* Typical comments about the autocrat were: *"he didn't let us do what we wanted to do"; "he wouldn't let us go behind the burlap"; "he was all right mostly—sort of dictator-like"; "we just had to do things; he wanted us to get it done in a hurry"; "he made us make masks, and the boys didn't like that"; "the other two guys suggested and we could do it or not, but not with him"; "we didn't have any fun with him—we didn't have any fights."* Typical comments about the democratic leader were: *"he was a good sport, worked along with us and thinks of things just like we do"; "he never did try to be the boss, but we always had plenty to do"; "just the right combination—nothing I didn't like about him"; "we all liked him; he let us tear down the burlap and everything."* These comments were almost uniformly dependent upon the rôle played by the leader, and were exactly reversed when he played a different rôle.

KURT LEWIN, RONALD LIPPITT, AND RALPH K. WHITE   285

As between the leaders in autocracy and *"laissez-faire,"* the preference was for the *"laissez-faire"* leader in seven cases out of ten.   The three boys who preferred the autocrat made such comments about the *"laissez-faire"* leader as: *"he was too easy-going"; "he had too few things for us to do"; "he let us figure things out too much";* in contrast the autocrat *"told us what to do, and we had something to do all the time."*   For the other seven, even disorder was preferable to rigidity: *"we could do what we pleased with him"; "he wasn't strict at all."*

Another form of aggression was outgroup hostility, as manifested especially in two "wars" between clubs meeting in the same large room at the same time.   Both wars seemed to be mainly in a spirit of play.   They were much more like snowball fights than serious conflicts.   (This is one more reason why in this case one should be

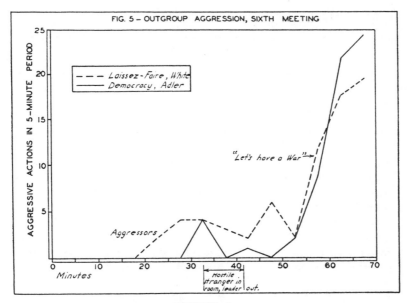

FIGURE 5

CONFLICT BETWEEN GROUPS AFTER INTRUSION OF HOSTILE STRANGER

After the stranger left, strong hostility developed between the two groups. Before the major conflict, minor hostilities had already occurred, with one or two members of the *laissez-faire* group playing the rôle of aggressors.

286   JOURNAL OF SOCIAL PSYCHOLOGY

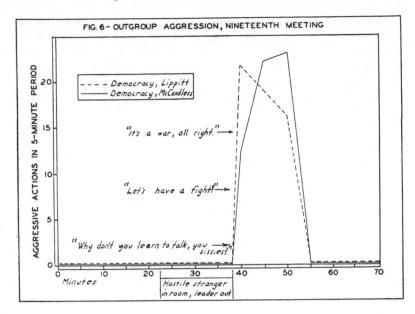

FIGURE 6

CONFLICT BETWEEN GROUPS AFTER INTRUSION OF HOSTILE STRANGER

The intrusion of a hostile stranger was followed by intergroup conflict (as in Figure 5). In this case the hostilities began suddenly, rising within four minutes almost to their maximum level.

cautious in comparing adult political phenomena directly with our data on small groups of children.) Our two small "wars" are interesting in their own right, however, especially since the same general constellation of factors seemed to be operating in both cases.

The curves of rising hostility, computed for five-minute intervals, are shown in Figures 5 and 6. From these curves it can be seen that the first "war" started gradually, with a long period of minor bickering and name calling, followed by a much steeper gradient of increasing hostility. The overt hostilities consisted of throwing water, small pieces of clay (which nearly always missed their mark), and sometimes water color paint, flicked from the end of a long paint brush. No one was hurt. The second conflict (Figure 6) began much more suddenly. Name calling began in the first minute after the "hostile stranger" left the room, and almost immediately the boys seemed to remember their previous conflict and to wish a repetition of it. Beginning with verbal aggression such as, *"Why don't you learn to talk, you sissies?"* they passed within three minutes to throwing small pieces of soap (small pieces of soap statuettes, which they had carved, were lying about), and within five minutes nearly all the boys on both sides were wholeheartedly participating. This difference in steepness of the hostility gradient was perhaps due in part to a higher level of tension or to weaker restraining forces on the later occasion, but it seemed to be due also to a cognitive difference. On the later occasion the pattern of intergroup conflict had been established; it was, by that time, a part of the boys' "cognitive structure"—a clearly defined region which they could enter or not as they chose; and since they had found the first "war" to be very pleasantly exciting, they readily and quickly entered the same region again when the general psychological situation was conducive to conflict. In this connection it may be noted that the second conflict was labelled verbally almost immediately, while the first one was not labelled until it was already well under way. On the first occasion the shout, *"Let's have a war!"* went up long after the minor hostilities had begun; on the second accasion, one boy shouted, *"Let's have a fight,"* only two minutes after the name calling began, and another one legalized it two minutes later with the words, *"It's a war all right."*

Certain similarities between the two days of conflict suggest some very tentative hypotheses as to the psychological factors conducive to this sort of conflict. In the first place, both occurred on days when, with the adult leader absent, a hostile stranger had been in the room and had criticized the work which the boys were doing. This had been deliberately planned as a "test situation"; a graduate student, playing the rôle of a janitor or an electrician, was the hostile stranger. It may be doubtful whether or not the term "substitute hate object" is an appropriate one here; but there was no question in the observers' minds that in both cases the intrusion of the stranger tended to disorganize the regular play activities of the clubs and to build up a tense, restless psychological condition which was conducive to intergroup conflict. In the second place, both conflicts started when no respected adult was present. In the first one the main aggressors were unquestionably the *laissez-faire* group (see Figure 5). Their leader was physically present at the time, but he was psychologically unimportant. The second conflict began when the leaders on both sides were out of the room, and by the time the leaders returned, it had gathered great momentum. In the third place, both conflicts occurred at a time when there was no absorbing group activity as an alternative. The first one began at a time when the members of the *laissez-faire* group seemed unusually bored and dissatisfied with their own lack of solid accomplishment. The second one began after the boys had become somewhat bored with their soap carving, and after this individualistic activity had been further disrupted by the criticisms of the stranger.

The free direct expression of aggression by the "wars" following frustration in the *laissez-faire* and democratic situations offers a contrast to several other patterns of expression which were observed in some of the authoritarian situations. These types of behavior might be briefly labelled: (*a*) a "strike"; (*b*) rebellious acts; (*c*) reciprocal aggression among all members; (*d*) scapegoat attack; (*e*) release behavior after a decrease in leader pressure; (*f*) aggression against impersonal "substitute hate objects."

Both the "strike" and symptoms of rebellious action occurred in the aggressive type of autocracy. About the middle of the series of six meetings the club members went to their teacher with a letter of resignation signed by four of them. They asked their teacher to give this to the leader when he came to get them after school. The teacher refused to act as a go-between, suggesting that the boys go to the leader directly, but when he appeared after school, courage seemed to wane and they all went to the meeting as usual. Overt rebellious acts were of the following nature: breaking a rule by carving on the posts in the clubroom (while casting sidelong glances at the leader), deliberately walking behind the burlap walls of the clubroom without permission (mentioned to an interviewer), leaving the club meeting early, and pretending not to hear when spoken to by the leader. The third and fourth kinds of behavior were also typical of aggressive authoritarianism and have been mentioned in describing the first experiment during which two scapegoats emerged. As has been mentioned, changes in amount of aggression while the leader was out, and days of transition to a freer atmosphere were especially good indicators of the existence of unexpressed tension in the apathetic autocracies.

KURT LEWIN, RONALD LIPPITT, AND RALPH K. WHITE   289

Two very interesting examples of what we have tentatively called "release behavior through an impersonal substitute hate object" are worthy of description. During the eleventh meeting of the first experiment the authoritarian group was given a chance to indicate by secret ballot whether they would like the club to stop or continue for several more meetings. We may go to an observer's record for further comments:

> Peculiar actions follow the leader's announcement that because of the vote there will be no more meetings after today. The leader asks *RO* and *J* to put the paper on the floor as usual. They put it down and then run and jump on it time and again in a wild manner. The group masks are divided among the members and *J* immediately begins to throw his around violently, pretending to jump on it. He throws it down again and again, laughing. *R* wants to know if it won't break, then starts to throw his down too. Later *J* and *RO* chase each other around the room wildly with streamers of towelling. . . .

Rather clearly the work products of this authoritarian atmosphere seemed to be the objects of aggressive attack rather than prideful ownership.

During a last meeting of the second experiment a rather similar burst of behavior occurred in one of the democratic groups. The group was highly involved in an activity of making an oil painting on glass. While the leader was out for a short time (by arrangement) a student in the janitor rôle came in to sweep. From the running accountist's record of the 20-second minute we find,

> He is making dirt fly and sweeping it toward the group. They all begin to cough but don't move from their work.

Several minutes later we find the comment,

> Janitor has almost swept them away, but still no hostile response. The project seems to have a very high valence.

Five minutes later the janitor had gotten them out of their chairs in order to sweep, then

> the janitor accidentally knocks a piece of their glass on the floor. They all yell and *R* makes as if to throw something at him. *F* says that if the leader were here he would beat up the janitor.

Five minutes later, after a number of comments criticizing the art work of the club, the janitor left. The members dropped their work completely, climbed the rafters and made considerable noise. On the thirty-sixth minute we find,

> R comes down from the rafter and begins to complain about the janitor, L joins him and they all complain bitterly and loudly.

Within three minutes the group began to destroy a large wooden sign upon which they had painted the club name. Such comments as this appear in the running account,

> F is wielding two hammers at once. . . . R is busy pulling out all the nails. . . . They are excited. . . . F knocks the first hole through it. . . . R tries to caution F for a minute, and then gets busy himself . . . their unexpressed aggression toward the janitor is taking a violent outlet . . . they are all very serious and vicious about the destruction of the sign . . . they seem to be getting a great deal of "pure animal pleasure" of the pillage.

The meeting ended with three or four minutes of pleasant conversation.

C. INTERPRETIVE COMMENTS

From the many theoretical problems involved we should like to discuss but one, namely, the problem of aggression and apathy. Even here we wish to show the complexity of the problem and its possible attack from a field theoretical point of view rather than to set forth a definite theory.

It is not easy to say what aggression is, that is, if one is not satisfied with mere verbal definition. One important aspect obviously is that one group or an individual within a group turns against another group (or individual). In case these groups are subgroups of one original group, it can be called aggression *within a group,* otherwise aggression *against an outgroup.*

Both kinds of aggression occurred in our experiments. All of these aggressions were spontaneous in character. In other words, it was not a situation where a group of people are ordered by a politically dominating power (like the state) to indulge in a certain type of directed activity called war. On the whole the aggression was the outcome of the momentary emotional situation, although

KURT LEWIN, RONALD LIPPITT, AND RALPH K. WHITE 291

in two cases the aggressions had definitely the character of a fight of one group against another group and showed a certain amount of coöperative organization within each group.

It is necessary to mention four points which seem to play a dominant rôle in the spontaneous aggressions: tension, the space of free movement, rigidity of group structure, and the style of living (culture).

1. *Tension*

An instance where tension was created by *annoying* experiences occurred when the group work was criticized by a stranger (janitor). There were two cases where fighting broke out immediately afterwards.

In the autocratic atmosphere the behavior of the leader probably annoyed the children considerably (to judge from the interviews reported above).

In addition, there were six times as many directing approaches to an individual by the leader in autocracy than in democracy (Figure 7). It is probably fair to assume that the bombardment

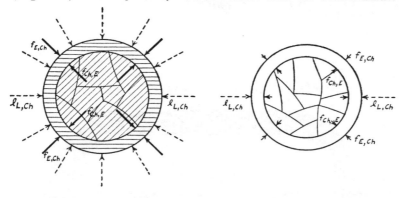

CHILD IN AUTOCRACY   CHILD IN DEMOCRACY

FIGURE 7

LEADER PRESSURE AND CHILD TENSION

In the authoritarian situation the leader makes six times as many directing approaches ($l_{L,Ch}$) to the child member as in the democratic situation. This creates social pressure (equivalent to forces $f_{E,Ch}$ of the environment on the child) and therefore a higher state of tension in the child in the autocratic group; this tension demands some sort of outlet toward the environment (equivalent to forces $f_{Ch,E}$).

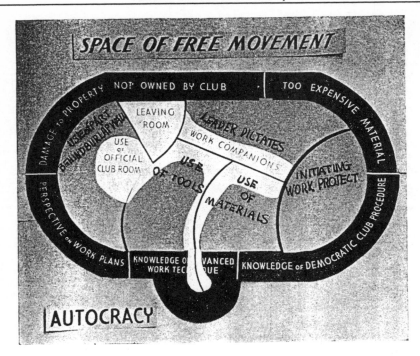

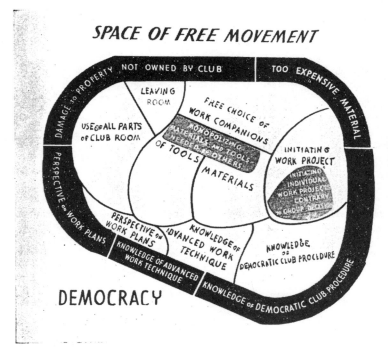

FIGURES 8 AND 9

SPACE OF FREE MOVEMENT IN AUTOCRACY AND DEMOCRACY

In the autocratic situation the space of free movement (white) was originally bounded only by the limitation in ability and knowledge (black) of the
members, but was soon limited much further by the social influence of
the leader (gray). In democracy the space was increased with the help
of the leader.

with such frequent ascendant approaches is equivalent to higher *pressure* and that this pressure created a higher tension.

2. *Narrow Space of Free Movement as a Source of Tension*

On the whole, even more important than this single annoying experience was the general atmosphere of the situation. Experiments in individual psychology (1) seemed to indicate that lack of space of free movement is equivalent to higher pressure; both conditions seem to create tension. This seemed particularly true if an originally larger space was narrowed down (one is reminded here of the physical tension created by decreasing volume, although one should not overstress the analogy).

Our experiments seemed to indicate that a similar relation between the narrow space of free movement and high tension holds also in regard to groups. The space of free movement in autocracy was smaller in relation to the activities permitted and the social status which could be reached (Figures 8 and 9). In *laissez-faire,* contrary to expectations, the space of free movement was not larger but smaller than in democracy, partly because of the lack of time perspective and partly because of the interference of the work of one individual with the activities of his fellows.

3. *Aggression as the Effect of Tension*

The annoying occurrences, the pressure applied by the leader, and the lack of space of free movement, are three basic facts which brought up a higher tension. Our experiments indicate that this higher tension might suffice to create aggression. This seems to be of theoretical importance; obviously some aggressive acts can be viewed mainly as a kind of "purposive" action (for instance, to destroy a danger), and one might ask whether or not this component is an essential part in the causation of any aggression. In our experiments, the two wars between the two outgroups can hardly be classified in this way. They seemed to be rather clear cases where aggression was "emotional expression" of an underlying tension.

4. *Rigidity of Group Structure*

However, to understand aggression one will have to realize that tension is only one of the factors which determine whether or not an aggressive action will take place. The building up of tension

294   JOURNAL OF SOCIAL PSYCHOLOGY

can be said to be equivalent to the creation of a certain type of need which might express itself in aggressive action. Tension sets up the driving force (2) for the aggression (in the two situations with which we are dealing). However, whether these driving forces actually lead to aggression or to some other behavior, for instance that of leaving the group, depends on additional characteristics of the situation as a whole. One of these seems to be the rigidity of the social position of the person within the group.

Aggression within a group can be viewed as a process by which one part of the group sets itself in opposition to another part of the group, in this way breaking the unity of the group. Of course, this separation is only of a certain degree.

In other words, if M indicates a member or subgroup and Gr the whole group, an aggression involves a force acting on the subgroup in the direction away from the main group $(f_{M,-Gr})$ or other part of the subgroup. From this it should follow theoretically

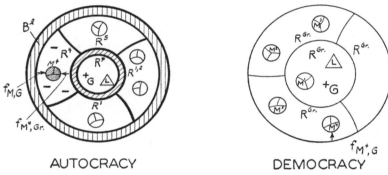

AUTOCRACY   DEMOCRACY

FIGURE 10

RIGIDITY OF GROUP STRUCTURE AS A TENSION FACTOR

In autocracy where each member or subgroup $(M^1, M^2 \ldots M^5)$ has a circumscribed region of activity $(R^1, R^2 \ldots R^5)$, and especially where the central regions of group life (policy formation R^p) are inaccessible to most members, rigid barriers (B) to own goals (G) continually frustrate members' efforts. The member's own position in the group structure (R^4) therefore acquires a negative valence, usually creating a force away from group membership $(f_{M^4,-Gr})$. But in rigid group structures a restraining barrier (B^l) keeps members or subgroups from leaving until a very high state of tension develops.

In democracy where all group regions (R^{Gr}) are accessible to all members $(M^1, M^2 \ldots M^5)$, their own goals (G) are more easily attained and no such frustrating situation develops.

KURT LEWIN, RONALD LIPPITT, AND RALPH K. WHITE   295

that if a subgroup can easily locomote in the direction away from the group it will do so in case this force shows any significant strength. In other words, a strong tension and an actual aggression will be built up only in case there exist forces which hinder the subgroup from leaving the group (Figure 10).

Cultural anthropology gives examples which might be interpreted from this angle. The Arapesh (7), for instance, are living in a society where everyone is a member of a great variety of different groups and seems to shift easily from one group to another; it is a society without rigidly fixed social position. The fact that they show extremely little aggression might well be linked with this lack of rigid social structure.

Another example might be seen in the fact that adolescents who have been kept within the family probably show more aggression; in other words, the more rigid the family structure the more difficult it is for them to move from childhood to adulthood.

An additional example is the well-known fact that narrow family ties which serve to make it difficult for husband and wife to leave each other may make aggression between them particularly violent.

In our experiment, autocracy provided a much more rigid social group than democracy. It was particularly difficult for the members of an autocracy to change their social status (3). On the other hand, in both groups the member did not like to leave the group as a whole because of the interest in the work project and the feeling of responsibility to the adult leader.

On the whole, then, the rigidity of the group will function as a restraining force (2) against locomotion away from the group, or from the position within the group. Sufficient strength of this restraining force seems to be one of the conditions for the building up of a tension which is sufficiently high to lead to aggression.

It can be seen easily that the barriers limiting the space of free movement may have a similar function. We mentioned above, that a narrow space of free movement seems to be equivalent to pressure, and, in this way, creates tension. At the same time, the barriers prevent locomotion, thus providing the restraining forces necessary for building up higher tension.

It was already mentioned that these restraining forces are particularly strong in our autocratic group (Figure 10).

5. *Style of Living (Culture)*

Whether or not a given amount of tension and given restraining forces will cause a person to become aggressive depends finally upon the particular patterns of action which are customarily used in the culture in which he lives. The different styles of living can be viewed as different ways a given problem is usually solved. A person living in a culture where a show of dominance is "the thing to do" under certain conditions will hardly think of any other way in which the solution of this problem may be approached. Such social patterns are comparable to "habits." Indeed, individual habits as well as cultural patterns have dynamically the character of restraining forces against leaving the paths determined by these patterns. In addition, they determine the cognitive structure which a given situation is likely to have for a given individual.

For the problem of aggression, this cultural pattern, determined by the group in which an individual lives and by his past history, is of great importance. It determines under what conditions aggression will be, for the individual concerned, the "distinguished path"

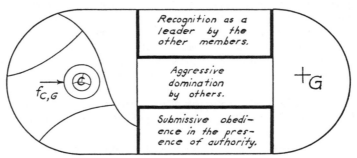

FIGURE 11

DIFFERENT STYLES OF LIVING AS REPRESENTED BY DIFFERENT DISTINGUISHED
PATHS (AGGRESSIVE AUTOCRACY)

The goal (G) of maximum social status and space of free movement can be reached by one or more of several procedures depending on actual possibilities and the prevailing mode of behavior in that group. In our "experimentally created cultures," the distinguished path to G was for a child (C) in aggressive autocracy that of aggressive domination of other members. In a similar situation the distinguished path for a member of democratic groups seemed to be that of gaining voluntary recognition of the other members as a leader through work and social efforts. In the situation of apathetic authoritarianism the path seemed to be that of submissive obedience to authority, which might win praise from the leader.

to the goal (2). It determines, furthermore, how easily a situation will show for him a cognitive structure where aggression appears to be one possible path for his action (Figure 11).

The factors named are sufficient to warn against any "one-factor" theory of aggression. Here, as in regard to any other behavior, it is the specific constellation of the field as a whole that determines whether or not aggression will occur. In every case one has to consider both the driving and the restraining forces and the cognitive structure of the field. Such a field theoretical approach seems to be rather arduous. On the other hand, only in this way will one be able to understand for instance the paradox of behavior that autocracy may lead either to aggression or to apathy. It was stated that aggression is partly to be viewed as an emotional outbreak due to tension and that this tension, in turn, is due to pressure and restraining forces (lack of space of free movement). We have apathy when the pressure and the restraining forces from without are kept stronger than the forces ($f_{Ch,E}$ in Figure 7) within the person which lead to the emotional expression, and are due to the tension. Whether or not the forces from without or those from within are stronger depends upon the absolute amount of pressure and also on the "willingness" of the person to "accept" the pressure.

The field theoretical approach also provides indications for the circumstances under which one might generalize the results of such experimental group studies. One must be careful of making too hasty generalization, perhaps especially in the field of political science. The varieties of democracies, autocracies, or *"laissez-faire"* atmospheres are, of course, very numerous. Besides, there are always individual differences of character and background to consider. On the other hand, it would be wrong to minimize the possibility of generalization. The answer in social psychology and sociology has to be the same as in an experiment in any science. The essence of an experiment is to create a situation which shows a certain pattern. What happens depends by and large upon this pattern and is largely although not completely independent of the absolute size of the field. This is one of the reasons why experiments are possible and worthwhile.

The generalization from an experimental situation should, therefore, go always to those life situations which show the same or sufficiently similar general patterns. This statement includes both the rights and the limitations of generalization.

D. SUMMARY

1. In a first experiment, Lippitt compared one group of five 10-year-old children, under autocratic leadership, with a comparable group under democratic leadership. In a second experiment, Lippitt and White studied four comparable clubs of 10-year-old boys, each of which passed successively through three club periods in such a way that there were altogether five democratic periods, five autocratic periods, and two *"laissez-faire"* periods.

2. In the second experiment, the factor of personality differences in the boys was controlled by having each group pass through autocracy and then democracy, or vice versa. The factor of leader's personality was controlled by having each of four leaders play the rôle of autocrat and the rôle of democratic leader at least once.

3. Records on each club meeting include stenographic records of conversation, quantitative symbolic records of group structure, quantitative symbolic records of all social interactions, and a continuous interpretive running account. Parents and teachers were interviewed; each boy was given the Rorschach ink blots, a Moreno-type questionnaire, and was interviewed three times. Analysis of causal relationships between these various types of data is still far from complete. As a preliminary report we are giving here a part of the data bearing upon one specific problem, that of aggression.

4. In the first experiment, hostility was 30 times as frequent in the autocratic as in the democratic group. Aggression (including both "hostility" and "joking hostility") was 8 times as frequent. Much of this aggression was directed toward two successive scapegoats within the group; none of it was directed toward the autocrat.

5. In the second experiment, one of the five autocracies showed the same aggressive reaction as was found in the first experiment. In the other four autocracies, the boys showed an extremely non-aggressive, "apathetic" pattern of behavior.

6. Four types of evidence indicate that this lack of aggression was probably not caused by lack of frustration, but by the repressive influence of the autocrat: (*a*) outbursts of aggression on the days of transition to a freer atmosphere; (*b*) a sharp rise of aggression when the autocrat left the room; (*c*) other indications of generalized apathy, such as an absence of smiling and joking; and (*d*) the fact that 19 out of 20 boys liked their democratic leader better than their

KURT LEWIN, RONALD LIPPITT, AND RALPH K. WHITE   299

autocratic leader, and 7 out of 10 also liked their *"laissez-faire"* leader better.

7. There were two wars," more or less playful, and without bodily damage, between clubs meeting in the same room at the same time. The first of these began gradually, the second suddenly. Three factors, present in both cases, seemed conducive to group conflict: (*a*) irritation and tension produced by a hostile stranger, (*b*) absence of a respected adult, and (*c*) lack of any absorbing alternative activity.

8. There were two striking instances of aggression against impersonal objects.

9. A general interpretation of the above data on aggression can be made in terms of four underlying factors: tension, restricted space of free movement, rigidity of group structure, and style of living (culture).

REFERENCES

1. LEWIN, K. A Dynamic Theory of Personality: Selected papers. Trans. by Donald K. Adams and Karl E. Zener. New York: McGraw-Hill, 1935. Pp. ix+286.

2. ———. The conceptual representation and the measurement of psychological forces. *Duke Univ. Contrib. Psychol. The.,* 1938, **1**, No. 4. Pp. 247.

3. ———. Experiments in social space. *Harvard Educ. Rev.,* 1939, **9**, No. 1.

4. LEWIN, K., & LIPPITT, R. An experimental approach to the study of autocracy and democracy: A preliminary note. *Sociometry,* 1938, **1**, 292-300.

5. ———. Field theory and experiment in social psychology. (Accepted for publication in the May issue of the American Journal of Sociology.)

6. LIPPITT, R. An experimental study of authoritarian and democratic group atmospheres. *Univ. Iowa Stud., Stud. Child Wel.,* 1939, **16**, No. 3. [In press.]

7. MEAD, MARGARET [ED.]. Coöperation and Competition among Primitive Peoples. New York: Macmillan, 1937. Pp. viii+325.

8. MORENO, J. L. Who Shall Survive? A new approach to the problem of human interrelations. (Nervous and Mental Disease Monograph Series No. 58.) Washington, D. C.: Nervous & Mental Disease Publishing Co., 1934. Pp. xvi+437.

Child Welfare Research Station
State University of Iowa
Iowa City, Iowa

[5]

III

A FACTORIAL STUDY OF THE LEADER BEHAVIOR DESCRIPTIONS[1]

by

ANDREW W. HALPIN, *University of Chicago*

and

B. JAMES WINER, *Purdue University*

The Leader Behavior Description Questionnaire described in the preceding section was modified for use in the study of Air Force personnel manning bombardment aircraft. The modification consisted of (1) preparing new instructions appropriate to describing the behavior of the aircraft commander, (2) changing the wording of the items, substituting "crew" for "group" and "crew member" for "group member" and (3) reducing the number of dimensions or characteristics to be described.

The number of items in the revised form was reduced from 150 to 130, eliminating 20 items which seemed inappropriate to the air crew situation. Scoring keys were prepared for the following characteristics of leader behavior: Membership (12 items), Communication (22 items), Organization (16 items), Production (12 items), Domination (19 items), Leadership Quality (31 items), Goal Direction (9 items), and Initiative (16 items, some of which were scored on other dimensions). The Leadership Quality dimension was made up of items which, in the previous section, were found to be highly correlated with several different dimensions. Hence, it might be regarded as a good measure of "halo effect" in the description of leadership.

In applying these 8 Keys, 111 of the 130 items were keyed once, 13 appeared in two keys and 6 appeared in none.

The LBDQ was administered to 52 air crews flying B-50 bombers. The leader behavior of the 52 air crew commanders was de-

---

[1] This study was sponsored jointly by the Human Resources Research Laboratories, Department of the Air Force, and The Ohio State University Research Foundation.

scribed by 300 crew members. The 300 descriptions of leader behavior were scored on the 8 keys described above. The intercorrelations among the 8 keys are shown in Table 1. The high intercorrelations among some of the keys indicated that there was considerable overlap between them. A modified Wherry-Doolittle (1) test selection procedure was applied to this rank of intercorrelations and it was found that 5 of the keys would account for almost all the total variance on the 8 keys. The 5 keys (numbers 2, 3, 4, 6 and 8) selected for further analysis and the intercorrelation among them are noted in Table 1. These 5 keys may be regarded as defining 5 factors, but since the keys show intercorrelations significantly greater than zero, they constitute an oblique set of factors.

TABLE 1—Intercorrelations Among Eight Dimension Keys

Dimension No.	(Key)	Dimension (Key)							
		1	2[a]	3[a]	4[a]	5	6[a]	7	8[a]
		r	r	r	r	r	r	r	r
1.	Leadership Quality		.61	.73	.40	.91	.81	.89	.87
2.	Domination[a]	.61		.30	—.18	.57	.61	.44	.49
3.	Organization	.73	.30		.60	.72	.47	.78	.69
4.	Production[a]	.40	—.18	.60		.41	.23	.54	.47
5.	Communication	.91	.57	.72	.41		.79	.84	.80
6.	Membership[a]	.81	.61	.47	.23	.79		.69	.66
7.	Goal Direction	.89	.44	.78	.54	.84	.69		.82
8.	Initiative[a]	.87	.49	.69	.47	.80	.66	.82	
	Mean	88.1	29.1	51.2	28.1	58.3	28.0	25.4	39.6
	Standard Deviation	20.0	9.1	8.3	5.9	11.6	7.8	6.4	8.2

N = 300.

[a] The least highly intercorrelated keys (2, 3, 4, 6 and 8) were selected for use on the factor analysis.

THE FACTOR ANALYSIS

The next step was to compute the correlations between each of the 130 items and each of these five keys. These item-key correlations were used to estimate the factor loadings of the items on each of the keys. These loadings were transformed from a set of oblique to a set of orthogonal reference axes. To accomplish this, a transformation matrix was computed from the matrix of key intercorrelations, and the matrix of oblique factor loadings was multiplied by this transformation matrix to yield the desired matrix of orthogonal factor loadings. The reference axes thus determined were rotated to meaningfulness for the four factors which emerged.

Three additional factors were extracted, but after the completion of rotation, it was found that these three factors accounted for only approximately 6.3 per cent of the variance common to the 7 factors. No meaningful interpretation could be made of the relatively unrepresented factors. Consequently, the additional factors were given no further consideration.

The remaining 4 factors were postulated to account for the intercorrelations. Approximately 32 per cent of the items have one-half or more of their total variance accounted for by the 4 factors. The

TABLE 2—Distribution of Communalities for 130 Items

Communalities	Number of Items	Cumulative Frequency	Cumulative Percentage
80–99	3	3	2.3
60–79	23	26	20.0
40–59	44	70	53.8
20–39	44	114	87.8
0–19	16	130	100.0

TABLE 3—Per Cent of Common Variance Accounted for by Four Factors

Factor Number	Factor Designation	Per Cent of Common Variance
I	Consideration	49.6
II	Initiating Structure	33.6
III	Production Emphasis	9.8
IV	Sensitivity (Social Awareness)	7.0

distribution of communalities is shown in Table 2, where it may be seen that 53.8 per cent of the items have 40 per cent or more of their total variance (communality) accounted for by the 4 factors.

Table 3 shows the per cent of common-factor variance accounted for by the 4 factors. In may be seen that Factors I and II account for 83.2 per cent of the common-factor variance. The factors were identified as Consideration, Initiating Structure, Production Emphasis, and Sensitivity (Social Awareness). Examination of the items with the highest loadings on each factor determined the name assigned to the factor.

Factor I, Consideration, which accounts for 49.6 per cent of the common factor variance is best represented by the items in Table 4.

42   LEADER BEHAVIOR: ITS DESCRIPTION AND MEASUREMENT

TABLE 4—Items With High Loadings on Factor I: Consideration

Item	Factor			
	I	II	III	IVa
	Factor Loadings			
Does personal favors for crew members	.68	—.05	.06	—.10
Looks out for personal welfare of crew members	.70	.15	.07	—.03
Refuses to explain his actions	—.77	.09	—.04	.14
Treats all crew members as his equal	.81	—.10	—.11	—.12
Is friendly and approachable	.81	.07	.00	.25
Finds time to listen to crew members	.81	.22	.03	—.08

a Reflected.

High positive loadings on this factor are associated with behavior indicative of friendship, mutual trust, respect, and warmth in the relationship between the aircraft commander and his crew. High negative loadings appear on items of behavior which indicate that the airplane commander is authoritarian and impersonal in his relations with the members of his crew. Tentatively, this factor has been designated as Consideration. It appears to mean the extent to which the aircraft commander, while carrying out his leadership functions, is considerate of the men on the crew. It does not imply laxity in the performance of his duties.

Factor II, Initiating Structure, is a close second to Factor I in that it accounts for 33.6 per cent of the common-factor variance. This factor is best represented by the items in Table 5.

TABLE 5—Items With High Loadings on Factor II: Initiating Structure

Item	Factor			
	I	II	III	IVa
	Factor Loadings			
Asks that crew follow S.O.P.	.03	.60	.15	—.01
Maintains definite standards of performance	.11	.75	.12	.17
Makes sure his part in the crew is understood	.18	.72	.22	.09
Tries out his new ideas on the crew	—.08	.62	.19	.27
Makes his attitude clear to the crew	.15	.63	.14	.22
Assigns crew members to particular tasks	—.07	.57	.20	.16

a Reflected.

The behaviors with high positive loadings on this factor are those which indicate that the aircraft commander, to a marked degree, organizes and defines the relationship between himself and the members of his crew. He tends to define the role which he expects each member of the crew to assume, and endeavors to establish well-defined patterns of organization, channels of communication, and ways of getting jobs done. This factor probably represents a basic and unique function of leadership. It is possible that other factors (including Consideration) may represent only facilitating means for accomplishing this end.

Factors I and II, in combination, account for 83.2 per cent of the common-factor variance. Because Factors III and IV account for only 16.8 per cent of this common factor variance, it is not possible at this point to define these factors with the same precision as the first two. This does not imply, however, that Factors III and IV are necessarily any less important than Factors I and II, since the original questionnaire may not have contained adequate samples of behaviors from the areas tapped by Factors III and IV.

Factor III, Production Emphasis, is best represented by the items in Table 6.

TABLE 6—Items With High Loadings on Factor III: Production Emphasis

Item	Factor			
	I	II	III	IVª
	Factor Loadings			
Encourages overtime work	—.28	.21	.51	.10
Stresses being ahead of competing crews	.00	.06	.53	.16
Treats crew members like cogs in a machine	—.68	.40	.62	—.03
Schedules the work to be done	.01	.57	.47	—.10
He"needles" crew members for greater effort	—.43	.39	.42	.32

ª Reflected.

This factor appears to measure a manner of motivating the crew to greater activity by emphasizing the mission or job to be done. Because of the dominance of Factors I and II, there are few "pure" items in this factor.

Factor IV, Sensitivity (Social Awareness), is best represented by the items in Table 7.

Again, as in the case of Factor III, there are relatively few items which have loadings on Factor IV without significant loading on Factors I or II. On the basis of somewhat incomplete data, this factor appears to measure the aircraft commander's sensitivity to and awareness of social interrelationships and pressures existing both

TABLE 7—Items With High Loadings on Factor IV: Sensitivity

Item	Factor			
	I	II	III	IVa
	Factor Loadings			
Resists changes in ways of doing things	.28	.25	—.22	—.49
Asks for sacrifices for good of entire crew	.16	.27	.02	.39
Aware of conflicts when they occur in the crew	.25	.45	—.09	.65
"Rides" the crew member who makes a mistake	.14	.32	.46	—.60
Waits for the crew to push new ideas	—.07	—.12	.01	—.32
Blames the same crew member when anything goes wrong	.17	—.05	.11	—.53

a Reflected.

inside and outside the crew. It may represent behaviors on the part of the aircraft commander which have often been referred to as "sizing up the situation." This factor does not indicate the extent to which the aircraft commander acts in accordance with these insights, but merely indicates his awareness of social pressures either within the crew or coming from outside the crew. It is important to note that this concept includes also awareness of social pressures which originate outside the crew, and have bearing upon the crew's behavior. There seems, however, to be a distinction between being aware of social pressures and taking appropriate action. Specifically, the aircraft commander's knowledge of the conflicts does not imply that he necessarily takes appropriate action to resolve them.

THE DEVELOPMENT OF SCORING KEYS

The next step was to use the item analysis findings for the construction of new keys. The two major dimensions which had emerged from the factor analysis were Consideration and Initiating Structure. The first objective, therefore, was to develop keys for these two dimensions. Because Factors III and IV contributed little to the common variance and were represented in "pure" form in only relatively few items, no attempt was made at this point to construct keys for these two less clearly delineated dimensions.

Inspection of the correlations of the items with the major dimensions of Consideration and Initiating Structure showed that the degree of association of certain items with one rather than the other of the dimensions was relatively unequivocal, but that in the case of other items, this relationship was not as clear-cut. Consequently, two keys were prepared for each dimension: a "pure" and a "complex." The "pure" key, as the name indicates, is one in which each item has a high correlation with the relevant dimension and a relatively low correlation with the other major dimension. The "complex" key is one in which the items do not possess this same unequivocal relation with the two dimensions, but in which the pattern of factor-loadings for any given item provides a logical basis for assigning the item to a particular dimension key.

Two questions guided the analysis at this point. First, in reviewing the 130 item LBDQ, could the "pure" and "complex" items for the Consideration and Initiating Structure dimensions be amalgamated into a single key for each dimension? Second, with a view to the future objective of constructing a shorter form of the LBDQ, would the choice and number of items in each of the "pure" keys, without the addition of the "complex" items, provide a sufficiently reliable factor key for each of these two dimensions?

Four scoring keys were constructed, consisting of 17 items scored for Consideration "Pure," 11 items scored for Consideration "Complex," 14 items scored for Structure "Pure," and 16 items scored for Structure "Complex." These keys were validated on a new sample of 100 cases, representing members of rather highly selected air crews. The intercorrelations among the 4 new keys are shown in Table 8. The correlation between Consideration "Pure" and Consideration "Complex" is .87, while the correlation between the Structure keys is .72. These correlations are high enough to suggest that the pure and complex keys might be combined if necessary. The correlation of .23 between Consideration "Pure" and Structure "Pure" suggests that these two keys are relatively independent. Lesser independence between these two "Complex" keys is indicated by a correlation of .47 between the two keys. In order to determine the correlation between the combined "pure" and "complex" Consideration keys and the combined "pure" and "complex" Initiating Structure keys, the formula for the correlation of sums was applied to the data in Table 8. This correlation is .42. Thus, the combination of the "complex" items with their respective "pure" items diminishes the independence of the dimension scores (from r=.23 to r=.42).

The reliability coefficients shown in Table 8 indicate a higher degree of reliability for the "pure" than for the "complex" forms.

TABLE 8—Intercorrelations of "Pure" and "Complex" Keys for Consideration and Initiating Structure: Reliability Coefficients for an Independent Sample of 100 Combat Aircrews

No. Key	Key			
	1	2	3	4
	r	r	r	r
1. Consideration "Pure"		.87	.23	.59
2. Consideration "Complex"	.87		.08	.47
3. Structure "Pure"	.23	.08		.72
4. Structure "Complex"	.59	.47	.72	
Reliability	.95	.89	.83	.79
Mean	47.1	30.2	43.1	47.3
Standard Deviation	11.9	7.8	5.5	6.4

The corrected reliability of .95 for Consideration "Pure" and of .83 for Structure "Pure" are high enough to indicate that these keys could be used in short forms of the questionnaires.

Both the intercorrelations among the 4 keys and the data on the reliability of the keys suggest that the "pure" keys alone should be used in constructing new dimension keys.

SHORT FORMS

The next step taken was to construct an 80-item form of the LBDQ. This form consisted of Consideration (15 items), Initiating Structure (15 items), Production Emphasis (25 items), and Social Awareness (25 items). It was hoped, by adding items to the Production Emphasis and Social Awareness Keys, to build up these scales. However, in spite of the attempt to improve them, the Production Emphasis and Social Awareness scales have continued to make only a minor contribution toward measuring the total factor variance. This result may be due in part to the nature of the new items that were added for their measurement in the 80-item form of the questionnaire. Whatever the cause, due to their negligible contribution, they were dropped from further consideration.

The 80-item form of the LBDQ consists, then, of 80 items, only 30 of which are scored. The 15 items scored on the Consideration Key and their factor loadings are shown in Table 9. The 15 items scored on the Initiating Structure Key are shown in Table 10.

It will be noted in Table 9 that the items have high loadings only on Factor I, Consideration. Some of the items have low positive

TABLE 9—Consideration Key: Factor Loadings Derived
From 130-Item Form

Form			Item	Scoring	Factor			
80—Item	130—Item	40—Item			I	II	III	IV
Item Number					Factor Loadings			
1	4	1	He does personal favors for crew members	+	.68	—.05	.06	.10
5	13	3	He does little things to make it pleasant to be a member of the crew	+	.74	—.10	.12	.11
9	18	6	He is easy to understand	+	.69	.12	—.01	.05
13	41	8	He finds time to listen to crew members	+	.81	.22	.03	.08
18	59	12	He keeps to himself	—	—.52	.07	.00	.05
19	74	13	He looks out for the welfare of individual crew members	+	.70	.15	.07	.03
31	87	18	He refuses to explain his actions	—	—.77	.09	—.04	—.14
33	95	20	He acts without consulting the crew	—	—.62	.06	—.02	—.11
34	101	21	He is slow to accept new ideas	—	—.67	—.07	.02	—.13
37	105	23	He treats all crew members as his equals	+	.81	—.10	—.11	.12
37	108	26	He is willing to make changes	+	.74	—.15	.05	.16
45	112	28	He is friendly and approachable	+	.81	.07	.00	.25
51	111	31	He makes crew members feel at ease when talking with him	+	.74	.23	.03	.11
58	114	34	He puts suggestions by the crew into operation	+	.67	.13	.11	—.11
63	124	38	He gets crew approval on important matters before going ahead	+	.63	.02	—.08	.00

loadings on Factors II, III and IV. Other items have negative loadings on Factors II, III or IV. Items with both positive and negative loadings on Factors II, III and IV were included with the aim of suppressing or cancelling out the effect of these three factors. It may be seen in Table 10 that the same principle was followed less successfully in selecting items for measuring Structure.

In the final form of the LBDQ, constructed recently, the number of items was reduced to 40, with 15 items for measuring Consideration, 15 items for measuring Structure, and 10 buffer items to maintain the "tone" of the questionnaire provided by the items intended to measure Factors III and IV. The item numbers of the items in the 40-item form are shown in Tables 9 and 10.

For a sample of 100 of the 80-item questionnaires, the odd-even estimates of reliability are .87 for Consideration and .75 for Initiating Structure. When the Spearman-Brown formula is applied to correct

TABLE 10—Initiating Structure Key: Factor Loadings Derived
From 130-Item Form

Form			Item	Scoring	Factor			
80—Item	130—Item	40—Item			I	II	III	IV
Item Number					Factor Loadings			
2	3	2	He makes his attitude clear to the crew	+	.15	.63	.14	—.22
6	9	4	He tries out his new ideas in the crew	+	—.08	.62	.19	—.27
10	11	7	He rules with an iron hand	+	—.66	.61	.27	—.22
14	14	9	He criticizes poor work	+	—.20	.55	.17	—.31
17	17	11	He speaks in a manner not to be questioned	+	—.05	.47	.14	—.10
21	31	14	He assigns crew members to particular tasks	+	—.07	.57	.20	—.16
25	24	16	He works without a plan	—	—.32	—.58	—.04	—.06
26	56	17	He maintains definite standards of performance	+	.11	.75	.12	.17
35	117	22	He emphasizes meeting deadlines	+	.18	.48	.05	—.25
38	121	24	He encourages the use of uniform procedures	+	.19	.66	.26	—.13
42	128	27	He makes sure his part in the crew is understood by members	+	.17	.72	.22	—.09
46	39	29	He asks that crew members follow standard operating procedures	+	.03	.60	.15	.01
52	129	32	He lets crew members know what is expected of them	+	.29	.58	.11	—.18
59	46	35	He sees to it that crew members are working up to capacity	+	—.12	.71	.34	—.12
64	102	39	He sees to it that the work of crew members is coordinated	+	.44	.60	.18	—.05

for attenuation, the reliabilities for these keys become .93 and .86, respectively. The 15-item keys are thus shown to exhibit usefully high reliabilities.

There remains the question as to whether or not complete independence was achieved between the Consideration and Structure scales. In one sample of 29 air crew commanders described by 201 crew members a correlation of .52 was found between the Consideration and Initiating Structure scores. When the same air crew commanders were later described on a different air base the correlation between the two scales was .45. For another sample of 249 aircraft commanders a correlation of .38 was found between the two scales. Although the factor analysis showed Consideration and Structure to be orthogonal factors, uncorrelated factor scores could not be obtained since few items were factorially pure. Some indi-

TABLE 11—Analysis of Variance of Consideration Scores of 29 Air Crew
Commanders Described by 201 Crew Members

Source of Variation	Sum of Squares	Degrees of Freedom	Estimate of Variance	F Ratio
Between Crews	11,409.27	28	407.47	4.07[a]
Within Crews	17,225.70	172	100.15	
Total	28,634.97	200		

[a] Significant at the .01 level.

viduals exhibit both forms of behavior. Reference to Table 10 shows
that the items for the measurement of Initiating Structure show moderately high loadings on Factors I, III and IV. Initiating Structure
appears to represent a complex form of behavior, difficult to measure independently of other behavioral dimensions. In addition, the
great variety of demands imposed by military life and operating conditions would appear to preclude the absolute separation of Consideration and Initiating Structure.

A further question remains relative to the extent to which several
persons describing the same leader, tend to describe him in the same
terms. In the samples under discussion, each air crew commander
was described by four or more crew members. It has been found in
several samples of subjects that different subordinates describing the
same leader tend to describe him in similar terms. However, different leaders are not described as similar. Results of the analysis
of variance among the description scores of 29 air crew commanders
described by 201 crew members are shown in Tables 11 and 12. The
variance in the descriptions of different leaders is found to be significantly greater than the variance in description of the same leader.

Comparison of Tables 11 and 12 reveals a tendency toward
greater agreement in describing the air crew commander's behavior
with respect to Consideration than in describing his behavior with
regard to Initiating Structure. In view of the significant F ratios

TABLE 12—Analysis of Variance of Initiating Structure Scores of 29 Air
Crew Commanders Described by 201 Crew Members

Source of Variation	Sum of Squares	Degrees of Freedom	Estimate of Variance	F Ratio
Between Crews	4,591.77	28	163.99	2.00[a]
Within Crews	14,118.60	172	82.09	
Total	18,710.37	200		

[a] Significant at the .01 level.

50   LEADER BEHAVIOR: ITS DESCRIPTION AND MEASUREMENT

for both dimensions, it was concluded that the crew mean Consideration and crew mean Initiating Structure scores could be used as indices for describing the leader behavior of the air crew commander as perceived by his crew.

THE RELATION OF LEADER BEHAVIOR DESCRIPTION SCORES TO OTHER MEASURES

Ratings of leadership effectiveness were available for the sample of 29 air crew commanders. These ratings were made by the administrative superiors of the commanders. Ratings were made on technical competence, effectiveness in working with other crew members, performance under stress, and the like. The correlations between these effectiveness ratings by superiors and the leader behavior of the air crew commanders as described by their subordinates are shown in Table 13. The last item in this table is a crew satisfaction index. This is on evaluation by the crew members of their satisfaction with the leadership of the air crew commander.

It will be seen in Table 13 that Consideration is correlated negatively with all the effectiveness ratings by superiors. This negative relationship is enhanced when Initiating Structure is partialled out. It is apparent that Consideration is not perceived as a form of beha-

TABLE 13—Correlations and Partial Correlations Between Effectiveness Ratings by Superiors and Leader Behavior Descriptions by Subordinates for 29 Air Crew Commanders

Effectiveness Rating	Consideration Score	Structure Score	Consideration with Structure Partialled out	Structure with Consideration Partialled out
	r	r	r	r
Technical Competence	—.22	.19	—.38[a]	.36[a]
Effectiveness of Working with Other Crew Members	—.13	.27	—.33	.40[a]
Conformity to Standard Operating Procedures	—.25	.32	—.52[b]	.54[b]
Performance Under Stress	—.12	.16	—.24	.26
Attitude and Motivation to be Effective	—.34	.16	—.50[b]	.42[a]
Over-all Effectiveness as a Combat Crew Member	—.23	.28	—.46[a]	.48[b]
Crew's Satisfaction Index	.64[b]	.35	.57[b]	—.03

[a] Significant at the .05 level.
[b] Significant at the .01 level.

vior which contributes directly toward leadership effectiveness. Initiating Structure is correlated positively with all the effectiveness ratings, significantly so for 4 items when Consideration is partialled out. Initiating Structure as described by subordinates is associated with leadership effectiveness as rated by superiors. Crew satisfaction, however, is more highly related to Consideration than to Initiating Structure. Consideration would, thus, appear to be a form of behavior which contributes toward crew morale rather than making a direct contribution to effectiveness.

SUMMARY

A Leader Behavior Description Questionnaire consisting of 130 items was administered to crew members who described air crew commanders. A factor analysis of the intercorrelations among 8 hypothesized dimensions of leader behavior resulted in the emergence of 4 factors. These factors were identified as Consideration, Initiating Structure, Production Emphasis, and Social Awareness.

Two factors, Consideration and Initiating Structure, accounted for 83 per cent of the total factor variance. Attempts to improve the contribution of the two remaining factors by increasing the number of items for their measurement proved unsuccessful. Efforts were therefore concentrated upon the task of developing the best possible short scales for describing Consideration and Initiating Structure.

In an 80-item form of the questionnaire, only the 15 items for measuring consideration and the 15 items for measuring Structure were keyed and scored. The reliabilities of these short keys were found to be satisfactorily high for practical use. The two scales are correlated to a moderate degree, but are sufficiently independent to permit the use of the Consideration and Initiating Structure scales as measures of different kinds of behavior. Different persons describing the same leader show significant similarity in their descriptions.

Consideration tends to be correlated negatively with leadership effectiveness ratings by superiors, while Initiating Structure is positively related to effectiveness ratings. Consideration is more highly related than Initiating Structure to an index of crew satisfaction.

References

1. Wherry, R. J. and Winer, B. J. A Method for Factoring Large Numbers of Items. Psychometrica, 1953, *18*, 161–179.

[6]

David G. Bowers and *Stanley E. Seashore*

Predicting Organizational Effectiveness with a Four-Factor Theory of Leadership

Recent research in the area of leadership seems to point to the existence of four basic dimensions of leadership: support, interaction facilitation, goal emphasis, and work facilitation. Data from a recent study of 40 agencies of one of the leading life insurance companies are used to evaluate the impact of both supervisory and peer leadership upon outcomes of satisfaction and factorial performance measures.

Results from the study suggest that this conceptual model is useful and that leadership's relation to organizational outcomes may best be studied when both leadership and effectiveness are multidimensional. Both peer and supervisory leadership measures relate to outcomes. In most instances, the ability to predict is enhanced by taking simultaneous account of certain nonleadership variables.

David G. Bowers is program associate at the Center for Research on the Utilization of Scientific Knowledge, The University of Michigan.

Stanley E. Seashore is professor of psychology and assistant director of the Institute for Social Research, The University of Michigan.

FOR centuries writers have been intrigued with the idea of specifying predictable relationships between what an organization's leader does and how the organization fares. In our own time, behavioral science has looked extensively at this question, yet incongruities and contradictory or unrelated findings seem to crowd the literature. It is the intent in this paper to locate and integrate the consistencies, to explore some neglected issues, and, finally, to generate and use a network of variables for predicting outcomes of organizational effectiveness.

Leadership has been studied informally by observing the lives of great men and formally by attempting to identify the personality traits of acknowledged leaders through assessment techniques. Review of the research literature from these studies, however, reveals few consistent findings.[1] Since the Second World War, research emphasis has shifted from a search for personality traits to a search for behavior that makes a difference in the performance or satisfaction of the followers. The conceptual scheme to be outlined here is an example of this approach.

In this paper, the primary concern is with leadership in businesses or industrial enterprises, usually termed "supervision" or "management," although most of the constructs of leadership to be used here apply equally well to social groups, clubs, and voluntary associations.

Work situations in business organizations in a technologically advanced society typically involve a comparatively small number of persons who receive direction from one person. This is the basic unit of industrial society and has been called the "organizational family."[2] In this modern organizational family, there is usually task interdependence and there is frequently social interdependence as well. The ideal is that of a group of people working effectively together toward the accomplishment of some common aim.

This paper presents a review of the conceptual structure resulting from several programs of research in leadership practices, followed by a reconceptualization that attempts to take into consideration all of these earlier findings. In an attempt to assess the usefulness of the reconceptualization, it is then applied to leadership and effectiveness data from a recent study.

[1] C. A. Gibb, "Leadership," in G. Lindzey, *Handbook of Social Psychology* (Cambridge, Mass.: Addison-Wesley Publishing Co., Inc., 1954), II, 877–917; R. M. Stogdill, Personal Factors Associated with Leadership: A Survey of the Literature, *Journal of Psychology*, 25 (1948), 35–71.

[2] F. C. Mann, "Toward an Understanding of the Leadership Role in Formal Organization," in R. Dubin, G. C. Homans, F. C. Mann, and D. C. Miller, *Leadership and Productivity* (San Francisco, Calif.: Chandler Publishing Company, 1965), pp. 68–103.

DIMENSIONS OF LEADERSHIP

It seems useful at the outset to isolate on a common-sense basis certain attributes of "leadership." First, the concept of leadership is meaningful only in the context of two or more people. Second, leadership consists of behavior; more specifically, it is behavior by one member of a group toward another member or members of the group, which advances some joint aim. Not all organizationally useful behavior in a work group is leadership; leadership behavior must be distinguished from the performance of noninterpersonal tasks that advance the goals of the organization. On a common-sense basis, then, leadership is organizationally useful behavior by one member of an organizational family toward another member or members of that same organizational family.

Defined in this manner, leadership amounts to a large aggregation of separate behaviors, which may be grouped or classified in a great variety of ways. Several classification systems from previous research have achieved considerable prominence, and are briefly described here.

Ohio State Leadership Studies

In 1945, the Bureau of Business Research at Ohio State University undertook the construction of an instrument for describing leadership. From extended conversations and discussions among staff members who represented various disciplines, a list of nine dimensions or categories of leadership behavior were postulated. Descriptive statements were then written and assigned to one or another of the nine dimensions, and after further refinement, 150 of these were selected as representing these nine dimensions and were incorporated into the Leader Behavior Description Questionnaire.

Two factor analyses attempted to simplify its conceptual framework further. Hemphill and Coons[3] intercorrelated and factor-analyzed group mean scores for 11 dimensions for a sample com-

[3] J. K. Hemphill and A. E. Coons, "Development of the Leader Behavior Description Questionnaire," in R. M. Stogdill and A. E. Coons (eds.) *Leader Behavior: Its Description and Measurement* (Research Monograph No. 88, Columbus, Ohio: Bureau of Business Research, the Ohio State University, 1957), pp. 6–38.

posed largely of educational groups,[4] and obtained three orthogonal factors.

1. *Maintenance of membership character.* Behavior of a leader which allows him to be considered a "good fellow" by his subordinates; behavior which is socially agreeable to group members.

2. *Objective attainment behavior.* Behavior related to the output of the group; for example, taking positive action in establishing goals or objectives, structuring group activities in a way that members may work toward an objective, or serving as a representative of group accomplishment in relation to outside groups, agencies, forces, and so on.

3. *Group interaction facilitation behavior.* Behavior that structures communication among group members, encouraging pleasant group atmosphere, and reducing conflicts among members.

Halpin and Winer[5] made an analysis using data collected from air-force crews, revising the original measuring instrument to adapt it to the respondent group. Only 130 items were used, with appropriate rewording, and the number of dimensions was reduced to eight. Treatment of the data indicated that five of the eight were sufficient for describing the entire roster, and the correlation of the 130 items with these five dimensions was regarded as a matrix of oblique factor loadings. These item loadings were then factor analyzed and the results rotated, producing four orthogonal factors.

1. *Consideration.* Behavior indicative of friendship, mutual trust, respect, and warmth.

2. *Initiating structure.* Behavior that organizes and defines relationships or roles, and establishes well-defined patterns of organization, channels of communication, and ways of getting jobs done.

3. *Production emphasis.* Behavior which makes up a manner of motivating the group to greater activity by emphasizing the mission or job to be done.

---

[4] The 11 dimensions were made up of the original 9, one of which (communication) had been subdivided, plus an overall leadership evaluation.

[5] A. W. Halpin and J. Winer, "A Factorial Study of the Leader Behavior Description Questionnaire," in R. M. Stogdill and A. E. Coons, *Leader Behavior, op. cit.*, pp. 39–51.

4. *Sensitivity (social awareness).* Sensitivity of the leader to, and his awareness of, social interrelationships and pressures inside or outside the group.

The Halpin and Winer analysis has been the more widely known and used. Because the investigators dropped the third and fourth factors as accounting for too little common variance, "consideration" and "initiating structure" have become to some extent identified as "the Ohio State" dimensions of leadership.

Early Survey Research Center Studies

Concurrent with the Ohio State studies was a similar program of research in human relations at the University of Michigan Survey Research Center. Approaching the problem of leadership or supervisory style by locating clusters of characteristics which (*a*) correlated positively among themselves and (*b*) correlated with criteria of effectiveness, this program developed two concepts called "employee orientation" and "production orientation."[6]

Employee orientation is described as behavior by a supervisor, which indicates that he feels that the "human relations" aspect of the job is quite important; and that he considers the employees as human beings of intrinsic importance, takes an interest in them, and accepts their individuality and personal needs. Production-orientation stresses production and the technical aspects of the job, with employees as means for getting work done; it seems to combine the Ohio State dimensions of initiating structure and production emphasis. Originally conceived to be opposite poles of the same continuum, employee-orientation and production-orientation were later reconceptualized,[7] on the basis of further data, as representing independent dimensions.

Katz and Kahn,[8] writing from a greater accumulation of find-

[6] D. Katz, N. Maccoby, and Nancy C. Morse, *Productivity, Supervision, and Morale in An Office Situation* (Detroit, Mich.: The Darel Press, Inc., 1950); D. Katz, N. Maccoby, G. Gurin, and Lucretia G. Floor, *Productivity, Supervision, and Morale Among Railroad Workers* (Ann Arbor, Mich.: Survey Research Center, 1951).

[7] R. L. Kahn, The Prediction of Productivity, *Journal of Social Issues*, 12 (1956), 41–49.

[8] D. Katz and R. L. Kahn, "Human Organization and Worker Motivation," in L. R. Tripp (ed.), *Industrial Productivity* (Madison, Wisc.: Industrial Relations Research Association, 1951), pp. 146–171.

ings, presented another conceptual scheme, with four dimensions of leadership.

1. *Differentiation of supervisory role.* Behavior by a leader that reflects greater emphasis upon activities of planning and performing specialized skilled tasks; spending a greater proportion of time in actual supervision, rather than performing the men's own tasks himself or absorption in impersonal paperwork.

2. *Closeness of supervision.* Behavior that delegates authority, checks upon subordinates less frequently, provides more general, less frequent instructions about the work, makes greater allowance for individuals to perform in their own ways and at their own paces.

3. *Employee orientation.* Behavior that gives major emphasis to a supportive personal relationship, and that reflects a personal interest in subordinates; being more understanding, less punitive, easy to talk to, and willing to help groom employees for advancement.

4. *Group relationships.* Behavior by the leader that results in group cohesiveness, pride by subordinates in their work group, a feeling of membership in the group, and mutual help on the part of those subordinates.

Differentiation of supervisory role corresponds in part to what the Ohio State studies refer to as initiating structure or objective attainment behavior, and clearly derives from the earlier concept of production orientation. Closeness of supervision, on the other hand, has something in common with maintenance of membership character, consideration, and employee-orientation, but also with objective attainment behavior, initiating structure, and production orientation. Employee orientation clearly corresponds to the earlier concept by the same name, while group relationships is to some extent similar to the interaction facilitation behavior and social sensitivity of the Ohio State studies.

In still another conceptualization, combining theory with review of empirical data, Kahn[9] postulated four supervisory functions.

9 R. L. Kahn, "Human Relations on the Shop Floor," in E. M. Hugh-Jones (ed.), *Human Relations and Modern Management* (Amsterdam, Holland: North-Holland Publishing Co., 1958), pp. 43–74.

1. *Providing direct need satisfaction.* Behavior by a leader, not conditional upon behavior of the employee, which provides direct satisfaction of the employee's ego and affiliative needs.

2. *Structuring the path to goal attainment.* Behavior that cues subordinates toward filling personal needs through attaining organizational goals.

3. *Enabling goal achievement.* Behavior that removes barriers to goal achievement, such as eliminating bottlenecks, or planning.

4. *Modifying employee goals.* Behavior that influences the actual personal goals of subordinates in organizationally useful directions.

Direct need satisfaction clearly resembles consideration and employee-orientation; enabling goal achievement seems similar to initiating structure or objective attainment behavior; structuring the path to goal attainment and modifying employee goals are probably closer to the Ohio State production emphasis factor.

Studies at the Research Center for Group Dynamics

Cartwright and Zander,[10] at the Research Center for Group Dynamics, on the basis of accumulated findings, described leadership in terms of two sets of group functions.

1. *Group maintenance functions.* Behavior that keeps interpersonal relations pleasant, resolves disputes, provides encouragement, gives the minority a chance to be heard, stimulates self-direction, and increases interdependence among members.

2. *Goal achievement functions.* Behavior that initiates action, keeps members' attention on the goal, develops a procedural plan, evaluates the quality of work done, and makes expert information available.

These descriptive terms clearly refer to broader constructs than consideration or initiating structure. Group maintenance functions, for example, include what has been termed consideration, maintenance of membership character, or employee-orientation, but they also include functions concerned with relationships among group members not in formal authority positions. This concept is in some ways similar to group interaction facilitation

[10] D. Cartwright and A. Zander, *Group Dynamics Research and Theory* (Evanston, Ill.: Row, Peterson & Co., 1960).

behavior in the Ohio State factor analysis of Hemphill and Coons.[11] Goal achievement functions seem to encompass what the Ohio State studies referred to as initiating structure and production emphasis or objective attainment behavior, and what early Survey Research Center studies called production orientation.

Mann's Three Skills

In subsequent work at the Survey Research Center built upon earlier findings, a recent classification, proposed by several writers and developed and operationalized by Floyd Mann,[12] treats leadership in terms of a trilogy of skills required of supervisors or managers. Although behaviors requiring particular skills and those skills themselves are not necessarily perfectly parallel, it seems reasonable to assume at least an approximate correspondence between the two. The three skills are:

1. *Human relations skill.* Ability and judgment in working with and through people, including knowledge of principles of human behavior, interpersonal relations, and human motivation.

2. *Technical skill.* Ability to use knowledge, methods, techniques, and equipment necessary for the performance of specific tasks.

3. *Administrative skill.* Ability to understand and act according to the objectives of the total organization, rather than only on the basis of the goals and needs of one's own immediate group. It includes planning, organizing the work, assigning the right tasks to the right people, inspecting, following up, and coordinating the work.

Likert's New Patterns of Management

Rensis Likert of the University of Michigan Institute for Social Research, building upon many of the findings of the Survey Research Center and the Research Center for Group Dynamics as well as upon his own early work in the same area for the Life Insurance Agency Management Association, describes five conditions for effective supervisory behavior.

[11] Hemphill and Coons, *op. cit.*
[12] Mann, *op. cit.*

1. *Principle of supportive relations.* The leadership and other processes of the organization must be such as to ensure a maximum probability that in his interactions and his relationships with the organization, each member will, in the light of his background, values, and expectations, view the experience as supportive, and as one that builds and maintains his sense of personal worth and importance.[13]

2. *Group methods of supervision.* Management will make full use of the potential capacities of its human resources only when each person in an organization is a member of one or more effectively functioning work groups that have a high degree of group loyalty, effective skills of interaction, and high performance goals.[14]

3. *High performance goals.* If a high level of performance is to be achieved, it appears to be necessary for a supervisor to be employee-centered, and at the same time to have high performance goals and a contagious enthusiasm as to the importance of achieving these goals.[15]

4. *Technical knowledge.* The (effective) leader has adequate competence to handle the technical problems faced by his group, or he sees that access to this technical knowledge is fully provided.[16]

5. *Coordinating, scheduling, planning.* The leader fully reflects and effectively represents the views, goals, values, and decisions of his group in those other groups where he is performing the function of linking his group to the rest of the organization. He brings to the group of which he is the leader the views, goals, and decisions of those other groups. In this way, he provides a linkage whereby communication and the exercise of influence can be performed in both directions.[17]

Comparison and Integration

These various research programs and writings make it clear that a great deal of conceptual content is held in common. In

---

[13] R. Likert, *New Patterns of Management* (New York: McGraw-Hill Book Co., 1961), p. 103.

[14] *Ibid.*, p. 104.

[15] *Ibid.*, p. 8.

[16] *Ibid.*, p. 171.

[17] *Ibid.*, p. 171.

fact, four dimensions emerge from these studies, which seem to comprise the basic structure of what one may term "leadership":

1. *Support.* Behavior that enhances someone else's feeling of personal worth and importance.

2. *Interaction facilitation.* Behavior that encourages members of the group to develop close, mutually satisfying relationships.

3. *Goal emphasis.* Behavior that stimulates an enthusiasm for meeting the group's goal or achieving excellent performance.

4. *Work facilitation.* Behavior that helps achieve goal attainment by such activities as scheduling, coordinating, planning, and by providing resources such as tools, materials, and technical knowledge.

This formulation is obviously very close, except in terminology, to that expressed by Rensis Likert and was, in fact, stimulated by it. Table 1 indicates how concepts from the various research programs relate to these four basic concepts of leadership. More important, however, is the fact that each of these four concepts appears, sometimes separately, sometimes in combination, in all but two (Katz, et al., 1950; Kahn, 1958) of the previous formulations listed. These four dimensions are not considered indivisible, but capable of further subdivision according to some regularity of occurrence in social situations or according to the conceptual preferences of investigators.

INDEPENDENCE OF LEADERSHIP AND POSITION

Traditional leadership research has focused upon the behavior of formally designated or recognized leaders. This is probably due, at least in part, to the historical influence of the hierarchical models of the church and the army. As a result, it has until recently been customary to study leadership either as an attribute of the person of someone who is authority-vested, or as an attribute of his behavior. More recently, attention has been paid to leadership in groups less formally structured, as illustrated by the work of Bass with leaderless group discussion, the work of Sherif, as well as some of the work of other researchers in the area of group dynamics.[18]

[18] B. M. Bass, *Leadership, Psychology, and Organizational Behavior* (New York: Harper & Bros., 1960); Cartwright and Zander, *op. cit.*; M. and Carolyn W. Sherif, *An Outline of Social Psychology* (New York: Harper & Bros., 1956).

Table 1. Correspondence of leadership concepts of different investigators.

Bowers and Seashore (1964)	Hemphill and Coons (1957)	Halpin and Winer (1957)	Katz et al. (1950)	Katz and Kahn (1951)	Kahn (1958)	Mann (1962)	Likert (1961)	Cartwright and Zander (1960)
Support	Maintenance of membership character	Consideration	Employee orientation	Employee orientation / Closeness of supervision	Providing direct need satisfaction	Human relations skills	Principle of supportive relationships	Group maintenance functions
Interaction facilitation	Group interaction facilitation behavior	Sensitivity		Group relationships		Human relations skills	Group methods of supervision	
Goal emphasis	Objective attainment behavior	Production emphasis	Production orientation		Structuring path to goal attainment / Modifying employee goals	Administrative skills	High-performance goals	Goal-achievement functions
Work facilitation	Objective attainment behavior	Initiating structure		Differentiation of supervisory role / Closeness of supervision	Enabling goal achievement	Technical skills	Technical knowledge, planning, scheduling	

In the previous section, leadership was conceptualized in terms of four social-process functions, four kinds of behavior that must be present in work groups if they are to be effective. The performance of these functions was deliberately not limited to formally designated leaders. Instead, it was proposed that leadership, as described in terms of support, goal emphasis, work facilitation, and interaction facilitation, may be provided by anyone in a work group for anyone else in that work group. In this sense, leadership may be either "supervisory" or "mutual"; that is, a group's needs for support may be provided by a formally designated leader, by members for each other, or both; goals may be emphasized by the formal leader, by members to each other, or by both; and similarly for work facilitation and interaction facilitation.

This does not imply that formally designated leaders are unnecessary or superfluous, for there are both common-sense and theoretical reasons for believing that a formally acknowledged leader through his supervisory leadership behavior sets the pattern of the mutual leadership which subordinates supply each other.

LEADERSHIP AND ORGANIZATIONAL EFFECTIVENESS

Leadership in a work situation has been judged to be important because of its connection, to some extent assumed and to some extent demonstrated, to organizational effectiveness. Effectiveness, moreover, although it has been operationalized in a variety of ways, has often been assumed to be a unitary characteristic. These assumptions define a commonly accepted theorem that leadership (if not a unitary characteristic, then a limited roster of closely related ones) is always salutary in its effect and that it always enhances effectiveness.

The pattern of the typical leadership study has been first, to select a criterion of effectiveness: sometimes a rating of overall effectiveness by superiors, at other times a questionnaire measure of "morale," on still other occasions a few measures such as output, absence, or accident rates. Next, an attempt is made to relate leadership to the criterion selected. When, in fact, a relationship is obtained, this is accepted. When no relationship or one opposite to that expected is obtained, the investigator often makes some statement referring to "error" or "further research."

It seems that a better strategy would be to obtain: (*a*) measures reflecting a theoretically meaningful conceptual structure of leadership; (*b*) an integrated set of systematically derived criteria; and (*c*) a treatment of these data, which takes account of the multiplicity of relationships and investigates the adequacy of leadership characteristics in predicting effectiveness variables.

In the present study an attempt is made to satisfy these conditions. A conceptual structure of leadership is developed, using empirical evidence. The four concepts of this structure are operationalized in terms of questionnaire items describing behavioral acts largely "loaded" on one or another of these constructs, and a systematically derived set of criteria of organizational effectiveness is obtained.

RESEARCH METHODS

Research Site

This study was conducted in 40 agencies of a leading life insurance company. These agencies are independently owned businesses, performing identical functions in their separate parts of the country. Only one or two hierarchical levels intervene between the regional manager, at the top of the hierarchy, and the sales agent at the bottom. The typical agency consists of an exclusive territory comprising a number of counties of a state or states. The regional manager ordinarily has headquarters in some principal city of his territory, and contracts with individuals to service the area as sales agents. He receives an "override" upon the commissions of policies sold by these agents, in addition to the full commissions from whatever policies he sells personally.

If geographical distance or volume of business is great enough, he may contract with individuals to serve as district managers. The district manager is given territorial rights for some subportion of the regional manager's territory, is permitted to contract agents to service the area, subject to the approval of the regional manager, and receives a portion of what would otherwise be the regional manager's override upon sales within his territory.

Although this is the usual arrangement, variations occur. Occasionally, for example, a territory will be so constituted as to prevent subdivision into districts. In these cases, the regional manager contracts directly with sales agents throughout his territory. In other cases, the territory is almost entirely urban, in which case the regional manager may substitute salaried or partially salaried supervisory personnel for district managers. In all cases, however, there are at least a regional manager and sales agents, and frequently, in addition, a district manager between these two parties.

In all, the company's field force comprises nearly 100 agencies. Of these, 40 were selected as being roughly representative of them all. Selection was made by company personnel, with an effort to select half of the 40 from the topmost part of the list of agencies ordered by performance, and the other half from among poorer performing agencies, omitting any having recent organizational disruption or change. Questionnaires were mailed out in April, 1961, to all contracted regional managers, district managers, sales agents, and supervisory personnel on full or part salary in these agencies; 83 percent were returned by June, 1961, for a total of 873 respondents.

Measurement

This report is concerned with 20 index measurements obtained through paper-and-pencil questionnaires, and 7 factorial measures of agency performance obtained from company records. A short description of each questionnaire variable appears in Table 2. These measures reflect perceptions of behavior rather than behavior itself, and are therefore no different from any other method of quantifying behavior: all involve the measurement of behavior, by some person and some mechanism. Close familiarity by the recipients of the behavior—and whatever systematic bias this introduces—is here considered as more desirable than the lack of information and large random error that an outside observer would very probably introduce.

In addition to these questionnaire measurements, the company provided some 70 measures of agency performance, which were then factor analyzed,[19] resulting in 7 orthogonal factors.

Factor I. Staff-clientele maturity. This factor reflects a difference in the kind of business produced by the agency attributable

[19] The factor analysis method used was that of a principal axes solution with varimax rotation.

Table 2. Content of variables used.

Area	Description of questionnaire variable
Leadership* Support	Importance of morale Willingness to make changes Friendliness Conversational ease Opinion acceptance
Goal emphasis	Importance of competitive position Extra work effort
Work facilitation	Stressing standard procedures Offering new approaches Checking works vs capacity Emphasis upon meeting deadlines
Satisfaction†	With company With fellow agents With income prospects With regional manager With office costs With job
Need for Affiliation	Importance of being liked Importance of being accepted
Regional manager's expert power	Respect for regional manager's competence and good judgment
Classical business ideology‡	Extent of agreement with statements of value and belief about nature of "best" economic society.
Rivalry among agents	Extent to which some agents are trying to advance at others' expense

* Items in the leadership area were adapted from two sources: items used in the Ohio State studies and those used in previous Survey Research Center studies.

† 11 items, 6 satisfaction areas.

‡ Items based upon conceptualization by F. X. Sutton, S. E. Harris, C. Kaysen, and J. Tobin, *American Business Creed* (Cambridge, Mass.: Harvard University Press, 1956).

to the age and experience of the agent staff and the clientele that they reach. A high score reflects a high average premium per thousand, collected relatively infrequently, with very little term insurance or graduated premium life insurance, a small proportion of the business from new or young agents, and greater profitability from business already on the books.

Factor II. Business growth. This seems to indicate in fairly uncomplicated fashion the growth of business volume over the years immediately preceding the year of measurement.

Factor III. Business costs. Although the principal loadings are on variables measuring the costs per unit of new business, some minor loadings occur on variables relating to costs of renewal business. This factor, therefore, seems to be a business-cost dimension.

Factor IV. Advanced underwriting. This seems to be a factor measuring the extent to which there is emphasis by the agent staff upon advanced underwriting. A high score on this factor reflects a large average face value per life and per policy, comparatively large premiums per collection, a fairly high ratio of cases rejected, very little prepayment, fairly high costs, and high profitability of new business. A low score, of course, reflects a reverse pattern.

Factor V. Business volume. A fairly straightforward dimension measuring the dollar volume of new business done by the agency.

Factor VI. Manpower turnover. A measure of the extent to which there was a change in personnel within the agency during 1959. This factor loads most heavily on the ratio of terminations plus appointments to manpower, and on the ratio of terminations alone to manpower.

Factor VII. Regional manager's personal performance. This factor differs from those above by representing the performance of the regional manager, not of the agency as a whole. It seems to reflect the extent to which he is putting energy into agency maintenance and development, as against taking short-run gain. It is, perhaps, an age factor, related in some measure to the regional manager's distance from retirement.

Four of these factors are measures of performance in the usual sense; that is, a positive and a negative value can be placed at opposite ends of these continua: business growth, business costs, business volume, and manpower turnover. Factor I (staff-clientele maturity) and Factor IV (advanced underwriting) are descriptive, rather than evaluative,[20] and Factor VII is peculiar to only one person in the agency.

There are, therefore, within this study multiple-criteria measures, both of satisfaction, described earlier, and of performance. Although the use of multiple-criteria measures has become more common in recent years, it is still infrequent enough to make the study somewhat unique.

From the data that resulted, the following questions suggest themselves:

1. Are both mutual and supervisory leadership measures useful; that is, are there differential effects from the various leadership dimensions such that some criteria are associated with certain measures or combinations of measures and some with others?

2. In what way are mutual leadership measures related to supervisory measures?

3. How adequately may criteria of effectiveness be predicted from leadership measures as compared to other kinds of measures?

The reader should from the outset be reminded of several problems of the analysis. First, the analytic model used in this study assumes a particular causal directionality. Since the data are from a single period of time, this directionality cannot be proved. As an operating assumption, it must be either accepted or rejected by the reader, and the relationships otherwise interpreted by him. The assumption of managerial behavior as an organizational prime mover is, however, a common one. Second, since the model starts from assumptions about the nature of leadership, the analysis considers first the relationships of leadership characteristics to criteria of effectiveness. Third, since this is an attempt to locate possible precursors of effectiveness, the analysis then considers the relationship of nonleadership variables to effectiveness, paying serious attention only to those nonleadership variables that can reasonably be interpreted as causes of effectiveness. Fourth, not all of either leadership or nonleadership variables with statistically

---

[20] It should be noted that these factors are interpreted by the authors on the basis of a single set of data. Data from other periods or other firms, as well as interpretations by life insurance experts, might differ from those presented here.

PREDICTING ORGANIZATIONAL EFFECTIVENESS   255

Table 3. Correlation of leadership with satisfactions.

Leadership measure	Satisfaction with				
	Company	Fellow agents	Job	Income	Manager
Peer					
Support	.03*	.68	.39	.29*	.47
Goal emphasis	.37	.77	.26*	.42	.62
Work facilitation	.29*	.68	.34	.51	.45
Interaction facilitation	.31	.72	.30*	.42	.55
Manager					
Support	.31	.65	.35	.45	.86
Goal emphasis	.11*	.71	.09*	.43	.31
Work facilitation	.31	.61	.24*	.36	.41
Interaction facilitation	.30*	.67	.10*	.53	.78

* All others significant beyond .05 level of confidence, 2-tail

significant relationships are used to predict effectiveness measures; only the one or two of each category that is most highly correlated.

RESULTS

Relation of Leadership to Effectiveness

Table 3 presents the correlation coefficients of leadership measures with measures of satisfaction. Table 4 presents similar correlations of leadership measures to performance factors. These

Table 4. Correlation of leadership with performance factors.

Leadership measure	Performance factor						
	I	II	III	IV	V	VI	VII
Peer							
Support	.26	−.02	−.27	−.21	.23	−.12	.27
Goal emphasis	.49*	−.05	−.45*	−.27	.15	.04	.04
Work facilitation	.33*	.14	−.41*	−.41*	.18	.00	.04
Interaction facilitation	.44*	−.13	−.44*	−.24	.11	.14	.05
Manager							
Support	.28	−.24	−.26	−.12	.25	.16	.10
Goal emphasis	.31*	.11	−.27	−.18	.41*	.03	−.19
Work facilitation	.43*	.13	−.37*	−.33*	.21	.16	−.12
Interaction facilitation	.42*	−.29	−.30	−.21	.13	.20	.01

* Significant beyond .05 level of confidence, 2-tail.

Table 5. Improvement of prediction of criteria of effectiveness by addition of other significantly related leadership characteristics.

Effectiveness measure	Best predictor	Other measures improving prediction
Satisfaction with		
Company	Peer goal emphasis	None
Fellow agents	Peer goal emphasis	None
Job	Peer support	None
Income	Manager interaction facilitation	Peer goal emphasis
Manager	Manager support	None
Factors*		
I Staff-clientele maturity	Peer goal emphasis	Peer work facilitation
III Business costs	Peer goal emphasis	None
IV Advanced underwriting	Peer work facilitation	None
V Business volume	Manager goal emphasis	None

* Performance Factors II, VI, and VII showed no significant relationships to leadership characteristics.

data indicate first, that the incidence of significant relationships of leadership to effectiveness is well above the chance level. Of 40 satisfaction-leadership coefficients, 30 are significant beyond the 5 percent level of confidence. Of 56 performance-leadership coefficients, 13 are significant beyond the 5 percent level of confidence. Second, the significant coefficients are not uniformly distributed throughout the matrix; instead, certain effectiveness criteria (e.g., satisfaction with income) and certain leadership measures (e.g., peer work facilitation) have many significant relationships, whereas others have few or none (e.g., performance factor VI). Third, significant coefficients are as often found in relation to peer as to managerial leadership characteristics.

For parsimony, the leadership characteristic with the largest coefficient in relation to each criterion measure is chosen as the analytic starting point in these matrices. To this is then added in turn each of the other significant leadership relationships by means of a two-predictor multiple-correlation technique. Because no r-to-z transformation of multiple correlation coefficients is possible, these cannot be compared with the original r value; there-

Table 6. Intercorrelation of managerial and peer leadership variables.*

Managerial variables	Peer leadership characteristics			
	Support	Goal emphasis	Work facilitation	Interaction facilitation
Support	.59	.67	.52	.58
Goal emphasis	.54	.65	.72	.59
Work facilitation	.49	.63	.82	.66
Interaction facilitation	.55	.71	.62	.74

* All coefficients significant beyond .05 level of confidence, 2-tail.

fore, seven correlation points are arbitrarily set as the criterion of significant improvement in prediction.[21]

It is apparent from Table 5, that, with two exceptions, adding other leadership characteristics that display somewhat smaller, but significant, correlations does not improve prediction. It is also apparent that peer goal emphasis plays a central role in this analysis: it is either the best predictor, or a significant additive, in five of the twelve cases.

Relation of Peer to Managerial Leadership

Before assessing the adequacy of leadership as a predictor of effectiveness, it seems advisable to answer the question posed earlier about the relationship between peer and managerial leadership. Table 6 presents the intercorrelation; all 16 coefficients in the table are statistically significant, indicating therefore that there is a close relationship between all managerial characteristics, on the one hand, and all peer characteristics on the other. Following the same method as that used for effectiveness, it appears that the best predictor of peer support is managerial support; of peer goal emphasis, managerial interaction facilitation; of peer work facilitation, managerial work facilitation, and of peer interaction facilitation, managerial interaction facilitation. With one exception, therefore, the best predictor of the peer characteristic is its managerial opposite number. Table 7 indicates that three predictions are improved by related managerial characteristics.

[21] The actual multiple correlation values require much space and are therefore omitted here. Copies of these tables of multiple correlation coefficients may be obtained upon request from the authors.

Table 7. Improvement of prediction of peer leadership characteristics by addition of other managerial leadership characteristics.

Peer measure	Managerial best predictor	Other managerial measures improving prediction
Support	Support	Goal emphasis
Goal emphasis	Interaction facilitation	Goal emphasis
Work facilitation	Work facilitation	None
Interaction facilitation	Interaction facilitation	Work facilitation

Assuming causation, one may say that if a manager wishes to increase the extent to which his subordinates support one another, he must increase his own support and his own emphasis upon goals. If he wishes to increase the extent to which his subordinates emphasize goals to one another, he must first increase his own facilitation of interaction and his emphasis upon goals. By increasing his facilitation of the work, he will increase the extent to which his subordinates do likewise, and if, in addition, he increases his facilitation of interaction, his subordinates will in turn facilitate interaction among themselves.

These data appear to confirm that there is in fact a significant and strong relationship between managerial and peer leadership characteristics. In general, the statement may be made that a forerunner of each peer variable is its managerial opposite number, and that substantial improvement is in most cases made by combining with this another managerial characteristic.

Adequacy of Prediction by Leadership Measures

Because this analysis has placed great emphasis on leadership constructs as predictors of organizational outcomes, it seems desirable to consider the extent to which prediction of these outcomes can be enhanced by the inclusion of nonleadership variables.[22] Table 8 summarizes the data on predictability of all criteria by nonleadership measurements. It seems likely from these data that some of the criteria may be much more successfully predicted using nonleadership variables than using leadership measures,

[22] Nonleadership variables comprised a large majority of the 214 items in the questionnaire.

Table 8. Prediction of criteria by nonleadership variables.

Criterion	Total no. of significant relations (N = 214)	No. of significant nonleadership variables	No. of significant nonleadership variables exceeding best leadership predictor	No. of possible causal variables*
Satisfaction with				
Company	56	52	33	23
Job	39	36	11	8
Manager	66	44	1	1
Fellow agents	56	34	0	0
Income	60	43	2	2
Factors				
Factor I	22	15	1	1
Factor II	19	19	19	17
Factor III	50	39	9	6
Factor IV	26	23	12	6
Factor V	19	17	5	1
Factor VI	17	13	13	0
Factor VII	11	9	9	0

* Based upon the judgment of the research staff.

that some others may be enhanced by using both, and that the predictability of still others is not improved by nonleadership characteristics.

The analysis at this point becomes somewhat complex, since relationships exist not only between leadership or nonleadership variables and criteria, but also among leadership and among nonleadership variables. In effect, therefore, the search for the best predictive model turns into a rather complicated examination of various chains and arrangements of constructs. To simplify this procedure, each criterion is presented separately, diagramming for each a plausible and statistically optimal "causal" schema.

Figure 1*a* presents the relationships of leadership and nonleadership variables to satisfaction with the company and with income. This diagram indicates that supportive managers make more satisfactory arrangements about the office expenses of their agents, and that these arrangements, in part, lead to greater satisfaction with the company as a whole. In addition, as managers facilitate the interaction of their agents, the goals of the company and needs or aspirations of the people who work for it come to be more

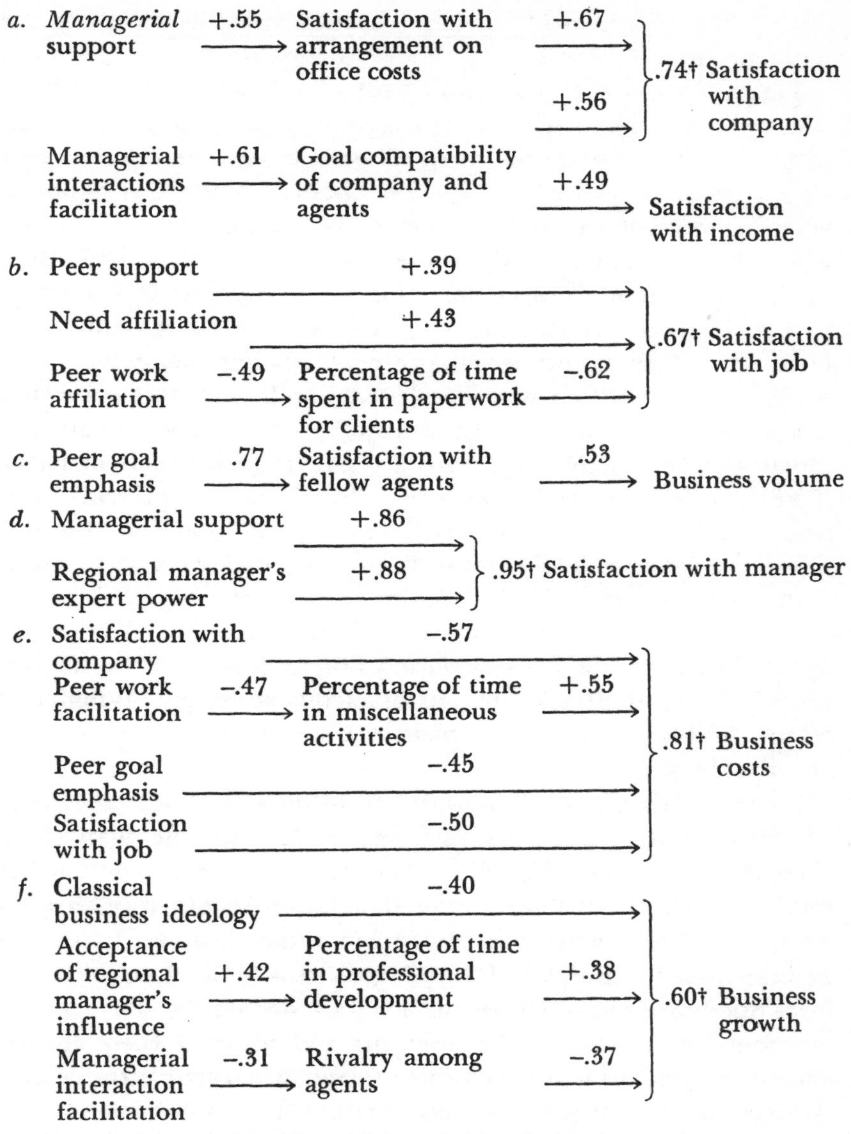

a. *Managerial* +.55 Satisfaction with +.67 ⎫
   support ⟶ arrangement on ⟶ ⎪ .74† Satisfaction
   office costs ⎬ with
   +.56 ⎪ company
   ⟶ ⎭

   Managerial +.61 Goal compatibility
   interactions ⟶ of company and +.49
   facilitation agents ⟶ Satisfaction
   with income

b. Peer support +.39
   ⟶ ⎫
   Need affiliation +.43 ⎪
   ⟶ ⎬ .67† Satisfaction
   Peer work −.49 Percentage of time −.62 ⎪ with job
   affiliation ⟶ spent in paperwork ⟶ ⎭
   for clients

c. Peer goal .77 Satisfaction with .53
   emphasis ⟶ fellow agents ⟶ Business volume

d. Managerial support +.86
   ⟶ ⎫
   Regional manager's +.88 ⎬ .95† Satisfaction with manager
   expert power ⟶ ⎭

e. Satisfaction with −.57
   company ⟶
   Peer work −.47 Percentage of time +.55
   facilitation ⟶ in miscellaneous ⟶
   activities ⎫
   Peer goal −.45 ⎬ .81† Business
   emphasis ⟶ ⎪ costs
   Satisfaction −.50
   with job ⟶

f. Classical −.40
   business ideology ⟶
   Acceptance Percentage of time
   of regional +.42 in professional +.38
   manager's ⟶ development ⟶ ⎬ .60† Business
   influence ⎪ growth
   Managerial −.31 Rivalry among −.37
   interaction ⟶ agents ⟶
   facilitation

† Multiple correlation of variables listed against the effectiveness measure.

Figure 1. Predicted measures: (*a*) satisfaction with company and with income; (*b*) satisfaction with job; (*c*) satisfaction with fellow agents; business volume; (*d*) satisfaction with manager; (*e*) business costs; (*f*) business growth.

PREDICTING ORGANIZATIONAL EFFECTIVENESS   261

compatible, which also leads to satisfaction with the company and with income.

Figure 1*b* presents a similar chain of relationships to satisfaction with the job itself. This diagram is interpreted to mean that as agents facilitate the work for each other, less time is spent by agents in paperwork for specific clients. When this happens, when agents behave more supportively toward each other, and when the agents are, on the whole, higher in need for affiliation, there is greater job satisfaction. Figure 1*c* presents relationships to two criteria: satisfaction with fellow agents and volume of business. When agents emphasize goals among themselves, they become more satisfied with each other; and when this condition exists, an agency does a greater volume of business. Figure 1*d* shows very succinctly that agents are satisfied with their manager if he is supportive and knowledgeable. Figure 1*e* presents relationships to business costs in diagram form. Earlier diagrams showed the network of relationships associated with satisfaction with the company and with the job; here, these two satisfaction states are associated with lower business costs. In addition, as agents facilitate the work for each other, they spend a smaller proportion of their time in miscellaneous activities. When this occurs, and when agents emphasize goals to one another, costs are also lower.

Figure 1*f* diagrams relationships to business growth. The relationships presented in this diagram are less reliable than those presented in earlier figures. They are, as a group, somewhat smaller in size than those found in relation to other criteria already described. With this caution in mind, however, they can be interpreted as follows: business growth is high when the agent force does *not* hold to a classical business ideology; when regional managers, by accepting the opinions and ideas of their agents, encourage professional development; and when managers reduce rivalries among agents by encouraging their interaction. Far from stressing growth attained by competitive effort, this paradigm presents a picture of growth through cooperative professionalism.

Two additional performance measures of effectiveness present one significant, reasonable "causal" relationship each: staff-clientele maturity is greater when agents have a higher level of aspiration, and more advanced underwriting occurs when agents have a higher level of education. Although significant correlations were presented earlier in relation to these two factors, the reasonable interpretation of them is that the leadership measures are either effects or coordinates, not causes, of these descriptive rather than evaluative performance factors.

That no reasonable, significant relationships to manpower turnover are to be found is extremely puzzling. In most investigations of the effect of social-psychological variables upon organizational behavior, it is assumed that performance measures which are more "person" than "production" oriented will show the highest relationships to questionnaire measurements. In the present case this assumption is not supported. No variations of analysis that were attempted produced any noticeable change. An attempt was made to assess curvilinear correlations, but no improvement over linear correlation resulted. It was also thought that the factorial measure of turnover might be too complicated and that a simpler measure of proportion of terminations might be more productive. This also produced no noticeable effect. Apparently, manpower turnover in this particular company or industry is related to forces in the individual, the environment, or perhaps the organizational situation not tapped by the questionnaire measurement used.

It is not surprising that no correlations are found with the regional manager's personal performance. It is, as explained earlier, the weakest factor, and differs from the other factors in being descriptive of a single individual rather than of the agency as a whole. It may well be affected more by variables such as the regional manager's distance from retirement than by factors assessed here.

DISCUSSION AND CONCLUSIONS

To what extent have the data demonstrated the usefulness of the conceptualization presented at the beginning of this article? It seems reasonable to state the following:

1. Seven of the eight leadership characteristics outlined above in fact play some part in the predictive model generated from the

PREDICTING ORGANIZATIONAL EFFECTIVENESS   263

data; only peer interaction facilitation seems to play no unique role.

2. Both managerial and peer leadership characteristics seem important.

3. There are plausible relationships of managerial to peer leadership characteristics.

4. The model is not a simple one of managerial leadership leading to peer leadership, which in turn leads to outcomes separately; instead, different aspects of performance are associated with different leadership characteristics, and, in some cases, satisfaction outcomes seem related to performance outcomes.

5. Some effectiveness measures are related to causal factors other than those tapped in this instrument.

6. The ability to predict outcomes with the variables selected varies from .95 to .00.

7. The role of leadership characteristics in this prediction varies in importance from strong, direct relationships in some cases (e.g., satisfaction with manager) to indirect relationships (e.g., business volume) to no relationship (e.g., advanced underwriting).

8. Leadership, as conceived and operationalized here, is not adequate alone to predict effectiveness; instead, additional and, in some cases, intervening constructs must be included to improve prediction. These "other" constructs are of several distinct types:

a. *Leadership-related.* Regional manager's expert power, regional manager's influence acceptance, and rivalry among agents.

b. *Work Patterns.* Percentage of time in miscellaneous activities, in paperwork for clients, in professional development.

c. *Personal and Motivational.* Education, level of aspiration, need for affiliation, goal compatibility of individual and organization, and classical business ideology.

[7]
The Managerial Dilemma

To see the dilemma of management in full perspective, it is necessary to examine first *what* is being managed. Since management takes place within an organizational system, attention must be turned first to what organization *is*. Then it will be possible to concentrate on an examination of the problems and possibilities involved in improving competence in managing *it*.[1]

ORGANIZATION UNIVERSALS

Several characteristics of organizations seem to be *universal*. They are present, in some degree, regardless of the specific product or line of work of the organization.[2] Effective management of these universals is the condition of efficient production through sound organization.

Purpose(s)

The first universal is *purpose(s)*.[3] Try to imagine a purposeless organization. Can you picture to yourself an organization that lacks purpose?

Those who have attempted to do so have been unable to identify an organization that does not have a purpose. Admittedly, it is not always easy to identify *what* the purpose is. Furthermore, the purpose for which the organization exists may, or may not, be the same as the purpose people experience as the basis for joining or remaining in it. Too frequently, organization and in-

5

6   THE MANAGERIAL GRID

dividual purpose may seem to be unconnected with one another, or even to be contradictory.

Although more or less specific purposes can be stated for educational, governmental, hospital, military, political, religious and family organizations, it is somewhat easier to describe the purpose of industrial organizations. Here, organization purpose is spoken of in terms of profit. Even the purpose of government is *to supply* service(s), not at a profit, but at the minimum necessary expense. The possibility of direct P/(L) (profit-loss) evaluation of human effort, particularly in service organizations, is not too common. Though P/(L) statements frequently are unavailable in service institutions, the organization's intention is consistent with profit motivation. Therefore, for this discussion, the equivalent of profit, that is, the production of *things or services,* will be regarded as the production aim of industrial and governmental organization — that is, those activities in which people engage toward organization purpose.

For the moment then, production can be accepted as an indication of organization purpose(s). It is to be regarded as universal of organizations.

People

Another characteristic of organization is *people.*[4] No organization is without them. It might be said that it would be desirable to eliminate people. Indeed, in some instances it seems wiser to replace people with technological procedures and automated processes, so that human energy is not being wasted in doing work that machine systems can do as well, or even better. But, if a peopleless arrangement were possible to achieve, it is unlikely that the word *organization* would be used to describe it. Other language already has been developed to picture machine operations of production that can be manned by one acting alone. The phrase *automated factory* depicts peopleless operations where organization, as we know it, has been eliminated.

Organization purpose then, cannot be achieved with-

THE MANAGERIAL DILEMMA 7

out people, nor does it exist under circumstances where one person is acting alone. To achieve it, others need to be drawn in. Needing more than one person to achieve a result such as production is what leads to the condition of organization.

Hierarchy

Hierarchy is a third attribute. Some people are bosses. Others are bossed. Some are more responsible for solving problems than others. That is the dimension of hierarchy.[5]

The process of achieving organization purpose (the first universal) through the efforts of several people (the second universal) results in some people attaining authority to supervise others; that is, to exercise the responsibility for planning, controlling and directing the activities of others through a hierarchical arrangement (the third universal).

While every organization has hierarchy and while many organizations have job descriptions that depict an individual's responsibility under his hierarchical position, the problem of boss-subordinate relations is far more complex than can possibly be pictured by a job description. But the foundation for understanding management is in recognizing that a boss' actions are dictated by certain *assumptions* he makes regarding how supervision should be exercised.[6]

Sometimes supervision is applied dramatically, such as when a boss tells others what he expects of them in no uncertain terms. But it also is possible that a person may not act like a boss. For instance he may not hold tight rein on subordinates. In those situations, then, people may not feel like they are being bossed at all; they have little or no feeling that influence is being exerted by those in the hierarchy, one level or more up. Yet the fact is that organizations, by necessity, are hierarchical. No matter how it is utilized, hierarchy is seen to be an essential condition of organization.[7]

Other universals of organization play an additional part in understanding problems of managerial competence. They are not introduced at this time, but one of them,

8   THE MANAGERIAL GRID

organizational culture and its significance on managerial behavior is discussed in Chapters 12 and 13.

This book is concerned with a fundamental inquiry regarding how these three organization properties are interrelated. The question is, "How are organization purposes achieved through people by bosses?"[8]

THE MANAGERIAL GRID

A variety of theories regarding managerial behavior can be identified. These theories—or sets of assumptions—are based on the way in which the three organization universals just discussed are connected to one another.[9]

One of the three is *concern for production;* the amount of emphasis supervision places on achieving production. A second is *concern for people;* the productive unit of organization. The third is *hierarchy;* the *boss* aspect. Whenever a man acts as a manager, he is in some way making assumptions about how to solve problems of achieving organization purposes of production through people.[10]

Dimensions of the Grid

Before going on let's define exactly what we mean by "concern for." This is not meant to indicate *how much* (such as, how much production, meaning quantity), nor is it intended to reflect the degree that the needs of people actually are met. Rather emphasis here is on the *degree* of "concern for" which is present in the *boss* because his *actions* are rooted in, and flow out of his own *basic attitudes.* What is significant is *how* a supervisor is concerned about production and *how* he concerns himself about people, and *how* these concerns intertwine.[11,12]

Concern for Production. The words *production* or *people* cover a range of considerations. Attitudes of concern toward production, for example, may be seen in the quality of policy decisions, the number of creative ideas that applied research turns into useful products, procedures or processes; number of accounts processed;

THE MANAGERIAL DILEMMA 9

quality and thoroughness of staff services; workload and efficiency measurements; volume of sales or units of physical output. Production as used here, is not limited to *things*. Its proper meaning covers whatever it is that organizations engage people to accomplish.

At the lowest level, it is true, concern for production may take the form of the number of units of things that can be counted or of time required to attain a certain production schedule. But at the top of an organization, concern for production may be demonstrated in the kind of policies which are established and the character of direction given to major programs of organization effort. Indeed, the concern for production at the top may be expressed through finding new directions or new products to sustain organization growth and development.

Concern for People. In a similar fashion, concern for people can be expressed in a variety of different ways. Included are concern for degree of personal commitment to completing a job one is responsible for; accountability based on trust rather than obedience; self esteem or the personal worth of an individual; establishing and maintaining good working conditions; maintaining an equitable salary structure and fringe benefits; desire for security in work; social relations or friendships with associates; etc.

As will be seen, *concern for production* and *concern for people* are expressed in vastly different ways, depending on the specific manner in which these two concerns are joined.[18]

"Pure" Theories

The *Managerial Grid*, depicted in Figure 1, shows these two concerns and a range of possible interactions between them. The horizontal axis indicates concern for production while the vertical axis indicates concern for people. Each is expressed as a nine-point scale of concern. The number *1* in each instance represents minimum concern. The *9* stands for maximum concern.

At the lower left corner of the Grid is the 1,1 style. This has a minimum of both concerns; that is, of con-

10   THE MANAGERIAL GRID

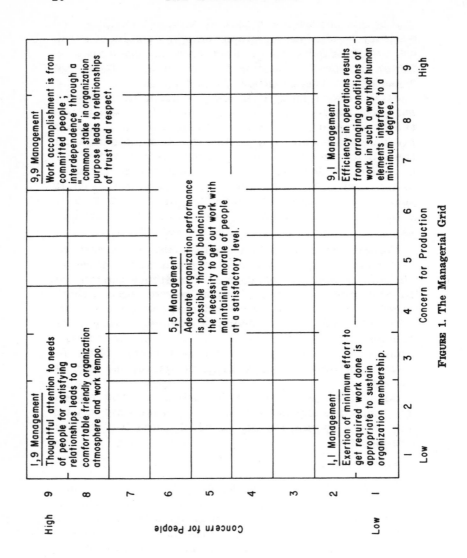

FIGURE 1. The Managerial Grid

cern for production and concern for people. At the top left corner of the Grid is found the 1,9 style. Here there is a minimum of concern for production but maximum concern for people. In the lower right corner is 9,1. This style has a maximum concern for production and a minimum for human aspects. In the upper right corner is the 9,9 style, where concern for both people and production reaches maximum. Then, in the center is the 5,5 style, which is a "middle of the road" or an intermediate amount of both kinds of concerns.

It should be emphasized that the manner in which these two concerns are linked together by a manager defines how he uses hierarchy. In addition, the character of *concern for* at different grid positions differs, even though the *degree* may be the same. For example, when high concern for people is coupled with a low concern for production, the type of people concern expressed (*i.e.,* that people be "happy") is far different from the type of high concern for people shown when a high concern for production is also evident (*i.e.,* that people be involved in the work and strive to contribute to organization purpose).

A number of additional managerial theories may be shown on this grid. Indeed, in a 9-point system such as is employed here, 81 "mixtures" of these two concerns might be pictured. However, emphasis first will be placed on analyzing the assumptions at the corners and midpoint. Each of these five theories defines a definite but different set of assumptions regarding how individuals, in fact, do orient themselves for managing situations of production that involve people.

As such, each theory can be seen as a set of possible assumptions for using hierarchy to link people into production. Each constitutes an alternative way of thinking. Each can be applied for analyzing how a given situation is being or might be managed. Each of the theories in actual practice is found, to some degree, in concrete situations in industrial and government organizations. Equally, the kinds of assumptions to be described are universal

12   THE MANAGERIAL GRID

and, in a certain sense, common throughout various cultures. But the important point here is that when a manager confronts a situation in which work is to be accomplished through people, there are, indeed, a *range* of alternative ways for him to go about supervising. To increase his managerial competence he needs to know them and to be able to select the best course of action for any given situation from among a number of possibilities.[14]

As in any field of applied endeavor, disagreement can arise between what is the best theory and what theory is most realistic for practical application in a "live" situation. However, as in any applied setting, the answer regarding what is best can only be given in the light of existing realities. There is no ideological way of saying what is best without reference to actual circumstances. But the choice is neither arbitrary nor random. The *results* a manager obtains will reflect, in predictable ways, the kinds of assumptions he applied in that situation.[15] If the assumptions do not "fit" the situation well, poorer results will be obtained than if they do. More will be said on this later.

Significance and Interpretation of Grid Positions

Should the five "pure" theories be viewed as defining a set of personality characteristics? If not, then in what manner should they be considered?

One answer is that these positions constitute anchorages for managerial attitudes and practices. Conceived of in this manner, aspects of the Grid are more accurately regarded as describing systems of pressures acting on an individual to manage in a certain fashion.[16] Such pressures arise:

1. From inside himself

2. From the immediate external situation, and/or

3. From characteristics of the organizational system including traditions, established practices and procedures.

Though most people seem to be predisposed to manage in one way or another, points on the Grid are *not* to be thought of as personality types that isolate a given individual's behavior. They do not slot him in a rigid and inflexible way into a certain place. Behavior is more changing and flexible than that.

In comparison with a mechanical explanation of managerial behavior, the Grid pictures a number of different sets of assumptions about how an individual *can* manage. Any set of assumptions is subject to change. Whenever a person changes his underlying managerial assumptions, his actual managerial practices shift accordingly, or else a gross discrepancy is present between the attitudes he expresses and the actions he takes. A given individual's style, then, may be viewed as a dominant set of assumptions.[17] These assumptions orient his thinking and his behavior in dealing with production/people relationships. Furthermore, he may or may not be aware of the assumptions that are guiding his actions.[18] The purpose of this book, and of much management training, is to aid an individual to become more knowledgeable regarding his own assumptions about how to manage.

Observe an individual's behavior in a variety of situations. It becomes clear that even the notion of one *dominant* style, a single set of managerial assumptions, is not sufficient to catch the full implication of a person's managerial approach. In addition to a dominant set of managerial assumptions, which are the most characteristic of the managerial style a person has adopted, the concept of a *backup* set of assumptions is a useful one. An individual's backup theory is the one he uses when his dominant theory fails to get the desired results. It is the style he falls back on. Any style may be a backup to any other theory as a dominant style.

Which managerial style is dominant for any given person in any particular situation can be determined by any one or several sets of conditions in combination.

Organization. Managerial behavior frequently is determined by situational factors, such as the organization in which a person operates. Thus, when organizational practices are so fixed or rigid as to permit only small variations in individual behavior, the managerial style

14   THE MANAGERIAL GRID

exhibited may reflect little of a man's personal thinking and much of his organization beliefs about "the right way to manage." Therefore, one section within each of the anchor positions in the following chapters is concerned with organization or situational requirements which are likely to call forth various managerial styles.

Situation. The situation itself may be the determining or overriding factor dictating which set of managerial assumptions are employed to deal with it. Management of people in the crisis of an explosion situation is likely to be different than it would be under circumstances that are routine.

Values. Any individual's choice of managerial assumptions may be based on values or beliefs he holds concerning the "right" way to treat people, or the way to manage to achieve "best" results. Any given set of assumptions can have a personal value attached to them which represents an individual's private conviction concerning the desirability of any managerial style as a dominant one.

Personality. The dominant managerial style may, to an important degree, result from deep-rooted personality characteristics which predispose an individual to prefer one approach over another. Thus, in the sections concerned with the five anchor positions (Figure 1), the personality dispositions likely to be found in conjunction with a given managerial style are presented.

Chance. Finally, a set of managerial assumptions may guide a person's behavior because he has not been confronted with, nor has discovered in his own experience, that other sets of assumptions about how to manage are available. "Chance," so to speak, has not helped him learn. But many managers, upon learning the variety of managerial styles available to them, do shift, sometimes rather dramatically, from one style to another, as they seek to integrate people into production. Seeing alternatives, they embrace a different set of assumptions.

The point to be emphasized here is that managerial styles are *not* fixed. They are not unchanging. They are determined by a range of factors. Many are subject to modification through formal instruction or self-training of the kind possible from this book.

PLAN OF THE BOOK

Primary emphasis is to be placed on analyzing managerial assumptions. Five sets of key managerial orientations are described in the first part of the book.

In these chapters, managerial actions are divided into several segments. Each chapter has sections that are concerned with goal setting, direction and control; boss-subordinate relationships, *i.e.*, those aspects of management traditionally connected with supervision, planning, execution and followup. Other topics include conflict; creativity; commitment; management development; and communications. Although the interconnections between each cluster are numerous, these aspects of managerial effort can be discussed separately with profit. Then, personality characteristics likely to predispose the selection of one dominant managerial style as against others are outlined. Finally, organization factors likely to prompt application of one style over another are discussed.

In the second section of the book, managerial *facades* are explored. These are deceptive ways of managing which are adopted to hide one's true motivation. Then, attention is turned to an examination of managerial practices where two or more theories are applied simultaneously or in succession within a given situation.

In the third section of the book, research which has been conducted to evaluate managerial styles of American managers of today is reported and interpreted. Also in this section, the scores you made on the instrument you completed, in Chapter 1, will be interpreted so that you can estimate the assumptions underlying your own managerial practices. This will give you a basis for thinking about any changes in your own approach you may wish to consider.

Finally, the significance of the organization culture itself as a critical ingredient influencing managerial behavior will be discussed. Strategies for increasing organization

16   THE MANAGERIAL GRID

effectiveness, which include individual management development as well as organization development, will be outlined. An assessment is provided of one such development effort.

References

1. The line of thinking that leads to the generalized version of the Managerial Grid is consistent with work by C. Argyris, *Personality and organization*. New York: Harper, 1957; K. D. Benne and P. Sheats, Functional Roles of Group Members. *Journal of Social Issues*, 2, 1948, 42-47; E. A. Fleishman, E. F. Harris, & H. E. Burtt, *Leadership and Supervision in Industry*. Columbus, Ohio: Bureau of Educational Research, Ohio State University, 1955; R. Likert, *New Patterns of Management*. New York: McGraw-Hill, 1961; D. McGregor, *The Human Side of Enterprise*. New York: McGraw-Hill, 1960; D. Moment & A. Zaleznik, *Role Development and Interpersonal Competence*. Boston: Harvard University, 1963; and, T. Parsons, R. F. Bales & E. A. Shils, *Working Papers in the Theory of Action*. Glencoe, Ill.: Free Press, 1953.

2. Sherif, M. & Sherif, C. *An Outline of Social Psychology*. (Rev. Ed.). New York: Harper & Bros., 1956, 143-180.

3. Simon, H. A. Recent Advances in Organization Theory. *Research Frontiers in Politics and Government*. Washington, D. C.: Brookings, 1955.

4. Allen, L. A. *Management and Organization*. New York: McGraw-Hill, 1958, 58.

5. Bavelas, A. Communication Patterns in Task-Oriented Groups. *Journal of the Acoustical Society of America*. 22, 1950, 725-730. Also in D. Cartwright & A. Zander, (Eds.), *Group Dynamics: Research and Theory*. Evanston, Ill.: Row, Peterson, 1956, 493-506. Pfiffner, J. M. & Sherwood, F. P. *Administrative Organization*. Englewood Cliffs, N. J.: Prentice-Hall, 1960, 52-73. Kelley, H. H. Communication in Experimentally Created Hierarchies. *Human Relations*, 4, 1951, 39-56.

6. Appley, L. A. *Management in Action*. New York: American Management Association, 1956, 20-22.

7. Likert, R. A Motivational Approach to a Modified Theory of Organization and Management. In M. Haire (Ed.), *Modern Organization Theory*. New York: Wiley, 1959, 184-217. Stanton, E. S. Company Policies and Supervisors' Attitudes Toward Supervision. *Journal of Applied Psychology*, 44, 1960, 22-26.

8. In this book, attention is not focused on organization and managerial principles and functions *per se;* such as unity of direction, span of control, delegation of authority, etc. Rather, consideration is limited to the assumptions a manager operates under when, for example, he delegates authority, or plans a given work activity. Organization principles and management functions are treated as neutral or as givens, whereas the *ways* in which they are applied under different managerial styles *are* subject to examination.

9. Blake, R. R., Mouton, J. S. & Bidwell, A. C. "The Managerial Grid," *Advanced Management—Office Executive*, 1, 1962, 12-15, 36.

THE MANAGERIAL DILEMMA 17

Blake, R. R., and Mouton, J. S. "The Developing Revolution in Management Practices, *ASTD Journal*, 16, 1962, 29-50.

10. McGregor, D. *The Human Side of Enterprise*. New York: McGraw-Hill, 1960, 6.

11. Bales, R. F. The Equilibrium Problem in Small Groups. In T. Parsons, R. F. Bales, & E. A. Shils, *Working Papers in the Theory of Action*. Glencoe, Ill.: Free Press, 1953, 111-161. Also, abridged in A. P. Hare, E. F. Borgatta, & R. F. Bales (Eds.), *Small Groups*. New York: Knopf, 1955, 425-456.

12. The two Grid dimensions, *concern for people and concern for purpose* (production in this particular context) toward which interaction is pointed appear to be basic variables. That is, essentially the same assumptions regarding the integration of people and purpose can be applied in a wide variety of settings; from the family situation to medical and educational institutions; from sales organizations to R&D facilities; from American to Asiatic cultures; etc.

13. It is possible to add a number of dimensions to the Grid; such as activity—passivity; unit of social action, from one to many; self *vs.* other or team orientation; degree of actual effectiveness (Reddin, W. *The Tri-Dimensional Grid*. University of New Brunswick: mimeograph). While these additional dimensions have research value, at this stage in development, they appear to add unduly to the complexity of the task of seeking a meaningful, systematic framework for managerial theories, which has direct application in concrete action situations. Thus, they will not be included further.

14. Shibutani, T. Reference Groups as Perspectives. *American Journal of Sociology*, 60, 1955, 562-570.

15. McGregor, D., *op. cit.*, 11.

16. Lewin, K. *A Dynamics Theory of Personality*. New York: McGraw-Hill, 1935. Lewin, K. *Field Theory in Social Science*. New York: Harper & Bros., 1951.

17. Mead, G. H. *Mind, Self, and Society*. Chicago: Univ. of Chicago 1934; Festinger, L. *A Theory of Cognitive Dissonance*. Evanston, Ill.: Row, Peterson, 1957.

18. Katz, D. The Functional Approach to the Study of Attitudes. *Public Opinion Quarterly*, 24, 1960, 163-204.

Part V
Contingency Theories

[8]

How Do You Make Leaders More Effective?

New Answers to an Old Puzzle

Fred E. Fiedler

Let's begin with a basic proposition: The organization that employs the leader is as responsible for his success or failure as the leader himself. Not that this is a new insight —far from it. Terman wrote in 1904 that leadership performance depends on the situation, as well as on the leader. Although this statement would not be questioned by anyone currently working in this area, it also has been widely ignored. Practically all formal training programs attempt to change the individual; many of them assume explicitly or implicitly that there is one style of leadership or one way of acting that will work best under all conditions. Most military academies, for example, attempt to mold the individual into a supposedly ideal leader personality. Others assume that the training should enable the individual to become more flexible or more sensitive to his environment so that he can adapt himself to it.

Before going further let's define a few terms. I will confine my discussion to *task groups* rather than the organization of which the group is a part. Furthermore, we will assume that anyone who is placed in a leadership position will have the requisite technical qualifications for the job. Just as the leader of a surgical team obviously has to have medical training, so a manager must know the essential administrative requirements of his job. We will here talk primarily about training *as a leader* rather than training as a specialist. The effectiveness of the leader will be defined in terms of how well his group or organization performs the primary tasks for which the group exists. We measure the effectiveness of a football coach by how many games his team wins and not by the character he builds, and the excellence of an orchestra conductor by how well his orchestra plays, not by the happiness of his musicians' or his ability as a musicologist. Whether the musicians' job satisfaction or the conductor's musicological expertness do, in fact, contribute to the orchestra's excellence is an interesting question in its own right, but it is not what people pay to hear. Likewise, the performance of a manager is here measured in terms of his department's or

3

group's effectiveness in doing its assigned job. Whether the accomplishment of this job is to be measured after a week or after five years depends, of course, upon the assignment the organization gives the group, and the accomplishments the organization considers important.

When we think of improving leadership, we almost automatically think of training the individual. This training frequently involves giving the man a new perspective on his supervisory responsibilities by means of role playing, discussions, detailed instructions on how to behave toward subordinates, as well as instruction in the technical and administrative skills he will need in his job. A training program might last a few days, a few months, or as in the case of college programs and military academies, as long as four years. What is the hard evidence that this type of training actually increases organizational performance?

Empirical studies to evaluate the effectiveness of various leadership training programs, executive development, and supervisory workshops have been generally disappointing. Certainly, the two field experiments and two studies of ongoing organizations conducted by my associates and me failed to show that training increases organizational performance.

The first experiment in 1966 was conducted at a Belgian naval training center. We chose 244 Belgian recruits and 48 petty officers from a pool of 546 men. These men were assembled into 96 three-men groups: 48 groups had petty officers and 48 groups had recruits as leaders. The recruits ranged in age from 17 to 24, and none had been in the service longer than six weeks. The petty officers ranged in age from 19 to 45 years, and had an average of ten years' experience. All petty officers had received a two-year technical and leadership training course at petty officer candidate school. Since most successful graduates enlist for a 20-year term, Belgian petty officers are not only well-trained but they are also truly motivated and committed career-men.

The petty officers were matched with the recruit leaders on intelligence and other relevant scores. Each group worked on four cooperative tasks which were considered fair samples of the type of work petty officers might perform. One task consisted of writing a recruiting letter urging young men to join the Belgian navy as a career; the second and third tasks required the groups to find the shortest route for a convoy first through ten and then through twelve ports; the fourth task required the leader to train his men without using verbal instructions in the disassembling and reassembling of a .45-caliber automatic pistol.

Despite the fact that the recruits had had no leadership experience or training, their groups performed as well as those led by petty officers.

To test whether these results were not simply due to the chance or to a fault in our experimental design, we conducted a second experiment at a leadership training workshop for officers of Canadian military colleges. This study compared the performance of groups led by captains and majors with groups led by enlisted men who had just finished their eight weeks of basic training. All of the officers were, themselves, graduates of a Canadian military college. In addition, the officers had from 5 to 17 years of leadership experience and training after graduation. The 32 enlisted men were basic trainees between 19 and 22 years of age, and their intelligence scores were substantially below those of the officers'. To reduce the possibility that they might feel anxious or inhibited by working with officers, the officers wore casual clothes and the enlisted men were told

4

that they would work with civilian instructors.

The officers and men worked as three-men groups on three different tasks. They were asked to (a) write a fable, (b) find the shortest route for a truck convoy, and (c) draw bar graphs from score distributions that first had to be converted from one scale to another. As in the Belgian study, the tasks were designed so that all three group members had to participate in the work. As in the Belgian study, the groups led by the trained and experienced officers performed no better than the groups led by untrained and inexperienced enlisted men.

It is, of course, possible that experimental tasks do not give realistic results. For this reason we further checked in real-life situations whether the amount of training influenced performance by a study of 171 managers and supervisors in U.S. post offices. The performance of each of these supervisors was rated by two to five of his superiors. Amount of training ranged from zero hours of training to three years, with a median of 45 hours. The number of hours of supervisory training received by these managers was totally unrelated to their rated performance. We also investigated whether the post offices with highly trained supervisors were more effective on such objective post office performance measures as target achievement in number of first-class pieces handled, indirect costs, mail processing, etc. However, 12 of the 15 correlations were slightly *negative;* none was significant. Thus, training apparently did not improve organizational performance.

Another study related the amount of training received by police sergeants with the performance ratings made by their supervisors and other sergeants. Here again, training was unrelated to performance. Thus, neither the two controlled experiments nor the two field studies provide any basis for assuming

that leadership training of the type given in these institutions, or in the training programs taken by postal managers or police sergeants, contributed to organizational performance.

I repeat that these findings are by no means unusual. Empirical studies to determine whether or not leadership training improves organizational performance have generally come up with negative findings. Newport, after surveying 121 large companies, concluded that not *one* of the companies had obtained any scientifically acceptable evidence that the leadership training for their middle management had actually improved performance.

T–group and sensitivity training, which has become fashionable in business and industry, has yielded similarly unsatisfactory results. Reviews of the literature by Campbell and Dunnette and by House found no convincing evidence that this type of training increased organizational effectiveness, and a well-known study at the International Harvester Company by Fleishman, Harris, and Burtt on the effects of supervisory training concluded that the effects of supervisory training in modifying behavior were very short-lived and did not improve performance.

Effect of Experience on Leadership

Let us now ask whether supervisory experience improves performance. Actually, since leadership experience almost always involves on-the-job training, we are dealing with a closely related phenomenon.

Interestingly enough, the literature actually contains few, if any, studies which attempt to link leadership experience to organizational effectiveness. Yet, there seems to be a firmly held expectation that leadership experience makes a leader more effective. We simply have more trust in experienced leaders. We   5 can infer this, for example, from the many regulations that require time in grade before promotion to the next higher level, as well as the many specifications of prior job in hiring executives for responsible positions.

We have already seen that the experienced petty officers and military academy officers did not perform more effectively than did the inexperienced enlisted men, nor did the more experienced officers or petty officers perform better than the less experienced.

In addition, we also analyzed data from various other groups and organizations. These included directors of research and development teams at a large physical research laboratory, foremen of craftshops, general foremen in a heavy machinery manufacturing company, managers of meat, and of grocery markets in a large supermarket chain as well as post office supervisors and managers, and police sergeants. For all these managers we could obtain reliable performance ratings or objective group effectiveness criteria. None of the correlations was significant in the expected direction. The median correlation relating leadership experience to leadership performance for all groups and organizations was –.12—certainly not significant in the positive direction!

To summarize the findings, neither orthodox leadership training nor leadership experience nor sensitivity training appear to contribute across the board to group or organizational effectiveness. It is, therefore, imperative first that we ask why this might be so, and second that we consider alternative methods for improving leadership performance.

The Contingency Model

6   The "Contingency Model," a recent theory of leadership, holds that the effectiveness of group performance is contingent upon (a) the leader's motivational pattern, and (b) the degree to which the situation gives the leader power and influence. We have worked with a leadership motivation measure called the "Esteem for the Least Preferred Coworker," or LPC for short. The subject is first asked to think of all the people with whom he has ever worked, and then given a simple scale on which he describes the one person in his life with whom he has been able to work *least well*. This "least preferred coworker" may be someone he knows at the time, or it may be someone he has known in the past. It does not have to be a member of his present work group.

In grossly oversimplified terms, the person who describes his least preferred coworker in relatively favorable terms is basically motivated to have close interpersonal relations with others. By contrast, the person who rejects someone with whom he cannot work is basically motivated to accomplish or achieve on the task, and he derives satisfaction from being recognized as having performed well on the task. The task-motivated person thus uses the task to obtain a favorable position and good interpersonal relations.

Classifying Leadership Situations

The statement that some leaders perform better in one kind of situation while some leaders perform better in different situations is begging a question. "What kinds of situations are best suited for which type of leader?" In other words, how can we best classify groups if we wish to predict leadership performance?

We can approach this problem by assuming that leadership is essentially a work relationship involving power and influence. It is easier to be a leader when you have complete control than when your control is weak

Figure 1
Cells or ''Octants''

	Very Favorable			Intermediate in Favorableness			Unfavorable	
	1	2	3	4	5	6	7	8
Leader-member relations	Good	Good	Good	Good	Poor	Poor	Poor	Poor
Task structure	High	High	Low	Low	High	High	Low	Low
Position power	Strong	Weak	Strong	Weak	Strong	Weak	Strong	Weak

and dependent on the good will of others. It is easier to be the captain of a ship than the chairman of a volunteer group organized to settle a school bussing dispute. The *job* may be more complex for the navy captain but *being in the leadership role* is easier for him than for the committee chairman. It is, therefore, not unreasonable to classify situations in terms of how much power and influence the situation gives the leader. We call this "situational favorableness." One simple categorization of groups on their situational favorableness classifies leadership situations on the basis of three major dimensions:

1. *Leader-member relations.* Leaders presumably have more power and influence if they have a good relationship with their members than if they have a poor relationship with them, if they are liked, respected, trusted, than if they are not. Research has shown that this is by far the most important single dimension.

2. *Task structure.* Tasks or assignments that are highly structured, spelled out, or programmed give the leader more influence than tasks that are vague, nebulous and unstructured. It is easier, for example, to be a leader whose task it is to set up a sales display according to clearly delineated steps than it is to be a chairman of a committee preparing a new sales campaign.

3. *Position power.* Leaders will have more power and influence if their position is vested with such prerogatives as being able to hire and fire, being able to discipline, to reprimand, and so on. Position power, as it is here used, is determined by how much power the leader has over his subordinates. If the janitor foreman can hire and fire, he has more position power in his own group than the chairman of a board of directors who, frequently, cannot hire or fire—or even reprimand his board members.

Using this classification method we can now roughly order groups as being high or low on each of these three dimensions. This gives us an eight-celled classification (Figure 1). This scheme postulates that it is easier to be a leader in groups that fall into Cell 1 since you are liked, have position power, and have a structured task. It is somewhat more difficult in Cell 2 since you are liked, have a structured task, but little position power, and so on to groups in Cell 8 where the leader is not liked, has a vague, unstructured task, and little position power. A good example of Cell 8 would be the disliked chairman of the volunteer committee we mentioned before.

The critical question is, "What kind of leadership does each of these different group situations call for?" Figure 2 sum-   7 marizes the results of 63 analyses based on a total of 454 separate groups. These included bomber and tank crews, antiaircraft artillery units, managements of consumer cooperative companies, boards of directors, open-hearth shops, basketball and surveying teams, and various groups involved in creative and problem-solving tasks.

The horizontal axis of the graph indicates the "situational favorableness," namely, the leader's control and influence as defined by the eight-fold classification shown in Figure 1. The vertical axis indicates the relationship between the leader's motivational pattern, as measured by the LPC score, and his group's performance. A median correlation above the midline shows that the relationship-motivated leaders tended to perform better than the task-motivated leaders. A correlation below the midline indicates that the task-motivated leaders performed better than the relationship-

motivated leaders. Figure 3 shows the predictions that the model would make in each of the eight cells.

These findings have two important implications for our understanding of what makes leaders effective. First, Figure 2 tells us that the task-motivated leaders tend to perform better than relationship-motivated leaders in situations that are very favorable and in those that are unfavorable. Relationship-motivated leaders tend to perform better than task-motivated leaders in situations that are intermediate in favorableness. Hence, both the relationship- and the task-motivated leaders perform well under some conditions and not under others. It is, therefore, not correct to speak of any person as generally a good leader or generally a poor leader. Rather, a leader may perform well in one situation but not in another. This is also borne out by the repeated findings that we cannot predict a

Figure 2

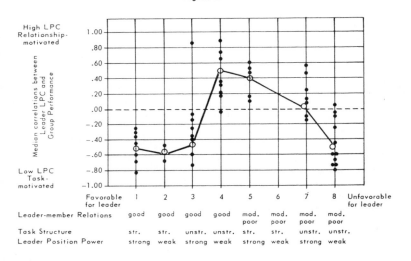

8

Figure 3

Prediction of the Performance of Relationship- and Task-Motivated Leaders

	1	2	3	4	5	6	7	8
Relationship-Motivated / High LPC				Good	Good	Some-what better	Some-what better	
Task-Motivated / Low LPC	Good	Good	Good					Good

leader's performance on the basis of his personality traits, or even by knowing how well he performed on a previous task unless that task was similar in situational favorableness.

Second, the graph on Figure 2 shows that the performance of a leader depends as much on the situational favorableness as it does on the individual in the leadership position. Hence, the organization can change leadership performance either by trying to change the individual's personality and motivational pattern or by changing the favorableness of the leader's situation. As we shall see, this is really what training is all about.

Before we go further, we must ask how valid the Contingency Model is. How well does it predict in new situations? There have been at least 25 studies to date that have tested the theory. These validation studies included research on grocery and meat markets, a physical science laboratory, a machinery plant, a hospital, an electronics company, and teams of volunteer public health workers in Central America, as well as various experimentally assembled groups in the laboratory. Of particular importance is a large experiment that used cadets at West Point to test the entire eight cells of the model. This study almost completely reproduced the curve shown on Figure 2. In all studies that were recently reviewed, 35 of the 44 obtained correlations were in the predicted direction—a finding that could have occurred by chance less than one time in 100. An exception is Cell 2, in which laboratory experiments—but not field studies—have yielded correlations showing the relationship-motivated leaders perform better than task-motivated leaders.

Effect of Leadership Training?

The main question of this paper is, of course, how we can better utilize leadership training and experience to improve leadership performance. While appropriate leadership training and experience apparently do not increase organizational performance, there is considerable evidence that they do affect the manager's attitudes, behavior, and of course, his technical skills and administrative know-how. These programs teach the leader better methods of getting along with his subordinates, more effective handling of administrative routines, as well as technical background required for the job. In other words, the leader who is trained or experienced will have considerably greater control and influence over his job and his subordinates than one who is untrained and inexperienced.

In contrast, the inexperienced and untrained leader confronts numerous problems that are new to him, and for which he does not have a ready answer. As a result, he 9

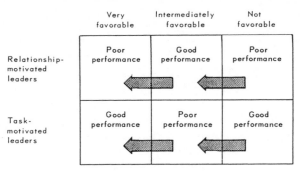

Figure 4

**Favorableness of the situation for the
trained or experienced leader**

Arrows indicate the predicted effect of experience and training.

cannot give clear and concise instructions to his subordinates. Moreover, since so many situations are novel, he will be more anxious and less sure of himself, which will tend to make him more dependent upon his group and others in the organization. Not even the most detailed manual of operating instructions will enable a new manager to step into his job and behave as if he had been there for years. Thus, situations will be correspondingly less favorable for the untrained and inexperienced leader than for the trained and experienced leader.

What we are really saying here is that leadership training and experience primarily improve the favorableness of the leadership situation. But, if the Contingency Model is right, a more favorable situation requires a different type of leadership than a less favorable situation. Hence, leadership training and experience that will improve the performance of one type of leader *will decrease the performance of the other*. On the average, it will have little or no measurable effect on organizational performance. This is

schematically shown by Figure 4. The arrows indicate that effect of training and experience in improving the favorableness of the leadership situation.

The headings on Figure 4 indicate the situational favorableness for the already trained or experienced leader. The untrained or inexperienced leader obviously would face a correspondingly less favorable situation. Thus, while the situation at the left of the table is very favorable for the trained leader, it is likely to be intermediate for the leader who lacks training and experience. The training or experience, as indicated by the arrow, would then change the untrained leader's situation from one which is intermediate to one which is very favorable. Likewise, if the trained leader's situation is intermediate in favorableness, the untrained leader's situation would be unfavorable. Training would, then, improve the untrained leader's situation from an unfavorable one to a situation which is intermediate in favorableness.

But why should an inexperienced and untrained leader perform better than

10

someone with training and experience? Under certain conditions this is not too difficult to see. An individual who is new on the job is likely to seek good interpersonal relations with his coworkers so that he can enlist their full cooperation. He is not likely to throw his weight around and he will, therefore, be less likely to antagonize his group members. In other words, the proposition is far from absurd, and it is quite compatible with the behavior of the manager who learns to rely on his staff of experts in making various decisions.

The proof of this theoretical pudding lies in various studies that bear out our suppositions.

STUDY OF SCHOOL PRINCIPALS

One study was conducted by McNamara on principals of rural elementary schools and of urban secondary schools in Canada. The performance of elementary principals was evaluated by means of ratings obtained from school superintendents and their staffs. The performance of secondary school principals was measured on the basis of province-wide achievement tests given to all students in the 11th grade. The average test score was used as the measure of the principal's effectiveness.

McNamara divided his group into task- and relationship-motivated principals, and again into inexperienced principals who had been on their job less than two years and those with three or more years of experience.

Let us now consider the favorableness of the leadership situation of elementary school principals. Their position power is reasonably high, and their task is fairly structured. The schools in McNamara's sample were quite small, the curricula of these schools are determined by the authorities of the province and by the school superintendent's office,

and the elementary school principal typically is not called upon to make many policy decisions or innovations. His task is, therefore, structured. Hence, the experienced principal will have a very favorable leadership situation, and we would expect the task-motivated principals to perform better than the relationship-motivated principals.

The inexperienced principal faces a considerably less favorable situation. While his position power is high, he does not know his teachers well, and many of the administrative problems that arise will have to be handled in a manner that is new to him. We would predict that his task is unstructured and that the situation is intermediate. Without much experience the relationship-motivated principals will, therefore, perform better than their task-motivated colleagues. That this is the case is shown on Figure 5.

The secondary principal also has high position power. However, his organization is considerably more complex. In McNamara's sample, the schools had from 25 to 40 teachers who, in turn, were supervised by department heads. Thus, the principal's control over the teachers is less direct. In addition, of course, the curriculum of a high school varies from school to school and the high school principal generally has to make a considerable number of policy decisions about the teaching program, his staff, as well as the activities and disciplinary problems of his students. For this reason, the experienced principals of secondary schools were judged to have a situation of intermediate favorableness. Relationship-motivated principals should perform best. The inexperienced high school principal will have to set new precedents and he will have to think through many of the problems for the first time as they arise. Hence, the situation will be relatively unfavorable. We would predict, therefore, that the task-motivated principals with less than two years' experience

11

will perform best in these situations. Here, again, the data follow the prediction. (See Figure 5.)

It is particularly important to note that the relationship-motivated elementary school principal with longer experience actually performed *less well* than the relationship-motivated elementary school principal with less experience. Likewise, the task-motivated secondary school principal with more experience had significantly *poorer* performance than the task-motivated principal with considerably less experience. Thus, for these particular administrators, the more extensive experience not only failed to improve their performance but actually decreased their effectiveness.

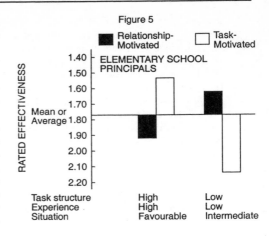

Figure 5

STUDY OF CONSUMER COOPERATIVES

Another study that illustrates the effect of training and experience was conducted some years ago on 32 member companies of a large federation of consumer cooperatives. The federation used two indices for measuring company effectiveness and managerial performance. These were (a) the operating efficiency of the company, that is, roughly the proportion of overhead to total sales, and (b) the proportion of net income to total sales. We used the three-year average of these measures for our study.

In a reanalysis of these data, the managers were divided into those with task- and relationship-motivated leadership patterns, and of these, the ten with the most and the ten with the least years of experience in the organization. Since the federation of the companies maintained a strong management development program, managers with long experience also tended to have the most extensive training.

The leadership situation for the expe-

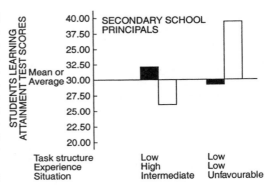

rienced managers was judged to be relatively favorable. They had considerable position power, and their job was relatively structured. As in the case of school administrators, the inexperienced and less well trained managers would, of course, face a larger number of problems that they had not encountered before,

Figure 6

Performance of relationship- and task-motivated managers with relatively high and relatively low levels of experience

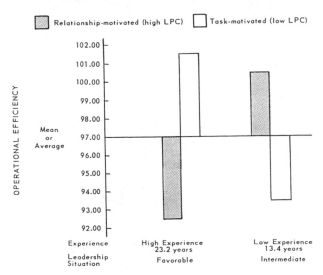

Relationship-motivated (high LPC)   Task-motivated (low LPC)

and the task would, therefore, be correspondingly less structured. Hence, for the inexperienced managers the situation would be intermediate in favorableness.

The Contingency Model would then predict that the experienced managers with task-oriented leadership patterns would perform better, as would the inexperienced managers with relationship-motivated leadership patterns. That this was the case is shown on Figure 6 for operating efficiency. Somewhat weaker results were obtained for the net income criterion. It is again apparent that the experienced and trained relationship motivated managers performed less well than did the relatively inexperienced and untrained managers who are relationship-motivated.

We have also studied the effect of training and experience on the performance of the post office managers and supervisors, police sergeants, and formal and informal leaders of company boards. These studies have yielded essentially similar results.

NEW STUDIES OF MILITARY LEADERSHIP

Two studies were recently conducted specifically for the purpose of testing the hypothesis on completely new data. These were of field artillery sections and navy aircraft maintenance shops. Training and experience data were available for the noncommissioned officers in charge of these groups. In these studies, groups were assigned to cells 1, 3, 5, and 8 of the model. (See Figure 7.) Just as predicted, the task-motivated leaders performed best in cells 1, 3, and 8, while the relationship-moti- 13

Figure 7

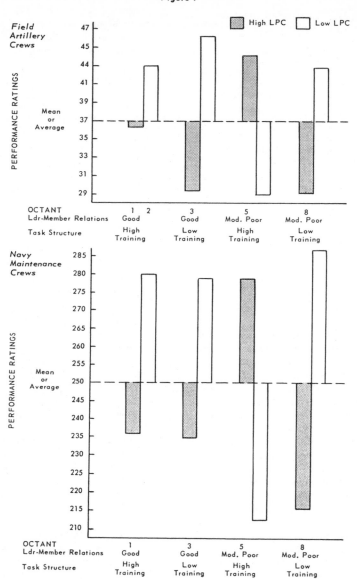

vated leaders performed best in cell 5. All findings were statistically significant.

To Train or Not to Train

What does all this mean for improving managerial performance, and how can we apply the findings that we have described?

In sum, if we want to improve leadership performance, we can either change the leader by training, or we can change his leadership situation. Common sense suggests that it is much easier to change various aspects of a man's job than to change the man. When we talk about leadership behavior, we are talking about fairly deeply ingrained personality factors and habits of interacting with others. These cannot be changed easily, either in a few hours or in a few days. In fact, as we have seen, not even four years of military academy and 5 to 17 years of subsequent experience enable a leader to perform significantly better on different tasks than someone that has had neither training nor experience.

We have seen that a leader's performance depends not only on his personality, but also on the organizational factors that determine the leader's control and influence, that—is, the "situational favorableness." As we have shown, appropriate training and experience improve situational favorableness. Whether or not they improve performance depends upon the match between the leader's motivational pattern and the favorableness of the situation. This means that a training program that improves the leader's control and influence may benefit the relationship-motivated managers, but it will be detrimental to the task-motivated managers, or vice versa, depending upon the situation.

The idea that we can improve a leader's performance by increasing the favorableness of his situation is, of course, far from

new. A poorly performing manager may be given more authority, more explicit instructions, more congenial coworkers in the hope that it will help him do a better job. Moreover, decreasing the favorableness of the situation in order to improve a manager's performance is also not quite as unusual as it might appear at first blush. If a man becomes bored, stale, or disinterested in his job, a frequent remedy is to transfer him to a more challenging job. As it turns out, "challenging" is just another way of saying that the job is less structured, has less position power, or requires working with difficult people. It is certainly well known that some men perform best under pressure and that they get into difficulty when life is too calm. These are the trouble shooters who are dispatched to branch offices or departments that need to be bailed out.

What, then, can an organization do to increase managerial performance? As a first step, it is necessary to determine which of the managers are task- and which are relationship-motivated. This can be accomplished by means of a short scale. Second, the organization needs to categorize carefully the situational favorableness of its managerial jobs. (Scales are available in Fiedler, F. E., *A Theory of Leadership Effectiveness*, McGraw-Hill, 1967.) Third, the organization can decide on a number of options in its management of executive personnel.

The least expensive and probably most efficient method is to develop a careful program of managerial rotation that moves some individuals from one job to another at a faster rate than it moves others. For example, it will be recalled that the relationship-motivated elementary school principals on the average became less effective after two years on the job. Moving these men to new jobs probably would have made them more effective than leaving them at the same school for many more years. Likewise, moving the   15

Fred E. Fiedler *is professor of psychology and of management and organization and director of the Organization Research Group at the University of Washington. He received his M.A. in 1947 and his Ph.D. in 1949 at the University of Chicago. From 1951 to 1969 he was professor of psychology at the University of Illinois and director of the Group Effectiveness Research Laboratory. In 1958–59 he was appointed Fulbright Research Scholar and Visiting Professor at the University of Amsterdam, and in 1963–1966 he received a Ford Faculty Research Award and served as guest professor at the University of Louvian, Belgium.*

Dr. Fiedler has published more than one hundred articles and papers on leadership, group processes, and organizational behavior. He is author of Leader Attitudes and Group Effectiveness (*University of Illinois Press, 1958*), *co-author of* Boards, Management and Company Success (*Interstate Publishers, Danville, Illinois, 1959*), *and* A Theory of Leadership Effectiveness (*McGraw-Hill, 1967*). *He has served as consulting editor for* Sociometry *and is currently a consulting editor for* Administrative Science Quarterly *and* The Journal of Applied Social Psychology.

Dr. Fiedler has served as a consultant to numerous governmental and private agencies and business concerns. Among them the U.S. Veterans Administration; the U.S. Naval Research Laboratory; the Walter Reed Army Institute of Research; the U.S. Post Office; the U.S. Military Academy, West Point; the U.S. Naval Academy, Annapolis; the U.S. Civil Service Commission; and the Battelle Northwest Memorial Institute. He has been the principal investigator in a number of large research programs sponsored by the Office of Naval Research, the Office of the Surgeon General of the Army, the Department of Health, Education and Welfare, and the Advanced Research Projects Agency.

task-motivated secondary school principals after two years probably would have increased their performance. In the case of the consumer cooperatives, it took 15 to 20 years in the organization (as employee and assistant manager, as well as manager) before the relationship-motivated managers began to go stale. How long a man should stay on a particular job must, of course, be determined empirically in each organization.

A second major option is management training. The problem here is whether to train only some people or all those who are eligible: training a task-motivated manager who is accepted by his group and has a

structured task is likely to improve his performance; training a relationship-motivated manager for the same job is likely to make him less effective. The organization would, therefore, be better off if it simply did not train relationship-motivated managers for these particular jobs. On the other hand, the relationship-motivated but not the task-motivated managers should be trained for jobs in which the situational favorableness is intermediate.

Leadership training should devote more effort to teaching leaders how to modify their environment and their own job so that they fit their style of leadership. We must get

16

rid of the implicit assumption that the environment and the organization, or a particular leadership position, are constant and unchanging. In addition to changes which occur as the leaders gain experience, they also continuously modify their leadership positions. They often speak of showing their men who is boss, presumably to assert their position power or of "being one of the boys" to de-emphasize it; they speak of getting to know their men, presumably to establish better relations with them; they speak of different approaches to their work; they look for certain types of assistants who complement their abilities; they demand more authority, or they play down the authority they already have; they ask for certain types of assignments and try to avoid others. The theory that has here been described merely provides a basis for a more rational modification of the leadership job.

How can we train leaders to determine the conditions under which they are most likely to succeed or fail, and how can they learn to modify their own leadership situation? The frequently negative relationship between leadership experience and leader performance undoubtedly stems in part from the difficulties in obtaining feedback about one's own leadership effectiveness. As research has shown, unless the group fails utterly in its task, most leaders are unable to say with any degree of accuracy how well their group performed in comparison with other groups.

Leadership training away from the organization should provide the prospective leader with a wide range of leadership situations in which he can get immediate feedback on how well he has performed. On the basis of these experiences, he must learn to recognize which situations fit his particular style of leadership and how he can best modify situations so that they will enable him to perform effectively. This may involve the development of six to eight short leadership tasks and situations, or adequately measured organizational tasks, in which each trainee is required to lead. He must then be given an objective appraisal of how well his group's performance compared with the performance of others under the same conditions.

The closest approximation to the all-around good leader is likely to be the individual who intuitively or through training knows how to manage his environment so that the leadership situation best matches his leadership style.

It may be desirable for various reasons to train all managers of a certain level, especially since being sent to executive training programs has in many organizations become a symbol of success. Men are sent to these training programs not because they need to learn, but because they need to be rewarded. If this is the case, the organization might do well to place the manager who completes the training program into a position that matches his leadership motivation pattern. For example, in the consumer cooperative companies, the relationship motivated managers might have been given staff jobs, or jobs with troubled companies at the conclusion of an extensive training program.

Conclusion

As a consequence of our research, we have both discredited some old myths and learned some new lessons.

The old myths:

• That there is one best leadership style, or that there are leaders who excel under all circumstances.

• That some men are born leaders, and that neither training, experience, or conditions can materially affect leadership skills.

17

The lessons, while more pedestrian and less dogmatic, are more useful. We know that people differ in how they respond to management situations. Furthermore, we know that almost every manager in an organization can perform effectively, providing that we place him in a situation that matches his personality, providing we know how to match his training and experience to the available jobs—and providing that we take the trouble.

SELECTED BIBLIOGRAPHY

The interested reader may wish to consult Fiedler's, *A Theory of Leadership Effectiveness,* McGraw-Hill, 1967, which presents a detailed summary of many of his studies as well as a fairly technical description of the theory. A more popular version of the theory is described in a *Harvard Business Review* article entitled, "Engineer the Job to Fit the Manager," September, 1965 and in *Psychology Today,* "Style or Circumstance: the Leadership Enigma," March 1969. A more technical and extensive summary of the work on leadership training will appear shortly in a forthcoming issue of *Administrative Science Quarterly*.

[9]

Journal of Contemporary Business   *Autumn 1974*

PATH-GOAL THEORY OF LEADERSHIP

ROBERT J. HOUSE
UNIVERSITY OF TORONTO

TERENCE R. MITCHELL
UNIVERSITY OF WASHINGTON

An integrated body of conjecture by students of leadership, referred to as the "Path-Goal Theory of Leadership," is currently emerging. According to this theory, leaders are effective because of their impact on subordinates' motivation, ability to perform effectively and satisfactions. The theory is called Path-Goal because its major concern is how the leader influences the subordinates' perceptions of their work goals, personal goals and paths to goal attainment. The theory suggests that a leader's behavior is motivating or satisfying to the degree that the behavior increases subordinate goal attainment and clarifies the paths to these goals.

HISTORICAL FOUNDATIONS

The path-goal approach has its roots in a more general motivational theory called expectancy theory.[1] Briefly, expectancy theory states that an individual's attitudes (e.g., satisfaction with supervision or job satisfaction) or behavior (e.g., leader behavior or job effort) can be predicted from: (1) the degree to which the job, or behavior, is seen as leading to various outcomes (expectancy) and (2) the evaluation of these outcomes (valences). Thus, people are satisfied with their job if they think it leads to things that are highly valued, and they work hard if they believe that effort leads to things that are highly valued. This type of theoretical rationale can be used to predict a variety of phenomena related to leadership, such as why leaders behave the way they do, or how leader behavior influences subordinate motivation.[2]

This latter approach is the primary concern of this article. The implication for leadership is that subordinates are motivated by leader behavior to the extent that this behavior influences expectancies, e.g., goal paths and valences, e.g., goal attractiveness.

Several writers have advanced specific hypotheses concerning how the
leader affects the paths and the goals of subordinates.[3] These writers
focused on two issues: (1) how the leader affects subordinates' expectations that effort will lead to effective performance and valued rewards,
and (2) how this expectation affects motivation to work hard and perform
well.

While the state of theorizing about leadership in terms of subordinates'
paths and goals is in its infancy, we believe it is promising for two
reasons. First, it suggests effects of leader behavior that have not yet
been investigated but which appear to be fruitful areas of inquiry. And,
second, it suggests with some precision the situational factors on which
the effects of leader behavior are contingent.

The initial theoretical work by Evans asserts that leaders will be effective by making rewards available to subordinates and by making these rewards contingent on the subordinate's accomplishment of specific goals.[4]
Evans argued that one of the strategic functions of the leader is to
clarify for subordinates the kind of behavior that leads to goal accomplishment and valued rewards. This function might be referred to as path
clarification. Evans also argued that the leader increases the rewards
available to subordinates by being supportive toward subordinates, i.e.,
by being concerned about their status, welfare and comfort. Leader sup-
portiveness is in itself a reward that the leader has at his or her disposal, and the judicious use of this reward increases the motivation of
subordinates.

Evans studied the relationship between the behavior of leaders and the
subordinates' expectations that effort leads to rewards and also studied
the resulting impact on ratings of the subordinates' performance. He
found that when subordinates viewed leaders as being supportive (considerate of their needs) and when these superiors provided directions and guidance
to the subordinates, there was a positive relationship between leader
behavior and subordinates' performance ratings.

However, leader behavior was only related to subordinates' performance
when the leader's behavior also was related to the subordinates' expectations

that their effort would result in desired rewards. Thus, Evans' findings suggest that the major impact of a leader on the performance of subordinates is clarifying the path to desired rewards and making such rewards contingent on effective performance.

Stimulated by this line of reasoning, House, and House and Dessler advanced a more complex theory of the effects of leader behavior on the motivation of subordinates.[5] The theory intends to explain the effects of four specific kinds of leader behavior on the following three subordinate attitudes or expectations: (1) the satisfaction of subordinates, (2) the subordinates' acceptance of the leader and (3) the expectations of subordinates that effort will result in effective performance and that effective performance is the path to rewards. The four kinds of leader behavior included in the theory are: (1) directive leadership, (2) supportive leadership, (3) participative leadership and (4) achievement-oriented leadership. Directive leadership is characterized by a leader who lets subordinates know what is expected of them, gives specific guidance as to what should be done and how it should be done, makes his or her part in the group understood, schedules work to be done, maintains definite standards of performance and asks that group members follow standard rules and regulations. Supportive leadership is characterized by a friendly and approachable leader who shows concern for the status, well-being and needs of subordinates. Such a leader does little things to make the work more pleasant, treats members as equals and is friendly and approachable. Participative leadership is characterized by a leader who consults with subordinates, solicits their suggestions and takes these suggestions seriously into consideration before making a decision. An achievement-oriented leader sets challenging goals, expects subordinates to perform at their highest level, continuously seeks improvement in performance *and* shows a high degree of confidence that the subordinates will assume responsibility, put forth effort and accomplish challenging goals. This kind of leader constantly emphasizes excellence in performance and simultaneously displays confidence that subordinates will meet high standards of excellence.

A number of studies suggest that these different leadership styles can be shown by the same leader in various situations.[6] For example, a leader may show directiveness toward subordinates in some instances and be participative or supportive in other instances.[7] Thus, the traditional method of characterizing a leader as either highly participative and

83

supportive *or* highly directive is invalid; rather, it can be concluded
that leaders vary in the particular fashion employed for supervising their
subordinates. Also, the theory, in its present stage, is a tentative explanation of the effects of leader behavior--it is incomplete because it
does not explain other kinds of leader behavior and does not explain the
effects of the leader on factors other than subordinate acceptance, satisfaction and expectations. However, tne theory is stated so that additional
variables may be included in it as new knowledge is made available.

PATH-GOAL THEORY

General Propositions

The first proposition of path-goal theory is that leader behavior is acceptable and satisfying to subordinates to the extent that the subordinates
see such behavior as either an immediate source of satisfaction or as-
instrumental to future satisfaction.

The second proposition of this theory is that the leader's behavior will
be motivational, i.e., increase effort, to the extent that (1) such behavior makes satisfaction of subordinate's needs contingent on effective
performance and (2) such behavior complements the environment of subordinates by providing the coaching, guidance, support and rewards necessary
for effective performance.

These two propositions suggest that the leader's strategic functions are
to enhance subordinates' motivation to perform, satisfaction with the job
and acceptance of the leader. From previous research on expectancy theory
of motivation, it can be inferred that the strategic functions of the leader
consist of: (1) recognizing and/or arousing subordinates' needs for outcomes over which the leader has some control, (2) increasing personal payoffs to subordinates for work-goal attainment, (3) making the path to those
payoffs easier to travel by coaching and direction, (4) helping subordinates
clarify expectancies, (5) reducing frustrating barriers and (6) increasing
the opportunities for personal satisfaction contingent on effective performance.

Stated less formally, the motivational functions of the leader consist
of increasing the number and kinds of personal payoffs to subordinates
for work-goal attainment and making paths to these payoffs easier to travel by clarifying the paths, reducing road blocks and pitfalls and increasing the opportunities for personal satisfaction en route.

Contingency Factors

Two classes of situational variables are asserted to be contingency
factors. A contingency factor is a variable which moderates the relationship between two other variables such as leader behavior and subordinate
satisfaction. For example, we might suggest that the degree of structure
in the task moderates the relationship between leaders' directive behavior
and subordinates' job satisfaction. Figure I shows how such a relationship might look. Thus, subordinates are satisfied with directive behavior
in an unstructured task and are satisfied with nondirective behavior in
a structured task. Therefore, we say that the relationship between leader
directiveness and subordinate satisfaction is contingent upon the structure of the task.

The two contingency variables are (a) personal characteristics of the
subordinates and (b) the environmental pressures and demands with which
subordinates must cope in order to accomplish the work goals and to
satisfy their needs. While other situational factors also may operate to determine the effects of leader behavior, they are not presently
known.

With respect to the first class of contingency factors, the characteristics of subordinates, path-goal theory asserts that leader behavior
will be acceptable to subordinates to the extent that the subordinates
see such behavior as either an immediate source of satisfaction or as
instrumental to future satisfaction. Subordinates' characteristics are
hypothesized to partially determine this perception. For example, Runyon[8]
and Mitchell[9] show that the subordinate's score on a measure called Locus of
Control moderates the relationship between participative leadership style
and subordinate satisfaction. The Locus-of-Control measure reflects the
degree to which an individual sees the environment as systematically responding to his or her behavior. People who believe that what happens to
them occurs because of their behavior are called internals; people who

85

Figure I

Hypothetical Relationship Between Directive Leadership
and Subordinate Satisfaction With Task
Structure as a Contingency Factor

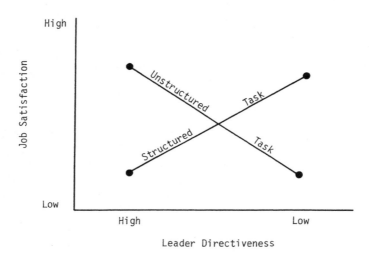

believe that what happens to them occurs because of luck or chance are
called externals. Mitchell's findings suggest that internals are more
satisfied with a participative leadership style and externals are more
satisfied with a directive style.

A second characteristic of subordinates on which the effects of leader
behavior are contingent is subordinates' perception of their own ability
with respect to their assigned tasks. The higher the degree of perceived
ability relative to task demands, the less the subordinate will view
leader directiveness and coaching behavior as acceptable. Where the subordinate's perceived ability is high, such behavior is likely to have
little positive effect on the motivation of the subordinate and to be
perceived as excessively close control. Thus, the acceptability of the
leader's behavior is determined in part by the characteristics of the
subordinates.

The second aspect of the situation, the environment of the subordinate,
consists of those factors that are not within the control of the subordinate but which are important to need satisfaction or to ability
to perform effectively. The theory asserts that effects of the leader's
behavior on the psychological states of subordinates are contingent on
other parts of the subordinates' environment that are relevant to subordinate motivation. Three broad classifications of contingency factors in
the environment are:

- The subordinates' tasks
- The formal authority system of the organization
- The primary work group.

Assessment of the environmental conditions makes it possible to predict
the kind and amount of influence that specific leader behaviors will have
on the motivation of subordinates. Any of the three environmental factors
could act upon the subordinate in any of three ways: first, to serve as
stimuli that motivate and direct the subordinate to perform necessary
task operations; second, to constrain variability in behavior. Constraints
may help the subordinate by clarifying expectancies that effort leads to
rewards or by preventing the subordinate from experiencing conflict and
confusion. Constraints also may be counterproductive to the extent that
they restrict initiative or prevent increases in effort from being associated positively with rewards. Third, environmental factors may serve

as rewards for achieving desired performance, e.g., it is possible for the subordinate to receive the necessary cues to do the job and the needed rewards for satisfaction from sources other than the leader, e.g., co-workers in the primary work group. Thus, the effect of the leader on subordinates' motivation will be a function of how deficient the environment is with respect to motivational stimuli, constraints or rewards.

With respect to the environment, path-goal theory asserts that when goals and paths to desired goals are apparent because of the routine nature of the task, clear group norms or objective controls of the formal authority systems, attempts by the leader to clarify paths and goals will be both redundant and seen by subordinates as imposing unnecessary, close control. Although such control may increase performance by preventing soldiering or malingering, it also will result in decreased satisfaction (see Figure I). Also with respect to the work environment, the theory asserts that the more dissatisfying the task, the more the subordinates will resent leader behavior directed at increasing productivity or enforcing compliance to organizational rules and procedures.

Finally, with respect to environmental variables the theory states that leader behavior will be motivational to the extent that it helps subordinates cope with environmental uncertainties, threats from others or sources of frustration. Such leader behavior is predicted to increase subordinates' satisfaction with the job context and to be motivational to the extent that it increases the subordinates' expectations that their effort will lead to valued rewards.

These propositions and specification of situational contingencies provide a heuristic framework on which to base future research. Hopefully, this will lead to a more fully developed, explicitly formal theory of leadership.

Figure II presents a summary of the theory. It is hoped that these propositions, while admittedly tentative, will provide managers with some insights concerning the effects of their own leader behavior and that of others.

Figure II

Summary of Path-Goal Relationships

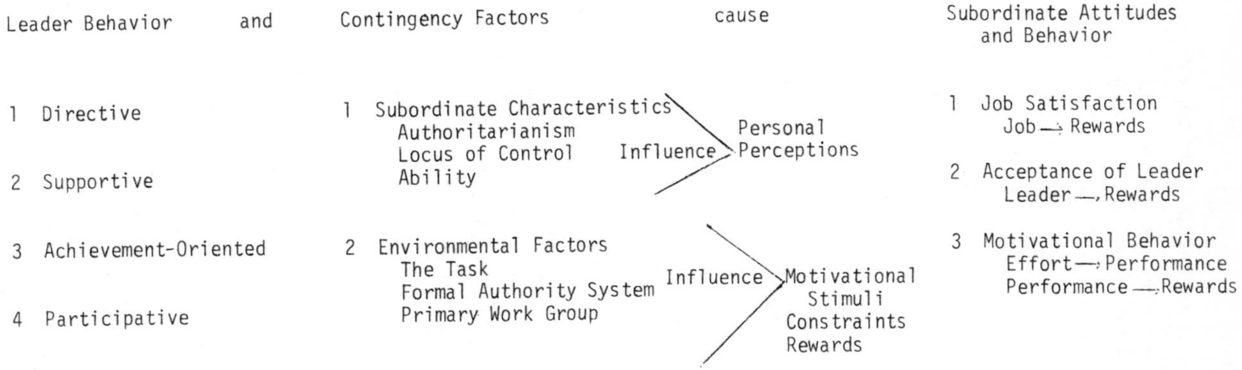

Leader Behavior	and	Contingency Factors	cause	Subordinate Attitudes and Behavior
1 Directive		1 Subordinate Characteristics Authoritarianism Locus of Control Ability	Personal Influence Perceptions	1 Job Satisfaction Job→ Rewards
2 Supportive				2 Acceptance of Leader Leader—→Rewards
3 Achievement-Oriented		2 Environmental Factors The Task Formal Authority System Primary Work Group	Influence Motivational Stimuli Constraints Rewards	3 Motivational Behavior Effort—→Performance Performance—→Rewards
4 Participative				

89

EMPIRICAL SUPPORT

The theory has been tested in a limited number of studies which have generated considerable empirical support for our ideas and also suggest
areas in which the theory requires revision. A brief review of these
studies follows.

Leader Directiveness

Leader directiveness has a positive correlation with satisfaction and
expectancies of subordinates who are engaged in ambiguous tasks and has
a negative correlation with satisfaction and expectancies of subordinates
engaged in clear tasks. These findings were predicted by the theory and
have been replicated in seven organizations. They suggest that when task
demands are ambiguous or when the organization procedures, rules and
policies are not clear, a leader behaving in a directive manner complements the tasks and the organization by providing the necessary guidance
and psychological structure for subordinates.[10] However, when task demands are clear to subordinates, leader directiveness is seen more as a
hindrance.

However, other studies have failed to confirm these findings.[11]
A study by Dessler[12] suggests a resolution to these conflicting findings--
he found that for subordinates at the lower organizational levels of a
manufacturing firm who were doing routine, repetitive, unambiguous tasks,
directive leadership was preferred by closed-minded, dogmatic, authoritarian subordinates and nondirective leadership was preferred by nonauthoritarian, open-minded subordinates. However, for subordinates at
higher organizational levels doing nonroutine, ambiguous tasks, directive
leadership was preferred for both authoritarian and nonauthoritarian
subordinates. Thus, Dessler found that two contingency factors appear to
operate siumultaneously: subordinate task ambiguity and degree of subordinate authoritarianism. When measured in combination, the findings
are as predicted by the theory; however, when the subordinate's personality is not taken into account, task ambiguity does not always operate
as a contingency variable as predicted by the theory. House, Burill and
Dessler recently found a similar interaction between subordinate authoritarianism and task ambiguity in a second manufacturing firm, thus adding
confidence in Dessler's original findings.[13]

Supportive Leadership

The theory hypothesizes that supportive leadership will have its most positive effect on subordinate satisfaction for subordinates who work on stressful, frustrating or dissatisfying tasks. This hypothesis has been tested in 10 samples of employees,[14] and in only one of these studies was the hypothesis disconfirmed.[15] Despite some inconsistency in research on supportive leadership, the evidence is sufficiently positive to suggest that managers should be alert to the critical need for supportive leadership under conditions where tasks are dissatisfying, frustrating or stressful to subordinates.

Achievement-Oriented Leadership

The theory hypothesizes that achievement-oriented leadership will cause subordinates to strive for higher standards of performance and to have more confidence in the ability to meet challenging goals. A recent study by House, Valency and Van der Krabben provides a partial test of this hypothesis among white collar employees in service organizations.[16] For subordinates performing ambiguous, nonrepetitive tasks, they found a positive relationship between the amount of achievement orientation of the leader and subordinates' expectancy that their effort would result in effective performance. Stated less technically, for subordinates performing ambiguous, nonrepetitive tasks, the higher the achievement orientation of the leader, the more the subordinates were confident that their efforts would pay off in effective performance. For subordinates performing moderately unambiguous, repetitive tasks, there was no significant relationship between achievement-oriented leadership and subordinate expectancies that their effort would lead to effective performance. This finding held in four separate organizations.

Two plausible interpretations may be used to explain these data. First, people who select ambiguous, nonrepetitive tasks may be different in personality from those who select a repetitive job and may, therefore, be more responsive to an achievement-oriented leader. A second explanation is that achievement orientation only affects expectancies in ambiguous situations because there is more flexibility and autonomy in such tasks. Therefore, subordinates in such tasks are more likely to be able to change in response to such leadership style. Neither of the above interpretations have been tested to date; however, additional research is currently under way to investigate these relationships.

91

Participative Leadership

In theorizing about the effects of participative leadership it is necessary to ask about the specific characteristics of both the subordinates
and their situation that would cause participative leadership to be viewed
as satisfying and instrumental to effective performance.

Mitchell recently described at least four ways in which a participative
leadership style would impact on subordinate attitudes and behavior as
predicted by expectancy theory.[17] First, a participative climate should
increase the clarity of organizational contingencies. Through participation in decision making, subordinates should learn what leads to what.
From a path-goal viewpoint participation would lead to greater clarity
of the paths to various goals. A second impact of participation would
be that subordinates, hopefully, should select goals they highly value.
If one participates in decisions about various goals, it makes sense that
this individual would select goals he or she wants. Thus, participation
would increase the correspondence between organization and subordinate
goals. Third, we can see how participation would increase the control
the individual has over what happens on the job. If our motivation is
higher (based on the preceding two points), then having greater autonomy
and ability to carry out our intentions should lead to increased effort
and performance. Finally, under a participative system, pressure towards
high performance should come from sources other than the leader or the organization. More specifically, when people participate in the decision
process they become more ego-involved; the decisions made are in some part
their own. Also, their peers know what is expected and the social pressure has a greater impact. Thus, motivation to perform well stems from
internal and social factors as well as formal external ones.

A number of investigations prior to the above formulation supported the
idea that participation appears to be helpful,[18] and Mitchell presents a
number of recent studies that support the above four points.[19] However,
it is also true that we would expect the relationship between a participative style and subordinate behavior to be moderated by both the personality characteristics of the subordinate and the situational demands.
Studies by Tannenbaum and Alport and Vroom have shown that subordinates
who prefer autonomy and self-control respond more positively to participative leadership in terms of both satisfaction and performance than

subordinates who do not have such preferences.[20] Also, the studies mentioned by Runyon[21] and Mitchell[22] showed that subordinates who were external in orientation were less satisfied with a participative style of leadership than were internal subordinates.

House also has reviewed these studies in an attempt to explain the ways in which the situation or environment moderates the relationship between participation and subordinate attitudes and behavior.[23] His analysis suggests that where participative leadership is positively related to satisfaction, regardless of the predispositions of subordinates, the tasks of the subjects appear to be ambiguous and ego-involving. In the studies in which the subjects' personalities or predispositions moderate the effect of participative leadership, the tasks of the subjects are inferred to be highly routine and/or nonego-involving.

House reasoned from this analysis that the task may have an overriding effect on the relationship between leader participation and subordinate responses, and that individual predispositions or personality character-istics of subordinates may have an effect only under some tasks. It was assumed that when task demands are ambiguous, subordinates will have a need to reduce the ambiguity. Further, it was assumed that when task demands are ambiguous, participative problem solving between the leader and the subordinate will result in more effective decisions than when the task demands are unambiguous. Finally, it was assumed that when the sub-ordinates are ego-involved in their tasks they are more likely to want to have a say in the decisions that affect them. Given these assumptions, the following hypotheses were formulated to account for the conflicting findings reviewed above:

● When subjects are highly ego-involved in a decision or a task and the decision or task demands are ambiguous, participative leadership will have a positive effect on the satisfaction and motivation of the subordinate, *regardless* of the subordinate's predisposition toward self-control, author-itarianism or need for independence.

● When subordinates are not ego-involved in their tasks and when task demands are clear, subordinates who are not authoritarian and who have high needs for independence and self-control will respond favorably to leader participation and their opposite personality types will respond less favorably.

These hypotheses were derived on the basis of path-goal theorizing; i.e., the rationale guiding the analysis of prior studies was that both task characteristics and characteristics of subordinates interact to determine the effect of a specific kind of leader behavior on the satisfaction, expectancies and performance of subordinates. To date, one major investigation has supported some of these predictions[24] in which personality variables, amount of participative leadership, task ambiguity and job satisfaction were assessed for 324 employees of an industrial manufacturing organization. As expected, in nonrepetitive, ego-involving tasks, employees (regardless of their personality) were more satisfied under a participative style than a nonparticipative style. However, in repetitive tasks which were less ego-involving the amount of authoritarianism of subordinates moderated the relationship between leadership style and satisfaction. Specifically, low authoritarian subordinates were *more satisfied* under a participative style. These findings are exactly as the theory would predict, thus, it has promise in reconciling a set of confusing and contradictory findings with respect to participative leadership.

SUMMARY AND CONCLUSIONS

We have attempted to describe what we believe is a useful theoretical framework for understanding the effect of leadership behavior on subordinate satisfaction and motivation. Most theorists today have moved away from the simplistic notions that all effective leaders have a certain set of personality traits or that the situation completely determines performance. Some researchers have presented rather complex attempts at matching certain types of leaders with certain types of situations, e.g., the articles written by Vroom and Fiedler in this issue. But, we believe that a path-goal approach goes one step further. It not only suggests what type of style may be most effective in a given situation--it also attempts to explain *why* it is most effective.

We are optimistic about the future outlook of leadership research. With the guidance of path-goal theorizing, future research is expected to unravel many confusing puzzles about the reasons for and effects of leader behavior that have, heretofore, not been solved. However, we add a word of caution: the theory, and the research on it, are relatively new to the literature of organizational behavior. Consequently, path-goal theory is offered more as a tool for directing research and stimulating insight than as a proven guide for managerial action.

FOOTNOTES

*This article is also to be reprinted in *Readings in Organizational and Industrial Psychology* by G. A. Yukl and K. N. Wexley, 2nd edition (1975). The research by House and his associates was partially supported by a grant from the Shell Oil Company of Canada. The research by Mitchell and his associates was partially supported by the Office of Naval Research Contract NR 170-761, N00014-67-A-0103-0032 (Terence R. Mitchell, Principal Investigator).

[1]T. R. Mitchell, "Expectancy Model of Job Satisfaction, Occupational Preference and Effort: A Theoretical, Methodological and Empirical Appraisal," *Psychological Bulletin* (1974, in press).

[2]D. M. Nebeker and T. R. Mitchell, "Leader Behavior: An Expectancy Theory Approach," *Organization Behavior and Human Performance*, 11(1974), pp. 355-367.

[3]M. G. Evans, "The Effects of Supervisory Behavior on the Path-Goal Relationship," *Organization Behavior and Human Performance*, 55(1970), pp. 277-298; T. H. Hammer and H. T. Dachler, "The Process of Supervision in the Context of Motivation Theory," Research Report No. 3 (University of Maryland, 1973); F. Dansereau, Jr., J. Cashman and G. Graen, "Instrumentality Theory and Equity Theory As Complementary Approaches in Predicting the Relationship of Leadership and Turnover Among Managers," *Organization Behavior and Human Performance*, 10(1973), pp. 184-200; R. J. House, "A Path-Goal Theory of Leader Effectiveness," *Administrative Science Quarterly*, 16, 3(September 1971), pp. 321-338; T. R. Mitchell, "Motivation and Participation: An Integration," *Academy of Management Journal*, 16, 4(1973), pp. 160-179; G. Graen, F. Dansereau, Jr. and T. Minami, "Dysfunctional Leadership Styles," *Organization Behavior and Human Performance*, 7(1972), pp. 216-236; _____, "An Empirical Test of the Man-in-the-Middle Hypothesis Among Executives in a Hierarchical Organization Employing a Unit Analysis," *Organization Behavior and Human Performance*, 8(1972), pp. 262-285; R. J. House and G. Dessler, "The Path-Goal Theory of Leadership: Some Post Hoc and A Priori Tests," to appear in J. G. Hunt, ed., *Contingency Approaches to Leadership* (Carbondale, Ill.: Southern Illinois University Press, 1974).

[4]M. G. Evans, "Effects of Supervisory Behavior"; _____, "Extensions of a Path-Goal Theory of Motivation," *Journal of Applied Psychology*, 59 (1974), pp. 172-178.

[5]R. J. House, "A Path-Goal Theory"; R. J. House and G. Dessler, "Path-Goal Theory of Leadership."

[6]R. J. House and G. Dessler, "Path-Goal Theory of Leadership"; R. M. Stogdill, *Managers, Employees, Organization* (Ohio State University, Bureau of Business Research, 1965); R. J. House, A. Valency and R. Van der Krabben, "Some Tests and Extensions of the Path-Goal Theory of Leadership" (in preparation).

[7]W. A. Hill and D. Hughes, "Variations in Leader Behavior As a Function of Task Type," *Organization Behavior and Human Performance* (1974, in press).

[8]K. E. Runyon, "Some Interactions Between Personality Variables and Management Styles," *Journal of Applied Psychology*, 57, 3(1973), pp. 288-294; T. R. Mitchell, C. R. Smyser and S. E. Weed, "Locus of Control: Supervision and Work Satisfaction," *Academy of Management Journal* (in press).

[9]T. R. Mitchell, "Locus of Control."

[10]R. J. House, "A Path-Goal Theory"; _____ and G. Dessler, "Path-Goal Theory of Leadership"; A. D. Szalagyi and H. P. Sims, "An Explora-tion of the Path-Goal Theory of Leadership in a Health Care Environment," *Academy of Management Journal* (in press); J. D. Dermer, "Supervisory Behavior and Budget Motivation" (Cambridge, Mass.: unpublished, MIT, Sloan School of Management, 1974); R. W. Smetana, "The Relationship Be-tween Managerial Behavior and Subordinate Attitudes and Motivation: A Contribution to a Behavioral Theory of Leadership" (Ph.D. diss, Wayne State University, 1974).

[11]S. E. Weed, T. R. Mitchell and C. R. Smyser, "A Test of House's Path-Goal Theory of Leadership in an Organizational Setting" (paper presented at Western Psychological Assoc., 1974); J. D. Dermer and J. P. Siegel, "A Test of Path-Goal Theory: Disconfirming Evidence and a Critique" (unpublished, University of Toronto, Faculty of Management Studies, 1973); R. S. Schuler, "A Path-Goal Theory of Leadership: An Empirical Investi-gation" (Ph.D. diss, Michigan State University, 1973); H. K. Downey, J. E. Sheridan and J. W. Slocum, Jr., "Analysis of Relationships Among Leader Behavior, Subordinate Job Performance and Satisfaction: A Path-Goal Approach" (unpublished mimeograph, 1974); J. E. Stinson and T. W. Johnson, "The Path-Goal Theory of Leadership: A Partial Test and Suggested Refinement," *Proceedings* (Kent, Ohio: 7th Annual Conference of the Midwest Academy of Management, April 1974), pp. 18-36.

[12]G. Dessler, "An Investigation of the Path-Goal Theory of Leadership" (Ph.D. diss, City University of New York, Bernard M. Baruch College, 1973).

[13]R. J. House, D. Burrill and G. Dessler, "Tests and Extensions of Path-Goal Theory of Leadership,I" (unpublished, in process).

[14]R. J. House, "A Path-Goal Theory"; _____ and G. Dessler, "Path-Goal Theory of Leadership"; A. D. Szalagyi and H. P. Sims, "Exploration of Path-Goal"; J. E. Stinson and T. W. Johnson, *Proceedings*; R. S. Schuler, "Path-Goal: Investigation"; H. K. Downey, J. E. Sheridan and J. W. Slocum, Jr., "Analysis of Relationships"; S. E. Weed, T. R. Mitchell and C. R. Smyser, "Test of House's Path-Goal."

[15]A. D. Szalagyi and H. P. Sims, "Exploration of Path-Goal."

[16]R. J. House, A. Valency and R. Van der Krabben, "Tests and Extensions of Path-Goal Theory of Leadership, II" (unpublished, in process).

[17]T. R. Mitchell, "Motivation and Participation."

[18]H. Tosi, "A Reexamination of Personality As a Determinant of the Effects of Participation," *Personnel Psychology*, 23(1970), pp. 91-99; J. Sadler "Leadership Style, Confidence in Management and Job Satisfaction," *Journal of Applied Behavioral Sciences*, 6(1970), pp. 3-19; K. N. Wexley, J. P. Singh and J. A. Yukl, "Subordinate Personality As a Moderator of the Effects of Participation in Three Types of Appraisal Interviews," *Journal of Applied Psychology*, 83 1(1973), pp. 54-59.

[19]T. R. Mitchell, "Motivation and Participation."

[20]A. S. Tannenbaum and F. H. Allport, "Personality Structure and Group Structure: An Interpretive Study of Their Relationship Through an Event-Structure Hypothesis," *Journal of Abnormal and Social Psychology*, 53(1956), pp. 272-280; V. H. Vroom, "Some Personality Determinants of the Effects of Participation," *Journal of Abnormal and Social Psychology*, 59(1959), pp. 322-327.

[21]K. E. Runyon, "Some Interactions Between Personality Variables and Management Styles," *Journal of Applied Psychology*, 57,3(1973), pp. 288-294.

[22]T. R. Mitchell, C. R. Smyser and S. E. Weed, "Locus of Control."

[23]R. J. House, "Notes on the Path-Goal Theory of Leadership" (University of Toronto, Faculty of Management Studies, May 1974).

[24]R. S. Schuler, "Leader Participation, Task Structure and Subordinate Authoritarianism (unpublished mimeograph, Cleveland State University, 1974).

RESEARCH

A New Look at Managerial Decision Making

Victor H. Vroom

*A*ll managers are decision makers. Furthermore, their effectiveness as managers is largely reflected in their "track record" in making the "right decisions." These "right decisions" in turn largely depend on whether or not the manager has utilized the right person or persons in the right ways in helping him solve the problem.

Our concern in this article is with decision making as a social process. We view the manager's task as determining how the problem is to be solved, not the solution to be adopted. Within that overall framework, we have attempted to answer two broad sets of questions: What decision-making processes should managers use to deal effectively with the problems they encounter in their jobs? What decision-making processes do they use in dealing with these problems and what considerations affect their decisions about how much to share their decision-making power with subordinates?

The reader will recognize the former as a normative or prescriptive question. A rational and analytic answer to it would constitute a normative model of decision making as a social process. The second question is descriptive, since it concerns how managers do, rather than should, behave.

Toward a Normal Model

About four years ago, Philip Yetton, then a graduate student at Carnegie-Mellon University, and I began a major research program in an attempt to answer these normative and descriptive questions.

We began with the normative question. What would be a rational way of deciding on the form and amount of participation in decision making that should be used in different situations? We were tired of debates over the relative merits of Theory X and Theory Y and of the truism that leadership depends upon the situation. We felt that it was time for the behavioral sciences to move beyond such generalities and to attempt to come to grips with the complexities of the phenomena with which they intended to deal.

Our aim was ambitious—to develop a set of ground rules for matching a man-

1

ager's leadership behavior to the demands of the situation. It was critical that these ground rules be consistent with research evidence concerning the consequences of participation and that the model based on the rules be operational, so that any manager could see it to determine how he should act in any decision-making situation.

Table I shows a set of alternative decision processes that we have employed in our research. Each process is represented by a symbol (e.g., AI, CI, GII) that will be used as a convenient method of referring to each process. The first letter in this symbol signifies the basic properties of the process (A stands for autocratic; C for consultative; and G for group). The Roman numerals that follow the first letter constitute variants on that process. Thus, AI represents the first variant on an autocratic process, and AII the second variant.

CONCEPTUAL AND EMPIRICAL BASIS OF THE MODEL

A model designed to regulate, in some rational way, choices among the decisions processess shown in Table I should be based on sound empirical evidence concerning the likely consequences of the styles. The more complete the empirical base of knowledge, the greater the certainty with which we can develop the model and the greater will be its usefulness. To aid in understanding the conceptual basis of the model, it is important to distinguish among three classes of outcomes that bear on the ultimate effectiveness of decisions. These are:

1) The quality or rationality of the decision.
2) The acceptance or commitment on the part of subordinates to execute the decision effectively.

Table 1.
TYPES OF MANAGEMENT DECISION STYLES

AI   You solve the problem or make the decision yourself, using information available to you at that time.

AII You obtain the necessary information from your subordinate(s), then decide on the solution to the problem yourself. You may or may not tell your subordinates what the problem is in getting the information from them. The role played by your subordinates in making the decision is clearly one of providing the necessary information to you, rather than generating or evaluating alternative solutions.

CI   You share the problem with relevant subordinates individually, getting their ideas and suggestions without bringing them together as a group. Then *you* make the decision that may or may not reflect your subordinates' influence.

CII You share the problem with your subordinates as a group, collectively obtaining their ideas and suggestions. Then *you* make the decision that may or may not reflect your subordinates' influence.

GII You share a problem with your subordinates as a group. Together you generate and evaluate alternatives and attempt to reach agreement (consensus) on a solution. Your role is much like that of chairman. You do not try to influence the group to adopt "your" solution and you are willing to accept and implement any solution that has the support of the entire group.

(GI is omitted because it applies only to more comprehensive models outside the scope of the article.)

3) The amount of time required to make the decision.

The effects of participation on each of these outcomes or consequences were summed up by the author in *The Handbook of Social Psychology* as follows:

> The results suggest that allocating problem solving and decision-making tasks to entire groups requires a greater investment of man hours but produces higher acceptance of decisions and a higher probability that the decision will be executed efficiently. Differences between these two methods in quality of decisions and in elapsed time are inconclusive and probably highly variable . . . It would be naive to think that group decision making is always more "effective" than autocratic decision making, or vice versa; the relative effectiveness of these two extreme methods depends both on the weights attached to quality, acceptance and time variables and on differences in amounts of these outcomes resulting from these methods, neither of which is invariant from one situation to another. The critics and proponents of participative management would do well to direct their efforts toward identifying the properties of situations in which different decision-making approaches are effective rather than wholesale condemnation or deification of one approach.

We have gone on from there to identify the properties of the situation or problem that will be the basic elements in the model. These problem attributes are of two types: 1) Those that specify the importance for a particular problem of quality and acceptance, and 2) those that, on the basis of available evidence, have a high probability of moderating the effects of participation on each of these outcomes. Table II shows the problem attributes used in the present form of the model. For each attribute a question is provided that might be used by a leader in diagnosing a particular problem prior to choosing his leadership style.

In phrasing the questions, we have held technical language to a minimum. Furthermore, we have phrased the questions in Yes-No form, translating the continuous variables defined above into dichotomous variables. For example, instead of attempting to determine how important the decision quality is to the effectiveness of the decision (attribute A), the leader is asked in the first question to judge whether there is any quality component to the problem. Similarly, the difficult task of specifying exactly how much information the leader possesses that is relevant to the decision (attribute B) is reduced to a simple judgment by the leader concerning whether or not he has sufficient information to make a high quality decision.

We have found that managers can diagnose a situation quickly and accurately by answering this set of seven questions concerning it. But how can such responses generate a prescription concerning the most effective leadership style or decision process? What kind of normative model of participation in decision making can be built from this set of problem attributes?

Figure 1 shows one such model expressed in the form of a decision tree. It is the seventh version of such a model that we have developed over the last three years. The problem attributes, expressed in question form, are arranged along the top of the figure. To use the model for a particular decision-making situation, one starts at the left-hand side and works toward the right asking oneself the question immediately above any box that is encountered. When a terminal node is reached, a number will be found designating the problem type and one of the decision-making processes appearing in Table I. AI is prescribed for four problem types (1, 2, 4, and 5); AII is prescribed for two problem types (9 and 10); CI is prescribed for only one problem type (8); CII is prescribed for four problem types (7, 11, 13, and 14); and GII is prescribed for three problem types (3, 6, and 12). The relative frequency with which

3

Table II
PROBLEM ATTRIBUTES USED IN THE MODEL

Problem Attributes	*Diagnostic Questions*
A. The importance of the quality of the decision.	Is there a quality requirement such that one solution is likely to be more rational than another?
B. The extent to which the leader possesses sufficient information/expertise to make a high-quality decision by himself.	Do I have sufficient information to make a high-quality decision?
C. The extent to which the problem is structured.	Is the problem structured?
D. The extent to which acceptance or commitment on the part of subordinates is critical to the effective implementation of the decision.	Is acceptance of decision by subordinates critical to effective implementation?
E. The prior probability that the leader's autocratic decision will receive acceptance by subordinates.	If you were to make the decision by yourself, is it reasonably certain that it would be accepted by your subordinates?
F. The extent to which subordinates are motivated to attain the organizational goals as represented in the objectives explicit in the statement of the problem.	Do subordinates share the organizational goals to be obtained in solving this problem?
G. The extent to which subordinates are likely to be in conflict over preferred solutions.	Is conflict among subordinates likely in preferred solutions?

each of the five decision processes would be prescribed for any manager would, of course, depend on the distribution of problem types encountered in his decision making.

Rationale Underlying the Model: The decision processes specified for each problem type are not arbitrary. The model's behavior is governed by a set of principles intended to be consistent with existing evidence concerning the consequences of participation in decision making on organizational effectiveness.

There are two mechanisms underlying the behavior of the model. The first is a set of seven rules that serve to protect the quality and the acceptance of the decision by

eliminating alternatives that risk one or the other of these decision outcomes. Once the rules have been applied, a feasible set of decision processes is generated. The second mechanism is a principle for choosing among alternatives in the feasible set where more than one exists.

Let us examine the rules first, because they do much of the work of the model. As previously indicated, the rules are intended to protect both the quality and acceptance of the decision. In the form of the model shown, there are three rules that protect decision quality and four that protect acceptance.

1. *The Information Rule.* If the quality of the decision is important and if the

Figure 1.
DECISION MODEL

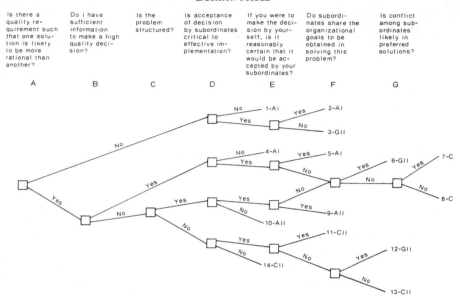

leader does not possess enough information or expertise to solve the problem by himself, AI is eliminated from the feasible set. (Its use risks a low-quality decision.)

2. *The Goal Congruence Rule.* If the quality of the decision is important and if the subordinates do not share the organizational goals to be obtained in solving the problem, GII is eliminated from the feasible set. (Alternatives that eliminate the leader's final control over the decision reached may jeopardize the quality of the decision.)

3. *The Unstructured Problem Rule.* In decisions in which the quality of the decision is important, if the leader lacks the necessary information or expertise to solve the problem by himself, and if the problem is unstructured, i.e., he does not know exactly what information is needed and where it is located, the method used must provide not only for him to collect the information but to do so in an efficient and effective manner.

Methods that involve interaction among all subordinates with full knowledge of the problem are likely to be both more efficient and more likely to generate a high-quality solution to the problem. Under these conditions, AI, AII, and CI are eliminated from the feasible set. (AI does not provide for him to collect the necessary information, and AII and CI represent more cumbersome, less effective, and less efficient means of bringing the necessary information to bear on the solution of the problem than methods that do permit those with the necessary information to interact.)

4. *The Acceptance Rule.* If the acceptance of the decision by subordinates is critical to effective implementation, and if it is not certain that an autocratic decision made by the leader would receive that acceptance, AI and AII are eliminated from the feasible set. (Neither provides an opportunity for subordinates to participate in the decision and both risk the necessary acceptance.)   5

5. *The Conflict Rule.* If the acceptance of the decision is critical, and an autocratic decision is not certain to be accepted, and subordinates are likely to be in conflict or disagreement over the appropriate solution, AI, AII, and CI are eliminated from the feasible set. (The method used in solving the problem should enable those in disagreement to resolve their differences with full knowledge of the problem. Accordingly, under these conditions, AI, AII, and CI, which involve no interaction or only "one-on-one" relationships and therefore provide no opportunity for those in conflict to resolve their differences, are eliminated from the feasible set. Their use runs the risk of leaving some of the subordinates with less than the necessary commitment to the final decision.)

6. *The Fairness Rule.* If the quality of decision is unimportant and if acceptance is critical and not certain to result from an autocratic decision, AI, AII, CI, and CII are eliminated from the feasible set. (The method used should maximize the probability of acceptance as this is the only relevant consideration in determining the effectiveness of the decision. Under these circumstances, AI, AII, CI, and CII, which create less acceptance or commitment than GII, are eliminated from the feasible set. To use them is to run the risk of getting less than the needed acceptance of the decision.)

6. *The Acceptance Priority Rule.* If acceptance is critical, not assured by an autocratic decision, and if subordinates can be trusted, AI, AII, CI, and CII are eliminated from the feasible set. (Methods that provide equal partnership in the decision-making process can provide greater acceptance without risking decision quality. Use of any method other than GII results in an unnecessary risk that the decision will not be fully accepted or receive the necessary commitment on the part of subordinates.)

Once all seven rules have been applied to a given problem, we emerge with a feasible set of decision processes. The feasible set for each of the fourteen problem types is shown in Table III. It can be seen that there are some problem types for which only one method remains in the feasible set, others for which two methods remain feasible, and still others for which five methods remain feasible.

Table III

PROBLEM TYPES AND THE FEASIBLE SET
OF DECISION PROCESSES

Problem Type	Acceptable Methods
1.	AI, AII, CI, CII, GII
2.	AI, AII, CI, CII, GII
3.	GII
4.	AI, AII, CI, CII, GII*
5.	AI, AII, CI, CII, GII*
6.	GII
7.	CII
8.	CI, CII
9.	AII, CI, CII, GII*
10.	AII, CI, CII, GII*
11.	CII, GII*
12.	GII
13.	CII
14.	CII, GII*

* Within the feasible set only when the answer to question F is Yes.

When more than one method remains in the feasible set, there are a number of ways in which one might choose among them. The mechanism we have selected and the principle underlying the choices of the model in Figure 1 utilizes the number of man-hours used in solving the problem as the basis for choice. Given a set of methods with equal likelihood of meeting both quality and acceptance requirements for the decision, it chooses that method that requires the least investment in man-hours. On the basis of the empirical evidence summarized earlier, this is deemed to be the method furthest to the left within the feasible set. For example, since AI, AII, CI, CII, and GII are all feasible as in Problem Types 1 and 2, AI would be the method chosen.

To illustrate application of the model in actual administrative situations, we will analyze four cases with the help of the model. While we attempt to describe these cases as completely as is necessary to permit the reader to make the judgments required by the model, there may remain some room for subjectivity. The reader may wish after reading the case to analyze it himself using the model and then to compare his analysis with that of the author.

CASE I. You are a manufacturing manager in a large electronics plant. The company's management has recently installed new machines and put in a new simplified work system, but to the surprise of everyone, yourself included, the expected increase in productivity was not realized. In fact, production has begun to drop, quality has fallen off, and the number of employee separations has risen.

You do not believe that there is anything wrong with the machines. You have had reports from other companies that are using them and they confirm this opinion. You have also had representatives from the firm that built the machines go over them and they report that they are operating at peak efficiency.

You suspect that some parts of the new work system may be responsible for the change, but this view is not widely shared among your immediate subordinates who are four first-line supervisors, each in charge of a section, and your supply manager. The drop in production has been variously attributed to poor training of the operators, lack of an adequate system of financial incentives, and poor morale. Clearly, this is an issue about which there is considerable depth of feeling within individuals and potential disagreement among your subordinates.

This morning you received a phone call from your division manager. He had just received your production figures for the last six months and was calling to express his concern. He indicated that the problem was yours to solve in any way that you think best, but that he would like to know within a week what steps you plan to take.

You share your division manager's concern with the falling productivity and know that your men are also concerned. The problem is to decide what steps to take to rectify the situation.

Analysis
Questions—
    A (Quality?) $=$ Yes
    B (Managers Information?) $=$ No
    C (Structured?) $=$ No
    D (Acceptance?) $=$ Yes
    E (Prior Probability of Acceptance?) $=$ No
    F (Goal Congruence?) $=$ Yes
    G (Conflict?) $=$ Yes
Problem Type—12
Feasible Set—GII
Minimum Man-Hours Solution (from Figure 1)—GII
Rule Violations—
    AI violates rules 1, 3, 4, 5, 7
    AII violates rules 3, 4, 5, 7
    CI violates rules 3, 5, 7
    CII violates rule 7

CASE II. You are general foreman in charge of a large gang laying an oil pipeline and have to estimate your expected rate of progress in order to schedule material deliveries to the next field site.

You know the nature of the terrain you will be traveling and have the historical data needed to compute the mean and variance in the rate of speed over that type of terrain. Given these two variables, it is a simple matter to calculate the earliest and latest times at which materials and support facilities will be needed at the next site. It is important that your estimate be reasonably accurate. Underestimates result in idle foremen and workers, and an overestimate results in tying up materials for a period of time before they are to be used.

Progress has been good and your five foremen and other members of the gang stand to receive substantial bonuses if the project is completed ahead of schedule.

Analysis
Questions—
  A (Quality?) = Yes
  B (Manager's Information?) = Yes
  D (Acceptance?) = No
Problem Type—4
Feasible Set—AI, AII, CI, CII, GII
Minimum Man-Hours Solution (from Figure 1)—AI
Rule Violations—None

CASE III. You are supervising the work of 12 engineers. Their formal training and work experience are very similar, permitting you to use them interchangeably on projects. Yesterday, your manager informed you that a request had been received from an overseas affiliate for four engineers to go abroad on extended loan for a period of six to eight months. For a number of reasons, he argued and you agreed that this request should be met from your group.

All your engineers are capable of handling this assignment and, from the standpoint of present and future projects, there is no particular reason why anyone should be retained over any other. The problem is somewhat complicated by the fact that the overseas assignment is in what is generally regarded as an undesirable location.

Analysis
Questions—
  A (Quality?) = No
  D (Acceptance?) = Yes
  E (Prior Probability of Acceptance?) = No
  G (Conflict?) = Yes
Problem Type—3
Feasible Set—GII
Minimum Man-Hours Solution (from Figure 1)—GII
Rule Violations—
  AI and AII violate rules 4, 5, and 6
  CI violates rules 5 and 6
  CII violates rule 6

CASE IV. You are on the division manager's staff and work on a wide variety of problems of both an administrative and technical nature. You have been given the assignment of developing a standard method to be used in each of the five plants in the division for manually reading equipment registers, recording the readings, and transmitting the scorings to a centralized information system.

Until now there has been a high error rate in the reading and/or transmittal of the data. Some locations have considerably higher error rates than others, and the methods used to record and transmit the data vary among plants. It is probable, therefore, that part of the error variance is a function of specific local conditions rather than anything else, and this will complicate the establishment of any system common to all plants. You have the information on error rates but no information on the local practices that generate these errors or on the local conditions that necessitate the different practices.

Everyone would benefit from an improvement in the quality of the data; it is used in a number of important decisions. Your contacts with the plants are through the quality-control supervisors who are responsi-

8

ble for collecting the data. They are a conscientious group committed to doing their jobs well, but are highly sensitive to interference on the part of higher management in their own operations. Any solution that does not receive the active support of the various plant supervisors is unlikely to reduce the error rate significantly.

Analysis
Questions—
    A (Quality?) = Yes
    B (Manager's Information?) = No
    C (Structured?) = No
    D (Acceptance?) = Yes
    E (Prior Probability of Acceptance?)
      = No
    F (Goal Congruence?) = Yes
Problem Type—12
Feasible Set—GII
Minimum Man-Hours Solution (from Figure 1)—GII
Rule Violations—
    AI violates rules 1, 3, 4, and 7
    AII violates rules 3, 4, and 7
    CI violates rules 3 and 7
    CII violates rule 7

Short Versus Long-Term Models

The model described above seeks to protect the quality of the decision and to expend the least number of man-hours in the process. Because it focuses on conditions surrounding the making and implementation of a particular decision rather than any long-term considerations, we can term it a short-term model.

It seems likely, however, that the leadership methods that may be optimal for short-term results may be different from those that would be optimal over a longer period of time. Consider a leader, for example, who has been uniformly pursuing an autocratic style (AI or AII) and, perhaps as a conse-

quence, has subordinates who might be termed "yes men" (attribute E) but who also cannot be trusted to pursue organizational goals (attribute F), largely because the leader has never bothered to explain them.

It appears likely, however, that the manager who used more participative methods would, in time, change the status of these problem attributes so as to develop ultimately a more effective problem-solving system. A promising approach to the development of a long-term model is one that places less weight on man-hours as the basis for choice of method within the feasible set. Given a long-term orientation, one would be interested in the possibility of a trade-off between man-hours in problem solving and team development, both of which increase with participation. Viewed in these terms, the time-minimizing model places maximum relative weight on man-hours and no weight on development, and hence chooses the style farthest to the left within the feasible set. A model that places less weight on man-hours and more weight on development would, if these assumptions are correct, choose a style further to the right within the feasible set.

We recognize, of course, that the minimum man-hours solution suggested by the model is not always the best solution to every problem. A manager faced, for example, with the problem of handling any one of the four cases previously examined might well choose more time-consuming alternatives on the grounds that the greater time invested would be justified in developing his subordinates. Similar considerations exist in other decision-making situations. For this reason we have come to emphasize the feasible set of decision methods in our work with managers. Faced with considerations not included in the model, the manager should consider any alternative within the feasible set, not opt automatically for the minimum man-hours solution.

9

Victor H. Vroom *joined the faculty at Yale University in September 1972 and was appointed chairman of the Department of Administrative Sciences and associate director of the Institution for Social and Policy Studies. For the last twenty years he has been involved in research and teaching on the psychological analysis of behavior in organizations. His 1964* book, Work and Motivation, *is regarded as a landmark in that field. He is also the author of six other books, including his forthcoming volume,* Leadership and Decision Making.

Born in 1932 in Montreal, Professor Vroom received his bachelor's and master's degrees from McGill University in 1953 and 1955, and went on to the University of Michigan to receive his Ph.D. in 1958. While in Canada, he was employed in personnel research and training at Canadair, Ltd., and at the Aluminium Company of Canada. After earning his doctorate he stayed at Michigan for two years as a study director in the Institute for Social Research and a lecturer in Psychology. He moved to the University of Pennsylvania

to become assistant professor of psychology and to the Carnegie Institute of Technology in 1963 as associate professor. In 1966, he was named full professor of psychology and industrial administration at Carnegie-Mellon's Graduate School of Industrial Administration.

He was the winner of the Ford Foundation Doctoral Dissertation Competition at Michigan and held the Foundation's faculty fellowship at Pennsylvania. In 1967 he was named winner in the McKinsey Foundation Research Design Competition, and was also appointed Fulbright Lecturer in the United Kingdom. He was given the James McKeen Cattell Award of the American Psychological Association in 1970.

Professor Vroom is a faculty principal of Management Analysis Center, Inc. (MAC), a faculty-based consulting firm headquartered in Cambridge, Massachusetts. He has been active as a consultant to over 30 major corporations including General Electric, Bell Telephone Laboratories, and Chemical Bank, and also served with the U.S. Department of Labor and the Ford Foundation. He serves on the Professional Advisory Committee of the Smith Richardson Foundation, the Council of Representatives of the American Psychology Association, and for nine years was consulting editor in the behavioral sciences for the Wadsworth Publishing Company.

As I am writing this, I have in front of me a "black box" that constitutes an electronic version of the normative model discussed on the preceding pages. (The author is indebted to Peter Fuss of Bell Telephone Laboratories for his interest in the model and his skill in developing the "black box.") The box, which is small enough to fit into the palm of one hand, has a set of seven switches, each appropriately labeled with the questions (A through G) used in Figure 1. A manager faced with a concrete problem or decision can "diagnose" that problem by setting each switch in either its "yes" or "no" position. Once the problem has been described, the

manager depresses a button that illuminates at least one or as many as five lights, each of which denotes one of the decision processes (AI, AII, etc.). The lights that are illuminated constitute the feasible set of decision processes for the problem as shown in Table III. The lights not illuminated correspond to alternatives that violate one or more of the seven rules previously stated.

In this prototype version of the box, the lights are illuminated in decreasing order of brightness from left to right within the feasible set. The brightest light corresponds to the alternative shown in Figure 1. Thus, if both CII and GII were feasible alternatives,

CII would be brighter than GII, since it requires fewer man-hours. However, a manager who was not under any undue time pressure and who wished to invest time in the development of his subordinates might select an alternative corresponding to one of the dimmer lights.

Toward a Descriptive Model of Leader Behavior

So far we have been concerned with the normative questions defined at the outset. But how do managers really behave? What considerations affect their decisions about how much to share their decision-making power with their subordinates? In what respects is their behavior different from or similar to that of the model? These questions are but a few of those that we attempted to answer in a large-scale research program aimed at gaining a greater understanding of the factors that influence managers in their choice of decision processes to fit the demands of the situation. This research program was financially supported by the McKinsey Foundation, General Electric Foundation, Smith Richardson Foundation, and the Office of Naval Research.

Two different research methods have been utilized in studying these factors. The first investigation utilized a method that we have come to term "recalled problems." Over 500 managers from 11 different countries representing a variety of firms were asked to provide a written description of a problem that they had recently had to solve. These varied in length from one paragraph to several pages and covered virtually every facet of managerial decision making. For each case, the manager was asked to indicate which of the decision processes shown in Table I they used to solve the problem. Finally, each manager was asked to answer the questions shown in Table II corresponding to the problem attributes used in the normative model.

The wealth of data, both qualitative and quantitative, served two purposes. Since each manager had diagnosed a situation that he had encountered in terms that are used in the normative model and had indicated the methods that he had used in dealing with it, it is possible to determine what differences, if any, there were between the model's behavior and his own behavior. Second, the written cases provided the basis for the construction of a standard set of cases used in later research to determine the factors that influence managers to share or retain their decision-making power. Each case depicted a manager faced with a problem to solve or decision to make. The cases spanned a wide range of managerial problems including production scheduling, quality control, portfolio management, personnel allocation, and research and development. In each case, a person could readily assume the role of the manager described and could indicate which of the decision processes he would use if he actually were faced with that situation.

In most of our research, a set of thirty cases has been used and the subjects have been several thousand managers who were participants in management development programs in the United States and abroad. Cases were selected systematically. We desired cases that could not only be coded unambiguously in the terms used in the normative model but that would also permit the assessment of the effects of each of the problem attributes used in the model on the person's behavior. The solution was to select cases in accordance with an experimental design so that they varied in terms of the seven attributes used in the model and variation in each attribute was independent of each other attribute. Several such standardized sets of cases have been developed, and over a thousand managers have now been studied using this approach.

11

To summarize everything we learned in the course of this research is well beyond the scope of this paper, but it is possible to discuss some of the highlights. Since the results obtained from the two research methods—recalled and standardized problems—are consistent, we can present the major results independent of the method used.

Perhaps the most striking finding is the weakening of the widespread view that participativeness is a general trait that individual managers exhibit in different amounts. To be sure, there were differences *among* managers in their general tendencies to utilize participative methods as opposed to autocratic ones. On the standardized problems, these differences accounted for about 10 percent of the total variance in the decision processes observed. These differences in behavior between managers, however, were small in comparison with differences *within* managers. On the standardized problems, no manager has indicated that he would use the same decision process on all problems or decisions, and most use all five methods under some circumstances.

Some of this variance in behavior within managers can be attributed to widely shared tendencies to respond to some situations by sharing power and others by retaining it. It makes more sense to talk about participative and autocratic situations than it does to talk about participative and autocratic managers. In fact, on the standardized problems, the variance in behavior across problems or cases is about three times as large as the variance across managers!

What are the characteristics of an autocratic as opposed to a participative situation? An answer to this question would constitute a partial descriptive model of this aspect of the decision-making process and has been our goal in much of the research that we have conducted. From our observations of behavior on both recalled problems and on standardized problems, it is clear that the decision-making process employed by a typical manager is influenced by a large number of factors, many of which also show up in the normative model. Following are several conclusions substantiated by the results on both recalled and standardized problems: Managers use decision processes providing less opportunity for participation (1) when they possess all the necessary information than when they lack some of the needed information, (2) when the problem that they face is well-structured rather than unstructured, (3) when their subordinates' acceptance of the decision is not critical for the effective implementation of the decision or when the prior probability of acceptance of an autocratic decision is high, and (4) when the personal goals of their subordinates are *not* congruent with the goals of the organization as manifested in the problem.

So far we have been talking about relatively common or widely shared ways of dealing with organizational problems. Our results strongly suggest that there are ways of "tailoring" one's approach to the situation that distinguish managers from one another. Theoretically, these can be thought of as differences among managers in decision rules that they employ about when to encourage participation. Statistically, they are represented as interactions between situational variables and personal characteristics.

Consider, for example, two managers who have identical distributions of the use of the five decision processes shown in Table I on a set of thirty cases. In a sense, they are equally participative (or autocratic). However, the situations in which they permit or encourage participation in decision making on the part of their subordinates may be very different. One may restrict the participation of his subordinates to decisions without a quality requirement, whereas the other may restrict their participation to problems with a quality requirement. The former would be more inclined to use participative decision processes (like GII) on such decisions as what color the walls should be painted or when the company picnic should be held. The latter would be more likely to encourage participation in decision making on decisions that have a clear and demonstrable impact on the organization's success in achieving its external goals.

Use of the standardized problem set permits the assessment of such differences in decision rules that govern choices among decision-making processes. Since the cases are selected in accordance with an experimental design, they can indicate differences in the behavior of managers attributable not only to the existence of a quality requirement in the problem but also in the effects of acceptance requirements, conflict, information requirements, and the like.

The research using both recalled and standardized problems has also enabled us to examine similarities and differences between the behavior of the normative model and the behavior of a typical manager. Such an analysis reveals, at the very least, what behavioral changes could be expected if managers began using the normative model as the basis for choosing their decision-making processes.

A typical manager says he would (or did) use exactly the same decision process as that shown in Figure 1 in 40 percent of the situations. In two thirds of the situations, his behavior is consistent with the feasible set of methods proposed in the model. In other words, in about one third of the situations his behavior violates at least one of the seven rules underlying the model.

The four rules designed to protect the acceptance or commitment of the decision have substantially higher probabilities of being violated than do the three rules designed to protect the quality or rationality of the decision. One of the acceptance rules, the Fairness Rule (Rule 6) is violated about three quarters of the time that it could have been violated. On the other hand, one of the quality rules, the Information Rule, (Rule 1) is violated in only about 3 percent of occasions in which it is applicable. If we assume for the moment that these two sets of rules have equal validity, these findings strongly suggest that the decisions made by typical managers are more likely to prove ineffective due to deficiencies of acceptance by subordinates than due to deficiencies in decision quality.

Another striking difference between the behavior of the model and of the typical manager lies in the fact that the former shows far greater variance with the situation. If a typical manager voluntarily used the model as the basis for choosing his methods of making decisions, he would become both more autocratic and more participative. He would employ autocratic methods more frequently in situations in which his subordinates were unaffected by the decision and participative methods more frequently when his subordinates' cooperation and support were critical and or their information and expertise were required.

It should be noted that the typical manager to whom we have been referring is merely a statistical average of the several thousand who have been studied over the last three or four years. There is a great deal of variance around that average. As evidenced by their behavior on standardized problems, some managers are already behaving in a manner that is highly consistent with the model, while others' behavior is clearly at variance with it.

A New Technology for
Leadership Development

The investigations that have been summarized here were conducted for research purposes to shed some light on the causes and conse- 13 quences of participation in decision making. In the course of the research, we came to realize, partly because of the value attached to it by the managers themselves, that the data collection procedures, with appropriate additions and modifications, might also serve as a valuable guide to leadership development. From this realization evolved an important by-product of the research activities—a new approach to leadership development based on the concepts in the normative model and the empirical methods of the descriptive research.

This approach is based on the assumption stated previously that one of the critical skills required of all leaders is the ability to adapt their behavior to the demands of the situation and that one component of this skill involves the ability to select the appropiate decision-making process for each problem or decision he confronts.

Managers can derive value from the model by comparing their past or intended behavior in concrete decisions with that prescribed by the model and by seeing what rules, if any, they violate. Used in this way, the model can provide a mechanism for a manager to analyze both the circumstances that he faces and what decisions are feasible under these circumstances.

While use of the model without training is possible, we believe that the manager can derive the maximum value from a systematic examination of his leadership style, and its similarities to and dissimilarities from the model, as part of a formal leadership development program.

During the past two years we have developed such a program. It is not intended to "train" participants in the use of the model, but rather to encourage them to examine their own leadership style and to ask themselves whether the methods they are using are most effective for their own organization. A critical part of the program involves the use of a set of standardized cases, each depicting a leader

faced with an administrative problem to solve. Each participant then specifies the decision-making process that he would use if faced with each situation. His responses are processed by computer, which generates a highly detailed analysis of his leadership style. The responses for all participants in the course are typically processed simultaneously, permitting the economical representation of differences between the person and other participants in the same program.

In its present form, a single computer printout for a person consists of three 15" x 11" pages, each filled with graphs and tables highlighting different features of his behavior. Understanding the results requires a detailed knowledge of the concepts underlying the model, something already developed in one of the previous phases of the training program. The printout is accompanied by a manual that aids in explaining results and provides suggested steps to be followed in extracting full meaning from the printout.

Following are a few of the questions that the printout answers:

1. How autocratic or participative am I in my dealings with subordinates in comparison with other participants in the program?

2. What decision processes do I use more or less frequently than the average?

3. How close does my behavior come to that of the model? How frequently does my behavior agree with the feasible set? What evidence is there that my leadership style reflects the pressure of time as opposed to a concern with the development of my subordinates? How do I compare in these respects with other participants in the class?

4. What rules do I violate most frequently and least frequently? How does this compare with other participants? On what cases did I violate these rules? Does my leadership style reflect more concern with getting decisions that are high in quality or

14

with getting decisions that are accepted?

5. What circumstances cause me to behave in an autocratic fashion; what circumstances cause me to behave participatively? In what respects is the way in which I attempt to vary my behavior with the demands of the situation similar to that of the model?

When a typical manager receives his printout, he immediately goes to work trying to understand what it tells him about himself. After most of the major results have been understood, he goes back to the set of cases to re-read those on which he has violated rules. Typically, managers show an interest in discussing and comparing their results with others in the program. Gatherings of four to six people comparing their results and their interpretation of them, often for several hours at a stretch, were such a common feature that they have recently been institutionalized as part of the procedure.

We should emphasize that the method of providing feedback to managers on their leadership style is just one part of the total training experience, but it is an important part. The program is sufficiently new so that, to date, no long-term evaluative studies have been undertaken. The short-term results, however, appear quite promising.

CONCLUSION

The efforts reported in this article rest on the conviction that social scientists can be of greater value in solving problems of organizational behavior if their prescriptive statements deal with the complexities involved in the phenomena with which they study. The normative model described in this paper is one step in that direction. Some might argue that it is premature for social scientists to be prescriptive. Our knowledge is too limited and the issues too complex to warrant pre-

scriptions for action, even those that are based on a diagnosis of situational demands. However, organizational problems persist, and managers cannot wait for the behavioral sciences to perfect their disciplines before attempting to cope with them. Is it likely that models that encourage them to deal analytically with the forces impinging upon them would produce less rational choices than those that they now make? We think the reverse is more probable—reflecting on the models will result in decisions that are more rational and more effective. The criterion for social utility is not perfection but improvement over present practice.

SELECTED BIBLIOGRAPHY

The interested reader may wish to consult *Leadership and Decision-Making* by Vroom and Yetton, which presents a more complete explication of the model, other models dealing with related aspects of the decision-making process, and their use in leadership development. This book will be published in June 1973 by the University of Pittsburgh Press. For another perspective on the normative questions with which this article deals, the leader should consult "How to Choose a Leadership Pattern" by Robert Tannenbaum and Warren Schmidt (*Harvard Business Review*, September 1958). The descriptive questions are explored by Frank Heller in his new book *Managerial Decision-Making* (Tavistock, 1971).

Finally, *Problem-Solving Discussions and Conferences* (McGraw-Hill 1963) by Norman R. F. Maier represents the most useful account of the conference leadership techniques and skills required to implement participative approaches to management.

The reader interested in exploring the approach to managerial training discussed in this article should contact Kepner-Tregoe and Associates, Research Road, P.O. Box 704, Princeton, New Jersey 08540.

15

Part VI
Transactional Approaches

[11]

Journal of Contemporary Business   *Autumn 1974*

PROCESSES OF LEADERSHIP EMERGENCE

EDWIN P. HOLLANDER*
STATE UNIVERSITY OF NEW YORK AT BUFFALO

Almost everything in organizational life is either a function of leadership or is, at least, associated with it. The leader undeniably plays a central role in this process and usually commands the greatest attention and influence. However, focussing solely on this person gives only a partial view of leadership because it is a process that involves distributed efforts.

For a long time leadership and the leader were virtually synonymous. That is still true when, for example, one asserts that "we need new leadership." Actually what is meant is that another leader, with different capabilities and style of operating, is desired. This is not merely a semantic point; rather, it is an indication of some lingering confusion of the process with the person.

Nevertheless, we have advanced considerably from a time when there was an insistent preoccupation with traits such as, "courage," "wisdom" and tenacity" which *made* a person a leader. History as well is built around accounts of the attainments and qualities of "great men." Although it may still hold some allure, the dictum that "leaders are born, not made" is now largely discredited.[1] Few organizations could subscribe to it in practice.

RECONSIDERING THE ORGANIZATIONAL LEADER'S ROLE

A role is a set of behaviors which are appropriate for a position which an individual fills. There may be differing perspectives on what is "appropriate," but this will do as a working definition here.

Roles are tied to functions that are part of the distributed efforts of the organization. A strict "situational view" of leadership would depict these functions as the major determinants of what a leader does and how effective he or she does it.[2] Thus, the leader's characteristics should mesh with these functional demands.

Unquestionably, the paramount role filled by the organizational leader
is that of executive or manager or supervisor, conveying the idea that the
leader directs the activities of others. Although there is no question that such a function is of central importance, this focus may
underplay other kinds of functions, or even entire roles, for the
organizational leader. Some of these are illustrated by the terms
"problem solver," "adjudicator," "advocate" and "change agent." These
need not be inconsistent with the executive role, but single-minded
attention to a leader's directive function tends to obscure the unique
requirements for other attributes.

Thus, the organizational leader may be influential in various capacities.
To place all of these functions within "direction of the enterprise"
does a disservice to the unique demands they make. In practice, this
may mean that someone is a first-rate, dependable manager, but a wash-
out in serving as an advocate for the unit. Or, consider the case of the
person who spervises a stable operation splendidly but proves inadequate
to the task of making needed changes in that operation.

Another consideration is that organizational leaders seem to "hold" a
position of authority. True enough, typically they are in charge of a
unit by the sanction of someone higher in the hierarchy than they, but
this portrays a very static view of the leader as the occupier of a
fixed position. It also tends to promote the concept of the leader and
followers as fitting into sharply demarcated categories. No wonder the
prevailing approach to organizational leadership seems largely absorbed
with stability rather than change and with position rather than influence. By comparison, less attention is given to the more dynamic
aspects of the leadership process which would embody a richer conception
of the leader's role and more consideration of leader-follower relations.

LEADER-FOLLOWER RELATIONS

It is commonly assumed that a cleavage exists between those who lead
and those who follow, and that being a follower is not being a leader.
But this simplistic view denies reality. All leaders, some of the time
and in varying degrees, are followers, and followers are not immutably
cast in nonleader roles. Often, they may, and do, become leaders.
Despite the appointment of some individuals to the status of leader, the
behavior attributes required of a leader in a particular time and place
are not confined to those persons alone.

Therefore, one of the most troublesome misconceptions is that only some members of a group have "leadership qualities" and that they will stand out as "leaders." Elsewhere, I have referred to this as the "pyramid model," with its peak made up of those chosen few and its base made up of everyone else.[3] Followers are treated essentially as "nonleaders," which is a relatively passive residual category. However, in two studies using sociometric choices of desired leaders and desired followers, extremely high correlations were found between these choices.[4] In short, the more desired leaders *and* followers tended to be the same individuals.

Although this evidence is merely suggestive, at the very least it calls into question the rather loose fashion in which leaders and followers are presumed to be sharply differentiated, usually on a dimension of activity-passivity. In fact, organizations expect responsiveness to be distributed throughout the hierarchy; no one can be literally inert without severe dislocations to the broader enterprise. Therefore, responding well as a "follower" may be associated with being effective as a "leader." But the converse should also be recognized, i.e., that being an effective follower is desirable in an incipient leader. Much as lip service is given to the importance of showing "leadership qualities," to be tapped as a leader, perhaps the "followership qualities" are really noted first.

This is not to dismiss very real distinctions between what is expected of leaders as opposed to followers. The most fundamental difference is centrality in the influence network. Leaders are likely to attempt to direct others' activities and also to have those directions accepted. Hemphill has aptly called this characteristic "initiation of structure," which is not just within the province of appointed leaders.[5]

LEADER EMERGENCE AND SOURCE OF AUTHORITY

Broadly speaking, there are two categories of leaders, each diverse within itself, yet not mutually exclusive with respect to their implications for one another. The first leader category encompasses appointed leaders within organizational frameworks; the second covers emergent leaders who achieve their role by the willing support of followers, as exemplified by election in the political realm and also in freely functioning "informal groups."

What matters especially is the leader's source of authority, i.e., how he or she receives validation as a leader. In traditional organizational structures that "how" is clear enough, at least from a formal perspective -- leaders are "put in charge" by subordinate authority. These more traditional roles are validated from above; the leader, by definition, is a person who is appointed to a position of authority.

However, even in such formal structures there are emergent leaders who gain influence from their peers. These leaders are validated by an informal process of acceptance of their influence through the impact of their personal qualities. In the military combat situation this is actualized in the phenomenon of "battlefield promotions"; within politics, emergent leadership takes the form of election -- the would-be leader is boosted through a process of nomination to candidacy and then seeks the support of a constituency.

A good deal is known about who becomes an emergent leader. The research literature reveals that the rate of interaction is one major determinant.[6] Talking in terms of quantity of output and less in terms of the quality of that output appears to place a person in a leader role.[7] In these studies, the usual definition of the "leader" is based on perceived and/or actual influence. However, quantity of participation may be related back to personal characteristics, such as age or social status.

A set of classic studies was conducted by Strodtbeck and his associates on simulated jury deliberations.[8] In the choice of a foreman, they found that those who initially sat at the ends of the jury table had a significantly higher probability of being selected by the others as foremen -- a positional effect. But further analysis revealed that those people who became foremen were higher up the socioeconomic scale with respect to education, occupation and income. Therefore, a reasonable inference is that sitting in the "leader's place" was a result of self-selection associated with these characteristics.

In groups where discussion skills are valued, people who *speak first* have a greater likelihood of being tapped as leaders. They enjoy the attention of others, and what they have to say provides a firmer basis for their assertion of influence. The research by Bass and his

22

colleagues with the Leaderless Group Discussion (LGD) technique amply indicates such regularities.[9] Their findings suggest that ascendant behavior, probably growing out of greater self-assurance from a past history of successful influence, gave some members a "leg-up" in becoming leader.

Various experiments have shown that it is possible to produce or otherwise modify leader behavior. Pepinsky, Hemphill and Shevitz identified male students who were low in speaking out and initiating structure in groups.[10] Then they were exposed to a contrived discussion in which the group indicated evident support for their assertions, which produced far more leader behavior from them in a subsequent discussion. The reverse procedure also was tried with similar students who were initially high on leader activity. They were exposed to evident disagreement with their statements by other group members and subsequently dropped markedly in leader activity.

Other work indicates that even the use of signal lights as reinforcers can have a significant effect on a person's proportion of talking time, as well as his or her perceived leadership status.[11] The lights not only produced an increase in leader acts, but also created the impression of greater influence. In a related vein, Rudraswamy led some subjects within a group to believe that they had higher status.[12] They attempted significantly more leader behavior than others in their group and even out-distanced members who had been given more task-relevant information in advance.

Therefore, when provided with a basis for acting as a leader, persons who otherwise might not will do so. However, this does not mean that there are not individual differences in the disposition to lead, even with favorable conditions. In one study with army squads, Gordon and Medland found that a measure of "aspiration to lead" was significantly related to positive peer evaluations on "leadership ability."[13] The causal direction of this relationship cannot be determined, but it seems reasonable to consider that the potential for acting as an emergent leader depends on self-evaluations which are consistent with the expectations of peers.

23

To return to an earlier point, the distinction between emergent and appointed leaders has some important psychological dimensions. For instance, there are indications that in appointing or electing a leader, different realities are created within which the leader and followers operate. Research on this topic shows that elected leaders are more vulnerable to being deposed than appointed leaders, but at the same time they experience a greater sense of their own efficacy in exerting influence.[14]

Of course, much depends on the source and circumstances of appointment; nonetheless, one interpretation from these results is that election may induce a greater vested interest in the leader and higher expectations by followers. The leader who is "put in charge" by appointment from above, is much less the responsibility of followers and, therefore, these followers may not have this same sense of investment. The appointed leader may "underperform" with greater impunity, but he or she also may operate with less group support.

There are also some noteworthy correlates of electing leaders which bear directly on the matter of emergence. One recent experiment found that, under comparable conditions, elected leaders were initially less in-fluential than appointed leaders.[15] However, after the groups exper-ienced apparent failure in their decision-making task, the result was reversed; elected leaders became more influential. This was presumed to be a "rallying around" effect, which was not found for the appointed leaders.

Especially noteworthy is the fact that before the groups knew how they were performing, there was one group member who was more influential than the elected leader and who typically emerged later as the group's choice for leader when a new election was held. Therefore, a new leader was "standing in the wings" awaiting his or her cue, after the crisis had run its course.

A TRANSACTIONAL PERSPECTIVE

Leadership is, in fact, a transactional process. That class of behaviors associated with a "leader" is not confined to one person who acts alone; there is a relationship with followers who perceive and evaluate the leader in the context of situational demands, whether that relationship is made explicit or not.

24

The situational approach helped to further the concept that the qualities of the leader were variously appropriate to the group's situation.
Hemphill[16] expressed its major theme in saying "there are no absolute
leaders, since successful leadership must always take into account the
specific requirements imposed by the nature of the group which is to be
led." Therefore, it took greater account of the actualities of daily
life by emphasizing that: leaders function in a particular time and
place; there are several pathways to becoming a leader, sometimes from
higher authority and sometimes from group consent; and leadership involves diverse functions among persons in varying roles.[17]

However, the situational view is open to the charge of overstatement in
several directions. Although no claim was made that different individuals are literally interchangeable in leader roles, some organizations
might interpret that to be the doctrine. Individual differences do
matter. Furthermore, the leader and the situation are not so sharply
disparate as they appear. From the followers' standpoint, the
leader is an element in the situation who also helps to shape and define
it for them.[18] There is also a problem inherent in the catch-all quality of the term "situation." It fails to distinguish adequately among
task demands, which are given the greatest play, and the structure, size
and resources of the group, including its organizational setting and its
history.

To specify the transactional quality of leadership more completely,
three determinants must be considered, i.e., "the 'leader,' with his (her)
personality, perceptions and resources relevant to goal attainment; the
'followers' with their personalities, perceptions, and relevant resources; and the situational context within which those variables function."[19]

These three elements are shown graphically in Figure I. The overlap
area represents the locus of "leadership" insofar as the leader and the
followers are bound together in a relationship within a situation. Each
of these elements has characteristics or components which can affect
leadership and its outcomes: none of them are entirely self-sufficient
because they are involved in an interacting system which can be treated
as mostly closed, though it obviously is partly open, to the outside
world.

Figure I
Some Relevant Attributes in Three
Leadership Elements*

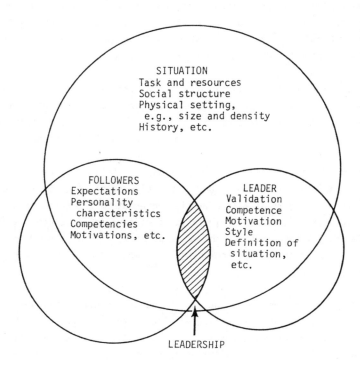

*(All terms should be interpreted liberally, not strictly.)

26

In the figure, the leader and followers are mainly within the situation, but not entirely so. This is intended to show that their involvement is one of partial, not total, inclusion. Furthermore, the leader does not stand apart from the followers but is represented as related to them in the area designated "leadership." Between them there is a process of social exchange.

For example, across many situations the leader is expected to set goals -- and not in isolation. Moreover, it is expected that these goals are to be effectively communicated. In a study bearing on this point, the leader's failure to provide goal orientations to the group provoked antagonism, tension and absenteeism.[20] These disruptive effects were especially marked if there had been clear agreement within the group about who was to serve as the leader; the followers' expectations had not been fulfilled.

Put in social exchange terms, the person in the role of leader who fulfills expectations and helps attain group goals provides rewards for others. These rewards then are reciprocated in the form of status, esteem and heightened influence; hence, the leader gives something and gets something in return.[21]

Leadership embodies a two-way influence relationship. Influence assertions from the leader to followers are reciprocated in demands made on the leader. Therefore, the integrity of the relationship depends on some yielding to influence on both sides.

This may seem an unduly idealized view, but it conveys a truth which is sufficiently general to bear upon many reaches of organizational functioning. Another way of seeing this is in resource allocation terms. When common ends are being sought, it is expected that each person will do his or her share. But the leader provides a unique resource which is consumed most obviously by activities directed toward the achievement of goals. The leader is also uniquely a "definer-of-reality" for the others by setting goals and also by communicating relevant information about progress, impediments and needed redirections.

27

If there is one consistent weakness evident across many organizational
settings, including government, it is the failure to share information
which defines the situation. Too often, "giving orders" substitutes
for "giving information" and, of course, the two are not mutually exclusive. The vacuum created by an absence of information can be filled
by other voices that are less familiar with the prevailing circumstances.
Therefore, in very practical terms, the leader's failure to provide a
realistic "definition of the situation" is an invitation for others to
do so. Indeed, giving perspective to events is what a large part of
political life is about, and its broader significance for organizational
leadership has long since been noted.[22]

INNOVATION AND CHANGE

A more "dynamic" view of leadership must take seriously the root meaning
of that term, which is change. This runs counter to the usual emphasis
on stasis, or equilibrium, still found in much of the organizational
literature. Although continuity and equilibration are of undeniable
importance, they may lead to an imbalance in the way leadership is
construed.

In general, the leader is not only influential but the one from whom
initiatives for change are expected. The leader's role usually embodies
the potential for taking innovative action in coping with new or altered
demands. But how successful the leader is as a change agent depends on
the perceptions that followers have of the leader's motivation and related actions. The concept of "idiosyncrasy credit" is intended to deal
with this innovative side of leadership.[23/]

The credit model takes off from the apparent paradox that leaders are
said to conform more to the group's norms, or standards of conduct, and
yet are also likely to be most influential in bringing about innovations.
Actually, these elements are easily reconciled when seen as a matter of
sequence. In the early contact between the leader, or would-be leader,
and relevant others, credits are gained by signs of a contribution to
the group's primary task and by a loyalty to the group's norms. In summary terms, these two factors are called "competence" and "conformity."

Credits exist only in the shared perceptions which group members gain of
the others over time. But credits have operational significance in

allowing later deviations which otherwise would be viewed negatively if a person did not have a sufficient balance to draw upon. Therefore, a newcomer to the group is poorly positioned to assert influence or take innovative action because the credits usually are not yet available. However, it should be added that a particular individual may bring derivative credit from another group under the general heading of a "favorable reputation."

Broadly speaking, when there are sufficient demonstrations of competence and conformity, the individual earns enough credits to arrive at a level of status sufficient to be a leader. At that point his or her assertions of influence become more acceptable. Moreover, there is the expectation that, once accumulated, credits will be used to take actions in the direction of needed innovation. A failure to do so may result in the loss of credits.

Experimental research with the credit model is reported elsewhere.[24] Suffice it to say, this work indicates that: early nonconformity by an otherwise competent group member blocks the acceptance of his or her influence, while later nonconformity is taken as the basis for alterations in the group's norms; and nonconformity to group norms is more readily accepted from someone already granted high accorded status than from someone who is low. An experiment by Alvarez also indicates that in "successful" organizations the higher-status person loses credits at a slower rate than the lower-status individual, for the same infractions of work rules.[25] In "unsuccessful" organizations, the opposite is true.

A final point concerns the applicability of the credit model to succession in leadership. Clearly, the new leader must establish a basis for support through the mechanisms indicated. But this depends on whether succession occurs from the "inside" or the "outside."

The insider has the advantage of already being known and, consequently, of having some credits. On the other hand, there are also perceived commitments involved, including the presence on the scene of proponents and opponents. The outsider needs to earn some credits and, at the same time, learn the terrain. There also are likely to be threats that need to be handled concerning some of the followers feelings. Although these appear to be serious disadvantages, they are counterbalanced by

29

other considerations. If the factor of reputation is at work, as it
usually is, some derivative credit is available. The outsider benefits
also from others' sense of curiosity and new beginnings. Furthermore, the
outsider enters the scene unencumbered with a past history of relationships and selective loyalties.

These points are merely suggestive of some considerations involved in
succession. There is obviously no one all-embracing generalization
about it which can hold across the board. Indeed, succession is an area
of leadership which urgently demands more study.

What prompted the introduction of succession here was a concern with
change as a feature of the leader's role. To round that out, the related
issue of style deserves to be mentioned. In particular, there are
leadership attributes, such as trust, loyalty and credibility, which
facilitate change and make it more palatable. In fact, these are not
the leader's characteristics, but are relational qualities, so named
because they grow out of a relationship between leaders and followers--
and are not easily created. Existence of these qualities depends on the
followers' perceptions of the leader's actions and assertions over time.

A major challenge in the study of leadership, emergent or otherwise, is
to arrive at a firmer understanding of these relational qualities and
the processes by which they grow or diminish, including the impact of
the leader's style. Unquestionably, there are individual differences at
work which may explain, at least in part, why style has seemed so neglected. The situational approach may have been taken too literally to
mean that "leaders don't count," but it never was aimed at disregarding
the leader's personal attributes.[26]

In conclusion, several points bear reiteration. There is a need to see
the leader's role as involving a variety of functions, not just the
direction of activity. The dichotomy between being a leader *or* a
follower is out-dated, and greater specification of the diverse components
of the situations in which leader-follower influence occurs is required.
More needs to be understood about the leader's function as a "definer-
of-reality" for followers. In general, the transactional features of
that relationship must be better appreciated, especially in such matters
as facilitating necessary innovations and change.

30

FOOTNOTES

*Portions of this paper served as the basis for a seminar presentation at Oxford University in June 1974. I am indebted to my colleagues there, especially Peter Collett and Mansur Lalljee, for their helpful comments. They are, of course, absolved of any responsibility for the final product. I also wish to express my appreciation for a Faculty Research Fellowship (7332A) from the University Awards Committee of the Research Foundation of State University of New York, which facilitated the preparation of this paper as well as some of the analyses upon which it is based.

[1] C. A. Gibb, "Leadership," in G. Lindzey and E. Aronson, eds., *The Handbook of Social Psychology*, 2nd ed., Vol. 4 (Reading, Mass.: Addison-Wesley, 1968), pp. 205-282.

[2] A. Bavelas, "Leadership: Man and Function," *Administrative Science Quarterly*, 4 (1960), pp. 491-498.

[3] E. P. Hollander, "Emergent Leadership and Social Influence," in L. Petrullo and B. M. Bass, eds., *Leadership and Interpersonal Behavior* (New York: Holt, Rinehart, and Winston, 1961), pp. 30-47.

[4] E. P. Hollander and W. B. Webb, "Leadership, Followership, and Friendship: An Analysis of Peer Nominations," *Journal of Abnormal and Social Psychology*, 50 (1955) pp. 163-167; A. J. Kubany, "Evaluation of Medical Student Clinical Performance: A Criterion Study," *Dissertation Abstracts*, 17 (1957), pp. 1119-1120.

[5] J. K. Hemphill, *Situational Factors in Leadership* (Columbus: Ohio State University, Bureau of Educational Research, 1949).

[6] A. P. Hare, *Handbook of Small Group Research* (New York: Free Press, 1962).

[7] See for example, R. F. Bales, "The Equilibrium Problem in Small Groups," in T. H. Parsons, R. F. Bales and E. A. Shils, eds., *Working Papers in the Theory of Action* (Glencoe, Ill.: The Free Press, 1953), pp. 111-161; H. W. Riecken, "The Effect of Talkativeness on Ability to Influence Group Solutions to Problems," *Sociometry*, 21 (1958) pp. 309-321; R. C. Regula and J. W. Julian, "The Impact of Quality and Frequency of Task Contributions on Perceived Ability," *Journal of Social Psychology*, 89 (1973) pp. 115-122.

[8] F. L. Strodtbeck, R. M. James and C. Hawkins, "Social Status in Jury Deliberations," in E. E. Maccoby, T. M. Newcomb and E. L. Hartley, eds., *Readings in Social Psychology*, 3rd Ed. (New York: Holt, 1958), pp. 379-388; F. L. Strodtbeck and L. H. Hook, "The Social Dimensions of a Twelve Man Jury Table," *Sociometry*, 24 (1961), pp. 397-415.

[9] B. M. Bass, et al., "Personality Variables Related to Leaderless Group Discussion Behavior," *Journal of Abnormal and Social Psychology*, 48 (1953), pp. 120-128.

[10] P. N. Pepinsky, J. K. Hemphill and R. N. Shevitz, "Attempts to Lead, Group Productivity and Morale under Conditions of Acceptance and Rejection," *Journal of Abnormal and Social Psychology*, 57 (1958), pp. 47-54.

[11] A. Bavelas, et al., "Experiments on the Alteration of Group Structure," *Journal of Experimental Social Psychology*, 1 (1965), pp. 55-70; S. M. Zdep and W. I. Oakes, "Reinforcement of Leadership Behavior in Group Discussion," *Journal of Experimental Social Psychology*, 3 (1967), pp. 310-320.

[12] V. Rudraswamy, "An Investigation of the Relationship between Perceptions of Status and Leadership Attempts," *Journal of the Indian Academy of Applied Psychology*, 1 (1964), pp. 12-19.

[13] L. V. Gordon and F. F. Medland, "The Cross-Group Stability of Peer Ratings of Leadership Potential," *Personnel Psychology*, 18 (1965), pp. 173-177.

[14] E. P. Hollander and J. W. Julian, "Studies in Leader Legitimacy, Influence and Innovation," in L. Berkowitz, ed., *Advances in Experimental Social Psychology*, Vol. 5 (New York: Academic Press, 1970), pp. 33-69.

[15] E. P. Hollander, B. J. Fallon and M. T. Edwards, "The Influence and Acceptability of Appointed and Elected Leaders under Conditions of Group Success or Failure," paper presented at the Eastern Psychological Association Convention (1974).

[16] J. K. Hemphill, "The Leader and his Group," *Education Research Bulletin*, 28 (1949), pp. 225-229; 245-246.

[17] E. P. Hollander, *Leaders, Groups and Influence* (New York: Oxford University Press, 1964), pp. 4-5.

[18] E. P. Hollander and J. W. Julian, "Contemporary Trends in the Analysis of Leadership Processes," *Psychological Bulletin*, 71 (1969), pp. 387-397.

[19] E. P. Hollander and J. W. Julian, "Leadership," in E. F. Borgatta and W. W. Lambert, eds., *Handbook of Personality Theory and Research* (Chicago: Rand McNally, 1968), pp. 890-899.

[20] P. J. Burke, "Authority Relations and Descriptive Behavior in Small Discussion Groups," *Sociometry*, 29 (1966), pp. 237-250.

[21] G. C. Homans, *Social Behavior: Its Elementary Forms* (New York: Harcourt, Brace and World, 1961).

[22] P. Selznick, *Leadership in Administration* (Evanston: Row, Peterson, 1957).

[23] E. P. Hollander, "Conformity, Status, and Idiosyncrasy Credit," *Psychological Review*, 65 (1958), pp. 117-127; _____, *Leaders, Groups and Influence*.

[24] E. P. Hollander, "Competence and Conformity in the Acceptance of Influence," *Journal of Abnormal and Social Psychology*, 61 (1960), pp. 361-365; "Some Effects of Perceived Status on Responses to Innovative Behavior," *Journal of Abnormal and Social Psychology*, 63 (1961), pp. 247-250.

[25] R. Alvarez, "Informal Reactions to Deviance in Simulated Work Organizations: A Laboratory Experiment," *American Sociological Review,* 33 (1968), pp. 895-912.

[26] See E. P. Hollander, "Style, Structure, and Setting in Organizational Leadership," *Administrative Science Quarterly*, 16 (1971), pp. 1-9.

[12]

A Role-Making Model of Leadership in Formal Organizations: A Developmental Approach

GEORGE GRAEN, JAMES F. CASHMAN
**University of Illinois
at Urbana-Champaign**

Role making is a set of processes by which an actor and a functionally interdependent other: (1) work through how each will behave in certain situations (interlocking behavior by reciprocal reinforcement), and (2) agree upon the general nature of their relationship (constructing relationship norms) against the background of the formal organization (Graen, 1975). These processes thus produce dyadic (two-person) social structures (Weick, 1969).

A special case of role making, namely, that involving the functional interdependence between a person in a leader position and one in a follower position, can be used to describe a vertical development process.[1] If our focus is restricted to these vertical dyad linkages (VDL), role-making processes can be used to describe the development of both interlocked behavior and relationship norms between leaders and each of their members. Moreover, by appropriately investigating the development of these dyadic linkages during periods when role-making processes are active, we may discover not only the nature of dyadic structures and the processes of becoming, but also the leadership-associated outcomes.[2]

Developmental Approach
A developmental approach focuses on early interactions among members

Preparation of this paper was supported in part by grant NE-G-00-3-0091 from the National Institute of Education (George Graen, principal investigator). We are also indebted to Fred Dansereau, Jr., and Wm. J. Haga for their many contributions on the natural experiment, and to Dan Gallagher, Steve Ginsburgh, and Bill Shiemann for their many contributions on the replications.

[1]Although not discussed in this study, other cases of role making which are under investigation are those involving peers in the same unit, peers in different units, and peers in different departments.

[2]In this study, we shall restrict our discussion to managerial units (units in which members are at least first-level supervisors).

of loosely knit dyads and searches for signs (early warning detectors) of the emerging dyadic social structures. These signs, once discovered, are used to predict over time the nature of the fully developed social structure and even the outputs of that structure. By accepting this approach, we make two basic assumptions about the leadership situation in managerial units. First, we assume that some interlocked behaviors must be shaped (successive approximation application of reinforcement) beginning early in the history of the VDL, e.g., critical tasks cannot be commanded of strangers or the consequences may harm the leader. Second, we assume that some relationships must be developed carefully over an extended period of time, e.g., mutual trust must be earned by both parties. Therefore, we expect that early interactions between a leader and a member will emit signs which can be used to predict the nature of the emergent leadership structure—the leader-member exchange.

A NATURAL EXPERIMENT

To examine the development of leader-member exchange within organizational units requires a setting where the parties to the vertical relationships are in the process of working through their respective roles (role making). By longitudinally studying a setting of this kind from several different points of view, the early indicators of leader-member exchange can be related to later behavioral outcomes.

Fortunately, a setting meeting these requirements was available for investigation. A large department of 60 managers was undergoing a complete reorganization. While 50 percent of the managers were in new positions and one-third were new to the organization, nearly 90 percent of the reporting relationships contained at least one new member. The development of leader-member exchanges was investigated over a nine-month period. Employing a wide array of instruments (incorporated into interview schedules), each of the 60 vertical dyad relationships was monitored from both the member's and the leader's points of view during four interview waves: (a) the second month after reorganization; (b) the fourth month; (c) the seventh month; and (d) the ninth month. (For further details on this natural experiment, see Dansereau, Graen, and Haga, 1975; Graen, 1975; Graen, et al., 1975; and Haga, Graen, and Dansereau, 1974.)

Design of the Study

Internal validity (Campbell and Stanley, 1963) of the results of a natural experiment are enhanced to the extent that plausible competing hypotheses are ruled out as possible explanations. These rival hypotheses can be controlled within a design through a number of events, including sampling, manipulation, and statistical adjustment. Sampling control occurs when the competing explanatory variables are found to be uncorrelated with the independent variable in a particular situation. In contrast, manipulation control occurs when the competing explanatory variables are made to be uncorrelated with the independent variable by modifying the structure of a particular situation. Finally, statistical control occurs when the competing variables are transformed to be uncorrelated with the independent variable by modifying the relationships of a particular situation.

Our sign (early warning detector) of the emerging dyadic social structure and the naturally occurring treatment variable of this experiment (independent variable) was called "negotiating latitude between a member and his leader." This measure attempted to assess the relative openness of a leader to individualized assistance for a member. The basic notion underlying this measure was that an early sign of the nature of the developing leader-member exchange is the member's evaluation of his relationship with his leader as a source of individualized assistance. A dyadic relationship characterized by a high degree of individualized assistance is more likely to produce negotiated exchanges between a member and a leader than one characterized by a low degree of this treatment variable. In fact, a necessary condition for the development of members may be the early application of individualized assistance. Only after a member comes to view his leader as open to dyadic exchanges with him can he be expected to propose, much less engage in, such exchanges. On the other hand, a leader may not be equally open to such exchanges with all of his members. Therefore, when a member indicates that his leader is open to his requests for individualized assistance, it is taken as a sign that dyadic negotiation is likely and that an in-group exchange is developing. In contrast, when a member indicates that his leader is relatively closed to such requests, it is taken as a sign that dyadic negotiation is unlikely and that an out-group exchange is developing.

The independent variable (our early warning detector) was dichotomized (by dividing at the median) into (high) in-group exchange and (low) out-group exchange and crossed with a classification variable called job type. Relationships analyzed using this design were predictive as opposed to concurrent or postdictive. Both the independent and the classification variables were defined based upon data collected at the second month, and the dependent variables were assessed subsequently four, seven, and nine months after reorganization. Job type showed no change during the study and our early warning detector was rather stable ($r_{tt} = .60$) from the second to the ninth and final month. Moreover, the classification of vertical relationships into out-group and in-group exchanges portended the development of two rather different kinds of situations faced by members. Job type was based upon the empirical classification of managerial tasks and reinforced by organizational documents (organizational charts, job descriptions, and the like). Our early warning detector was essentially uncorrelated with job type (showing nearly equal frequencies between in- and out-groups within each of the three job types). Using this design, our early warning detector effects are not confounded with type of job (sampling control).

The internal validity of this natural experiment was further enhanced by the findings that our independent variable (negotiating latitude) was not reliably related to education, job experience, job tenure, age, sex, level in the hierarchy, job complexity, or any other structural or demographic variable assessed (sampling control).

Unit Composition

Consider the distribution of in-group and out-group exchanges within units (a unit consists of all members who report to the same leader). The traditional assumption of an average leadership style approach is that each leader will develop homogeneous exchanges with his members. Within a unit, all will be in-group exchanges or all will be out-group exchanges, but none will be mixed. The vertical dyad linkage approach, in contrast, assumes that many units will be mixed. Only 15 percent of the units showed all exchanges the same. The remaining 85 percent of the units showed mixtures. This result is more compatible with the assumption of heterogeneous vertical relationships within units.

Job Type

Job type was viewed as a validating dimension for our measures of role behavior and job problems. Managers in functionally different types of jobs can be expected to perform their roles using different involvement patterns and to confront different job problems (e.g., resistance to change, red-tape delays, and inadequate authority to do the job). Therefore, our measures of involvement in activities and job problems severity should demonstrate differences among job types. Gratifyingly, job type showed reliable differences on three of the four dimensions of job problems as reported by managers and as reported by superiors. Only the factor dealing with supervisory problems failed to differentiate among job types; however, as we shall see, this was the job problem dimension relevant to leadership. Finally although job type demonstrated reliable differences on job attitudes, it failed to show such differences on leadership measures.

Leader-Member Exchange

Classification of leader-member exchanges based upon the extent of negotiating latitude during the second month after reorganization revealed two quite different developing situations. In terms of the positional resources of the leader and working relationship with the leader, those classified at two months as showing early in-group exchanges received consistently over time greater amounts of all resources assessed and more supportive and sensitive treatment than did those showing out-group exchanges. In-group members received greater latitude in developing their roles, more inside information, greater influence in decision making, stronger support for their actions, and more consideration for their feelings than did out-group members. On the member's side of the exchange, those members showing in-group exchanges indicated greater involvement in administering and communicating activities than did out-group members.

Output of Exchanges

In addition, leaders indicated that in-group members acted consistently according to the leader's expectations, while the out-group members acted progressively more deviant from the leader's expectations. Out-group members thus deviated further and further from what the leader wanted. Other outcomes from these two types of exchanges were indicated by the job problems confronting the managers and by the work attitudes of the managers. Although job problems clustered into four separate factors, only one factor dealing with supervisory problems differentiated the in-group from the out-group. From both the members' and the leaders' reports, out-group members faced more severe problems with their superiors than did in-group members. On work attitudes, the in-group showed more positive attitudes toward the job situation in general, the work itself, technical supervision, interpersonal supervision, and job performance rewards.

In summary, the results formed a consistent network of reliable re-lationships. This network was quite consistent with the model: leaders do routinely differentiate their units by developing in-group exchanges with selected members and out-group exchanges with their remaining members. Furthermore, in addition to developing more effective relationships, members developing in-group exchanges with their leaders assume greater involvement in unit activities and receive greater positional resources from their leader than do their out-group colleagues.

Boss-Leader Exchange

Classification of boss-leader exchanges based upon the latitude of the leaders with their respective bosses during the second month showed predictable differences in the situations confronting both the leaders and their members. Those leaders showing early in-group exchanges with their bosses reported receiving more inside information. They also showed greater participation in decisions and were given greater job latitude. Their relation-ships demonstrated more support and greater consideration for their feelings than those reported by their out-group colleagues. In addition, these differences were mirrored in the work attitudes of the leaders, especially in attitudes toward supervision and job performance rewards.

Reports of members revealed that leaders who establish in-group exchanges with their bosses can influence events beyond the boundaries of their units and hence can facilitate the programs of their members to a greater extent than can those leaders who fail to develop such exchanges with their bosses. Consequently, members' reports of problems dealing with extra-unit issues were strongly related to their leader's exchange with his boss. This difference in the instrumental value of the leader for the members was reflected in the members' work attitudes. Leaders who established in-group exchanges with their own bosses were seen as more technically competent and as possessing greater reward potential than those failing to develop such exchanges.

Thus, a boss-leader exchange to which a member is not a party can influence the members' job situation for good or ill. If his leader develops an in-group exchange with his boss, a member may find that his own effectiveness is enhanced and his frustrations are reduced compared with his peer whose leader fails to develop such an exchange with his boss. Although a member may rejoice in his good fortune or curse his misfortune, he can do very little to change this parameter of his situation. In this sense, the exchange relationship of a leader with his boss is an important variable describing the structure of a member's situation.

G. Graen, J. F. Cashman

IMPLICATIONS FOR LEADERSHIP RESEARCH

An immediate reaction to this study might be to consider the findings quaint and the model interesting (perhaps even exciting); however, it certainly does not demonstrate a new approach. Rather, it may be seen as a special case of a class of studies already in the mainstream of leadership. In contrast, a scholarly evaluation of this approach requires that comparisons be made between characteristics of this vertical dyad approach and those of other, more traditional approaches. As indicated in Table 1, differences between approaches can be analyzed according to assumptions underlying models, operations, and interpretations, as well as units of analysis.

Table 1

CHARACTERISTICS OF THREE APPROACHES TO LEADERSHIP

Characteristic	Average Leadership Style	Mixed Model	Vertical Dyad Linkage
1. *Model Assumes*:			
Leader's behavior toward members . . .	homo-geneous	homo-geneous	hetero-geneous
Member's reaction to leader's behavior . . .	homo-geneous	hetero-geneous	hetero-geneous
2. *Operations Assume*:			
Leader's behavior toward members . . .	homo-geneous	(?)	hetero-geneous
Member's reaction to leader's behavior . . .	homo-geneous	hetero-geneous	hetero-geneous
3. *Interpretation Assumes*:			
Leader's behavior toward members . . .	homo-geneous	homo-geneous	hetero-geneous
Member's reaction to leader's behavior . . .	homo-geneous	hetero-geneous	hetero-geneous
4. *Unit of Analysis* . . .	unit-level	individual-level	vertical dyad-level

Note: In reference to leader's behavior, homogeneous indicates that behavior is stylistic and basically similar toward all members, whereas heterogeneous indicates that behavior is situationally dependent and identifiably different toward members. In reference to members' reactions, homogeneous denotes reactions which are essentially similar, while heterogeneous denotes reactions which are situationally dependent and identifiably different between members.

A ROLE-MAKING MODEL OF LEADERSHIP   149

Perhaps the most widely used and most straight-forward of the contemporary endeavors is the "average leadership style" approach (Fleishman and Simmons, 1970). The model, in this instance, is one of a supervisor whose behaviors can be described as varying over relatively few dimensions, two in most cases. These behavioral patterns are assumed to be stylistic for a particular supervisor and thus similarly applied to all unit members. Further, this simplifying assumption is also made regarding the reaction of unit members. All subordinates within a unit will respond approximately the same to various levels of consideration or initiating structure, for example. Operationally, the integrity of the model is maintained. The leader's behavior is assessed by averaging across the unit members on responses to an instrument such as the Leader Behavior Description Questionnaire (LBDQ) (Fleishman and Hunt, 1973) or a derivative thereof. Members' reactions are operationalized in terms of overall unit performance, average morale, etc. The results, in turn, are analyzed at the unit level and interpreted similarly.

In an effort to overcome the more critical weaknesses of the "average style" approach, as noted by Korman (1966), among others, a more complex approach to understanding the dynamics of leadership has been utilized by a number of researchers (e.g., House, 1973; House, Filley, and Kerr, 1971; House and Kerr, 1973). We will call this the "mixed model" of leadership behavior. The assumptions underlying this model, its operationalization, and interpretation appear to be very different from its predecessor. Most importantly, the approach rejects the assumption of the homogeneity of unit members' reactions to the leader's behavior. This, in fact, is the very core of the approach. Leader behaviors are assumed to be most relevant in their impact upon the psychological states of their subordinates as individuals operating within particular structures (task autonomy, role clarity, etc.). Consistent with this assumption, the data are analyzed at the level of the individual.

But what about the leader's behavior? Apparently both the model and interpretation assume that these behaviors are homogeneous across unit members. The leader's behavior is described as instrumental or supportive, and frequently related to studies using the "average style" approach (House and Dessler, 1974); however, the effects of these *patterns* (styles) of behavior may vary across levels of numerous intervening situational and/or personality variables. Operationally, the assumption about the behavior of leaders toward group members is vague. The "mixed model," at least in the studies which have come to our attention, never attempts to directly measure this variable. Only subordinate *perceptions* of that behavior are measured. Thus, at the operational level, we are dealing with a variable which may be very different from that described in the model. Further, even dealing at the perceptual level, the nature of the assumption is unclear. The items used to define the various factors of perceived leader behavior are predominantly of the type which indicate a homogeneous behavioral pattern. Samples of such items are: "He asks that *group members* follow standard rules and regulations"; "He puts suggestions made by the *group* into operation"; "He looks out for the personal welfare of *group* members"; "Before taking action he consults with his *subordinates*." Factors consisting of these types of items suggest that the leader's style could be estimated appropriately by averaging across members of each unit. This operation would be consistent with interpretations typically given to the results of the "mixed model." This has not been done. Instead, the behavioral perceptions are averaged across members of various work groups. On the basis of this procedure, it would seem that leaders' behaviors are actually heterogeneous across unit members. If this is so, the interpretations referring back to the leader's style would be inappropriate because we never know what this style actually is.

The present approach differs from its predecessors in that it assumes heterogeneous behaviors from both the supervisor and unit member. Unlike the "average leadership style" approach, the "vertical dyad linkage" approach does not assume that supervisory behavior is consistent across unit members or that members' reactions to it are essentially the same. The unit is not the appropriate level of analysis for this approach. Unlike the "mixed model," this approach does not assume that leader behavior is merely a perceptual variable operating solely within the heads of unit members. Further, the present approach does not assume that these perceptions, analyzed at the individual level, allow interpretation back to the supervisor's style of behavior. Rather, the present approach assumes that supervisors may act differentially toward unit members and that these members may differ in their reactions to him. The appropriate level of analysis is not the work unit or the individual, but the vertical dyad.

If a case can be made that the present approach is new and different, then it appears necessary to determine the extent to which it may facilitate future research. Bluntly, to what extent may we expect this model to guide research rather than control it, and how useful will it be in leading to an understanding of the phenomenon of interest?

Korman (1974), in his incisive overview in *Contingency Approaches to Leadership*, provides a framework which may be useful in attempting to assess the relative strengths and weaknesses of the present approach. He argues that presently there exists a widening gap between the complexity and sophistication of theoretical formulations and the simplicity and primitiveness of the data base. In order to improve leadership theory, he suggests that six steps be taken. These steps include renewed emphasis on measurement, movement to a longitudinal view of the leadership process, discovery of causal mechanisms, multiple hypotheses testing, and notes of caution concerning both the dangers inherent in contingency variables and our overly eager usage of personality constructs. According to Korman, "measurement and theory go hand-in-hand and the development of one without the other is a waste of time for all concerned" (p. 194).

How do we go about improving our measurement? Over the past twenty years, the prevailing notion appears to have been to concentrate on developing a single reliable measure of leadership before we can deal with questions of validity. The danger inherent in this notion is that when a leadership measure bears no consistent relationship to the construct of leadership, a more consistent ordering of responses (improved reliability) can be of little value. The most reliable thermometer can tell us little about barometric pressure. In contrast, construct validity requires that we continually strive to establish network validities of leadership. Until we develop several

A ROLE-MAKING MODEL OF LEADERSHIP   151

different measures of our leadership construct and establish that these different measures form a consistent network of relationships, we can have little confidence in whatever our measure of leadership is really tapping. In short, any single measure of leadership must be suspect because it may be contaminated wholly or in part with method variance; it may be assessing one or more of a large number of extraneous constructs

The quality of our data base must be improved through attempts to ask these hard questions and to minimize various sources of error and invalidity in our data collection procedures (Graen, 1975). This means that we should scrutinize our theoretical formulations for possible untested assumptions which may produce invalidity in our measures. This also means that we should expend more energy attempting to build validity into our measures by establishing quality controls over our measurement procedures. Establishing such controls requires research designs which will allow professional interrogation over time and triangulation of information between different informants and different methods of measurement over time. Such controls can reduce misinterpretations of certain scales by subjects, or that of certain responses by interviewers through the development of a common language. In addition, such controls can reduce both the frequency and severity of various response sets to the extent that unbiased answers are made the least stressful responses. Procedures exist to interrogate different subjects regarding particular events and to identify areas of agreement and disagreement. Moreover, multimethod procedures are available to estimate method variance and convergent validity. Though designs employing these controls tend to be quite expensive, improvement in the quality of the data base must precede any real improvement in leadership theory.

But high-quality data alone will provide only a small increment in our understanding of leadership. High-quality data must be complemented with strategies which are as broadly systematic as the leadership phenomenon. If, as Korman (1974) suggests, leadership should be viewed as a process, then we must move from a static view to a longitudinal view. Only in this manner will we be able to investigate and document the stability and changes which occur in the development of this leadership process.

Causal mechanisms for leadership effects also need to be discovered and documented. Static correlations between input and outcome variables as moderated by a third structural or personality variable are compatible with the operation of a large number of rival mechanisms. Such empirical correlations indicate nothing about the direction of influence. Therefore, an interaction of an outcome variable may lead to an input variable, an interaction of an input variable may lead to an outcome variable, or an interaction of one or more of a large number of outside variables may lead to a relationship between input and outcome variables. The number of equally plausible (based upon these correlations) rival mechanisms that can be proposed is limited only by one's imagination. What is needed is not a longer list of rival mechanisms, but research designed to reduce the list through "Strong Inference" (Platt, 1964).

In sharp contrast to other leadership theories, the vertical dyad linkage model has incorporated these suggestions about design and instrumentation into its basic strategy. The results from the initial study were gratifyingly rich. The costs of time and material resources were high, but the outcomes may not have been reached through the alternative "bargain" strategies.

A THEORETICAL INTERPRETATION OF THE INITIAL STUDY

Team Building

The model (shown in Table 2) which emerges from our role-making studies of managerial dyads within formal organizations is one of team building within units based upon different leader-member exchanges. Leaders of managerial units, when faced with the task of developing new working relationships with most of the members they lead, responded in manners which served to differentiate their units. Only with some of their subordinate managers did leaders attempt to develop special exchange relationships which transcended the formal employment contract. All subordinate managers so selected may or may not have accepted such a

Table 2

A DEVELOPMENTAL MODEL OF ROLE MAKING IN VERTICAL DYADS

	Model Components	
Input	Process	Output
Member's Characteristics:		
Education		
Job Experience		
Job Tenure	*Leader-Member Exchange*	
Age		
Sex	1. Interlocked Behavior	*Job Performance*
Other	(a) member behavior: tasks	(rating)
	(b) leader behavior: resources	
Leader's Characteristics:		*Job Satisfaction*
Education	2. Working Relationship	Overall
Job Experience	(a) support	Work
Job Tenure	(b) sensitivity	Supervision—
Age	(c) trust	Interpers. Relations
Sex		Supervision—
Other		Tech. Competence
		Performance Rewards
Early Dyadic		*Job Problems*
Relationship:		Member Report
Negotiating		Superior Report
Latitude		

Note: Some characteristics of a member combine with some characteristics of a leader in a role-making process which leads to a leader-member exchange of one kind (in-group) or another (out-group, middle-group), and subsequently to performance, satisfaction, and problems.

special exchange relationships. But those who did consummate such an exchange promised to develop into members of the leader's trusted in-group. In contrast, those who either were not given the opportunity, or who declined the opportunity of the special exchange, became members of the leader's out-group. Thus, the units became differentiated over time into two distinct subgroups. Clearly, the key to this model is leader-member exchange.

Leader-Member Exchange

A distinction made by Jacobs (1970) between "leadership" and "supervision" exchanges aptly describes some of the differences between in-group and out-group leader-member exchanges. Using Jacobs' labels, leadership exchange involves the influence of members without resort to authority derived from an employment contract, whereas supervision exchange involves the influence of members through the exercise of contractual obligation. In developing a leadership exchange with his member, a leader does not rely upon the power of the employment contract. Rather, he seeks an alternative basis of influence—one anchored in the interpersonal exchange between leader and member. But what can the leader exchange with his member that is not covered by the employment contract?

Interlocking of Behavior Between Leader and Member

A leader, by virtue of his superior position in a hierarchy, possesses certain resources which are not available to his members. If these so-called positional resources (Graen, et al., 1973) are or can be made attractive outcomes for his members, a leader may exchange these resources on his own authority. A leader need not wait for formal approval from higher officials to exchange these resources, as he must do with contractual outcomes, such as salary increases, promotions, and the like. Further, this immediacy of exchange probably enhances the attractiveness of these outcomes. What resources does a leader possess that can be transformed into outcomes having either intrinsic or instrumental value for members?

A leader of a managerial unit usually has considerable discretion in task assignment, especially with nonroutine tasks. He may assign a member: (a) to a task that the member may find too difficult, hence he becomes frustrated and fails; or (b) to a task that the member may find too easy, hence he becomes bored; or (c) to a task that the member may find challenging, hence he grows. Moreover, a leader, through his own actions, can adjust the difficulty level of an assigned task. He can provide or withhold necessary information and support. He also can mediate the consequences of the member's actions by appropriate intervention. A leader may allow a member to participate in decision making regarding not only his own situation, but that of his entire unit. Being a gatekeeper of information from higher up in the hierarchy, a leader can provide or withhold "inside" information from his members. By virtue of his position on a higher rung of the ladder, a superior may mediate the visibility of his members with other superiors. In addition to the above, even the leader's interpersonal behavior as a person can become a positional resource by virtue of his position. His confidence in and consideration for a member may become attractive outcomes for that member.

A leader may share a portion of some or all of these positional resources with his members. If these resources are or can be made sufficiently attractive to members, they can serve as a leader's contribution to an exchange. If they cannot be made attractive enough to members, such an exchange is unlikely.

What can a member exchange in return for a share of the leader's positional resources? A member can reciprocate with greater than required expenditures of time and energy, the assumption of greater responsibility and risk, and concern for, if not commitment to, the success of the entire unit or organization. A member, in short, can enlarge the area of his vested interest to encompass that of his leader. If these outcomes are sufficiently attractive to a leader, a leader may attempt to establish such an exchange.

Benefits and Costs of an In-Group Exchange

For a leader, some of the costs of entering into such an in-group exchange are greater dependence upon that member and a reduction in control over him. Under such an exchange, a member gains greater capacity to make the leader appear effective or ineffective. Although a leader can delegate critical tasks to such a member, the leader maintains primary responsibility for the accomplishment of these tasks. If the member fails, the leader also fails. With this greater dependence upon a member, a leader must relinquish some degree of control over him. A leader must allow this member more latitude and provide him with the confidence and support required to perform adequately. This may mean actually negotiating with the member on unit-wide issues. Without resorting to authority, some actions cannot be commanded. They must be worked through—taking precious time to arrive at decisions. Resorting to authority on occasion may not be too damaging to a leadership exchange; however, indiscriminant use of formal authority to gain compliance from a member threatens to transform leadership into supervision. Of course, the benefits of more efficient and effective performance by in-group members may well be worth these potential costs.

Entering into a leadership exchange can also be costly for a member. Although under a supervision exchange a member receives only a minimal amount of his leader's various positional resources (those required to perform his duties adequately), he is required to perform only specified duties and to assume only specified responsibilities as conditions of employment. His compensation is equitable only under the terms of his contract. If a member assumes greater responsibility without changing the contract, he is placing his trust in his leader. On the other hand, his payoffs should be worth this risk. He should receive higher performance ratings, experience less severe problems with supervision, and feel greater satisfaction with the job situation than his out-group colleague.

To summarize the model shown in Table 2, the inputs to team development are the characteristics of each member and those of their leader. These characteristics are harnessed to outputs, such as member performance, satisfaction, and job problems, through their interactions with leader-member exchanges. Based upon the compatibility of some combination of member's characteristics and some combination of leader's characteristics, a leader initiates either an in-group or an out-group exchange with his member early in the life of the dyadic relationship. Our early warning detector of the signs of these exchanges (negotiating latitude) focuses upon the relative openness of a leader to extend individualized assistance to his member and is an attempt to tap dyadic negotiation. Over a period of time, the leader-member exchanges develop into distinct social structures of very different kinds. In-group exchanges involve interlocking different task behaviors and forming different working relationships than do out-group exchanges. Specifically, in-group exchanges will involve first, the interlocking of more responsible tasks accepted by members and higher levels of assistance provided by leaders; and second, working relationships will be characterized by greater support, sensitivity, and trust than occurs in out-group exchanges. Furthermore, the mechanism of this interlocking of member and leader behavior probably is reciprocal reinforcement (member task behavior reinforces leader resource allocation behavior; leader resource allocation behavior reinforces member task behavior—and the cycle repeats). These leader-member exchange *structures* are strongly and consistently related to the outputs of member performance, job satisfaction, and job problems. In addition, once these structures emerge, they demonstrate high stability over time. Thus, until the nature of the linkage becomes altered, both member and leader behavior can be both understood and predicted over time.

REPLICATIONS

While the finding of a consistent network of reliable relationships increases our confidence in the internal validity of a set of results, a replication of these results in another study is required to increase our confidence in the external validity of this finding (Campbell and Stanley, 1963).

Our attempts to replicate the results of the above study took place in three semiautonomous departments of a large organization, and in one large department of a medium-sized organization. Each of the four departments was investigated using the basic design of the natural experiment. That is, we used many of the instruments developed in the former study and employed the dyadic interview scheme at four points in time extending over a nine-month period. In addition to attempting to replicate our earlier results, these four studies were designed to facilitate the refinement of our measurement instrument and to extend our network of findings into new domains of content. We sought to refine our measure of negotiating latitude, for example, by including new items designed to augment its core, and by triangulating it through the use of a multimethod-multisource matrix (Campbell and Fiske, 1959). New domains of content included were: (a) communication activities—how frequently each manager communicated with each other manager regarding technical, administrative, planning, or other matters, and the percentage of time each manager initiated these communications; (b) bases of influence (French and Raven, 1959)—referent, expert, reward, coercive, and bureaucratic power; and (c) dyadic loyalty (Jennings, 1967)—behaviors indicating trust in one's leader.

Analysis of the data from the three departments within the same organization has advanced beyond the preliminary stage. Data collection in the fourth department was performed six months later than that in the other three departments. Analysis on these three departments indicates no consistent department-by-leadership interactions. Therefore, the results will be shown for the total of 109 vertical dyads.

Vertical Dyadic Linkages

Results indicate that vertical dyad relationships can be classified reliably into leadership exchanges and supervision exchanges, based upon the negotiating latitude measure. Moreover, we were able to successfully augment the negotiating latitude scale. Again, negotiating latitude (our early warning detector) was found to be quite stable ($r_{tt} = .73$) over a seven-month period. Measurement validity of this scale was supported by a multimethod-multisource analysis. Employing this procedure, two rather different methods were used to assess leadership and supervision exchanges. One method used a set of structured questions with fixed and ordered response alternatives (psychometric scale method). The other method simply asked each participant to draw a map of the vertical working relationships within his or her unit (VDL map method). Using this map method, each participant was asked to designate for each vertical relationship one of three categories: (1) ineffective, (2) intermediate in effectiveness, or (3) effective. These two methods were assessed from the perspective of both the manager and his superior.

Correlations involving data derived from the two methods (scale and map), and the two sources (member and superior) are presented in Table 3. Also shown in this table are correlations involving data from the peers using the map method. Each method produced comparable agreement between member and superior (.50 for the scale and .41 for the map). Notably, peers demonstrated comparable coefficients of agreement with both member ratings (.51) and superior ratings (.57). These agreement coefficients between different sources and within the same method must be interpreted in the light of existing measurement technology. For example, compared with the assessments of job performance, the present agreement coefficients rank well above the average of those reported (Borman, 1974). This may indicate that the signs of leader-member exchange are no less intersubjectively reliable than those of job performance. However, it should be noted that these data were collected during the final waves of a longitudinal investigation. Data collected in a oneshot, cross-sectional study, even using the present measurement procedures, may not be precise enough to replicate these results.

Equally important are the coefficients of convergent validity. If the measurement of negotiating latitude was completely subjective (residing only in a member's head), its correlation with that from a superior or peers can be expected to be unreliable. Moreover, to the extent that the measurement capitalizes on method variance, correlations within the same method (monomethod) can be expected to be stronger than those between different methods (heteromethod). Correlations between different methods for the same source (member .43, and superiors .53) are comparable with those

Table 3

MULTIMETHOD-MULTISOURCE CORRELATION MATRIX

Method Source	Scale		Map		
	Member	Superior	Member	Superior	Peers
1. *Scale*:					
Member	1.00				
Superior	.50	1.00			
2. *Map*:					
Member	.43	.36	1.00		
Superior	.40	.53	.41	1.00	
Peers	.34	.46	.51	.57	1.00

Note: All correlation coefficients are statistically reliable ($p < .01$). N = 109. Stability coefficients (unadjusted) were .82, .81, and .73 for member scale, and .66, .83, and .71 for superior scale between four and seven, seven and nine, and four and nine months, respectively. Spearman-Brown homogeneity coefficients were .80 and .61 at seven months, and .84 and .68 at nine months, for member scale and superior scale, respectively.

within the same method and between different sources. Even the most severe condition of between-different-methods and between-different-sources showed correlations comparable with the other two conditions. Clearly, these results increase our confidence in the measurement validity of negotiating latitude.

Unit Composition

Another finding from the VDL map data was that the approximation used in the natural experiment of a median (50-50 split) between in-group and out-group was imprecise. Rather, the map data suggested that a trichotomy of 25 percent (high-negotiation) in-group, 50 percent (medium-negotiation) middle-group, and 25 percent (low-negotiation) out-group is a closer approximation. Recall that participants generated their own distributions of vertical relationships by designating a given number in each of the three categories. Thus, we have three independent estimates of this distribution: self-ratings, superior ratings, and peer ratings. As in the original investigation, the traditional assumption of an average leadership style was incompatible with the results on the homogeneity of vertical exchanges within units. Employing the above trichotomy on the data from the map method, average peer ratings showed only 15 percent of the units with homogeneous exchanges and 85 percent with heterogeneous exchanges. Self-ratings showed 19 percent homogeneous and 81 percent heterogeneous. Finally, superior ratings showed 26 percent homogeneous and 74 percent heterogeneous. Clearly, these results are more in line with the assumptions of heterogeneous vertical relationships within units.

Instrumentation

The question of whether the instruments used in the natural experiment would prove useful in different situations was answered in the affirmative. Even the two sets of variables most dependent upon structural variation demonstrated relevance in the new settings. Our measures of the severity of various job problems (21 items) factored into the same four problem dimensions. In addition, our measures of relative involvement in various job activities (26 items) factored into five clearly defined dimensions: (a) Managing activities involved interactions with subordinates; (b) Boundary Spanning activities consisted of interactions with outsiders; (c) Administering activities dealt with decision-making processes; (d) Planning activities involved developing alternative paths; and (e) Liaison activities consisted of coordinating with other units.

As in the natural experiment, job type was employed as a validating dimension for both job problems and activities. As in the natural experiment, job type showed reliable differences on structural job problems as reported by members ($p < .02$), and as reported by superiors ($p < .03$). Similarly, job type, shown in Table 4, demonstrated reliable differences on four of the five dimensions of managerial behavior and on three of the five dimensions of involvement in activities superiors expected. These results support the sensitivity of these dimensions to differences in the formal structure of the situation.

Leader-Member Exchange

Classification of leader-member exchanges based upon extent of negotiating latitude during the second wave replicated and extended the reliable relationships found in the natural experiment. Overall, these replications demonstrated even stronger relationships than the original study. For example, managerial role behavior produced the results shown in Table 4. According to these results, in-, middle-, and out-groups demonstrated reliable differences on all five dimensions of member reports, and on four of the five dimensions of superior expectations. Almost all relationships showed monotonically increasing trends from out-group to in-group. Based upon member reports, in-group members showed greater time and effort expended in boundary activities, administering, planning, and liaison activities than that shown by the average middle-group and out-group members. Based upon superior reports, in-group members showed greater involvement on all except managing activities than did the average middle-group and out-group members. It should be noted that the trichotomy produced stronger relationships than those produced by a median dichotomy (50-50 split). (As was found in the natural experiment, the independent variable of negotiating latitude was not reliably related to any of the many structural or demographic variables assessed.) In terms of positional resources and working relationships, the trends were monotonically increasing from out-group to in-group regarding all resources assessed from the members' perspective. In-group members received greater latitude in their roles, more inside information, greater influence in decision making, stronger support for their actions, and more consideration for their feelings than did members of the other two groups.

Table 4

INVOLVEMENT IN MANAGERIAL BEHAVIOR BY THREE LEADERSHIP GROUPS

Activity	Mean Involvement						Probability		
	4 months			9 months					
	Out	Middle	In	Out	Middle	In	Exchange	Job Type	Time
1. Member Reported:									
Managing Boundary	9.92	11.07	11.43	10.42	11.12	11.87	.030	.008	.06
Spanning	8.23	8.90	10.48	8.31	9.35	10.96	.004	.001	.12
Administering	7.54	8.83	9.91	7.19	8.85	9.96	.0005	.003	.81
Planning	12.38	12.55	14.83	11.69	13.07	14.52	.006	.0001	.99
Liaison	7.62	8.13	8.91	7.35	8.57	9.30	.002	.08	.12
2. Superior Expected:									
Managing Boundary	12.27	12.42	12.87	12.50	12.58	12.61	.91	.0001	.83
Spanning	9.65	10.73	12.17	9.81	10.50	12.30	.006	.020	.92
Administering	8.23	9.16	10.04	7.62	8.67	10.17	.020	.0003	.13
Planning	14.69	15.51	16.70	14.54	14.50	16.70	.001	.260	.37
Liaison	9.12	9.33	9.96	8.86	8.98	10.47	.020	.110	.65

Note: No consistent pattern of interactions among the independent variables was found Group sizes were out-group (n = 26), middle-group (n = 60), and in-group (n = 23), for leader-member exchange, and type I (n = 29), type II (n = 27), type III (n = 26), type IV (n = 26), and type V (n = 27) for job type.

160   *G. Graen, J. F. Cashman*

Output

In-group members received higher performance ratings from their respective superiors than did members of the other two groups. As expected, out-group members received lower performance ratings than did members of the other two groups. Of the four job problem dimensions, the same single factor dealing with supervisory problems was reliably related to the trichotomy. Based upon reports of both members and superiors, out-group members were confronted with more severe problems with their superiors than were members of the other two groups. As expected, all job satisfaction scales showed strong and reliable relationships with the trichotomy. Again, all relationships were monotonically increasing from out-group to in-group.

Bases of Influence

One hypothesis that was derived directly from the heuristic model without benefit of antecedent evidence concerned the bases of influence (French and Raven, 1959) for each of the exchange relationships. According to this hypothesis, leadership exchange (in-group) will typically involve expert and referent power and little coercive power. In contrast, supervision exchange (out-group) will involve less expert and referent power and more coercive power. This hypothesis was derived from the assumption that the working relationship dimension of leader-member exchange varies from mutual trust and respect on one pole, to mutual distrust and control at the opposite pole.

Results relevant to this hypothesis are shown in Table 5. As shown, both the reports of members and those of superiors demonstrate reliable differences between in-groups and out-groups on both referent and expert bases of influence. In-group members' reports showed higher endorsement than those of out-group members, indicating that both reference and expertise factors influenced their acceptance of their leader's suggestions. In agreement, reports of superiors indicated that both reference and expertise factors were more instrumental in influencing in-group than out-group members. In addition, member reports showed reliable ($p < .003$) differences on coercive influence, but superior reports failed to demonstrate such reliable ($p = .31$) differences. Trends on coercive influence for both member and superior reports showed higher means for the out-group than for the in-group. With the single exception of the failure of superior reports on coercive influence, results were reliable and in the predicted directions.

Another way to view these results on bases of influence is according to rank-order. On members' reports, in-group and middle-group rank-orders were identical; but rank-orders for the out-group showed the rank of reference (3) and the rank of coercive (5) were transposed. On superiors' reports, the in-group rank-order was (1) expertise, (2) bureaucratic, (3) *reference*, (4) reward, and (5) *coercive*; whereas, the out-group rank-order was (1) bureaucratic, (2) expertise, (3) reward, (4) *coercive*, and (5) *reference*. Overall, the rank-orders of members and superiors were not too discrepant.

Dyadic Loyalty: Trust

Jennings (1967) maintains that a leader of a managerial unit often

Table 5

BASES OF INFLUENCE

Influence Base	Mean			Probability
	Out-Group (n = 26)	Middle (n = 60)	In-Group (n = 23)	
1. *Member Report:*				
Reference	2.00(5)	2.87(3)	3.83(3)	.001
Expertise	2.81(2)	3.71(2)	4.04(2)	.001
Reward	2.53(4)	2.78(4)	3.17(4)	.110
Coercive	2.69(3)	2.02(5)	1.74(5)	.003
Bureaucratic	4.23(1)	4.27(1)	4.13(1)	.800
2. *Superior Report:*				
Reference	2.65(5)	2.97(4)	3.43(3)	.007
Expertise	3.11(2)	3.55(2)	3.83(1)	.020
Reward	3.08(3)	3.02(3)	3.04(4)	.970
Coercive	2.73(4)	2.48(5)	2.35(5)	.310
Bureaucratic	3.96(1)	4.08(1)	3.52(2)	.040

Note: Number in parentheses indicates rank-order of that particular base of influence, with (1) indicating highest and (5) lowest ranking source of pressure to comply with a superior's requests. On each scale, response alternatives varied from strongly disagree (1) to strongly agree (5).

differentiates his subordinates into those who become his "crucial" subordinates and those who do not, and that the basis of this differentiation is dyadic loyalty. In agreement with these observations by a perceptive student of management practices, the role-making model of leadership hypothesizes that differentiation of subordinates is a natural consequence of leadership in managerial units, and that dyadic loyalty will differentiate in-group exchanges and out-group exchanges from the viewpoints of both members and superiors. In fact, the characteristics suggested by Jennings as illustrating dyadic loyalty can be used to test the above hypothesis. These characteristics are: (a) a focal member's openness to ideas and suggestions from his superior; (b) a focal member's willingness to share his ideas with his superior; (c) a focal member's availability to give support to his superior; (d) a superior's propensity to support his focal's decision; and (e) a focal member's propensity to protect his superior from others. The stronger the endorsement of this set of indices, the higher the dyadic loyalty.

As predicted, leader-member exchange showed reliable differences on dyadic loyalty measures as reported by members and superiors. As shown in Table 6, members' reports demonstrated reliable differences on sharing ideas ($p < .004$), defending decisions ($p < .001$), and protecting ($p < .001$). In all cases, the trend in endorsement was monotonically increasing from out-group to in-group. In addition, superior reports demonstrated reliable differences on all five measures. A comparison of member and superior reports indicates that the major discrepancies were that out-group members

Table 6

DYADIC LOYALTY

Dyadic Loyalty	Mean			Probability	
	Out-Group (n = 26)	Middle-Group (n = 60)	In-Group (n = 23)	Exchange	Job Type
1. *Member Report:*					
Focal is open to suggestions from superior . . .	4.00	4.02	4.31	.22	.70
Focal shares ideas with superior . . .	3.69	4.02	4.48	.004	.17
Focal is available to give support to superior . . .	4.28	4.22	4.53	.070	.72
Superior will defend focal's decisions . . .	3.25	3.81	4.46	.001	.17
Focal will not expose superior's mistakes . . .	3.69	3.99	4.37	.001	.24
2. *Superior Report:*					
Focal is open to suggestions from superior . . .	3.45	4.09	4.40	.002	.45
Focal shares ideas with superior . . .	3.19	4.00	4.67	.001	.27
Focal is available to give support to superior . . .	3.56	4.10	4.54	.002	.04
Superior will defend focal's decisions . . .	3.74	3.95	4.67	.001	.66
Focal will not expose superior's mistakes . . .	3.28	3.93	4.22	.001	.17

Note: On each scale, response alternatives varied from strongly disagree (1) to strongly agree (5).

tended to report higher endorsement levels than those reported by their superiors, except for defending members' decisions. In other words, out-group members tended to report higher loyalty on their part and lower loyalty from their superiors than that reported by their superiors.

The results on dyadic loyalty are clear. Both parties to the exchange agree that in-group exchanges are characterized by stronger bonds of dyadic loyalty than those of out-group exchanges. In-group exchanges exhibit greater openness to ideas, more reciprocal support, and a higher propensity to protect one's partner than out-group exchanges. In sum, an underlying dimension of mutual trust appears to define in-group exchanges, while a mutual lack of trust seems to characterize out-group exchanges.

In summary, these results replicate and extend the consistent set of reliable relationships found in the natural experiment. These results support the generalizability (external validity) of the finding that leaders routinely differentiate their units by developing and maintaining leadership exchanges with selected members and supervision exchanges with other members. These results also support the generalizability of the nature of these leader-member exchanges involving (as they do) member involvement in activities interlocked with the leader's distribution of positional resources and the nature of the supporting relationship.

IMPLICATIONS FOR ORGANIZATIONS

Should this model of leadership prove under further testing to provide valid descriptions of leadership processes, it may have implications for training leaders and members in team-building skills (Campbell, et al., 1970). It seems reasonable to expect that the outcomes of team building may be enhanced by coaching both parties to the leader-member exchange both before and during the process. In addition, it may have implications for normative models of operating. For example, the decision-making model of Vroom and Yetton (1973) may need to be modified to include considerations of team structure. It may change the prescriptive decision of whether or not to let a member who holds needed information participate in a decision. Within this normative program, the leader-member exchange may become a crucial contingency factor.

Given that leaders of managerial units must be granted adequate latitude to build a team to deal with many unprogrammable contingencies, few positive programs exist to improve the processes or to correct mistakes in the process. Seldom are leaders trained adequately to assess, select, and develop talent for maximum efficiency. Without a positive program, few alternative opportunities may be made available to even the more talented out-group members. One promising development along these lines is the experimental program within American Telephone and Telegraph, which is part of a program to train managers to assess and select talent through management assessment center procedures (Bray, 1974). This special program allows potential out-group members to request to be more objectively assessed and, if found deserving, to be given an opportunity to prove themselves in a new position.

164   *G. Graen, J. F. Cashman*

Results reported in this paper suggest the fruitfulness of our decision to forsake the traditional path to leadership (involving the assumption of homogeneous vertical dyads) for the relatively unexplored role-making path (allowing heterogeneous vertical dyads). We hope that the fruits of this role-making approach to leadership will convince others to view these processes as developmental phenomena and seek to understand them through longitudinal and "open systems" designs (Graen 1975).

Once leadership is viewed as part of a larger developmental process it begins to lose much of its mystique. For example, the influence of a leader need not be attributed to some mysterious inner power called charisma. Rather, it can be viewed as developing within vertical dyads into leader-member exchanges which contain interlocking behavior and relationship norms. Of course, these processes may not be active at all times. More likely, they are activated by appropriate sets of events, complete their sequences, and become dormant until activated anew. Only by monitoring these processes when they are active can we hope to document their nature. Cross-sectional studies of the dormant period can only reveal residual traces of these events and foster further mystery.

It seems apparent that to enhance the positive outcomes of managerial team building we must achieve a better understanding of these developmental processes. We must discover the conditions which activate these processes and learn to guide them toward desired outcomes and away from undesired outcomes. At the present time we have a beginning—only a beginning.

REFERENCES

Borman, W. C. "The Rating of Individuals in Organizations: An Alternative Ap-
1974   proach." *Organizational Behavior and Human Performance*, 12:105–24.

Bray, D. W. "Maximizing Human Resource Utilization with Sophisticated Selection
1974   Techniques." Paper presented at the American Psychological Association
Symposium. New Orleans, La.

Campbell, D. T., and D. W. Fiske. "Convergent and Discriminant Validation by the
1959   Multitrait-Multimethod Matrix." *Psychological Bulletin*, 56:81–105.

Campbell, D. T., and J. C. Stanley. *Experimental and Quasi-Experimental Designs
1963   for Research*. Chicago: Rand McNally.

Campbell, J. P., M. D. Dunnette, E. E. Lawler, and K. E. Weick, Jr. *Managerial
1970   Behavior, Performance and Effectiveness*. New York: McGraw-Hill.

Dansereau, F., G. Graen, and W. J. Haga. "A Vertical Dyad Linkage Approach to
1975   Leadership within Formal Organizations." *Organizational Behavior and
Human Performance*, 13:46–78.

Fleishman, E. A. "The Description of Supervisory Behavior." *Journal of Applied
1953   Psychology*, 37:1–6.

Fleishman, E. A., E. F. Harris, and H. E. Burtt. *Leadership and Supervision in Industry*.
1955   Columbus, Ohio: Bureau of Educational Research, Ohio State University.

Fleishman, E. A., and J. G. Hunt (eds.) *Current Developments in the Study of
1973   Leadership*. Carbondale, Ill.: Southern Illinois University Press.

Fleishman, E. A., and J. Simmons. "Relationship Between Leadership Patterns
1970   and Effectiveness Ratings Among Israeli Foremen." *Personnel Psychology*,
23:169–72.

French, J. R. P., and B. H. Raven. "The Bases of Social Power." In D. Cartwright
1959   (ed.) *Studies in Social Power:* 118–49. Ann Arbor, Mich.: University of
Michigan Press.

Graen, G.   "Role Making Processes within Complex Organizations." In M. D.
1975   Dunnette (ed.), *Handbook of Industrial and Organizational Psychology*
          Chapt. 28. Chicago: Rand McNally.

Graen, G., F. Dansereau, W. Haga, and J. Cashman.   *The Invisible Organization*
1975   Boston: Shenkman Publishing Company (in press)

Graen, G., F. Dansereau, T. Minami, and J. Cashman.   "Leadership Behaviors as
1973   Cues to Performance Evaluation." *Academy of Management Journal*,
          16:611—23.

Haga, W. J., G. Graen, and F. Dansereau.   "Professionalism and Role Making within
1974   a Service Organization." *American Sociological Review*. 39:122—33.

House, R. J.   "A Path-Goal Theory of Leader Effectiveness." in E. A. Fleishman and
1973   J. G. Hunt (eds.), *Current Developments in the Study of Leadership*.
          Carbondale, Ill.: Southern Illinois University Press. Originally published
          in *Administrative Science Quarterly*, 16:321—38 (1971).

House, R. J., and G. Dessler.   "The Path-Goal Theory of Leadership: Some Post
1974   Hoc and A Priori Tests." In J. G. Hunt and L. L. Larson (eds.), *Contingency
          Approaches to Leadership*. Carbondale, Ill.: Southern Illinois University
          Press.

House, R. J., A. C. Filley, and S. Kerr.   "Relation of Leader Consideration and
1971   Initiating Structure to R and D Subordinates' Satisfaction." *Administrative
          Science Quarterly*, 16:19—30.

House, R. J., and S. Kerr.   "Organizational Independence, Leader Behavior and
1973   Managerial Practices: A Replicated Study." *Journal of Applied Psychology*.
          58:173—80.

Jacobs, T. O.   *Leadership and Exchange in Formal Organizations*. Alexandria, Va.
1970   Human Resources Research Organization.

Jennings, E. E.   *The Mobile Manager: A Study of the New Generation of Top
1967   Executives*. New York: McGraw-Hill.

Korman, A. K.   "Contingency Approaches to Leadership: An Overview." In J. G. Hunt
1974   and L. L. Larson (eds.), *Contingency Approaches to Leadership*:189—95.
          Carbondale, Ill.: Southern Illinois University Press.

————   "Consideration, Initiating Structure and Organizational Criteria: A
1966   Review." *Personnel Psychology*, 19:349—61.

Platt, J. R.   "Strong Inference." *Science*, 146:347—52.
1964

Vroom, V. H., and P. W. Yetton.   *Leadership and Decision-Making*. Pittsburgh:
1973   University of Pittsburgh Press.

Weick, K. E.   *The Social Psychology of Organizing*. Reading, Mass.: Addison-
1969   Wesley Publishing Co.

Part VII
Transformational Leadership

[13]

The transformational leader uses charisma, individualized consideration, and intellectual stimulation to inspire employees to make extraordinary efforts.

Leadership: Good, Better, Best

Bernard M. Bass

What does Lee Iacocca have that many other executives lack? Charisma. What would have happened to Chrysler without him? It probably would have gone bankrupt. Here are two more questions: How much does business and industry encourage the emergence of leaders like Iacocca? And how much effort has organizational psychology put into research on charismatic leadership? The answers are that business and industry have usually discouraged charismatic leadership and that, for the most part, organizational psychology has ignored the subject. It has been customary to see leadership as a method of getting subordinates to meet job requirements by handing out rewards or punishments.

Take a look at Barry Bargainer. Barry considers himself to be a good leader. He meets with subordinates to clarify expectations—what is required of them and what they can expect in return. As long as they meet his expectations, Barry doesn't bother them.

Cynthia Changer is a different kind of leader. When facing a crisis, Cynthia in-

This article is a digest of portions of the author's forthcoming book, *Leadership and Performance Beyond Expectations*, to be published in March 1985, by The Free Press.

spires her team's involvement and participation in a "mission." She solidifies it with simple words and images and keeps reminding her staff about it. She has frequent one-to-one chats with each of her employees at his or her work station. She is consultant, coach, teacher, and mother figure.

Barry Bargainer, a transactional leader, may inspire a reasonable degree of involvement, loyalty, commitment, and performance from his subordinates. But Cynthia Changer, using a transformational approach, can do much more.

The first part of this article contrasts transactional and transformational leadership styles and the results that are obtained when managers select each approach. The second section reports on surveys of personnel in the military and in industry and examines factors in both approaches to leadership, as they emerged from the survey results. Transformational leadership is presented as a way to augment transactional approaches to management, since it is often more effective in achieving higher levels of improvement and change among employees.

A New Paradigm

For half a century, leadership research has been devoted to studying the effects of democratic and autocratic approaches. Much investigative time has gone into the question of who should decide — the leader or the led. Equally important to research has been the distinction between task orientation and relations orientation. Still another issue has been the need of the leader to "initiate structure" for subordinates and to be considerate of them. At the same time, increasing attention has been paid to the ability to promote change in individuals, groups, and organizations.

The need to promote change and deal with resistance to it has, in turn, put an emphasis on democratic, participative, re-

lations-oriented, and considerate leadership. Contingent rewards have been stressed in training and research with somewhat limited results.

In the past, we have mostly considered how to marginally improve and maintain the quantity or quality of performance, how to substitute one goal for another, how to shift attention from one action to another, how to reduce resistance to particular actions, or how to implement decisions. But higher-order changes are also possible. Increases in effort and the rate at which a group's speed and accuracy improve can sometimes be accelerated. Such higher-order changes also may involve larger shifts in attitudes, beliefs, values, and needs. Quantum leaps in performance may result when a group is roused out of its despair by a leader with innovative or revolutionary ideas and a vision of future possibilities. Leaders may help bring about a radical shift in attention. The context may be changed by leaders. They may change what the followers see as figure and what they see as ground or raise the level of maturity of their needs and wants. For example, followers' concerns may be elevated from their need for safety and security to their need for recognition and achievement.

The lower order of improvement — changes in degree or marginal improvement — can be seen as the result of leadership that is an exchange process: a *transaction* in which followers' needs are met if their performance measures up to their explicit or implicit contracts with their leader. But higher-order improvement calls for *transformational* leadership. There is a great deal of difference between the two types of leadership.

Transactional Leadership in Action

Transactional leaders like Barry Bargainer recognize what actions subordinates must take to achieve outcomes. Transactional leaders clarify these role and task require-   27

ments for their subordinates so that they are confident in exerting necessary efforts. Transactional leaders also recognize subordinates' needs and wants and clarify how they will be satisfied if necessary efforts are made. (See Exhibit 1.) This approach is currently stressed in leadership training, and it is good as far as it goes; however, the transactional approach has numerous shortcomings.

First, even after training, managers do not fully utilize transactional leadership. Time pressures, poor appraisal methods, doubts about the efficacy of positive reinforcement, leader and subordinate discomfort with the method, and lack of management skills are all partly responsible: How reinforcements are scheduled, how timely they are, and how variable or consistent they are all mediate the degree of their influence.

Some leaders, practicing management by exception, intervene only when things go wrong. In this instance, the manager's discomfort about giving negative feedback is even more self-defeating. When surpervisors attribute poor performance to lack of ability, they tend to "pull their punches" by distorting feedback so that it is more positive than it should be.

Another common problem occurs when supervisors say and actually believe they are giving feedback to their subordinates, who feel they are not receiving it. For example, Barry Bargainer may meet with his group of subordinates to complain that things are not going well. Barry thinks he is giving negative feedback while his subordinates only hear Barry grumbling about conditions. Barry may give Henry a pat on the back for a job he thinks has been well done. Henry may feel that he knows he did a good job, and it was condescending for Barry to mention it.

People differ considerably in their preference for external reinforcement or self-reinforcement. Task-oriented and experi-

Bernard M. Bass *is professor of organizational behavior at the State University of New York at Binghamton. He is past president of the Division of Organizational Psychology of the International Association of Applied Psychology.*

Dr. Bass is author of several hundred publications. Books that he has authored or co-authored include Leadership, Psychology, and Organizational Behavior *(Harper, 1960);* Psychology of Learning for Managers *(American Foundation for Management Research, 1964);* Organizational Psychology *(Allyn & Bacon, 1965);* Training in Industry: The Management of Learning *(Wadsworth, 1966);* Assessment of Managers: An International Comparison *(The Free Press, 1979);* People, Work, and Organizations *(Allyn & Bacon, 1981);* Stogdill's Handbook of Leadership *(The Free Press, 1981);* Interpersonal Communication in Organizations *(Academic Press, 1982);* Organizational Decision Making *(Richard D. Irwin, 1983); and* Leadership and Performance Beyond Expectations *(Free Press, 1985).*

The author has consulted with many of the Fortune 500 companies and has lectured and conducted management workshops in over 40 countries.

enced subordinates generally are likely to be self-reinforcing. They may say: "If I have done something well, I know it without other people telling me so," and "As long as I think that I have done something well, I am not too concerned about what other people think I have done."

Subordinates and supervisors attach differing importance to various kinds of feedback. Many subordinates attach more importance than do supervisors to their own success or failure with particular tasks, and to their own comparisons with the work of others. Subordinates are also likely to attach more importance than do supervisors to coworkers' comments about their work. Supervisors tend to put the most weight on their own comments to their subordinates, and to recommendations for rewards they, as supervisors, can make, such as raises, promotions, and more interesting assignments.

Transactional leadership often fails because the leaders lack the reputation for being able to deliver rewards. Transactional leaders who fulfill the self-interested expectations of their subordinates gain and maintain the reputation for being able to deliver pay, promotions, and recognition. Those that fail to deliver lose their reputation and are not considered to be effective leaders.

Transactional leadership may be abandoned by managers when noncontingent rewards (employees are treated well, regardless of performance) will work just as well to boost performance. For example, in a large, nonprofit organization, a study by Phillip Podsakoff et al. showed that contingent rewards (those given only if performance warrants them) did contribute to employee performance, but noncontingent rewards were correlated almost as strongly with performance as contingent rewards.

Noncontingent rewards may provide a secure situation in which employees' self-reinforcement serves as a consequence for good performance (for example, IBM's straight salaries for all employees). An employee's feeling of obligation to the organization for providing noncontingent rewards fuels his or her effort to perform at least adequately. The Japanese experience is exemplary; in the top third of such Japanese firms as Toyota, Sony, and Mitsubishi, employees and the companies feel a mutual sense of lifetime obligation. Being a good family member does not bring immediate pay raises and promotions, but overall family success will bring year-end bonuses. Ultimately, opportunities to advance to a higher level and salary will depend on overall meritorious performance.

When the contingent reinforcement used is aversive (reinforcement that recipients prefer to avoid), the success of the transactional leader usually plummets. In the same not-for-profit organization studied by Podsakoff et al., neither contingent reprimand, disapproval, nor punishment had any effect on performance or overall employee satisfaction. The same results have been observed in other organizations. Contingent approval and disapproval by results-oriented leaders did improve subordinates' understanding of what was expected of them but failed to have much effect on motivation or performance. In general, reprimand may be useful in highlighting what not to do, but usually it does not contribute to positive motivation, particularly when subordinates are expected to be innovative and creative.

Even when it is based solely on rewards, transactional leadership can have unintended consequences. When expounding on the principles of leadership, Vice Admiral James B. Stockdale argued that people do not like to be programmed:

. . . . You cannot persuade [people] to act in their own self-interest all of the time. A good leader appreciates contrariness.

. . . . some men all of the time and all men some of the time knowingly will do what is clearly to their disadvantage if only because they do not like to be suffocated by carrot-and-stick coercion. I will not be a piano key; I will not bow to the tyranny of reason.

In working subtly against transactional leadership, employees may take short-

30

Exhibit 1

Transactional Leadership (L = Leader; F = Follower)

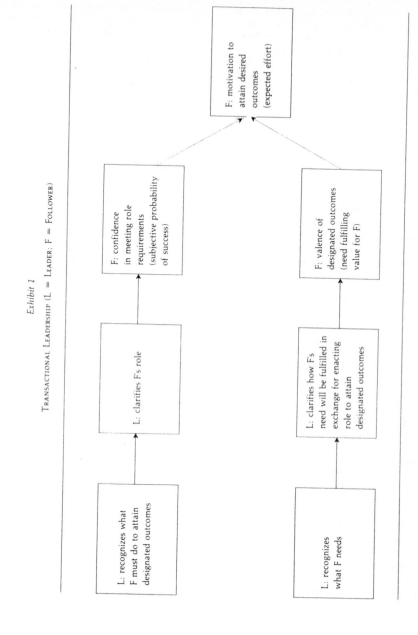

cuts to complete the exchange of reward for compliance. For instance, quality may suffer if the leader does not monitor it as closely as he or she does the quantity of output. The employee may begin to react defensively rather than adequately; in some cases, reaction formation, withdrawal, hostility, or "game playing" may result.

The Alternative: Add Transformational Leadership to the Manager-Employee Relationship

James McGregor Burns, the biographer of Franklin D. Roosevelt and of John F. Kennedy, was the first to contrast transactional with transformational leadership. The transformational leader motivates us to do more than we originally expected to do. Such a transformation can be achieved in the following ways:

1. Raising our level of consciousness about the importance and value of designated outcomes and ways of reaching these outcomes.

2. Getting us to transcend our own self-interests for the sake of the team, organization, or larger polity.

3. Raising our need level on Abraham Maslow's hierarchy from, say, the need for security to the need for recognition, or expanding our portfolio of needs by, for example, adding the need for self-actualization to the need for recognition.

Cynthia Changer is a transformational leader; Barry Bargainer is not. Exhibit 2 is a model of transformational leadership that starts with a current level of effort based on a follower's current level of confidence and desire for designated outcomes. A transactional leader contributes to such confidence and desire by clarifying what performance is required and how needs will be satisfied as a consequence. The transformational leader induces additional effort by directly increasing the follower's confidence as well as by elevat-

ing the value of outcomes through expanding his or her transcendental interests and level or breadth of needs in Maslow's hierarchy.

The need for more transformational leaders in business and industry was illustrated in an in-depth interview survey of a representative national sample of 845 working Americans. The survey found that while most employees liked and respected their managers, they felt their managers really didn't know how to motivate employees to do their best. Although 70% endorsed the work ethic, only 23% said they were working as hard as they could in their jobs. Only 9% agreed that their performance was motivated by transaction; most reported that there actually was little connection between how much they earned and the level of effort they put into the job.

Report on a Study of Transformational Leadership

I set out to find evidence of transformational leadership and its effects at various levels in industrial and military organizations, *not just at the top*.

I defined transformational leadership for 70 senior executives. Then, I asked them to describe in detail a transformational leader whom they had encountered at any time during their career. All respondents claimed to have known at least one such person. Most cited a former immediate supervisor or higher-level manager in the organization. A few mentioned family members, consultants, or counselors.

This transformational leader induced respondents to work ridiculous hours *and to do more than they ever expected to do*. Respondents reported that they aimed to satisfy the transformational leader's expectations and to give the leader all the support asked of them. They wanted to emulate the   31

Exhibit 2

TRANSFORMATIONAL LEADERSHIP (L = LEADER; F = FOLLOWER)

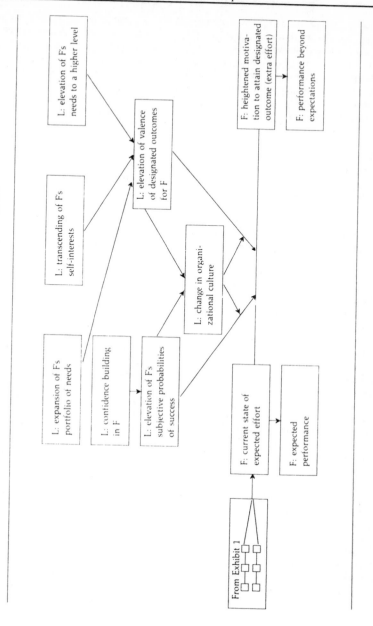

leader. The transformational leader increased their awareness of and promoted a higher quality of performance and greater innovativeness. Such a leader convinced followers to extend themselves and to develop themselves further. Total commitment to and belief in the organization emerged as consequences of belief in the leader and heightened self-confidence.

Many respondents (all were male) indicated that the transformational leader they could identify in their own careers was like a benevolent father who remained friendly and treated the respondent as an equal despite the leader's greater knowledge and experience. The leader provided a model of integrity and fairness and also set clear and high standards of performance. He encouraged followers with advice, help, support, recognition, and openness. He gave followers a sense of confidence in his intellect, yet was a good listener. He gave followers autonomy and encouraged their self-development. He was willing to share his greater knowledge and expertise with them. Yet he could be formal and firm and would reprimand followers when necessary. Most respondents, however, were inclined to see the transforming leader as informal and accessible. Such a leader could be counted on to stand up for his subordinates. Along with the heightened and changed motivation and awareness, frequent reactions of followers to the transforming leader included trust, strong liking, admiration, loyalty, and respect.

In conducting a second survey, I used the descriptions from the first to create a questionnaire of 73 behavioral items. Responses to each item were on a five-point frequency scale. A total of 176 senior U. S. Army officers completed the questionnaire describing the behavior of their immediate superiors. Five factors emerged from a statistical factor analysis of the data. Two dealt with transactional leadership, the ex-change relationship between superior and subordinate: contingent reward, by which subordinates earned benefits for compliance with the leader's clarification of the paths toward goals, and management by exception, by which the leader gave negative feedback for failure to meet agreed-upon standards. Three of the factors dealt with transformational leadership—the broadening and elevating of goals and of subordinates' confidence in their ability to go beyond expectations. These factors were (1) charismatic leadership (leaders aroused enthusiasm, faith, loyalty, and pride and trust in themselves and their aims); (2) individualized consideration (leaders maintained a developmental and individualistic orientation toward subordinates); and (3) intellectual stimulation (leaders enhanced the problem-solving capabilities of their associates). An interesting sidelight was that more transformational leadership was observed (by respondents) in combat units than in support units.

As expected, the three transformational factors were more highly correlated with perceived unit effectiveness than were the two transactional factors. Parallel results were obtained for subordinates' satisfaction with their leader. Charismatic, considerate, and intellectually stimulating leaders were far more satisfying to work for than were those who merely practiced the transactions of contingent reinforcement. I obtained similar results from a survey of 256 business managers, 23 educational administrators, and 45 professionals. Moreover, in these latter samples, respondents reported that they made greater efforts when leaders were charismatic, individualizing, and intellectually stimulating. Contingent reward was also fairly predictive of extra effort, but management by exception was counterproductive. Further analysis of the data by my colleague, David Waldman, supported the model shown in Exhibit 2. The analysis demonstrated that

33

when a leader displayed transformational abilities and engaged in transactional relationships, extra effort made by subordinates was above and beyond what could be attributed to transactional factors alone.

TRANSACTIONAL FACTORS: CONTINGENT REINFORCEMENT AND MANAGEMENT-BY-EXCEPTION

According to our questionnaire surveys, positive and aversive contingent reinforcement are the two ways managers in organized settings engage in transactional leadership to influence employee performance. Ordinarily, contingent reward takes two forms: praise for work well done and recommendations for pay increases, bonuses, and promotion. In addition, this kind of reward can take the form of commendations for effort or public recognition and honors for outstanding service.

Contingent punishment can take several forms as a reaction to a deviation from norms — when, for example, production falls below agreed-upon standards or quality falls below acceptable levels. The manager may merely call attention to the deviation. Being told of one's failure to meet standards may be sufficient punishment to change behavior. Being told why one has failed can be helpful, particularly to the inexperienced or inexpert subordinate, especially if the negative feedback is coupled with further clarification about what kind of performance is expected. While other penalties — such as fines, suspensions without pay, loss of leader support, or discharge — may be imposed, these are less frequently used and are less likely to promote effectiveness.

When the manager, for one reason or another, chooses to intervene only when failures, breakdowns, and deviations occur,

he or she is practicing management by exception. The rationale of those who use this practice is, "If it ain't broke, don't fix it!" The research studies I have completed with military officers, business executives, professionals, and educational administrators generally indicate that as a steady diet, management by exception can be counterproductive. But contingent rewards yield a fairly good return in terms of subordinate effort and performance. Nevertheless, in the aggregate, there will be additional payoff when the transformational factors appear in a leader's portfolio.

Charismatic and Inspirational Leadership

Charisma is not exclusively the province of world-class leaders or a few generals or admirals. It is to be found to some degree in industrial and military leaders throughout organizations. Furthermore, charisma is the most important component in the larger concept of transformational leadership. In my study I found that many followers described their military or industrial leader as someone who made everyone enthusiastic about assignments, who inspired loyalty to the organization, who commanded respect from everyone, who had a special gift of seeing what was really important, and who had a sense of mission that excited responses. Followers had complete faith in the leaders with charisma, felt proud to be associated with them, and trusted their capacity to overcome any obstacle. Charismatic leaders served as symbols of success and accomplishment for their followers.

Charisma is one of the elements separating the ordinary manager from the true leader in organizational settings. The leader attracts intense feelings of love (and sometimes hatred) from his or her subordinates. They want to identify with the leader. Although feelings about ordinary

34

managers are bland, relations are smoother and steadier. Like most intimate relationships, the relations between the charismatic leader and his or her followers tend to be more turbulent.

There may be a scarcity of charismatic leaders in business and industry because managers lack the necessary skills. On the other hand, managers who have the skills may not recognize opportunity or may be unwilling to risk what is required to stand out so visibly among their peers. More charismatic leaders potentially exist in organizational settings; furthermore, they may be necessary to an organization's success.

The ability to inspire — arouse emotions, animate, enliven, or even exalt — is an important aspect of charisma. Inspirational leadership involves the arousal and heightening of motivation among followers. Followers can be inspired by a cold, calculating, intellectual discourse, the brilliance of a breakthrough, or the beauty of an argument. Yet it is the followers' emotions that ultimately have been aroused. Followers may hold an intellectual genius in awe and reverence, but the inspirational influence on them is emotional.

Consider the specific leadership behaviors Gary Yukl used to illustrate what he meant by inspirational leadership:

> My supervisor held a meeting to talk about how vital the new contract is for the company and said he was confident we could handle it if we all did our part. My boss told us we were the best design group he had ever worked with and he was sure that this new product was going to break every sales record in the company.

The inspiring supervisor was not dispassionate. The supervisor talked about how *vital* the new contract was to the company. He said he was *confident* in his people. He told them they were the *best* group he had *ever* worked with. He was sure the product would *break every record.*

In summary, as a consequence of his or her self-confidence, absence of inner conflict, self-determination, and requisite abilities, a leader will be held in high esteem by followers, particularly in times of trouble. He or she can generally inspire them by emotional support and appeals that will transform their level of motivation beyond original expectations. Such a leader can sometimes also inspire followers by means of intellectual stimulation. The charismatic leader can do one or the other, or both.

Individualized Consideration

The transformational leader has a developmental orientation toward followers. He evaluates followers' potential both to perform their present job and to hold future positions of greater responsibility. The leader sets examples and assigns tasks on an individual basis to followers to help significantly alter their abilities and motivations as well as to satisfy immediate organizational needs.

Delegating challenging work and increasing subordinate responsibilities are particularly useful approaches to individualized development. As General Omar Bradley pointed out, there is no better way to develop leadership than to give an individual a job involving responsibility and let him work it out. A survey of 208 chief executives and senior officers by Charles Margerison reported that important career influences on them before age 35 included being "stretched" by immediate bosses and being given leadership experience, overall responsibility for important tasks, and wide experience in many functions.

The transformational leader will consciously or unconsciously serve as a role model for subordinates. For example, in the Margerison survey, the executives attributed their own successful development as man- 35 agers to having had early on in their careers managers who were models.

Managerial training supports the idea that managers profit from role models. What may be different in what I propose, however, is that the transformational leader emphasizes *individualism*. Personal influence and the one-to-one superior–subordinate relationship is of primary importance to the development of leaders. An organizational culture of individualism, even of elitism, should be encouraged; an organization should focus attention on identifying prospective leaders among subordinates.

Individualized attention is viewed as especially important by the new military commander of a unit. The commander is expected to learn the names of all those in the units at least two levels below his and to become familiar with their jobs. *Military leaders need to avoid treating all subordinates alike.* They must discover what best motivates each individual soldier or sailor and how to employ him most effectively. They must be generous in the use of their time. But as General Eugene Meyer notes, the leaders' interest must be genuine.

Individualized consideration implies that seniors maintain face-to-face contact or at least frequent telephone contact with juniors. The Intel Corporation accepted the fact that recently graduated engineers are more up to date on the latest advances in technology than are experienced executives of greater power and status in the firm. Therefore, the firm has consciously encouraged frequent contact and open communication between the recent college graduates and the senior executives through leveling arrangements. Senior executives and junior professionals are all housed in small, unpretentious, accessible offices that share common facilities. The organization stresses that influence is based on knowledge rather than power. In other well-managed firms, "walk-around

36

management" promotes individual contact and communication between those low and high in the hierarchy.

In another study of a high-tech company, Rudi Klauss and Bernard Bass found that project engineers were most influenced by and gained most of their information relevant to decision making from informal contact and individual discussion rather than from written documentation. This company did not believe that the aggregated data from management information systems were the most important inputs for decision making. Rather, two-thirds to three-quarters of the total work time of managers was spent in oral communication. It was the immediate, timely tidbits of gossip, speculation, opinion, and relevant facts that was most influential, not generalized reports reviewing conditions over a recent period of time. Individualized attention of superior to subordinate provided this opportunity for inputs of current and timely information.

Managers are most likely to make face-to-face contact with colleagues at their same organizational level (or by telephone for such colleagues at a distance physically). For superiors and subordinates, written memos are more frequently used. Yet regular, face-to-face debriefing sessions to disseminate important information from superior to subordinate will provide a better basis for organizational decision making and make the superior better equipped to deal with the erratic flow of work and demands on his or her time and the speed that decision making often requires. Unfortunately, unless personal contact becomes a matter of policy (such as walk-around management), communications from superior to subordinate are more likely to be on paper — or now, no doubt, increasingly on computer — rather than face-to-face.

Individualized consideration is reflected when a manager keeps each employee fully informed about what is happening and why — preferably in a two-way conversation rather than a written memo. Employees come to feel that they are on the inside of developments and do not remain bystanders. Sudden changes of plan are less likely to surprise them. If the interaction is two-way, employees have the opportunity to ask questions to clarify understanding. At the same time, managers learn first-hand their subordinates' concerns.

Individualized consideration is also demonstrated when the senior executive or professional takes time to serve as mentor for the junior executive or professional. A mentor is a trusted counselor who accepts a guiding role in the development of a younger or less experienced member of the organization. The mentor uses his or her greater knowledge, experience, and status to help develop his or her protégé and not simply to pull the protégé up the organization ladder on the mentor's coattails. This relationship is different from one in which a manager is supportive or provides advice when asked for it. Compared with the formal, distant relationship most often seen between a high-level executive and a junior somewhere down the line, the mentor is paternalistic or maternalistic and perhaps is a role model for the junior person.

A follow-up of 122 recently promoted people in business indicated that two-thirds had had mentors. This popularity

of mentoring in business, government, and industry reflects the current interest on the part of both individuals and organizations in the career development of the individual employee.

Intellectual Stimulation

The statement, "These ideas have forced me to rethink some of my own ideas, which I had never questioned before," sums up the kind of intellectual stimulation that a transformational leader can provide. Intellectual stimulation can lead to other comments like, "She enables me to think about old problems in new ways," or "He provides me with new ways of looking at things that used to be a puzzle for me."

Intellectual stimulation arouses in followers the awareness of problems and how they may be solved. It promotes the hygiene of logic that is compelling and convincing. It stirs the imagination and generates thoughts and insights. It is not the call to immediate action aroused by emotional stimulation. This intellectual stimulation is seen in a discrete leap in the followers' conceptualization, comprehension, and discernment of the nature of the problems they face and their solutions.

Executives should and can play a role as transforming leaders to the degree that they articulate what they discern, comprehend, visualize, and conceptualize to their

"An organizational culture of individualism, even of elitism, should be encouraged; an organization should focus attention on identifying prospective leaders . . ."

37

colleagues and followers. They should articulate what they see as the opportunities and threats facing their organization (or unit within it) and the organization's strengths, weaknesses, and comparative advantages. Leadership in complex organizations must include the ability to manage the problem-solving process in such a way that important problems are identified and solutions of high quality are found and carried out with the full commitment of organization members.

The intellectual component may be obscured by surface considerations. Accused of making snap decisions, General George Patton commented: "I've been studying the art of war for 40-odd years . . . [A] surgeon who decides in the course of an operation to change its objective is not making a snap decision but one based on knowledge, experience, and training. So am I."

The importance of a leader's technical expertise and intellectual power, particularly in high-performing systems, often is ignored in comparison with the attention paid to his or her interpersonal competence. Where would Polaroid be without Edwin Land? What kind of corporation would Occidental Petroleum be without Armand Hammer?

In this intellectual sphere, we see systematic differences between transformational and transactional leaders. The transformational leader may be less willing to accept the status quo and more likely to seek new ways of doing things while taking maximum advantage of opportunities. Transactional managers will focus on what can clearly work, will keep time constraints in mind, and will do what seems to be most efficient and free of risk.

What may intellectually separate the two kinds of leaders is that transformational leaders are likely to be more proactive than reactive in their thinking, more creative, novel, and innovative in their ideas, and less inhibited in their ideational search for solutions. Transactional leaders may be equally

bright, but their focus is on how best to keep running the system for which they are responsible; they react to problems generated by observed deviances and modify conditions as needed while remaining ever mindful of organizational constraints.

TRANSFORMATIONAL LEADERSHIP: BENEVOLENT OR MALEVOLENT?

Charismatic leadership, individualized consideration, and intellectual stimulation have been clearly seen in the moving and shaking that took place between 1982 and 1984 in a number of firms, such as General Electric, Campbell Soup, and Coca Cola. In each instance, the transformation could be attributed to a newly appointed chief. These transformational leaders were responsible for iconoclastic changes of image, increased organizational flexibility, and an upsurge of new products and new approaches. In each case, the transformational leadership of John F. Welch, Jr. of General Electric, Gordon McGovern of Campbell Soup, and Roberto Goizueta of Coca Cola paid off in invigoration and revitalization of their firms and an acceleration in business success.

Clearly, heads may be broken, feelings hurt, and anxieties raised with the advent of transformational leaders such as Welch, McGovern, or Goizueta. "Business as usual" is no longer tolerated. Such transformations may be moral or immoral.

For James Burns, transformational leadership is moral if it deals with true needs and is based on informed choice. The moral transformational leader is one who is guided by such universal ethical principles as respect for human dignity and equal rights. The leadership mobilizes and directs support for "more general and comprehensive values that express followers' more fundamental and enduring needs" (*Leadership*, Harper, 1978). Moral leadership helps followers to see the real conflict between competing values, the

38

inconsistencies between espoused values and behavior, the need for realignments in values, and the need for changes in behavior or transformations of institutions. Burns argued that if the need levels elevated by transformational leaders were not authentic, then the leadership was immoral.

The well-being of organizational life will be better served in the long run by moral leadership. That is, transformations that result in the fulfillment of real needs will prove to be more beneficial to the organization than transformations that deal with manufactured needs and group delusions. Organizational leaders should subscribe to a code of ethics that is accepted by their society and their profession.

The ethical transformational leader aims toward and succeeds in promoting changes in a firm — changes that strengthen firm viability, increase satisfaction of owners, managers, employees, and customers, and increase the value of the firm's products. But transformational leaders can be immoral if they create changes based on false images that cater to the fantasies of constituencies. Firms can be driven into the ground by such leaders. A transformational leader can lull employees and shareholders alike with false hopes and expectations while he or she is preparing to depart in a golden parachute after selling out the company's interests.

Whether transformational or transactional leadership will take hold within an organization will depend to some extent on what is happening or has happened outside of it. Welch, McGovern, and Goizueta all came into power to transform firms that were in danger of failing to keep pace with changes in the marketplace. Transformational leadership is more likely to emerge in times of distress and rapid change.

The personalities of followers will affect a leader's ability to be transformational. Charisma is a two-way process. A leader is seen as charismatic if he or she has followers who imbue him or her with extraor-dinary value and personal power. This is more easily done when subordinates have highly dependent personalities. On the other hand, subordinates who pride themselves on their own rationality, skepticism, independence, and concern for rules of law and precedent are less likely to be influenced by a charismatic leader or the leader who tries to use emotional inspiration. Subordinates who are egalitarian, self-confident, highly educated, self-reinforcing, and high in status are likely to resist charismatic leaders.

Which Kind of Leadership Should Managers Use?

Managers need to appreciate what kind of leadership is expected of them. Current leadership training and management development emphasize transactional leadership, which is good as far as it goes, but clearly has its limits. Transactional leaders will let their subordinates know what is expected of them and what they can hope to receive in exchange for fulfilling expectations. Clarification makes subordinates confident that they can fulfill expectations and achieve mutually valued outcomes. But subordinates' confidence and the value they place on potential outcomes can be further increased, through transformational leadership. Leadership, in other words, can become an inspiration to make extraordinary efforts.

Charismatic leadership is central to the transformational leadership process. Charismatic leaders have great referent power and influence. Followers want to identify with them and to emulate them. Followers develop intense feelings about them, and above all have trust and confidence in them. Transformational leaders may arouse their followers emotionally and inspire them to extra effort and greater accomplishment. As subordinates become competent with the mainly transformational leader's encouragement and support, contingent reinforce- 39 ment may be abandoned in favor of self-reinforcement.

Clearly, there are situations in which the transformational approach may not be appropriate. At the same time, organizations need to draw more on the resources of charismatic leaders, who often can induce followers to aspire to and maintain much higher levels of productivity than they would have reached if they had been operating only through the transactional process.

SELECTED BIBLIOGRAPHY

For more of the limitations of transactional leadership, reliance on contingent reinforcement, and the extent to which manipulative leadership is counterproductive, see "Management Styles Associated with Organizational, Task, Personal and Interpersonal Contingencies," by Bernard Bass, Enzo Valenzi, Dana Farrow, and Robert Solomon (*Journal of Applied Psychology*, December 1975); "Dimensionality of Leader-Subordinate Interactions: A Path-Goal Investigation," by Janet Fulk and Eric Wendler (*Organizational Behavior and Human Performance*, October 1982); "Evaluation of Feedback Sources as a Function of Role and Organizational Development," by Martin Greller (*Journal of Applied Psychology*, February 1980); "Performance Attributional Effects on Feedback from Supervisors," by Daniel Ilgen and William Knowlton (*Organizational Behavior and Human Performance*, June 1980); "Applied Behavior Analysis," by Judi Komacki (*The Industrial Psychologist*, February 1981); "Effect of Leader Contingent and Non-Contingent Reward and Punishment Behaviors on Subordinate Performance and Satisfaction," by Phillip Podsakoff, William Todor, and Richard Skov (*Academy of Management Journal*, December 1982); and "A Role Set Analysis of Managerial Reputation," by Ann Tsui (*Proceedings of the Academy of Management*, August 1982).

Admiral Stockdale's quotation can be found in "The Principles of Leadership" (*American Educator*, April 1981). General Patton's comment is in *Before the Colors Fade: Portrait of a Soldier: George S. Patton* (Houghton-Mifflin, 1964), by Frederick Ayer, Jr. General Meyer's comment is in "Leadership: A Return to Basics," by Edward Meyer (*Military Review*, July 1980).

For the seminal discussion on transformational leadership, see *Leadership* by James Burns (Harper & Row, 1978). For more on the impact or potential impact of transformational leadership, see *In Search of Excellence*, by Thomas Peters and Robert Waterman (Harper & Row, 1982); *Leadership in Organizations*, by Gary Yukl (Prentice-Hall, 1981); "Managers and Leaders: Are They Different?" by Abraham Zaleznik (*Harvard Business Review*, May/June 1977); and "Leadership Transforms Vision into Action," by Warren Bennis (*Industry Week*, May 31, 1982).

For more on communications between executives and employees, see *The Nature of Managerial Work*, by Henry Mintzberg (Harper & Row, 1973) and *Interpersonal Communication in Organizations*, by Rudi Klauss and Bernard Bass (Academic Press, 1982). A discussion of the Intel Corporation appears in Klauss and Bass' book.

Information on mentoring and managerial development may be found in *Problem Solving and the Executive Mind, Symposium: Functioning of the Executive Mind* by David Kolb (Case Western Reserve University, April 1982); *The Seasons of a Man's Life*, by Daniel Levinson, Charlotte Darrow, Edward Klein, Maria Levinson, and Braxton McKee (Knopf, 1978); *How Chief Executives Succeed*, by Charles Margerison (MCB Publications, Bradford, England, 1980); "A Theory of Human Motivation," by Abraham Maslow (*Psychological Review*, July 1943); and "Moving Up: Role Models, Mentors and the Patron System," by Eileen Shapiro, Florence Haseltine, and Mary Row (*Sloan Management Review*, Spring 1978).

Details about the impact of John F. Welch, Gordon McGovern, and Roberto Goizueta had on their companies can be found in the September 17, 1984 issue of the *Wall Street Journal*.

Part VIII
Charismatic Leadership

[14]

IV. CHARISMATIC AUTHORITY

10: The Principal Characteristics of Charismatic Authority and Its Relation to Forms of Communal Organization

The term 'charisma' will be applied to a certain quality of an individual personality by virtue of which he is set apart from ordinary men and treated as endowed with supernatural, superhuman, or at least specifically exceptional powers or qualities. These are such as are not accessible to the ordinary person, but are regarded as of divine origin or as exemplary, and on the basis of them the individual concerned is treated as a leader. In primitive circumstances this peculiar kind of deference is paid to prophets, to people with a reputation for therapeutic or legal wisdom, to leaders in the hunt, and heroes in war. It is very often thought of as resting on magical powers. How the quality in question would be ultimately judged from any ethical, aesthetic, or other such point of view is naturally entirely indifferent for purposes of definition. What is alone important is how the individual is actually regarded by those subject to charismatic authority, by his 'followers' or 'disciples.'

For present purposes it will be necessary to treat a variety of different types as being endowed with charisma in this sense. It includes the state of a 'berserker' whose spells of maniac passion have, apparently wrongly, sometimes been attributed to the use of drugs. In Medieval Byzantium a group of people endowed with this type of charismatic war-like passion were maintained as a kind of weapon. It includes the 'shaman,' the kind of magician who in the pure type is subject to epileptoid seizures as a means of falling into trances. Another type is that of Joseph Smith, the founder of Mormonism, who, however, cannot be classified in this way with absolute certainty since there is a possibility that he was a very sophisticated type of deliberate swindler. Finally it includes the type of intellectual, such as Kurt Eisner,[36] who is carried away with his own demagogic success. Sociological analysis, which must abstain from value judgments, will treat all these on the same level as the men who, according to conventional judgments, are the 'greatest' heroes, prophets, and saviours.

1. It is recognition on the part of those subject to authority which is decisive for the validity of charisma. This is freely given and guaranteed by what is held to be a 'sign' or proof,[37] originally always a miracle, and consists in devotion to the corresponding revelation, hero worship, or absolute trust in the leader. But where charisma is genuine, it is not this which is the basis of the claim to legitimacy. This basis lies rather in the conception that it is the *duty* of those who have been called to a charismatic mission to recognize its quality and to act accordingly. Psychologically this 'recognition' is a matter of complete personal devotion to the possessor of the quality, arising out of enthusiasm, or of despair and hope.

No prophet has ever regarded his quality as dependent on the attitudes

---

[36] The leader of the communistic experiment in Bavaria in 1919.—ED.

[37] *Bewährung.*

of the masses toward him. No elective king or military leader has ever treated those who have resisted him or tried to ignore him otherwise than as delinquent in duty. Failure to take part in a military expedition under such leader, even though recruitment is formally voluntary, has universally been met with disdain.

2. If proof of his charismatic qualification fails him for long, the leader endowed with charisma tends to think his god or his magical or heroic powers have deserted him. If he is for long unsuccessful, above all if his leadership fails to benefit his followers, it is likely that his charismatic authority will disappear. This is the genuine charismatic meaning of the 'gift of grace.' [38]

Even the old Germanic kings were sometimes rejected with scorn. Similar phenomena are very common among so-called 'primitive' peoples. In China the charismatic quality of the monarch, which was transmitted unchanged by heredity, was upheld so rigidly that any misfortune whatever, not only defeats in war, but drought, floods, or astronomical phenomena which were considered unlucky, forced him to do public penance and might even force his abdication. If such things occurred, it was a sign that he did not possess the requisite charismatic virtue, he was thus not a legitimate 'Son of Heaven.'

3. The corporate group which is subject to charismatic authority is based on an emotional form of communal relationship.[39] The administrative staff of a charismatic leader does not consist of 'officials'; at least its members are not technically trained. It is not chosen on the basis of social privilege nor from the point of view of domestic or personal dependency. It is rather chosen in terms of the charismatic qualities of its members. The prophet has his disciples; the war lord his selected henchmen; the leader, generally, his followers. There is no such thing as 'appointment' or 'dismissal,' no career, no promotion. There is only a 'call' at the instance of the leader on the basis of the charismatic qualification of those he summons. There is no hierarchy; the leader merely intervenes in general or in individual cases when he considers the members of his staff inadequate to a task with which they have been entrusted. There is no such thing as a definite sphere of authority and of competence, and no appropriation of official powers on the basis of social privileges. There may, however, be territorial or functional limits to charismatic powers and to the individual's 'mission.' There is no such thing as a salary or a

[38] *Gottesgnadentum.*
[39] Weber uses the term *Gemeinde*, which is not directly translatable.—ED.

benefice. Disciples or followers tend to live primarily in a communistic relationship with their leader on means which have been provided by voluntary gift. There are no established administrative organs. In their place are agents who have been provided with charismatic authority by their chief or who possess charisma of their own. There is no system of formal rules, of abstract legal principles, and hence no process of judicial decision oriented to them. But equally there is no legal wisdom oriented to judicial precedent. Formally concrete judgments are newly created from case to case and are originally regarded as divine judgments and revelations. From a substantive point of view, every charismatic authority would have to subscribe to the proposition, 'It is written . . . , but I say unto you. . .'[40] The genuine prophet, like the genuine military leader and every true leader in this sense, preaches, creates, or demands *new* obligations. In the pure type of charisma, these are imposed on the authority of revolution by oracles, or of the leader's own will, and are recognized by the members of the religious, military, or party group, because they come from such a source. Recognition is a duty. When such an authority comes into conflict with the competing authority of another who also claims charismatic sanction, the only recourse is to some kind of a contest, by magical means or even an actual physical battle of the leaders. In principle, only one side can be in the right in such a conflict; the other must be guilty of a wrong which has to be expiated.

Charismatic authority is thus specifically outside the realm of everyday routine and the profane sphere.[41] In this respect, it is sharply opposed both to rational, and particularly bureaucratic, authority, and to traditional authority, whether in its patriarchal, patrimonial, or any other form. Both rational and traditional authority are specifically forms of everyday routine control of action; while the charismatic type is the direct antithesis of this. Bureaucratic authority is specifically rational in the sense of being bound to intellectually analysable rules; while charismatic authority is specifically irrational in the sense of being foreign to all rules. Traditional authority is bound to the precedents handed down from the past and to this extent is also oriented to rules. Within the

[40] Something contrary to what was written, as Jesus said in opposition to the Scribes and Pharisees.—Ed.

[41] Weber used the antithesis of *Charisma* and *Alltag* in two senses. On the one hand, of the extraordinary and temporary as opposed to the everyday and routine; on the other hand, the sacred as opposed to the profane. See the editor's *Structure of Social Action*, ch. xvii.—Ed.

sphere of its claims, charismatic authority repudiates the past, and is in this sense a specifically revolutionary force. It recognizes no appropriation of positions of power by virtue of the possession of property, either on the part of a chief or of socially privileged groups. The only basis of legitimacy for it is personal charisma, so long as it is proved; that is, as long as it receives recognition and is able to satisfy the followers or disciples. But this lasts only so long as the belief in its charismatic inspiration remains.

The above is scarcely in need of further discussion. What has been said applies to the position of authority of such elected monarchs as Napoleon, with his use of the plebiscite. It applies to the 'rule of genius,' which has elevated people of humble origin to thrones and high military commands, just as much as it applies to religious prophets or war heroes.

4. Pure charisma is specifically foreign to economic considerations. Whenever it appears, it constitutes a 'call' in the most emphatic sense of the word, a 'mission' or a 'spiritual duty.' In the pure type, it disdains and repudiates economic exploitation of the gifts of grace as a source of income, though, to be sure, this often remains more an ideal than a fact. It is not that charisma always means the renunciation of property or even of acquisition, as under certain circumstances prophets and their disciples do. The heroic warrior and his followers actively seek 'booty'; the elective ruler or the charismatic party leader requires the material means of power. The former in addition requires a brilliant display of his authority to bolster his prestige. What is despised, so long as the genuinely charismatic type is adhered to, is traditional or rational everyday economizing, the attainment of a regular income by continuous economic activity devoted to this end. Support by gifts, sometimes on a grand scale involving foundations, even by bribery and grand-scale honoraria, or by begging, constitute the strictly voluntary type of support. On the other hand, 'booty,' or coercion, whether by force or by other means, is the other typical form of charismatic provision for needs. From the point of view of rational economic activity, charisma is a typical anti-economic force. It repudiates any sort of involvement in the everyday routine world. It can only tolerate, with an attitude of complete emotional indifference, irregular, unsystematic, acquisitive acts. In that it relieves the recipient of economic concerns, dependence on property income can be the economic basis of a charismatic mode of life for some groups; but that is not usually acceptable for the normal charismatic 'revolutionary.'

The fact that incumbency of church office has been forbidden to the Jesuits is a rationalized application of this principle of discipleship. The fact that all the 'virtuosi' of asceticism, the mendicant orders, and fighters for a faith belong in this category, is quite clear. Almost all prophets have been supported by voluntary gifts. The well-known saying of St. Paul, 'If a man does not work, neither shall he eat,' was directed against the swarm of charismatic missionaries. It obviously has nothing to do with a positive valuation of economic activity for its own sake, but only lays it down as a duty of each individual somehow to provide for his own support. This because he realized that the purely charismatic parable of the lilies of the field was not capable of literal application, but at best 'taking no thought for the morrow' could be hoped for. On the other hand, in such a case as primarily an artistic type of charismatic discipleship, it is conceivable that insulation from economic struggle should mean limitation of those who were really eligible to the 'economically independent'; that is, to persons living on income from property. This has been true of the circle of Stefan George, at least in its primary intentions.

5. In traditionally stereotyped periods, charisma is the greatest revolutionary force. The equally revolutionary force of 'reason' works from without by altering the situations of action, and hence its problems finally in this way changing men's attitudes toward them; or it intellectualizes the individual. Charisma, on the other hand, may involve a subjective or internal reorientation born out of suffering, conflicts, or enthusiasm. It may then result in a radical alteration of the central system of attitudes and directions of action with a completely new orientation of all attitudes toward the different problems and structures of the 'world.' [42] In prerationalistic periods, tradition and charisma between them have almost exhausted the whole of the orientation of action.

---

[42] Weber here uses *Welt* in quotation marks, indicating that it refers to its meaning in what is primarily a religious context. It is the sphere of 'worldly' things and interests as distinguished from transcendental religious interests.—ED.

[15]

A 1976 Theory of Charismatic Leadership

Robert J. House

Charisma is the term commonly used in the sociological and political science literature to describe leaders who by force of their personal abilities are capable of having profound and extraordinary effects on followers.[1] These effects include commanding loyalty and devotion to the leader and of inspiring followers to accept and execute the will of the leader without hesitation or question or regard to one's self interest. The term charisma, whose initial meaning was 'gift', is usually reserved for leaders who by their influence are able to cause followers to accomplish outstanding feats. Frequently such leaders represent a break with the established order and through their leadership major social changes are accomplished.

Most writers concerned with charisma or charismatic leadership begin their discussion with Max Weber's conception of charisma. Weber describes as charismatic those leaders who 'reveal a transcendent mission or course of action which may be in itself appealing to the potential followers, but which is acted on because the followers believe their leader is extraordinarily gifted' (Weber, 1947, p. 358). Transcendence is attributed implicitly to both the qualities of the leader and the content of his mission, the former being variously described as 'supernatural, superhuman or exceptional' (Weber, 1947, p. 358).

Shils (1965) points out that Weber conceived of charismatic leadership as one of the processes through which routinized social processes, norms and legal rules are changed. Weber distinguished innovators and creators from maintainers and attributed the 'gift' of charisma in part to the creative or innovative quality of the leader's goals.

Several writers contend that charismatic leadership can and does exist in formal complex organizations (Dow, 1969; Oberg, 1972; Runciman, 1963; Shils, 1965). Yet despite the profound effects that charismatic leaders are presumed to have on followers' commitment, motivation, and performance, discussions of charisma have been speculative in nature and almost exclusively theoretical. To the knowledge of this writer none of the theoretical notions in the sociological or political science literature have been subjected to empirical test, despite the fact that many of these notions are implicitly testable.

In this chapter the sociological and political science literature on charisma will be reviewed and, where possible, the major assertions in this literature will be restated as propositions in an attempt to make them testable. In addition, selected literature from the discipline of social psychology will be reviewed and propositions which the writer believes are relevant to the concept of charisma will be inferred from the literature.

The outcome of this analysis is a speculative theoretical explanation of charisma from a psychological perspective rather than from a sociological or political science perspective. Hopefully, such an explanation will help us to have greater insight into how charismatic leadership emerges and its effects in modern organizations. Further, it is hoped that such an explanation will provide testable propositions with which to further leadership research.

In the remainder of this presentation the concept of charisma will be examined under the following topics: charismatic effects, characteristics of charismatic leaders, behavior of charismatic leaders, situational factors associated with the emergence and effectiveness of charismatic leaders. While these topics will be addressed separately, they are necessarily intertwined. Thus, at times a discussion of one topic will have implications for the other topics, and reference will be made to such implications.

The Effects of Charismatic Leadership

In the current literature the term charismatic leadership is generally defined and described in terms of the effects of the leader on followers, or in terms of the relationship between leaders and followers. For example Oberg (1972) states that 'the test for charisma . . . is the degree of devotion and trust the object (charismatic leader) inspires and the degree to which it enables the individual to transcend his own finiteness and alienation and feel made whole' (p. 22). Tucker (1968) refers to both 'charismatic following' and the 'charismatic relationship'.

> Often times, the relationship of the followers to the charismatic leader is that of disciples to a master, and in any event he is revered by them. They do not follow him out of fear or monetary inducement, but out of love, passionate devotion, enthusiasm. They are not as a rule concerned with career, promotion, salary, or benefice. The charismatic following is a non-bureaucratic group (p. 735).

It appears that most, if not all, writers agree that the effects of charismatic leadership are more emotional than calculative in that the follower is inspired enthusiastically to give unquestioned obedience, loyalty, commitment and devotion to the leader and to the cause that the leader represents.

The charismatic leader is also implicitly assumed to be an object of identification by which the followers emulate the leader's values, goals, and behavior. Thus, one of the effects of the charismatic leader is to cause followers to model their behavior, feelings, and cognitions after the leader (Friedrich, 1961). Through the articulation of a transcendent goal the leader is assumed to clarify or specify a mission for the followers. By the leader's expression of self-confidence, and through the exhibition of confidence in followers, the leader is also assumed to inspire self-confidence in the followers. Thus the charismatic leader is asserted to clarify followers' goals, cause them to set or accept higher goals, and have greater confidence in their ability to contribute to the attainment of such goals.

Finally, according to the political science and sociological literature on charisma, the charismatic leader is assumed to have the effect of bringing about rather radical change by virtue of beliefs and values that are different from the established order. Thus Oberg (1972) speaks of the 'change agent' function of the charismatic leader.

The above review of the effects of charismatic leadership suggests several dependent variables for a theory of charisma. Some of these effects are: follower trust in the correctness of the leader's beliefs, similarity of followers' beliefs to those of the leader, unquestioning acceptance of the leader, affection for the leader, willing obedience to the leader, identification with and emulation of the leader, emotional involvement of the follower in the mission, heightened goals of the follower, and the feeling on the part of followers that they will be able to accomplish, or contribute to the accomplishment of, the mission. This large number of charismatic effects is consistent with Etzioni's definition of charisma as 'the ability of an actor to exercise diffuse and intensive influence over the normative (ideological) orientations of other actors' (Etzioni, 1961, p. 203).

The charismatic effects listed above constitute an *initial* list of variables that can be used as preliminary dependent variables for a theory of charisma. While this number of variables lacks parsimony as the defining criteria of a charismatic leader, this list of presumed 'charismatic effects' provides a starting point for empiric research on charisma. If one were to identify a number of persons in a population (say military or industrial leaders in a given population) who informed observers (such as superiors or peers) could agree on as being clearly charismatic, it would be possible to identify these leaders' effects by measuring the degree to which their followers' responses to them are different from responses of followers of other leaders randomly selected from the same population. The major differences in follower responses could then be clustered into primary groups and scaled. The scores of the followers on these groups could then serve as the basis for a more accurate, complete and parsimonious operational definition of charismatic effects. Leaders who have such effects on followers could be identified in subsequent samples. Such leaders could then be classified as charismatic leaders. Their personality characteristics and behaviors could be compared with those of other leaders (who do not have such effects) to identify characteristics and behaviors which differentiate the charismatic leaders from others. This process of operationally defining charismatic leadership permits one to identify leaders in a population who have the charismatic effects described in the political science and sociological literature and thereby specify an operational set of dependent variables for a theory of leadership.

Some of the above effects have also been the dependent variables in social-psychological research. Specifically, the ability of one person to arouse needs and enhance self-esteem of others, and the ability of one person to serve successfully as a behavioral model for another have been the subject of substantial empirical investigation by psychologists. Later in this chapter we will review this research in an attempt to identify and describe the specific situational factors and leader behaviors that result in such 'charismatic' effects.

Defining charismatic leadership in terms of its effects permits one to identify charismatic leaders only after they have had an impact on followers. Such a definition says nothing about the personal characteristics, behaviors, or situational factors that bring about the charismatic effects. This is the scientific challenge that must be addressed if the mysterious quality of charismatic leadership is to be explained and charismatic effects are to be made predictable. We now turn to a discussion of these issues.

Definition of Charismatic Leadership

Throughout this chapter the term charismatic leadership will be used to refer to any leader who has the above 'charismatic effects' on followers to an unusually high degree.[2] The operational definition of a given charismatic leader awaits research which will allow one to scale the above specific 'charismatic effects'. While it is not likely that all charismatic leaders have all of the above 'charismatic effects', there are many possibilities that can be examined. For example, such effects may be present in a complex interacting manner. Alternatively it may be the sum of, or some absolute level of, selected effects that do indeed differentiate charismatic leaders from others.

Characteristics of the Charismatic Leader

Both the literature concerning charismatic leadership and the opinions of laymen seem to agree that the charismatic leader can be described by a specific set of personal characteristics. According to Weber (1947), the charismatic leader is accepted by followers because both the leader and the follower perceive the leader as possessing a certain extraordinary gift. This 'gift' of charisma is seldom specified and generally held to be some mysterious quality that defies definition. In actuality the 'gift' is likely to be a complex interaction of personal characteristics, the behavior the leader employs, characteristics of followers, and certain situational factors prevailing at the time of the assumption of the leadership role.

The literature on charismatic leadership repeatedly attributes three personal characteristics to leaders who have charismatic effects, namely: extremely high levels of self-confidence, dominance, and a strong conviction in the moral righteousness of his/her beliefs.[3] It is interesting to note that these three characteristics are also attributed to charismatic leaders by laymen as well as by scholars. As a classroom exercise I have on three occasions asked students to form into small groups and to discuss the characteristics of some charismatic leader that they have personally known or to whom they have been exposed. These groups repeatedly described the charismatic leaders that they selected for discussion as possessing dominance, self-confidence, and a strong conviction in their beliefs and ideals.

While the consensus of political science and sociological writers and the results of my own informal experiment are not evidence that leaders who have charismatic effects do indeed possess these characteristics, the argument is certainly subject to an empiric test with self-report measures of personality traits, beliefs, and values.

In addition to the characteristics discussed above it is hypothesized here that leaders who have charismatic effects have a high need to have influence over others. Such a need seems intuitively likely to characterize leaders who have such effects because without such a need they are unlikely to have developed the necessary persuasive skills to influence others and also are unlikely to obtain satisfaction from the leadership role. Uleman (1972) has developed a measure of the need for influence that can be used to test the above hypotheses.

The following proposition summarizes the above discussion:

Proposition 1. Characteristics that differentiate leaders who have charismatic effects on subordinates from leaders who do not have such charismatic effects are dominance and self-confidence, need for influence, and a strong conviction in the moral righteousness of their beliefs.[4]

Behavior of Charismatic Leaders

The sociological and political science literature offer some hints about the behavior of charismatic leaders.

Role Modeling

First it is suggested that leaders who have charismatic effects express, by their actions, a set of values and beliefs to which they want their followers to subscribe. That is, the leader 'role models' a value system for the followers. Gandhi constitutes an outstanding example of such systematic and intentional role modeling. He preached self-sacrifice, brotherly love, and nonviolent resistance to British rule. Repeatedly he engaged in self-sacrificing behaviors, such as giving up his lucrative law practice to live the life of a peasant, engaging in civil disobedience, fasting, and refusing to accept the ordinary conveniences offered to him by others.

The importance of the role modeling as a leadership strategy is illustrated by Gandhi's proposed leadership policies for the self-governance of India. 'Most important for Gandhi was the example that leaders set for their followers . . . "No leader of an independent India will hesitate to give an example by cleaning out his own toilet box"' (Collins & LaPierre, 1975, 234–35).

Concerning role modeling, a study by Joestling and Joestling (1972) is suggestive of the effects that a high status role model can have on the self-esteem of observers. Male and female students were asked to rate the value of being a woman. Half of the students were enrolled in the class taught by a qualified female instructor. Twenty-six percent of the women subjects in the class taught by a male thought there was nothing good about being a woman. In contrast, only five percent of the women subjects in the class taught by a qualified female had similar negative attitudes toward being a woman.

While role modeling often proves successful, success does not always occur. The question then is what permits a leader to be a successful role model, i.e., to be emulated by the followers.

There is substantial evidence that a person is more likely to be modeled to the extent that that person is perceived as nurturant (i.e., helpful, sympathetic, approving) and as being successful or possessing competence.

There is evidence that role modeling can have profound effects. Behavior resulting from modeling may be very specific such that the individual can be said to imitate or mimic the behavior of the model. Or, the behavior may be more general, taking the form of innovative behavior, generalized behavior orientations, and applications of principles for generating novel combinations of responses (Bandura, 1968).

Bandura (1968) reviews a substantial body of experimental evidence that shows that: (a) model's emotional responses to rewards or punishments elicit similar emotional responses in observers (p. 240); (b) stable changes in the valences (a measure of attractiveness) subjects assign to outcomes and changes in long-standing attitudes often result from the role modeling (pp. 243–44); and (c) modeling is capable of developing generalized conceptual and behavioral properties of observers such as moral judgement orientations and delay-of-gratification patterns of behavior (p. 252).

Of particular significance for the study of leadership are the diverse kinds of attitudes, feelings, and behavior and the diversity of subjects involved in prior studies. Role modeling has been shown to influence the degree to which: (a) undergraduate females learn assertive behavior in assertiveness training programs (Young, Rimm & Kennedy, 1973); (b) mentally disturbed patients assume independence in their personal life (Goldstein, Martins, Hubben, Van Belle, Schaaf, Wiersma, & Goedhart, 1973); (c) undergraduates are willing to disclose unfavorable or favorable anxiety-related information to others (Sarason, Ganzer & Singer, 1972); (d) personal changes and learning outcomes result from adult t-groups (Peters, 1973); (e) individuals are willing to induce punishment (electric shock) to others (Baron, 1971); (f) nurses experience fear of tuberculosis (DeWolfe, 1967); (g) subjects adopt biased attitudes toward minority ethnic groups (Kelman, 1958; Stotland and Patchen, 1961).

Many of the subjects in the above studies were either college students or adults. Thus, the findings are not limited to young children but are also relevant to persons in full-time occupations. Further, the dependent variables are all of significance for effective organizational or group performance. Feelings of fear, willingness to disclose information unfavorable to self, stereotyping, willingness to administer punishment, prejudicial attitudes, learning of interpersonal skills, and learning independence are relevant to interpersonal relations within organizations. Similarly, these cognitions and behaviors are relevant to the establishment of trust, to adequacy of communication, and to experiences that are satisfying in organizational life.

Thus it is argued here that role modeling is one of the processes by which leaders bring about charismatic effects. Furthermore, it is likely that the feelings, cognitions and behavior that are modeled frequently determine subordinates' adjustment to organizational life, their job satisfaction, and their motivation to work. With respect to motivation, the above findings suggest that leaders can have an effect on the values (or valences) subordinates attach to the outcomes of their effort as well as their expectations. And, as will be discussed below, leaders can also have an effect on subordinates' self-esteem, and their goal levels. Based on the above review of the literature concerned with role modeling, the following proposition is advanced:

Proposition 2. The more favorable the perceptions of the potential follower toward a leader the more the follower will model: (a) the valences of the leader; (b) the expectations of the leader that effective performance will result in desired or undesired outcomes for the follower; (c) the emotional responses of the leader to work related stimuli; (d) the attitudes of the leader toward work and toward the organization. Here 'favorable perceptions' is defined as the perceptions of the leader as attractive, nurturant, successful, or competent.

Image Building

If proposition 2 is valid, then it can be speculated that leaders who have charismatic effects not only model the values and beliefs they want followers to adopt, but also that such leaders take actions consciously designed to be viewed favorably by followers. This speculation leads to the following proposition:

Proposition 3. Leaders who have charismatic effects are more likely to engage in behaviors designed to create the impression of competence and success than leaders who do not have such effects.

This proposition is consistent with the traditional literature on charismatic leadership. Weber (1947) speaks of the necessity of the charismatic leader to 'prove' his extraordinary powers to the followers. Only as long as he can do so will he be recognized. While Weber and others have argued that such 'proof' lies in actual accomplishments, the above proposition stresses the *appearance* of accomplishments and asserts that charismatic leaders engage in behaviors to gain such an appearance.

Goal Articulation

In the traditional literature on charisma it is frequently asserted that charismatic leaders articulate a 'transcendent' goal which becomes the basis of a movement or a cause. Such a goal is ideological rather than pragmatic and is laden with moral overtones. Alternatively, if a movement is already in effect, one behavior of the emergent leader is the articulation of the goal of the movement with conviction and exhortation of the moral rightness of the goal (Tucker, 1968, p. 738).

Examples of such goals are Martin Luther King's 'I have a dream', Hitler's 'Thousand-year Reich' and his 'lebensraum', or Gandhi's vision of an India in which Hindus and Moslems would live in brotherly love, independent from British rule.

Berlew (1974, p. 269) states:

> The first requirement for . . . charismatic leadership is a common or shared vision for what the future *could be*. To provide meaning and generate excitement, such a common vision must reflect goals or a future state of affairs that is valued by the organizations' members and thus important to them to bring about. . . . All inspirational speeches or writings have the common element of some vision or dream of a better existence which will inspire or excite those who share the author's values. This basic wisdom too often has been ignored by managers.

Thus the following proposition is advanced:

Proposition 4. Leaders who have charismatic effects are more likely to articulate ideological goals than leaders who do not have such effects.

Exhibiting High Expectations and Showing Confidence

Leaders who communicate high performance expectations for subordinates and exhibit confidence in their ability to meet such expectations are hypothesized to enhance subordinates' self-esteem and to affect the goals subordinates accept or set for themselves. Some examples of this kind of charismatic leader behavior are Churchill's statement that England's air defense in World War II was 'England's finest hour', Hitler's claim that aryans were 'the master race', black leaders' exhortation that 'Black is beautiful', and Martin Luther King's prediction that 'We shall overcome'. All of these statements imply high expectations and confidence in the followers.

There is substantial evidence that the expectation that one can accomplish one's goals is positively related to motivation and goal attainment. Persons with high self-esteem are more likely than persons with low self-esteem to seek higher personal rewards for performance (Pepitone, 1964), and to choose occupations that are congruent with self-perceived traits (Korman, 1966) and self-perceived ability level (Korman, 1967). Further, Korman (1968) has shown experimentally that for high self-esteem subjects there is a positive relationship between task performance and satisfaction, but that no such relationship exists for low self-esteem subjects. Raben and Klimoski (1973) have also shown experimentally that high self-esteem subjects are more likely than low self-esteem subjects to rise to the challenge of doing a task for which they believe they are not qualified. Thus, it is argued here that, to the extent the leader can affect the self-esteem of subordinates, leader behavior will have an effect on the kinds of rewards subordinates seek, their satisfaction with the rewards they obtain, and their motivation to perform effectively.

The effect of leader behavior on subordinate self-esteem has been given little attention in the leadership literature.[5] The assertion that leaders can affect subordinates' self-esteem is derived from two lines of research: research concerning the role-modeling effects and research concerned with reality testing.

We have already argued that through role modeling leaders can have a rather profound effect on subordinates' beliefs. One of these beliefs is self-esteem which is defined by Lawler (1971, p. 107) as the belief that subordinates have with respect to their own general level of ability to cope with and control their environment. Is is argued here that subordinates' self-perceptions are likely to be modeled after the leader's perceptions of the subordinates.[6] Thus if the leader communicates high performance expectations and shows confidence in subordinates, they will in turn set or accept a higher goal for themselves and have greater confidence in themselves.[7]

The second line of research suggesting that leaders affect subordinates' self-esteem is that research concerned with 'reality testing'. In social situations where interpersonal evaluation is highly subjective, individuals tend to 'reality test', i.e., to test their notions of reality against the opinions of others (Deutsch & Gerard, 1955; Festinger, 1950). Consequently, to the extent that the leader shows followers that he/she believes them to be competent and personally responsible, the followers are hypothesized also to perceive themselves as competent. This self-perception is hypothesized to enhance motivation, performance, and satisfaction. Some indirect evidence in support of this line of reasoning is found in the results of studies by Berlew and Hall (1966), Stedry and Kay (1966), Korman (1971), Rosenthal and Jacobson (1968), Seaver (1973), and Meichenbaum, Bowers, and Ross (1969). Berlew and Hall (1966) and Stedry and Kay (1966) in field studies both found that individual performance increased as a function of the level of expectation superiors communicated to the individuals. Similarly, Korman (1971) showed in a laboratory study that the performance of students on creative tasks was a direct positive function of the expectations that other college students had for the laboratory subjects. Korman (1971) also showed that ratings of subordinates' performance in two field settings and self-ratings of motivation in three field settings were all significantly correlated with the degree to which subordinates perceived their leaders' practices to reflect confidence in the subordinates.

These findings are consistent with those studies conducted in educational settings in which the expectations of teachers have been shown to be reflected in the performance of students (Meichenbaum, et al., 1969; Rosenthal & Jacobson, 1968; Seaver, 1973). In these studies teachers were induced to believe that certain students were more competent than others. This belief, or expectancy, on the part of the teacher was shown to be associated with higher student performance. However, there are also studies conducted in educational settings which have failed to demonstrate an effect of teachers' expectancies of students' performance (Anderson & Rosenthal, 1968; Collins, 1969; Conn, Edwards, Rosenthal & Crowne, 1968; Evans & Rosenthal, 1969; Fiedler, Cohen & Finney, 1971). Seaver (1973) points out that in all of these disconfirming studies and also in the Rosenthal and Jacobson study which is the subject of much controversy, the means of inducing teacher expectations were weak and thus 'failure to find expectancy effects may be attributable solely to their failure to induce the desired expectancy in teachers' (p. 341).

If it is assumed that the leader's expectation of subordinates affects the subordinates' self-esteem and their self-esteem in turn affects their performance, then the above studies all provide indirect support for the assertion that leader's expectations affect subordinates' performance.

The *combination* of leader's confidence and high expectations, rather than high expectations alone, should be emphasized here. It is possible that leaders might set high performance standards, thus implying high expectations of subordinates, while at the same time showing low confidence in the subordinates' ability to meet such expectations. An example of this would be the leader who scores high on such questionnaire items as 'he needles foremen for production'.[8] While such leader behavior may motivate subordinates to strive for high performance in order to avoid punishment, it is also likely to induce fear of failure. Such a state in turn will likely be accompanied by efforts to avoid accountability on the part of the subordinates, strong feelings of dissatisfaction, low acceptance of the leader, and resistance to the leader's influence attempts in the long run.

Thus, while leader expectations are considered to have a significant effect on the reactions of subordinates, high expectations are hypothesized to have a positive effect *only* when subordinates' perceive the superior to also have confidence in their (the subordinates') ability to meet such expectations.

Effect on Followers' Goals

In addition to affecting the self-esteem of subordinates, leader expectations and confidence are also hypothesized to affect several important characteristics of the subordinates' goals. In the following paragraphs we review the research concerned with goal characteristics.

In a series of laboratory studies, Locke and his associates (Bryan & Locke, 1967a, 1967b; Locke & Bryan, 1966a, 1966b) have demonstrated that when subjects are given specific goals by the experimenter they perform at significantly higher levels than those given the instruction to 'do your best'. Two field studies (Mace, 1935; Mendleson, 1971) also offer support for the generalizability of these laboratory findings to natural field settings. Thus, it is argued here that, if laboratory experimenters can influence the goal characteristics of experimental subjects, it seems reasonable that leaders can have similiar influence on the goal characteristics of subordinates.

Specific and high expectations of leaders are hypothesized to clarify subordinates' performance goals. Further, it is hypothesized that the more the leader shows confidence in the subordinates' ability to meet goals, the more subordinates are likely to accept them as realistic and attainable.

Specific and high leader expectations are likely to provide a standard against which subordinates can evaluate their own performance. Accordingly, it is hypothesized here that leaders' expectations also serve as a basis on which subordinates may derive feedback. Finally, it is hypothesized that, when the leader's expectations are both high and clear to the subordinate and when the leader shows confidence in the subordinate's ability to meet such expectations, the subordinates will set and/or accept higher goals for themselves than would otherwise be the case, and will have more confidence that they will be able to meet the goals.

The above hypotheses concerning the leaders' effect on followers' self-esteem and goals can be summarized in the following proposition:

Proposition 5. Leaders who simultaneously communicate high expectations of, and confidence in followers are more likely to have followers who accept the goals of the leader and believe that they can contribute to goal accomplishment and are more likely to have followers who strive to meet specific and challenging performance standards.

Motive Arousal Leader Behavior

One explanation for the emotional appeal of the charismatic leader may be the specific content of the messages he communicates to followers. It is speculated here that charismatic leaders communicate messages that arouse motives that are especially relevant to mission accomplishment. For example Gandhi's exhortations of love and acceptance of one's fellow man likely aroused the need for affiliation, a need (or motive) especially relevant to the goal of uniting Hindus, Moslems, and Christians.

Military leaders often employ symbols of authoritarianism and evoke the image of the enemy, thus arousing the power motive, a motive especially relevant to effective combat performance. For example Patton, when addressing infantry recruits, would do so against the background of a large American flag, dressed with medals of his accomplishments, and wearing a shining helmet displaying the four stars indicating the status of general.

Miner's research is relevant to defining some of the conditions under which the arousal of the need for power is associated with successful performance. Miner found that individuals who were high on a projective (sentence completion) measure of the power need were more likely to be successful in hierarchical bureaucratic organizations than individuals low on the power need. These findings did not hold true in egalitarian non-bureaucratic organizations however (Miner, 1965).

Industrial leaders and leaders of scientists frequently stress excellence of performance as a measure of one's worth, thus arousing the need for achievement, a motive especially relevant to the assumption of personal responsibility, persistence, and pride in high-quality work performance. Varga (1975) has shown that the need for achievement is positively associated with economic and technical performance among research and development project leaders. He has also shown that the need for power is a strong factor contributing to such success when in conjunction with the need for achievement, but a factor making for failure when possessed by leaders low on the need for achievement.

There is some evidence that formally appointed leaders in a laboratory situation are capable of arousing subordinates' need for achievement (Litwin & Stringer, 1968). There is also a substantial amount of evidence that the achievement, affiliation, and power needs can be aroused from experimental inductions. For example the need for achievement has been aroused for males by suggesting to subjects that the experimental task is a measure of personal competence, or that the task is a standard against which one can measure his general level of ability (Heckhausen, 1967; McClelland, 1953; McClelland, Clarke, Roby & Atkinson, 1958; Raynor, 1974).

The need for affiliation has been aroused by having fraternity members rate one another, while all were present, on a sociometric friendship index (Shipley & Veroff, 1952) while at the same time requiring each brother to stand and be rated by the other members of the fraternity on a list of trait adjectives.

The power need has been aroused experimentally by (a) evoking the image of, or reminding one of, an enemy, (b) having subjects observe the exercise of power by one person over another, or (c) allowing subjects to exercise power over another (Winter, 1973). Thus it is hypothesized that needs can be, and often are, similarly aroused by leaders in natural settings. By stressing the challenging aspects of tasks, making group members' acceptance of each other salient to performance appraisal, or talking about competition from others, it is hypothesized that leaders can and frequently do arouse the needs for achievement, affiliation, and power. Further it is hypothesized that, to the extent that such motives are associated with task-required performance, the arousal of these motives will result in increased effectiveness on the part of subordinates. Thus the performance consequence of motive arousal is contingent on the task contingencies. For example, when task demands of subordinates require assumption of calculated risks, achievement oriented initiative, assumption of personal responsibility, and persistence toward challenging goals, the arousal of the need for achievement will facilitate task accomplishment. Further, there is evidence that when subordinates' need for achievement is high, task accomplishment will lead to satisfaction. When subordinates' need for achievement is low, task accomplishment will not be related to satisfaction (Steers, 1975).

When the task demands of subordinates require them to be persuasive, assert influence over or exercise control of others, or be highly competitive or combative, the arousal of the power motive is hypothesized to be related to effective performance and satisfaction. For example, on competitive tasks, or tasks requiring persuasion or aggression, the arousal of the power motive is hypothesized to lead to effective performance.

Finally, when task demands require affiliative behavior, as in the case of tasks requiring cohesiveness, team work, and peer support, the arousal of the affiliative motive becomes highly relevant to performance and satisfaction. An example of such tasks would be tasks that are enriched by assignment of major work goals to groups rather than individuals (Trist & Bamforth, 1951).

These speculations are summarized with the following proposition:

Proposition 6. Leaders who have charismatic effects are more likely to engage in behaviors that arouse motives relevant to the accomplishment of the mission than are leaders who do not have charismatic effects.[9]

Social Determinants of Charismatic Leadership

The sociological literature (Weber, 1947) stresses that charismatic leadership is born out of stressful situations. It is argued that such leaders express sentiments deeply held by followers. These sentiments are different from the established order and thus their expression is likely to be hazardous to the leader (Friedland, 1964). Since their expression is hazardous, the leader is perceived as courageous. Because of other 'gifts' attributed to the leader, such as extraordinary competence, the followers believe that the leader will bring about social change and will thus deliver them from their plight.

Thus it can be hypothesized that a strong feeling of distress on the part of followers is one situational factor that interacts with the characteristics and behavior of leaders to result in charismatic effects.

However Shils (1965) argues that charisma need not be born out of distress. Rather, according to Shils, charisma is dispersed throughout the formal institutions of society.

Accordingly, persons holding positions of great power will be perceived as charismatic because of the 'awe-inspiring' quality of power. Shils' only requirement is that the expression of power must appear to be integrated with a transcendent goal.

The above controversy suggests the hypothesis that leaders are more likely to have charismatic effects in situations stressful for followers than in non-stressful situations. Further it can be hypothesized that persons with the characteristics of dominance, self-confidence, need for influence, and strong convictions will be more likely to emerge as leaders under stressful conditions. Whether or not follower distress is a necessary condition for leaders to have charismatic effects or for persons with such characteristics to emerge as leaders is an empirical question that remains to be tested.

While there is lack of agreement as to whether or not leaders can have charismatic effects under nonstressful situations, all writers do seem to agree that charisma must be based on the articulation of an ideological goal. Opportunity to articulate such a goal, whether in stressful or nonstressful situations, thus can be hypothesized as one of the situational requirements for a person to have charismatic effects. This hypothesis suggests that, whenever the roles of followers can be defined as contributing to ideological values held by the follower, a leader can have some degree of charismatic effect by stressing such values and engaging in the specific behaviors described in the above propositions.

The question then is under what circumstances are roles definable in terms of ideological values. Clearly the roles of followers in political or religious movements can be defined in terms of ideological values. In addition, Berlew (1974) argues that since man seeks meaning in work there are many such ideological values to be stressed in modern formal organizations. Specifically he argues that any of the value-related opportunities listed in Table 1 can have a charismatic effect.

*Table 1   Sources of meaning in organizations: opportunities and related values**

Type of Opportunity	Related Need or Value
1. A chance to be tested; to make it on one's own	Self-reliance Self-actualization
2. A social experiment, to combine work, family, and play in some new way	Community Integration of life
3. A chance to do something *well* – e.g., return to real craftsmanship; to be really creative	Excellence Unique accomplishment
4. A chance to do something *good* – e.g., run an honest, no rip-off business, or a youth counselling center	Consideration Service
5. A chance to change the way things are – e.g., from Republican to Democrat or Socialist, from war to peace, from unjust to just	Activism Social responsibility Citizenship

Source: Berlew, 1974, with permission by Prentice-Hall.

There are some work roles in society which do not lend themselves to ideological value orientation. These are generally the roles requiring highly routine, nonthinking effort in institutions directed exclusively to economic ends. It is hard to conceive of clerks or assembly-line workers in profit-making firms as perceiving their roles as ideologically oriented. However the same work when directed toward an ideological goal could lend itself to charismatic leadership. For example in World War II, 'Rosie the Riveter' expressed the ideological contribution of an assembly-line worker. And such menial efforts as stuffing envelopes frequently are directed toward ideological goals in political or religious organizations. The following proposition summarizes the above argument:

Proposition 7. A necessary condition for a leader to have charismatic effects is that the role of followers be definable in ideological terms that appeal to the follower.

Summary and Overview

Figure 1 presents a diagramatic overview of the theory presented above. It is hypothesized that leaders who have charismatic effects are differentiated from others by some combination (possibly additive and possibly interactive) of the four personal characteristics shown in the upper right box: dominance, self-confidence, need for influence, and a strong conviction in the moral righteousness of his or her beliefs. Charismatic leaders are hypothesized to employ these characteristics with the following specific behaviors: goal articulation, role modeling, personal image building, demonstration of confidence and high expectations for followers, and motive arousal behaviors. Goal articulation and personal image building are hypothesized to result in favorable perceptions of the leader by followers. These favorable perceptions are asserted to enhance followers' trust, loyalty, and obedience to the leader and also to moderate the relationships between the remaining leader behaviors and the follower responses to the leader. The follower responses are hypothesized to result in effective performance if the aroused behavior is appropriate for their task demands.

Conclusion – Why a 1976 Theory

This chapter presents a '1976' theory of charismatic leadership. The date, 1976, is attached to the title to reflect the philosophy of science of the writer. The theory is advanced for the purpose of guiding future research and not as a conclusive explanation of the charismatic phenomenon. As such it includes a set of propositions that are hopefully testable. Admittedly tests of the theory will require the development and validation of several new scales. However it is hoped that the propositions are at least presently testable in principle. 'A theory that cannot be mortally endangered cannot be alive' (cited in Platt, 1964, from personal communication by W.A.H. Rustin).

The results of empiric tests of the theory will undoubtedly require revision of the theory. It is believed by the writer that theories, no matter how good at explaining a set of phenomena, are ultimately incorrect and consequently will undergo modification over time. Thus as MacKenzie and House (1975) have stated 'the fate of the better theories is to become explanations that hold for some phenomena in some limited condition'. Or, as Hebb (1969,

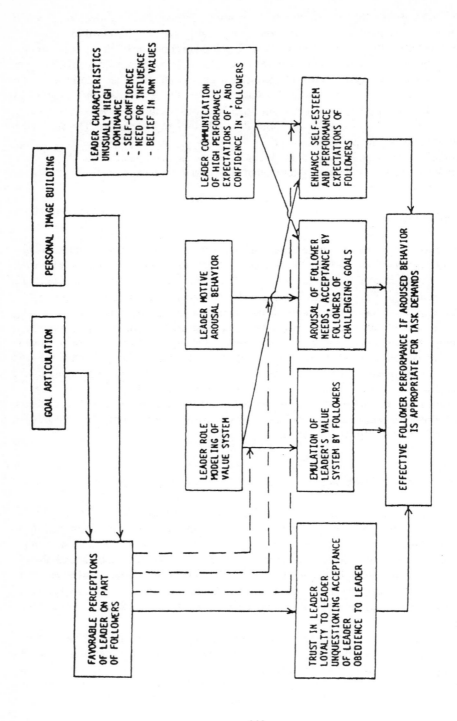

Figure 1. A model of charismatic leadership. (Dotted lines indicate that favorable perceptions moderate the relationship between leader and follower responses)

p. 21) asserts, 'A good theory is one that holds together long enough to get you to a better theory'.

Hopefully at some future date this theory will have led to a better theory.

Notes

1. The author is indebted to Hugh J. Arnold, Martin G. Evans, Harvey Kolodny, Stephan J. Motowidlo, John A. Dearness, and William Cooper for their helpful critiques of this chapter. The literature review on which this chapter is based was conducted while the author was visiting professor at Florida International University, April–July, 1975.
2. This definition would be tautological if the 'charismatic effects' were not operationally discovered using two independent operations. However, since the discovery of the 'charismatic effects' involves having charismatic leaders identified by one set of observers (peers or superiors) and specification of their effects by an independent set of observers (namely their followers), such a definition avoids the tautological problem.
3. It is entirely possible that charismatic leaders present themselves as highly confident and as having a strong conviction in the moral righteousness of their beliefs but do not indeed believe in either themselves or their beliefs. Some leaders may thus have charismatic effects because of their ability to *act as though* they have such confidence and convictions. The writer is indebted to Ed Locke for pointing out this alternative hypothesis.
4. Sashkin, in his commentary on the present chapter, points out that earlier research has shown eminent leaders possess the traits of 'intellectual fortitude and integrity of character' and speech fluency (or 'capacity for ready communication'). While these traits were not specified in the earlier version of this presentation which Professor Sashkin reviewed, they are not in contradiction to the earlier literature on charismatic leadership and rather consistent with the general description of the charismatic personality advanced in this literature. Thus I would accept these characteristics, along with those in proposition 1, as possible characteristics that differentiate leaders who have charismatic effects from other leaders.
5. The argument that the enhancement of subordinate self-esteem is an important charismatic effect grew out of earlier conversations between the writer and David E. Berlew. See Berlew (1974) for further elaboration of this argument.
6. Such modeling, of course, will be a function of the degree to which the subordinate holds favorable perceptions of the leader, as specified in proposition 2.
7. It is possible that such leader behavior will have a positive effect on subordinates' task-related self-esteem only (i.e., on the subordinates' confidence in their ability to accomplish task goals). It is also possible that such leader behavior will result in enhanced chronic and generalized self-esteem of subordinates. Whether leaders can indeed have such a powerful effect on subordinates' self-perceptions is of course a question that requires empiric investigation.
8. Fleishman, E.A. *Manual For the Supervisory Behavior Description Questionnaire*. Washington, D.C.: American Institutes for Research, 1972.
9. The ability of the leader to arouse motives of subordinates is hypothesized to be a function of the degree to which subordinates hold favorable perceptions of the leader, as specified in proposition 2.

References

Anderson, D. F., & Rosenthal, R. Some effects of interpersonal expectancy and social interaction on institutionalized retarded children. *Proceedings of the 76th Annual Convention of the American Psychological Association*, 1968, *3*, 479–80.

Bandura, A. Social learning theory and identificatory process. In David A. Goslin (Ed.), *Handbook of socialization theory and research*. Chicago: Rand McNally, 1968.

Baron, Robert A. Exposure to an aggresive model and apparent probability of retaliation from the victim as determinants of adult aggressive behavior. *Journal of Experimental and Social Psychology*, 1971, *1*, 343–55.

Berlew, D. E. Leadership and organizational excitement. In D. A. Kolb, I. M. Rubin, and J. M. McIntyre (Eds.), *Organizational psychology: A book of readings. (2nd ed.)*. Englewood Cliffs, N.J.: Prentice Hall, 1974.

Berlew, D. E., & Hall, D. T. The socialization of managers: Effects of expectations on performance. *Administrative Science Quarterly*, 1966. *11*, 207–23.

Bryan, J. F., & Locke, E. A. Parkinson's law as a goal-setting phenomenon. *Organizational Behavior and Human Performance*, 1967, *2*, 258–75. (a)

Bryan, J. F., & Locke, E. A. Goal-setting as a means of increasing motivation. *Journal of Applied Psychology*, 1967, *51*, 274–77. (b)

Collins, L., & LaPierre, D. *Freedom at midnight*. New York: Simon and Schuster, 1975.

Collins, W. L. Expectancy effects in the classroom: A failure to replicate. *Journal of Educational Psychology*, 1969, *60*, 377–83.

Conn, L. K., Edwards, C. N., Rosenthal, R., & Crowne, D. Perception of emotion and response to teachers' expectancy by elementary school children. *Psychological Reports*, 1968, *22*, 27–34.

Deutsch, M., & Gerard, H. A study of normative and informational social influence upon individual judgment. *Journal of Abnormal and Social Psychology*, 1955, *51*, 629–36.

DeWolfe, A. S. Identification and fear decrease. *Journal of Consulting Psychology*, 1967, *31*, 259–63.

Dow, T. E. The theory of charisma. *Sociological Quarterly*, 1969, *10*, 306–18.

Etzioni, A. *A comparative analysis of complex organizations*. New York: Free Press, 1961.

Evans, J. T., & Rosenthal, R. Interpersonal self-fulfilling prophecies: Further extrapolations from the laboratory to the classroom *Proceedings of the 77th Annual Convention of the American Psychological Association*, 1969, *4*, 371–72.

Festinger, L. Informal social communication. *Psychological Review*, 1950, *57*, 271–82.

Fiedler, F. E., Cohen, R. D., & Finney, S. An attempt to replicate the teacher expectancy effect. *Psychological Reports*, 1971, *29*, 1223–28.

Friedland, W. H. For a sociological concept of charisma. *Social Forces*, 1964, *43*, 18–26.

Friedrich, C. J. Political leadership and the problem of the charismatic power. *The Journal of Politics*, 1961, *23*, 3–24.

Goldstein, A. P., Martins, J., Hubben, J., Van Belle, H. A., Schaab, W., Wiersma, H., & Goedhart, A. The use of modelling to increase independent behavior. *Behavior Research and Therapy*, 1973, *11*, 31–42.

Hebb, D. O. Hebb on hocus-pocus: A conversation with Elizabeth Hall. *Psychology Today*, 1969, *3* (6), 20–28.

Heckhausen, H. *The anatomy of achievement motivation*. New York: Academic Press, 1967.

Joestling, J. and Joestling, R. Sex differences in group belongingness as influenced by instructor's sex. *Psychological Reports*, 1972, *31*, 717–18.

Kelman, H. C. Compliance, identification, and internalization: Three processes of attitude change. *Journal of Conflict Resolution*, 1958, *2*, 51–60.

Korman, A. K. Consideration, initiating structure and organizational criteria—A review. *Personnel Psychology*, 1966, *19*, 349–61. (a)

Korman, A. K. Self-esteem variable in vocational choice. *Journal of Applied Psychology*, 1966, *50*, 479–86. (b)

Korman, A. K. Self-esteem as a moderator of the relationship between perceived abilities and vocational choice. *Journal of Applied Psychology*, 1967, *51*, 65–67.

Korman, A. K. Task success, task popularity, and self-esteem. *Journal of Applied Psychology*, 1968, *52*, 484–90.

Korman, A. K. Expectancies as determinants of performance. *Journal of Applied Psychology*, 1971, *55*, 218–22.

Lawler, E. E., III. *Pay and organizational effectiveness: A psychological view*. New York: McGraw-Hill, 1971.

Litwin, G. H., & Stringer, R. A., Jr. *Motivation and organization climate*. Division of Research, Graduate School of Business Administration, Harvard University, Cambridge, Mass., 1968.

Locke, E. A., & Bryan, J. F. Cognitive aspects of psychomotor performance: The effects of performance goals on level of performance. *Journal of Applied Psychology*, 1966, *50*, 286–91. (a)

Locke, E. A., & Bryan, J. F. The effects of goal-setting, rule-learning and knowledge of score on performance. *American Journal of Psychology*, 1966, *79*, 451–57. (b)

Mace, C. A. Incentives: Some experimental studies. Report No. 72. London: Industrial Health Research Board, 1935.

McClelland, D. C. *The achievement motive*. New York: Appleton-Century-Crofts, 1953.

McClelland, D. C., Clarke, R. A., Roby, T. B., and Atkinson, J. W. The effect of the need for achievement on thematic apperception. In J. W. Atkinson (Ed.), *Motives in fantasy, action, and society*. New York: Van Nostrand, 1958.

Mackenzie, K. D., & House, R. J. Paradigm development in the social sciences: A proposed research strategy. Working Paper No. 75–03, Faculty of Management Studies, University of Toronto, 1975.

Meichenbaum, D. H., Bowers, K. S., & Ross, R. R. A behavioral analysis of teacher expectancy effect. *Journal of Personality and Social Psychology*, 1969, *13*, 306–16.

Mendleson, J. Managerial goal setting: An exploration into its meaning and measurement. Unpublished doctoral dissertation. Michigan State University, East Lansing, 1971.

Miner, J. B. *Studies in managerial education*. New York: Springer, 1965.

Oberg, W. Charisma, commitment, and contemporary organization theory. *Business Topics*, 1972, *20* (2), 18–32.

Pepitone, A. *Attraction and hostility*. New York: Atherton, 1964.

Peters, D. R. Identification and personal learning in t-groups. *Human Relations*, 1973, *26*, 1–21.

Platt, J. R. Strong inference. *Science*, 1964, *146*, 347–53.

Raben, C. S., & Klimoski, R. J. The effects of expectations upon task performance as moderated by levels of self-esteem. *Journal of Vocational Behavior*, 1973, *3*, 475–83.

Raynor, J. O. Future orientation in the study of achievement motivation. In J. W. Atkinson, and J. O. Raynor (Eds.), *Motivation and achievement*. New York: Wiley, 1974.

Rosenthal, R., & Jacobson, L. *Pygmalion in the classroom: Teacher expectations and pupils' intellectual development*. New York: Holt, Rinehart, and Winston, 1968.

Runciman, W. G. Charismatic legitimacy and one-party rule in China. *Archives Europeenes de Sociologic*, 1963, *4*, 148–65.

Sarason, I. B., Ganzer, V. J., & Singer, M. Effects of modeled self disclosure on the verbal behavior of persons differing in defensiveness. *Journal of Counseling and Clinical Psychology*, 1972, *39*, 483–90.

Seaver, W. B. Effects of naturally induced teacher expectancies. *Journal of Personality and Social Psychology*, 1973, *28*, 333–42.

Shils, E. A. Charisma, order, and status. *American Sociological Review*, 1965, *30*, 199–213.

Shipley, T. E., & Veroff, J. A projective measure of need affiliation. *Journal of Experimental*

Psychology, 1952, *43*, 349–56.

Stedry, A. C., & Kay, E. The effects of goal difficulty on performance: A field experiment. *Behavioral Science*, 1966, *11*, 459–70.

Steers, R. M. Task-goal attributes, n-achievement, and supervisory performance. *Organizational Behavior and Human Performance*, 1975, *13*, 392–403.

Stotland, E., & Patchen, M. Identification and changes in prejudice and authoritarianism. *Journal of Abnormal and Social Psychology*, 1961, *62*, 265–74.

Trist, E. L., & Bamforth, K. W. Some social and psychological consequences of the longwall method of coal-getting. *Human Relations*, 1951, *4*, 3–38.

Tucker, R. C. The theory of charismatic leadership. *Daedulus*, 1968, *97*, 731–56.

Uleman, J. S. The need for influence: Development and validation of a measure and comparison with the need for power. *Genetic Psychology Monographs*, 1972, *85*, 157–214.

Varga, K. n-Achievement, n-Power and effectiveness of research and development. *Human Relations*, 1975, *28*, 571–90.

Weber, M. *The theory of social and economic organization.* In A. M. Henderson and T. Parsons (Trs.). Glencoe, Ill.: Free Press, 1947.

Winter, D. G. *The power motive.* New York: Free Press, 1973

Young, E. R., Rimm, D. C., & Kennedy, T. D. An experimental investigation of modification of assertive behavior. *Behavioral Research and Therapy*, 1973, *11*, 317–19.

Part IX
Power Approaches

[16]

THE BASES OF SOCIAL POWER

John R. P. French, Jr. and Bertram Raven

The processes of power are pervasive, complex, and often disguised in our society. Accordingly one finds in political science, in sociology, and in social psychology a variety of distinctions among different types of social power or among qualitatively different processes of social influence (1, 6, 14, 20, 23, 29, 30, 38, 41). Our main purpose is to identify the major types of power and to define them systematically so that we may compare them according to the changes which they produce and the other effects which accompany the use of power. The phenomena of power and influence involve a dyadic relation between two agents which may be viewed from two points of view: (a) What determines the behavior of the agent who exerts power? (b) What determines the reactions of the recipient of this behavior? We take this second point of view and formulate our theory in terms of the life space of P, the person upon whom the power is exerted. In this way we hope to define basic concepts of power which will be adequate to explain many of the phenomena of social influence, including some which have been described in other less genotypic terms.

Recent empirical work, especially on small groups, has demonstrated the necessity of distinguishing different types of power in order to account for the different effects found in studies of social influence. Yet there is no doubt that more empirical knowledge will be needed to make final decisions concerning the necessary differentiations, but this knowledge will be obtained only by research based on some preliminary theoretical distinctions. We present such preliminary concepts and some of the hypotheses they suggest.

POWER, INFLUENCE, AND CHANGE

Psychological Change

Since we shall define power in terms of influence, and influence in terms of psychological change, we begin with a discussion of change. We want to define change at a level of generality which includes changes in behavior, opinions, attitudes, goals, needs, values and all other aspects of the person's psychological field. We shall use the word "system" to refer to any such part of the life space.[1] Following Lewin (26, p. 305) the state of a system at time 1 will be denoted $s_1(a)$.

Psychological change is defined as any alteration of the state of some system a over time. The amount of change is measured by the size of the difference between the states of the system a at time 1 and at time 2: $ch(a) = s_2(a) - s_1(a)$.

Change in any psychological system may be conceptualized in terms of psychological forces. But it is important to note that the change must be coordinated to the resultant force of all the forces operating at the moment. Change in an opinion, for example, may be determined jointly by a driving force induced by another person, a restraining force corresponding to anchorage in a group opinion, and an own force stemming from the person's needs.

Social Influence

Our theory of social influence and power is limited to influence on the person, P, produced by a social agent, O, where O can be either another person, a role, a norm, a group or a part of a group. We do not consider social influence exerted on a group.

The influence of O on system a in the life space of P is defined as the resultant force on system a which has its source in an act of O. This resultant force induced by O consists of two components: a force to change the system in the direction induced by O and an opposing resistance set up by the same act of O.

By this definition the influence of O does not include P's own forces nor the forces induced by other social agents. Accordingly the "influence" of O must be clearly distinguished from O's "control" of P (Chapter 11). O may be able to induce strong forces on P to carry out an activity (i.e., O exerts strong influence on P); but if the opposing forces induced by another person or by P's own needs are stronger, then P will locomote in an opposite direction (i.e., O does not have control over P). Thus psychological change in P can be taken as an operational definition of the social influence of O on P only when the effects of other forces have been eliminated.

It is assumed that any system is interdependent with other parts of the life space so that a change in one may produce changes in others. However, this theory focuses on the primary changes in a system which are produced directly

---

[1] The word "system" is here used to refer to a whole or to a part of the whole.

by social influence; it is less concerned with secondary changes which are indirectly effected in the other systems or with primary changes produced by nonsocial influences.

Commonly social influence takes place through an intentional act on the part of O. However, we do not want to limit our definition of "act" to such conscious behavior. Indeed, influence might result from the passive presence of O, with no evidence of speech or overt movement. A policeman's standing on a corner may be considered an act of an agent for the speeding motorist. Such acts of the inducing agent will vary in strength, for O may not always utilize all of his power. The policeman, for example, may merely stand and watch or act more strongly by blowing his whistle at the motorist.

The influence exerted by an act need not be in the direction intended by O. The direction of the resultant force on P will depend on the relative magnitude of the induced force set up by the act of O and the resisting force in the opposite direction which is generated by that same act. In cases where O intends to influence P in a given direction, a resultant force in the same direction may be termed positive influence whereas a resultant force in the opposite direction may be termed negative influence.

If O produces the intended change, he has exerted positive control; but if he produces a change in the opposite direction, as for example in the negativism of young children or in the phenomena of negative reference groups, he has exerted negative control.

Social Power

The *strength of power* of O/P in some system *a* is defined as the maximum potential ability of O to influence P in *a*.

By this definition influence is kinetic power, just as power is potential influence. It is assumed that O is capable of various acts which, because of some more or less enduring relation to P, are able to exert influence on P.[2] O's power is measured by his maximum possible influence, though he may often choose to exert less than his full power.

An equivalent definition of power may be stated in terms of the resultant of two forces set up by the act of O: one in the direction of O's influence at-

---

[2] The concept of power has the conceptual property of *potentiality;* but it seems useful to restrict this potential influence to more or less enduring power relations between O and P by excluding from the definition of power those cases where the potential influence is so momentary or so changing that it cannot be predicted from the existing relationship. Power is a useful concept for describing social structure only if it has a certain stability over time; it is useless if every momentary social stimulus is viewed as actualizing social power.

tempt and another resisting force in the opposite direction. Power is the maximum resultant of these two forces:

$$\text{Power of O/P (a)} = (f_{a,x} - f_{\overline{a,x}})^{\text{max}}$$

where the source of both forces is an act of O.

Thus the power of O with respect to system *a* of P is equal to the maximum resultant force of two forces set up by any possible act of O: (a) the force which O can set up on the system *a* to change in the direction x, (b) the resisting force [3] in the opposite direction. Whenever the first component force is greater than the second, positive power exists; but if the second component force is greater than the first, then O has negative power over P.

It is necessary to define power with respect to a specified system because the power of O/P may vary greatly from one system to another. O may have great power to control the behavior of P but little power to control his opinions. Of course a high power of O/P does not imply a low power of P/O; the two variables are conceptually independent (Chapter 11).

For certain purposes it is convenient to define the range of power as the set of all systems within which O has power of strength greater than zero. A husband may have a broad range of power over his wife, but a narrow range of power over his employer. We shall use the term "magnitude of power" to denote the summation of O's power over P in all systems of his range.

The dependence of *s*(*a*) on O.

Several investigators have been concerned with differences between superficial conformity and "deeper" changes produced by social influence (1, 5, 6, 11, 12, 20, 21, 22, 23, 26, 36, 37). The kinds of systems which are changed and the stability of these changes have been handled by distinctions such as "public vs. private attitudes," "overt vs. covert behavior," "compliance vs. internalization," and "own vs. induced forces." Though stated as dichotomies, all of these distinctions suggest an underlying dimension of the degree of dependence of the state of a system on O.

We assume that any change in the state of a system is produced by a change in some factor upon which it is functionally dependent. The state of an

---

[3] We define resistance to an attempted induction as a force in the opposite direction which is set up by the same act of O. It must be distinguished from opposition which is defined as existing opposing forces which do not have their source in the same act of O. For example, a boy might resist his mother's order to eat spinach because of the manner of the induction attempt, and at the same time he might oppose it because he didn't like spinach.

opinion, for example, may change because of a change either in some internal factor such as a need or in some external factor such as the arguments of O. Likewise the maintenance of the same state of a system is produced by the stability or lack of change in the internal and external factors. In general, then, psychological change and stability can be conceptualized in terms of dynamic dependence. Our interest is focused on the special case of dependence on an external agent, O (31).

In many cases the initial state of the system has the character of a quasi-stationary equilibrium with a central force field around $s_1(a)$ (26, p. 106). In such cases we may derive a tendency toward retrogression to the original state as soon as the force induced by O is removed.[4] Let us suppose that O exerts influence producing a new state of the system, $s_2(a)$. Is $s_2(a)$ now dependent on the continued presence of O? In principle we could answer this question by removing any traces of O from the life space of P and by observing the consequent state of the system at time 3. If $s_3(a)$ retrogresses completely back to $s_1(a)$, then we may conclude that maintenance of $s_2(a)$ was completely dependent on O; but if $s_3(a)$ equals $s_2(a)$, this lack of change shows that $s_2(a)$ has become completely independent of O. In general the degree of dependence of $s_2(a)$ on O, following O's influence, may be defined as equal to the amount of retrogression following the removal of O from the life space of P:

$$\text{Degree of dependence of } s_2(a) \text{ on } O = s_2(a) - s_3(a).$$

A given degree of dependence at time 2 may later change, for example, through the gradual weakening of O's influence. At this later time, the degree of dependence of $s_4(a)$ on O, would still be equal to the amount of retrogression toward the initial state of equilibrium $s_1(a)$. Operational measures of the degree of dependence on O will, of course, have to be taken under conditions where all other factors are held constant.

Consider the example of three separated employees who have been working at the same steady level of production despite normal, small fluctuations in the work environment. The supervisor orders each to increase his production, and the level of each goes up from 100 to 115 pieces per day. After a week of producing at the new rate of 115 pieces per day, the supervisor is removed for a week. The production of employee A immediately returns to 100 but B and C return to only 110 pieces per day. Other things being equal, we can infer that A's new rate was completely dependent on his supervisor whereas

---

[4] Miller (33) assumes that all living systems have this character. However, it may be that some systems in the life space do not have this elasticity.

the new rate of B and C was dependent on the supervisor only to the extent of 5 pieces. Let us further assume that when the supervisor returned, the production of B and of C returned to 115 without further orders from the supervisor. Now another month goes by during which B and C maintain a steady 115 pieces per day. However, there is a difference between them: B's level of production still depends on O to the extent of 5 pieces whereas C has come to rely on his own sense of obligation to obey the order of his legitimate supervisor rather than on the supervisor's external pressure for the maintenance of his 115 pieces per day. Accordingly, the next time the supervisor departs, B's production again drops to 110 but C's remains at 115 pieces per day. In cases like employee B, the degree of dependence is contingent on the perceived probability that O will observe the state of the system and note P's conformity **(5, 6, 11, 12, 23)**. The level of observability will in turn depend on both the nature of the system (e.g., the difference between a covert opinion and overt behavior) and on the environmental barriers to observation (e.g., O is too far away from P). In other cases, for example that of employee C, the new behavior pattern is highly dependent on his supervisor, but the degree of dependence of the new state will be related not to the level of observability but rather to factors inside P, in this case a sense of duty to perform an act legitimately prescribed by O. The internalization of social norms is a related process of decreasing degree of dependence of behavior on an external O and increasing dependence on an internal value; it is usually assumed that internalization is accompanied by a decrease in the effects of level of observability **(37)**.

The concepts "dependence of a system on O" and "observability as a basis for dependence" will be useful in understanding the stability of conformity. In the next section we shall discuss various types of power and the types of conformity which they are likely to produce.

THE BASES OF POWER

By the basis of power we mean the relationship between O and P which is the source of that power. It is rare that we can say with certainty that a given empirical case of power is limited to one source. Normally, the relation between O and P will be characterized by several qualitatively different variables which are bases of power **(30**, Chapter 11). Although there are undoubtedly many possible bases of power which may be distinguished, we shall here define five which seem especially common and important. These five bases of O's power are: (1) reward power, based on P's perception that

O has the ability to mediate rewards for him; (2) coercive power, based on P's perception that O has the ability to mediate punishments for him; (3) legitimate power, based on the perception by P that O has a legitimate right to prescribe behavior for him; (4) referent power, based on P's identification with O; (5) expert power, based on the perception that O has some special knowledge or expertness.

Our first concern is to define the bases which give rise to a given type of power. Next, we describe each type of power according to its strength, range, and the degree of dependence of the new state of the system which is most likely to occur with each type of power. We shall also examine the other effects which the exercise of a given type of power may have upon P and his relationship to O. Finally, we shall point out the interrelationships between different types of power, and the effects of use of one type of power by O upon other bases of power which he might have over P. Thus we shall both define a set of concepts and propose a series of hypotheses. Most of these hypotheses have not been systematically tested, although there is a good deal of evidence in favor of several. No attempt will be made to summarize that evidence here.

Reward Power

Reward power is defined as power whose basis is the ability to reward. The strength of the reward power of O/P increases with the magnitude of the rewards which P perceives that O can mediate for him. Reward power depends on O's ability to administer positive valences and to remove or decrease negative valences. The strength of reward power also depends upon the probability that O can mediate the reward, as perceived by P. A common example of reward power is the addition of a piece-work rate in the factory as an incentive to increase production.

The new state of the system induced by a promise of reward (for example the factory worker's increased level of production) will be highly dependent on O. Since O mediates the reward, he controls the probability that P will receive it. Thus P's new rate of production will be dependent on his subjective probability that O will reward him for conformity minus his subjective probability that O will reward him even if he returns to his old level. Both probabilities will be greatly affected by the level of observability of P's behavior. Incidentally, a piece rate often seems to have more effect on production than a merit rating system because it yields a higher probability of reward for conformity and a much lower probability of reward for nonconformity.

The utilization of actual rewards (instead of promises) by O will tend over time to increase the attraction of P toward O and therefore the referent power of O over P. As we shall note later, such referent power will permit O to induce changes which are relatively independent. Neither rewards nor promises will arouse resistance in P, provided P considers it legitimate for O to offer rewards.

The range of reward power is specific to those regions within which O can reward P for conforming. The use of rewards to change systems within the range of reward power tends to increase reward power by increasing the probability attached to future promises. However, unsuccessful attempts to exert reward power outside the range of power would tend to decrease the power; for example if O offers to reward P for performing an impossible act, this will reduce for P the probability of receiving future rewards promised by O.

Coercive Power

Coercive power is similar to reward power in that it also involves O's ability to manipulate the attainment of valences. Coercive power of O/P stems from the expectation on the part of P that he will be punished by O if he fails to conform to the influence attempt. Thus negative valences will exist in given regions of P's life space, corresponding to the threatened punishment by O. The strength of coercive power depends on the magnitude of the negative valence of the threatened punishment multiplied by the perceived probability that P can avoid the punishment by conformity, i.e., the probability of punishment for nonconformity minus the probability of punishment for conformity (11). Just as an offer of a piece-rate bonus in a factory can serve as a basis for reward power, so the ability to fire a worker if he falls below a given level of production will result in coercive power.

Coercive power leads to dependent change also; and the degree of dependence varies with the level of observability of P's conformity. An excellent illustration of coercive power leading to dependent change is provided by a clothes presser in a factory observed by Coch and French (3). As her efficiency rating climbed above average for the group the other workers began to "scapegoat" her. That the resulting plateau in her production was not independent of the group was evident once she was removed from the presence of the other workers. Her production immediately climbed to new heights.[5]

[5] Though the primary influence of coercive power is dependent, it often produces secondary changes which are independent. Brainwashing, for example, utilizes coercive power to produce many primary changes in the life space of the prisoner, but these dependent changes can lead to identification with the aggressor and hence to secondary changes in ideology which are independent.

At times, there is some difficulty in distinguishing between reward power and coercive power. Is the withholding of a reward really equivalent to a punishment? Is the withdrawal of punishment equivalent to a reward? The answer must be a psychological one—it depends upon the situation as it exists for P. But ordinarily we would answer these questions in the affirmative; for P, receiving a reward is a positive valence as is the relief of suffering. There is some evidence that conformity to group norms in order to gain acceptance (reward power) should be distinguished from conformity as a means of forestalling rejection (coercive power) (5).

The distinction between these two types of power is important because the dynamics are different. The concept of "sanctions" sometimes lumps the two together despite their opposite effects. While reward power may eventually result in an independent system, the effects of coercive power will continue to be dependent. Reward power will tend to increase the attraction of P toward O; coercive power will decrease this attraction (11, 12). The valence of the region of behavior will become more negative, acquiring some negative valence from the threatened punishment. The negative valence of punishment would also spread to other regions of the life space. Lewin (25) has pointed out this distinction between the effects of rewards and punishment. In the case of threatened punishment, there will be a resultant force on P to leave the field entirely. Thus, to achieve conformity, O must not only place a strong negative valence in certain regions through threat of punishment, but O must also introduce restraining forces, or other strong valences, so as to prevent P from withdrawing completely from O's range of coercive power. Otherwise the probability of receiving the punishment, if P does not conform, will be too low to be effective.

Legitimate Power

Legitimate power is probably the most complex of those treated here, embodying notions from the structural sociologist, the group-norm and role oriented social psychologist, and the clinical psychologist.

There has been considerable investigation and speculation about socially prescribed behavior, particularly that which is specific to a given role or position. Linton (29) distinguishes group norms according to whether they are universals for everyone in the culture, alternatives (the individual having a choice as to whether or not to accept them), or specialties (specific to given positions). Whether we speak of internalized norms, role prescriptions and expectations (34), or internalized pressures (15), the fact remains that each individual sees certain regions toward which he should locomote, some regions toward which he should not locomote, and some regions toward which he may locomote if they are generally attractive for him. This applies to specific behaviors in which he may, should, or should not engage; it applies to certain attitudes or beliefs which he may, should, or should not hold. The feeling of "oughtness" may be an internalization from his parents, from his teachers, from his religion, or may have been logically developed from some idiosyncratic system of ethics. He will speak of such behaviors with expressions like "should," "ought to," or "has a right to." In many cases, the original source of the requirement is not recalled.

Though we have oversimplified such evaluations of behavior with a positive-neutral-negative trichotomy, the evaluation of behaviors by the person is really more one of degree. This dimension of evaluation, we shall call "legitimacy." Conceptually, we may think of legitimacy as a valence in a region which is induced by some internalized norm or value. This value has the same conceptual property as power, namely an ability to induce force fields (**26,** p. 40-41). It may or may not be correct that values (or the superego) are internalized parents, but at least they can set up force fields which have a phenomenal "oughtness" similar to a parent's prescription. Like a value, a need can also induce valences (i.e., force fields) in P's psychological environment, but these valences have more the phenomenal character of noxious or attractive properties of the object or activity. When a need induces a valence in P, for example, when a need makes an object attractive to P, this attraction applies to P but not to other persons. When a value induces a valence, on the other hand, it not only sets up forces on P to engage in the activity, but P may feel that all others ought to behave in the same way. Among other things, this evaluation applies to the legitimate right of some other individual or group to prescribe behavior or beliefs for a person even though the other cannot apply sanctions.

Legitimate power of O/P is here defined as that power which stems from internalized values in P which dictate that O has a legitimate right to influence P and that P has an obligation to accept this influence. We note that legitimate power is very similar to the notion of legitimacy of authority which has long been explored by sociologists, particularly by Weber (**42**), and more recently by Goldhammer and Shils (**14**). However, legitimate power is not always a role relation: P may accept an induction from O simply because he had previously promised to help O and he values his word too much to break the promise. In all cases, the notion of legitimacy involves some sort of code or standard, accepted by the individual, by virtue of which the external agent can assert his power. We shall attempt to describe a few of these values here.

Bases for legitimate power. Cultural values constitute one common basis for the legitimate power of one individual over another. O has characteristics which are specified by the culture as giving him the right to prescribe behavior for P, who may not have these characteristics. These bases, which Weber **(42)** has called the authority of the "eternal yesterday," include such things as age, intelligence, caste, and physical characteristics. In some cultures, the aged are granted the right to prescribe behavior for others in practically all behavior areas. In most cultures, there are certain areas of behavior in which a person of one sex is granted the right to prescribe behavior for the other sex.

Acceptance of the social structure is another basis for legitimate power. If P accepts as right the social structure of his group, organization, or society, especially the social structure involving a hierarchy of authority, P will accept the legitimate authority of O who occupies a superior office in the hierarchy. Thus legitimate power in a formal organization is largely a relationship between offices rather than between persons. And the acceptance of an office as *right* is a basis for legitimate power—a judge has a right to levy fines, a foreman should assign work, a priest is justified in prescribing religious beliefs, and it is the management's prerogative to make certain decisions **(10)**. However, legitimate power also involves the perceived right of the person to hold the office.

Designation by a legitimizing agent is a third basis for legitimate power. An influencer O may be seen as legitimate in prescribing behavior for P because he has been granted such power by a legitimizing agent whom P accepts. Thus a department head may accept the authority of his vice-president in a certain area because that authority has been specifically delegated by the president. An election is perhaps the most common example of a group's serving to legitimize the authority of one individual or office for other individuals in the group. The success of such legitimizing depends upon the acceptance of the legitimizing agent and procedure. In this case it depends ultimately on certain democratic values concerning election procedures. The election process is one of legitimizing a person's right to an office which already has a legitimate range of power associated with it.

Range of legitimate power of O/P. The areas in which legitimate power may be exercised are generally specified along with the designation of that power. A job description, for example, usually specifies supervisory activities and also designates the person to whom the job-holder is responsible for the duties described. Some bases for legitimate authority carry with them a very broad range. Culturally derived bases for legitimate power are often especially broad. It is not uncommon to find cultures in which a member of a given caste can legitimately prescribe behavior for all members of lower castes in practically all regions. More common, however, are instances of legitimate power where the range is specifically and narrowly prescribed. A sergeant in the army is given a specific set of regions within which he can legitimately prescribe behavior for his men.

The attempted use of legitimate power which is outside of the range of legitimate power will decrease the legitimate power of the authority figure. Such use of power which is not legitimate will also decrease the attractiveness of O (11, 12, 36).

Legitimate power and influence. The new state of the system which results from legitimate power usually has high dependence on O though it may become independent. Here, however, the degree of dependence is not related to the level of observability. Since legitimate power is based on P's values, the source of the forces induced by O include both these internal values and O. O's induction serves to activate the values and to relate them to the system which is influenced, but thereafter the new state of the system may become directly dependent on the values with no mediation by O. Accordingly this new state will be relatively stable and consistent across varying environmental situations since P's values are more stable than his psychological environment.

We have used the term legitimate not only as a basis for the power of an agent, but also to describe the general behaviors of a person. Thus, the individual P may also consider the legitimacy of the attempts to use other types of power by O. In certain cases, P will consider that O has a legitimate right to threaten punishment for nonconformity; in other cases, such use of coercion would not be seen as legitimate. P might change in response to coercive power of O, but it will make a considerable difference in his attitude and conformity if O is not seen as having a legitimate right to use such coercion. In such cases, the attraction of P for O will be particularly diminished, and the influence attempt will arouse more resistance (11). Similarly the utilization of reward power may vary in legitimacy; the word "bribe," for example, denotes an illegitimate reward.

Referent Power

The referent power of O/P has its basis in the identification of P with O. By identification, we mean a feeling of oneness of P with O, or a desire for such an identity. If O is a person toward whom P is highly attracted, P will have a desire to become closely associated with O. If O is an attractive group, P will have a feeling of membership or a desire to join. If P is already closely associated with O he will want to maintain this relationship (39, 41).

P's identification with O can be established or maintained if P behaves, believes, and perceives as O does. Accordingly O has the ability to influence P, even though P may be unaware of this referent power. A verbalization of such power by P might be, "I am like O, and therefore I shall behave or believe as O does," or "I want to be like O, and I will be more like O if I behave or believe as O does." The stronger the identification of P with O the greater the referent power of O/P.

Similar types of power have already been investigated under a number of different formulations. Festinger (7) points out that in an ambiguous situation, the individual seeks some sort of "social reality" and may adopt the cognitive structure of the individual or group with which he identifies. In such a case, the lack of clear structure may be threatening to the individual and the agreement of his beliefs with those of a reference group will both satisfy his need for structure and give him added security through increased identification with his group (16, 19).

We must try to distinguish between referent power and other types of power which might be operative at the same time. If a member is attracted to a group and he conforms to its norms only because he fears ridicule or expulsion from the group for nonconformity, we would call this coercive power. On the other hand if he conforms in order to obtain praise for conformity, it is a case of reward power. The basic criterion for distinguishing referent power from both coercive and reward power is the mediation of the punishment and the reward by O: to the extent that O mediates the sanctions (i.e., has means control over P) we are dealing with coercive and reward power; but to the extent that P avoids discomfort or gains satisfaction by conformity based on identification, regardless of O's responses, we are dealing with referent power. Conformity with majority opinion is sometimes based on a respect for the collective wisdom of the group, in which case it is expert power. It is important to distinguish these phenomena, all grouped together elsewhere as "pressures toward uniformity," since the type of change which occurs will be different for different bases of power.

The concepts of "reference group" (40) and "prestige suggestion" may be treated as instances of referent power. In this case, O, the prestigeful person or group, is valued by P; because P desires to be associated or identified with O, he will assume attitudes or beliefs held by O. Similarly a negative reference group which O dislikes and evaluates negatively may exert negative influence on P as a result of negative referent power.

It has been demonstrated that the power which we designate as referent power is especially great when P is attracted to O (2, 7, 8, 9, 13, 23, 30).

In our terms, this would mean that the greater the attraction, the greater the identification, and consequently the greater the referent power. In some cases, attraction or prestige may have a specific basis, and the range of referent power will be limited accordingly: a group of campers may have great referent power over a member regarding campcraft, but considerably less effect on other regions (30). However, we hypothesize that the greater the attraction of P toward O, the broader the range of referent power of O/P.

The new state of a system produced by referent power may be dependent on or independent of O; but the degree of dependence is not affected by the level of observability to O (6, 23). In fact, P is often not consciously aware of the referent power which O exerts over him. There is probably a tendency for some of these dependent changes to become independent of O quite rapidly.

Expert Power

The strength of the expert power of O/P varies with the extent of the knowledge or perception which P attributes to O within a given area. Probably P evaluates O's expertness in relation to his own knowledge as well as against an absolute standard. In any case expert power results in primary social influence on P's cognitive structure and probably not on other types of systems. Of course changes in the cognitive structure can change the direction of forces and hence of locomotion, but such a change of behavior is secondary social influence. Expert power has been demonstrated experimentally (8, 33). Accepting an attorney's advice in legal matters is a common example of expert influence; but there are many instances based on much less knowledge, such as the acceptance by a stranger of directions given by a native villager.

Expert power, where O need not be a member of P's group, is called "informational power" by Deutsch and Gerard (4). This type of expert power must be distinguished from influence based on the content of communication as described by Hovland et al. (17, 18, 23, 24). The influence of the content of a communication upon an opinion is presumably a secondary influence produced after the *primary* influence (i.e., the acceptance of the information). Since power is here defined in terms of the primary changes, the influence of the content on a related opinion is not a case of expert power as we have defined it, but the initial acceptance of the validity of the content does seem to be based on expert power or referent power. In other cases, however, so-called facts may be accepted as self-evident because they fit into P's cognitive structure; if this impersonal acceptance of the truth of the fact is independent of the more or less enduring relationship between O and P, then P's acceptance of the fact is not an actualization of expert power. Thus we distinguish between expert power based on the credibility of O and informational influence which is based on charactertistics of the stimulus such as the logic of the argument or the "self-evident facts."

Wherever expert influence occurs it seems to be necessary both for P to think that O knows and for P to trust that O is telling the truth (rather than trying to deceive him).

Expert power will produce a new cognitive structure which is initially relatively dependent on O, but informational influence will produce a more independent structure. The former is likely to become more independent with the passage of time. In both cases the degree of dependence on O is not affected by the level of observability.

The "sleeper effect" (18, 24) is an interesting case of a change in the degree of dependence of an opinion on O. An unreliable O (who probably had negative referent power but some positive expert power) presented "facts" which were accepted by the subjects and which would normally produce secondary influence on their opinions and beliefs. However, the negative referent power aroused resistance and resulted in negative social influence on their beliefs (i.e., set up a force in the direction opposite to the influence attempt), so that there was little change in the subjects' opinions. With the passage of time, however, the subjects tended to forget the identity of the negative communicator faster than they forgot the contents of his communication, so there was a weakening of the negative referent influence and a consequent delayed positive change in the subjects' beliefs in the direction of the influence attempt ("sleeper effect"). Later, when the identity of the negative communicator was experimentally reinstated, these resisting forces were reinstated, and there was another negative change in belief in a direction opposite to the influence attempt (24).

The range of expert power, we assume, is more delimited than that of referent power. Not only is it restricted to cognitive systems but the expert is seen as having superior knowledge or ability in very specific areas, and his power will be limited to these areas, though some "halo effect" might occur. Recently, some of our renowned physical scientists have found quite painfully that their expert power in physical sciences does not extend to regions involving international politics. Indeed, there is some evidence that the attempted exertion of expert power outside of the range of expert power will reduce that expert power. An undermining of confidence seems to take place.

Summary

We have distinguished five types of power: referent power, expert power, reward power, coercive power, and legitimate power. These distinctions led to the following hypotheses.

1. For all five types, the stronger the basis of power the greater the power.

2. For any type of power the size of the range may vary greatly, but in general referent power will have the broadest range.

3. Any attempt to utilize power outside the range of power will tend to reduce the power.

4. A new state of a system produced by reward power or coercive power will be highly dependent on O, and the more observable P's conformity the more dependent the state. For the other three types of power, the new state is usually dependent, at least in the beginning, but in any case the level of observability has no effect on the degree of dependence.

5. Coercion results in decreased attraction of P toward O and high resistance; reward power results in increased attraction and low resistance.

6. The more legitimate the coercion the less it will produce resistance and decreased attraction.

REFERENCES

1. Asch, S. E. *Social psychology.* New York: Prentice-Hall, 1952.

2. Back, K. W. Influence through social communication. *J. abnorm. soc. Psychol.,* 1951, **46**, 9-23.

3. Coch, L., & French, J. R. P., Jr. Overcoming resistance to change. *Hum. Relat.,* 1948, **1**, 512-32.

4. Deutsch, M., & Gerard, H. B. A study of normative and informational influences upon individual judgment. *J. abnorm. soc. Psychol.,* 1955, **51**, 629-36.

5. Dittes, J. E., & Kelley, H. H. Effects of different conditions of acceptance upon conformity to group norms. *J. abnorm. soc. Psychol.,* 1956, **53**, 100-107.

6. Festinger, L. An analysis of compliant behavior. In Sherif, M., & Wilson, M. O., (Eds.). *Group relations at the crossroads.* New York: Harper, 1953, 232-56.

7. Festinger, L. Informal social communication. *Psychol. Rev.,* 1950, **57**, 271-82.

8. Festinger, L., Gerard, H. B., Hymovitch, B. Kelley, H. H., & Raven, B. H. The influence process in the presence of extreme deviates. *Hum. Relat.,* 1952, **5**, 327-346.

9. Festinger, L., Schachter, S., & Back, K. The operation of group standards. In Cartwright, D., & Zander, A. *Group dynamics: research and theory.* Evanston: Row, Peterson, 1953, 204-23.

10. French, J. R. P., Jr., Israel, Joachim & As, Dagfinn "Arbeidernes medvirkning i industribedriften. En eksperimentell undersøkelse." Institute for Social Research, Oslo, Norway, 1957.

11. French, J. R. P., Jr., Levinger, G., & Morrison, H. W. The legitimacy of coercive power. In preparation.

12. French, J. R. P., Jr., & Raven, B. H. An experiment in legitimate and coercive power. In preparation.

13. Gerard, H. B. The anchorage of opinions in face-to-face groups. *Hum. Relat.*, 1954, **7**, 313-325.

14. Goldhammer, H., & Shils, E. A. Types of power and status. *Amer. J. Sociol.*, 1939, **45**, 171-178.

15. Herbst, P. G. Analysis and measurement of a situation. *Hum. Relat.*, 1953, **2**, 113-140.

16. Hochbaum, G. M. Self-confidence and reactions to group pressures. *Amer. soc. Rev.*, 1954, **19**, 678-687.

17. Hovland, C. I., Lumsdaine, A. A., & Sheffield, F. D. *Experiments on mass communication*. Princeton: Princeton Univer. Press, 1949.

18. Hovland, C. I., & Weiss, W. The influence of source credibility on communication effectiveness. *Publ. Opin. Quart.*, 1951, **15**, 635-650.

19. Jackson, J. M., & Saltzstein, H. D. The effect of person-group relationships on conformity processes. *J. abnorm. soc. Psychol.*, 1958, **57**, 17-24.

20. Jahoda, M. Psychological issues in civil liberties. *Amer. Psychologist*, 1956, **11**, 234-240.

21. Katz, D., & Schank, R. L. *Social psychology*. New York: Wiley, 1938.

22. Kelley, H. H., & Volkart, E. H. The resistance to change of group-anchored attitudes. *Amer. soc. Rev.*, 1952, **17**, 453-465.

23. Kelman, H. Three processes of acceptance of social influence: compliance, identification and internalization. Paper read at the meetings of the American Psychological Association, August 1956.

24. Kelman, H., & Hovland, C. I. "Reinstatement" of the communicator in delayed measurement of opinion change. *J. abnorm. soc. Psychol.*, 1953, **48**, 327-335.

25. Lewin, K. *Dynamic theory of personality*. New York: McGraw-Hill, 1935, 114-170.

26. Lewin, K. *Field theory in social science*. New York: Harper, 1951.

27. Lewin, K., Lippitt, R., & White, R. K. Patterns of aggressive behavior in experimentally created social climates. *J. soc. Psychol.*, 1939, **10**, 271-301.

28. Lasswell, H. D., & Kaplan, A. *Power and society: A framework for political inquiry*. New Haven: Yale Univer. Press, 1950.

29. Linton, R. *The cultural background of personality*. New York: Appleton-Century-Crofts, 1945.

30. Lippitt, R., Polansky, N., Redl, F., & Rosen, S. The dynamics of power. *Hum. Relat.*, 1952, **5**, 37-64.

31. March, J. G. An introduction to the theory and measurement of influence. *Amer. polit. Sci. Rev.*, 1955, **49**, 431-451.

32. Miller, J. G. Toward a general theory for the behavioral sciences. *Amer. Psychologist*, 1955, **10**, 513-531.

33. Moore, H. T. The comparative influence of majority and expert opinion. *Amer. J. Psychol.*, 1921, **32**, 16-20.

34. Newcomb, T. M. *Social psychology*. New York: Dryden, 1950.

35. Raven, B. H. The effect of group pressures on opinion, perception, and communication. Unpublished doctoral dissertation, University of Michigan, 1953.

36. Raven, B. H., & French, J. R. P., Jr. Group support, legitimate power, and social influence. *J. Person.*, 1958, **26**, 400-409.

37. Rommetveit, R. *Social norms and roles.* Minneapolis: Univer. Minnesota Press, 1953.

38. Russell, B. *Power: A new social analysis.* New York: Norton, 1938.

39. Stotland, E., Zander, A., Burnstein, E., Wolfe, D., & Natsoulas, T. Studies on the effects of identification. University of Michigan, Institute for Social Research. Forthcoming.

40. Swanson, G. E., Newcomb, T. M., & Hartley, E. L. *Readings in social psychology.* New York: Henry Holt, 1952.

41. Torrance, E. P., & Mason, R. Instructor effort to influence: an experimental evaluation of six approaches. Paper presented at USAF-NRC Symposium on Personnel, Training, and Human Engineering. Washington, D. C., 1956.

42. Weber, M. *The theory of social and economic organization.* Oxford: Oxford Univer. Press, 1947.

Journal of Applied Psychology
1990, Vol. 75, No. 2, 132–140

Influence Tactics and Objectives in Upward, Downward, and Lateral Influence Attempts

Gary Yukl and Cecilia M. Falbe
Management Department
State University of New York at Albany

Two studies were conducted to replicate and extend previous exploratory research by Kipnis, Schmidt, and Wilkinson (1980) on influence tactics and objectives in organizations. A new questionnaire was developed that included measures of important influence tactics and objectives omitted in the earlier research. Whereas the earlier research used only agent self-reports of influence behavior, the present research used both agent and target reports. Differences in downward, lateral, and upward influence attempts were replicated more for data from agents than for data from targets. Direction of influence had a stronger effect on influence objectives than on influence tactics. Despite some differences due to data source and direction of influence, the relative frequency of use for the 8 influence tactics was remarkably similar across conditions. Consultation and rational persuasion were the tactics used most frequently, regardless of the direction of influence.

One of the most important determinants of managerial effectiveness is success in influencing subordinates, peers, and superiors. Despite the obvious importance of this subject, there has been very little empirical research on the influence behavior of managers. Considerable research has been conducted on sources of managerial power (see Podsakoff & Schriesheim, 1985), but only a few studies have examined issues such as the types of influence tactics used by managers and the objectives of their influence attempts (Kipnis, Schmidt, & Wilkinson, 1980; Mowday, 1978; Schilit & Locke, 1982).

In the exploratory study by Kipnis et al. (1980), a questionnaire was developed to measure categories of influence behavior (called *influence tactics*) and common reasons for making influence attempts in organizations (called *influence objectives*). The questionnaire was administered to a sample of night students, and each respondent described how often he or she used the influence tactics in influence attempts with a particular subordinate, peer, or superior. On the basis of the results of their exploratory research, Kipnis et al. concluded that managers tend to use different tactics and to have somewhat different objectives depending on the direction of influence. This study was an important first step but, like all exploratory research, the findings need to be verified and the potential limitations examined. Up until now the conclusions have been reported in many textbooks as established facts about influence tactics in organizations rather than as tentative findings from a single exploratory study. Moreover, subsequent studies have used the influence questionnaire to examine other types of research questions (Ansari & Kapoor, 1987; Erez & Rim, 1982) and as the basis for developing a typology of managers based on patterns of tactics (Kipnis & Schmidt, 1988).

There are a number of limitations and potential problems in the Kipnis et al. study. First, the items in their questionnaire

were based on examples described by students, and the range of influence tactics measured by the questionnaire is too narrow. Their questionnaire does not include some influence tactics found to be relevant for leadership effectiveness. Second, their list of influence objectives needs to be extended to include others central to managerial work. Third, the research examined only self-perception of influence tactics and objectives. The possibility of systematic biases in these self-reports has not been examined. For example, respondents may have exaggerated their use of socially desirable influence tactics, such as rational persuasion, and understated their use of less acceptable tactics, such as coercive pressure. Likewise, respondents may have been biased to select as their target someone toward whom they were more likely to use socially desirable influence tactics.

The present research had the following two major objectives: (a) to determine if the major findings in the Kipnis et al. study could be replicated with differences in methodology, and (b) to extend the research to include additional types of influence behavior and objectives. This article describes preliminary research to develop new measures and two studies designed to address the potential limitations in the earlier research by Kipnis et al.

Development of the Measures

Influence Tactics

Preliminary research was conducted to pretest and refine a more comprehensive questionnaire for measuring influence tactics. All of the items in our questionnaire were new, but included among them were items representing six of the eight scales in the Kipnis et al. study: assertiveness, rationality, ingratiation, exchange, upward appeals, and coalitions. Two of their scales ("sanctions" and "blocking") were not represented in our questionnaire because of conceptual problems and infrequent use. Most of their sanctions items (e.g., giving a pay increase or promotion, suspending or firing the target) are reactions to something the target has already done rather than specific, pro-

Correspondence concerning this article should be addressed to Gary Yukl, Management Department, School of Business, SUNY, Albany, New York 12222.

active influence attempts. In their study, sanctions were used infrequently with subordinates (the mean item score in their study was 1.3 on a scale of 1 to 5) and not at all with peers or superiors (the mean item score was 1.0). Their blocking tactic was used infrequently with coworkers (mean item score was 1.7) and almost never with superiors and subordinates (mean item scores were 1.1). The three blocking items with highest factor loadings appear to be examples of pressure tactics (threaten to stop working with the person, engage in work slowdown, threaten to notify an outside agency). In their more recent research, Kipnis and his associates (Kipnis & Schmidt, 1988) no longer include blocking as one of their influence tactics. Thus, there seemed little point to include either sanctions or blocking when the questionnaire space could be devoted to more relevant influence tactics.

The new questionnaire included items representing two influence tactics not found in the Kipnis et al. questionnaire but likely to be important, namely, inspirational appeals and consultation. The major source of behavior examples for items representing these tactics was the literature on managerial leadership. Inspirational appeals to values and emotions are an important aspect of charismatic and transformational leadership (Bass, 1985; Bennis & Nanus, 1985; Conger & Kanungo, 1988; House, 1977; Tichy & Devanna, 1986). Inspirational appeals include (a) use of emotional, symbolic language to emphasize the importance of a new project or task, (b) appeals to the target person's sense of justice, humanitarianism, or organizational loyalty, and (c) appeals to the person's desire to excel, to beat competitors, or to accomplish an important, challenging task. Research on inspirational behavior by leaders is still in the exploratory stage, but there is strong indication that this influence tactic may be an effective approach for gaining subordinate commitment to a leader's objectives and strategies.

Consultation is a form of leadership behavior that has been studied extensively during the last 3 decades (Bass, 1985; Yukl, 1989). It is widely accepted that managers are sometimes able to influence people to accept a decision by involving them in the process of making it, or at least in the process of planning how to implement it (Bradford & Cohen, 1984; Cotton, Vollrath, Froggatt, Lengnick-Hall, & Jennings, 1988; Vroom & Jago, 1988; Vroom & Yetton, 1973). The mechanism for influence through participation is not very well understood, but when a person is invited to help decide what to do and how to do it, the person is likely to identify with the decision and try to make it successful. Although consultation is not always successful, it is an important, widely used tactic for influencing commitment to a decision (Heller, 1971).

As in the Kipnis et al. study, the response choices for each item in our questionnaire indicated the frequency of use for the type of influence behavior described by the item. The preliminary questionnaire was administered to a sample of 293 target respondents that included both night master's of business administration (MBA) students and managers in several companies. Respondents were asked to use the questionnaire to describe the influence behavior of a peer or their boss. The questionnaire was revised and shortened after a variety of analyses, including factor analysis, item analysis, Q-sorts, and classification of items into predetermined scales by judges. Because the purpose was to replicate and extend the Kipnis et al. research,

Table 1
Scale Definitions of Influence Tactics

Scale	Definition
Pressure Tactics	The person uses demands, threats, or intimidation to convince you to comply with a request or to support a proposal. (Similar to *assertiveness*)
Upward Appeals	The person seeks to persuade you that the request is approved by higher management, or appeals to higher management for assistance in gaining your compliance with the request. (Similar to *upward appeal*)
Exchange Tactics	The person makes an explicit or implicit promise that you will receive rewards or tangible benefits if you comply with a request or support a proposal, or reminds you of a prior favor to be reciprocated. (Similar to *exchange*)
Coalition Tactics	The person seeks the aid of others to persuade you to do something or uses the support of others as an argument for you to agree also. (Similar to *coalitions*)
Ingratiating Tactics	The person seeks to get you in a good mood or to think favorably of him or her before asking you to do something. (Similar to *ingratiation*)
Rational Persuasion	The person uses logical arguments and factual evidence to persuade you that a proposal or request is viable and likely to result in the attainment of task objectives. (Similar to *rationality*)
Inspirational Appeals	The person makes an emotional request or proposal that arouses enthusiasm by appealing to your values and ideals, or by increasing your confidence that you can do it.
Consultation Tactics	The person seeks your participation in making a decision or planning how to implement a proposed policy, strategy, or change.

the grouping of items into scales was strongly influenced by their scale definitions and item content.

The revised questionnaire had scales measuring eight influence tactics, the definitions of which are shown in Table 1. The correlations among scales (see Table 2) indicate that the eight tactics are sufficiently independent to be regarded as distinct forms of influence behavior.

Each of the scales in the revised questionnaire had four or five items. Parallel versions of the questionnaire were developed for agents and targets. Both versions had the same items, but minor changes in wording were needed to make the questionnaire suitable for respondents to describe someone else's influence tactics rather than their own. The only other difference between the two versions was a *not applicable* option in the target version that did not appear in the agent version. The following response choices were used in the target version of the revised questionnaire:

NA   Not applicable; the behavior is something this person cannot do in my organization.

1   Never uses this tactic under any circumstances

2   Seldom uses this tactic (only once or twice a year)

3   Uses this tactic occasionally (several times a year)

Table 2
Intercorrelations of Influence Tactics

Variable	1	2	3	4	5	6	7	8
1. Pressure tactics	—							
2. Upward appeals	.50	—						
3. Exchange tactics	.11	.18	—					
4. Coalition tactics	.16	.31	.15	—				
5. Ingratiating tactics	.19	.17	.44	.27	—			
6. Rational persuasion	.03	.10	.20	.51	.25	—		
7. Inspirational appeals	.20	.11	.31	.37	.44	.49	—	
8. Consultation	-.24	-.16	.15	.37	.18	.52	.36	—

4   Uses this tactic moderately often (every few weeks)
5   Uses this tactic very often (almost every week)

A sample item from each scale in the target version is listed as follows:

1. Confronts you and demands that you carry out a requested action promptly. (pressure)

2. Complains to someone in higher authority if you do not carry out a requested action. (upward appeal)

3. Indicates that he/she will do a favor for you in return for doing what he/she wants. (exchange)

4. Gets other people to provide evidence to you supporting a plan or proposal that he/she wants you to help implement. (coalition)

5. Compliments you on past accomplishments before asking you to do another task. (ingratiation)

6. Provides evidence that the actions he/she is proposing will lead to the successful completion of a task or project. (rational persuasion)

7. Describes a proposed task or project with enthusiasm and conviction that it is important and worthwhile. (inspirational appeal)

8. Tells you what he/she is trying to accomplish and asks if you know a good way to do it. (consultation)

Influence Objectives

Another purpose of the preliminary research was to develop a more comprehensive and relevant list of influence objectives. Studies on the nature of managerial work (Kanter, 1982; Kaplan, 1986; Kotter, 1982; McCall & Segrist, 1980; Mintzberg, 1973; Pavett & Lau, 1983) suggest that an important component of this work is influencing other members of the organization. A manager's effectiveness depends on success in influencing others to (a) modify their plans and schedules, (b) approve and support the manager's plans and proposals, (c) provide additional resources needed to accomplish major tasks, (d) accept and carry out new assignments, and (e) provide relevant and timely information. Some of these influence objectives are not represented as separate items in the Kipnis et al. questionnaire.

The preliminary questionnaire had 12 influence objectives. This list was shortened and revised after examination of frequency scores, intercorrelations among objectives, and judges' ratings of relevance. The following eight objectives were selected for the revised questionnaire, as compared with only five in the Kipnis et al. study:

1. Ask the person to do a new task or work on a new project or account.

2. Ask the person to do a task faster or better.

3. Ask the person to change his/her policies, plans, or procedures to accommodate your needs.

4. Ask the person to provide advice or help in solving a problem.

5. Ask the person to give or loan you additional resources such as funds, supplies, materials, or use of equipment, facilities, or personnel.

6. Ask the person to give a formal approval or signoff on a proposal, product, report, or document.

7. Ask the person to support your proposals in a meeting with other managers or clients.

8. Ask for information needed to do your work.

The questions about influence objectives appeared in a separate section of the questionnaire following the section on influence tactics. Respondents were asked to indicate how often their influence attempts have each type of objective. Response choices in the revised version were as follows:

NA   Not applicable
1   Never
2   Seldom (only once or twice a year)
3   Occasionally (several times a year)
4   Moderately often (every few weeks)
5   Very often (almost every week)

For both the influence tactics and objectives, a *Not Applicable* response was recoded as 1 before doing any analyses.

Study 1

This study is essentially a replication of the Kipnis et al. (1980) research on agent self-reports of influence attempts, using a new questionnaire with a broader range of influence tactics and objectives. As in their research, the primary design in this study was a comparison of influence tactics used in upward, downward, and lateral relations.

Hypotheses

The exploratory research by Kipnis et al. did not propose formal hypotheses, and their findings on directional differences were not interpreted. In any replication there is the implicit hypothesis that the same relationships will be found, but it is useful to consider whether there is a credible rationale for these findings. Prior theory and research were examined to determine if sufficient basis existed for making a priori hypotheses. Although prior research suggests the feasibility of the eight influence tactics for influence attempts in all three directions, there was a credible rationale for proposing six hypotheses about expected directional differences.

Hypothesis 1: Pressure tactics are used most often in downward influence attempts and least often in upward influence attempts. Pressure tactics are based on coercive power, and there is growing evidence that coercive power is used more frequently with subordinates than with peers or superiors (e.g., Kim & Yukl, 1989). The strongest directional difference found by Kipnis et al. was for assertiveness, which is similar to pressure tactics. Hypothesis 1 reflects their findings.

Hypothesis 2: Upward appeals are used more often in downward and lateral influence attempts than in upward influence attempts. Upward appeals are an attempt to invoke the authority and power of higher management by (a) telling the target you are acting on behalf of higher management, (b) threatening to go over the target's head (also a pressure tactic), or (c) directly asking superiors to help you influence the target (also a coalition tactic). Upward appeals are easier to use with subordinates and peers and are more likely to be successful (Sayles, 1989). When an agent claims to have the approval of higher management and the target is the agent's boss, the target is more likely to question the agent's credibility. Threats to go over the target's head and overt attempts at upward bypassing are more likely to have unfavorable repercussions for future relationships if the target is one's own boss rather than a peer or subordinate.

Hypothesis 3: Exchange tactics are used more often in downward and lateral influence attempts than in upward influence attempts. The concept of exchange implies that there is something of value to be traded. Managers usually have control over resources desired by subordinates, but it is less common for subordinates to control resources desired by a superior. Furthermore, it is awkward for subordinates to initiate an exchange with a superior, because resources under subordinate control are usually things they are expected to provide without additional rewards. With peers, the potential for exchange depends on the extent of task interdependence between them and their control over complementary resources. The potential for using exchange tactics is considerable when peers depend on each other for information, assistance, resources, approvals, political support, and cooperation to accomplish their task and personal objectives (Cohen & Bradford, 1989; Kaplan, 1984).

Hypothesis 4: Coalition tactics are used more often in upward and lateral influence attempts than in downward influence attempts. Managers usually have sufficient power and authority to influence subordinates without using coalitions. However, for (a) introducing innovations in an organization, (b) convincing superiors to change an unpopular policy or plan, and (c) influencing a peer over whom one has no authority, coalitions may be one of the most effective influence strategies (Izraeli, 1975; Kanter, 1982; Kotter, 1985; Mechanic, 1962; Pfeffer, 1981; Strauss, 1962).

Hypothesis 5: Inspirational appeals are used more often in downward influence attempts than in lateral or upward influence attempts. Inspirational appeals appear to be most appropriate for influencing somebody to (a) support an innovative proposal or change in strategy, (b) accept a difficult task or as-

signment, or (c) increase efforts on a task for which success is in doubt. The first type of influence objective may occur in downward, lateral, or upward influence attempts, but the latter two objectives are more likely to occur in downward influence attempts (Kipnis et al., 1980). Thus, inspirational appeals are most likely to be used in influence attempts with subordinates.

Hypothesis 6: Consultation is used most often in downward influence attempts and least often in upward influence attempts. Consultation appears to be most appropriate when a manager has authority to make a decision that must be implemented or supported by the target person (Vroom & Yetton, 1973). Because of the nature of authority relationships in hierarchical organizations, this situation is most likely to occur for a manager in relation to subordinates and least likely to occur in relation to superiors.

With regard to influence objectives, theoretical support was found for five hypotheses about directional differences. In formal organizations, work objectives and standards are usually determined by a top-down process, and influence attempts concerning them tend to follow the chain of command. Most managers have the authority to assign work to subordinates and establish performance standards for them. However, it is rare for work assignments to be made in an upward direction, and it is awkward for subordinates to request faster or better performance by their boss. In the case of interdependent units, a manager may have authority to ask peers to carry out their part of a joint activity, and the inputs provided by peers may be evaluated according to established standards of performance. Thus, the following two hypotheses appear reasonable and are consistent with results from the Kipnis et al. study.

Hypothesis 7: Requests to get someone to do a new task occur most often in downward influence attempts and least often in upward influence attempts.

Hypothesis 8: Requests for faster or better performance occur most often in downward influence attempts and least often in upward influence attempts.

The target of influence attempts involving resource allocation and approvals is usually the person who has authority to make these decisions. In hierarchical organizations, the authority to allocate resources, authorize decisions, and give formal approvals is greatest for managers in relation to subordinates, and least in relation to superiors. Although these objectives were not included in the Kipnis et al. research, the following hypotheses are reasonable.

Hypothesis 9: Requests for resources occur most often in upward influence attempts and least often in downward influence attempts.

Hypothesis 10: Requests for approvals or signoffs occur most often in upward influence attempts and least often in downward influence attempts.

The process of coalition formation includes attempts to get others to support one's proposals in meetings where the proposals will be accepted or rejected (Cohen & Bradford, 1989; Stevenson, Pearce, & Porter, 1985). Support is more likely to be sought from people who have considerable political power. Thus, the following hypothesis is proposed.

Hypothesis 11: Managers seek support for proposals more often from superiors and peers than from subordinates.

136   GARY YUKL AND CECILIA M. FALBE

Table 3
Mean Frequency of Influence Tactics as Reported by Agents

	Direction of influence attempt				
Influence tactic	Downward $(N = 62)$	Lateral $(N = 75)$	Upward $(N = 60)$	$F(2, 194)$	Eta^2
Pressure tactics	2.2$_a$	1.9$_b$	1.5$_c$	17.4**	15%
(Assertiveness)	(2.4$_a$)	(1.6$_b$)	(1.4$_c$)	(243.9**)	
Upward appeals	2.1$_a$	2.2$_a$	1.6$_b$	16.4**	14%
(Upward appeal)	(1.8$_a$)	(1.7$_a$)	(1.4$_b$)	(37.2**)	
Exchange tactics	1.6$_a$	1.7$_a$	1.4$_b$	6.5**	6%
(Exchange)	(2.0$_a$)	(2.0$_a$)	(1.7$_b$)	(13.5**)	
Coalition tactics	2.2	2.2	2.3	0.2	
(Coalitions)	(2.2)	(2.2)	(2.3)	0.1	
Ingratiating tactics	2.6$_a$	2.6$_a$	2.2$_b$	6.1**	6%
(Ingratiation)	(2.6$_a$)	(2.7$_a$)	(2.4$_b$)	(16.7**)	
Rational persuasion	3.3	3.2	3.3	0.5	
(Rationality)	(3.5$_b$)	(3.4$_b$)	(3.7$_a$)	(7.2**)	
Inspirational appeals	2.9$_a$	2.8$_{ab}$	2.5$_b$	4.2*	4%
Consultation	3.6$_a$	3.4$_{ab}$	3.3$_b$	3.7*	4%

Multivariate *F* test

Pillais criterion	5.2**
Hotelling's trace criterion	5.4**
Wilks's lambda	5.3**

Note. Means with different subscripts differ significantly at the .05 level by the Duncan multiple range test.
Results from Kipnis, Schmidt, and Wilkinson (1980) are shown in parentheses.
* $p < .05$. ** $p < .01$.

Method

The sample consisted of 197 respondents, including evening MBA students who worked in regular jobs during the day and managers who were attending management development courses. Respondents filled out the agent self-report version of the revised influence questionnaire in class. Respondents were asked to describe their own influence attempts with an upward, lateral, or downward target. The direction of influence in each case was determined randomly by the researchers. People not in their current job for at least 6 months were instructed not to answer the questionnaire. Respondents were assured that their responses would remain confidential.

Results

Scale reliabilities for the eight influence tactics, computed in terms of Cronbach's alpha, were as follows: .67 for pressure tactics, .67 for upward appeals, .61 for exchange, .70 for coalition tactics, .63 for ingratiation, .70 for rational persuasion, .79 for inspirational appeals, and .71 for consultation. The scale reliabilities are comparable with those found in the Kipnis et al. study. Table 3 shows the results for the multivariate and univariate analyses of variance (MANOVAs and ANOVAs). Results from the Kipnis et al. study for corresponding scales (expressed in terms of mean item scores) are also shown in Table 3 to facilitate comparison.

Most of the results found by Kipnis et al. for influence tactics were successfully replicated. Consistent with Hypothesis 1, pressure tactics were used most frequently in downward influence attempts and least frequently in upward influence attempts. Consistent with Hypotheses 2 and 3, upward appeals and exchange tactics were used less often in upward influence attempts than in downward or lateral influence attempts. Con-

trary to Hypothesis 4, but consistent with the findings by Kipnis et al., there were no significant directional differences for coalition tactics. Results for rational persuasion were also nonsignificant, and they failed to replicate the Kipnis et al. finding that this tactic was used more in upward influence attempts.

The eta squared values in Table 3 indicate the percentage of variance in each influence tactic accounted for by direction of influence. Kipnis et al. did not report effect magnitudes for their ANOVA. However, estimates of eta squared values based on their means and standard deviations suggest that, except for assertiveness, the effect magnitudes were smaller in their study than in ours, despite their larger *F* values.

Turning to the two new scales not included in the Kipnis et al. research, significant differences were found in each case. Consistent with Hypotheses 5 and 6, inspirational appeals and consultation were used more frequently in downward influence attempts than in upward ones, with results for lateral influence attempts in between.

Results for influence objectives are shown in Table 4 and are compared with results for objectives in the Kipnis et al. study. Consistent with the Kipnis et al. research and Hypotheses 7 and 8, assigning work and requesting faster or better performance were most likely to occur in downward influence attempts and least likely to occur in upward influence attempts. Requests for resources were significantly more likely to be made in upward and lateral influence attempts than in downward attempts, which is partially consistent with Hypothesis 9. This objective is closest to requests for benefits in the Kipnis et al. study, although the benefits in our study are job-related resources, not things like a better job or a pay increase.

Other results for objectives were less consistent with the re-

INFLUENCE TACTICS AND OBJECTIVES

Table 4

Mean Frequency of Influence Objectives as Reported by Agents

Influence objective	Direction of influence attempt			$F(2, 194)$	Eta^2
	Downward ($N = 62$)	Lateral ($N = 75$)	Upward ($N = 60$)		
Assign task or project	3.6$_a$	2.8$_b$	1.9$_c$	39.9**	29%
(Assign work)	(4.1$_a$)	(2.5$_b$)	(1.9$_c$)	(329.7**)	
Request better performance	3.3$_a$	2.5$_b$	1.8$_c$	28.9**	23%
(Improve performance)	(3.9$_a$)	(2.9$_b$)	(2.4$_c$)	(135.2**)	
Request changes	2.7$_a$	2.4$_{ab}$	2.1$_b$	4.4**	4%
(Seek changes)	(3.5$_a$)	(3.3$_b$)	(3.5$_a$)	(6.7*)	
Request advice or help	3.6	3.6	3.5	0.1	
(Seek assistance)	(3.2$_a$)	(2.8$_b$)	(2.1$_c$)	(64.4**)	
Request resources	1.7$_b$	2.4$_a$	2.6$_a$	11.9**	11%
(Request benefits)	(1.3$_c$)	(1.7$_b$)	(2.4$_a$)	(90.4**)	
Request approval/signoff	1.9$_c$	2.7$_b$	3.2$_a$	17.7**	15%
Request proposal support	2.0$_b$	2.5$_a$	2.6$_a$	4.1*	4%
Request information	4.0	3.7	3.5	2.9	

Multivariate F test

Pillais criterion	7.7**
Hotelling's trace criterion	10.5**
Wilks's lambda	9.1**

Note. Means with different subscripts differ significantly at the .05 level by the Duncan multiple range test. Results from Kipnis, Schmidt, and Wilkinson (1980) are shown in parentheses.
* $p < .05$. ** $p < .01$.

sults found by Kipnis et al., although the discrepancies may be due to subtle differences in the definition of objectives. In our study, requests for changes in plans and procedures occurred most often in downward influence attempts and least often in upward attempts. In the Kipnis et al. study, trying to get someone to change the way the work is done or to accept an innovation occurred more often in upward and downward influence attempts than in lateral ones. In our study, no significant differences were found with respect to requests for advice or help in solving problems. In the Kipnis et al. study, the objective "assist me on my job" occurred most often in downward influence attempts and least often in upward influence attempts. However, their objective included getting the target person to "do some of your work."

With regard to the three influence objectives not included in the Kipnis et al. study, requests for approvals were made most often in upward influence attempts and least often in downward influence attempts, consistent with Hypothesis 10. Attempts to gain support for the agent's proposals occurred more frequently with peers and superiors than with subordinates, consistent with Hypothesis 11. No significant directional differences were found with respect to frequency of requests for information.

In summary, a large majority of the results found by Kipnis et al. for influence tactics and objectives were replicated, despite the many differences in methodology between the studies and the much lower power of our study (197 respondents vs. 754). The results also indicate that some relevant tactics and objectives were missing in the Kipnis et al. research. Consultation and inspirational appeals were among the tactics people reported using most frequently in their influence attempts. Among the influence objectives, requests for information

ranked first in terms of frequency, regardless of the direction of influence, and the other new objectives had moderately high frequency scores.

Study 2

The major purpose of the second study was to determine if the results could be replicated with a data source other than agent self-reports. Study 2 was carried out at the same time as Study 1, but with a different sample. The research design was similar, and the same hypotheses were tested. However, all data in Study 2 were obtained from targets of influence attempts rather than from agents.

Method

The sample consisted of 237 respondents, including evening MBA students with regular jobs during the day and managers in management development courses. Respondents filled out the target version of the questionnaire anonymously in class. All respondents were asked to describe the influence behavior and objectives of an agent designated as a superior, a peer, or a subordinate. The type of agent to be described by each respondent was randomly assigned by the researchers. If the agent was a peer or subordinate, the respondent was asked to select a person with whom he or she had interacted frequently over the past 6 months. When the agent was a superior, respondents were asked to describe their immediate supervisor if they had worked under that person for at least 6 months. People who were new on their jobs were instructed not to answer the questionnaire.

Results

Scale reliabilities for the influence tactics, computed in terms of Cronbach alphas, were as follows: .65 for pressure tactics, .45

Table 5
Mean Frequency of Influence Tactics as Reported by Targets

Influence tactic	Direction of influence attempt			$F(2, 234)$	Eta^2
	Downward ($N = 87$)	Lateral ($N = 71$)	Upward ($N = 79$)		
Pressure tactics	2.0$_a$	1.5$_b$	1.5$_b$	12.9**	10%
Upward appeals	1.7$_a$	1.7$_a$	1.5$_b$	5.6**	5%
Exchange tactics	1.4	1.5	1.4	1.0	
Coalition tactics	1.9	1.9	2.0	0.1	
Ingratiating tactics	2.5	2.4	2.2	2.5	
Rational persuasion	2.8	2.7	2.9	2.1	
Inspirational appeals	2.7$_a$	2.2$_b$	2.4$_b$	6.4**	5%
Consultation	3.2	3.1	3.1	0.3	
Multivariate *F* test					
Pillais Criterion				5.0**	
Hotellings Trace Criterion				5.0**	
Wilks's Lambda				5.0**	

Note. Means with different subscripts differ significantly at the .05 level by the Duncan multiple range test.
* $p < .05$. ** $p < .01$.

for upward appeals, .65 for exchange tactics, .57 for coalition tactics, .56 for ingratiation, .62 for rational persuasion, .70 for inspirational appeals, and .75 for consultation. Reliabilities were within acceptable limits for most of the scales but on the low side for a few scales.

Table 5 presents the mean scale scores for influence tactics used in downward, lateral, and upward influence attempts, as reported by targets, and the results for the MANOVAS and ANOVAs. In general, the data from target respondents yielded fewer significant differences than data from agent respondents. The results provide partial support for Hypotheses 1, 2, and 5, but Hypotheses 3, 4, and 6 were not supported. Significant differences consistent with those in Study 1 were found for pressure tactics, upward appeals, and inspirational appeals. The nonsignificant differences for coalition tactics and rational persuasion are consistent with the findings in Study 1. Contrary to Study

1, there were no significant differences for exchange tactics, ingratiation, or consultation.

Table 6 shows results for objectives of influence attempts, as reported by targets. There were significant differences for most influence objectives, and most of the hypotheses about objectives received at least partial support. Assigning work and requesting faster or better performance were more likely to occur in downward influence attempts than in lateral or upward influence attempts, which is partially consistent with Hypotheses 7 and 8. Requests for resources and approvals were more likely to occur in upward influence attempts than in downward influence attempts, which is partially consistent with Hypotheses 9 and 10.

The other four influence objectives yielded less consistent results for agents and targets. Directional differences involving requests for information and requests for advice were signifi-

Table 6
Mean Frequency of Influence Objectives as Reported by Targets

Influence objective	Direction of influence attempt			$F(2, 234)$	Eta^2
	Downward ($N = 87$)	Lateral ($N = 71$)	Upward ($N = 79$)		
Assign task or project	3.7$_a$	2.3$_b$	2.2$_b$	49.0**	30%
Request better performance	2.5$_a$	1.5$_b$	1.7$_b$	20.0**	15%
Request change in plans	2.7$_a$	2.1$_c$	2.4$_b$	6.7**	5%
Request advice or help	3.4$_b$	3.3$_b$	4.1$_a$	12.8**	10%
Request resources	1.4$_b$	2.0$_a$	2.3$_a$	15.7**	12%
Request approval/signoff	2.1$_b$	2.0$_b$	3.1$_a$	15.9**	12%
Request proposal support	2.0	1.9	2.2	1.2	
Request information	3.7$_b$	3.1$_c$	4.1$_a$	17.1**	13%
Multivariate *F* test					
Pillais criterion				13.1**	
Hotelling's trace criterion				14.7**	
Wilks's lambda				13.9**	

Note. Means with different subscripts differ significantly at the .05 level by the Duncan multiple range test.
* $p < .05$. ** $p < .01$.

Table 7
Rank Order of Tactic Frequencies

	Downward		Lateral		Upward	
Influence tactic	Agents	Targets	Agents	Targets	Agents	Targets
Consultation	1	1	1	1	2	1
Rational persuasion	2	2	2	2	1	2
Inspirational appeals	3	3	3	4	3	3
Ingratiating tactics	4	4	4	3	5	4
Coalition tactics	5	6	5	5	4	5
Pressure tactics	6	5	7	7	7	6
Upward appeals	7	7	6	6	6	7
Exchange tactics	8	8	8	8	8	8

Note. Kendall's coefficient of concordance, $W = .96$, $p < .001$. Ranks were based on means carried out to two decimal places.

cant for the target data but not for the agent data. Directional differences involving requested support for a proposal were significant for the agent data but not for target data. Directional differences involving requested changes in plans or procedures were significant for both data sources, but the results for the target data actually supported the Kipnis et al. findings better than the results for agent data.

Supplementary Analyses in Studies 1 and 2

The focus so far has been on results from the ANOVA comparing downward, lateral, and upward influence attempts. An alternative focus is to examine the relative frequency of the eight influence tactics. Table 7 shows the rank order of scale means in each condition for Studies 1 and 2. It is evident that substantial agreement occurred between agents and targets on the relative use of the influence tactics. Kendall's coefficient of concordance among the rankings was .96 (Siegel, 1956). The four tactics used most frequently were consultation, rational persuasion, inspirational appeals, and ingratiation. Exchange tactics were used least often. Except for the distortion caused by the greater use of pressure tactics in downward relations, the frequency ranking of tactics was remarkably similar regardless of data source or direction of influence. Looking more closely at the Kipnis et al. results, we discovered a similar pattern of frequency rankings. This pattern in their results may have been obscured by their computation of scale scores as the sum of the items in a scale rather than as the mean item score; it is difficult to compare scale sums when the number of scale items varies from 2 to 6.

With regard to the frequency rankings for influence objectives, there was no consistent pattern across conditions. Requests for information and requests for advice or help were most common, but beyond this there was little similarity in rank order for objectives across data sources and directions of influence. Likewise, in the Kipnis et al. study, frequency rankings for influence objectives varied considerably across conditions.

Discussion

The Kipnis et al. conclusion that managers have different reasons for influencing subordinates, peers, and superiors was strongly supported, and the nature of these differences was fur-

ther clarified by use of a more specific and comprehensive list of objectives derived from descriptive accounts of managerial work. Most hypotheses about directional differences for influence objectives were supported by data from both agents and targets. The results are consistent with prevailing conceptions about role relationships and the distribution of authority in organizations. The larger number of influence objectives in our study fills in some gaps in the list proposed by Kipnis et al. and provides a clearer picture of the variety and mix of influence attempts made by managers.

Our research only partially replicated the Kipnis et al. findings for differences in upward, downward, and lateral use of influence tactics. Contrary to their findings, no significant directional differences were found for rational persuasion, not even for agents. The directional differences they found for exchange and ingratiation were replicated for agents, but the effects were weak and could not be replicated for targets. Of the six influence tactics from their study, only pressure and upward appeals had significant results for both agents and targets. The relatively weak effects due to direction of influence were overshadowed by the similarity in frequency rankings for the influence tactics. The overall pattern of results suggests that the Kipnis et al. conclusions for influence tactics are considerably overstated. The big story is not directional differences but rather the discovery that some tactics are used more than others, regardless of whether the target is a subordinate, peer, or superior.

The present research also demonstrated that consultation and inspirational appeals are an important addition to the list of influence tactics identified by Kipnis et al. Agent and target respondents agreed that these two tactics were among the ones used most frequently by managers, regardless of the direction of influence. Consultation and inspirational appeals are relevant and meaningful influence tactics that help to bridge the gap between power research and research on leadership. These tactics appear to be important for understanding the process by which leaders influence follower commitment to new objectives, strategies, and projects.

Although many results were consistent for agents and targets, some inconsistent results also occurred. Social desirability biases in the agent self-reports are one possible reason for these discrepancies. However, to account for the obtained pattern of results, the biases would have to differ depending on the direction of influence attempt, and there is no evidence of such an interaction. A more likely possibility is that the target data were generally less accurate because of attributions and judgmental errors made when respondents retrospectively described the influence behavior and intentions of another person. This explanation is consistent with the finding that pairwise comparisons for agent data usually provided stronger support for the hypotheses than the corresponding comparisons for target data. Also consistent with this explanation is the finding that scale reliabilities were usually higher for agent data than for target data. However, the reason for inconsistent findings across the two data sources is still only a matter of speculation. Additional research is needed to resolve and explain the discrepancies, and this research may have to use another method of data collection, such as diaries or observation.

Future research should examine the relative effectiveness of different influence tactics for different objectives, targets, and situations. The relevance of the eight tactics identified in our research should be further substantiated by direct evidence that use of these tactics has important consequences for individuals and organizations.' Finally, researchers should consider the sequences and combinations of influence tactics used in different situations, not just the relative frequency of individual tactics.

References

Ansari, M. A., & Kapoor, A. (1987). Organizational context and upward influence tactics. *Organizational Behavior and Human Decision Processes, 40,* 39–49.

Bass, B. (1985). *Leadership and performance beyond expectations.* New York: Free Press.

Bennis, W., & Nanus, B. (1985). *Leaders: The strategies for taking charge.* New York: Harper & Row.

Bradford, D., & Cohen, A. (1984). *Managing for excellence: The guide to developing high performance organizations.* New York: Wiley.

Cohen, A., & Bradford, D. (1989). Influence without authority: The use of alliances, reciprocity and exchange to accomplish work. *Organizational Dynamics, 17,* 5–17.

Conger, J., & Kanungo, R. (1988). *Charismatic leadership: The elusive factor in organizational effectiveness.* San Francisco: Jossey-Bass.

Cotton, J., Vollrath, D., Froggatt, K., Lengnick-Hall, M., & Jennings, K. (1988). Employee participation: Diverse forms and different outcomes. *Academy of Management Review, 12,* 8–22.

Erez, M., & Rim, Y. (1982). The relationship between goals, influence tactics, and personal and organizational variables. *Human Relations, 35,* 871–878.

Heller, F. (1971). *Managerial decision-making: A study of leadership style and power sharing among senior managers.* London: Tavistock.

House, R. (1977). A 1976 theory of charismatic leadership. In J. Hunt & L. Larson (Eds.), *Leadership: The cutting edge* (pp. 189–207). Carbondale, IL: Southern Illinois University Press.

Izraeli, D. (1975). The middle manager and the tactics of power expansion: A case study. *Sloan Management Review, 16,* 57–70.

Kanter, R. (1982). The middle manager as innovator. *Harvard Business Review, 60,* 95–105.

Kaplan, R. E. (1984). Trade routes: The manager's network of relationships. *Organizational Dynamics, 12*(4). 37–52.

Kaplan, R. (1986). *The warp and woof of the general manager's job* (Technical Rep. No. 27). Greensboro, NC: Center for Creative Leadership.

Kim, H., & Yukl, G. (1989). The importance of different types of power for influencing subordinates, peers, and superiors. In W. A. Ward & E. G. Gomolka (Eds.), *Managing for performance: Proceedings of the 26th annual meeting* (pp. 4–6). Portland, ME: Eastern Academy of Management.

Kipnis, D., & Schmidt, S. (1988). Upward influence styles: Relationship with performance evaluation, salary and stress. *Administrative Science Quarterly, 33,* 528–542.

Kipnis, D., Schmidt, S. M., & Wilkinson, I. (1980). Intraorganizational influence tactics: Explorations in getting one's way. *Journal of Applied Psychology, 65,* 440–452.

Kotter, J. (1982). *The general managers.* New York: Free Press.

Kotter, J. (1985). *Power and influence: Beyond formal authority.* New York: Free Press.

McCall, M., & Segrist, C. (1980). *In pursuit of the manager's job: Building on Mintzberg* (Technical Rep. No. 14). Greensboro, NC: Center for Creative Leadership.

Mechanic, D. (1962). Sources of lower participants in complex organizations. *Administrative Science Quarterly, 7,* 349–364.

Mintzberg, H. (1973). *The nature of managerial work.* New York: Harper & Row.

Mowday, R. (1978). The exercise of upward influence in organizations. *Administrative Science Quarterly, 23,* 137–156.

Pavett, C., & Lau, A. (1983). Managerial work: The influence of hierarchical level and functional specialty. *Academy of Management Journal, 26,* 170–177.

Pfeffer, J. (1981). *Power in organizations.* Boston: Pitman.

Podsakoff, P., & Schriesheim, C. (1985). Field studies of French and Raven's bases of power: Critique, reanalysis, and suggestions for future research. *Psychological Bulletin, 97,* 387–411.

Sayles, L. (1989). *Leadership: Managing in real organizations.* New York: McGraw-Hill.

Schilit, W., & Locke, E. (1982). A study of upward influence in organizations. *Administrative Science Quarterly, 27,* 304–316.

Siegel, S. (1956). *Nonparametric statistics for the behavioral sciences.* New York: McGraw-Hill.

Stevenson, W., Pearce, J., & Porter, L. (1985). The concept of "coalition" in organization theory and research. *Academy of Management Review, 10,* 256–268.

Strauss, G. (1962). Tactics of lateral relationship: The purchasing agent. *Administrative Science Quarterly, 7,* 161–186.

Tichy, N., & Devanna, M. (1986). *The transformational leader.* New York: Wiley.

Vroom, V., & Jago, A. (1988). *The new leadership: Managing participation in organizations.* Englewood Cliffs, NJ: Prentice-Hall.

Vroom, V., & Yetton, P. (1973). *Leadership and decision-making: A revised normative model.* Pittsburgh, PA: University of Pittsburgh Press.

Yukl, G. (1989). *Leadership in organizations* (2nd ed.). Englewood Cliffs, NJ: Prentice-Hall.

Received May 17, 1989
Revision received October 3, 1989
Accepted October 3, 1989 ∎

Part X
Cognitive Approaches

[18]

Leadership:
The Management of Meaning

LINDA SMIRCICH
GARETH MORGAN

The concept of leadership permeates and structures the theory and practice of organizations and hence the way we shape and understand the nature of organized action, and its possibilities. In fact, the concept and practice of leadership, and variant forms of direction and control, are so powerfully ingrained into popular thought that the absence of leadership is often seen as an absence of organization. Many organizations are paralyzed by situations in which people appeal for direction, feeling immobolized and disorganized by the sense that they are not being led. Yet other organizations are plagued by the opposite situation characterized in organizational vernacular as one of "all chiefs, no Indians"—the situation where the majority aspire to lead and few to follow. Thus, successful acts of organization are often

seen to rest in the synchrony between the initiation of action and the appeal for direction; between the actions of leaders and the receptivity and responsiveness of followers.

In this paper we focus on understanding the phenomenon of leadership, not merely to improve the practice of leadership, but as a means for understanding the phenomenon of organization. For, in leading, managers enact a particular form of social reality with far-reaching, but often poorly understood and appreciated, consequences. We engage in our analysis to reveal how concepts and ideas that dominate management theory and ideology shape managerial practice and the reality of organization. Our approach is to analyze leadership as a

The Journal of Applied Behavioral Science,
Volume 18, Number 3, Pages 257-273
Copyright © 1982 by JAI Press Inc.
All rights of reproduction in any form reserved.
ISSN: 0021-8863

Linda Smircich is an associate professor of organizational behavior in the School of Business Administration, University of Massachusetts, Amherst, Massachusetts 01003. Gareth Morgan is an associate professor of organizational behavior in the Faculty of Administrative Studies of York University, Toronto, Ontario, Canada.

258   THE JOURNAL OF APPLIED BEHAVIORAL SCIENCE Vol. 18/No. 3/1982

distinctive kind of social practice, present a case study of leadership in an organizational context, and analyze its consequences for understanding the basic nature of modern corporate life.

THE PHENOMENON OF LEADERSHIP

Leadership is realized in the process whereby one or more individuals succeeds in attempting to frame and define the reality of others. Indeed, leadership situations may be conceived as those in which there exists an *obligation* or a perceived *right* on the part of certain individuals to define the reality of others.

This process is most evident in unstructured group situations where leadership emerges in a natural and spontaneous manner. After periods of interaction, unstructured leaderless groups typically evolve common modes of interpretation and shared understandings of experience that allow them to develop into a social organization (Bennis & Shepard, 1965). Individuals in groups that evolve this way attribute leadership to those members who structure experience in meaningful ways. Certain individuals, as a result of personal inclination or the emergent expectations of others, find themselves adopting or being obliged to take a leadership role by virtue of the part they play in the definition of the situation. They emerge as leaders because of their role in framing experience in a way that provides a viable basis for action, e.g., by mobilizing meaning, articulating and defining what has previously remained implicit or unsaid, by inventing images and meanings that provide a focus for new attention, and by consolidating, confronting, or changing prevailing wisdom (Peters, 1978; Pondy, 1976).

Through these diverse means, individual actions can frame and change situations, and in so doing enact a system of shared meaning that provides a basis for organized action. The leader exists as a formal leader only when he or she achieves a situation in which an obligation, expectation, or right to frame experience is presumed, or offered and accepted by others.

Leadership, like other social phenomena, is socially constructed through interaction (Berger & Luckmann, 1966), emerging as a result of the constructions and actions of both leaders and led. It involves a complicity or process of negotiation through which certain individuals, implicitly or explicitly, surrender their power to define the nature of their experience to others. Indeed, leadership depends on the existence of individuals willing, as a result of inclination or pressure, to surrender, at least in part, the powers to shape and define their own reality. If a group situation embodies competing definitions of reality, strongly held, no clear pattern of leadership evolves. Often, such situations are characterized by struggles among those who aspire to define the situation. Such groups remain loosely coupled networks of interaction, with members often feeling that they are "disorganized" because they do not share a common way of making sense of their experience.

Leadership lies in large part in generating a point of reference, against which a feeling of organization and direction can emerge. While in certain circumstances the leader's image of reality may be hegemonic, as in the case of charismatic or totalitarian leaders who mesmerize their followers, this is by no means always the case. For the phenomenon of leadership in being interactive is by nature dialectical. It is shaped through the interaction of at least two points of reference, i.e., of leaders and of led.

This dialectic is often the source of powerful internal tensions within leadership situations. These manifest themselves in the conflicting definitions of those who aspire to define reality and in the fact that while the leader of a group may forge a unified pattern of meaning, that very same pattern often provides a point of reference for the negation of leadership (Sennett, 1980). While individuals may look to a leader to frame and concretize their reality, they may also react against, reject, or change the reality thus defined. While leadership often emerges as a result of expectations projected on the emergent leader by the led, the surrender of power involved provides the basis for negation of the situation thus created. Much of the tension in leadership situations stems from this source. Although leaders draw their power from their ability to define the reality of others, their inability to control completely provides seeds of disorganization in the organization of meaning they provide.

The emergence of leadership in unstructured situations thus points toward at least four important aspects of leadership as a phenomenon. First, leadership is essentially a social process defined through interaction. Second, leadership involves a process of defining reality in ways that are sensible to the led. Third, leadership involves a dependency relationship in which individuals surrender their powers to interpret and define reality to others.[1] Fourth, the emergence of formal leadership roles represents an additional stage of institutionalization, in which rights and obligations to define the nature of experience and activity are recognized and formalized.

LEADERSHIP IN FORMALIZED SETTINGS

The main distinguishing feature of formal organization is that the way in which experience is to be structured and defined is built into a stock of taken for granted meanings, or "typifications" in use (Schutz, 1967) that underlie the everyday definition and reality of the organization. In particular, a formal organization is premised upon shared meanings that define roles and authority relationships that institutionalize a pattern of leadership. In essence, formal organization truncates the leadership process observed in natural settings, concretizing its characteristics as a mode of social organization into sets of predetermined roles, relationships, and practices, providing a blueprint of how the experience of organizational members is to be structured.

Roles, for example, institutionalize the interactions and definitions that shape the reality of organizational life. Rules, conventions, and work practices present ready-made typifications through which experience is to be made sensible. Authority relationships legitimize the pattern of dependency relations that characterize the process of leadership, specifying who is to define organizational reality, and in what circumstances. Authority relationships institutionalize a hierarchical pattern of interaction in which certain individuals are expected to define the experience of others—to lead, and others to have their experience defined—to follow. So powerful is this process of institutionalized leadership and the expectation that someone has the right and obligation to define reality, that leaders are held to account if they do not lead "effectively." Those expecting to be led, for example, often rationalize their own inaction or ineffectiveness by scapegoating through statements such as "she is a poor manager" or "he is messing things up." On the other hand, occupancy of an authority role presents the leader in every situation with an existential dilemma—how to define and structure the element of organizational reality encountered at a given time. Formal organizations are often heavily populated by those who feel obliged to define the reality and experience of others in a way that is consistent with their idea of "being a good leader." To fail in this obligation is to fail in one's organizational role.

In these ways, patterns of formal organization institutionalize aspects of the leadership process within the context of a unified structure that specifies patterns of desired interaction, sense making, and dependency. As in the case of leadership as an emergent process, formal structures of organized action also contain a dialectical tension between the pattern of action and meaning that the structure seeks to establish, and the tendency of individuals to reinterpret, or even react against, the structure thus defined. While submitting to the dominant pattern of meaning, individuals frequently strive to develop patterns of their own, a phenomenon well documented in studies of the so-called "informal organization" (Roethlisberger & Dickson, 1939).

It is this inherent tension that calls for the development of a mediating form of leadership, bridging the gulf between the requirements of institutionalized structure and the natural inclinations of its human agents. It is this form of leadership that we most often recognize as leadership in informal organizations—the interpersonal process linking structure and the human beings who inhabit this struc-

ture. The person that is most easily recognized as an organizational leader is one who rises above and beyond the specification of formal structure to provide members of the organization with a sense that they are organized, even amidst an everyday feeling that at a detailed level everything runs the danger of falling apart.

Similarly, successful corporate leaders who give direction to the organization in a strategic sense frequently do so by providing an image or pattern of thinking in a way that has meaning for those directly involved (Quinn, 1980). This is reflected in part in Selznick's (1957) conception of leadership as involving the embodiment of organizational values and purpose. Strategic leadership, in effect, involves providing a conception and direction for organizational process that goes above and beyond what is embedded in the fabric of organization as a structure, i.e., a reified and somewhat static pattern of meaning.

Formal organization thus embodies at least two distinctive, yet complementary aspects of the phenomenon of leadership: (1) the structure of organization institutionalizes the leadership process into a network of roles, often in an overconcretized and dehumanizing form; (2) mediating or interpersonal leadership—what is most evident as leadership in action, operationalizes the principles of leadership as an emergent process within the context of the former. This is usually as a means of transcending the limitations of the former for containing the dialectical tension that it embodies, and as a means of giving the whole coherence and direction over time. These two aspects of leadership have been well recognized in leadership research (Katz & Kahn, 1966) and are frequently interpreted and studied in terms of a relationship between "initiating structure" and "consideration" (e.g., Stogdill, 1974).

The phenomenon of leadership in formal organizations has been conceptualized and studied in many ways. Leadership research has sought for an understanding of leadership in terms of the personal traits of leaders (Mann, 1959), in terms of situations in which they lead (Fiedler, 1967), in terms of what they do (Mintzberg, 1973) or some combination thereof. Such approaches to the study of leadership tap into important attributes of what leadership may involve in day to day practice, particularly in terms of action requirements, and identify those practices most likely to work in different situations. Other approaches have viewed leadership as a process of exchange and influence (Barnard, 1938; Jacobs, 1971), and attempts have been made to understand the nature of the interactions and transactions necessary for effective leadership to occur (Bougon, Note 1). In the remainder of this paper, we wish to supplement these views with an approach to studying leadership that focuses on the way detailed interactive situations acquire meaningful form.

LEADERSHIP AS THE MANAGEMENT OF MEANING

A focus on the way meaning in organized settings is created, sustained, and changed provides a powerful means of understanding the fundamental nature of leadership as a social process. In understanding the way leadership actions attempt to shape and interpret situations to guide organizational members into a common interpretation of reality, we are able to understand how leadership

works to create an important foundation for organized activity. This process can be most easily conceptualized in terms of a relationship between figure and ground. Leadership action involves a moving figure—a flow of actions and utterances (i.e., what leaders do) within the context of a moving ground—the actions, utterances, and general flow of experience that constitute the situation being managed. Leadership as a phenomenon is identifiable within its wider context as a form of action that seeks to shape its context.

Leadership works by influencing the relationship between figure and ground, and hence the meaning and definition of the context as a whole. The actions and utterances of leaders guide the attention of those involved in a situation in ways that are consciously or unconsciously designed to shape the meaning of the situation. The actions and utterances draw attention to particular aspects of the overall flow of experience, transforming what may be complex and ambiguous into something more discrete and vested with a specific pattern of meaning. This is what Schutz (1967) has referred to as a "bracketing" of experience, and Goffman (1974) as a "framing" of experience, and Bateson (1972) and Weick (1979) as the "punctuation of contexts." The actions and utterances of leaders frame and shape the context of action in such a way that the members of that context are able to use the meaning thus created as a point of reference for their own action and understanding of the situation.

This process can be represented schematically in terms of the model presented in Figure 1. When leaders act they punctuate contexts in ways that provide a focus for the creation of

262   THE JOURNAL OF APPLIED BEHAVIORAL SCIENCE Vol. 18/No. 3/1982

Figure 1. Leadership: A Figure-Ground Relationship Which
Creates Figure-Ground Relationships

Framing Experience ⟶	*Interpretation* ⟶	*Meaning and Action*
Leadership action creates a focus of attention within the ongoing stream of experience which characterizes the total situation.	The action assumes significance, i.e., is interpreted within its wider context. The leader has a specific figure-ground relation in mind in engaging in action; other members of the situation construct their own interpretation of this action.	Action is grounded in the interpretive process which links figure and ground.
Such action "brackets" and "frames" an element of experience for interpretation and meaningful action.		

meaning. Their action isolates an element of experience, which can be interpreted in terms of the context in which it is set. Indeed, its meaning is embedded in its relationship with its context. Consider, for example, the simple situation in which someone in a leadership role loses his or her temper over the failure of an employee to complete a job on time. For the leader this action embodies a meaning that links the event to context in a significant way, e.g., "This employee has been asking for a reprimand for a long time"; "This was an important job"; "This office is falling apart." For the employees in the office, the event may be interpreted in similar terms, or a range of different constructions placed upon the situation, e.g., "Don't worry about it, he always loses his temper from time to time"; "She's been under pressure lately because of problems at home."

The leader's action may generate a variety of interpretations that set the basis for meaningful action. It may serve to redefine the context into a situation where the meeting of deadlines assumes greater significance, or merely serves as a brief interruption in daily routine, soon forgotten. As discussed earlier, organized situations are often characterized by complex patterns of meaning, based on rival interpretations of the situation. Different members may make sense of situations with the aid of different interpretive schemes, establishing "counter-realities," a source of tension in the group situation that may set the basis for change of an innovative or disintegrative kind. These counter-realities underwrite much of the political activities within organizations, typified by the leader's loyal lieutenants—the "yes men" accepting and reinforcing the leader's definition of the situation and the "rebels" or "out" groups forging and sustaining alternative views.

Effective leadership depends upon the extent to which the leader's definition of the situation, e.g., "People in this office are not working hard enough," serves as a basis for action by others. It is in this sense that effective leadership rests heavily on the framing of the experience of others, so that action can be guided by common conceptions as to what should occur. The key challenge for a leader is to manage meaning in such a way that individuals orient themselves to the achievement of desirable ends. In this endeavor the use of language, ritual, drama, stories, myths, and symbolic construction of all kinds may play an important role (Pfeffer, 1981; Pondy,

Frost, Morgan & Dandridge, 1982; Smircich, 1982). They constitute important tools in the management of meaning. Through words and images, symbolic actions and gestures, leaders can structure attention and evoke patterns of meaning that give them considerable control over the situation being managed. These tools can be used to forge particular kinds of figure-ground relations that serve to create appropriate modes of organized action. Leadership rests as much in these symbolic modes of action as in those instrumental modes of management, direction, and control that define the substance of the leader's formal organizational role.

A CASE STUDY IN THE MANAGEMENT OF MEANING

In order to illustrate the way leadership involves the management of meaning, we present here a case study drawn from an ethnographic study of the executive staff of an insurance company. The company was a division of a larger corporation (10,000 employees), was 11 years old, and employed 200 people. The case focuses on the way the president of the insurance company, Mr. Hall, sought to structure the experience of staff members by creating a particular figure-ground relationship—"Operation June 30th" (OJ30). OJ30 emerged as a prominent organizational event during the fieldwork and provided a focus for studying the process of leadership in action, in this instance, one of limited success.

Methodology

The research was conducted by one of the authors during the summer of 1979. An agreement was reached whereby the researcher was invited to spend six weeks in the insurance company as an observer of the executive staff. The purpose of the research was to learn about the ways of life within the 10-member top management group, to uncover the structures of meaning in use in the setting, and to synthesize an image of the group's reality.

The specific techniques used to gather data in the setting, consistent with the ethnographic tradition (Bogdan & Taylor, 1975; Schatzman & Strauss, 1973; Smircich, Note 2), were oriented toward understanding the realms of intersubjective meaning which gave that organization a semblance of unity and character to its membership.

In this study the researcher maintained the work hours of the organization. Early on she met individually with each of the staff members and explained the project as an attempt to learn about their organization. Each day's activity consisted of observing the management staff in a variety of situations: staff meetings, planning sessions, interactions with their subordinates, on coffee breaks, and in casual conversation. The guiding principle in this endeavor was to obtain a multisided view of the situation in order to build a holistic image of the group's understanding of itself. Toward the end of the stay in the company, tape recorded conversations/interviews were held with all staff members, including the president. The raw data from this study consist of daily field notes, documents, tapes of conversations, and the researcher's experience of the situation.

During the field work, the organization was in the midst of OJ30, and it was a prominent topic of discussion by the staff and in the researcher's con-

264   THE JOURNAL OF APPLIED BEHAVIORAL SCIENCE Vol. 18/No. 3/1982

versations with the staff. For the purposes of this paper, the data were culled for all references to the OJ30 program so that an account of the situation from multiple viewpoints could be presented.

Ideally, the research would have proceeded in a way that allowed the researcher to reflect back to the group the many-sided image of the meaning system in use that had emerged. As the case study shows, the president's unwillingness to proceed with this aspect of the research was representative of the way of life he strived to maintain in the organization and in that sense provides a form of validation for some of the data presented here.

The background to Operation June 30th

"Operation June 30th" was instigated by Mr. Hall, the president, in direct response to complaints by the district sales managers that the agents in the field were not getting adequate service from the home office. Insurance claims, applications, endorsements, and renewals were not being handled promptly. The agents were getting complaints from their custom-

ers about long delays; consequently, they submitted second and third work requests that only served to make the volume of paperwork greater. The slowdown in processing of paperwork also meant that the agents' commission checks were slow in going out so that they did not receive their commissions in the month of sale.

After hearing the frustration of the Sales Department, Hall considered what might be done.[2] He conferred with the vice-president of administrative operations and the vice-president of claims and asked them if they thought it would be possible to have processing operations current by June 30th, the end of the fiscal year. President Hall then wrote an announcement (Figure 2), showed it to the vice-presidents for their comments and approval, and released it to the district sales managers.

With the initiation of OJ30, makeshift posters proclaiming "Operation June 30th Goals Week of June ____" were attached to file cabinets in the operations area. To bring the workflow up to date, overtime work (evenings and Saturdays) was expected, and other departments were encouraged to help out wherever possible by

Figure 2. Operation June 30

WHAT:	A special program designed to bring all insurance processing activities up to date by June 30, 1979.
WHY:	The present work backlog is having an adverse impact on total insurance operations.
HOW:	1. All departments will make a concerted effort to eliminate all backlogs. The goal is to have work conditions current in all departments by June 30.
	2. All insurance home office employees who have the time will be expected to "volunteer" to assist other departments by performing certain assigned processing tasks until June 30. Procedures relative to this will be developed.
TIMING:	Operation June 30 will commence on Monday, May 14 and will terminate on Saturday, June 30.
PRIORITY:	This program has the highest priority. Nothing else in insurance is of more importance.
REPORTS:	Each staff member will report in writing weekly to Mr. Hall on the status of work conditions in his or her department.

loaning people during the week or by urging their people to come in on the weekends. Each week at the staff meeting a status report was made by the vice-president of operations on the number of files that had been processed through each of the operating units.

At Hall's staff meeting of July 2nd, the vice-president of operations declared OJ30 a "success." During that meeting an energetic discussion about how to express gratitude to the employees took place. The company ultimately provided a free lunch for the employees to thank them for their efforts, and a written statement of progress was prepared for the district sales managers. But privately some staff members expressed quite differing views about what had occurred. In fact some held the opinion that the whole affair was a failure because it did not address the real problems in the company.

OJ30 was a focus for the construction of different interpretations of reality. While the president and some of his staff constructed the situation in one way, other members forged their own view of the situation through the interplay of quite a different figure-ground relationship. It is instructive to examine the way the dynamics of the leadership process in this situation are reflected in the constructions of those involved.

Operation June 30: An attempt to manage meaning

How OJ30 structured meaning is reflected in the way it was created, named, and managed as a significant event within day to day work life. OJ30 was presented to staff members in a way that attempted to orient attention away from the current situation to a desired future state. No attempt was made to analyze or interpret the significance of the backlog of work; the intent was just to eliminate it. This is reflected in the president's choice of language in the creation and naming of Operation June 30th. In the announcement the backlog was labelled "adverse," but not otherwise interpreted. The backlog is defined as the problem, and OJ30 was conceived as a military style operation to overcome it, implying a gathering of troops for an all-out assault. The name chosen by the president was not oriented to an explanation of the present conditions (e.g., "Operation Backlog" or "Operation Clean Sweep") but instead served to focus attention on a desired future state. Moreover, the inclusion of a date gave the program the status of a concrete event with an end point.

In this effort the president chose to emphasize certain temporal, perceptual ("special program," "highest priority") and interpersonal horizons ("concerted effort," "volunteer") to serve as context. By choosing a future time horizon, a perceptual space of tightness/closeness to respond to urgency, and an interpersonal horizon of smoothness and nonconflict, the president implied that the message of Operation June 30th was one of a forward focus. He placed no blame for current conditions and viewed the organization as a team, each member having an important role. When the vice-president of operations declared Operation June 30th a success, Hall saw the free lunch as an appropriate way to draw the event to a close.

This same pattern of emphasis was reflected in other examples of the president's talk, as in this instance of elaborating his management philosophy:

We all need each other. You really don't go very far unless everybody's got their shoulder to the wheel. . . . You can't overdo this (teamwork) to the point where you threaten to suppress some spirited debate in an organization. . . . You could have people not speaking their minds just because they feel they might undermine the teamwork philosophy, or the image you're trying to build. That would be wrong, because you've got to have some confrontation between people as you go along, as long as it doesn't get personal. This is what I keep saying to the staff. You can't get personal about these things, because once you get personal and take on a person individually and affect your relationship, then you've injected a little poison into the outfit. But as long as you're sincere and you're talking about the issues instead of personalities, then debate should be encouraged if you're going to make the best decisions . . . and the main thing is just to keep the personalities out of it.

The president does not speak of his role in terms of charting the direction of the organization but instead focuses his efforts at establishing and maintaining internal harmony. His approach toward OJ30 was quite consistent with this focus.

The staff members' reactions

Although the president sought to shape a reality of cooperation and urgency in the face of adverse conditions, it is apparent from the talk of executive staff that he did not succeed in generating these feelings among these staff members. Indeed, the reality for them was basically one of disharmony, disaffection, and noninvolvement. This is evidenced by remarks of the vice-president of operations, whose department was the main focus of Operation June 30th.

> Tom (the president) talks about "sprinting to the finish," "we all have to put our shoulder to the wheel," but you know nobody responds. . . . To tell you the truth, I'm pretty fed up, I'm agitated by working every Saturday that I've been working, and to see very few other people who are helping or anything. . . ."

The vice-president of operations maintained a chart to keep track of who had been helping during Operation June 30th and expressed dissatisfaction with what it showed. "See, Director of Personnel, all dashes by his name, he hasn't helped out. . . . We have no team around here."

The president's use of military imagery was noted by the director of personnel but not seen as effective.

> It's (OJ30) probably a good thing in a lot of ways because say somebody attacked our country, we got called into a world war. . . . I kind of thought that when this initially came out it would serve as a common cause, a unification of the different forces we have in the company. It started off in that direction, but it's eased up quite a bit.

There was no urgency about OJ30 for the staff members. "We'll be in the same boat on July 30th," said one executive and he explained why.

> As long as . . . the president or someone else that has some involvement with that department doesn't challenge them, everyone's going to think everything is fine. And it will be, until some agents or some insured . . . begin to ask more questions as to why this isn't being done. I know for a fact that they aren't up-to-date. I could go over there and find errors.

But at the July 2nd staff meeting this same executive did not question the vice-president of operations' description of OJ30 as a success, justifying his own behavior by saying his department was not directly involved and that it was the president's responsibility to check and ask questions. But he believed the president incapable of doing so because he didn't know what to look for. In his own way, this executive also participated in burying the problems, but he saw that as the only option available to him.

The staff members' interpretations

The executive staff members rejected the meaning that the president sought to attach to the OJ30 program. They made sense of the project not in terms of some desired future state of task performance, but against the background of what they knew and felt about their organization.[3]

They were not a team, but instead a group in which conflict was repressed but close to the surface. Their group enacted a continued pattern of not dealing with problems effectively. The executive staff attributed this pattern to the preferences and style of the president. They considered him "too trusting" and "not wanting to hear if things are bad." Although he espoused that "you have to have some confrontation between people," he and the staff participated in avoiding confrontation.

To the executive staff, OJ30 was symbolic of the way of life in their organization. It represented one more instance of the president's continued reluctance to deal fully and directly with problems. He may have labelled OJ30 "highest priority" and attempted to mobilize their energies, but he got little more than business as usual. For the staff did not interpret it as an occasion in which to behave in tight and helpful coordination. They made sense of OJ30, not as an organizational imperative emphasizing interdependence, but as an organizational malaise encouraging an isolationist response.

The executive staff expressed feelings of powerlessness; they saw no way to do things differently. For them it was a choice of resigning or going along with the way it is. Neither alternative seemed attractive. They shared a common understanding of the expected mode of behavior, basically a passive posture and a shared perception of the president's preferences. Paradoxically, the president's attempt to manage the meaning of OJ30 ("everybody get their shoulder to the wheel") was actually sabotaged by his staff's adherence to what they saw as the "real" organizational value—the value which Hall, to them, embodied: If you do nothing, no harm will come to you.

The competing interpretations of reality

Figure 3 presents a summary of the competing interpretive schemes through which the president and his executive staff made sense of the OJ30 project. For the president, OJ30 sought to define the situation in a way that created a high priority, future-oriented program addressed to the question, "What do we do now?" His interpretation of the final "success" of the program was framed against the relative success of OJ30 in getting rid of the backlog of work. For the staff, OJ30 was framed against an understanding of why they were "in a mess" and had a very different significance. It was just another sign of the inadequate way the fragmented organization was being run. They saw it as the act of a manager who was afraid to confront the real issues, who insisted on seeing the organization as a team, whereas the reality was that of a poorly managed group characterized by narrow self-interest, and noncooperation at anything but a surface level. OJ30 for

Figure 3. Competing Interpretations of OJ30

Framing Experience	Interpretation	Meaning and Action
OJ30 frames significant elements of work experience (work backlog, customer and staff complaints) in a form that makes them amenable to action.	*The President's Interpretation* — OJ30 provides an opportunity for the company to work together in the resolution of a problem. It will solve the problem and help develop a cooperative spirit.	*For the President* — OJ30 does much to clear the backlog of work and can be judged a success. Meaning framed against an *idealized image*
	The Staff Members' Interpretation — OJ30 represents another futile act which will do nothing to solve the organization's basic problems. It symbolizes the way we do things here.	*For Staff Members* — Will call for no more than minimal action; do not take too seriously for it can't do much to remedy the basic problem. Meaning framed against *past history*

them was symbolic of the status quo, and hence they were not effectively mobilized into action.

IMPLICATIONS FOR THE THEORY AND PRACTICE OF CONTEMPORARY ORGANIZATION

The OJ30 case illustrates a leadership action concerned with managing the meaning of a particular situation. As an action designed to catch up on a work-flow problem, OJ30 was partially successful, for it did generate extra work from many staff who felt obliged to do something in conformity with the president's wishes. As an action designed to define the meaning of a situation, it was for the most part a failure, for it was interpreted by the executive staff in a manner that ran counter to what the president desired. Indeed the president's most powerful impact on the pattern of meaning within the organization was of a negative kind—his inaction and avoidance of problems creating an atmosphere of drifting and inaction.

At the surface our analysis may lead to the conclusion that Hall was a weak and ineffective leader. But to quickly judge him so is to risk losing sight of the larger dynamics that are at work in this leadership situation. Although Hall's view of organizational reality is not shared by the executive staff, he exerted a major impact on the broader definition of the situation. His style and presence provided the most powerful point of reference for action. The executive staff in this case adopts a passive nonconfronting posture, living a somewhat uncomfortable organizational reality defined and symbolized by the president. Hall provides evidence of how even weak leadership, by its

fundamental nature, involves the definitions of situations.

Leaders symbolize the organized situation in which they lead. Their actions and utterances project and shape imagery in the minds of the led, which is influential one way or another in shaping actions within the setting as a whole. This is not to deny the importance of the voluntary nature of the enactments and sense-making activities initiated by members of the situation being managed. Rather, it is to recognize and emphasize the special and important position accorded to the leader's view of the situation in the frame of reference of others. Leaders, by nature of their leadership role, are provided with a distinctive opportunity to influence the sense making of others. Our case study illustrates the importance of the leader recognizing the nature of his or her influence and managing the meaning of situations in a constructive way. At a minimum this involves that he or she (a) attempt to deal with the equivocality that permeates many interactive situations; (b) attend to the interpretive schemes of those involved, and (c) embody through use of appropriate language, rituals, and other forms of symbolic discourse, the meanings and values conducive to desired modes of organized action. A focus on leadership as the management of meaning encourages us to develop a theory for the practice of leadership in which these three generalizations are accorded a central role.

Our analysis also draws attention to the role of power as a defining feature of the leadership process. With the OJ30 case we see the way the power relations embedded in a leadership role oblige others to take particular note of the sense-making activities emanating from that role. We have characterized this in terms of a dependency relation between leaders and led, in which the leader's sense-making activities assume priority over the sense-making activities of others.

The existence of leadership depends on and fosters this dependency, for insofar as the leader is expected to define the situation, others are expected to surrender that right. As we have noted, leadership as a phenomenon depends upon the existence of people who are prepared to surrender their ability to define their reality to others. Situations of formal leadership institutionalize this pattern into a system of rights and obligations whereby the leader has the prerogative to define reality, and the led to accept that definition as a frame of reference for orienting their own activity.

Organized action in formal settings constitutes a process of enactment and sense making on the part of those involved, but one shaped in important ways by the power relations embedded in the situation as a whole. Leadership and the organizational forms to which it gives rise enact a reality that expresses a power relationship. An understanding of the power relationship embedded in all enactment processes is thus fundamental for understanding the nature of organization as an enacted social form, for enactments express power relationships.

Thus our analysis of the leadership process tells us much about the nature of organization as a hierarchical phenomenon. Most patterns of formal organization institutionalize the emergent characteristics of leadership into roles, rules, and relations that give tangible and enduring form to relationships between leaders and led. Our analysis of leadership as a social phenomenon based on interaction, sense

making, and dependency implies a view of much modern organization in which these factors are seen as defining features. To see leadership as the management of meaning is to see organizations as networks of managed meanings, resulting from those interactive processes through which people have sought to make sense of situations.

This view of leadership and organization provides a framework for reconsidering the way leadership has been treated in organizational research. By viewing leadership as a relationship between traits, roles, and behaviors and the situations in which they are found, or as a transactional process involving the exchange of rewards and influence, most leadership research has focused upon the dynamics and surface features of leadership as a tangible social process. The way leadership as a phenomenon involves the structuring and transformation of reality has with notable exceptions (e.g., Burns, 1978), been ignored, or at best approached tangentially. The focus on the exchange of influence and rewards has rarely penetrated to reveal the way these processes are embedded in, and reflect a deeper structure of power-based meaning and action. Leadership is not simply a process of acting or behaving, or a process of manipulating rewards. It is a process of power-based reality construction and needs to be understood in these terms.

The concept of leadership is a central building block of the conventional wisdom of organization and management. For the most part the idea that good organization embodies effective leadership practice passes unquestioned. Our analysis here leads us to question this wisdom and points toward the unintended consequences that leadership situations often generate.

The most important of these stem from the dependency relations that arise when individuals surrender their power and control over the definition of reality to others. Leaders may create situations in which individuals are crippled by purposelessness and inaction when left to guide efforts on their own account. Leadership may actually work against the development of self-responsibility, self-initiative, and self-control, in a manner that parallels Argyris's (1957) analysis of the way the characteristics of bureaucratic organization block potentialities for full human development. These blocks arise whenever leadership actions divert individuals from the process of defining and taking responsibility for their own action and experience.

Leadership situations may generate a condition of "trained inaction" in the led, a variant form of Veblen's (1904) "trained incapacity," observed by Merton (1968) as a dominant characteristic of the bureaucratic personality. This trained inaction is clearly illustrated in the OJ30 study where the executive staff experienced problems in their work situation as something beyond their control. The situation here emanates from the way a relatively weak leader defines the situation; but it is equally evident in situations of strong, dominating leadership illustrated in a graphic but extreme way in situations such as the tragedy in Jonestown, Guyana.

An awareness of the dependency relationships that characterize leadership situations sensitizes us to potentially undesirable consequences and also points toward ways in which leadership action can be directed for the avoidance of such states through the crea-

tion of patterns of meaning construction that facilitate constructive tension and innovation rather than passivity. In this regard our analysis points toward an important focus for both the practice of contemporary organization and for future research—on the processes through which the management of meaning in organized situations can develop in ways that enhance, rather than deny, the ability of individuals to take responsibility for the definition and control of their world.

It is important to investigate forms of organized action that depart from the traditional leadership model. We are persuaded to suggest that the study of nonleadership situations would focus attention on a phenomenon of some importance.

Patterns of organization that replace hierarchical leadership with patterns of more equalized interaction in which each has an obligation to define what is happening, and respond accordingly, changes the very basis of organization. Such arrangements increase the adaptive capacity of organization through what Emery and Trist (1972) have described as a redundancy of functions. These embody a model of human development in line with the ability of human beings to take responsibility for their actions. In situations characterized by hierarchical dependency, those in leadership roles are obliged to interpret and assimilate all that there is to observe and understand about a situation before initiating the action of others. In situations of more equalized power, this obligation and ability is more widely spread. Members of a situation are unable to look to authority relations to solve problems; adaptive capacities have to be developed at the level at which they are needed, increasing the learning and adaptive ability of the whole. Autonomous work groups and leaderless situations of all kinds present concrete opportunities for the study of emergent principles of organization that offer alternatives to the dependency relations that have permeated Western culture as an organizational norm.

The conventional wisdom that organization and leadership are by definition intertwined has structured the way we see and judge alternative modes of organized action. Approaching this subject from a perspective that treats organization as a phenomenon based on the management of meaning, we can begin to see and understand the importance of developing and encouraging alternative means through which organized action can be generated and sustained.

NOTES

1. A minor qualification is appropriate here in that certain charismatic leaders may inspire others to restructure their reality in creative ways. The dependency relation is evident, however, in that the individual takes the charismatic leader as a point of reference in this process.

2. The president of the insurance company had been involved in the day to day management of the company for 18 months. Previously, all nine executive staff members had reported to an executive vice-president so that the president could devote his attention to external relationships. When the executive vice-president died in January 1978, a decision was made not to replace him. Instead, all executive staff members reported directly to the president. The executive staff was a stable group; all had been employed in the company for no less than seven years.

3. The staff members were concerned about the equivocality surrounding the cause of the backlog. In a conversation with the researcher, the director of sales asked himself, "How did the company get into this position?" And replied, "It started two years ago with the decision to microfilm. It ate us up. I could have my head handed to me for this, the president backed

it." The sales director expressed the view that the past decision to install microfilming equipment and to microfilm all stored records as well as microfilm all incoming work had been the major factor in the operating department's falling so far behind in the processing of work. The other executives agreed with this interpretation.

REFERENCE NOTES

1. Bougon, M. *Schemata, leadership, and organizational behavior.* Doctoral dissertation, Cornell University, 1980.
2. Smircich, L. Studying organizations as cultures. In G. Morgan (Ed.), *Organizational research strategies: Links between theory and method.* Unpublished manuscript.

REFERENCES

Argyris, C. *Personality and organization.* New York: Harper, 1957.
Barnard, C. *The functions of the executive.* Cambridge, Mass.: Harvard University Press, 1938.
Bateson, G. *Steps to an ecology of mind.* New York: Ballantine Books, 1972.
Bennis, W. G., & Shepherd, H. A. A theory of group development. *Human Relations,* 1965, *9,* 415–457.
Berger, P., & Luckmann, T. *The social construction of reality.* New York: Anchor Books, 1966.
Bogdan, R., & Taylor, S. J. *Introduction to qualitative methods.* New York: Wiley, 1975.
Burns, J. M. *Leadership.* New York: Harper & Row, 1978.
Emery, F. E., & Trist, E. L. *Towards a social ecology.* Harmondsworth: Penguin, 1973.
Fiedler, F. E. *A theory of leadership effectiveness.* New York: McGraw-Hill, 1967.
Goffman, E. *Frame analysis.* New York: Harper Colophon Books, 1974.
Jacobs, T. O. *Leadership and exchange in formal organizations.* Alexandria, Va.: Human Resources Organization, 1971.
Katz, D., & Kahn, R. L. *The social psychology of organizations.* New York: Wiley, 1966.
Mann, R. D. A review of the relationships between personality and performance in small groups. *Psychological Bulletin,* 1959, *56,* 241–270.
Merton, R. K. *Social theory and social structure.* (enlarged ed.). New York: Free Press, 1968.
Mintzberg, H. *The nature of managerial work.* Englewood Cliffs, N.J.: Prentice-Hall, 1973.

Peters, T. J. Symbols, patterns and settings: An optimistic case for getting things done. *Organizational Dynamics,* 1978, 3–22.

Pfeffer, J. Management as symbolic action: The creation and maintenance of organizational paradigms. *Research in Organizational Behavior,* 1981, *3,* 1–52.

Pondy, L. R. Leadership is a language game. In M. McCall & M. Lombardo (Eds.), *Leadership: Where else can we go?* Durham, N.C.: Duke University Press, 1976.

Pondy, L. R., Frost, P., Morgan, G., & Dandridge, T. (Eds.). *Organizational symbolism.* Greenwich, Conn.: JAI Press, 1982.

Quinn, J. B. *Strategies for change.* New York: Irwin, 1980.

Roethlisberger, F. J., & Dickson, W. J. *Management and the worker.* Cambridge, Mass.: Harvard University Press, 1939.

Schatzman, L., & Strauss, A. *Fieldwork.* Englewood Cliffs, N.J.: Prentice-Hall, 1973.

Schutz, A. *Collected papers I: The problem of social reality.* (2nd ed.). The Hague: Martinus Nijhoff, 1967.

Selznick, P. *Leadership in administration.* New York: Harper & Row, 1957.

Sennett, R. *Authority.* New York: Knopf, 1980.

Smircich, L. Organizations as shared meanings. In Pondy, L. R., Frost, P., Morgan, G. & Dandridge, T. (Eds.). *Organizational symbolism.* Greenwich , Conn.: JAI Press, 1982.

Stogdill, R. M. *Handbook of leadership: A survey of theory and research.* New York: The Free Press, 1974.

Veblen, T. *The theory of business enterprise.* Clifton, N.J.: Augustus M. Kelly, 1975 (originally published 1904).

Weick, K. *The social psychology of organizing.* Reading, Mass.: Addison-Wesley, 1979.

[19]

An Attribution Theory of Leadership

Bobby J. Calder

The study of leadership is one of the few areas of social science which has had a truly cumulative history of research and thought. This work has not always been at the forefront of advances in methodology and theory, but neither has it been subject to the ebb and flow of attention characteristic of many other areas. The pattern of leadership research has been one of discarding, extending, and introducing ideas as the limitations of existing ideas are realized. A progression of different orientations has guided modern psychological studies of leadership. From the turn of the century to the 1940s, researchers attempted to identify the personal attributes and personality traits which leaders possess. Hundreds of studies compared leaders and nonleaders on variables such as height, intelligence, and dominance, but failed to establish any strong relationship between these variables and leadership. The many inadequacies of this work were revealed by the reviews of Stogdill (1948), Hemphill (1949), Gibb (1954), and Mann (1959). Most important, the trait approach failed to distinguish between leadership as a process and the leader as a person. Research was not able to detect traits associated with leadership across situations or even to obtain high correlations within a given situation.

The next orientation shifted from the characteristics of leaders to the actual behavior of leaders and their style of leadership. Bales (1950) developed a methodology for observing group discussions and recording member actions. He found two kinds of leadership styles which he termed "task" and "maintenance" (interpersonal) behaviors. Similar categories of leader behavior, initiation of structure and consideration, were obtained by Shartle and his co-workers (1952). These categories were obtained from factor analyses of a questionnaire (the Leader

Behavior Description Questionnaire) containing items referring to more specific behaviors. Scores on this test, still a subject of research activity, have been found to correlate with measures of leadership effectiveness and to support the importance of structure and consideration. A related line of research by Kahn and Katz (1960) sought to determine those patterns of supervision (e.g., closeness of supervision and employee orientation) most related to productivity and morale. Although the behavioral approach did point out some important aspects of leadership, its descriptive orientation did not really provide an explanation of leadership processes.

The trait and behavioral approaches to leadership were followed by an explicit recognition of the importance of the situational context in which leadership occurs. Fiedler (1964, 1967, 1971a, 1971b) proposed a "contingency model" which hypothesizes that leadership effectiveness depends on the relationship between the leader's task versus interpersonal orientation and the favorableness of the situation. Although empirical support for this model has been mixed (see e.g., Hunt, 1967; Graen, Alvares, Orris, and Martella, 1970; Fiedler, 1971b, 1971c; Chemers and Skrzypek, 1972), it has clearly been valuable in stimulating research concerned with more than just the distinguishing characteristics of leaders. Katz and Kahn's (1966) discussion of leadership has also been influential in emphasizing the interaction of style and task demands in determining leadership effectiveness.

Recently an even broader view of leadership has begun to emerge, one fully recognizing the multiple contingencies of the leadership process. Hollander and Julian (1968, 1969, 1970) have developed a "transactional" approach to leadership which emphasizes the exchange relations between leaders and followers. The leader provides resources in achieving group goals and in return receives status, esteem, influence, and legitimacy. Gibb (1969a, 1969b), along the same lines, has discussed an "interactional" approach. Leadership is viewed as "a concept applied to the *inter*action of two or more persons, when the evaluation of one, or of some of the parties to the interaction is such that he, or they, come to control and direct the actions of the others in the pursuit of common ends" (Gibb, 1969a, p. 221). This general orientation has perhaps had the most impact in the narrower form of "path-goal" theory (Evans, 1970, 1974; House, 1971; House and Mitchell, 1974). Utilizing an expectancy theory framework, House argues that the leader attempts to influence the valences and expectancies of subordinates regarding their organizational performance. The leader may increase the value of work-goal attainment or clarify path-goal instrumental relationships. It is suggested that, for an unstructured task situation, enhancing the value of work goals is more likely to increase effectiveness than path-goal clarification, while the reverse is true for a structured task. Although such theories are not fully interactional, they do attempt to specify just what it is that leaders provide followers. As such, they are a step beyond descriptions of what leaders do.

Given this evolutionary pattern, one would expect that judgments of the contribution of leadership research would have been less harsh than they have been. Stogdill (1974), in a recent compendium of research findings, concludes that:

> It is difficult to know what, if anything, has been convincingly demonstrated by replicated research. The endless accumulation of empirical data has not produced an integrated understanding of leadership (p. vii).

This view is probably shared by a majority of social scientists, with research on leadership being held in vague disrepute. Nor does there appear to be any great optimism that the accumulation of research is really heading anywhere.

What is to be made of this paradox? On the one hand, even a superficial examination of the history of leadership research conveys the sense of steady progress in theoretical sophistication and data collection. Yet there is little sense of really having achieved anything in the way of a new or profound understanding of leadership beyond that available from everyday knowledge. It is suggested here that a new, alternative orientation to leadership is needed. While attention is directed at a particular theoretical perspective, namely attribution theory, this perspective is not suggested in the context of simply extending current leadership research. While it might be possible simply to graft attribution theory onto one or more present approaches to leadership, the objective here is to propose a reorientation of the entire leadership area in which attribution would become the central construct. Indeed, in this reorientation, leadership itself would cease to be a scientific construct.

First- and Second-degree Constructs

Ideas about leadership may be used at two levels of analysis. One is the level of social science theory which we have been examining. Explanatory terms derived at this level are sometimes called second-degree constructs. They are supposed to be of a high degree of abstraction and to be supported by scientific evidence. In contrast, first-degree constructs belong to the world of everyday explanation. They are the terms and language we use to give meaning to the events of everyday life. A powerful criticism of social science in general has been advanced by ethnomethodologists such as Circourel (1964) and by phenomenologists such as Schutz (1967, originally 1932). All too often social science theory confuses first-degree constructs with those of the second-degree. Explanations of everyday life are implicitly assumed to have some scientific status. The validity of these first-degree constructs, however, lies only in the social construction of reality by a group of actors.

In our view, the paradoxical state of leadership research stems from just such a confusion of first- and second-degree constructs. The major problem is with the construct of leadership itself. Certainly leadership is a meaningful part of our language for describing and explaining everyday events. As will be discussed shortly, this language is very rich indeed. It is institutionalized and taught to very young children, complete with colorful examples of presumed historical significance. The thinking of social scientists has of late even contributed to this language. But none of this necessarily implies the validity of leadership as a second-degree construct.

Faced with a social construction of reality stressing the importance of leadership, researchers have directly adopted the language and ideas of everyday explanation in their zeal to study the phenomenon of leadership. Unfortunately, this "phenomenon" still exists principally as a first-degree construct. There has been almost no attempt to define what a leader is in truly psychological, sociological, or anthropological terms. Instead, the reference of the construct is to our everyday conception of leadership. In turn, leadership research may be seen as an attempt to make even further use of our implicit notions that leaders possess certain traits, that the behavior of leaders is different from followers, that different tasks require different leadership styles, and the like. We should point out that this criticism does not deny that intuition may be a source of scientific theory. It does deny that the constructs and logic of everyday language can be accepted as scientific without additional support. Leadership research has not provided this support. *The paradox of leadership research is resolved by the realization that what has been attempted is not the development of scientific theory but the systematic and consistent use of everyday thought.*

The problem with leadership research does not lie specifically with leadership theories. It lies with the metatheory of leadership. At the heart of the problem is *conceptualization*. Science consists of the interrelationships of concepts (Bunge, 1967). The real world is too complex to be understood in and of itself. Conceptualization seeks to represent the real world in a simple enough way to allow understanding. Scientific concepts are abstracted forms and represent only limited aspects of real world objects and behaviors. As shown in figure 1a, two types of reference relationships are crucial to conceptualiza-

FIGURE 1   Metatheoretical Reference Relationships

(a) The Nature of Scientific Theory

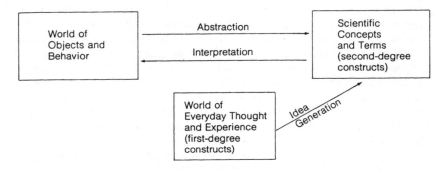

(b) The Nature of Leadership Theories

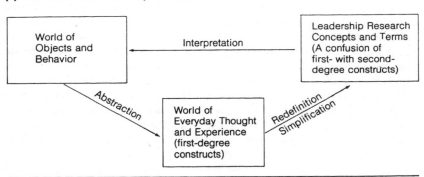

tion. Scientific concepts and the terms referring to them are abstractions of the real world in the sense that they are classes of objects depending on some common property or relation between the objects (Reichenbach, 1947). Concepts, in other words, are simplifications and idealizations of reality. The scientific process must work in reverse, too. We must be able to use scientific concepts to *interpret* the real world, to say whether real objects possess the properties or relations embodied in a conceptualization. Ostensive interpretation is the ability to name or point to real objects on the basis of conceptualization. Operational interpretation is more sophisticated. It is the ability to use a concept to measure real objects (Bunge, 1967).

The critical issue here is the nature of scientific concepts. In all of science the origin of concepts is somewhat problematic (Kaplan, 1964). How do we develop concepts? Where do they come from? Part of the answer seems to be that good theory spawns its own concepts (the best example being particle physics). There is also the process of reformulating old concepts in the face of empirical evidence. Still, there must be an external origin at some point in theory development, and this origin is the world of everyday thought and experience. In normal scientific discourse, this everyday world bears some unknown and largely irrelevant relationship to the real world. And its relationships to scientific conceptualization, when acknowledged at all, is meant to be limited to generating ideas, or "bootstrapping" (see figure 1a). Scientific concepts originating in this way are expected to be immediately subject to the most rigorous tests of interpretation and further abstraction.

When one looks at leadership research from the standpoint of metatheory, one is struck by its divergence from the philosophy-of-science view of conceptualization. Figure 1b attempts to characterize the problem in terms of the relationships of abstraction and interpretation. What has happened is that researchers have begun with an *unusually* strong bias toward the ideas of everyday thought and experience, or what we have called first-degree constructs. These constructs are in fact abstractions, albeit nonscientific ones, of the real world. As discussed more fully later, everyday conceptualizations of leadership represent people's nonscientific efforts to understand and give meaning to their world. The problem is that these everyday concepts have assumed such significance in our society that they seem to possess a higher-order legitimacy and credibility. The aura surrounding these concepts has led leadership researchers to adapt them with only minor redefinitions in terminology, but with even further simplification. Whereas everyday conceptualizations are highly situational in meaning, leadership researchers have tried to simplify them so that they are generalizable across situations. These overly-simplified everyday abstractions are the ostensible "second-degree" concepts of leadership research. Our point is that these "second-degree" concepts represent a confusion of first- with second-degree concepts and fundamental distortion of the scientific method. This confusion and distortion accounts for the failures of leadership research. The ostensible second-degree constructs of leadership research are difficult to use scientifically even for ostensive interpretation.

This basic problem has been compounded many times over by an unwillingness to change or discard leadership research concepts in the normal scientific way for fear of moving too far away from the original everyday ideas. This fear is natural since the presumed significance of leadership research stems directly from the clear importance of these everyday ideas. There are indications that leadership researchers are not entirely oblivious to this problem. Some researchers have implicitly begun to look for new ideas. Oldham (1976), for instance, addresses leadership in terms of the motivationl strategies of supervisors: "Personally Rewarding," "Personally Punishing," "Setting Goals," "Designing Feedback Systems," "Placing Personnel," "Designing Job Systems," "Materially Rewarding," "Materially Punishing," and "Designing Reward Systems." Approaches such as this may be seen, from our perspective, as efforts to move away from first-degree constructs while preserving the illusion that one is studying what it is that is important about those first-degree constructs. This need not be an illusion. It could be a viable research strategy, but to be so would require explicit attention to the relationship between first- and second-degree constructs. In any event, the strategy of trying to maintain some connection with the imagery of leadership while developing truly second-degree concepts is in fact a roundabout route back to the normal scientific relationships of figure 1a. While this strategy might have some pedagogical merit, it is far from optimal in moving toward scientific understanding. The more direct strategy of being unencumbered, beyond the idea-generation state, by second-degree constructs seems preferable.

What happens if we attempt to disentangle the second-degree constructs in leadership research from the first-degree? Although this is no doubt a matter for extended analysis, it seems clear that whatever second-degree constructs and hypotheses remain are not likely to be unique to the leadership area. They would in fact be those associated with other, more general models of behavior and interaction. The question, for instance, of what traits leaders possess becomes the question of whether trait models explain certain behaviors. The imagery of leadership may fit these behaviors, but this is irrelevant to the second-degree explanation. Leadership is a label applied in everyday life to the behaviors. Likewise, the transactional nature of leader-follower interaction reduces to models of interpersonal influence. In short, a scientific understanding of "leadership" does not depend on the construct of leadership. Now it may well be that general models, such as trait theory itself, also confuse first- and second-degree constructs. We would contend, though, that the hypotheses and constructs specific to the leadership area are the more blatant offenders.

It is not proposed that leadership research be abandoned as a unique line of inquiry. Acceptance of our view, however, does necessitate a basic reorientation. One possibility, as illustrated by Oldham's work, is the gradual drift away from second-degree leadership constructs toward new constructs which still implicitly bear on the everyday meaning of leadership. Unfortunately, researchers moving away from traditional concepts have fallen into the same trap. They tend to tie their new concepts to the world of everyday experience, producing the same confusion of first- and second-degree constructs. Perhaps the best example of this tendency is the work of Vroom and Yetton (1973). This work may be interpreted as an attempt actually to systematize everyday thinking in an overtly prescriptive fashion. Their model takes the form of a set of rules for managers to use in deciding how participative to be with their subordinates. The focus is "normative," but this may best be understood as "socially normative," rather than "scientifically normative" or "objectively optimal." This approach in fact dodges the confusion of first- and second-degree constructs by limiting itself to the former, the prescriptions of experience. The danger is that the scientific trappings associated with such models (e.g., basing rules at least partially on leadership research) do not make them any more scientific than any other statement of "principles of management."

A more viable reorientation for scientific inquiry is to make the everyday constructs and hypotheses of leadership an *object* of study. How people make inferences about and react to leadership is itself an important behavior to explain. To use a common analogy, we may investigate the behavior of people as "naïve scientists" of leadership. The term "naïve scientists" is apt, if a little too condescending, in view of our own use of "naïve" theory. Although there are several schools of thought (e.g., enthnomethodology and sociological phenomenology) relevant to this perspective, the "naïve psychology" of Fritz Heider (1958) seems best suited as a basis for our discussion.

Heider was concerned chiefly with interpersonal perception, the process through which people infer dispositions in others. An individual's actions may be attributed to a variety of causes, both environmental and personal, but according to Heider the common-sense rules of everyday explanation bias us strongly toward seeing people as the cause of their own behavior. The fact that a behavior has occurred at all tends to "engulf the field" of potential causes. Even so, people do make distinctions in the extent to which they assign responsibility for an action to the actor. Dispositions are inferred more strongly if external (situational) forces are weak and if the actor seems to have both the ability and the motivation to perform an action. Attributions to the actor serve to make the perceiver's world more predictable and managable. Heider's framework has subsequently been extended to make up the theoretical perspective called "attribution theory." Before turning to this theory, it may be useful to point up some of the subjective features of our everyday "naïve psychology" of leadership.

The Naïve Psychology of Leadership

Leadership is a prime manifestation of our bias toward perceiving personal causes for behavior. It is first of all something we say about other people, possibly including ourselves. It is not necessary to embrace the Whorf-Sapir hypothesis that thought depends on language to see that our language serves as a ready conduit for such statements. Leadership is a label which can be applied to behavior. It locates the reason for that behavior squarely in the personal dispositional nature of the actor. Certain inherent qualities of the actor are taken as causing both the behavior and its intended effects. These qualities concern both the ability and motivation of the actor. These qualities, however, are not invariant. This is an important point. Consider the following descriptions of two people.

Person 1	*Person 2*
Problem-solver	Physically imposing
Likeable	Shrewd
Warm speaker	Manipulative speaker
Selfless	Egotistical
Modest	Power-loving

Although the qualities of each person are very different, both in ability and motivation, the semantic constraints associated with our naïve concept of "leader" easily encompass each description. Both people could, given some behavior, be called a leader. That we might further specify the first person to be a "benevolent leader" and the second an "autocratic leader" is irrelevant. The point is that our naïve construct of leadership is very fuzzy. In general usage it refers only to some degree of personal potency. More specific qualitative meanings are largely situationally defined. It is not surprising that leadership has proven elusive as a scientific construct.

Judgments about leadership are made on the basis of observed behavior. An individual who labels another as a leader has no direct knowledge of the other's internal qualities. The other person's behavior must serve as evidence for the existence of these qualities.

Knowledge of this behavior comes either from direct observation or through indirect sources. The behavioral evidence itself may be only symptomatic, in that it is taken as reflecting the likelihood of more significant behaviors. That is, cues such as style of speech and physical attractiveness may be used as surrogate behaviors for judging leadership. In any case, leadership is an inference. An individual may be more or less confident about this inference. The central problem for the individual in inferring leadership is the adequacy of the behavioral evidence available.

The behaviors accepted as evidence of leadership depend on the particular set of actors involved. At the very least, the predominant social class composition of a group of actors and the purpose of the group's interaction renders some behaviors more appropriate than others for leadership inferences. Members of a street corner gang obviously focus on behaviors which are very different from those which are salient in the corporate board room. It may well be, as contended in leadership research, that there are dimensions of these behaviors which are the same, such as the structuring of group activities, but this should not be allowed to obscure what are very real qualitative differences. The meaning of leadership depends on the qualitative nature of the behavior taken as evidence of leadership. The meaning of leadership for members of the street corner gang is not nearly so fuzzy as indicated by the general usage of "leadership." This meaning is lost entirely in second-degree classifications of types of leader behavior.

Not only do evidential behaviors differ across groups of actors, but they are also distinct from other behaviors occurring within the group. If all the behaviors performed in a group were similar, there would be no basis for inferring leadership. The important point is that evidential behaviors must be *typical* of a class of behaviors which are *different* from those of most group members. Leaders, like deviates, cannot conform in their behaviors, otherwise there would be no basis for judging them different. Yet leaders are not deviates. Their behavior is perceived to belong to a special class of functionally positive behaviors. Hollander (1958) has advanced the well-known premise that leaders obtain "idiosyncrasy credits," that is, implicit permission to differ in their behavior in order to benefit the group. Granting of these credits is related to the supposed earlier conformity of leaders. This notion is clearly compatible with the present orientation. In our view, however, leaders are not in fact leaders until there is some basis for distinguishing their behavior.

Perhaps one of the most frequent distinguishing characteristics of evidential behavior is simply the extremity of that behavior. People who do more of something are likely to be perceived as leaders (or else as deviates). There is no better example of this than sheer verbal participation. Research indicates that people who talk more are more likely to be judged leaders. Consider a well-known experimental investigation by Bavelas, Hastorf, Gross, and Kite (1965). Industrial engineering and industrial psychology students were placed in four-person groups to discuss three human relations problems. The primary concern of the experiments was to modify one member's verbal output with operant conditioning techniques and to observe the effects of this behavioral difference on the perceptions of other group members. Each subject had in front of him a red and a green light which only he could see. The red light served as a negative reinforcer, flashing whenever the subject's comments supposedly hindered the discussion. The green light served as a positive reinforcer, flashing whenever the subject's comments supposedly contributed to the discussion. On the basis of the first discussion, the subject who ranked next to last in participation was selected as a target person (TP). Reinforcements were delivered during the second discussion to increase the TP's participation. During the third discussion, as in the first discussion, no reinforcements were delivered.

In the first experiment reported by Bavelas et al., the TP was positively reinforced and the other group members were negatively reinforced. The TP's participation increased significantly in the second discussion and remained higher during the third discussion. These increases were accompanied by increases on a questionnaire measure of the perception of the TP as a leader by the group members. A second experiment obtained the same effects when the reinforcements were delivered after some of the TP's remarks. Subsequent experiments failed to alter the TP's participation when only positive or only negative reinforcement was used. Zdep and Oakes (1967) replicated the Bavelas et al. findings and demonstrated that the presence or absence of the initial leadership questionnaire exerts no effect on the TP's leadership status.

According to a naïve psychology of leadership (which was not the perspective of this research), subjects employed talking as an evidential behavior—as an appropriate basis for inferring leadership. This is not at all surprising, considering what is known about verbal participation. Studies have shown that verbal behavior is strikingly systematic; it is plausible to speculate that people may well be aware of this regularity. The highest participator in a group usually accounts for about 40 percent of the total communication over a range of group sizes. Moreover, if the remaining group members are ranked in terms of participation, the percentages of participation for adjacent ranks approximate a constant ratio, and mathematical functions can be written to describe the data (Bales, Strodtbeck, Mills, and Roseborough, 1951; Stephan and Mishler, 1952; Coleman, 1960; Kadane and Lewis, 1969). Such regularities suggest that people may come to expect variations in verbal behavior and may use these variations along with other behavior to infer leadership.

Evidential behaviors must be typical as well as different. Not all behavioral variation in a group implies leadership. Certain classes of variation are even associated with deviance. Inferences about leadership are made only from differences in behavior which fit expectations of how leaders typically behave. As already noted, such expectations are different for different groups of actors. Just what these leadership expectations are is an empirical question. To imply leadership, an observed behavior must be typical in the sense that the differentiated behavior falls within a set of behaviors associated with leadership expectations.

According to Heider, the perception of personal causes of behavior may be tempered by the perception of situational forces. Certainly the meaning of leadership is particular to a given group of actors *and* their situational context over time. Heider's thought suggests, moreover, that the situation constitutes a potential alternative explanation of behavior. A given evidential behavior can be attributed not to leadership as a personal, internal cause but to external, situational forces. For example, if subjects knew that a target person's verbal participation was artificially raised by external reinforcement, this behavior would not result in the perception of leadership. Internal qualities would be discounted as a cause of the behavior.

The importance of situational factors as alternative explanations in the perception of leadership can be seen by contrasting "leadership" and "headship." Researchers have generally reserved "leadership" for social influence which is not based on formal authority (cf. Kochan, Schmidt, and De Cotiss, 1975). With headship, individuals acquire the right to exercise certain legitimate forms of influence in an organization as a consequence of occupying a certain position in the organization. It is widely supposed that such legitimate influence should not be confused with leadership, which is based on personal initiative and the voluntary compliance of others. The same assumption applies, though more loosely, in the naïve psychology of leadership. Behaviors which might otherwise constitute evidence of leadership are discounted in favor of the situational explanation that they are enacted because it is the individual's duty to perform them. In general, the perception of leadership is less likely whenever the role demands of other people are salient as causes of behavior. But the distinction between leadership and headship is not so rigid as researchers have tried to make it. (It is not a scientific distinction). Unless role demands are highly salient, people follow their bias toward personal causation. The fire chief who goes with a group of firemen into a burning building probably will be perceived as a leader even if going into the building is his duty.

Extreme behaviors sometimes "engulf the field" of perception to the extent that even highly plausible situational explanations are ignored. The executive who contributes heavily to a company task force may be perceived as a leader by members even though they know that this behavior is likely to earn the executive a large bonus.

In sum, the naïve psychology of leadership provides participants in a group with an understanding of their behavior. As a scientific construct, leadership is hopelessly ambiguous, as documented by Pfeffer's (in press) discussion of treatments in the literature. At the level of situational meaning for a given set of actors, leadership provides a rich, internal, personal explanation of behavior.

Attribution Theory Perspectives

Naïve psychology is presently being investigated under the rubric of attribution theory. While there has been little attempt to operationally define the term "attribution," the construct refers to the cognitive processes through which individuals infer causation from observed behavior. Attribution is a second-degree construct. It is less vague than the notion of "interpersonal perception," though both refer to the psychological processes underlying naïve psychology. Attribution studies rely heavily on two theoretical perspectives, one due to Kelley (1967, 1971, 1972), and the other to Jones and Davis (1965).

We have preceded our discussion of attribution theory with an informal overview of the naïve psychology of leadership, because in our view the two main attribution theory perspectives are not capable of providing a complete analysis. These perspectives do not address all of the complexities entailed in the attribution of leadership. Attribution theories are by no means a ready-made vehicle for the reorientation of leadership research which we have advocated.

Both major theoretical perspectives dwell on conditions which determine whether a behavior is attributed to internal, personal causes or to situational forces. Kelley posits an intuitive "analysis of variance" model. In inferring an internal state such as leadership from another person's observed behaviors, an individual analyzes the covariation between the behaviors and a possible internal state. There are four dimensions of possible covariation. Are the behaviors (1) "distinctive" in that an observer does not tend to attribute the internal state to most people? (If he does, the observer must make an internal attribution that he reacts to most people in a similar way rather than an external attribution that there is something different about the person observed.) Is there consistency over (2) time and (3) place (modality) in the observation of the behaviors? Is there consistency over (4) people by way of a consensus that the behaviors reflect the internal state? To the extent that behavior exhibits distinctiveness and consistency over time, place, and the reactions of others, it is accepted as evidence of a personal disposition such as leadership. Otherwise the behavior is

---

FIGURE 2 An Extension (shaded areas)
of Jones and Davis' Treatment of Behaviors and Effects

Effects

	Observed	Unobserved
Observed	Jones and Davis' Correspondence Possible	Unnatural Description
Unobserved	Correspondence Possible	No Correspondence Possible

Behaviors

---

discounted and attributed to situational factors. The former is termed an "internal" attribution, the latter, an "external" attribution. Although the consistency-across-other-people dimension appears to be more complex than the theory indicates, data from laboratory experiments generally support the theory (e.g., McArthur, 1972).

Jones and Davis cast their approach in terms of how an observer can be sure that the language he uses to describe a behavior is also descriptive of the personal dispositions of the performer. Their term for the match between observed behaviors and inferred dispositions is "correspondence." The problem for the observer is whether any disposition corresponds to the observer's description of another person's behavior. Correspondence depends on certain variables. These variables concern the "effects" produced by a behavior rather than the behavior itself. Jones and Davis rule out effects for which behaviors are unobserved as evidence of dispositions—that is, as candidates for possible correspondence. This restriction seems unnecessary. The theory may readily be extended, as shown in the shaded areas in figure

2. Correspondence is certainly possible where both behaviors and effects are observed. Jones and Davis do not allow, however, for the possibility that behavior can be assumed in the face of observed effects. If this logic is pursued, it becomes apparent that one of the main contributions of the theory lies in suggesting that attributions may be made on the basis of knowledge about the effects of a person's actions *even though these actions were not themselves observed.* To see the importance of this for the attribution of leadership, consider the situation in which a person is placed in a supervisory position and the performance results of his subordinates suddenly improve. Although no one may ever observe behaviors on the part of the supervisor which could have produced the improved results, these effects are still typically used as a basis for attributions.

Instances in which behavior is observed but effects are not are more problematic. The physical, or otherwise objective, description of behavior is rarely in itself meaningful. Behavior only acquires meaning when suppositions about effects and purposes are part of the description. Otherwise the description is unnatural, for the very reason that correspondence is precluded. One of the main values of Jones and Davis' work is to point up the sterility of any attribution theory that does not recognize the nonobjective nature of the description of behavioral observations. These descriptions are so weighted toward effects that the actual observation of behavior is hardly a necessary condition for correspondence.

Jones and Davis also limit their analysis to intended effects. Again we must recognize the weight given to effects in descriptions. Even unintended or accidental effects color descriptions. An observer might know that a successful new supervisor could not logically have produced all the improvement in his subordinates' performance, but these performance effects are part of the description of that supervisor's behavior anyway. Existing attribution theories are quite weak in capturing the meaningfulness of such descriptions. It is an oversimplification to focus separately on either behavior or effects.

Two key variables, according to Jones and Davis, affect correspondence: the number of noncommon effects produced by a choice, and the social desirability of a choice. The choice may be between implicit or explicit alternatives. In either case, the chosen alternative is associated with a set of observed effects, *and* each of the unchosen alternatives is associated with a set of effects which would have been the consequences had they been chosen. To the extent that the effects associated with the chosen alternative do not overlap with those of the unchosen alternatives, a stronger attribution can be made. For example, if a woman chooses to marry one of three boyfriends, where all three are handsome but the chosen one is richer while the other two are more intelligent and personable, the chosen alternative possesses fewer noncommon effects (being rich is the sole noncommon effect), and the attribution should be strong that the woman is materialistic, and so forth. The strength of an attribution is also increased if the assumed social desirability of the effects associated with the chosen alternative is low. People may choose what is socially desirable rather than personally desirable. If most people would have preferred the effects of the choice, it is less revealing of an internal, nonsituational cause than a choice involving less socially desirable effects.

FIGURE 3   An Analysis of Leadership Attributions
Based on Jones and Davis' Theory of Correspondent Inferences

		Assumed Social Desirability of Effects	
		High	Low
Number of Noncommon Effects	High	Ambiguous and Doubtful Leadership	Interesting but Ambiguous Leadership
	Low	Doubtful Leadership	Correspondent Leadership

Jones and Davis' theory is not well developed. It does not recognize, for instance, the fact that selection of a set of alternatives involves as much choice as the final selection among alternatives. That is, the fact that all of a woman's boyfriends are handsome must surely affect attributions, even though the theory eliminates this effect because it is common within the choice set at a particular point. The theory has stimulated interesting research, however. In an experimental paradigm originated by Jones, Davis, and Gergen (1961), a subject observes a job interview and then makes attributions about the interviewee. The interviewee is either consistent with the role demands of this job (in-role) or is inconsistent (out-of-role). Out-of-role behavior presumably encompasses fewer noncommon effects and has lower social desirability. As predicted, attributions about the interviewee's personality traits are stronger for out-of-role behavior. Figure 3 displays a summary of the impact of the number of noncommon effects and the social desirability of effects on the attribution of leadership. Correspondent inferences are possible only when both variables are low. In this case, observers can be more confident that behavior which can be described in the language of leadership also reflects personal leadership qualities.

Attribution theories are not as mechanistic as our discussion indicates. The active nature of the perceiver's role is usually handled in terms of observer biases. Jones and Davis emphasize the possible consequences of an action for the observer. The effects on which an inference about correspondence is based may be interpreted differently, depending on the involvement of the observer. The effects may be "hedonically relevant" in that they constitute positive or negative outcomes for the observer; or they may involve "personalism" in that they are perceived to be directed at the observer personally. Both hedonic relevance and personalism may strengthen what would otherwise be a weak attribution. In general, if behavior is observed during the course of an ongoing interaction, the goals of that interaction will in part shape the nature of the attributions made (cf. Jones and Thibaut, 1958). Such biases are likely to be particularly important for the attribution of leadership in groups where goal compatibility among members is absent. If the goals embodied in an observed behavior conflict with an observer's own goals, the observer is less likely to make a leadership attribution regardless of the nature of the observed behavior.

An Attribution Theory of Leadership

We may now draw together our discussion in the form of a tentative attribution theory of leadership. As noted, it is felt that the theoretical perspectives of Kelley and Jones and Davis do not in themselves provide a complete approach. The present perspective seeks to point up the full complexities of the naïve psychology of leadership. Figure 4 provides an overview of the model.

Leadership is defined as a first-degree construct. It refers to a set of personal qualities which are described in ordinary language. These qualities and the words used to describe them differ for different groups of actors and situations. The investigation of the naïve psychology of leadership presumes some knowledge of the qualities and language which constitute the meaning of leadership. The scientific problem at issue is the explanation of how a set of actors, for whom leadership is situationally defined, infer leadership from observing each other's behavior. The internal qualities associated with leadership are not directly knowable. The individual who uses the first-degree construct of leadership must work backward from behavior and can never know with certainty whether or not leadership qualities actually exist as a personal cause of behavior.

FIGURE 4   Flow Diagram of the Attribution Model

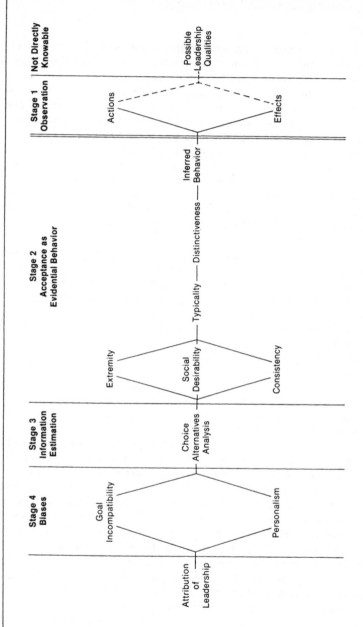

Leadership is a disposition and cannot itself be observed. The first stage in the attribution of leadership is therefore the observation of behavior by another and the effects of this behavior. (Note that the stages in fig. 4 are given from right to left to connote that the individual is working backward.) In the simplest instance, the individual observes both actual physical behavior and its consequences. The observation of physical behavior, however, is not a necessary condition for the attribution of leadership. Many behaviors are private or otherwise unobservable. Often description is available only second-hand from others. As discussed in connection with Jones and Davis' work, individuals may also rely heavily on knowledge about effects which are associated with a person, even though the requisite behavior for these effects has not been observed. If an effect is not in actuality due to a person, this is a source of attributional error.

Observed actions and effects may also imply entirely different behaviors which have no basis at all in actual observation. Individuals may infer the existence of important behaviors from observations which are trivial in themselves. Earlier we saw that simply observing the amount of time talking increased the likelihood of attributing leadership. Such relationships probably depend on the fact that such simple observations imply the existence of otherwise unobserved behaviors. Someone who talks a lot in a group probably makes relatively more money, knows important people, and so forth. These "inferred observations" supply indirect evidence to the attribution process. It is explicitly recognized in the next stage of our model that individuals may base their attributions on more information than they have in fact observed.

In the second state of the attribution process, actual and inferred observations are either accepted or rejected as evidence of leadership. Observations are first examined for distinctiveness. The actions and effects associated with a focal person are compared with other actors in the group. To be acceptable as evidence, the focal person's behavior must be distinguishable. By definition, leadership cannot describe everyone in the group; its very meaning calls for distinctive behavior. The process we have in mind is similar to Kelley's notion of distinctiveness. There the emphasis was on how a person sorts out his own reactions to people. Does he always react in a particular way to most people or is his reaction to a certain person distinctive? Only if the reaction is distinctive should it be attributed to some property of the focal person. Our contention is that a somewhat simpler notion will do.

An individual examines the variability in behavior across the group. If little variability exists, then there is no information on which to base inferences about leadership. With greater variability, more potential evidence is available to the attribution process.

Once potential evidence is detected, it is matched against expectations about how leaders should act. Figure 5 characterizes the nature of these "typicality" inferences. The meaning of leadership for a group is represented as a set of beliefs linking leadership qualities to specific behaviors. The individual has what amounts to an implicit theory of leadership. That is, he believes that personal leadership qualities

FIGURE 5   Processes Underlying Typicality Inferences

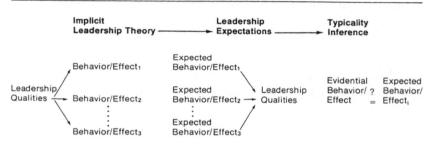

produce certain behaviors and effects. These beliefs are at the core of the first-degree qualitative meaning of leadership. The individual uses his implicit leadership theory to interpret potential evidential behaviors and effects. He does this by reversing the causal direction of his beliefs. As depicted in figure 5, expectations are formed by assuming that the behaviors and effects believed to be caused by leadership qualities themselves provide causal evidence for the existence of these qualities. That is, the belief that a certain leadership quality produces a certain behavior is transformed into the expectation that an instance of the behavior implies the existence of the quality. Logically this is to assert that if A implies B, then B implies A. While logically incorrect, these expectations provide a psychological basis for interpreting observed behavior. A potential evidential behavior or effect is compared with expected behaviors and effects. If the former is similar to the latter, a typicality inference is made. The inference is that the potential evidence, standing alone, implies leadership qualities.

It may be helpful to illustrate the psychologic of the putative typicality inference process. Remember that, by our account, leadership has meaning only as defined by a particular group of actors. Let us look at, what is for leadership research, a somewhat unusual group— apartment house janitors in Chicago. Intensive interviews by Gold (1964) suggest the tenor of the janitor's everyday life. "Cut-throating", for instance, is common. This is the practice of trying to force another janitor out of a building by reporting violations of union rules (e.g., the other janitor's wife helps him do the work), sabotaging the other janitor's building or equipment, and even going directly to the other janitor's boss to ask for that janitor's building. Now we might imagine that these janitors, in their interaction, have certain ideas about leadership, or personal potency. Suppose that this group thinks of leadership in terms of qualities such as manliness, aggressiveness, shrewdness, and egotisticalness. Whatever their own language for these traits, this constellation underlies the meaning of leadership for them.

The meaning of leadership must further depend on a set of beliefs which explain certain behaviors on the basis of these qualities. Corresponding to the first step in figure 5, suppose that the janitors' implicit theory of leadership looked something like that shown in figure 6 (arrows indicate that a quality leads to a behavior).

FIGURE 6   Janitors' Implicit Theories of Leadership

Qualities	Behavior
Manliness	Tries to cut-throat other janitors
	Engages in intimidating rough-housing
Aggressiveness	Makes fun of some janitors
	Takes up for his janitor friends
Shrewdness	Talks a lot about his exploits
Egotisticalness	Stands up to tenants

When janitors observe each others' behavior, their implicit theory of leadership is used in reverse. That is, they assume, corresponding to the second step in figure 5, that trying to cut-throat other janitors implies the qualities of aggressiveness and shrewdness. (That such underhandedness might indicate the opposite of leadership in some groups is irrelevant.) Engaging in intimidating rough-housing indicates manliness and aggressiveness, and so on for the other behaviors. Such reversals create leadership expectations. If a given observed behavior is judged distinctive (see fig. 4), it is compared with these expectations (the third step in fig. 5). If the two are similar—the observed behavior is *typical* of the expected—then the observed behavior is taken, other things being equal, to indicate leadership.

Typicality inferences are not sufficient for the attribution of leadership, however. Look back at figure 4. The next step is the determination of whether or not there are alternative explanations of the observed behavior which would discount the typicality inference. This is the major concern of most attribution theorists, and Kelley's ideas are important here. Although all possible alternative explanations can never be ruled out, not even psychologically, it is possible for the individual to examine the evidence for spuriousness, the possibility that the ostensible behavior-leadership link is actually due to some extraneous factor. The work of Kelley, discussed earlier, suggests three major dimensions for such an intuitive analysis. If the evidence does not hold up over time or across relevant situations, or if it is not supported by the opinions of other relevant actors, it may plausibly be attributed to nonpersonal situational sources. "Standing up to a tenant" on one occasion is not attributed to a janitor's leadership qualities unless this behavior is validated so as to minimize the possibility of spuriousness. Along with Kelley's validation dimensions, we would explicitly add Jones and Davis' criteria of social desirability. Group pressure is a powerful alternative explanation which must be ruled out in the attribution of leadership.

Coupled with the consistency evaluation of potential evidence in figure 4 is the evaluation of extremity. This is thought to be important in two ways. First, it is possible that evidence may not be judged extreme or important enough to imply leadership qualities. The nature of leadership is such that individuals may have quantitative standards for leadership. Even behaviors and effects which are distinctive and typical may not automatically be assumed to indicate leadership. Potential evidence is discounted unless certain cutoffs are exceeded. Standing up to a tenant might have to entail telling the tenant what he can and cannot request rather than merely a less extreme, passive refusal to comply with a request.

The extremity evaluation is also important as a possible bypass for consistency alternative explanations. This is why in figure 4 it is depicted as operating in parallel with consistency and social desirability. Any behavior or effect which is sufficiently extreme can override alternative explanations. This is the phenomenon Heider called "engulfing the field" of perception. It probably occurs frequently in the attribution of leadership. The rumor of a janitor's having once punched a tenant in the nose might be extreme enough to override any consideration of validity.

The third stage postulated in the attribution process involves what is termed "information estimation." The prior acceptance stage determines whether potential evidence should be interpreted as indicating leadership or should be discounted. Evidence, however, may be acceptable and still not be specifically informative about leadership qualities. Following Jones and Davis, the informativeness of the evidence is thought to depend on an analysis of the alternative behaviors presumably open to a focal person. For any behavior that a focal person performs, it is possible to construe various alternative behaviors and the effects associated with them. At a minimum there is the alternative of not performing the behavior. By comparing the evidential behavior and effects with hypothesized alternatives, the information value of the evidence can be estimated. Jones and Davis' notion of noncommon effects is illustrative in many ways of the process we have in mind.

Although a full analysis of the information estimation stage is beyond the scope of this discussion, what is plausible is that an observer evaluates the evidential worth of observed behavior and effects by comparing them to what he construes to be the *personal* alternatives of the actor. He compares the behavior performed with other things the actor might have done. The likelihood that an observed behavior is caused by leadership qualities as opposed to other qualities can be evaluated from these alternatives. A different sort of validity is at stake here, one more akin to what we might think of in scientific parlance as "construct" validity. The question is whether there is any evidence for "leadership" qualities causing the observed behavior versus other, perhaps unsuspected, qualities. The acceptance stage dealt with spuriousness, not the legitimacy of the inferred qualities themselves. It is informative in the latter regard to believe that the person observed could have performed other behaviors with different effects, which would have implicated nonleadership qualities. This is particularly true to the extent that the observed behavior could be explained by these same nonleadership qualities as well as possible leadership qualities. If a janitor were known to have other options for making extra money (for example, working part-time for his brother-in-law), but the janitor seemed to choose cut-throating instead, an observer would feel far more confident that the underlying qualities involved in cut-throating were aggressiveness and shrewdness, which are leadership qualities, rather than greediness, which is common to both behaviors. While the previous stage ruled out nonpersonal alternative explanations, in this stage more or less confidence in the evidential behavior results from attemps to rule out competing personal explanations which do not involve leadership qualities.

The final state shown in figure 4 recognizes the potential of individual biases to affect attributions. The major sources of bias have already been discussed. There is the broad class of goal incompatibility, which subsumes hedonic relevance, and the more specific effect of personalism. It is our hypothesis that the latter effect generally produces only minor distortions in comparison with goal incompatibility. It would seem very difficult to attribute leadership to someone whose goals run against one's own. On the other hand, the attribution of leadership would seem much easier if it facilitates attainment of one's goals.

Conclusions

Parts of the theoretical discussion here have of necessity been speculative. There are, to our mind, wide gaps in attribution theorizing. Moreover, attribution theorists in social psychology have never confronted the need for rich, qualitative understanding which their work implies. It is hoped that the present theory, and our comments on the naïve psychology of leadership, suggest a way in which it is possible, finally, to subject that aspect of everyday experience we call leadership to scientific scrutiny.

An attribution theory of leadership is likely to strike many as mere sophistry. They may feel that somehow there is nothing really new in it. There have long been studies of the perception of leadership. While true, this should not obscure the central point of the proposed theory: Leadership *exists* only as a perception. Leadership is not a viable scientific construct. It is, however, extremely important as naïve psychology. Attribution theory seeks to provide a scientific analysis of this naïve psychology. The problem for future research is not merely what variables affect the perception of leadership. Research must be directed at the underlying nature of the leadership attribution process. The theoretical proposals set forth in this chapter are intended to stimulate such research.

Attribution theory also has important implications for leadership training. Leadership cannot be taught as a skill. Skills may certainly help a person to perform more effectively, but leadership depends on how this performance and its effects are perceived by others. To teach leadership is to sensitize people to the perceptions of others—that is, to sensitize them to the everyday common-sense thinking of a group of people. The transfer of leadership from one group of actors to another thus becomes highly problematic. The would-be-leader must respond to attributions based on the meaning of leadership for each group with which he interacts.

If it does nothing more than call attention to the need for understanding the everyday, nonscientific, meaning of leadership for specific groups of actors, attribution theory represents an advance for both leadership research and training.

References

Bales, R. F. *Interaction Process Analysis: A Method for the Study of Small Groups.* Reading: Addison-Wesley, 1950.

Bales, R., Strodtbeck, F., Mills, T., and Roseborough, M. Channels of communication in small groups. *American Sociological Review,* 1951, *16,* 461-68.

Bavelas, A., Hastorf, A. H., Gross, A. E., and Kite, W. R. Experiments on the alternation of group structure. *Journal of Experimental Social Psychology,* 1965, *1,* 55-70.

Bunge, M. *Scientific Research I: The Search for System.* Berlin: Springer, 1967.

Chemers, M. M. and Skrzypek, G. J. Experimental test of the contingency model of leadership effectiveness. *Journal of Personality and Social Psychology,* 1972, *24,* 172-77.

Cicourel, A. *Method and Measurement in Sociology.* New York: Free Press, 1964.

Coleman, J. The mathematical study of small groups. In H. Solomon (ed.), *Mathematical thinking in the measurement of behavior,* Glencoe, Illinois: The Free Press of Glencoe, 1960.

Evans, M. The effects of supervisory behavior on the path-goal relationship. *Organization Behavior and Human Performance,* 1970, *55,* 277-98.

————. Extensions of a path-goal theory of motivation. *Journal of Applied Psychology,* 1974, *59,* 172-78.

Fiedler, F. E. A contingency model of leadership effectiveness. In L. Berkowitz (ed.), *Advances in experimental social psychology,* vol. I, Academic Press, 1964.

————. *A Theory of Leadership Effectiveness.* New York: McGraw-Hill, 1967.

————. Validation and extension of the contingency model of leadership effectiveness: A review of empirical findings. *Psychological Bulletin,* 1971a, *76,* 128-48.

————. *Leadership.* New York: General Learning Press, 1971b.

Gibb, C. A. Leadership. In G. Lindzey (ed.), *Handbook of Social Psychology,* vol. 2, Reading: Addison-Wesley, 1954, p. 877-920.

————. An interactional view of the emergence of leadership. In C. A. Gibb (ed.), *Leadership,* Baltimore: Penguin Books, 1969a, p. 214-22.

————. Leadership. In G. Lindzey and E. Aronson (eds.), *The Handbook of Social Psychology* (2nd ed.), vol 4, Reading: Addison-Wesley, 1969b, p. 205-82.

Gold, R. In the basement—The apartment building janitor. In P. Berger (ed.), *The Human Shape of Work: Studies in the Sociology of Occupations,* New York: Macmillan, 1964, pp. 1-49.

Graen, G., Alvares, K., Orris, J. B., Martella, J. A. Contingency model of leadership effectiveness: Antecedent and evidential results. *Psychological Bulletin,* 1969, *74,* 285-96.

Heider, F. *The Psychology of Interpersonal Relations,* New York: Wiley, 1958.

Hemphill, J. K. The leader and his group. *Educational Research Bulletin,* 1949, *28,* 225-29.

Hollander, E. Conformity, status, and idiosyncracy credit. *Psychological Review,* 1958, *65,* 117-27.

Hollander, E. P. and Jullian, J. W. Leadership. In E. F. Borgatta and W. W. Lambert (eds.), *Handbook of Personality Theory and Research,* Chicago: Rand McNally, 1968, p. 890-99.

————. Contemporary trends in the analysis of leadership processes. *Psychological Bulletin,* 1969, *71,* 387-97.

————. Studies in leader legitimacy, influence, and innovation. In L. Berkowitz (ed.), *Advances in Experimental Social Psychology,* vol. 5, New York: Academic Press, 1970, p. 34-69.

House, R. A path-goal theory of leader effectiveness. *Administrative Science Quarterly,* 1971, *16,* 321-38.

House, R., and Mitchell, T. Path-goal theory of leadership. *Journal of Contemporary Business,* 1974, *3,* 81-97.

Hunt, J. G. Fiedler's leadership contingency model: An empirical test in three organizations. *Organizational Behavior and Human Performance,* 1967, *2,* 290-308.

Jones, E. E. and Davis, K. E. From acts to dispositions. In L. Berkowitz (ed.), *Advances in Experimental Social Psychology,* vol. 2, New York: Academic Press, 1965.

Jones, E., Davis, K., and Gergen, K. Role playing variations and their informational value for person perception. *Journal of Abnormal and Social Psychology,* 1961, *63,* 302-10.

Jones, E. and Thibout, J. Interaction goals as bases of inference in person perception. In R. Taguiri and L. Petrullo (eds.), *Person Perception and Interpersonal Behavior,* Stanford: Stanford University Press, 1958.

Kadane, J. B., and Lewis, G. H. The distribution of participation in group discussions: An empirical and theoretical reappraisal. *American Sociological Review,* 1969, *34,* 710-23.

Kahn, R., and Katz, D. Leadership practices in relation to productivity and morale. In D. Cartwright and A. Zander (eds.), *Group dynamics,* Evanston, Ill.: Row, Peterson, and Co., 1960.

Kaplan, A. *The Conduct of Inquiry: Methodology for Behavioral Science,* New York: Intext Educational Publishers, 1964.

Katz, D., and Kahn, R. L. *The Social Psychology of Organizations.* New York: Wiley, 1966.

Kelley, H. Attribution theory in social psychology. *Nebraska Symposium on Motivation,* 1967, *15,* 192-238.

———. *Attribution in Social Interaction.* Morriston, N. J.: General Learning Press, 1971.

———. *Causal Schemata and the Attribution Process.* Morristown, N. J.: General Learning Press, 1972.

Kochan, T., Schmidt, S., and De Cotiis, T. Superior-subordinate relations: Leadership and headship. *Human Relations,* 1975, *28,* 279-94.

Mann, R. D. A review of the relationships between personality and performance in small groups. *Psychological Bulletin,* 1959, *56,* 241-70.

MacArthur, L. The how and what of why: Some determinants and consequences of causal attribution. *Journal of Personality and Social Psychology,* 1972, *22,* 171-93.

Oldham, G. The motivational strategies used by supervisors: Relationships to effectiveness indicators. *Organizational Behavior and Human Performance,* 1976, *15,* 66-86.

Pfeffer, J. *The ambiguity of leadership. Academy of Management Review,* in press.

Reichenbach, H. *Elements of Symbolic Logic.* New York: The Free Press, 1947.

Schutz, A. *The Phenomenology of the Social World.* Evanston, Ill.: Northwestern University Press, 1967.

Shartle, C. *Executive Performance and Leadership.* Columbus: Ohio State University Research Foundation, 1952.

Stephan, F., and Mishler, E. The distribution of participation in small groups: An exponential approximation. *American Sociological Review,* 1952, *17,* 598-608.

Stogdill, R. Personal factors associated with leadership. *Journal of Psychology,* 1948, *25,* 35-71.

Vroom, V., and Yetton, P. *Leadership and Decision-Making.* Pittsburgh: University of Pittsburgh Press, 1973.

Zdep, S. M., and Oakes, W. F. Reinforcement of leadership behavior in group discussion *Journal of Experimental Social Psychology,* 1967, *3,* 310-20.

Part XI
Role of Followers

[20]

The Effects of Varying Combinations of Authoritarian and Equalitarian Leaders and Followers[1]

William Haythorn, The RAND Corporation, Arthur Couch, Harvard University, Don Haefner, Peter Langham, University of Rochester and Launor Carter, The RAND Corporation

Recently attention has been focused on the relationships between the personality characteristics of group members and the nature of the leadership that emerges from the interaction of these individuals with each other and their tasks (3, 8). The behavior of leaders in groups is determined not only by their own personalities, but also by the underlying needs, role expectations, and values of the group members. Conversely, the behavior of group members is partly determined by the personality of the leaders, particularly in interaction with their own needs and expectations. Of particular interest are groups in which there is some modal similarity or dissimilarity of the leader's and followers' personalities, creating situations where the interaction of different needs, expectations, perceptions, and values can be studied systematically. The present study was designed to investigate a specific case of the interaction between leader's and followers' personalities in the determination of behavior in groups.

This paper is the second report describing the results of a study of the behavior of authoritarian and equalitarian personalities in small groups. The California F scale was used as the principal measure of the authoritarian personality (1). In the first paper (11), behavioral differences between groups composed of individuals homogeneously high on the F scale and individuals homogeneously low on the F scale were reported. An analysis was made of the differences between these groups with respect to rated behavioral traits, recorded behavioral acts, and responses to a Post-Meeting Reaction Sheet. Significant differences between high-F and low-F Ss in the predicted directions were found, indicating that a more 'democratic' group culture prevailed in the low-F groups, and the low-F groups were more effective in dealing with the task problem. Significant differences – more marked than those distinguishing the groups as a whole – were found between the emergent leaders of the two kinds of groups, indicating that a qualitatively different kind of leadership occurs in groups composed of personalities at opposite ends of the authoritarian–equalitarian dimension. Emergent leaders in the low-F groups were more sensitive to others, more effective leaders, more prone to making suggestions for action subject to group sanction, and less likely to give direct orders to others.

To permit experimental manipulation of the leadership structure, these same subjects were subsequently assembled with appointed leaders in the study reported here. Half of the groups were composed with appointed leaders who had F scores similar to those of the other group members, while in the other half the appointed leaders had scores at the opposite end of the distribution. This design permitted an investigation of the effects of assembling groups with leaders whose personalities were similar to those of other group members, as compared with groups whose leaders' personalities were unlike those of other members. The major hypotheses examined were as follows:

　　1. *Hypothesis 1.* F-plus *leaders* (a) engage in less equalitarian behavior than F-minus leaders; (b) are less concerned with group approval for their actions; (c) engage in more autocratic behavior; and (d) show less sensitivity to others than do F-minus leaders.

　　2. *Hypothesis 2.* F-plus *followers* (a) engage in less equalitarian behavior; (b) show less sensitivity to others; (c) are more satisfied with appointed leaders; (d) are less critical of their own group; and (e) are more submissive toward appointed leaders than F-minus followers.

　　3. *Hypothesis 3. Under F-minus leadership,* followers (a) have more influence on group processes; (b) develop a less formal group structure; and (c) express greater differences of opinion than under F-plus leadership.

　　4. *Hypothesis 4. With F-minus followers,* leaders (a) are not likely to engage in as much autocratic behavior; and (b) are not as distinct from other group members as are leaders with F-plus followers. That is, leaders with F-plus followers are thought, when under pressure, to take decisive, directive action in order to get the job done, because of the expectations on the part of F-plus followers regarding the role of an appointed leader.

　　5. *Hypothesis 5. In groups composed of leaders and followers with similar F-Scale scores,* (a) followers are more secure; (b) followers are more motivated to achieve the common group goal; (c) followers are more satisfied with the appointed leadership; (d) there is less personality conflict within the group; (e) there is less conflict between the leader and group members; and (f) there is higher group morale and productivity than in groups composed of leaders and followers with dissimilar F-scale scores.

Method

Subjects

The subjects (Ss) for the experiments consisted of (a) 32 male undergraduate students who were high on the F scale, 'conservative' as judged by the Cattell Q_1 scale, and relatively normal as estimated by the MMPI; and (b) 32 male undergraduate students who had low F-scale scores, were liberal as determined by the Q_1 scale, and were also 'normal' as judged by the MMPI. The mean F-scale scores for the two groups were 124.5 and 66.9, respectively, using the 30-item, 7-points-per-item scale described in the *Authoritarian Personality* (1).[2]

The Task

The task given the groups was the discussion and composition of a short script involving a human relations problem. Complete instructions were read to the Ss before they began working, to the effect that they were to help E in developing a test of human relations skills. They were to be shown a film of a human relations problem, after which they were to answer a number of questions about how the problem had been handled, how it should have been handled, etc. When they finished answering the questions as individuals, they were to discuss similar questions as a group and arrive at answers to which they all agreed. Following completion of this phase of the task, they were to compose dialogue for similar films. Once their script was completed, they were to record it on a magnetic tape recorder. After reading the instructions, E showed the film, then left the room. He did not return until the group had completed all phases of the procedure outlined in the instructions. A typed copy of the latter was left on the table with the Ss.

Observation Procedures

While Ss worked on the task in the experimental room, observers watched through one-way vision mirrors from an adjacent room. Four Os (first- and second-year graduate students) recorded their observations in three ways, as follows:

1. While observing, Os categorized and 'typed out' behavioral units as they occurred, using a Stenotype system of interaction recording described in an earlier paper (4). The category system was revised, however, to fit the needs of this study.

2. At the end of 30 minutes of recording, the pair of Os was relieved by another pair. Immediately after being relieved, Os rated each S on 16 behavioral characteristics, defined in the previous report (11), as follows: striving for individual prominence, friendliness, security, influence, equalitarianism, striving for group approval, submissiveness, striving for goal achievement, self-isolating behavior, effective intelligence, sensitivity to others, leadership, aggressiveness, autocratic behavior, social ability, and nonadaptability. These ratings had an average interobserver reliability of .75, with a range from .31 to .91. Since the group sessions varied in length from two to four hours, each S was rated by each O at least once in each group, and usually two or more times.

3. At the end of each group session, all four Os and E filled out a Post-Meeting Reaction Sheet (PMRS) designed to describe aspects of the group not easily attributed to single individuals. Examples of the items on the PMRS are:

   a. This group was not serious enough – there was too much playing around.

   b. The group effectiveness was interfered with by personality clashes between members.

   There were 37 such items, to each of which Os indicated the extent of their agreement, using a 7-point scale.

4. In addition, Ss were asked to fill out a very similar PMRS, and to rate the degree to which they were satisfied with their group, the extent to which they thought the group had been productive, to rank the group members in order of how well they were liked, and to rank group members in terms of their relative contributions to the achievement of group goals.

'Emergent' Group Sessions

The Ss were scheduled to come to the laboratory work room in groups of four. In their first session – results of which are described in the previous paper (11) – each of the sixteen groups was composed of Ss homogeneous with regard to F-scale scores. In this session, there was no experimental structuring of leadership.

Appointed Leader Sessions

After the emergent sessions, all individuals were reassembled with three members from their original emergent groups and another member from a different group. The alien member was appointed as leader (by telling him he was to take charge of group activities that day and would be responsible for getting the job done). In half of the groups the leader had an F score similar to that of group members, and in half it was dissimilar. Thus there were four groups with F-plus leaders and F-plus followers, four with F-plus leaders and F-minus followers, four with F-minus leaders and F-plus followers, and four with F-minus leaders and F-minus followers.

In Session III, two of the original emergent-group members who had been together in Session II were reassembled with the member who had been withdrawn during Session II. In addition, an alien member was introduced as the leader for that session. Groups having had an F-plus leader in Session II were given an F-minus leader in Session III, and vice versa.

Characteristics of Appointed Leaders

The experimental design required that 32 of the 64 Ss be appointed as leaders, 16 in Session II and 16 in Session III. Two were chosen from each of the original groups as follows: The men in each group were assigned ranks on the basis of the leadership nominations made by Ss in their PMRS, and also on the basis of leadership ratings made by Os. Finally, in the F-minus groups each S was ranked on the basis of the equalitarian ratings given by Os, while in the F-plus groups they were ranked on the basis of ratings by Os of autocratic behavior. These three sets of ranks were averaged, and the two individuals (Ranks I and II) with the lowest average ranks were selected to serve as appointed leaders in subsequent groups. A later check showed that this procedure, designed to assure as nearly as possible that the appointed leaders would behave in an authoritarian or equalitarian manner, resulted in selecting the same leaders as would have been chosen by subject ratings alone if ties were broken by observer ratings.

Analysis of data obtained in the emergent sessions (11) indicated significant behavioral differences between the individuals chosen from the F-plus groups and those chosen from the F-minus. In summary, leaders chosen from the F-minus groups were rated as being more friendly, more secure, more equalitarian, less striving for group approval, more submissive, less self-isolating, showing more effective intelligence, showing greater sensitivity to others, and showing greater leadership. The pattern of results generally agrees with current opinion concerning the differences between authoritarian and equalitarian leaders, except that the differences in aggressiveness and autocratic behavior failed to reach statistical significance.

Observers were not informed of the composition of the groups during the experiment, and were unable to guess the composition pattern significantly more accurately than chance. This finding may be attributed to an observer expectation that authoritarian individuals would be more aggressive, argumentative, and generally uncompromising towards others. Instead, in the emergent sessions they were rated as being significantly more concerned with group approval than were the F-minus Ss. Such concern for group approval in groups having no formal authority structure is theoretically a central facet of the authoritarian personality structure (1), underlying the tendency to conform to social mores. However, our Os apparently tended to identify pleasant social behavior as evidence of equalitarianism and consequently made many errors in attempting to estimate group composition. The fact that analyses generally supported our hypotheses in spite of observer failure to distinguish the groups is presumptive evidence that results to be reported are not attributable to bias.

Results

Trait Ratings of Appointed Leaders

The experimental design, a 2 × 2 factorial design with leaders' and followers' personalities as the main effects, permitted testing of several sources of variance. Group means and results of the analyses of variance of ratings by Os are presented in Table 1. Only the ratings yielding significant F ratios are included, in order to conserve space. Seven of the 16 rating variables did not yield significant F ratios for any of the three sources on either session.

The data entered in Table 1 are mean ratings of the appointed leaders, averaged over four Os. The four groups are F-plus leaders with F-minus followers, etc. The within-group variance is taken as the best estimate of error, or variance not attributable to experimental conditions. The 'effects on leaders' are divided into three sources: F scores of the followers, F scores of the leaders, and whether the leader and followers were homogeneous or heterogeneous with regard to F scores (the latter is the leader-by-follower interaction in the analysis of variance).

Trait Ratings of Followers

Analysis of the ratings of followers' behavior by Os parallels that for ratings of leaders. The main effects are the F scores of the followers and of the leaders. Again the interaction mean square indicates the effects of homogeneity vs. heterogeneity of leader–follower combinations. Only seven of the 16 variables yielded significant F ratios. These are presented in Table 2, with the group means and the within-group variance estimates.

There were three followers in each of the 16 groups in each session. Thus, each of the means of the four conditions are based on ratings of 12 individuals. However, in an earlier study (9) it was shown that the ratings of individuals within a group are not independent. Therefore, the average rating of the three followers in each group was computed and these averages used in computing means and within-group variance. Each condition mean is based on the averages of four groups. This procedure results in 15 degrees of freedom (16 − 1), distributed as follows: 1 for leaders' F scores, 1 for followers' F scores, 1 for interaction, and 12 for within-group variance. The estimate of significance so derived is believed to be very conservative.

Table 1 *Trait-Rating Results: Appointed Leadership Sessions (Leaders)*

| Analysis of Variance | | Leader Means | | | | | Effect on Leaders of: | | |
| | | F+ leaders | | F− leaders | | | | | |
Trait names	Session	$(F+F)^{\dagger}$	$(F-F)^{\dagger}$	$(F+F)$	$(F-F)$	s^2w	F+ vs. F− followers F ratio	Leader's personality F ratio	Group's composition F ratio
I. Individual Prominence	II	4.76	3.19	4.08	4.13	0.16	14.574 (F+)**	0.028 (F−)	1.097 (Homo)
	III	4.51	3.08	4.28	3.52	0.77	6.298 (F+)*	0.056 (F−)	0.572 (Homo)
V. Equalitarianism	II	3.56	4.76	5.29	4.82	0.70	0.747 (F−)	4.569 (F−)	3.954 (Hetero)
	III	3.27	4.04	4.89	5.48	1.00	1.837 (F−)	9.350 (F−)*	0.033 (Hetero)
VI. Striving for Group Approval	II	3.89	3.62	4.49	4.26	0.25	1.039 (F+)	6.264 (F−)*	0.008 (Homo)
	III	4.12	3.31	4.42	4.24	0.72	1.360 (F+)	2.068 (F−)	0.567 (Homo)
VII. Submissiveness	II	3.03	3.28	3.43	2.75	0.59	0.325 (F+)	0.026 (F+)	1.462 (Hetero)
	III	2.57	3.77	3.34	3.07	0.41	2.100 (F−)	0.011 (F−)	5.165 (Hetero)*
IX. Aggressiveness	II	2.98	1.78	1.92	2.49	0.39	1.013 (F+)	0.329 (F+)	8.037 (Homo)*
	III	2.95	1.63	1.96	1.34	0.51	7.441 (F+)*	3.223 (F+)	0.964 (Homo)
X. Autocratic	II	3.64	1.99	2.21	2.61	0.56	2.773 (F+)	1.150 (F+)	7.459 (Homo)*
	III	3.56	1.98	2.20	1.64	0.43	10.821 (F+)*	6.877 (F+)*	2.471 (Homo)
XI. Effective Intelligence	II	4.32	4.46	5.23	4.92	0.31	0.095 (F+)	5.963 (F−)*	0.653 (Hetero)
	III	4.21	3.90	4.96	5.42	0.53	0.038 (F−)	9.759 (F−)**	1.099 (Homo)
XII. Sensitivity	II	3.27	4.26	4.89	4.47	0.77	0.423 (F−)	4.361 (F−)	2.607 (Hetero)
	III	3.28	3.85	4.80	5.39	0.83	1.616 (F−)	11.304 (F−)**	0.001 (Homo)
XV. Nonadaptability	II	2.01	1.38	1.31	1.70	0.14	0.407 (F+)	1.055 (F+)	7.469 (Homo)*
	III	1.45	1.75	1.45	1.08	0.60	0.008 (F+)	0.759 (F+)	0.759 (Hetero)

Notes:
* p (.05) = 4.75: $df\,^1/_{12}$.
** p (.01) = 9.33.
† (F + F), (F − F), refers to the personality of Followers, (F+ Followers) (F− Followers), respectively.

390

Table 2 Trait-Rating Results: Appointed Leadership Sessions (Followers)

Analysis of Variance		Group Means					F+ vs. F− leadership F ratio	Effect on Followers of:	
		F+ followers		F− followers				Follower's personality F ratio	Group's composition F ratio
Trait names	Session	(F + L)†	(F − L)†	(F + L)	(F − L)	s²w			
III. Security	II	3.90	4.54	4.10	4.25	0.17	3.678 (F−)	0.046 (F+)	1.428 (Hetero)
	III	4.54	4.30	4.17	4.78	0.07	2.146 (F−)	0.196 (F−)	10.484 (Homo)**
IV. Influence	II	3.85	3.91	3.92	3.81	0.09	0.028 (F+)	0.014 (F+)	0.310 (Hetero)
	III	4.03	4.11	3.73	4.28	0.06	6.544 (F−)*	0.262 (F+)	3.671 (Homo)
V. Equalitarianism	II	2.62	3.16	3.57	3.52	0.45	0.525 (F−)	3.831 (F−)	0.777 (Hetero)
	III	2.64	2.61	2.94	3.99	0.32	3.211 (F−)	8.711 (F−)*	3.600 (Homo)
VI. Striving for Group Approval	II	3.12	3.16	2.72	3.04	0.16	0.823 (F−)	1.717 (F+)	0.480 (Homo)
	III	3.50	3.30	2.94	3.45	0.08	1.241 (F−)	2.046 (F+)	6.165 (Homo)*
VIII. Striving for Goal Achievement	II	3.34	3.63	3.94	3.90	0.27	0.218 (F−)	2.827 (F−)	0.398 (Hetero)
	III	3.90	3.84	3.90	4.64	0.13	3.628 (F−)	4.881 (F−)*	4.881 (Homo)*
XI. Effective Intelligence	II	3.25	3.48	3.97	3.62	0.20	0.072 (F+)	3.636 (F−)	1.702 (Hetero)
	III	3.42	3.44	3.47	4.25	0.11	5.589 (F−)*	6.537 (F−)*	5.244 (Homo)*
XII. Sensitivity	II	2.83	3.07	3.67	3.36	0.42	0.001 (F+)	3.093 (F−)	0.726 (Hetero)
	III	2.92	2.96	3.30	4.08	0.31	2.184 (F−)	7.338 (F−)*	1.780 (Homo)

Notes:
* p (.05) = 4.75: df ¹/₁₂.
** p (.01) = 9.33.
† (F + L), (F − L), refers to personality of leaders: (F + Leaders) (F − Leaders), respectively.

Behavioral Category Indices for Followers

It will be recalled that Os categorized and recorded behavioral acts as they occurred. Forty-three categories were used, but in order to simplify the analysis and increase the frequency of acts per category, these were combined into 17 category indices: I. Friendly acts; II. Positive affect acts; III. Direction-taking acts; IV. Self-emphasizing acts; V. Asking for suggestion or sanction; VI. Asking for group evaluation; VII. 'Democratic' acts; VIII. Directive acts; IX. Expressions of confusion or lack of orientation; X. Hostile acts; XI. Negative affect acts; XII. Initiating and integrating acts; XIII. Diagnosing and clarifying acts; XIV. General task participation acts; XV. Self-isolating acts; XVI. Withdrawing and out-of-field activity; and XVII. Tension release and out-of-field activity. These indices are not independent, in that some categories of behavior were included in more than one index. For a more complete description of the categories and indices, the reader is invited to consult the earlier report (11). Results of the analysis of these indices are presented in Table 3.

Subjects' Post-Meeting Reaction

At the end of each session, all four Ss were asked to complete a Post-Meeting Reaction questionnaire, asking them to express the degree to which they agreed to a number of statements about the group. Agreement was expressed on a 7-point scale with the middle point missing to eliminate noncommital responses (except the items on motivation and productivity, which had 9 points). Items on the questionnaire were grouped on a priori grounds into indices, and the means of the three followers in each group were computed. These follower means were then analyzed in the same way as previous data. Results of this analysis for all indices yielding significant F ratios are given in Table 4. No significant results were obtained for 12 of the 21 indices from the Ss' PMRS. These 12 were: II. Degree of equal participation; III. Degree of personality conflict; IV. Degree of informal friendliness; VII. Satisfaction with leadership; VIII. Degree of conflict within group; IX. Competence of members; X. Morale; XV. Formation of cliques; XVI. Personality conflict between leader and group members; XXI. Differences of opinion; XXII. Competition among members; and XXIII. Lack of cooperation.

Observers' Post-Meeting Reactions

Four Os also completed the PMRS. The same indices were computed, with the exception that Os answered questions regarding the formality of group structure and communication effectiveness, and did not answer the question concerning relative efficiency of leadership. Results of the Os' PMRS analysis are presented in Table 5. Nineteen of the 23 indices yielded at least one significant F ratio. Those that did not were: XVIII. Degree of goal-oriented control by appointed leader; XIX. Domination by appointed leader; and XXII. Competition among members.

Experimental Findings

The results, in general, support the hypotheses stated at the beginning of the paper. With regard to Hypothesis 1, F-plus leaders were rated as being less equalitarian, less concerned with group

Table 3 *Behavior Category Indices: Appointed Leadership Sessions (Followers)*

Analysis of Variance		Group Means					Effect on Followers of:		
		F+ followers		F- followers			F+ vs. F- leadership *F* ratio	F+ vs. F- personality *F* ratio	Group's composition *F* ratio
Index names	Session	(F+L)	(F−L)	(F+L)	(F−L)	s^2w			
VI. Asking for Group Evaluation (14, 11)	II	1.28	1.86	2.83	2.58	0.66	0.16 (F−)	7.87 (F−)*	1.07 (Hetero)
	III	2.87	1.73	1.93	2.60	3.18	0.07 (F+)	0.00	1.03 (Homo)
VII. 'Democratic' Acts (34, 12, 14, 11)	II	2.24	2.67	3.71	3.68	1.11	0.14 (F−)	5.54 (F−)*	0.20 (Hetero)
	III	5.00	2.78	3.22	3.37	6.85	0.62 (F+)	0.20 (F+)	0.82 (Homo)
IX. Expressions of Confusion or Lack of Orientation (22, 33, 61)	II	1.43	2.28	1.58	1.40	0.56	0.81 (F−)	0.96 (F+)	1.91 (Hetero)
	III	2.75	0.89	1.29	1.97	1.01	1.38 (F+)	0.14 (F+)	6.35 (Homo)*
XIII. Diagnosing and Clarifying Acts (35, 38)	II	2.21	3.12	5.90	4.38	2.32	0.16 (F+)	10.60 (F−)**	2.56 (Homo)*
	III	2.47	1.57	3.04	3.87	3.76	0.00	2.18 (F−)	0.80 (Homo)
XVI. Withdrawing and Out-of-field Activity (75, 76)	II	20.21	7.09	5.01	8.06	45.06	1.87 (F+)	5.08 (F+)*	5.18 (Homo)*
	III	8.93	12.74	7.31	14.97	79.93	1.65 (F−)	0.00	0.19 (Homo)
XVII. Tension Release and Out-of-field Activity (8, 76)	II	51.74	21.24	11.45	11.92	258.73	3.49 (F+)	9.51 (F+)**	3.70 (Homo)
	III	32.14	39.39	22.68	28.56	276.56	0.62 (F−)	1.49 (F+)	0.01 (Hetero)

Notes:
* p (.05) = 4.75; df ¹/₁₂.
** p (.01) = 9.33.

Table 4 Subjects' Post-Meeting Reaction Sheet Indices: Appointed Leadership Sessions (Followers)

Analysis of Variance		Group Means					F+ vs. F− leadership F ratio	Effect on Followers of:	
		F+ followers		F− followers				Follower's personality F ratio	Group's composition F ratio
Index names	Session	(F + L)†	(F − L)†	(F + L)	(F − L)	s^2w			
I. Dissatisfaction with Goal Progress	II	3.13	2.30	2.52	2.92	0.23	0.81 (F+)	0.00	6.53 (Homo)*
	III	2.53	3.28	2.50	2.38	0.25	1.59 (F−)	3.45 (F+)	2.97 (Hetero)
V. Definiteness of Leadership	II	5.17	5.35	3.98	4.00	0.10	0.42 (F−)	62.18 (F+)**	0.27 (Hetero)
	III	4.40	4.31	4.33	3.64	0.10	6.03 (F+)*	5.40 (F+)*	3.70 (Hetero)
VI. Striving for Equal Participation	II	5.96	5.75	4.42	5.21	0.36	0.95 (F−)	12.06 (F+)**	2.77 (Homo)
	III	5.96	5.79	4.54	5.42	0.65	0.77 (F−)	4.93 (F+)*	1.67 (Homo)
XI. Group Productivity	II	6.83	7.83	6.75	5.92	0.55	0.05 (F−)	7.26 (F+)*	6.10 (Hetero)*
	III	7.25	6.67	6.92	6.75	1.15	0.49 (F+)	0.05 (F+)	0.15 (Homo)
XIV. Motivation Towards Group Goal	II	5.50	5.17	3.83	4.00	1.62	0.02 (F+)	4.96 (F+)*	0.15 (Homo)
	III	5.58	5.33	4.25	4.58	1.11	0.01 (F−)	3.90 (F+)	0.31 (Homo)
XVII. Relative Efficiency of Leadership	II	5.50	5.50	6.08	4.25	0.68	4.94 (F+)*	0.65 (F+)	4.94 (Hetero)*
	III	5.41	3.55	4.16	5.41	0.58	0.60 (F+)	0.60 (F−)	15.46 (Homo)**
XVIII. Degree of Goal-oriented Control by Appointed Leader	II	4.83	6.04	5.44	4.94	0.39	1.28 (F−)	0.64 (F+)	7.43 (Hetero)*
	III	5.56	4.41	4.69	5.00	0.48	1.34 (F+)	0.16 (F+)	4.10 (Homo)
XIX. Domination by Appointed Leader	II	3.21	3.46	2.29	2.67	0.17	2.27 (F−)	16.97 (F+)**	0.09 (Homo)
	III	2.79	2.72	2.42	2.04	0.68	0.27 (F+)	1.50 (F+)	0.12 (Hetero)
XX. Satisfaction with Appointed Leader	II	4.58	5.67	4.50	3.50	0.78	0.01 (F−)	6.45 (F+)*	5.53 (Hetero)*
	III	5.25	5.22	3.91	3.66	1.34	0.05 (F+)	5.79 (F+)*	0.03 (Hetero)

Notes:
* p (.05) F ($^1/_{12}$) = 4.75.
** p (.01) = 9.33.
† (F + L), (F − L), refers to personality of leaders (F + leaders), (F − leaders), respectively.

394

Table 5 Observers' Post-Meeting Reaction Sheet Indices: Appointed Leadership Sessions (Groups)

Analysis of Variance Index names	Session	Group Means					Effect on 'Groups' of: Followers		
		F+ 'Groups'		F− 'Groups'		s²w	F+ vs. F− leadership F ratio	F+ vs. F− personality F ratio	Group's composition F ratio
		(F+L)	(F−L)	(F+L)	(F−L)				
I. Dissatisfaction with Goal Progress	II	3.85	2.48	2.52	2.92	0.76	1.23 (F+)	1.04 (F+)	4.10 (Homo)
	III	3.23	3.81	2.21	2.21	0.81	0.42 (F−)	8.50 (F+)*	0.42 (Hetero)
II. Degree of Equal Participation	II	2.88	3.02	3.17	3.08	1.20	0.01 (F−)	0.10 (F−)	0.04 (Hetero)
	III	3.38	3.48	2.28	3.78	0.33	7.71 (F−)*	1.93 (F+)	5.90 (Homo)*
III. Degree of Personality Conflict	II	3.73	3.48	2.90	3.58	0.64	0.29 (F−)	0.83 (F+)	1.35 (Homo)
	III	3.21	4.22	3.54	2.54	0.20	0.00	9.29 (F+)*	20.59 (Hetero)*
IV. Degree of Informal Friendliness	II	4.73	4.62	4.90	4.40	0.68	0.56 (F+)	0.00	0.22 (Hetero)
	III	5.00	4.47	4.32	5.48	0.36	1.11 (F−)	0.31 (F−)	7.98 (Homo)*
V. Definiteness of Leadership	II	5.52	5.14	4.04	5.06	0.40	1.00 (F−)	6.04 (F+)*	4.93 (Homo)*
	III	5.09	4.84	4.58	4.60	0.42	0.12 (F+)	1.34 (F+)	0.18 (Homo)
VI. Striving for Equal Participation	II	3.40	4.85	2.88	3.53	0.75	7.81 (F−)*	2.51 (F−)	0.30 (Hetero)
	III	3.98	4.72	4.32	5.78	0.89	5.43 (F−)*	2.20 (F−)	0.55 (Homo)
VII. Satisfaction with Leadership	II	4.95	5.04	5.60	4.85	0.68	0.13 (F+)	0.01 (F−)	2.58 (Homo)
	III	5.70	4.35	5.10	5.80	0.26	1.61 (F+)	2.75 (F−)	16.01 (Homo)**
VIII. Degree of Conflict Within Group	II	3.26	3.29	2.69	4.09	0.73	2.77 (F−)	0.07 (F−)	2.58 (Homo)
	III	2.81	3.76	3.18	2.38	0.40	0.06 (F−)	2.64 (F+)	7.71 (Hetero)*
IX. Competence of Members	II	4.70	5.85	5.58	5.15	0.34	1.50 (F−)	0.10 (F−)	7.32 (Hetero)*
	III	4.93	4.60	5.60	6.18	0.37	0.17 (F−)	13.85 (F−)*	2.30 (Homo)
X. Morale	II	4.30	4.70	4.48	3.92	0.84	0.03 (F+)	0.43 (F+)	1.12 (Hetero)
	III	4.80	4.00	4.45	5.72	0.21	1.06 (F−)	9.04 (F−)*	20.68 (Homo)**
XI. Group Productivity	II	6.15	7.35	6.25	5.50	1.60	0.16 (F−)	1.81 (F+)	2.26 (Hetero)
	III	6.20	5.15	6.50	7.90	0.78	0.16 (F−)	11.99 (F−)**	7.74 (Homo)*

Table 5 Continued

Index names	Session	Group Means				s²w	Effect on 'Groups' of:		
		F+ 'Groups'		F− 'Groups'			Followers		Group's composition F ratio
		(F+L)	(F−L)	(F+L)	(F−L)		F+ vs. F− leadership F ratio	F+ vs. F− personality F ratio	
XII. Formality of Group Structure	II	3.10	2.25	2.50	2.40	0.44	0.97 (F+)	1.29 (F+)	0.46 (Homo)
	III	2.85	2.30	2.90	2.00	0.34	6.26 (F+)*	0.19 (F+)	7.69 (Homo)*
XIII. Communication Effectiveness	II	5.40	5.40	5.50	4.90	0.49	0.74 (F+)	0.33 (F+)	0.74 (Hetero)
	III	5.40	4.95	4.75	5.95	0.35	1.59 (F−)	0.35 (F−)	7.69 (Homo)*
XIV. Motivation Towards Group Goal	II	3.65	5.15	4.90	5.05	0.90	3.03 (F−)	1.47 (F−)	2.03 (Hetero)
	III	3.80	4.00	4.55	5.95	0.44	5.75 (F−)*	16.38 (F−)**	3.24 (Homo)
XV. Formation of Cliques	II	2.90	3.60	2.90	3.45	1.32	1.18 (F−)	0.02 (F+)	0.02 (Hetero)
	III	1.90	3.20	2.30	2.10	0.30	3.99 (F−)	1.62 (F+)	7.42 (Hetero)*
XVI. Personality Conflict Between Leader and Group Members	II	2.72	3.15	2.33	3.03	0.84	1.52 (F−)	0.30 (F+)	0.08 (Homo)
	III	2.12	3.83	3.05	2.15	0.23	2.86 (F−)	2.41 (F+)	29.38 (Hetero)**
XX. Satisfaction with Appointed Leader	II	3.15	2.25	3.55	4.35	1.06	4.37 (F−)	0.06 (F−)	0.29 (Homo)
	III	3.35	4.00	3.50	5.65	1.52	5.15 (F−)*	2.13 (F−)	1.48 (Homo)
XXI. Difference of Opinion	II	3.15	3.70	2.60	4.65	0.87	7.76 (F−)*	0.18 (F−)	2.58 (Homo)
	III	2.75	3.62	3.22	2.52	0.43	0.07 (F−)	0.92 (F+)	5.82 (Hetero)*
XXIII. Lack of Cooperation	II	4.05	3.25	3.10	3.75	1.19	0.02 (F+)	0.17 (F+)	1.77 (Homo)
	III	3.25	4.30	3.70	2.30	0.41	0.30 (F+)	5.82 (F+)*	14.55 (Hetero)**

Notes:
* p (.05) F ($^1/_{12}$) = 4.75.
** p (.01) = 9.33.

396

approval, more autocratic, and less sensitive to others than F-minus leaders (Table 1). They were also rated as showing less effective intelligence (Table 1). The latter result is believed to be partially a function of the particular task given the groups, in this case a task requiring analysis of basic values which is presumably alien to F-plus personalities.

F-plus followers, as predicted from Hypothesis 2, were rated as being less equalitarian behaviorally, and as showing less sensitivity to others (Table 2). They were also rated as showing less goal motivation (Table 2). Again, the latter results were probably highly contingent on the task. The category indices supported these results by indicating that F-plus followers engaged in less asking for group evaluation and 'democratic' acts than did F-minus followers (Table 3).

F-plus followers were also found to be more satisfied with appointed leaders than F-minus followers, and were apparently less critical of their own groups in the sense that they rated their groups as more productive and more motivated to achieve the group goal than did the F-minus followers (Table 4). That this result is due to differential response tendencies is suggested by the fact that *O*s rated the groups with F-minus followers as showing more group productivity and goal striving (Table 5), and recorded more withdrawing and out-of-field activity for F-plus followers (Table 3).

Hypothesis 2*e*, that F-plus followers would be more submissive toward appointed leaders, was not supported by *O*s' ratings of submissiveness nor by the recorded 'direction-taking' behaviors. There was some support for this hypothesis from the PMRS analyses, however, where F-plus followers rated their groups as having more definite leadership and as being more dominated by the appointed leader (Table 4), and *O*s rated groups with F-plus followers as having more definite leadership (Table 5).

It was hypothesized (3*a*) that under F-minus leaders, followers – whether they were F-plus or F-minus – would exert more influence on group processes. This prediction was supported by ratings of 'influence' and 'effective intelligence' (Table 2). The hypothesis is further supported by the finding that *O*s rated groups with F-minus leaders as having a significantly higher degree of equal participation (Table 5).

Hypothesis 3*b* – that groups with F-minus leaders would develop a less formal group structure – was supported by the results with *O*s' PMRS rating (Table 5). By 'formal group structure' *O*s attempted to describe the extent to which the leader played his task role in a stilted manner. This finding does not imply any differences in the level or definiteness of leadership. Rather, it seems that the crucial differences here are in the style in which authoritarian and equalitarian personalities display leadership.

Hypothesis 3*c*, that followers would express greater differences of opinion under F-minus than under F-plus leaders, was supported by *O*s' ratings on the PMRS (Table 5), but not by the *S*s' PMRS ratings and not by the behavioral category index of 'negative affect acts', which subsumes the category 'disagrees'. The category index results were in the predicted direction, but did not approach statistical significance. Hypothesis 3*c* is, therefore, considered of doubtful tenability.

Hypothesis 4 stated that leaders with F-minus followers would differ from those with F-plus followers by (*a*) engaging in less autocratic behavior, and (*b*) being less distinct from other group members. These predictions were both supported by findings that leaders with F-plus followers were rated higher on autocratic behavior (Table 1), that *S*s and *O*s both rated groups with F-plus followers as having more definite leadership (Tables 4 and 5), and that F-plus followers rated their groups as being more dominated by the appointed leader (Table 4). (The latter results were offered as support for Hypothesis 2*e* above. Their repetition here is indicative of the interactive nature of the hypothesis investigated.)

Hypothesis 5*a* – that followers are more secure in homogeneous groups – was supported by the difference in rating of 'security' by *O*s (Table 2). Followers in homogeneously composed groups were also rated as 'striving for goal achievement' more than those in heterogeneous groups (Table 2), in support of Hypothesis 5*b*.

The hypothesis that followers would be more satisfied with the appointed leaders in homogeneous groups was not supported. In fact, quite the opposite was found, i.e., followers in the heterogeneous groups rated themselves as significantly more satisfied with their appointed leader. No satisfactory explanation of this result has been achieved, but inspection of the means indicates that the largest differences in satisfaction were between F-plus followers with F-minus leaders and F-minus followers with F-minus leaders. The latter were relatively quite dissatisfied with their leaders. To what extent this finding is due to differential response tendencies cannot be determined with the data obtained.

Hypothesis 5*d* – that there is less personality conflict in homogeneous groups – was supported by *O*s' PMRS ratings (Table 5), but not by *S*s' ratings. *O*s' ratings are believed to provide better tests of hypotheses involving *overt* behavior (because of the broader framework in which the *O*s were indoctrinated before the experiment), and the hypothesis is tenable within that context. However, if 'personality conflict' is taken to imply subjective reactions, the hypothesis is not supported. High-F persons are probably less sensitive to personality clashes than are low-F and probably are not as likely to perceive conflicts between themselves and others as are low-F persons.

The *O*s' ratings of conflict between leaders and group members support the hypothesis that there is less such conflict in homogeneous groups (Table 5). Again, this difference was not found with *S*s' ratings of their own groups.

Finally, ratings by *S*s and *O*s yielded conflicting and inconclusive results with regard to hypothesis 5*f*, that homogeneous groups are more productive and have higher morale. With regard to productivity and motivation, nothing very tenable can be concluded. From the observers' point of view, however, it appears that the homogeneous groups had higher morale, higher communication effectiveness, less conflict, and better cooperation than the heterogeneous groups (Table 5).

Discussion

The results, then, support most of the hypotheses tested, indicating significant differences for each of the five major comparisons. Two of these – the comparison of F-plus and F-minus leaders and the comparison of F-plus and F-minus followers – are rather conventional types of comparisons. They simply indicate that the behavior of individuals can be predicted, to some extent, from measures of those individuals' attitudes or personality characteristics.

The other three major comparisons, however, are quite different. Each of these suggests that to some extent the behavior of individuals in groups is dependent on the personalities of other group members. We found, for example, that there were differences between leaders with F-plus followers and leaders with F-minus followers. This finding indicates that the behavior of leaders is, to a significant degree, a function of the attitudes or personality characteristics of the followers. Conversely, the behavior of followers is found to be significantly a function of the attitudes or personality characteristics of the leaders. The latter, of course, is almost a *sine qua non* for the concept of leadership, but the former has received less attention theoretically and almost none empirically.

Finally, the significant interactions indicate that differences between F-plus and F-minus leaders are contingent on whether the followers are high or low F, and vice versa. This result supports the so-called interaction theory of leadership (8) even more forcefully than the observations referred to in the preceding paragraph. Separating the effects of followers on leader behavior from the interaction effects directs attention to the mutually dependent, adaptive nature of small-group behavior, and appears to facilitate our ability to predict.

The cautious reader will have noted the authors' tendency to reject the null hypothesis occasionally on tenuous bases. There are two relatively noticeable kinds of inconsistencies in the results – those between Session II and Session III, and those between *O*s' and *S*s' ratings. These have been resolved in the discussion by accepting significant results in one session if the other session was not highly contradictory, and to accept *O*s' ratings as more descriptive of the overt behavior and *S*s' as more descriptive of the subjective feelings involved.

Previous evidence (5) has indicated that appointing an individual to a position of leadership in laboratory groups results in his behaving differently from other group members. Another study (10) has shown that group characteristics can be predicted from behavioral and personality measures of individual group members. The present study indicates that conclusions drawn from these previous studies must be tempered by considerations of the interaction among group members, and particularly that between leaders and other group members. All of these findings, of course, are probably contingent on such specifics as the kind of task considered, the population studied, and the nature of the leadership appointment.

Summary

Four-man groups were required to perform on a task in which *S*s discussed specific human relations problems presented by film, then composed and recorded dialogue for similar problems. One of the four men in each group was appointed as leader. The California F scale was administered to all *S*s, and group composition was varied systematically to yield four conditions: (*a*) high-F leaders with high-F followers; (*b*) high-F leaders with low-F followers; (*c*) low-F leaders with high-F followers; and (*d*) low-F leaders with low-F followers. Observations of behavior were recorded by: (*a*) ratings of individuals on 16 behavioral characteristics, (*b*) an interaction recording technique using a classification of behavior acts into 43 categories, and (*c*) responses by *O*s and *S*s to a Post-Meeting Reaction Sheet involving questions about the group.

Five major comparisons were made: (*a*) F-plus leaders with F-minus leaders; (*b*) F-plus followers with F-minus followers; (*c*) leaders of F-plus followers with leaders of F-minus followers; (*d*) followers with F-plus or F-minus leaders; and (*e*) groups in which leader and followers were homogeneous as compared to groups in which they were heterogeneous with regard to F-scale scores. For each comparison, significant differences were found consistent with a number of hypotheses drawn from the theory of the 'authoritarian personality'.

Results indicate that F-plus appointed leaders differ behaviorally from F-minus leaders, and that F-plus followers differ from F-minus followers. These two comparisons are conventional tests of behavioral differences related to personality characteristics. In addition, interaction analyses indicated that the behavior of leaders was a function of whether their followers were F-plus or F-minus, and the behavior of followers depended on the F-scale scores of their leaders. Several significant individual and group differences were found between heterogeneously and homogeneously composed groups. The implications of these results for an interaction theory of leadership, and for the prediction of behavior from personality measures of individuals, are discussed.

Notes

1. The work described in this paper was done under a contract between the U. S. Navy, Office of Naval Research, and the University of Rochester. Dr. Launor F. Carter was the responsible investigator for that contract.
2. Further details regarding the selection of subjects are given in Reference 11.

References

1. Adorno, T.W., E. Frenkel-Brunswick, D.J. Levinson and R.N. Sanford (1950), *The authoritarian personality*, New York: Harper.
2. Blum, R. (1953), *The Study of groups*, Washington, D.C.: Human Resources Research Office, Staff Memorandum, 1 August.
3. Carter, L.F. (1953), 'Leadership and small-group behavior', in M. Sherif and M.W. Wilson (eds), *Group relations at the crossroads*, New York: Harper.
4. Carter, L.F., W. Haythorn, B. Meirowitz and J. Lanzetta (1951), 'Note on a new technique of interaction recording', *J. abnorm. soc. Psychol.*, **46**, 258–60.
5. Carter, L.F., W. Haythorn, B. Shriver and J. Lanzetta (1951), 'The behavior of leaders and other group members', *J. abnorm. soc. Psychol.*, **46**, 589–95.
6. Cattell, R.B., D.R. Saunders and G. Stice (1949), *Handbook for the sixteen personality factor questionnaire*, Champaign, Ill.: Institute for Personality and Ability Testing.
7. Dorris, R.J., D.J. Levinson and E. Hanfmann (1954), 'Authoritarian personality studied by a new variation of the sentence completion technique', *J. abnorm. soc. Psychol.*, **49**, 99–108.
8. Gibb, C.A. (1950), 'The research background of an interactional theory of leadership', *Aust. J. Psychol.*, **2**, 19–42.
9. Haythorn, W. (1952), 'The influence of the individual group members on the behavior of co-workers and on the characteristics of groups', unpublished doctor's dissertation, University of Rochester.
10. Haythorn, W. (1953), 'The influence of individual members on the characteristics of small groups', *J. abnorm. Soc. Psychol.*, **48**, 276–84.
11. Haythorn, W., A. Couch, D. Haefner, P. Langham and L.F. Carter (1956), 'The behavior of authoritarian and equalitarian personalities in small groups', *Hum. Relat.*, **9**, 57–74.
12. Stogdill, R.M. (1948), 'Personal factors associated with leadership: survey of the literature', *J. Psychol.*, **25**, 35–71.

[21]

Journal of Applied Psychology
1975, Vol. 60, No. 2, 187–193

The Reciprocal Nature of Influence Between Leader and Subordinate

Charles N. Greene
Graduate School of Business, Indiana University

Possible directions of causality between leader behavior (consideration and initiating structure) and subordinate performance and satisfaction were investigated in a longitudinal study over three 1-month intervals. First-line managers ($N = 103$) from three organizations completed a version of the Leader Behavior Description Questionnaire, while two subordinates of each manager completed a four-item "work satisfaction" questionnaire from Stogdill's Job Expectation Questionnaire. Subordinate peers rated subordinate performance. Inferences of causality were obtained by an examination of cross-lagged correlations, static correlations, and dynamic correlations between the variables. The results strongly suggest that (a) consideration caused subordinate satisfaction, (b) subordinate performance caused changes in leader emphasis on both consideration and structure, and (c) consideration moderated the initiating structure–performance relationship such that with highly considerate leaders, emphasis on structure caused higher subordinate performance.

Researchers and practitioners would agree that leader behavior is an important variable related to organizational effectiveness. Much of the empirical evidence on organizational leadership has come from the numerous field studies investigating the relationships between leadership styles (e.g., initiating structure and consideration) and subordinate performance and satisfaction (see Fleishman, 1973b). The majority of these studies have employed static correlational techniques or have contrasted the leader behavior of high- and low-productivity groups, which do not allow inferences of the direction of causality. To what extent does the leader influence the subordinate? To what extent does the subordinate influence the leader's behavior? Further, to what extent are there reciprocal effects? There is a need for more studies investigating such directional relationships between leader and group behavior (see e.g., Fleishman, 1973a).

Most often, the *importance* attributed to leader behavior stems from the presumed effect of the leader's behavior on his subordinates' performance and job satisfaction (Likert, 1961). There is evidence that leadership style affects subordinate performance and attitudes. For example, Day and Hamblin (1964) found subordinate performance varied according to the leader's use of punishment and closeness of supervision. More recently, Dawson, Messe, and Phillips (1972) have shown that experimental variation in the leader's consideration and structure produces changes in group behavior, and Jones, Gergen, Gumpert, and Thibaut (1965) have shown that leader attitudes do get translated into group attitudes.

Other studies investigating the possible effects of subordinate performance on leadership style have had mixed results. Jackson (1953) found that supervisors' leadership styles remained unchanged even though the performance characteristics of the different groups they managed varied substantially—thus indicating that subordinate performance did not affect subsequent leader behavior. In contrast, however, Hawthorne, Couch, Haefner, Langham, and Carter (1956), Lowin and Craig (1968), Farris and Lim (1969), and Crowe, Bochner, and Clark (1972) provided evidence that subordinate performance caused changes in leader behavior.

This research was supported by a Graduate School of Business research grant, Indiana University.

The author wishes to thank Ralph M. Stogdill for the useful suggestions he provided during the formulation stage of this research.

Requests for reprints should be sent to Charles N. Greene, Graduate School of Business, Indiana University, Bloomington, Indiana 47401.

There are sound theoretical bases (a number of which are reviewed by Lowin and Craig, 1968) from which one can argue that subordinate performance and, in addition, subordinate satisfaction can cause the leader to vary his style of leadership. For example, Katz and Stotland (1959) in their "functional view of attitudes" postulate that a person will develop positive attitudes toward objects which are instrumental to the satisfaction of his needs. This proposition can be applied to leader–subordinate relationships to the degree that the organization makes rewards bestowed on the leader contingent upon his subordinates' performance; in such an organization, the leader may develop more positive attitudes toward his high-performing subordinates. The expectation is that the person whose behavior causes another to be positively reinforced will in return be rewarded by the other. A further expectation is that low performance by a subordinate will cause the leader to restrict or to further specify the subordinate's work activities (both are forms of increased initiating structure) in attempting to improve his performance and, further, to express disapproval (a form of reduced consideration). Conversely, the leader would be expected to see little need for structure and thus engage in less structuring behavior with the high-performing subordinate and, further, to show greater approval and concern for the subordinate's own interests (both are forms of increased consideration). Similar predictions can be made about the influence of subordinate satisfaction on leader behavior to the extent that a subordinate's expression of satisfaction with work is perceived as reinforcing to the leader. Of the few studies which have examined such causality questions, none were designed to examine the extent to which causation may be reciprocal. When longitudinal data are obtained, as an alternative to experimental designs, there are means for inferring the strength and direction of causality, without requiring the actual manipulation of variables. Two methods for longitudinal data collection are the cross-lagged panel correlational technique and dynamic correlational analysis.

The purpose of this research was to assess, by means of these two techniques, questions of the direction of causal influence in relationships between leader and follower variables. Does a manager's leadership style (in particular, consideration and structure) have greater effect on his subordinate's performance and satisfaction or is the opposite direction of causality stronger? Further, to what extent are the relationships reciprocal?

METHOD

Sample

The data were collected from 103 first-line managers and for each manager, two of his immediate subordinates. The sample of first-line managers included: 42 department heads employed at either the corporate headquarters or a regional office of an insurance company; 31 project managers representing the research and engineering functions of a manufacturer of industrial and electronics equipment; and 30 first-line managers employed in the financial and marketing divisions of a chemical products firm.

Measures

Both the cross-lagged and dynamic correlational techniques require that identical measurements of the four variables — leader initiating structure (IS) and consideration (C) and subordinate performance (P) and satisfaction (S) — be obtained at least at two points in time with the same respondents. In the present study, the measures were taken on three separate occasions (Time 1, Time 2, and Time 3), each approximately 1 month apart.

Subordinates' perceptions of their leader's emphasis on initiating structure and consideration were measured by means of the Ohio State Leader Behavior Description Questionnaire—Form XII (Stogdill, 1965a). The subordinate's satisfaction with work was assessed by means of a four-item work satisfaction factor from Stogdill's (1965b) Job Expectation Questionnaire, which required the subordinate to compare present satisfaction with his work in relation to prior expectations about his work. Reliability of this measure (split-half), for six different samples, is reported to be about .80.

Two peers provided evaluations of the current performance of the subordinate. To ensure that raters were familiar with the subordinate's performance, the leader was asked to provide a list of names of several of the subordinate's peers who would be familiar with the subordinate's performance. Selection of the two peers who rated the subordinate's performance was made randomly from this list by the investigator. In no instances were the raters also subjects in the study. Two identical 7-point scales were utilized by the raters to indicate their evaluations of both the quantity and quality of the subordinate's performance. The responses were scaled 1 (extremely low quantity or quality of performance) to 7 (extremely high quantity or quality of performance). Analysis of the ratings revealed high levels of interrater agreement in all three organizations; the values of the reliability coefficient (corrected by the Spearman-Brown formula) for quantity and quality of performance were, respectively, .75 and .81 for Time 1, .76 and .89 for Time 2, and .80 and .88 for Time 3. Combining the ratings on both performance dimensions resulted in Spearman-Brown coefficients of .80 for Time 1, .86 for Time 2, and .84 for Time 3. As a consequence, both sets of peer ratings were averaged to provide one comprehensive measure of the subordinate's performance. The range of mean averaged peer ratings over all three time periods extended from 2.37 to 6.69.

Analytical Procedures

The cross-lagged correlational model, proposed initially by Simon (1954), has been discussed and applied more recently by a number of researchers, for example, Campbell (1963), Lawler and Suttle (1972), and Greene (1973). As noted earlier, use of this technique requires that identical measurements of the four variables be taken at least for two points in time and then (in the case of two time intervals) six correlation coefficients are computed for each pair of variables (e.g., $r\text{IS}_1\text{P}_1$, $r\text{IS}_1\text{P}_2$, $r\text{IS}_1\text{IS}_2$, $r\text{P}_1\text{IS}_2$, $r\text{P}_2\text{IS}_2$, $r\text{P}_1\text{P}_2$).

Inference of causality concerning, for example, the relationships among subordinate performance and initiating structure was made from the observed pattern between four of the six correlations — the two cross-lagged coefficients ($r\text{IS}_1\text{P}_2$ and $r\text{P}_1\text{IS}_2$) and the two static correlations ($r\text{IS}_1\text{P}_1$ and P_2S_2). To support a hypothesis that subordinate performance causes leader emphasis on initiating structure, the present (Time 1) state of subordinate performance should be more highly related to the future (Time 2) state of initiating structure than it is to the present state of initiating structure. Further, the correlation between the present performance and future initiating structure should exceed the correlation between the present initiating structure and future performance. Thus, if subordinate performance does cause initiating structure, the magnitudes of the correlations should be such that $r\text{P}_1\text{IS}_2 > (r\text{IS}_1\text{P}_1 = r\text{IS}_2\text{P}_2) > r\text{IS}_1\text{P}_2$. Conversely, if initiating structure is the causal variable, then one would expect that $r\text{IS}_1\text{P}_2 > (r\text{IS}_1\text{P}_1 = r\text{IS}_2\text{P}_2) > r\text{P}_1\text{IS}_2$. The relative magnitudes of the two cross-lagged coefficients ($r\text{IS}_1\text{P}_2$ and $r\text{P}_1\text{IS}_2$) provide indication of the extent to which causation is reciprocal.

Pelz and Andrews (1964) have noted that a deviation in the relative magnitudes of the static correlations ($r\text{IS}_1\text{P}_1$ and $r\text{IS}_2\text{P}_2$) from the pattern predicted by the model does not affect the ability to infer causality but simply suggests that the interval of measurement was not consistent with the true causal interval. Differences in relative strengths of the cross-lagged correlations ($r\text{IS}_1\text{P}_2$ and $r\text{P}_1\text{IS}_2$) still provide the basis for inferring causal direction. The correlational coefficients, not yet discussed ($r\text{IS}_1\text{IS}_2$ and $r\text{P}_1\text{P}_2$), provide information about the stability of the two variables over time and, thus, are not directly concerned with inference of causality.

While the cross-lagged correlation technique does have substantial advantages over static correlational techniques, it nonetheless cannot provide information which would enable the researcher to rule out the possibility of a third variable or additional variables causing the variables of interest to covary. Vroom (1966) has suggested one way to determine if this has occurred. In the example of the relationship between initiating structure and subordinate performance, a dynamic correlation coefficient is computed by correlating the difference in initiating structure from Time 1 to Time 2 with the difference in subordinate performance from Time 1 to Time 2. In other words, the change in initiating structure over time is correlated with the change in subordinate performance over time. Given a pattern of cross-lagged correlations showing, for example, that subordinate performance causes initiating structure, a large, highly significant, dynamic correlation would strongly support the case for causality.

The collection of data on three separate occasions, allowing for the 1- and 2-month time intervals between data collections, provided (a) time intervals seemingly long enough to be sensitive to changes in interactions between leader and subordinate, and (b) a sufficient number of separate data collections to determine if causation was reciprocal. Shorter time periods and more frequent data collections were avoided because of the increased possibility of encountering learning effects and response bias which would have contaminated the data.

RESULTS AND DISCUSSION

Since the analysis revealed no significant differences between the correlations obtained in the three companies (all zs < 1.64, $p > .10$), only the results for the total sample are reported. Furthermore, the measures of stability of the variables over time — the correlations among the *same* variables over the three 1-month time periods (e.g., $r\text{C}_1\text{C}_2$, $r\text{C}_2\text{C}_3$, and $r\text{C}_1\text{C}_3$) — were all significant (all ps $< .001$). The magnitudes of these stability coefficients extended from .58 to .73 on initiating structure, .68 to .78 on consideration, .60 to .76 on subordinate performance, and .57 to .69 on subordinate work satisfaction. In general, the magnitudes of these coefficients offer evidence of some stability of the variables, and yet clearly they are low enough to indicate that changes in each of the variables occurred over the 1- and 2-month time intervals.

Consideration and Satisfaction

The pattern of cross-lagged coefficients, presented in Table 1A, is generally what

190   CHARLES N. GREENE

TABLE 1

CORRELATIONS AMONG LEADER CONSIDERATION, INITIATING STRUCTURE, AND
SUBORDINATE WORK SATISFACTION AND PERFORMANCE

Time period	Cross-lagged coefficients	Static coefficients	Dynamic coefficients
A. Consideration and Subordinate Satisfaction			
T1 and T2	$rC_1S_2 = .40^{***}$ $rS_1C_2 = .16$	$rC_1S_1 = .18$ $rC_2S_2 = .22^*$	$r\Delta_{C_1-C_2}\Delta_{S_1-S_2} = .42^{***}$
T2 and T3	$rC_2S_3 = .34^{***}$ $rS_2C_3 = .19^*$	$rC_2S_2 = .22^*$ $rC_3S_3 = .20^*$	$r\Delta_{C_2-C_3}\Delta_{S_1-S_3} = .50^{***}$
T1 and T3	$rC_1S_3 = .45^{***}$ $rS_1C_3 = .12$	$rC_1S_1 = .18$ $rC_3S_3 = .20^*$	$r\Delta_{C_1-C_2}\Delta_{S_1-S_3} = .48^{***}$
B. Consideration and Subordinate Performance			
T1 and T2	$rC_1P_2 = .05$ $rP_1C_2 = .37^{***}$	$rC_1P_1 = .05$ $rC_2P_2 = .07$	$\Delta r_{C_1-C_2}\Delta_{P_1-P_2} = .59^{***}$
T2 and T3	$rC_2P_3 = .17$ $rP_2C_3 = .45^{***}$	$rC_2P_2 = .07$ $rC_3P_3 = .15$	$r\Delta_{C_2-C_3}\Delta_{P_2-P_3} = .57^{***}$
T1 and T3	$rC_1P_3 = .07$ $rP_1C_3 = .33^{***}$	$rC_1P_1 = .05$ $rC_3P_3 = .15$	$r\Delta_{C_1-C_2}\Delta_{P_1-P_3} = .50^{***}$
C. Initiating Structure and Subordinate Satisfaction			
T1 and T2	$rIS_1S_2 = -.08$ $rS_1IS_2 = -.12$	$rIS_1S_1 = .10$ $rIS_2S_2 = .05$	$r\Delta_{IS_1-IS_2}\Delta_{S_1-S_2} = .47^{***}$
T2 and T3	$rIS_2S_3 = .15$ $rS_2IS_3 = -.20^*$	$rIS_2S_2 = .05$ $rIS_3S_3 = -.07$	$r\Delta_{IS_2-IS_3}\Delta_{S_2-S_3} = .45^{***}$
T1 and T3	$rIS_1S_3 = .14$ $rS_1IS_3 = -.07$	$rIS_1S_1 = .10$ $rIS_3S_3 = -.07$	$r\Delta_{IS_1-IS_3}\Delta_{S_1-S_3} = .39^{***}$
D. Initiating Structure and Subordinate Performance			
T1 and T2	$rIS_1P_2 = -.12$ $rP_1IS_2 = -.33^{***}$	$rIS_1P_1 = .07$ $rIS_2P_2 = -.14$	$r\Delta_{IS_1-IS_2}\Delta_{P_1-P_2} = .47^{***}$
T2 and T3	$rIS_2P_3 = -.15$ $rP_2IS_3 = -.37^{***}$	$rIS_2P_2 = -.14$ $rIS_3P_3 = -.17$	$r\Delta_{IS_2-IS_3}\Delta_{P_1-P_3} = .49^{***}$
T1 and T3	$rIS_1P_3 = -.16$ $rP_1IS_3 = -.36^{***}$	$rIS_1P_1 = .07$ $rIS_3P_3 = -.17$	$r\Delta_{IS_1-IS_3}\Delta_{P_1-P_3} = .45^{***}$

$^*\ p < .05.$
$^{**}\ p < .01.$
$^{***}\ p < .001.$

would be expected if leader emphasis on consideration *caused* subordinate satisfaction. The "consideration-causes-subordinate satisfaction" coefficients were relatively strong (.40, .34, and .45, for the three respective time periods; all $ps < .001$) and considerably stronger than the corresponding S → C cross-lagged coefficients. Examination of the static (simultaneous) and the dynamic coefficients, however, somewhat reduces the confidence in such causal inference.

The static correlations consistently were of lesser magnitudes than the C → S cross-lagged correlations, yet four of the six were significant ($p < .05$). These significant correlations suggest that the time intervals between measurements may have been inconsistent with the true time intervals between the cause and the effect. In addition, the significant but rather *moderate* dynamic correlations (rs extended from .42 to .50, all $ps < .001$) indicate that a third variable and, more likely, several additional variables may have contributed to the covariance between consideration and satisfaction. This particular finding is not surprising, however, since there are other known causes of satisfaction with work. Thus, one interpretation that can be made from these results is that leader emphasis on consideration constitutes one of several likely causes of subordinate satisfaction.

Consideration and Performance

The coefficients reported in Table 1B provided rather strong indications that subordinate performance *causes* leader emphasis on consideration. The only significant correlations were the $P \rightarrow C$ cross-lagged coefficients: $rs = .37, .45,$ and $.33$, respectively; all $ps < .001$. All of the remaining correlations, including the $C \rightarrow P$ cross-lagged coefficients, were low and did not approach significance. These results help confirm the findings of Lowin and Craig's (1968) experiment and, further, can be interpreted as supporting the theoretical proposition that the leader's attitude toward his subordinates, and its expression, is contingent upon their performance. The leader may be expected, for example, to support and show his approval of those subordinates who have positively reinforced him by their good performance and to be less considerate of subordinates who negatively reinforce him by their low performance. The dynamic coefficients, also noted in Table 1B, were significant ($rs = .59, .57$ and $.50$; all $ps < .001$) but of insufficient magnitudes to rule out the effects of "other" variables.

Initiating Structure and Satisfaction

The correlations testing the relationships between leader initiating structure and subordinate work satisfaction, presented in Table 1C, provide little evidence of causality. With one exception, none of the correlations was significant. The values of r extended from $-.20$ to $.15$. As one would expect, given the low cross-lagged correlations, the dynamic correlations were much too low ($.37, .45,$ and $.39$) to rule out the possibility of "other" variables affecting the cross-lagged correlations obtained.

Initiating Structure and Performance

As noted in Table 1D, the only significant correlations obtained in the cross-lagged analysis of relationships between leader initiating structure and subordinate satisfaction were the moderate, though significant, $P \rightarrow IS$ cross-lagged coefficients ($-.33, -.37,$ and $-.36$). Consistent with the theory discussed earlier, the most apparent explanation of these findings (given the negative signs of all of the coefficients) is that low performance by a subordinate caused the leader to engage in more structuring behavior. High subordinate performance, on the other hand, would appear to lead to reduced emphasis on initiating structure. The dynamic coefficients were significant but, as before, too low to exclude the possibility of additional variables affecting the relationships found.

The results concerning the proposition about the moderating effects of consideration were suggested earlier by Fleishman and Harris (1962) who did provide evidence of one such "additional variable." This earlier work by Fleishman and Harris demonstrated that leadership styles may interact so that high emphasis on consideration allows the leader to initiate more structure to achieve organizational objectives. Thus, high turnover and grievances were related to low consideration and high structure. However, supervisors with high consideration could increase structure without adverse effects on grievance and turnover. Supervisors with low structure had high turnover and grievances regardless. Thus, Fleishman and Harris (1962) found consideration to be an important moderator variable of the leader structure – group performance relationship. Cummins (1971) later replicated these results using "quality" as a group output measure.

In testing this proposition with the present data, the sample was trichotomized on the basis of leaders' scores on consideration for each time period. As can be noted in Table 2, the results are consistent with the proposition and with the findings of Fleishman and Harris (1962). For leaders perceived to be high on consideration, the "initiating structure-causes-subordinate performance" cross-

TABLE 2

CORRELATIONS AMONG LEADER INITIATING STRUCTURE
AND SUBORDINATE PERFORMANCE
MODERATED BY LEADER
CONSIDERATION

Time period (T)	Cross-lagged coefficients	Static coefficients
Low consideration		
T1 and T2	$r\mathrm{IS}_1\mathrm{P}_2 = -.18$	$r\mathrm{IS}_1\mathrm{P}_1 = -.22$
	$r\mathrm{P}_1\mathrm{IS}_2 = -.40^{**}$	$r\mathrm{IS}_2\mathrm{P}_2 = -.13$
T2 and T3	$r\mathrm{IS}_2\mathrm{P}_3 = -.22$	$r\mathrm{IS}_2\mathrm{P}_2 = -.13$
	$r\mathrm{P}_2\mathrm{IS}_3 = -.44^{***}$	$r\mathrm{IS}_3\mathrm{P}_3 = -.25^{*}$
T1 and T3	$r\mathrm{IS}_1\mathrm{P}_3 = -.21$	$r\mathrm{IS}_1\mathrm{P}_1 = -.22$
	$r\mathrm{P}_1\mathrm{IS}_3 = -.41^{***}$	$r\mathrm{IS}_3\mathrm{P}_3 = -.25^{*}$
Medium consideration		
T1 and T2	$r\mathrm{IS}_1\mathrm{P}_2 = -.05$	$r\mathrm{IS}_1\mathrm{P}_1 = .03$
	$r\mathrm{P}_1\mathrm{IS}_2 = -.12$	$r\mathrm{IS}_2\mathrm{P}_2 = -.19$
T2 and T3	$r\mathrm{IS}_2\mathrm{P}_3 = -.17$	$r\mathrm{IS}_2\mathrm{P}_2 = -.19$
	$r\mathrm{P}_2\mathrm{IS}_2 = -.29^{*}$	$r\mathrm{IS}_3\mathrm{P}_3 = -.09$
T1 and T3	$r\mathrm{IS}_1\mathrm{P}_3 = -.10$	$r\mathrm{IS}_1\mathrm{P}_1 = .03$
	$r\mathrm{P}_1\mathrm{IS}_3 = -.22$	$r\mathrm{IS}_3\mathrm{P}_3 = -.09$
High consideration		
T1 and T2	$r\mathrm{IS}_1\mathrm{P}_2 = .25^{*}$	$r\mathrm{IS}_1\mathrm{P}_1 = .19$
	$r\mathrm{P}_1\mathrm{IS}_2 = -.09$	$r\mathrm{IS}_2\mathrm{P}_2 = .21$
T2 and T3	$r\mathrm{IS}_2\mathrm{P}_3 = .30^{**}$	$r\mathrm{IS}_2\mathrm{P}_2 = .21$
	$r\mathrm{P}_2\mathrm{IS}_3 = -.05$	$r\mathrm{IS}_3\mathrm{P}_3 = .10$
T1 and T3	$r\mathrm{IS}_1\mathrm{P}_3 = .29^{*}$	$r\mathrm{IS}_1\mathrm{P}_1 = .19$
	$r\mathrm{P}_1\mathrm{IS}_3 = -.06$	$r\mathrm{IS}_3\mathrm{P}_3 = .10$

* $p < .10$.
** $p < .05$.
*** $p < .01$.

lagged coefficients were positive, significant, and substantially higher than the corresponding P → IS coefficients. Conversely, significant results in exactly the opposite direction were obtained when the leader was perceived as not emphasizing a high degree of consideration. Here, all of the correlations were negative and the *patterns* of coefficients rather strongly indicated that performance caused initiating structure, particularly in the low consideration group. While of substantially lesser magnitudes, the negative signs of the IS → P cross-lagged coefficients in the low consideration group are supportive of the contention that high emphasis on structure may be counterproductive when the leader shows little consideration.

Limitations of the Results

One apparent limitation of the results, which should be acknowledged, concerns the magnitudes of the dynamic correlations reported in Table 1. While all of these correlations were significant, none were strong enough to exclude the possibility of "other" variables causing the variables of interest to covary. Given other known causes of several of these variables, this finding is not surprising. It, nonetheless, does represent a constraint which reduces somewhat the confidence with which causal inference can be made, and suggests the need for additional research.[1]

SUMMARY

The results of this investigation have provided indications that consideration causes subordinate satisfaction and, conversely, that subordinate performance causes both leader consideration and structure across conditions. However, when the relationship between initiating structure and subordinate performance was moderated by consideration, there was evidence of reciprocal causation. In particular, the results indicate how a leader might positively affect subordinate performance by increased emphasis on both consideration and structure.

[1] Another limitation of cross-lagged correlational analysis is its inability to provide information about which of the two variables caused one of the two cross-lagged correlations to be stronger than the other. Yee and Gage (1968) devised a rather unusual technique, the Frequency-of-Change-in-Product-Moment technique (FCP) which overcomes this limitation. The data reported in this study were also analyzed using the FCP technique as an alternative, but the results are not reported here because of space limitations. The results using the FCP technique are consistent with the cross-lagged correlational results and their interpretations discussed in this paper. The FCP results may be obtained from the author by request.

REFERENCES

Campbell, D. T. From description to experimentation: Interpreting trends as quasi-experiments. In C. W. Harris (Ed.), *Problems in measuring change.* Madison: University of Wisconsin Press, 1963.

Crowe, B. J., Bochner, S., & Clark, A. W. The effects of subordinates' behavior on managerial style. *Human Relations*, 1972, *25*, 215–237.

Cummins, R. C. Relationship of initiating structures and job performance as moderated by consideration. *Journal of Applied Psychology,* 1971, *55,* 489–490.

Dawson, J. E., Messe, L. A., & Phillips, J. L. Effect of instructor–leader behavior on student performance. *Journal of Applied Psychology,* 1972, *56,* 369–376.

Day, R. C., & Hamblin, R. L. Some effects of close and punitive styles of supervision. *American Journal of Sociology,* 1964, *69,* 499–510.

Farris, G. F., & Lim, G. F., Jr. Effects of performance on leadership cohesiveness, influence, satisfaction and subsequent performance. *Journal of Applied Psychology,* 1969, *53,* 490–497.

Fleishman, E. A. Overview. In E. A. Fleishman & J. G. Hunt (Eds.), *Current developments in the study of leadership.* Carbondale: Southern Illinois University Press, 1973. (a)

Fleishman, E. A. Twenty years of consideration and structure. In E. A. Fleishman & J. G. Hunt Eds.), *Current developments in the study of leadership.* Carbondale: Southern Illinois University Press, 1973. (b)

Fleishman, E. A., & Harris, E. F. Patterns of leadership related to employee grievances and turnover. *Personnel Psychology,* 1962, *15,* 43–56.

Greene, C. N. Causal connections among managers' merit pay, satisfaction, and performance. *Journal of Applied Psychology,* 1973, *58,* 95–100.

Hawthorne, W. W., Couch, A., Haefner, D., Langham, P., & Carter, L. F. The effects of varying combinations of authoritarian and equalitarian leaders and followers. *Journal of Personality and Social Psychology,* 1956, *53,* 210–219.

Jackson, J. M. The effect of changing the leadership of small work groups. *Human Relations,* 1953, *6,* 25–44.

Jones, E. E., Gergen, K. J., Gumpert, P., & Thibaut, J. W. Some conditions affecting the use of ingratiation to influence performance evalua-

tion. *Journal of Personality and Social Psychology,* 1965, *1,* 613–625.

Katz, D., & Stotland, E. A preliminary statement to a theory of attitude structure and change. In S. Koch (Ed.), *Psychology: A study of science* (Vol. 3). New York: McGraw-Hill, 1959.

Lawler, E. E., & Suttle, J. L. A causal correlational test of the need hierarchy concept. *Organizational Behavior and Human Performance,* 1972, *3,* 265–287.

Likert, R. *New patterns of management.* New York: McGraw-Hill, 1961.

Lowin, A., & Craig, J. R. The influence of level of performance on managerial style: An experimental object lesson in the ambiguity of correlational data. *Organizational Behavior and Human Performance,* 1968, *3,* 441–458.

Pelz, D. C., & Andrews, F. M. Detecting causal priorities in panel study data. *American Sociological Review,* 1964, *29,* 836–848.

Simon, H. A. Spurious correlation: A causal interpretation. *Journal of the American Statistical Association,* 1954, *49,* 467–479.

Stogdill, R. M. *Manual for job description and job expectation questionnaire—Form XII.* Columbus: Ohio State University, Bureau of Business Research, 1965. (a)

Stogdill, R. M. *Manual for job description and job expectation questionnaire.* Columbus: Ohio State University, College of Administrative Science, Program for Research in Leadership and Organization, 1965. (b)

Vroom, V. H. A comparison of static and dynamic correlation methods in the sudy of organizations. *Organizational Behavior and Human Performance,* 1966, *1,* 55–70.

Yee, A. H., & Gage, N. L. Techniques for estimating the source and direction of causal influence in panel data. *Psychological Bulletin,* 1968, *2,* 115–126.

(Received June 21, 1974)

Part XII
Leader Substitutes

[22]

ORGANIZATIONAL BEHAVIOR AND HUMAN PERFORMANCE 22, 375–403 (1978)

Substitutes for Leadership: Their Meaning and Measurement

STEVEN KERR

University of Southern California

AND

JOHN M. JERMIER

The Ohio State University

Current theories and models of leadership seek to explain the influence of the hierarchical superior upon the satisfaction and performance of subordinates. While disagreeing with one another in important respects, these theories and models share an implicit assumption that while the style of leadership likely to be effective may vary according to the situation, *some* leadership style will be effective *regardless* of the situation. It has been found, however, that certain individual, task, and organizational variables act as "substitutes for leadership," negating the hierarchical superior's ability to exert either positive or negative influence over subordinate attitudes and effectiveness. This paper identifies a number of such substitutes for leadership, presents scales of questionnaire items for their measurement, and reports some preliminary tests.

A number of theories and models of leadership exist, each seeking to most clearly identify and best explain the presumedly powerful effects of leader behavior or personality attributes upon the satisfaction and performance of hierarchical subordinates. These theories and models fail to agree in many respects, but have in common the fact that none of them systematically accounts for very much criterion variance. It is certainly true that data indicating strong superior-subordinate relationships have sometimes been reported. In numerous studies, however, conclusions have had to be based on statistical rather than practical significance, and hypothesis support has rested upon the researcher's ability to show that the trivially low correlations obtained were not the result of chance.

Current theories and models of leadership have something else in common: a conviction that hierarchical leadership is always important. Even situational approaches to leadership share the assumption that while the *style* of leadership likely to be effective will vary according to the situation, *some* leadership style will *always* be effective *regardless* of the situation. Of course, the extent to which this assumption is explicated varies greatly, as does the degree to which each theory is dependent upon

Requests for reprints should be sent to Dr. Steven Kerr, Department of Management, University of Southern California, Los Angeles, CA 90007.

the assumption. Fairly explicit is the Vertical Dyad Linkage model developed by Graen and his associates (Graen, Dansereau, & Minami, 1972; Dansereau, Cashman, & Graen, 1973), which attributes importance to hierarchical leadership without concern for the situation. The Fiedler (1964, 1967) Contingency Model also makes the general assumption that hierarchical leadership is important in situations of low, medium, and high favorableness, though predictions about relationships between LPC and performance in Octants VI and VII are qualified (Fiedler & Chemers, 1974, p. 82). Most models of decision-centralization (e.g., Tannenbaum & Schmidt, 1958; Heller & Yukl, 1969; Vroom & Yetton, 1973; Bass & Valenzi, 1974) include among their leader decision-style alternatives one whereby subordinates attempt a solution by themselves, with minimal participation by the hierarchical superior. Even in such cases, however, the leader is responsible for initiating the method through delegation of the problem, and is usually described as providing (structuring) information.

The approach to leadership which is least dependent upon the assumption articulated above, and which comes closest to the conceptualization to be proposed in this paper, is the Path-Goal Theory (House, 1971; House & Mitchell, 1974). Under circumstances when both goals and paths to goals may be clear, House and Mitchell (1974) point out that "attempts by the leader to clarify paths and goals will be both redundant and seen by subordinates as imposing unnecessary, close control." They go on to predict that "although such control may increase performance by preventing soldiering or malingering, it will also result in decreased satisfaction."

This prediction is supported in part by conclusions drawn by Kerr, Schriesheim, Murphy, and Stogdill (1974) from their review of the consideration-initiating structure literature, and is at least somewhat consistent with results from a few recent studies. A most interesting and pertinent premise of the theory, however, is that even unnecessary and redundant leader behaviors will have an impact upon subordinate satisfaction, morale, motivation, performance, and acceptance of the leader (House & Mitchell, 1974; House & Dessler, 1974). While leader attempts to clarify paths and goals are therefore recognized by Path-Goal Theory to be unnecessary and redundant in certain situations, in no situation are they explicitly hypothesized by Path-Goal (or any other leadership theory) to be irrelevant.

This lack of recognition is unfortunate. As has already been mentioned, data from numerous studies collectively demonstrate that in many situations these leader behaviors *are* irrelevant, and hierarchical leadership (as operationalized in these studies) per se does not seem to matter. In fact, leadership variables so often account for very little criterion variance that a few writers have begun to argue that the leadership construct is sterile altogether, that "the concept of leadership itself has outlived its usefulness" (Miner, 1975, p. 200). This view is also unfortunate, however, and fails to take note of accurate predictions by leadership theorists even as such theorists fail to conceptually reconcile their inaccurate predictions.

What is clearly needed to resolve this dilemma is a conceptualization adequate to explain both the occasional successes and frequent failures of the various theories and models of leadership.

SUBSTITUTES FOR LEADERSHIP

A wide variety of individual, task, and organizational characteristics have been found to influence relationships between leader behavior and subordinate satisfaction, morale, and performance. Some of these variables (for example, job pressure and subordinate expectations of leader behavior) act primarily to influence which leadership style will best permit the hierarchical superior to motivate, direct, and control subordinates. The effect of others, however, is to act as "substitutes for leadership," tending to negate the leader's ability to either improve or impair subordinate satisfaction and performance.

Substitutes for leadership are apparently prominent in many different organizational settings, but their existence is not explicated in any of the dominant leadership theories. As a result, data describing formal superior-subordinate relationships are often obtained in situations where important substitutes exist. These data logically ought to be, and usually are, insignificant, and are useful primarily as a reminder that when leadership styles are studied in circumstances where the choice of style is irrelevant, the effect is to replace the potential power of the leadership construct with the unintentional comedy of the "Law of the instrument."[1]

What is needed, then, is a taxonomy of situations where we should not be studying "leadership" (in the formal hierarchical sense) at all. Development of such a taxonomy is still at an early stage, but Woodward (1973) and Miner (1975) have laid important groundwork through their classifications of control, and some effects of nonleader sources of clarity have been considered by Hunt (Note 2) and Hunt and Osborn (1975). Reviews of the leadership literature by House and Mitchell (1974) and Kerr *et al.* (1974) have also proved pertinent in this regard, and suggest that individual, task, and organizational characteristics of the kind outlined in Table 1 will help to determine whether or not hierarchical leadership is likely to matter.

---

[1] Abraham Kaplan (1964, p. 28) has observed: "Give a small boy a hammer, and he will find that everything he encounters needs pounding."

TABLE 1
SUBSTITUTES FOR LEADERSHIP

Characteristic	Will tend to neutralize	
	Relationship-Oriented, Supportive, People-Centered Leadership: Consideration, Support, and Interaction Facilitation	Task-Oriented, Instrumental, Job-Centered Leadership: Initiating Structure, Goal Emphasis, and Work Facilitation
of the subordinate		
1. ability, experience, training, knowledge		X
2. need for independence	X	X
3. "professional" orientation	X	X
4. indifference toward organizational rewards	X	X
of the task		
5. unambiguous and routine		X
6. methodologically invariant		X
7. provides its own feedback concerning accomplishment		X
8. intrinsically satisfying	X	
of the organization		
9. formalization (explicit plans, goals, and areas of responsibility)		X
10. inflexibility (rigid, unbending rules and procedures)		X
11. highly-specified and active advisory and staff functions		X
12. closely-knit, cohesive work groups	X	X
13. organizational rewards not within the leader's control	X	X
14. spatial distance between superior and subordinates	X	X

Conceptual domain of substitutes for leadership. Since Table 1 is derived from previously-conducted studies, substitutes are only suggested for the two leader behavior styles which dominate the research literature. The substitutes construct probably has much wider applicability, however, perhaps to hierarchical leadership in general.

It is probably useful to clarify some of the characteristics listed in Table 1. "Professional orientation" is considered a potential substitute for leadership because employees with such an orientation typically cultivate horizontal rather than vertical relationships, give greater credence to peer review processes, however informal, than to hierarchical evaluations, and tend to develop important referents external to the employing organization (Filley, House, & Kerr, 1976). Clearly, such attitudes and behaviors can sharply reduce the influence of the hierarchical superior.

"Methodologically invariant" tasks may result from serial interdependence, from machine-paced operations, or from work methods which are highly standardized. In one study (House, Filley, & Kerr, 1971, p. 26), invariance was found to derive from a network of government contracts which "specified not only the performance requirements of the end product, but also many of the management practices and control techniques that the company must follow in carrying out the contract."

Invariant methodology relates to what Miner (1975) describes as the "push" of work. Tasks which are "intrinsically satisfying" (another potential substitute listed in Table 1) contribute in turn to the "pull" of work. Miner believes that for "task control" to be effective, a force comprised of both the push and pull of work must be developed. At least in theory, however, either type alone may act as a substitute for hierarchical leadership.

Performance feedback provided by the work itself is another characteristic of the task which potentially functions in place of the formal leader. It has been reported that employees with high growth need strength in particular derive beneficial psychological states (internal motivation, general satisfaction, work effectiveness) from clear and direct knowledge of the results of performance (Hackman & Oldham, 1976; Oldham, 1976). Task-provided feedback is often: (1) the most immediate source of feedback given the infrequency of performance appraisal sessions (Hall & Lawler, 1969); (2) the most accurate source of feedback given the problems of measuring the performance of others (Campbell, Dunnette, Lawler, & Weick, 1970); and (3) the most self-evaluation evoking and intrinsically motivating source of feedback given the controlling and informational aspects of feedback from others (DeCharms, 1968; Deci, 1972, 1975; Greller & Herold, 1975). For these reasons, the formal leader's function as a provider of role structure through performance feedback may be insignificant by comparison.

Cohesive, interdependent work groups and active advisory and staff personnel also have the ability to render the formal leader's performance feedback function inconsequential. Inherent in mature group structures are stable performance norms and positional differentiation (Bales & Strodtbeck, 1951; Borgatta & Bales, 1953; Stogdill, 1959; Lott & Lott, 1965; Zander, 1968). Task-relevant guidance and feedback from others may be provided directly by the formal leader, indirectly by the formal leader through the primary work group members, directly by the primary work group members, by staff personnel, or by the client. If the latter four instances prevail, the formal leader's role may be quite trivial. Cohesive work groups are, of course, important sources of affiliative need satisfaction.

Programming through impersonal modes has been reported to be the most frequent type of coordination strategy employed under conditions of low-to-medium task uncertainty and low task interdependence (Van de Ven, Delbecq, & Koenig, 1976). Thus, the existence of written work goals, guidelines, and groundrules (organizational formalization) and rigid rules and procedures (organizational inflexibility) may serve as substitutes for leader-provided coordination under certain conditions. Personal and group coordination modes involving the formal leader may become important only when less costly impersonal strategies are not suitable.

The measurement of substitutes for leadership. This section will discuss the assessment of leadership substitutes through the administration of a questionnaire. Such an approach obviously will provide information about respondent perceptions, not "objective" properties, of the variables under study. It is not the intention of this paper to enter into the controversy over the relative merits of paper-and-pencil and other approaches, or the investigation of "psychological" rather than "actual" attributes. In common with most other variables in the behavioral sciences, potential substitutes for leadership can be measured in more than one way, and when feasible these ways should be employed in combination.

In seeking to devise a questionnaire to measure the potential substitutes listed in Table 1, it was initially assumed that scales already in existence would probably be adequate. This turned out not to be the case. To understand why, consider the following items, taken from scales which strongly relate to the substitutes construct:

—I feel certain about how much authority I have.
—I know exactly what is expected of me (from the "Role Clarity" scale, Rizzo, House, & Lirtzman, 1970).
—The mission of work groups is clearly defined.
—Objectives are clearly communicated and understood (from the "Goal Consensus and Clarity" scale, House & Rizzo, 1972).
—Schedules, programs, or project specifications are used to guide work.
—Group rules or guidelines to direct efforts are very clear (from the "Formalization" scale, House & Rizzo, 1972).
—How much are you required to depend on your superior for the nonfinancial resources (information, supplies, etc.) necessary for the performance of your job?

—To what extent are you able to act independently of your superior in performing your job duties? (from the ''Job Autonomy/ Independence from Others'' scale, Wigdor, Note 4).

The problem with such items is that it is impossible to determine whether they refer to substitutes of the kind suggested in Table 1, or whether they refer to leadership itself. For example, suppose we learn that respondents must depend on the leader for information, and cannot act independently in performing job duties. Is this a commentary on their level of training and experience, or does it tell us instead about the leader's managerial style? Similarly, if subordinates express certainty about how much authority they have, does such certainty arise from organizational formalization, or from frequent access to and communications with the leader?

Such questions should not be taken as criticism of the scales mentioned above. Since theories have not been concerned with substitutes for leadership, scales used in leadership research have not been required to distinguish leader-provided autonomy, goal and role clarity, etc., from autonomy and clarity which stem from other sources. It may become necessary in the future to make such distinctions, however, and the scales described in Table 2 have been constructed for this purpose. These scales are presented in the same order as the listing of characteristics in Table 1 to which they refer. It should be noted that the measure of Organizational Formalization is very similar to House and Rizzo's (1972) Formalization scale, and some items in the Organization Rewards not Within the Leader's Control scale derive from Wigdor's (Note 4) measure of Job Autonomy/Independence from Others. Unlike early scales, however, those in Table 2 have been written so as to permit a distinction between effects which are the result of leadership and those which stem from substitutes for leadership.

TELEVISION SCRIPT PRETEST

Administration of the questionnaire. To learn something about scale properties, nine subscales in Table 2 were administered to 153 male and female juniors and seniors who were enrolled in a first course in organizational behavior.[2] Complete and usable information was obtained from 148 of them. The administration was intended to (a) provide information about the subscales' internal reliabilities; (b) assess their degree of interdependence; and (c) permit at least a crude validation of responses, by examin-

---

[2] The Task-Provided Feedback Concerning Accomplishment, Organizational Inflexibility. Spatial Distance, and Need for Independence scales were not included in this administration.

TABLE 2

QUESTIONNAIRE ITEMS FOR THE MEASUREMENT OF SUBSTITUTES FOR LEADERSHIP*

(1) *Ability, experience, training, and knowledge*

—Because of my ability, experience, training or job knowledge, I have the competence to act independently of my immediate superior in performing my day-to-day duties.

—Because of my ability, experience, training or job knowledge, I have the competence to act independently of my immediate superior in performing unusual and unexpected job duties.

—Due to my lack of experience and training, I must depend upon my immediate superior to provide me with necessary data, information, and advice. (R)

(2) *Professional orientation*

—For feedback about how well I am performing I rely on people in my occupational specialty, whether or not they are members of my work unit or organization.

—I receive very useful information and guidance from people who share my occupational speciality, but who are not members of my employing organization.

—My job satisfaction depends to a considerable extent on people in my occupational speciality who are not members of my employing organization.

(3) *Indifference toward organizational rewards*

—I cannot get very enthused about the rewards offered in this organization, or about the opportunities available.

—This organization offers attractive payoffs to people it values. (R)

—In general, most of the things I seek and value in this world cannot be obtained from my job or my employing organization.

(4) *Unambiguous, routine, and methodologically invariant tasks*

—Because of the nature of the tasks I perform, on my job there is little doubt about the best way to get the work done.

—Because of the nature of the work I do, I am often required to perform nonroutine tasks. (R)

—Because of the nature of my work, at the beginning of each work day I can predict with near certainty exactly what activities I will be performing that day.

—There is really only one correct way to perform most of my tasks.

—My job duties are so simple that almost anyone could perform them after a little bit of instruction and practice.

—It is so hard to figure out the correct approach to most of my work problems that second-guessers would have a field day. (R)

(5) *Task-provided feedback concerning accomplishment*

—After I've done something on my job I can tell right away from the results I get whether I've done it correctly.

—My job is the kind where you can make a mistake or an error and not be able to see that you've made it. (R)

—Because of the nature of the tasks I perform, it is easy for me to see when I've done something exceptionally well.

TABLE 2—*Continued*

(6) *Intrinsically satisfying tasks*

—I get a great deal of personal satisfaction from the work I do.

—It is hard to imagine that anyone could enjoy performing the tasks that I perform on my job. (R)

—My job satisfaction depends to a considerable extent on the nature of the actual tasks I perform on the job.

(7) *Organizational formalization*

—Clear, written goals and objectives exist for my job.

—My job responsibilities are clearly specified in writing.

—In this organization, performance appraisals are based on written standards.

—Written schedules, programs and work specifications are available to guide me on my job.

—My duties, authority, and accountability are documented in policies, procedures, and job descriptions.

—Written rules and guidelines exist to direct work efforts.

—Written documents (such as budgets, schedules, and plans) are used as an essential part of my job.

—There are contradictions and inconsistencies among the written statements of goals and objectives. (R)

—There are contradictions and inconsistencies among the written guidelines and ground-rules. (R)

(8) *Organizational inflexibility*

—In this organization the written rules are treated as a bible, and are never violated.

—People in this organization consider the rulebooks and policy manuals as general guide-lines, not as rigid and unbending. (R)

—In this organization anytime there is a policy in writing that fits some situation, everybody has to follow that policy very strictly.

(9) *Advisory and staff functions*

—For feedback about how well I am performing, I rely on staff personnel inside the organization, based outside my work unit or department.

—In my job I must depend on staff personnel located outside of my work unit or department to provide me with data, reports, and informal advice necessary for my job performance.

—I receive very useful information and guidance from staff personnel who are based outside my work unit or department.

(10) *Closely-knit, cohesive, interdependent work groups*

—For feedback about how well I am performing I rely on members of my work group other than my superior.

—The quantity of work I turn out depends largely on the performance of members of my work group other than my superior.

—The quality of work I turn out depends largely on the performance of members of my work group other than my superior.

384   KERR AND JERMIER
                                          TABLE 2—*Continued*

—I receive very useful information and advice from members of my work group other than
my superior.

—I am dependent on members of my work group other than my superior for important
organizational rewards.

—My job satisfaction depends to a considerable extent on members of my work group
other than my superior.

(11) *Organizational rewards not within the leader's control*

—On my job I must depend on my immediate superior to provide the necessary financial
resources (such as budget and expense money). (R)

—On my job I must depend on my immediate superior to provide the necessary nonfinancial resources (such as file space and equipment). (R)

—My chances for a promotion depend on my immediate superior's recommendation. (R)

—My chances for a pay raise depend on my immediate superior's recommendation. (R)

—My immediate superior has little say or influence over which of his or her subordinates
receives organizational rewards.

—The only performance feedback that matters to me is that given me by my immediate
superior. (R)

—I am dependent on my immediate superior for important organizational rewards. (R)

(12) *Spatial distance between superior and subordinates*

—The nature of my job is such that my immediate superior is seldom around me when I'm
working.

—On my job my most important tasks take place away from where my immediate superior
is located.

—My immediate superior and I are seldom in actual contact or direct sight of one another.

(13) *Subordinate need for independence*

—I like it when the person in charge of a group I am in tells me what to do. (R)

—When I have a problem I like to think it through myself without help from others.

—It is important for me to be able to feel that I can run my life without depending on
people older and more experienced than myself.

* Response choices to each item include:
(5) Almost always true or almost completely true,
(4) Usually true, or true to a large extent,
(3) Sometimes true, sometimes untrue or true to some extent,
(2) Usually untrue, or untrue to a large extent, and
(1) Almost always untrue or almost completely untrue.
(R) indicates reflected item.

ing them with reference to work units whose characteristics and mode of
leadership were already known, and whose type and strength of leadership substitutes were systematically different. To accomplish "c", rather
than being asked to describe past or present work experiences, respon-

dents were asked to take on the role of one of the following television characters, and to reply to the questions from the vantage point of that character:

—Mary Richards, working for Lou Grant (*The Mary Tyler Moore Show*).
—Hawkeye Pierce, working for Colonel Sherman Potter (*M.A.S.H.*).
—Archie Bunker, working for the loading dock supervisor in his plant (*All in the Family*).

Respondents who were unfamiliar with all three characters were asked to reply from the vantage point of "a low-level assembly line worker, working for a foreman in an automobile plant."

It should be emphasized that the credibility of these data is limited. Respondents undoubtedly are differentially familiar with the various television characters, and assembly line worker "replies" were obviously based mainly on stereotypes. Furthermore, inferences had to be made with regard to questions which could not unequivocably be answered from the television scripts. These problems could have been partially resolved by asking respondents to reply from the perspectives of characters in a written case study. However, it is unlikely that a case study could create as much completeness and richness of characterization as is provided by a continuing television series.

Subscale properties. Reliabilities and intercorrelations for the nine subscales are shown in Table 3. As can be seen from the table, all reliabilities are above .7, and five exceed .8.

Table 3 also suggests that the subscales may be considered, in this sample at least, to be essentially independent. Only one of 36 intercorrelations is greater than .5. On the other hand, 14 are below .1, and 29 are less than .3. Furthermore, all relatively high intercorrelations are readily comprehensible from a conceptual standpoint. Those which exceed .4 are:

Intrinsically Satisfying Tasks,
—positively with Ability, Experience, Training and Knowledge
—negatively with Indifference toward Organizational Rewards
—negatively with Unambiguous, Routine, and Methodologically Invariant Tasks

Ability, Experience, Training, and Knowledge,
—negatively with Unambiguous, Routine, and Methodologically Invariant Tasks

Professional Orientation,
—positively with Advisory and Staff Functions

Subscale means and standard deviations. Table 4 summarizes means and standard deviations, by character, for each potential leadership sub-

TABLE 3
SUBSCALE RELIABILITIES AND INTERCORRELATIONS

Subscale title	Reliability*	(Pretest sample = 148)								
		1	2	3	4	5	6	7	8	9
(1) Ability, experience, training, and knowledge	.85	1								
(2) Professional orientation	.74	.06	1							
(3) Indifference toward organizational rewards	.85	-.07	-.08	1						
(4) Unambiguous, routine, and methodologically invariant tasks	.78	-.45	-.26	.03	1					
(5) Intrinsically satisfying tasks	.85	.41	.07	-.47	-.56	1				
(6) Organizational formalization	.77	-.21	.04	-.29	.32	.06	1			
(7) Advisory and staff functions	.80	.03	.45	-.26	-.34	.26	.17	1		
(8) Closely-knit, cohesive interdependent work groups	.78	-.18	.20	-.03	.00	.03	.09	.14	1	
(9) Organizational rewards not within the leader's control	.81	.15	.18	.29	-.16	-.06	-.17	.07	-.12	1

* Reliabilities were calculated using the Kuder–Richardson Formula 8.

stitute. Despite the crudeness of the data in Table 4, some interesting insights emerge.

For our hypothetical assembly line worker, the characteristic with the greatest potential to negate the leader's influence is the routine and unam-· biguous nature of the job duties (mean = 4.3). According to Table 1, whether the leader behaves in a structuring manner may in this situation be an irrelevant question. Scale means show no strong substitutes for leader-provided consideration, however, and questions relating to relationship-oriented behavior by the hierarchical superior may therefore by highly relevant.

For Mary Richards, the strongest potential leadership substitute is the intrinsic satisfaction she (presumably) obtains from the tasks she performs (mean = 4.3). Table 1 suggests that this could act as a substitute for leader-provided consideration, and on the show she does seem happy in her work despite the erratic attempts at warmth and collegiality displayed by her superior.[3] She is also seen as able and knowledgeable (mean = 4.0), and under some circumstances might for this reason be unresponsive to leader-provided structure as well. However, Table 4 also shows that she is very interested in organizational rewards (least indifferent of the four characters described), and that her superior is seen as controlling these rewards to a high degree (more than the superior of any other character). As a consequence, hierarchical leadership is probably not irrelevant in this situation. (This point will be elaborated upon shortly).

For Hawkeye Pierce, the strongest substitute for hierarchical leadership is his personal skill, training, and job knowledge (mean = 4.2). Table 1 indicates that these qualities should obviate the need for leader-provided structure, and he does in fact perform his work decisively and competently on the show despite the fact that his superior gives him virtually no structure. Pierce is also indifferent to organizational rewards (more so than the other characters), and in any case his superior is seen as lacking control over such rewards. In Pierce's case, no clear alternatives to leader-provided consideration behavior appear in Table 4, perhaps because such likely substitutes for a surgeon as "professional orientation" and "intrinsic satisfaction from tasks performed" are less likely to be salient under combat conditions. Pierce might therefore welcome and benefit from relationship-oriented leader behavior. For the most part, however, it is not evident from either Table 4 or the television show that hierarchical leadership exerts much influence upon Hawkeye Pierce's performance or satisfaction.

---

[3] On one occasion her superior, encountering a situation clearly crying out for some show of supportive leadership, finally and reluctantly exhorted his staff to "keep up the fair work!"

388   KERR AND JERMIER

TABLE 4
Means and Standard Deviations, by Character

	Mary Richards		Hawkeye Pierce		Archie Bunker		Assembly-Line Worker	
	(N = 27)		(N = 60)		(N = 41)		(N = 20)	
Subscale title	M^*	SD	M	SD	M	SD	M	SD
(1) Ability, experience, training, and knowledge	4.0	.73	4.2	.69	4.1	.82	2.5	.82
(2) Professional orientation	3.1	.73	3.0	.78	2.3	.87	2.4	.67
(3) Indifference toward organizational rewards	2.2	.48	3.7	1.00	2.9	.88	3.6	.72
(4) Unambiguous, routine, and methodologically invariant tasks	2.7	.50	2.8	.69	3.4	.60	4.3	.66
(5) Intrinsically satisfying tasks	4.3	.50	3.4	.88	3.5	.82	2.2	.96
(6) Organizational formalization	2.9	.56	2.5	.69	2.8	.49	3.1	.74
(7) Advisory and staff functions	3.1	.73	2.6	.91	2.1	.68	1.9	.61
(8) Closely-knit, cohesive, interdependent work groups	3.5	.55	3.3	.72	3.3	.91	3.7	.46
(9) Organizational rewards not within the leader's control	2.1	.53	3.1	.74	2.3	.62	2.3	.82

* A scale mean of 5.0 would indicate that the characteristic is perceived to be present to the maximum degree, while a 1.0 would suggest its virtual absence. The closer any scale mean comes to 5.0, the more likely it is that the characteristic will act as a substitute for hierarchical leadership.

The data pertaining to Archie Bunker should be viewed with particular caution since *All in the Family*, unlike the other shows used for this study, focuses upon the character's home rather than work environment. Table 4 scale means suggest that for Archie, as for Hawkeye Pierce, the strongest potential substitute for leadership is his own experience and job knowledge. Similarity between Pierce's and Bunker's situation is not, however, very great. Pierce's personal competence probably stems from extensive formal training, while Bunker's is the result of his having spent many years in essentially the same position. Furthermore, the job which Bunker is competent at is, according to Table 4, much more routine and methodologically invariant. An important final difference is that compared to Pierce, Bunker is much more concerned with organizational rewards, and his superior is seen as controlling rewards to a great degree. This would probably cause Bunker to be at least somewhat influenced by his hierarchical superior's leadership style.

Summarizing what has been discussed in this section of the paper, the data presented in Tables 3 and 4 suggest that in this sample at least, the nine subscales administered are essentially independent and have adequate internal reliabilities. They also yield readily-interpretable data which plausibly describe the presence or absence of substitutes for leadership in the work situations of those who are (hypothetically) responding.

FIELD STUDIES

To further demonstrate the validity and reliability of the constructs developed in this paper, and to investigate their importance in actual organizational settings, two field studies were conducted. Data were gathered using the 55-item substitutes for leadership questionnaire presented in Table 2[4], and various leader behavior-subordinate outcome measures.

Samples and procedure. In both of the organizational studies, police officers in a large Midwestern city filled in the questionnaire during normal working hours. Police organizations provide settings to severely test the import of leader substitutes since formal rank and command control are essential elements which enhance the police supervisor's role (Wilson & McLaren, 1972). If important leader substitutes are found in these settings, their presence in other organizations could reasonably be assumed.

In the first study, 54 sworn University police officers of rank less than sergeant participated; in the second study, 113 sworn City police officers of rank less than sergeant participated. Subjects were guaranteed anonymity prior to filling in the questionnaire.

Subscale properties. Internal reliability and correlation coefficients for the 13 subscales are presented in Table 5. Nearly all of the subscales exhibit a satisfactory level of internal consistency in both samples. Where the estimates of reliability are less than .7 for a measure in one sample (task-provided feedback, inflexibility, and organizational rewards not within the leader's control), adequate levels of reliability were obtained in the other sample. Thus, these subscales meet acceptable standards of reliability for preliminary research, and may be employed to further assess the validity of the substitutes for leadership construct.

As in the student sample discussed above, subscale intercorrelations (Table 5) are modest, suggesting that these conceptually distinct varieties of leader substitutes tap relatively unique content domains.

In the sample of City police, only four of 78 correlations coefficients exceed .3, and only two are in excess of .4. In the sample of University police, 14 of 66 correlations exceed .3, but only three are in excess of .4.

---

[4] In the University police sample the Need for Independence scale was not included.

TABLE 5

SUBSCALE RELIABILITIES AND INTERCORRELATIONS**

Subscale title	Reliability*		1	2	3	4	5	6	7	8	9	10	11	12	13
	University police	City police					Field studies								
1. AETK***	.83	.85		-.06	-.08	-.07	.14	.16	.02	-.06	.10	-.13	-.02	.20	.14
2. PROF	.81	.81	.32		.00	.28	.20	-.01	.19	.15	.55	.33	-.24	-.28	-.05
3. INDOR	.82	.82	-.26	-.10		-.04	-.16	-.48	-.10	.07	.00	.13	.18	.06	.05
4. ROUTIN	.74	.70	-.08	-.18	-.12		.06	-.07	.27	.27	.03	.06	-.17	-.21	-.02
5. TSKFB	.79	.67	.28	.14	-.20	.38		.21	.22	.01	.23	.18	-.18	.11	-.12
6. INSAT	.80	.72	.28	.26	-.36	-.27	.32		.23	.05	.12	.02	-.11	.20	-.09
7. ORFORM	.85	.77	-.17	.16	-.21	.39	.47	.21		.34	.30	.04	-.26	.07	-.02
8. INFLEX	.53	.70	.04	-.27	.01	.33	.14	-.12	.29		.03	.20	-.12	-.02	-.12
9. ADSTF	.80	.76	.28	.29	-.39	-.15	.02	.08	.07	.10		.27	-.17	.06	-.10
10. CLOSE	.79	.79	.09	.54	-.23	-.15	.24	.44	.36	-.03	.40		-.20	-.02	-.09
11. ORNWLC	.81	.63	.22	.05	.17	.11	-.07	-.23	-.14	-.09	-.05	-.31		-.02	.07
12. SPDIST	.85	.82	.04	.10	.31	-.23	-.04	.04	-.11	-.13	-.13	.19	-.04		.03
13. NINDEP	—	.76	—	—	—	—	—	—	—	—	—	—	—	—	—

* Reliabilities were calculated using the Kuder–Richardson Formula 8.
** City police sample above diagonal ($n=113$); University Police sample below diagonal ($n=49$).

$p < .05$ if $r \geq .20$ $p < .05$ if $r \geq .29$
$p < .01$ if $r \geq .25$ $p < .01$ if $r \geq .38$

*** See Table 2 for Legend.

Subscale means and standard deviations. Table 6 presents means and standard deviations for potential leadership substitutes in both police samples. While quite similar on most characteristics, some interesting differences among groups did emerge.

For example, City police perceived their organization to be significantly more formalized and rule-inflexible ($p < .01$) than did University police. This probably reflects the fact that the University policing function is a relatively new addition to the criminal justice system in the city. Standardized rules and policies are less prevalent, and are somewhat less likely to be enforced, in an organization at this stage of development. Also, the relatively small size of the University force makes coordination by rules and standard operating procedures less necessary.

University police also reported, on average, greater indifference toward organizational rewards, but higher dependence upon their formal supervisor to administer rewards. They perceived their supervisor to be more spatially distant (with less direct contact) than did City police.

A partial explanation for the finding concerning reward indifference is that University police are better educated (many with college credit toward degrees) than City police (roughly 70% with no college or technical school training). In general, reward packages specific to any organization tend to be less important to those who are externally mobile as a result of previous training and well-developed skills.

There was no relationship between Spatial Distance and Organizational Rewards Not Within the Leader's Control in either sample (Table 5). This indicates that the leader's reward power is perceived to be essentially independent of the amount of direct contact between himself and his subordinates. The leader is apparently able to exert outcome control through reward distribution even when behavioral control through direct contact is not possible (Ouchi, 1977).

Thus supervisors among the University police, though characterized as more spatially distant from subordinates than those in the City police organization, nevertheless are perceived to be more influential with respect to organizational reward power. However, given differences in attractiveness of extrinsic rewards to subordinates between the two organizations, one might question whether University police supervisors can transform reward power into interpersonal influence any more effectively than their City police counterparts.

Predictive validity. In a preliminary attempt to assess the criterion-related validity of the substitutes for leadership subscales, City police data were regression analyzed and interpreted. Recall that earier in this paper it was argued that the emphasis upon hierarchical leadership variables (though they have often failed to share much criterion variance) has retarded attempts to understand subordinate behavior and attitudes.

TABLE 6
MEANS AND STANDARD DEVIATIONS

	Field studies University police (n = 49)		City police (n = 113)	
Subscale title	M	SD	M	SD
1. AETK	4.3	.61	4.1	.64
2. PROF	2.9	.88	2.7	.76
3. INDOR	3.5	.99	3.0	.77
4. ROUTIN	2.4	.65	2.7	1.08
5. TSKFB	3.5	.75	3.6	.58
6. INSAT	3.8	.76	3.6	.62
7. ORFORM	2.9	.72	3.2	.53
8. INFLEX	2.6	.60	3.2	.63
9. ADSTF	2.7	.84	2.7	.71
10. CLOSE	3.3	.65	2.9	.60
11. ORNWLC	2.8	.80	3.5	.53
12. SPDIST	4.0	.84	3.5	.82
13. NINDEP	—	—	3.6	.60

Police departments, usually characterized by quasi-military organization where the formal leadership function is assumed to be of paramount importance (Bordua & Reiss, 1966; McNamara, 1967) are a case in point. Important leadership substitutes undoubtedly exist, but are usually excluded as predictors of subordinate morale and performance since their contribution is thought to be dwarfed by leadership variables. This portion of the study examines that assumption within the systematic framework presented above, focusing upon the relative predictive power of various substitutes for leadership as well as leader behaviors[5].

In addition to the *leadership substitutes* discussed above, two subordinate outcomes (organizational commitment, role ambiguity) and four varieties of leader behavior were measured. Porter, Steers, Mowday, and Boulian's (1974) *Organizational Commitment* scale measures expressed willingness to strive toward internalized organizational goals and desire to remain a member. Rizzo, House, and Lirtzman's (1970) *Role Ambiguity* scale was chosen as the other criterion variable because of its demonstrated reliability and consistent relationships with job satisfaction, tension/anxiety, and performance, as well as its frequent inclusion in

---

[5] Note that sample size rules out a full-scale test of the interactive influence of several substitutes upon hierarchical leadership. Ideally cases would be selected where substitutes are abundant, then where they are scarce, and then subsamples compared. The validity coefficient where substitutes are abundant should then be relatively low, suggesting that hierarchical leadership influence upon subordinate outcomes has been neutralized.

leadership research (Schuler, Aldag, & Brief, 1977). The KR-8 reliability coefficients for these two criterion variables were .86 and .90, respectively.

Instrumental and *Supportive leader behaviors* were measured using a set of scales designed specifically for use in Path-Goal Theory hypothesis testing (Schriesheim, Note 3). The Instrumental leader behaviors which were measured included: (1) clarification of what is expected of subordinates in their work roles (*Role Clarification* KR-8 = .92, 5 items); assignment of subordinates to specific tasks (*Work Assignment* KR-8 = .64, 5 items); and rule, procedural, and method specification relevant to task execution (*Specification of Procedures* KR-8 = .72, 5 items). It has been shown that these varieties of instrumental leadership are perceived distinctly by subordinates, and that they differentially relate to criteria (Bish & Schriesheim, Note 1; Schriesheim, Note 4). *Supportive leader behavior* is indicative of warmth, friendship, trust, and concern for the subordinate's personal welfare (KR-8 = .95, 11 items). These dimensions of leader behavior are discussed in House and Mitchell (1974) and House and Dessler (1974).

Table 7 displays the validity coefficients between subordinate role ambiguity and organizational commitment and selected leadership and substitutes for leadership variables. As may be seen, even in a police command bureaucracy, where the formal leader's role is traditionally afforded high significance, leader behaviors account for only a small portion of the criterion variance. Indeed, role clarification is the only leader behavior which exerts a significant independent effect upon the subordinate outcome variables.

High organizational commitment tends to be associated with intrinsically satisfying tasks where performance feedback is readily available as much as with leader role clarification. Similarly, the independent contributions of task and organizational variables (organizational formalization, task routinization, intrinsically satisfying tasks) toward explaining role ambiguity are not overshadowed by the leadership predictors. Again only leader role clarification provides a statistically significant, independent contribution among the leader behaviors.

As shown in the reduced models, parsimonius predictor sets may be selected which account for meaningful portions of criterion variance. When powerful leader substitutes such as intrinsically satisfying work and task-provided performance feedback exist, the leader's supportive behaviors fail to contribute significantly in predicting organizational commitment. The function of leader work assignment and specification of procedures in reducing role ambiguity may be seen to be superfluous given the importance of organizational structure and task variables, though no important substitutes for leader role clarification were found.

TABLE 7
MULTIPLE REGRESSION EQUATIONS: ORGANIZATIONAL COMMITMENT AND ROLE
AMBIGUITY REGRESSED UPON LEADER BEHAVIORS AND LEADERSHIP SUBSTITUTES

(City police $n=113$)
Organizational commitment

Predictor	Full model simple r	Beta weight	F ratio	Reduced model Beta weight	F ratio
AETK	.20*	.08	1.0		
PROF	.09	−.03	0.1		
ROUTIN	.10	.13	2.3		
TSKFB	.32**	.15	3.2	.19*	6.3
INSAT	.56**	.46**	28.7	.45**	32.1
ORFORM	.22	.00	0.0		
INFLEX	−.04	−.09	0.9		
ADSTF	.20*	.12	1.3		
CLOSE	.01	−.01	0.0		
NINDEP	−.15	−.09	1.1		
ILBROLCL	.39**	.22*	5.0	.22**	7.5
ILBWA	.06	−.03	0.1		
ILBSPEC	−.03	−.01	0.0		
SUPPORT	.21*	−.07	0.6		

| $R = .66**$. | | | | $R = .63**$. | |

Role ambiguity

AETK	−.07	.00	0.0		
PROF	−.06	.12	1.9		
ROUTIN	−.40**	−.29**	15.4	−.29**	18.6
TSKFB	−.28**	−.11	2.2		
INSAT	−.41**	−.24**	10.9	−.25**	13.5
ORFORM	−.53**	−.29**	13.1	−.30**	18.8
INFLEX	−.19	−.03	0.2		
ADSTF	−.08	.02	0.0		
CLOSE	−.03	−.04	0.4		
NINDEP	.11	.02	0.1		
ILBROLCL	−.55**	−.36**	17.6	−.35**	26.0
ILBWA	−.18	−.03	0.1		
ILBSPEC	−.06	.00	0.0		
SUPPORT	−.24*	−.04	0.2		

| $R = .77**$. | ($*p < .05$ $**p < .01$). | | | $R = .75**$. | |

This latter finding may be partially explained by recognizing that information about work goals, authority and responsibility, and job performance standards may be difficult to transmit except by personal modes, while work assignment and specification of procedures can readily be transmitted by central dispatching and standard operating procedures, respectively (see Bordua & Reiss, 1966).

ELABORATION OF THE CONSTRUCT

Table 1 was designed to capsulize our present knowledge with respect to possible substitutes for hierarchical leadership. Since present knowledge is the product of past research, and since past research was primarily unconcerned with the topic, the table is probably oversimplified and incomplete in a number of respects. Rigorous elaboration of the substitutes construct must necessarily await additional research, but we would speculate that such research would show the following refinements to be important.

Distinguishing between "substitutes" and "neutralizers." A "neutralizer" is defined by Webster's as something which is able to "paralyze, destroy, or counteract the effectiveness of" something else. In the context of leadership, this term may be applied to characteristics which make it effectively *impossible* for relationship and/or task-oriented leadership to make a difference. Neutralizers are a type of moderator variable when uncorrelated with both predictors and the criterion, and act as suppressor variables when correlated with predictors but not the criterion (Zedeck, 1971; Wherry, 1946).

A "substitute" is defined to be "a person or thing acting or used in place of another." In context, this term may be used to describe characteristics which render relationship and/or task-oriented leadership not only impossible but also *unnecessary*.[6] Substitutes may be correlated with both predictors and the criterion, but tend to improve the validity coefficient when included in the predictor set. That is, they will not only tend to affect which leader behaviors (if any) are influential, but will also tend to impact upon the criterion variable.

The consequences of neutralizers and substitutes for previous research have probably been similar, since both act to reduce the impact of leader behaviors upon subordinate attitudes and performance. For this reason it is not too important that such summaries of previous research as Table 1 distinguish between them. Nevertheless, an important theoretical distinction does exist. It is that substitutes do, but neutralizers do not, provide a "person or thing acting or used in place of" the formal leader's negated influence. The effect of neutralizers is therefore to create an "influence vacuum," from which a variety of dysfunctions may emerge.

As an illustration of this point, look again at the characteristics outlined in Table 1. Since each characteristic has the capacity to counteract leader influence, all 14 may clearly be termed neutralizers. It is *not* clear, however, that all 14 are substitutes. For example, subordinates' perceived "ability, experience, training, and knowledge" tend to impair the leader's influence, but may or may not act as substitutes for leadership. It is

[6] This potentially important distinction was first pointed out by M. A. Von Glinow in a doctoral seminar.

known that individuals who are high in task-related self-esteem place high value upon non-hierarchical control systems which are consistent with a belief in the competence of people (Korman, 1970). The problem is that subordinate perceptions concerning ability and knowledge may not be accurate. Actual ability and knowledge may therefore act as a substitute, while false perceptions of competence and unfounded self-esteem may produce simply a neutralizing effect.

"Spatial distance," "subordinate indifference toward organizational rewards," and "organizational rewards not within the leader's control" are other examples of characteristics which do not render formal leadership unnecessary, but merely create circumstances in which effective leadership may be impossible. If rewards are clearly within the control of some other person this other person can probably act as a substitute for the formal leader, and no adverse consequences (except probably to the leader's morale) need result. When no one knows where control over rewards lies, however, or when rewards are linked rigidly to seniority or to other factors beyond anyone's control, or when rewards are perceived to be unattractive altogether, the resulting influence vacuum would almost inevitably be dysfunctional.

Distinguishing between direct and indirect leader behavior effects. It is possible to conceptualize a *direct effect* of leadership as one which occurs when a subordinate is influenced by some leader behavior *in and of itself.* An *Indirect effect* may be said to result when the subordinate is influenced by the *implications* of the behavior for some future consequence. Attempts by the leader to influence subordinates must always produce direct and/or indirect effects or, when strong substitutes for leadership exist, no effect.

This distinction between direct and indirect effects of leader behavior has received very little attention, but its importance to any discussion of leadership substitutes is considerable. For example, in their review of Path-Goal theory, House and Dessler (1974, p. 31) state that "subordinates with high needs for affiliation and social approval would see friendly, considerate leader behavior as an immediate source of satisfaction" (direct effect). As Table 1 suggests, it is conceivable that fellow group members could supply such subordinates with enough affiliation and social approval to eliminate dependence on the leader. With other subordinates, however, the key "may be not so much in terms of what the leader does but may be in terms of how it is *interpreted* by his members" (Graen *et al.*, 1972, p. 235). Graen *et al.* concluded from their data that "consideration is interpreted as the leader's evaluation of the member's role behavior. . ." (p. 233). For these subordinates, therefore, consideration seems to have been influential primarily because of its perceived implications for the likelihood of receiving future rewards. In this case the effect is an indirect one, for which group member approval and affiliation probably cannot substitute.

In the same vein, we are told by House and Dessler (1974, pp. 31–32) that:

> Subordinates with high needs for achievement would be predicted to view leader behavior that clarifies path-goal relationships and provides goal oriented feedback as satisfying. Subordinates with high needs for extrinsic rewards would be predicted to see leader directiveness or coaching behavior as instrumental to their satisfaction if such behavior helped them perform in such a manner as to gain recognition, promotion, security, or pay increases.

It is apparent from House and Dessler's remarks that the distinction between direct and indirect effects need not be limited to relationship-oriented behaviors. Such characteristics of the task as the fact that it "provides its own feedback" (listed in Table 1 as a potential substitute for task-oriented behavior) may provide achievement-oriented subordinates with immediate satisfaction (direct effect), but fail to negate the superior's ability to help subordinates perform so as to obtain future rewards (indirect effect). Conversely, subordinate experience and training may act as substitutes for the indirect effects of task-oriented leadership, by preventing the leader from improving subordinate performance, but may not offset the direct effects.

Indentifying other characteristics and other leader behaviors. Any elaboration of the substitutes construct must necessarily include the specification of other leader behaviors, and other characteristics which may act as substitutes for leader behaviors. As was mentioned earlier, most previous studies of leadership were concerned with only two of its dimensions. This approach is intuitively indefensible. Richer conceptualizations of the leadership process already exist, and almost inevitably underscore the importance of additional leader activities. As these activities are delineated in future research, it is likely that substitutes for them will also be identified.

Table 8 is offered as a guide to research. It portrays a state of increased sophistication of the substitutes construct, assuming future development along lines suggested in this section. Substitutes would be differentiated from neutralizers, and direct effects of leadership empirically distinguished from indirect effects. The columns on the right are intended to represent as-yet-unexplored leader behaviors, and the dotted lines on the bottom indicate the presence of additional characteristics which may act either as neutralizers, or as true substitutes for leadership.

Distinguishing between cause and effect in leader behavior. Another area where the substitutes construct appears to have implications for leadership research concerns the question of causality. It is now evident from a variety of laboratory experiments and longitudinal field studies

TABLE 8
SUBSTITUTES FOR LEADERSHIP: A THEORETICAL EXTENSION

Will Act as a substitute for

Characteristic	Relationship-Oriented, Supportive, People-Centered Leadership (Consideration, Support, and Interaction Facilitation): Directly	Indirectly	Task-Oriented, Instrumental, Job-Centered Leadership (Initiating Structure, Goal Emphasis, and Work Facilitation): Directly	Indirectly	(Other leader behaviors . . .): Directly	Indirectly
Substitutes						
of the subordinate						
1. ability		X		X	?	?
3. "professional" orientation		X		X	?	
of the task						
5. unambiguous and routine			X	X	?	
7. provides its own feedback concerning accomplishment			X		?	?
8. intrinsically satisfying	X				?	?
of the organization						
12. closely-knit, cohesive work groups	X		X	X	?	
Neutralizers						
4. indifference toward organizational rewards		X		X	?	
13. organizational rewards not within the leader's control		X		X	?	

. . . .

that leader behavior may result from as well as cause subordinate attitudes and performance. It is possible to speculate upon the effect that leadership substitutes would have on the relative causal strength of superior- and subordinate-related variables. This paper has tried to show that such substitutes act to reduce changes in subordinates' attitudes and performance which are *caused* by leader behaviors. On the other hand, there seems no reason why leadership substitutes should prevent changes in leader behavior which *result* from different levels of subordinate performance, satisfaction, and morale. The substitutes for leadership construct may therefore help to explain why the direction of causality is sometimes predominantly from leader behavior to subordinate outcomes, while at other times the reverse is true.

Specification of interaction effects among substitutes and neutralizers. From the limited data obtained thus far, it is not possible to differentiate at all among leadership substitutes and neutralizers in terms of relative strength and predictive capability. We have received some indication that the strength of a substitute, as measured by its mean level, is not strongly related to its predictive power. Substitutes for leadership as theoretically important as intrinsic satisfaction, for example, apparently need only be present in moderate amounts (as is the case with the City Police; see Table 6) to have potent substituting effects (see Table 7). Other, less important substitutes and neutralizers, might have to be present to a tremendous degree before their effects might be felt. Clearly, the data reported in this study are insufficient to determine at what point a particular substitute becomes important, or at what point several substitutes, each fairly weak by itself, might combine to collectively impair hierarchical leader influence. Multiplicative functions involving information on the strength and predictive power of substitutes for leadership should be able to be specified as evidence accumulates.

CONCLUSIONS

The research literature provides abundant evidence that for organization members to maximize organizational and personal outcomes, they must be able to obtain both guidance and good feelings from their work settings. Guidance is usually offered in the form of role or task structuring, while good feelings may stem from "stroking" behaviors,[7] or may be derived from intrinsic satisfaction associated with the task itself.

The research literature does *not* suggest that guidance and good feelings must be provided by the hierarchical superior; it is only necessary that they somehow be provided. Certainly the formal leader represents a po-

---

[7] "Stroking" is used here, as in transactional analysis, to describe "any type of physical, oral, or visual recognition of one person by another" (Huse, 1975, p. 288).

tential source of structuring and stroking behaviors, but many other organization members do too, and impersonal equivalents also exist. To the extent that other potential sources are deficient, the hierarchical superior is clearly in a position to play a dominant role. In these situations the opportunity for leader downward influence is great, and formal leadership ought to be important. To the extent that other sources provide structure and stroking in abundance, the hierarchical leader will have little chance to exert downward influence. In such cases it is of small value to gain entree to the organization, distribute leader behavior questionnaires to anything that moves, and later debate about which leadership theory best accounts for the pitifully small percentage of variance explained, while remaining uncurious about the large percentage unexplained.

Of course, few organizations would be expected to have leadership substitutes so strong as to totally overwhelm the leader, or so weak as to require subordinates to rely entirely on him. In most organizations it is likely that, as was true here, substitutes exist for some leader activities but not for others. Effective leadership might therefore be described as the ability to supply subordinates with needed guidance and good feelings which are not being supplied by other sources. From this viewpoint it is inaccurate to inform leaders (say, in management development programs) that they are incompetent if they do not personally provide these things regardless of the situation. While it may (or may not) be necessary that the organization as a whole function in a "9-9" manner (Blake & Mouton, 1964), it clearly is unnecessary for the manager to behave in such a manner unless no substitutes for leader-provided guidance and good feelings exist.

Dubin (1976, p. 33) draws a nice distinction between "proving" and "improving" a theory, and points out that "if the purpose is to prove the adequacy of the theoretical model . . . data are likely to be collected for values on only those units incorporated in the theoretical model. This usually means that, either experimentally or by discarding data, attention in the empirical research is focused solely upon values measured on units incorporated in the theory."

In Dubin's terms, if we are really interested in improving rather than proving our various theories and models of leadership, a logical first step is that we stop assuming what really needs to be demonstrated empirically. The criticality of the leader's role in supplying necessary structure and stroking should be evaluated in the broader organizational context. Data pertaining to both leadership and possible substitutes for leadership (Table 1) should be obtained, and both main and interaction effects examined. A somewhat different use of information about substitutes for leadership would be as a "prescreen," to assess the appropriateness of a potential sample for a hierarchical leadership study.

What this all adds up to is that, if we really want to know more about the sources and consequences of guidance and good feelings in organizations, we should be prepared to study these things *whether or not* they happen to be provided through hierarchical leadership. For those not so catholic, whose interest lies in the derivation and refinement of theories of formal leadership, a commitment should be made to the importance of developing and operationalizing a *true* situational theory of leadership, one which will explicitly limit its propositions and restrict its predictions *to those situations* where hierarchical leadership theoretically ought to make a difference.

REFERENCES

Bales, R., & Strodtbeck, F. Phases in group problem solving. *Journal of Abnormal and Social Psychology*, 1951, **46**, 485–495.

Bass, B., & Valenzi, E. Contingent aspects of effective management styles. In J. G. Hunt & L. L. Larson (Eds.), *Contingency approaches to leadership*. Carbondale: Southern Illinois Press, 1974.

Blake, R., & Mouton, J. *The managerial grid*. Houston: Gulf, 1964.

Bordua, D., & Reiss, A. Command, control, and charisma: Reflections on police bureaucracy. *American Journal of Sociology*, 1966, **72**, 68–76.

Borgatta, E., & Bales, R. Task and accumulation of experience as factors in the interaction of small groups. *Sociometry*, 1953, **16**, 239–252.

Campbell, J., Dunnette, E., Lawler, E., & Weick, K. *Managerial behavior, performance and effectiveness*. New York: McGraw–Hill, 1970.

Dansereau, F., Cashman, J., & Graen, G. Instrumentality theory and equity theory as complementary approaches in predicting the relationship of leadership and turnover among managers. *Organizational Behavior and Human Performance*, 1973, **10**, 184–200.

DeCharms, R. *Personal causation*. New York: Academic Press, 1968.

Deci, E. Intrinsic motivation, extrinsic reinforcement, and inequity. *Journal of Personality and Social Psychology*, 1972, **22**, 113–120.

Deci, E. *Intrinsic motivation*. New York: Plenum, 1975.

Dubin, R. Theory building in applied areas. In M. Dunnette (Ed.), *Handbook of industrial and organizational psychology*. Chicago: Rand–McNally, 1976.

Fiedler, F. E. A contingency model of leadership effectiveness. In L. Berkowitz (Ed.), *Advances in experimental social psychology*. New York: Academic Press, 1964.

Fiedler, F. E. *A theory of leadership effectiveness*. New York: McGraw–Hill, 1967.

Fiedler, F. E., & Chemers, M. M. *Leadership and effective management*. Glenview, IL: Scott, Foresman, 1974.

Filley, A. C., House, R. J., & Kerr, S. *Managerial process and organizational behavior* (2nd ed.). Glenview, IL: Scott, Foresman, 1976.

Graen, G., Dansereau, F., Jr., & Minami, T. Dysfunctional leadership styles. *Organizational Behavior and Human Performance*, 1972, **7**, 216–236.

Greller, M., & Herold, D. Sources of feedback: A preliminary investigation. *Organizational Behavior and Human Performance*, 1975, **13**, 244–256.

Hackman, R., & Oldham, G. Motivation through the design of work: Test of a theory. *Organizational Behavior and Human Performance*, 1976, **16**, 250–279.

Hall, D., & Lawler, E. Unused potential in R and D labs. *Research Management*, 1969, **12**, 339–354.

Heller, F. A., & Yukl, G. Participation, managerial decision-making, and situational variables. *Organizational Behavior and Human Performance*, 1969, **4**, 227–234.

House, R. J. A path-goal theory of leader effectiveness. *Administrative Science Quarterly*, 1971, **16**, 321–338.

House, R. J., & Dessler, G. The path-goal theory of leadership: Some post hoc and a priori tests. In J. G. Hunt & L. L. Larson (Eds.), *Contingency approaches to leadership*. Carbondale: Southern Illinois University Press, 1974.

House, R. J., Filley, A. C., & Kerr, S. Relation of leader consideration and initiating structure to R and D subordinates' satisfaction. *Administrative Science Quarterly*, 1971, **16**, 19–30.

House, R. J., & Mitchell, T. R. Path-goal theory of leadership. *Journal of Contemporary Business*, 1974, **3**, 81–97.

House, R. J., & Rizzo, J. R. Toward the measurement of organizational practices: Scale development and validiation. *Journal of Applied Psychology*, 1972, **56**, 288–296.

Hunt, J. G., & Osborn, R. N. An adaptive-reactive theory of leadership: The role of macro variables in leadership research. In J. G. Hunt & L. L. Larson (Eds.), *Leadership frontiers*. Carbondale: Southern Illinois University Press, 1975.

Huse, E. F. *Organization development and change*. St. Paul: West, 1975.

Kaplan, Abraham. *The conduct of inquiry*. San Francisco: Chandler, 1964.

Kerr, S., Schriesheim, C., Murphy, C. J., & Stogdill, R. M. Toward a contingency theory of leadership based upon the consideration and initiating structure literature. *Organizational Behavior and Human Performance*, 1974, **12**, 62–82.

Korman, A. Toward a hypothesis of work behavior. *Journal of Applied Psychology*, 1970, **54**, 31–41.

Lott, A., & Lott, B. Group cohesiveness as interpersonal attraction: A review of relationships with antecedent and consequent variables. *Psychological Bulletin*, 1965, **64**, 259–302.

McNamara, J. Uncertainties in police work: The relevance of police recruits' backgrounds and training. In D. Bordua (Ed.), *The police: Six sociological essays*. New York: Wiley, 1967.

Miner, J. The uncertain future of the leadership concept: An overview. In J. G. Hunt & L. L. Larson (Eds.), *Leadership frontiers*. Carbondale: Southern Illinois Press, 1975.

Oldham, G. Job characteristics and internal motivation: The moderating effect of interpersonal and individual variables. *Human Relations*, 1976, **29**, 559–570.

Ouchi, W. The relationship between organizational structure and organizational control. *Administrative Science Quarterly*, 1977, **22**, 95–113.

Porter, L., Steers, R., Mowday, R., & Boulian, P. Organizational commitment, job satisfaction, and turnover among psychiatric technicians. *Journal of Applied Psychology*, 1974, **59**, 603–609.

Rizzo, J. R., House, R. J., & Lirtzman, S. I. Role conflict and ambiguity in complex organizations. *Administrative Science Quarterly*, 1970, **15**, 150–163.

Schuler, R., Aldag, R., & Brief, A. Role conflict and ambiguity: A scale analysis. *Organizational Behavior and Human Performance*, 1977, **20**, 111–128.

Stogdill, R. *Individual behavior and group achievement*. New York: Oxford University Press, 1959.

Tannenbaum, R., & Schmidt, W. How to choose a leadership pattern. *Harvard Business Review*, 1958, **36**, 95–101.

Van de Ven, A., Delbecq, A., & Koenig, R. Determinants of coordination modes within organizations. *American Sociological Review*, 1976, **41**, 322–338.

Vroom, V., & Yetton, P. *Leadership and decision making*. Pittsburgh: University of Pittsburgh Press, 1973.

Wherry, R. Test selection and suppressor variables. *Psychometrika*, 1946, 11, 239–247.

Wilson, O., & McLaren, R. *Police administration* (3rd ed.). New York: McGraw–Hill, 1972.

Woodward, J. Technology, material control, and organizational behavior. In A. Negandhi (Ed.), *Modern organization theory*. Kent: Kent State University, 1973.

Zander, A. Group aspirations. In D. Cartwright & A. Zander (Eds.), *Group dynamics: Research and theory* (3rd ed.). New York: Harper & Row, 1968.

Zedeck, S. Problems with the use of "moderator" variables. *Psychological Bulletin*, 1971, 76, 295–310.

REFERENCE NOTES

1. Bish, J., & Schriesheim, C. *An exploratory analysis of Form XII of The Ohio State Leadership Scales*. Paper presented at the National Academy of Management Conference, 1974.

2. Hunt, J. *Different nonleader clarity sources as alternatives to leadership*. Paper presented at the Eastern Academy of Management Conference, 1975.

3. Schriesheim, C. *The development and validation of instrumental and supportive leadership scales and their application to some tests of path-goal theory of leadership hypotheses*. Unpublished doctoral dissertation, The Ohio State University, 1978.

4. Wigdor, L. *Effectiveness of various management and organizational characteristics on employee satisfaction and performance as a function of the employee's need for job independence*. Unpublished doctoral dissertation, City University of New York, 1969.

RECEIVED: August 19, 1976

Part XIII
Organizational Culture

[23]

Minerva, the Roman goddess of wisdom, is said to have sprung full-blown from the forehead of Zeus. Similarly, an organization's culture begins life in the head of its founder—springing from the founder's ideas about truth, reality, and the way the world works.

The Role of the Founder in Creating Organizational Culture

Edgar H. Schein

How do the entrepreneur/founders of organizations create organizational cultures? And how can such cultures be analyzed? These questions are central to this article. First I will examine what organizational culture is, how the founder creates and embeds cultural elements, why it is likely that first-generation companies develop distinctive cultures, and what the implications are in making the transition from founders or owning families to "professional" managers.

The level of confusion over the term *organizational culture* requires some defini-
tions of terms at the outset. An organizational culture depends for its existence on a definable organization, in the sense of a number of people interacting with each other for the purpose of accomplishing some goal in their defined environment. An organization's founder simultaneously creates such a group and, by force of his or her personality, begins to shape the group's culture. But that new group's culture does not develop until it has overcome various crises of growth and survival, and has worked out solutions for coping with its external problems of adapta-

Organizational Dynamics, Summer 1983. © *1983, Periodicals Division, American Management Associations. All rights reserved. 0090–2616/83/0014–0013/$02.00/0*

tion and its internal problems of creating a workable set of relationship rules.

Organizational culture, then, is the pattern of basic assumptions that a given group has invented, discovered, or developed in learning to cope with its problems of external adaptation and internal integration —a pattern of assumptions that has worked well enough to be considered valid and, therefore, to be taught to new members as the correct way to perceive, think, and feel in relation to those problems.

In terms of external survival problems, for example, I have heard these kinds of assumptions in first-generation companies:

> The way to decide on what products we will build is to see whether we ourselves like the product; if *we* like it, our customers will like it.

> The only way to build a successful business is to invest no more than 5 percent of your own money in it.

> The customer is the key to our success, so we must be totally dedicated to total customer service.

In terms of problems of internal integration the following examples apply:

> Ideas can come from anywhere in this organization, so we must maintain a climate of total openness.

> The only way to manage a growing business is to supervise every detail on a daily basis.

> The only way to manage a growing business is to hire good people, give them clear responsibility, tell them how they will be measured, and then leave them alone.

Several points should be noted about the definition and the examples. First, culture is not the overt behavior or visible artifacts one might observe on a visit to the company. It is not even the philosophy or value system that the founder may articulate or write down in various "charters." Rather, it is the assumptions that underlie the values and determine not only behavior patterns, but also such visible artifacts as architecture, office layout, dress codes, and so on. This

14

Edgar H. Schein *received his Ph.D. in social psychology from the Harvard Department of Social Relations in 1952. Following three years at the Walter Reed Institute of Research, he joined M.I.T.'s Sloan School, where he has been ever since. He is the author of a basic text entitled* Organizational Psychology *(Prentice-Hall, Inc., 1980), which is now in its third edition, the book* Process Consultation *(Addison-Wesley, 1969) and, most recently, the book* Career Dynamics *(Addison-Wesley, 1978). Currently Sloan Fellows Professor of Management at the Sloan School, he is pursuing research on the dynamics of organizational culture.*

distinction is important because founders bring many of these assumptions with them when the organization begins; their problem is how to articulate, teach, embed, and in other ways get their own assumptions across and working in the system.

Founders often start with a theory of how to succeed; they have a cultural paradigm in their heads, based on their experience in the culture in which they grew up. In the case of a founding *group*, the theory and paradigm arise from the way that group reaches consensus on their assumptions about how to view things. Here, the evolution of the culture is a multi-stage process reflecting the several stages of group formation. The ultimate organizational culture will always reflect the complex interaction between (1) the assumptions and theories that founders bring to the group initially and (2) what the group learns subsequently from its own experiences.

Figure 1
EXTERNAL AND INTERNAL PROBLEMS

Problems of External Adaptation and Survival

1. Developing consensus on the *primary task, core mission, or manifest and latent functions of the group* — for example, strategy.

2. Consensus on *goals*, such goals being the concrete reflection of the core mission.

3. Developing consensus on the *means to be used* in accomplishing the goals — for example, division of labor, organization structure, reward system, and so forth.

4. Developing consensus on the *criteria to be used in measuring how well the group is doing against its goals and targets* — for example, information and control systems.

5. Developing consensus on *remedial or repair strategies* as needed when the group is not accomplishing its goals.

Problems of Internal Integration

1. *Common language and conceptual categories.* If members cannot communicate with and understand each other, a group is impossible by definition.

2. Consensus on *group boundaries and criteria for inclusion and exclusion.* One of the most important areas of culture is the shared consensus on who is in, who is out, and by what criteria one determines membership.

3. Consensus on *criteria for the allocation of power and status.* Every organization must work out its pecking order and its rules for how one gets, maintains, and loses power. This area of consensus is crucial in helping members manage their own feelings of aggression.

4. Consensus on *criteria for intimacy, friendship, and love.* Every organization must work out its rules of the game for peer relationships, for relationships between the sexes, and for the manner in which openness and intimacy are to be handled in the context of managing the organization's tasks.

5. Consensus on *criteria for allocation of rewards and punishments.* Every group must know what its heroic and sinful behaviors are; what gets rewarded with property, status, and power; and what gets punished through the withdrawal of rewards and, ultimately, excommunication.

6. Consensus on *ideology and "religion."* Every organization, like every society, faces unexplainable events that must be given meaning so that members can respond to them and avoid the anxiety of dealing with the unexplainable and uncontrollable.

WHAT IS ORGANIZATIONAL CULTURE ABOUT?

Any new group has the problem of developing shared assumptions about the nature of the world in which it exists, how to survive in it, and how to manage and integrate internal relationships so that it can operate effectively and make life livable and comfortable for its members. These external and internal problems can be categorized as shown in Figure 1.

The external and internal problems are always intertwined and acting simultaneously. A group cannot solve its external survival problem without being integrated to some degree to permit concerted action, and it cannot integrate itself without some successful task accomplishment vis-à-vis its survival problem or primary task.

The model of organizational culture that then emerges is one of shared solutions to problems which work well enough to begin to be taken for granted — to the point where they drop out of awareness, become unconscious assumptions, and are taught to new members as a reality and as the correct way to view things. If one wants to identify the elements of a given culture, 15

1. *The organization's relationship to its environment.* Reflecting even more basic assumptions about the relationship of humanity to nature, one can assess whether the key members of the organization view the relationship as one of dominance, submission, harmonizing, finding an appropriate niche, and so on.

2. *The nature of reality and truth.* Here are the linguistic and behavioral rules that define what is real and what is not, what is a "fact," how truth is ultimately to be determined, and whether truth is "revealed" or "discovered"; basic concepts of time as linear or cyclical, monochronic or polychronic; basic concepts such as space as limited or infinite and property as communal or individual; and so forth.

3. *The nature of human nature.* What does it mean to be "human," and what attributes are considered intrinsic or ultimate? Is human nature good, evil, or neutral? Are human beings perfectible or not? Which is better, Theory X or Theory Y?

4. *The nature of human activity.* What is the "right" thing for human beings to do, on the basis of the above assumptions about reality, the environment, and human nature: to be active, passive, self-developmental, fatalistic, or what? What is work and what is play?

5. *The nature of human relationships.* What is considered to be the "right" way for people to relate to each other, to distribute power and love? Is life cooperative or competitive; individualistic, group collaborative, or communal; based on traditional lineal authority, law, or charisma; or what?

---

one can go down the list of issues and ask how the group views itself in relation to each of them: What does it see to be its core mission, its goals, the way to accomplish those goals, the measurement systems and procedures it uses, the way it remedies actions, its particular jargon and meaning system, the authority system, peer system, reward system, and ideology? One will find, when one does this, that there is in most cultures a deeper level of assumptions which ties together the various solutions to the various problems, and this deeper level deals with more ultimate questions. The real cultural essence, then, is what members of the organization assume about the issues shown in Figure 2.

In a fairly "mature" culture—that is, in a group that has a long and rich history—one will find that these assumptions are patterned and interrelated into a "cultural paradigm" that is the key to understanding how members of the group view the world. In an organization that is in the process of formation, the paradigm is more likely to be found only in the founder's head, but it is im-

portant to try to decipher it in order to understand the biases or directions in which the founder "pushes" or "pulls" the organization.

HOW DO ORGANIZATIONAL CULTURES BEGIN? THE ROLE OF THE FOUNDER

Groups and organizations do not form accidentally or spontaneously. They are usually created because someone takes a leadership role in seeing how the concerted action of a number of people could accomplish something that would be impossible through individual action alone. In the case of social movements or new religions, we have prophets, messiahs, and other kinds of charismatic leaders. Political groups or movements are started by leaders who sell new visions and new solutions. Firms are created by entrepreneurs who have a vision of how a concerted effort could create a new product or service in the marketplace. The process of culture formation in the organization begins with the founding of the group. How does this happen?

16

In any given firm the history will be somewhat different, but the essential steps are functionally equivalent:

1. A single person (founder) has an idea for a new enterprise.

2. A founding group is created on the basis of initial consensus that the idea is a good one: workable and worth running some risks for.

3. The founding group begins to act in concert to create the organization by raising funds, obtaining patents, incorporating, and so forth.

4. Others are brought into the group according to what the founder or founding group considers necessary, and the group begins to function, developing its own history.

In this process the founder will have a major impact on how the group solves its external survival and internal integration problems. Because the founder had the original idea, he or she will typically have biases on how to get the idea fulfilled —biases based on previous cultural experiences and personality traits. In my observation, entrepreneurs are very strong-minded about what to do and how to do it. Typically they already have strong assumptions about the nature of the world, the role their organization will play in that world, the nature of human nature, truth, relationships, time, and space.

Three Examples

Founder A, who built a large chain of supermarkets and department stores, was the dominant ideological force in the company until he died in his seventies. He assumed that his organization could be dominant in the market and that his primary mission was to supply his customers with a quality, reliable product. When A was operating only a corner store with his wife, he built customer relations through a credit policy that displayed trust in the customer, and he always took products back if the customer was not satisfied. Further, he assumed that stores had to be attractive and spotless, and that the only way to ensure this was by close personal supervision. He would frequently show up at all his stores to check into small details. Since he assumed that only close supervision would teach subordinates the right skills, he expected all his store managers to be very visible and very much on top of their jobs.

A's theory about how to grow and win against his competition was to be innovative, so he encouraged his managers to try new approaches, to bring in consulting help, to engage in extensive training, and to feel free to experiment with new technologies. His view of truth and reality was to find it wherever one could and, therefore, to be open to one's environment and never take it for granted that one had all the answers. If new things worked, A encouraged their adoption.

Measuring results and fixing problems was, for A, an intensely personal matter. In addition to using traditional business measures, he went to the stores and, if he saw things not to his liking, immediately insisted that they be corrected. He trusted managers who operated on the basis of similar kinds of assumptions and clearly had favorites to whom he delegated more.

Authority in this organization remained very centralized; the ultimate source of power, the voting shares of stock, remained entirely in the family. A was interested in developing good managers throughout the organization, but he never assumed that sharing ownership through some kind of stock option plan would help in that process. In fact, he did not even share ownership with several key "lieutenants" who had been with the company through most of its life but were not in the family. They were well paid, but received no stock. As a result, peer relationships were officially de- 17 fined as competitive. A liked managers to compete for slots and felt free to get rid of "losers."

A also introduced into the firm a number of family members who received favored treatment in the form of good developmental jobs that would test them for ultimate management potential. As the firm diversified, family members were made division heads even though they often had relatively little general management experience. Thus peer relationships were highly politicized. One had to know how to stay in favor, how to deal with family members, and how to maintain trust with nonfamily peers in the highly competitive environment.

A wanted open communication and high trust levels, but his own assumptions about the role of the family, the effect of ownership, and the correct way to manage were, to some degree, in conflict with each other, leading many of the members of the organization to deal with the conflicting signals by banding together to form a kind of counter-culture within the founding culture. They were more loyal to each other than to the company.

Without going into further detail, I want to note several points about the "formation" of this organization and its emerging culture. By definition, something can become part of the culture only if it works. A's theory and assumptions about how things "should be" worked, since his company grew and prospered. He personally received a great deal of reinforcement for his own assumptions, which undoubtedly gave him increased confidence that he had a correct view of the world. Throughout his lifetime he steadfastly adhered to the principles with which he started, and did everything in his power to get others to accept them as well. At the same time, however, A had to share concepts and assumptions with a great many other people. So as his company grew and learned from its own experience, A's assumptions gradually had to be modified, or A had to withdraw from certain areas of running the business. For example, in their diversification efforts, the management bought several production units that would permit backward integration in a number of areas—but, because they recognized that they knew little about running factories, they brought in fairly strong, autonomous managers and left them alone.

A also had to learn that his assumptions did not always lead to clear signals. He thought he was adequately rewarding his best young general managers, but could not see that for some of them the political climate, the absence of stock options, and the arbitrary rewarding of family members made their own career progress too uncertain. Consequently, some of his best people left the company—a phenomenon that left A perplexed but unwilling to change his own assumptions in this area. As the company matured, many of these conflicts remained and many subcultures formed around groups of younger managers who were functionally or geographically insulated from the founder.

Founder B built a chain of financial service organizations using sophisticated financial analysis techniques in an urban area where insurance companies, mutual funds, and banks were only beginning to use these techniques. He was the conceptualizer and the salesman in putting together the ideas for these new organizations, but he put only a small percentage of the money up himself, working from a theory that if he could not convince investors that there was a market, then the idea was not sound. His initial assumption was that he did not know enough about the market to gamble with his own money—an assumption based on experience, according to a story he told about the one enterprise in which he had failed miserably. With this enterprise, he had trusted his own judgment on what customers would want, only to be proven totally wrong the hard way.

B did not want to invest himself heavily in his organizations, either financially or personally. Once he had put together a package, he tried to find people whom he trusted to administer it. These were usually people who, like himself, were fairly open in their approach to business and not too hung up on previous assumptions about how things should be done. One can infer that B's assumptions about concrete goals, the means to be used to achieve them, measurement criteria, and repair strategies were pragmatic: Have a clear concept of the mission, test it by selling it to investors, bring in good people who understand what the mission is, and then leave them alone to implement and run the organization, using only ultimate financial performance as a criterion.

B's assumptions about how to integrate a group were, in a sense, irrelevant since he did not inject himself very much into any of his enterprises. To determine the cultures of those enterprises, one had to study the managers put into key positions by B—matters that varied dramatically from one enterprise to the next. This short example illustrates that there is nothing automatic about an entrepreneur's process of inserting personal vision or style into his or her organization. The process depends very much on whether and how much that person wants to impose himself or herself.

Founder C, like A, was a much more dominant personality with a clear idea of how things should be. He and four others founded a manufacturing concern several years ago, one based on the founder's product idea along with a strong intuition that the market was ready for such a product. In this case, the founding group got together because they shared a concept of the core mission, but they found after a few years that the different members held very different assumptions about how to build an orga-

nization. These differences were sufficient to split the group apart and leave C in control of the young, rapidly growing company.

C held strong assumptions about the nature of the world—how one discovers truth and solves problems—and they were reflected in his management style. He believed that good ideas could come from any source; in particular, he believed that he himself was not wise enough to know what was true and right, but that if he heard an intelligent group of people debate an idea and examine it from all sides, he could judge accurately whether it was sound or not. He also knew that he could solve problems best in a group where many ideas were batted around and where there was a high level of mutual confrontation around those ideas. Ideas came from individuals, but the testing of ideas had to be done in a group.

C also believed very strongly that even if he knew what the correct course of action was, unless the parties whose support was critical to implementation were completely sold on the idea, they would either misunderstand or unwittingly sabotage the idea. Therefore, on any important decision, C insisted on a wide debate, many group meetings, and selling the idea down and laterally in the organization; only when it appeared that everyone understood and was committed would he agree to going ahead. C felt so strongly about this that he often held up important decisions even when he personally was already convinced of the course of action to take. He said that he did not want to be out there leading all by himself if he could not count on support from the troops; he cited past cases in which, thinking he had group support, he made a decision and, when it failed, found his key subordinates claiming that he had been alone in the decision. These experiences, he said, taught him to ensure commitment before going ahead on anything, even if doing so was time-consuming and frustrating.

19

While C's assumptions about how to make decisions led to a very group-oriented organization, his theory about how to manage led to a strong individuation process. C was convinced that the only way to manage was to give clear and simple individual responsibility and then to measure the person strictly on those responsibilities. Groups could help make decisions and obtain commitment, but they could not under any circumstance be responsible or accountable. So once a decision was made, it had to be carried out by individuals; if the decision was complex, involving a reorganization of functions, C always insisted that the new organization had to be clear and simple enough to permit the assignment of individual accountabilities.

C believed completely in a proactive model of man and in man's capacity to master nature; hence he expected of his subordinates that they would always be on top of their jobs. If a budget had been negotiated for a year, and if after three months the subordinate recognized that he would overrun the budget, C insisted that the subordinate make a clear decision either to find a way to stay within the budget or to renegotiate a larger budget. It was not acceptable to allow the overrun to occur without informing others and renegotiating, and it was not acceptable to be ignorant of the likelihood that there would be an overrun. The correct way to behave was always to know what was happening, always to be responsible for what was happening, and always to feel free to renegotiate previous agreements if they no longer made sense. C believed completely in open communications and the ability of people to reach reasonable decisions and compromises if they confronted their problems, figured out what they wanted to do, were willing to marshal arguments for their solution, and scrupulously honored any commitments they made.

On the interpersonal level, C assumed "constructive intent" on the part of all members of the organization, a kind of rational loyalty to organizational goals and to shared commitments. This did not prevent people from competitively trying to get ahead—but playing politics, hiding information, blaming others, or failing to cooperate on agreed-upon plans were defined as sins. However, C's assumptions about the nature of truth and the need for every individual to keep thinking out what he or she thought was the correct thing to do in any given situation led to frequent interpersonal tension. In other words, the rule of honoring commitments and following through on consensually reached decisions was superseded by the rule of doing only what you believed sincerely to be the best thing to do in any given situation. Ideally, there would be time to challenge the original decision and renegotiate, but in practice time pressure was such that the subordinate, in doing what was believed to be best, often had to be insubordinate. Thus people in the organization frequently complained that decisions did not "stick," yet had to acknowledge that the reason they did not stick was that the assumption that one had to do the correct thing was even more important. Subordinates learned that insubordination was much less likely to be punished than doing something that the person knew to be wrong or stupid.

C clearly believed in the necessity of organization and hierarchy, but he did not trust the authority of position nearly so much as the authority of reason. Hence bosses were granted authority only to the extent that they could sell their decisions; as indicated above, insubordination was not only tolerated, but actively rewarded if it led to better outcomes. One could infer from watching this organization that it thrived on intelligent, assertive, individualistic people —and, indeed, the hiring policies reflected this bias.

So, over the years, the organization

C headed had a tendency to hire and keep the people who fit into the kind of management system I am describing. And those people who fit the founder's assumptions found themselves feeling increasingly like family members in that strong bonds of mutual support grew up among them, with C functioning symbolically as a kind of benign but demanding father figure. These familial feelings were very important, though quite implicit, because they gave subordinates a feeling of security that was needed to challenge each other and C when a course of action did not make sense.

The architecture and office layout in C's company reflected his assumptions about problem solving and human relationships. He insisted on open office landscaping; minimum status differentiation in terms of office size, location, and furnishings (in fact, people were free to decorate their offices any way they liked); open cafeterias instead of executive dining rooms; informal dress codes; first-come, first-serve systems for getting parking spaces; many conference rooms with attached kitchens to facilitate meetings and to keep people interacting with each other instead of going off for meals; and so forth.

In summary, C represents a case of an entrepreneur with a clear set of assumptions about how things should be, both in terms of the formal business arrangements and in terms of internal relationships in the organization—and these assumptions still reflect themselves clearly in the organization some years later.

Let us turn next to the question of how a strong founder goes about embedding his assumptions in the organization.

How Are Cultural Elements Embedded?

The basic process of embedding a cultural element—a given belief or assumption—is a "teaching" process, but not necessarily an explicit one. The basic model of culture formation, it will be remembered, is that someone must propose a solution to a problem the group faces. Only if the group shares the perception that the solution is working will that element be adopted, and only if it continues to work will it come to be taken for granted and taught to newcomers. It goes without saying, therefore, that only elements that solve group problems will survive, but the previous issue of "embedding" is how a founder or leader gets the group to do things in a certain way in the first place, so that the question of whether it will work can be settled. In other words, embedding a cultural element in this context means only that the founder/leader has ways of getting the group to try out certain responses. There is no guarantee that those responses will, in fact, succeed in solving the group's ultimate problem. How do founder/leaders do this? I will describe a number of mechanisms ranging from very explicit teaching to very implicit messages of which even the founder may be unaware. These mechanisms are shown in Figure 3.

As the above case examples tried to show, the initial thrust of the messages sent is very much a function of the personality of the founder; some founders deliberately choose to build an organization that reflects their own personal biases while others create the basic organization but then turn it over to subordinates as soon as it has a life of its own. In both cases, the process of culture formation is complicated by the possibility that the founder is "conflicted," in the sense of having in his or her own personality several mutually contradictory assumptions.

The commonest case is probably that of the founder who states a philosophy of delegation but who retains tight control by feeling free to intervene, even in the smallest and most trivial decisions, as A did. Because the owner is granted the "right" to 21

Figure 3
How Is Culture Embedded and Transmitted?

Each of the mechanisms listed below is used by founders and key leaders to embed a value or assumption they hold, though the message may be very implicit in the sense that the leader is not aware of sending it. Leaders also may be conflicted, which leads to conflicting messages. A given mechanism may convey the message very explicitly, ambiguously, or totally implicitly. The mechanisms are listed below from more or less explicit to more or less implicit ones.

1. *Formal statements of organizational philosophy, charters, creeds, materials used for recruitment and selection, and socialization.*

2. *Design of physical spaces, facades, buildings.*

3. *Deliberate role modeling, teaching, and coaching by leaders.*

4. *Explicit reward and status system, promotion criteria.*

5. *Stories, legends, myths, and parables about key people and events.*

6. *What leaders pay attention to, measure, and control.*

7. *Leader reactions to critical incidents and organizational crises* (times when organizational survival is threatened, norms are unclear or are challenged, insubordination occurs, threatening or meaningless events occur, and so forth).

8. *How the organization is designed and structured.* (The design of work, who reports to whom, degree of decentralization, functional or other criteria for differentiation, and mechanisms used for integration carry implicit messages of what leaders assume and value.)

9. *Organizational systems and procedures.* (The types of information, control, and decision support systems in terms of categories of information, time cycles, who gets what information, and when and how performance appraisal and other review processes are conducted carry implicit messages of what leaders assume and value.)

10. *Criteria used for recruitment, selection, promotion, leveling off, retirement, and "excommunication" of people* (the implicit and possibly unconscious criteria that leaders use to determine who "fits" and who doesn't "fit" membership roles and key slots in the organization).

run his or her own company, subordinates will tolerate this kind of contradictory behavior and the organization's culture will develop complex assumptions about how one runs the organization "in spite of" or "around" the founder. If the founder's conflicts are severe to the point of interfering with the running of the organization, buffering layers of management may be built in or, in the extreme, the board of directors may have to find a way to move the founder out altogether.

The mechanisms listed in Figure 3 are not equally potent in practice, but they can reinforce each other to make the total message more potent than individual components. In my observation the most important or potent messages are role modeling by leaders (item 3), what leaders pay attention to (item 6), and leader reactions to critical events (item 7). Only if we observe these leader actions can we begin to decipher how members of the organization "learned" the right and proper things to do, and what model of reality they were to adopt.

To give a few examples, A demonstrated his need to be involved in everything at a detailed level by frequent visits to stores and detailed inspections of what was going on in them. When he went on vacation, he called the office every single day at a set time and wanted to know in great detail what was going on. This behavior persisted into his period of semi-retirement, when he would still call *daily* from his retirement home, where he spent three winter months.

A's loyalty to his family was quite evident: He ignored bad business results if a family member was responsible, yet punished a non-family member involved in such results. If the family member was seriously damaging the business, A put a competent manager in under him, but did not always give that manager credit for subsequent good results. If things continued to go badly, A would finally remove the family member, but always with elaborate rationalizations to protect the family image. If challenged on this kind of blind loyalty, A would assert that owners had certain rights that could not be challenged. Insubordination from a family member was tolerated and excused, but the same kind of insubordination from a non-family member was severely punished.

In complete contrast, B tried to find competent general managers and turn a business over to them as quickly as he could. He involved himself only if he absolutely had to in order to save the business, and he pulled out of businesses as soon as they were stable and successful. B separated his family life completely from his business and had no assumptions about the rights of a family in a business. He wanted a good financial return so that he could make his family economically secure, but he seemed not to want his family involved in the businesses.

C, like B, was not interested in building the business on behalf of the family; his preoccupation with making sound decisions overrode all other concerns. Hence C set out to find the right kinds of managers and then "trained" them through the manner in which he reacted to situations. If managers displayed ignorance or lack of control of an area for which they were responsible, C would get publicly angry at them and accuse them of incompetence. If managers overran a budget or had too much inventory and did not inform C when this was first noticed, they would be publicly chided, whatever the reason was for the condition. If the

manager tried to defend the situation by noting that it developed because of actions in another part of the same company, actions which C and others had agreed to, C would point out strongly that the manager should have brought that issue up much earlier and forced a rethinking or renegotiation right away. Thus C made it clear through his reactions that poor ultimate results could be excused, but not being on top of one's situation could never be excused.

C taught subordinates his theory about building commitment to a decision by systematically refusing to go along with something until he felt the commitment was there, and by punishing managers who acted impulsively or prematurely in areas where the support of others was critical. He thus set up a very complex situation for his subordinates by demanding on the one hand a strong individualistic orientation (embodied in official company creeds and public relations literature) and, on the other, strong rules of consensus and mutual commitment (embodied in organizational stories, the organization's design, and many of its systems and procedures).

The above examples highlighted the differences among the three founders to show the biases and unique features of the culture in their respective companies, but there were some common elements as well that need to be mentioned. All three founders assumed that the success of their business(es) hinged on meeting customer needs; their most severe outbursts at subordinates occurred when they learned that a customer had not been well treated. All of the official messages highlighted customer concern, and the reward and control systems focused heavily on such concerns. In the case of A, customer needs were even put ahead of the needs of the family; one way a family member could really get into trouble was to mess up a customer relationship.

All three founders, obsessed with 23

product quality, had a hard time seeing how some of their own managerial demands could undermine quality by forcing compromises. This point is important because in all the official messages, commitment to customers and product quality were uniformly emphasized – making one assume that this value was a clear priority. It was only when one looked at the inner workings of A's and C's organizations that one could see that other assumptions which they held created internal conflicts that were difficult to overcome – conflicts that introduced new cultural themes into the organizations.

In C's organization, for example, there was simultaneously a concern for customers and an arrogance toward customers. Many of the engineers involved in the original product designs had been successful in estimating what customers would really want – a success leading to their assumption that they understood customers well enough to continue to make product designs without having to pay too much attention to what sales and marketing were trying to tell them. C officially supported marketing as a concept, but his underlying assumption was similar to that of his engineers, that he really understood what his customers wanted; this led to a systematic ignoring of some inputs from sales and marketing.

As the company's operating environment changed, old assumptions about the company's role in that environment were no longer working. But neither C nor many of his original group had a paradigm that was clearly workable in the new situation, so a period of painful conflict and new learning arose. More and more customers and marketing people began to complain, yet some parts of the organization literally could not hear or deal with these complaints because of their belief in the superiority of their products and their own previous assumptions that they knew what customers wanted.

In summary, the mechanisms shown in Figure 3 represent *all* of the possible ways in which founder messages get communicated and embedded, but they vary in potency. Indeed, they may often be found to conflict with each other – either because the founder is internally conflicted or because the environment is forcing changes in the original paradigm that lead different parts of the organization to have different assumptions about how to view things. Such conflicts often result because new, strong managers who are not part of the founding group begin to impose their own assumptions and theories. Let us look next at how these people may differ and the implications of such differences.

FOUNDER/OWNERS VS. "PROFESSIONAL MANAGERS"

Distinctive characteristics or "biases" introduced by the founder's assumptions are found in first-generation firms that are still heavily influenced by founders and in companies that continue to be run by family members. As noted above, such biases give the first-generation firm its distinctive character, and such biases are usually highly valued by first-generation employees because they are associated with the success of the enterprise. As the organization grows, as family members or non-family managers begin to introduce new assumptions, as environmental changes force new responses from the organization, the original assumptions begin to be strained. Employees begin to express concern that some of their "key" values will be lost or that the characteristics that made the company an exciting place to work are gradually disappearing.

Clear distinctions begin to be drawn between the founding family and the "professional" managers who begin to be brought into key positions. Such "professional" managers are usually identified as non-family

24

and as non-owners and, therefore, as less "invested" in the company. Often they have been specifically educated to be managers rather than experts in whatever is the company's particular product or market. They are perceived, by virtue of these facts, as being less loyal to the original values and assumptions that guided the company, and as being more concerned with short-run financial performance. They are typically welcomed for bringing in much-needed organizational and functional skills, but they are often mistrusted because they are not loyal to the founding assumptions.

Though these perceptions have strong stereotypic components, it's possible to see that much of the stereotype is firmly based in reality if one examines a number of first-generation and family-owned companies. Founders and owners do have distinctive characteristics that derive partly from their personalities and partly from their structural position as owners. It is important to understand these characteristics if one is to explain how strongly held many of the values and assumptions of first-generation or family-owned companies are. Figure 4 examines the "stereotype" by polarizing the founder/owner and "professional" manager along a number of motivational, analytical, interpersonal, and structural dimensions.

The main thrust of the differences noted is that the founder/owner is seen as being more self-oriented, more willing to take risks and pursue non-economic objectives and, by virtue of being the founder/owner, more *able* to take risks and to pursue such objectives. Founder/owners are more often intuitive and holistic in their thinking, and they are able to take a long-range point of view because they are building their own identities through their enterprises. They are often more particularistic in their orientation, a characteristic that results in the building of more of a community in the early organizational stages. That is, the initial

founding group and the first generation of employees will know each other well and will operate more on personal acquaintance and trust than on formal principles, job descriptions, and rules.

The environment will often be more political than bureaucratic, and founder-value biases will be staunchly defended because they will form the basis for the group's initial identity. New members who don't fit this set of assumptions and values are likely to leave because they will be uncomfortable, or they will be ejected because their failure to confirm accepted patterns is seen as disruptive.

Founder/owners, by virtue of their position and personality, also tend to fulfill some *unique functions* in the early history of their organizations:

1. *Containing and absorbing anxiety and risk.* Because they are positionally more secure and personally more confident, owners more than managers absorb and contain the anxieties and risks that are inherent in creating, developing, and enlarging an organization. Thus in times of stress, owners play a special role in reassuring the organization that it will survive. They are the stakeholders; hence they do have the ultimate risk.

2. *Embedding non-economic assumptions and values.* Because of their willingness to absorb risk and their position as primary stakeholders, founder/owners are in a position to insist on doing things which may not be optimally efficient from a short-run point of view, but which reflect their own values and biases on how to build an effective organization and/or how to maximize the benefits to themselves and their families. Thus founder/owners often start with humanistic and social concerns that become reflected in organizational structure and process. Even when "participation," or "no layoffs," or other personnel practices such as putting marginally competent family 25

Figure 4
How Do Founder/Owners Differ from "Professional Managers"?

Motivation and Emotional Orientation

Entrepreneurs/founders/owners are . . .	*Professional managers are . . .*
Oriented toward creating, building.	Oriented toward consolidating, surviving, growing.
Achievement-oriented.	Power- and influence-oriented.
Self-oriented, worried about own image; need for "glory" high.	Organization-oriented, worried about company image.
Jealous of own prerogatives, need for autonomy high.	Interested in developing the organization and subordinates.
Loyal to own company, "local."	Loyal to profession of management, "cosmopolitan."
Willing and able to take moderate risks on own authority.	Able to take risks, but more cautious and in need of support.

Analytical Orientation

Primarily intuitive, trusting of own intuitions.	Primarily analytical, more cautious about intuitions.
Long-range time horizon.	Short-range time horizon.
Holistic; able to see total picture, patterns.	Specific; able to see details and their consequences.

Interpersonal Orientation

"Particularistic," in the sense of seeing individuals as individuals.	"Universalistic," in the sense of seeing individuals as members of categories like employees, customers, suppliers, and so on.
Personal, political, involved.	Impersonal, rational, uninvolved.
Centralist, autocratic.	Participative, delegation-oriented.
Family ties count.	Family ties are irrelevant.
Emotional, impatient, easily bored.	Unemotional, patient, persistent.

Structural/Positional Differences

Have the privileges and risks of ownership.	Have minimal ownership, hence fewer privileges and risks.
Have secure position by virtue of ownership.	Have less secure position, must constantly prove themselves.
Are generally highly visible and get close attention.	Are often invisible and do not get much attention.
Have the support of family members in the business.	Function alone or with the support of non-family members.
Have the obligation of dealing with family members and deciding on the priorities family issues should have relative to company issues.	Do not have to worry about family issues at all, which are by definition irrelevant.
Have weak bosses, Boards that are under their own control.	Have strong bosses, Boards that are not under their own control.

members into key slots are "inefficient," owners can insist that this is the only way to run the business and make that decision stick in ways that professional managers cannot.

3. *Stimulating innovation.* Because of their personal orientation and their secure position, owners are uniquely willing and able to try new innovations that are risky, often with no more than an intuition that things will improve. Because managers must document, justify, and plan much more carefully, they have less freedom to innovate.

As the organization ages and the founder becomes less of a personal force, there is a trend away from this community feeling toward more of a rational, bureaucratic type of organization dominated by general managers who may care less about the original assumptions and values, and who are not in a position to fulfill the unique functions mentioned above. This trend is often feared and lamented by first- and second-generation employees. If the founder introduces his or her own family into the organization, and if the family assumptions and values perpetuate those of the founder, the original community feeling may be successfully perpetuated. The original culture may then survive. But at some point there will be a complete transition to general management, and at that point it is not clear whether the founding assumptions survive, are metamorphosed into a new hybrid, or are displaced entirely by other assumptions more congruent with what general managers as an occupational group bring with them.

4. *Originating evolution through hybridization.* The founder is able to impose his or her assumptions on the first-generation employees, but these employees will, as they move up in the organization and become experienced managers, develop a range of new assumptions based on their own experience. These new assumptions will be congruent with some of the core assumptions of the original cultural paradigm, but

will add new elements learned from experience. Some of these new elements or new assumptions will solve problems better than the original ones because external and internal problems will have changed as the organization matured and grew. The founder often recognizes that these new assumptions are better solutions, and will delegate increasing amounts of authority to those managers who are the best "hybrids": those who maintain key old assumptions yet add relevant new ones.

The best example of such hybrid evolution comes from a company that was founded by a very free-wheeling, intuitive, pragmatic entrepreneur: "D" who, like C in the example above, believed strongly in individual creativity, a high degree of decentralization, high autonomy for each organizational unit, high internal competition for resources, and self-control mechanisms rather than tight, centralized organizational controls. As this company grew and prospered, coordinating so many autonomous units became increasingly difficult, and the frustration that resulted from internal competition made it increasingly expensive to maintain this form of organization.

Some managers in this company, notably those coming out of manufacturing, had always operated in a more disciplined, centralized manner—without, however, disagreeing with core assumptions about the need to maximize individual autonomy. But they had learned that in order to do certain kinds of manufacturing tasks, one had to impose some discipline and tight controls. As the price of autonomy and decentralization increased, D began to look increasingly to these manufacturing managers as potential occupants of key general management positions. Whether he was conscious of it or not, what he needed was senior general managers who still believed in the old system but who had, in addition, a new set of assumptions about how to run things that were more in 27 line with what the organization now needed. Some of the first-generation managers were quite nervous at seeing what they considered to be their "hardnosed" colleagues groomed as heirs apparent. Yet they were relieved that these potential successors were part of the original group rather than complete outsiders.

From a theoretical standpoint, evolution through hybrids is probably the only model of culture change that can work, because the original culture is based so heavily on community assumptions and values. Outsiders coming into such a community with new assumptions are likely to find the culture too strong to budge, so they either give up in frustration or find themselves ejected by the organization as being too foreign in orientation. What makes this scenario especially likely is the fact that the *distinctive* parts of the founding culture are often based on biases that are not economically justifiable in the short run.

As noted earlier, founders are especially likely to introduce humanistic, social service, and other non-economic assumptions into their paradigm of how an organization should look, and the general manager who is introduced from the outside often finds these assumptions to be the very thing that he or she wants to change in the attempt to "rationalize" the organization and make it more efficient. Indeed, that is often the reason the outsider is brought in. But if the current owners do not recognize the positive functions their culture plays, they run the risk of throwing out the baby with the bath water or, if the culture is strong, wasting their time because the outsider will not be able to change things anyway.

The ultimate dilemma for the first-generation organization with a strong founder-generated culture is how to make the transition to subsequent generations in such a manner that the organization remains adaptive to its changing external environment without destroying cultural elements

that have given it its uniqueness, and that have made life fulfilling in the internal environment. Such a transition cannot be made effectively if the succession problem is seen only in power or political terms. The thrust of this analysis is that the *culture* must be analyzed and understood, and that the founder/owners must have sufficient insight into their own culture to make an intelligent transition process possible.

ACKNOWLEDGMENTS AND SELECTED BIBLIOGRAPHY

The research on which this paper is based was partly sponsored by the Project on the Family Firm, Sloan School of Management, M.I.T., and by the Office of Naval Research, Organizational Effectiveness Research Programs, under Contract No. N00014-80-C-0905, NR 170-911.

The ideas explored here have been especially influenced by my colleague Richard Beckhard and by the various entrepreneurs with whom I have worked for many years in a consulting relationship. Their observations of themselves and their colleagues have proved to be an invaluable source of ideas and insights.

Earlier work along these lines has been incorporated into my book *Career Dynamics* (Addison-Wesley, 1978). Further explication of the ideas of an organizational culture can be found in Andrew M. Pettigrew's article "On Studying Organizational Cultures" (*Administrative Science Quarterly*, December 1979), Meryl Louis's article "A Cultural Perspective on Organizations" (*Human Systems Management*, 1981, 2, 246-258), and in H. Schwartz and S. M. Davis's "Matching Corporate Culture and Business Strategy" (*Organizational Dynamics*, Summer 1981).

The specific model of culture that I use was first published in my article "Does Japanese Management Style Have a Message for American Managers?" (*Sloan Management Review*, Fall 1981) and is currently being elaborated into a book on organizational culture.

Part XIV
Gender and Leadership

[24]

Psychological Bulletin
1990, Vol. 108, No. 2, 233–256

Gender and Leadership Style: A Meta-Analysis

Alice H. Eagly and Blair T. Johnson
Purdue University

Research comparing the leadership styles of women and men is reviewed, and evidence is found for both the presence and the absence of differences between the sexes. In contrast to the gender-stereotypic expectation that women lead in an *interpersonally oriented* style and men in a *task-oriented* style, female and male leaders did not differ in these two styles in *organizational studies*. However, these aspects of leadership style were somewhat gender stereotypic in the two other classes of leadership studies investigated, namely (a) *laboratory experiments* and (b) *assessment studies*, which were defined as research that assessed the leadership styles of people not selected for occupancy of leadership roles. Consistent with stereotypic expectations about a different aspect of leadership style, the tendency to lead *democratically or autocratically,* women tended to adopt a more democratic or participative style and a less autocratic or directive style than did men. This sex difference appeared in *all three classes* of leadership studies, including those conducted in organizations. These and other findings are interpreted in terms of a social role theory of sex differences in social behavior.

In recent years many social scientists, management consultants, and other writers have addressed the topic of gender and leadership style. Some authors with extensive experience in organizations who write nontechnical books for management audiences and the general public have argued for the presence of sex differences in leadership style. For example, Loden (1985) maintained that there is a masculine mode of management characterized by qualities such as competitiveness, hierarchical authority, high control for the leader, and unemotional and analytic problem solving. Loden argued that women prefer and tend to behave in terms of an alternative feminine leadership model characterized by cooperativeness, collaboration of managers and subordinates, lower control for the leader, and problem solving based on intuition and empathy as well as rationality. Loden's writing echoes the androgynous manager theme developed earlier by Sargent (1981), who accepted the idea that women and men, including those who are managers in organizations, behave stereotypically to some extent. Sargent advocated that managers of each sex adopt "the best" of the other

sex's qualities to become more effective, androgynous managers. In a somewhat different rendition of this sex-difference theme, Hennig and Jardin (1977) also acknowledged sex-differentiated managerial behavior, which they ascribed to personality traits acquired in early socialization, particularly through differing male and female resolutions of the Oedipus complex.

In contrast to these generalizations about gender-stereotypic leadership styles promulgated in books written primarily for practicing managers and the general public, social scientists have generally maintained that there are in fact no reliable differences in the ways that women and men lead. Although a few social scientists have acknowledged that there is some evidence for sex differences in leadership style among research participants who have not been selected for occupancy of leadership roles in natural settings (e.g., Brown, 1979; Hollander, 1985), most have agreed that women and men who occupy leadership roles in organizations do not differ (but see Shakeshaft, 1987, for a contrasting opinion). Illustrating this consensus among social scientists are the following representative statements summarizing research comparing the styles of female and male leaders: "The preponderance of available evidence is that no consistently clear pattern of differences can be discerned in the supervisory style of female as compared to male leaders" (Bass, 1981, p. 499); "Contrary to notions about sex specialization in leadership styles, women leaders appear to behave in similar fashion to their male colleagues" (Nieva & Gutek, 1981, p. 91); "There is as yet no research evidence that makes a case for sex differences in either leadership aptitude or style" (Kanter, 1977a, p. 199); "In general, comparative research indicates that there are few differences in the leadership styles of female and male designated leaders" (Bartol & Martin, 1986, p. 278).

Underlying this divergence in the opinions voiced in popular and social scientific writings is the fact that authors in these two camps have based their conclusions on quite different kinds of data. Authors such as Loden (1985) who have written books for managers and the general public based their conclusions pri-

This research was supported by National Science Foundation Grants BNS-8605256 and BNS-8807495. Preliminary reports of this research were presented at the Annual Meetings of the Eastern Psychological Association, April 1988; the Midwestern Psychological Association, April 1988; the International Congress of Psychology, September 1988; and the American Psychological Association, August 1989. A table showing the effect sizes and study characteristics for each study included in the meta-analysis is available from the first author.

We thank Anna Fairchild for assistance in locating studies and in recording and checking data. We also thank Judith Hall, Edwin P. Hollander, Judi Komaki, Louis Sternberg, Howard Weiss, and Wendy Wood for comments on a draft of the article and Katherine Markee for help in conducting computer-based information searches.

Blair T. Johnson is now at Syracuse University.

Correspondence concerning this article should be addressed to Alice H. Eagly, Department of Psychological Sciences, Purdue University, West Lafayette, Indiana 47907.

marily on their own experience in organizations as well as on the impressions they gleaned from interviews with practicing managers. Social scientists typically based their conclusions on more formal studies of managerial behavior in which data were gathered via questionnaires or behavioral observations and then analyzed quantitatively. In view of these contrasting methods, it is tempting for social scientists to dismiss the generalizations that are based on personal experience and interviews, and to accept as valid only those conclusions that stem from more formal empirical research on leadership. However, the generalizations that social scientists appear to have accepted in this area, which stem from reviews of empirical research (e.g., Bartol & Martin, 1986), are quite vulnerable to error because of the relatively informal methods by which reviewers have drawn conclusions from the available research. With only one exception,[1] these reviews were traditional, narrative reviews and, therefore, were not based on any clear rules about how one derives conclusions from research findings. Moreover, none of the existing reviews was based on more than a small proportion of the available studies. For example, both Bartol and Martin (1986) and Dobbins and Platz (1986) based their generalizations on eight studies that compared the leadership styles of men and women, yet we located 162 studies pertaining only to the four types of leadership style we included in our meta-analysis (see *Method*). Moreover, prior reviewers did not state the criteria by which they selected their small samples of studies. As we became aware of these selection problems and of the severe underuse of available research on gender and leadership style, we decided that a thorough survey of this domain was long overdue. Our meta-analysis thus provides a systematic, quantitative integration of the available research in which the leadership styles of men and women were compared and statistical analyses were performed on the resulting data.

Theoretical Analysis of Sex Differences in Leadership Style

Leaving aside the claims of both the social scientists and the management experts who have written about gender and leadership style, we face a topic of considerable complexity that we analyze from several perspectives. One of our perspectives takes into account existing knowledge about sex differences in social behaviors such as aggression, helping, and conformity as well as numerous nonverbal and communicative behaviors. Large numbers of laboratory and field studies have been performed on such behaviors, primarily by social psychologists, and in many of these studies female and male behavior has been compared. Quantitative reviews of this research have established the presence rather than the absence of overall sex differences (see overviews by Eagly, 1987; Eagly & Wood, in press; Hall, 1984). These differences, although typically not large, tend to be comparable in magnitude to most other findings reported in social psychological research. On the average, sex appears to be a variable that has neither especially impactful nor especially weak effects on social behavior and that produces findings consistent with laypeople's ideas about how the sexes differ (see Eagly, 1987).

Reasons to expect the absence of sex differences in leadership style. Despite the gender-stereotypic findings generally pro-

duced in studies of social behavior, similar results would not necessarily be obtained for leaders and managers because of important differences between leadership research and typical research in social psychology. In particular, the majority of leadership studies have been performed in organizations. In contrast, most social psychological research has been carried out in experimental laboratories and to a lesser extent in field settings not embedded within organizations (e.g., on street corners). In such environments, subjects interact with strangers on a short-term basis, and the constraints of organizational and familial roles are generally minimal or absent. Consequently, there is often considerable ambiguity about how one should behave, and people may react in terms of quite global and readily observable attributes of themselves and others (e.g., sex, age, race, and general physical appearance). In situations of this type, gender roles, which are rules about how one should behave as a male or female, may provide more guidance than they otherwise would and thus produce gender-stereotypic behavior.

Behavior may be less stereotypic when women and men who occupy the same managerial role are compared because these organizational leadership roles, which typically are paid jobs, usually provide fairly clear guidelines about the conduct of behavior. Managers become socialized into their roles in the early stages of their experience in an organization (see Feldman, 1976; Graen, 1976; Terborg, 1977; Wanous, 1977). In addition, male and female managers have presumably been selected by organizations (and have selected themselves into these roles) according to the same set of organizationally relevant criteria, further decreasing the likelihood that the men and women who occupy these roles differ substantially in their style. Thus, reasonable assumptions about socialization into leadership roles and selection for these roles suggest that male and female leaders *who occupy the same organizational role* should differ very little. Managers of both sexes are presumably more concerned about managing effectively than about representing sex-differentiated features of societal gender roles.

This argument that organizational roles should override gender roles is consistent with Kanter's (1977a) structural interpretation of organizational behavior. Kanter argued that apparent sex differences in the behavior of organizational leaders are in fact a product of the differing structural positions of the sexes within organizations. Because women are more often in positions of little power or opportunity for advancement, they behave in ways that reflect their lack of power. Kanter's reasoning thus suggests that women and men who are equivalent in terms of status and power would behave similarly, even though sex differences may appear to be substantial when women and

---

[1] The one available quantitative review of sex differences in leadership style (Dobbins & Platz, 1986) unfortunately included studies with designs not suited for examining these differences. These inappropriate studies investigated bias in subjects' perceptions of leaders by equalizing the behavior of male and female leaders and varying only the leader's sex (Butterfield & Powell, 1981; Lee & Alvares, 1977). Because equivalence of male and female behavior was ensured in these studies, they cannot be regarded as assessing sex differences in leadership style.

men are compared without control of their organizational status.

Reasons to expect the presence of sex differences in leadership style. Despite these reasons for arguing that differences between female and male organizational leaders should be minimal, other perspectives suggest that sex differences may be common, especially in some types of leadership research. As our reasoning has already implied, the social structural rationale for the absence of differences between occupants of the same managerial role within organizations is fully consistent with the presence of differences in leadership studies that compare women and men in other circumstances. In the leadership literature, there are two major types of studies that did not examine organizational leaders—namely, laboratory experiments, usually conducted with college students, and assessment studies, which we defined as research assessing the styles of people who were not selected for occupancy of leadership positions. Because the social structural rationale for the absence of differences between women and men in the same organizational role is not relevant to studies of these two types, sex-differentiated leadership styles are likely to be prevalent in such research, just as gender-stereotypic behavior is commonly found in social psychological research more generally.

There are, in addition, several reasons to suggest that male and female organizational leaders, even those who occupy the same positions, may differ to some extent in their leadership style despite the structural forces for minimizing differences that we have already noted. One such reason acknowledges the possibility of ingrained sex differences in personality traits and behavioral tendencies, differences that are not nullified by organizational selection or socialization. For example, some psychologists have maintained that sex differences in adult social behavior are in part a product of biological influences such as the greater prenatal androgynization of males (e.g., Money & Ehrhardt, 1972). Other psychologists have emphasized the importance of childhood events that are different for the sexes such as experiences that occur in sex-segregated play groups in which girls and boys play in different styles and use different methods of influencing one another (Maccoby, 1988). Thus, it is possible that biological sex differences and sex-differentiated prior experiences cause men and women to be somewhat different kinds of people, even if they do occupy the same managerial role. It may not be possible to find men and women who are so nearly equivalent that trait-level differences disappear entirely, even though sex differences in the behavior of organizational leaders may be smaller than those in the general population. In particular, men and women may come to managerial roles with a somewhat different set of skills. Especially relevant is the evidence meta-analyses have provided for women's social skills: Women as a group, when compared with men as a group, can be described as friendly, pleasant, interested in other people, expressive, and socially sensitive (see Eagly, 1987; Hall, 1984). To the extent that such findings reflect ingrained sex differences that are not leveled by organizational selection or socialization, male and female managers may behave differently, despite structural forces toward sameness.

Another perspective suggesting that leader behavior may be somewhat sex differentiated in organizations postulates *gender-role spillover*, which is "a carryover into the workplace of gender-based expectations for behavior" (Gutek & Morasch, 1982, p. 58; see also Nieva & Gutek, 1981). The spillover concept suggests that gender roles may contaminate organizational roles to some extent and cause people to have different expectations for female and male managers. In support of this idea, Russell, Rush, and Herd (1988) found that university women described an effective female (vs. male) leader as exhibiting higher levels of both the interpersonally oriented and the task-oriented aspects of leadership (i.e., higher in consideration and initiation of structure; see discussion of these variables in next subsection).[2]

Consistent with the idea that gender roles spill over to organizational roles, several social scientists have claimed that female leaders and managers experience conflict between their gender role and their leadership role (see Bass, 1981; Bayes & Newton, 1978; Kruse & Wintermantel, 1986; O'Leary, 1974). This conflict arises for female leaders because the stereotype of manager and the normative expectations associated with being a good manager include more masculine than feminine qualities (see Powell, 1988). The idea that women are subjected to incompatible expectations from the managerial and the female role thus presumes that gender roles are important within organizations.

Another manifestation of the spillover of gender roles onto organizational roles is that people who hold positions in organizations tend to have negative attitudes about women occupying managerial roles. Reflecting the subordinate status of women in the society, numerous studies have shown that people are often reluctant to have a female supervisor and think that women are somewhat less qualified for leadership and that female managers would have negative effects on morale (see reviews by O'Leary, 1974; Riger & Galligan, 1980; Terborg, 1977). Because these attitudes and beliefs raise questions about women's competence, ability to lead, and potential for advancement, female managers often face a less supportive environment than male managers. Sex differences in leadership style might result from this aspect of gender-role spillover as well as from the other aspects we have noted.

Finally, some of the fine-grained features of the structural interpretation of organizational behavior suggest other possible sources of sex differences in the behavior of organizational leaders. One such consideration is that, as Kanter (1977b) pointed out, women in managerial roles often have the status of *token* because of their rarity in such positions. Thus, female managers commonly are members of a numerically small minority, whereas their male counterparts are members of a majority group. As Kanter and others argued, token status increases one's visibility (Taylor, Fiske, Etcoff, & Ruderman, 1978) and can have a number of negative implications for how one is perceived and treated, especially when the token is a woman (Crocker & McGraw, 1984; Ott, 1989; Yoder & Sinnett, 1985). In

---

[2] Whereas the belief that effective female managers are especially concerned about relationships may reflect stereotypic beliefs about women in general, the belief that effective female managers are especially concerned about task accomplishment may reflect a more complex theory about women having to perform extremely well to succeed as managers.

addition. even those female and male leaders who occupy the same organizational role may differ systematically in seniority, salary, the availability of mentoring and informal collegial support, and other characteristics that convey some of the subtleties of organizational status. Women, especially as relative newcomers in many managerial roles, tend to have less status in these ways. and this difference may be reflected in their behavior.

In summary, ingrained sex differences in traits and behavioral tendencies, a spillover of gender roles onto organizational roles, and subtle differences in the structural position of women and men could cause leadership behavior to be somewhat sex-differentiated even when occupants of the same organizational role are compared. Therefore, some evidence of sex differences in leadership style in organizational studies would not be surprising. Nonetheless. our reasoning that organizational roles are more important than gender roles led us to predict that differences between men and women occupying the same leadership role in organizations would be smaller than differences between men and women observed in other types of leadership research. namely laboratory experiments and assessment studies.

Design of the Meta-Analysis

Types of leadership style. The fact that investigators have examined many facets of leadership style (see Bass, 1981) requires that reviewers decide which facets to include and how to organize them into types. In examining this issue, we found that the majority of the studies had assessed the extent to which leaders or managers were concerned with two aspects of their work. The first of these aspects we termed *task accomplishment,* (or, for brevity, task style)—that is, organizing activities to perform assigned tasks. The second aspect we termed *maintenance of interpersonal relationships* (or, for brevity, interpersonal style)—that is, tending to the morale and welfare of the people in the setting.

This distinction between task and interpersonal styles was first represented in leadership research by Bales (1950), who proposed two categories of leaders, those with an orientation to task accomplishment and those with a socioemotional orientation indicative of concern for morale and relationships among group members. This distinction was developed further in the Ohio State studies on leadership (e.g., Halpin, 1957; Halpin & Winer, 1957; Hemphill & Coons, 1957; Stogdill, 1963). In this research, task orientation, labeled *initiation of structure,* included behavior such as having subordinates follow rules and procedures, maintaining high standards for performance, and making leader and subordinate roles explicit. Interpersonal orientation, labeled *consideration,* included behavior such as helping and doing favors for subordinates, looking out for their welfare, explaining procedures, and being friendly and available. Task and interpersonal orientations are typically regarded as separate, relatively orthogonal dimensions (e.g., in the Leader Behavior Description Questionnaire [LBDQ] constructed by the Ohio State researchers; Halpin & Winer, 1957). Less commonly, these orientations are treated as two ends of a single continuum (e.g., in the Least Preferred Co-Worker [LPC] instrument; Fiedler, 1967).[3]

Task and interpersonal styles in leadership research are obviously relevant to gender because of the stereotypes people have about sex differences in these aspects of behavior (see Ashmore, Del Boca, & Wohlers, 1986; Eagly & Steffen, 1984). Men are believed to be more self-assertive and motivated to master their environment (e.g., more aggressive, independent, self-sufficient, forceful, dominant). In contrast, women are believed to be more selfless and concerned with others (e.g., more kind, helpful, understanding, warm, sympathetic, aware of others' feelings). In research on gender, these two orientations have been labeled *masculine* and *feminine, instrumental* and *expressive,* and *agentic* and *communal.* Although the task and interpersonal dimensions studied in leadership research are not as broad as these very general tendencies examined in gender stereotype research, the ideas are quite similar. Therefore, leadership research provides an excellent opportunity to determine whether the behavior of leaders is gender stereotypic.

The only other aspect of leadership style studied frequently enough to allow us to represent it in our meta-analysis is the extent to which leaders (a) behave democratically and allow subordinates to participate in decision making, or (b) behave autocratically and discourage subordinates from participating in decision-making.[4] The dimension of *democratic* versus *autocratic* leadership (or participative vs. *directive* leadership) follows from early experimental studies of leadership style (e.g., Lewin & Lippitt, 1938) and has been developed since that time by a number of researchers (e.g., Likert, 1961; Vroom & Yetton, 1973). Although democratic versus autocratic style is a different (and narrower) aspect of leader behavior than task-oriented and interpersonally oriented styles (see Bass, 1981), the democratic–autocratic dimension also relates to gender stereotypes, because one component of the agentic or instrumental aspect of these stereotypes is that men are relatively dominant and controlling (i.e., more autocratic and directive than women).

Methods of assessing leadership style. The diversity of the methods that have been used to assess style complicates the task of integrating research in this area. Moreover, a substantial methodological literature criticizes and compares these measures (see Bass, 1981). Because the methodological issues that have been raised remain largely unresolved by leadership researchers, we did not attempt to settle these issues in order to base our meta-analytic generalizations on only those measures that we or other investigators might regard as most valid. Instead, we included all measures that researchers regarded as assessing task-oriented and interpersonally oriented styles or

---

[3] Although the Least Preferred Co-Worker Scale has been given a variety of interpretations, the view that low-LPC people are task oriented and high-LPC people are relationship oriented seems to be the most widely accepted of these interpretations (see Rice, 1978).

[4] Although Bass (1981) distinguished between (a) democratic versus autocratic leadership and (b) participative versus directive leadership, we treated these measures as a single class because we found this distinction difficult to maintain when categorizing measures. We refer to this single class as *democratic versus autocratic* style. Researchers have treated this style as a single, bipolar dimension because democratic and autocratic styles presumably are incompatible. In contrast, interpersonal and task styles apparently are not incompatible, as suggested by the preference of most researchers for treating these styles as separate, relatively orthogonal dimensions.

autocratic versus democratic style. We coded our studies on a number of these measures' features, many of which may be regarded as having implications for the quality of the measures. For example, measures differed in how directly or indirectly they assessed leadership style; the most direct measures were based on observers' coding of ongoing leadership behavior, and the most indirect measures were based on leaders' responses to questionnaire measures of attitudes or personality. Representing such features in our coding scheme (see *Method*) allowed us to determine whether they covaried with sex differences in leadership style.

Congeniality of leadership roles for men and women. When we thought about gender in relation to the available studies of leadership style, we were struck by the variation in the extent to which the leadership roles investigated in this research (e.g., elementary school principal, nursing supervisor, military officer) would be perceived as congenial mainly for women or men. For leadership roles that are typically regarded as especially suitable for women, negative attitudes toward female leaders presumably would not be prevalent, nor would conflict between the female and the leader role be an issue. Presumably women would be under less pressure to adopt male-stereotypic styles of leadership in such positions.

To enable us to take account of the gender congeniality of leadership roles, we conducted a questionnaire study to obtain judgments of each role, and analyzed these judgments to estimate the extent to which women or men were more interested in each role and believed themselves more competent to perform it. In addition, because people associate task-oriented qualities with men and interpersonally oriented qualities with women, we also determined the extent to which each role was judged to require each set of these gender-stereotypic qualities. These features of our meta-analysis allowed us to determine whether the ascription of gender-stereotypic qualities to leadership roles related to sex differences in the styles by which people carry out these roles.

Predictions for meta-analysis. As we have already stated, our major prediction is that gender-stereotypic sex differences in leadership style are less pronounced in organizational studies comparing occupants of the same managerial role than in leadership studies of other types. Beyond this prediction, our purposes as reviewers are primarily descriptive and exploratory, even though other predictions might follow from the issues we have discussed. For example, if, as we suggested, female managers often face a less supportive environment than do male managers, these women might strive so hard to overcome antifemale prejudices that they behave counterstereotypically as a result. Additional complexities enter if we reason that ratings of leaders' behavior could produce findings that are more stereotypic than those produced by measures grounded more firmly in behavior. Rather than set forth a series of speculative hypotheses that take these and other considerations into account, we prefer to present our review and to discuss such issues as they become relevant to interpreting our meta-analytic findings.

Method

Sample of Studies

Computer-based information searches were conducted using the keywords *leadership style* as well as *leader* and *leadership* when paired with terms such as *gender, sex, sex differences,* and *women.* These keywords were searched in the following data bases: *Psychological Abstracts* (PsycINFO: 1967 to April, 1987), *Dissertation Abstracts International* (DISS: 1961 to May, 1987), Educational Resources Information Center (ERIC: 1966 to November, 1986), Social Science Citation Index (Social SciSearch: 1971 to October, 1986), *Sociological Abstracts* (1963 to October, 1986), and a worldwide business and management data base (ABI/INFORM: 1971 to February, 1987). We also searched through the reference lists of numerous review articles, chapters, and books as well as the reference lists of all located studies.

Criteria for including studies in the sample were that (a) the study included one or more measures that assessed task- and interpersonally oriented styles or autocratic versus democratic style; (b) subjects were adults or adolescents from the United States or Canada who were not sampled from abnormal populations; (c) the study assessed the leadership style of at least five people of each sex; and (d) the reported results were sufficient either to calculate a sex-of-subject effect size or to determine the statistical significance or direction of the sex difference. This last criterion eliminated studies that provided only a multiple regression equation in which sex appeared as one of the predictors (e.g., Gustafson, 1982) as well as studies that provided only a multivariate analysis of variance on leadership style combined with other measures (e.g., Martinez, 1982; Rice, Instone, & Adams, 1984).

Studies were omitted if the people whose leadership style was assessed[5] had been selected to equalize their status on a personality or attitudinal variable (e.g., an index of masculinity or feminity) that probably correlates with both sex and leadership style (e.g., Sirianni-Brantley, 1985; Stake, 1981); accurate estimation of any sex difference in leadership style is not possible from such studies. In addition, studies were rejected if the leadership measure assessed only a narrow aspect of style such as methods of dealing with poorly performing subordinates or managing conflict (e.g., Dobbins, 1986; Dobbins, Pence, Orban, & Sgro, 1983; Koberg, 1985; Renwick, 1977). If leadership was assessed on several narrow indexes (e.g., Baugher, 1983; Lanning, 1982), these were combined, when appropriate, into a measure of one of the styles considered in this article (e.g., task orientation), based on our independent choices of the indexes that best matched the item content of the most popular measures of the broader style. The indexes were combined using Rosenthal and Rubin's (1986) suggested formula and assuming that the average interindex correlation was .25. This correlation was estimated by averaging the interitem correlations given (or derived from coefficient alphas) for multiple-item style measures used in the studies included in the meta-analysis. These combined measures aggregated five indexes whenever possible (and fewer otherwise). If the report was not sufficiently detailed to allow such combinations, the study was eliminated (e.g., Hughes, Copeland, Ford, & Heidt, 1983; Moore, Shaffer, Goodsell, & Baringoldz, 1983).

Studies were also eliminated if the only measures of leadership style assessed ideal rather than actual style (e.g., Arcy, 1980). Studies were omitted if they assessed, not people's naturally occurring styles, but the impact of treatments designed to instill a certain leadership style (e.g., Crudge, 1983; Hall, 1983; Heft & Deni, 1984). Finally, we excluded studies of T groups, encounter groups, and therapy groups (e.g., Hurst, Stein, Korchin, & Soskin, 1978), because their measures of leader behavior reflected a tradition quite different from that of the other leadership style research we located. Application of these criteria yielded 162 studies reported in 161 documents (see Appendix).

---

[5] References to *people whose leadership style was assessed* (and, for brevity, sometimes merely *people*) in this article designate leaders only in organizational and laboratory studies; in assessment studies, people not selected for leadership (e.g., samples of undergraduates or nonmanagerial employees of business firms) responded to measures of leadership style.

238   ALICE H. EAGLY AND BLAIR T. JOHNSON

Variables Coded From Each Study

The following general information was coded from each report: (a) date of publication; (b) publication form (journal article; other published document; dissertation or master's thesis; other unpublished document); (c) percentage of male authors; (d) sex of first author; (e) number of observations;[6] (f) level of data aggregation (i.e., number of observations aggregated into each data point in the study's statistical analysis);[7] (g) confounding of male–female comparison with variables such as seniority, education, and age (controlled via matching; known to be confounded on some variables; unknown whether confounded and confounding likely; unknown whether confounded and confounding unlikely);[8] (h) type of study (organizational; assessment; laboratory); (i) type of setting or subject population (see Table 3 for categories); and (j) size of group or organization in which leadership occurred (laboratory group of given size; small organization, defined as less than 500 long-term participants; large organization; mixed or unknown size of organization; people not selected for leadership).

In addition, the following characteristics of the leaders and their roles were coded: (a) level of leadership (first or line; second or middle; third or higher; ambiguous, mixed, or unknown; people not selected for leadership); (b) age of people whose leadership style was assessed; (c) percentage of men among people whose leadership style was assessed (estimated from census tables and other information if not stated in report); (d) percentage of men among subordinates (also estimated if not stated in report; unknown when subordinates not specifically identified); (e) basis of selection of people whose style was assessed (random sample or entire population; unsuccessful random sample, i.e., effort to obtain random sample or entire population but less than 80% participation; self-selected; unknown); and (f) basis for laboratory leadership (appointed randomly; appointed based on own qualifications; emerged; mixed or unclear).

Finally, the following attributes of the measures of leadership style were coded: (a) type of style assessed (interpersonal; task; interpersonal versus task; democratic versus autocratic); (b) identity of raters (people rated selves; supervisors rated leaders; subordinates rated leaders; peers rated leaders; judges not related organizationally to leaders rated leaders; mixed or unclear); (c) type of rating for style measure (responses to attitude or personality scale; responses to hypothetical leadership situations; presumed observation of leader's behavior without control of behaviors available for observation; actual observation of leader's behavior based on behaviors made available during study);[9] (d) basis of selection of raters (random sample or entire population; unsuccessful random sample, i.e., effort to obtain random sample or entire population but less than 80% participation; self-selected; unknown); (e) percentage of men among raters; (f) name of style measure (see Table 2 for categories); and (g) reliability of style measure (reported value; unknown).[10]

These variables were coded independently by the authors, with a median agreement of 97%; "basis of selection of people whose style was assessed" yielded the lowest agreement (77%). Disagreements were resolved by discussion.

Variables Constructed From Questionnaire Respondents' Judgments of Leadership Roles

As noted early in the article we conducted a questionnaire study to generate measures of gender-relevant aspects of the leadership roles investigated in the organizational and laboratory studies. To assess the perceived congeniality of the roles for women and men, we calculated sex differences in respondents' self-reported competence to perform each role and interest in performing each role as well as respondents' beliefs about differences in average men's and women's interest in performing each role.[11] Other measures assessed respondents' judgments

of the extent to which each role requires interpersonally oriented ability and task-oriented ability.

Respondents. The sample consisted of 125 female and 181 male Purdue University undergraduates who received partial course credit for participation.

Procedure. Respondents participated in groups of about 15 and in sessions conducted by a female or male experimenter. Each respondent completed one of three versions of a questionnaire that took approximately one hour to complete. Each of the three versions contained brief descriptions of each of the 119 leadership roles investigated in the organizational or laboratory studies. Examples of descriptions used for organizational studies are principal of an elementary school, manager in the communications division of a company, supervisor of state agency caseworkers who determine if particular workers are disabled, and director of intercollegiate athletics in a major university. Examples of descriptions used for laboratory studies are leader of a laboratory discussion group attempting to reach consensus about a decision that all group members had first made individually, manager of a simulated engineering department of a large oil refinery (the manager is given the responsibility of bolstering productivity), and leader of a laboratory group trying to decide which items to take along in order to survive in a desert.

In one version of the questionnaire, respondents judged the roles in response to two questions eliciting self-reports of their competence and interest in relation to each role: (a) How competent would you be as

---

[6] The number of observations (n) for the statistical analysis typically represented either the number of people whose style was assessed or the number of raters (e.g., subordinates) who described the leaders.

[7] For example, each data point might represent 5 observers' ratings of a leader on 10 items, yielding 50 judgments aggregated into each data point. To the extent that measures were based on multiple judgments of leaders' styles, they should yield more reliable estimates of sex differences, in the manner that the number of items in a test relates to the reliability of the total test (e.g., Ghiselli, 1964).

[8] Most organizational studies examined occupants of a given role (e.g., elementary school principals), but a few examined broader classifications of managers (e.g., middle managers of an organization). Even when occupants of the identical role were examined, the equivalence of the men and women in terms of attributes such as age, education, and job seniority is not ensured. Therefore, this aspect of our coding scheme took account of confounding between sex and other attributes of leaders. Some organizational and assessment studies did use samples of men and women who were matched on various attributes, and other studies included data revealing the presence or absence of confounding. When such data were absent in organizational studies, we ordinarily coded confounding as unknown and likely. However, when such data were absent and the people whose style was assessed were students, we coded confounding as unknown and unlikely.

[9] The following list provides an example of the standard measures classified into each category: responses to attitude or personality scale, Least Preferred Co-Worker; responses to hypothetical leadership situations, Leadership Effectiveness and Adaptability Description; presumed observation of leader's behavior without control of behaviors available for observation, Leader Behavior Description Questionnaire; observation of leader's behavior based on behaviors made available during study, Interaction Process Analysis. See Table 2 for information about these measures.

[10] The reliability of the measure was reported for only 14% of the sex comparisons, precluding any corrections or weighting based on reliability information.

[11] In this article, the term *respondents* designates people who participated in the questionnaire study and not those who participated in the studies included in the meta-analysis.

a [role description given]? and (b) How interested would you be in becoming a [role description given]? For the competence question, respondents were told to assume that they could obtain required training or education, and for the interest question, they were told that they had obtained the training or education. In a second version of the questionnaire, respondents judged the roles in response to two questions assessing their beliefs about women's and men's interest in the roles: (a) How interested would the *average woman* be in becoming a [role description given]? and (b) How interested would the *average man* be in becoming a [role description given]? These respondents were told to assume that these average women and men could obtain required training or education. In a third version of the questionnaire, respondents judged the roles in response to two questions assessing their beliefs about the abilities each role required: (a) How much *ability to cooperate and get along with other people* is needed to be an effective [role description given]? and (b) How much *ability to direct and control people* is needed to be an effective [role description given]?

All ratings were made on 15-point scales. Each version of the questionnaire was divided into two parts, both of which elicited respondents' judgments of all of the roles in relation to one of the questions. The order of the two parts was counterbalanced. Within each part, the descriptions of the behaviors appeared in one of two random orders.

Analysis of ratings. For the two questions in the first version of the questionnaire, mean scores for each role were computed separately for female and male respondents. For each role, the female respondents' mean was subtracted from the male respondents' mean to yield a mean sex difference, which was standardized by dividing it by the pooled (within-sex) standard deviation. For the two questions in the second version of the questionnaire, the respondents' mean rating of the average woman for each role was subtracted from their mean rating of the average man to yield a mean stereotypic sex difference, which was standardized by dividing it by the standard deviation of the differences between the paired ratings. For the two questions in the third version of the questionnaire, a mean of all the respondents' ratings of each role was calculated. These five mean scores thus described each of the leadership roles in the organizational and laboratory studies. For studies reporting findings aggregated over several roles, ratings of the relevant roles were averaged (e.g., Birdsall, 1980; Gupta, Jenkins, & Beehr, 1983).

Computation and Analysis of Effect Sizes

The effect size calculated is *g*, the difference between the leadership style of the men and women, divided by the pooled standard deviation (see Hedges & Olkin, 1985). A positive sign was given to stereotypic differences (i.e., women more interpersonally oriented, men more task oriented, women more democratic and less autocratic) and a negative sign to counterstereotypic differences.

Multiple effect sizes from single studies. Some studies yielded more than one effect size, most commonly because more than one type of style was assessed. Specifically, if the data report was sufficient, separate effect sizes were calculated when (a) different types of leadership styles were assessed in a study (most frequently interpersonal and task styles); (b) distinctively different measures were used to assess the same type of style (e.g., LBDQ and unique investigator-constructed measure); or (c) different groups of raters responded to the same measure (e.g., leaders, subordinates). Separate effect sizes were also calculated when different groups of leaders were assessed within an organization (e.g., line managers, middle managers) or samples were taken within different types of organizations (e.g., high schools, elementary schools) or different populations of people (e.g., undergraduates, business school graduate students). If the reported findings were sufficient in laboratory studies, separate effect sizes were calculated when experimental manipulations resulted in (a) leaders obtaining their roles on

different bases (e.g., appointed randomly, emerged); (b) groups of subordinates differing in sex composition (e.g., all-male, all-female, mixed sex); or (c) groups working on different tasks (e.g., high vs. low task clarity). Although the computation of more than one effect size from some of the studies created some nonindependence in our data set, the questions we desired to address could not be answered without partitioning the data in these ways. As a result, 31 studies yielded only one effect size, 79 studies yielded two effect sizes, 10 studies yielded three, 19 yielded four, 3 yielded six, and 2 yielded eight, for a total of 329 effect sizes. In addition, 18 studies produced no effect sizes (but did yield a report of the significance or direction of one or more sex comparisons).

Computation of effect sizes. The computation of the 329 *g*s was based on (a) means and standard deviations or error terms for 149 of the *g*s, (b) *F* and *t* for 80, (c) correlations or chi-squares for 45, (d) proportions of men and women manifesting particular styles for 48,[12] and (e) exact *p*s or level *p*s (e.g., *p* < .05) for 7. For 41 of the 370 available sex comparisons, the report lacked enough statistical detail to allow an effect size to be computed.

The pooled standard deviation that is the denominator of the effect size was estimated, whenever possible, only from the portion of each study's data entering into the effect size. When the pooled standard deviation was estimated from the mean square error of an analysis of variance (ANOVA), this error term was reconstituted by adding into the sum of squares error all (available) between-groups sums of squares except that for sex. One-way designs are approximated by this procedure, which has been recommended by Hedges and Becker (1986) and Glass, McGaw, and Smith (1981).

To reduce computational error, each of us calculated effect sizes independently. The statistical significance and direction of the sex comparisons were also recorded; this information provided the only record of the sex comparison for studies that provided insufficient information to calculate effect sizes. When the raters who provided the leadership style measure were different from the leaders or managers rated (e.g., they were subordinates) and these ratings were reported separately for the male and female raters, effect sizes were calculated separately for the male and female raters (and the significance and direction of the sex comparison were recorded separately). These additional effect sizes, calculated separately for raters of each sex, supplemented the effect sizes that were combined over both sexes of raters and were used in most analyses.

Analysis of effect sizes. The *g*s were converted to *d*s by correcting them for bias (i.e., *g*'s overestimate of the population effect size, which occurs especially for small samples; see Hedges, 1981; Hedges & Olkin, 1985). To obtain an overall estimate of the sex difference reported in the available research, we then combined the study outcomes by averaging the *d*s. To determine whether each set of *d*s shared a common effect size (i.e., was consistent across the studies), we calculated a homogeneity statistic, *Q*, which has an approximate chi-square distribution with *k* − 1 degrees of freedom, where *k* is the number of effect sizes (Hedges, 1981; Hedges & Olkin, 1985).

---

[12] Measures such as Hersey and Blanchard's (1977) Leadership Effectiveness and Adaptability Description (see Table 2), which ordinarily classify leaders into the four quadrants formed by task and interpersonal dimensions of style, were analyzed to yield the proportions of each sex in the two high-task quadrants (for a measure of task-oriented style) and the proportions of each sex in the two high-interpersonal quadrants (for a measure of interpersonally oriented style). These proportions as well as other proportions we encountered were transformed to effect sizes by treating each proportion as the mean of a distribution of 0's and 1's (McNemar, 1962). Thus, the effect size was the difference between the male and female proportions divided by the pooled standard deviations of the samples of 0's and 1's.

In the absence of homogeneity, we accounted for variability in heterogeneous effect sizes by relating them to the attributes of the studies. To determine the relation between these study characteristics and the magnitude of the effect sizes, both categorical and continuous models were tested (Hedges, 1982a, 1982b; Hedges & Olkin, 1985). Categorical models, which are analogous to ANOVAs, may show that heterogeneous effect sizes are homogeneous within the subgroups established by dividing studies into classes based on study characteristics. The techniques for calculating categorical models provide a between-classes effect (analogous to a main effect in an ANOVA) and a test of the homogeneity of the effect sizes within each class. The between-classes effect is estimated by Q_B, which has an approximate chi-square distribution with $p - 1$ degrees of freedom, where p is the number of classes. The homogeneity of the effect sizes within each class is estimated by Q_{Wi}, which has an approximate chi-square distribution with $m - 1$ degrees of freedom, where m is the number of effect sizes in the class. The tables reporting tests of categorical models also include the mean weighted effect size for each class, calculated with each effect size weighted by the reciprocal of its variance, and an indication of whether this mean differed significantly from the 0.00 value that indicates exactly no sex difference.

The continuous models are least squares simple linear regressions, calculated with each effect size weighted by the reciprocal of its variance. Each such model yields a test of the significance of a predictor as well as a test of model specification, which evaluates whether significant systematic variation remains unexplained in the regression model (Hedges, 1982b; Hedges & Olkin, 1985). The sum of squares error statistic, Q_E, which provides this test of model specification, has an approximate chi-square distribution with $k - p - 1$ degrees of freedom, where k is the number of effect sizes and p is the number of predictors (not including the intercept). If correctly specified models are not achieved when implementing continuous models (or homogeneity is not achieved within the classes when implementing categorical models), the results of these analyses cannot be interpreted as confidently as they would otherwise be.

As an alternative analysis to predicting effect sizes using categorical and continuous models, we attained homogeneity by identifying outliers among the effect sizes and sequentially removing those that reduced the homogeneity statistic by the largest amount (see Hedges & Olkin, 1985). Using such a procedure, Hedges (1987) found for several meta-analyses on psychological topics that the removal of up to 20% of the outliers in a group of heterogeneous effect sizes usually resulted in a high degree of homogeneity. Inspection of the percentage of effect sizes removed to attain homogeneity allows one to determine whether the effect sizes are homogeneous aside from the presence of relatively few aberrant values. Under such circumstances, the mean attained after removal of such outliers may better represent the distribution of effect sizes than the mean based on all of the effect sizes.

Results

Characteristics of Studies

Before considering the sex differences reported in studies of leadership style, we examined the characteristics of these studies. Table 1 shows 18 of these study characteristics aggregated over all of the 370 sex comparisons that we encountered as well as summarized separately within each of the types of leadership style.

As shown by the central tendencies of the characteristics listed in Table 1, studies typically (a) were published relatively recently; (b) were published as dissertations; (c) based the statistical analysis on a moderate number of observations; (d) aggregated a moderate number of observations into each data point; (e) compared the sexes in such a way that some confounding with other variables was likely; and (f) were carried out in organizations. In addition, these studies typically (a) assessed middle managers; (b) assessed adults in their thirties; (c) assessed people in male-dominated roles or from populations with male majorities; (d) assessed leaders with predominantly female subordinates; and (e) unsuccessfully attempted random sampling of the people whose style was assessed or randomly selected them. Finally, the measuring instruments typically (a) had people rate their own leadership styles or had subordinates rate their leaders; and (b) used ratings presumably based on observation of leaders' behavior but without control of the behaviors available for observation.

The means for the last five characteristics represent the variables constructed from questionnaire respondents' judgments of the leadership roles examined in the studies. As shown by these means, women judged themselves as significantly more competent in these leadership roles and as more interested in occupying the roles than men did. In addition, respondents of both sexes judged the average woman more interested in occupying the roles than the average man.[13] They also judged that the roles required "quite a lot" of both interpersonal and task ability.[14]

When these study characteristics were examined separately within the types of leadership style (see Table 1), notable exceptions to these overall patterns were that (a) journal articles were especially common in studies of autocratic versus democratic style, (b) measures of interpersonal versus task style and democratic versus autocratic style were based more exclusively on self-ratings, and (c) measures of interpersonal versus task style were based primarily on responses to attitude scales.

Table 2 lists the measuring instruments that assessed leadership style and names all measures that were used for two or more of the sex comparisons. As Table 2 shows, the majority of the studies used standard instruments; the Leader Behavior Description Questionnaire, which places task and interpersonal orientations on separate dimensions, received the most use. The Least Preferred Co-Worker instrument predominated

---

[13] The greater congeniality of these leadership roles for women compared with men should be interpreted in terms of the distribution of organizational settings given in Table 3. In particular, a large number of studies in our sample examined elementary school principals, a role our data suggested that women find congenial.

[14] The mean ratings on these 15-point scales fell in the range anchored by the term "quite a lot." Suggesting that our student respondents were able to discriminate between the interpersonal and task requirements of leadership roles, mean ratings showed that some roles were thought to require considerably more interpersonal than task ability (e.g., "leader of a laboratory discussion group attempting to reach consensus about a decision that all group members had first made individually"; "elected leader of a student organization in a college") and that other roles were thought to require considerably more task than interpersonal ability (e.g., "platoon leader at West Point" and other military roles; "president of a corporation").

Table 1
Summary of Study Characteristics

Variable and class	All comparisons ($n = 370$)	Interpersonal style comparisons ($n = 153$)	Task style comparisons ($n = 154$)	Interpersonal vs. task style comparisons ($n = 35$)	Democratic vs. autocratic style comparisons ($n = 28$)
Median date of publication	1981	1981	1981	1981	1980
Publication form					
Journal article	91	34	35	6	16
Other published document	10	4	5	0	1
Dissertation	256	110	109	27	10
Unpublished document	13	5	5	2	1
Median no. of observations for analysis	88	88	81	105	84
Median no. of observations aggregated into					
each data point	12	12	12	16	15
Confounding of male–female comparison					
Controlled via matching	42	20	20	2	0
Known	92	38	38	9	7
Unknown and likely	175	79	77	12	7
Unknown and unlikely	61	16	19	12	14
Type of study					
Organizational	289	131	128	17	13
Assessment	56	15	15	16	10
Laboratory	25	7	11	2	5
Level of leadership					
First or line	58	23	27	4	4
Second or middle	184	84	83	7	10
Third or higher	11	3	3	4	1
Ambiguous, mixed, or unknown	61	28	26	4	3
People not selected for leadership	56	15	15	16	10
Mean age of people whose style was					
assessed (years)	37.85	39.26	38.39	32.80	31.24
Median percentage of men among people					
whose style was assessed	73.00	73.00	73.00	61.60	61.84
Median percentage of men among					
subordinates	16.32	16.17	16.25	25.49	18.66
Basis of selection for people whose style					
was assessed					
Random sample	103	42	42	11	8
Unsuccessful random sample	131	59	57	10	5
Self-selected	58	21	23	6	8
Unknown	78	31	32	8	7
Identity of raters for style measure					
People rated selves	197	73	72	34	18
Supervisors rated leaders	15	8	7	0	0
Subordinates rated leaders	120	57	58	1	4
Peers rated leaders	4	1	1	0	2
Judges rated leaders	22	8	11	0	3
Mixed or unclear	12	6	5	0	1
Type of rating for style measure					
Responses to attitude or personality scale	67	17	17	31	2
Responses to hypothetical leadership					
situations	62	27	26	2	7
Presumed observation of leader's					
behavior	205	97	95	1	12
Actual observation of leader's behavior	36	12	16	1	7
Mean respondent judgments of roles					
Competence sex difference[a]	−0.11*	−0.12*	−0.11*	−0.06	−0.10
Interest sex difference	−0.09*	−0.09*	−0.09*	−0.02	−0.05
Stereotypic interest difference	−0.10*	−0.11*	−0.10*	−0.02	−0.06
Interpersonal ability rating[b]	11.04	11.05	11.06	10.94	10.91
Task ability rating	10.88	10.91	10.90	10.83	10.54

Note. For categorical variables, numbers in table represent frequency of sex comparisons in each class. Summaries of continuous variables are based on reports for which information was available on each variable.
[a] For the first three variables constructed from judgments of the leadership roles, values are positive for differences in the masculine direction (greater male estimates of competence and of interest; ascription of greater interest to average men). [b] For the last two variables constructed from judgments of the leadership roles, values are larger to the extent that a role was judged to require more interpersonal or task ability (on 15-point scales with 15 indicating high ability).
* Differs significantly ($p < .05$ or smaller) from 0.00 (exactly no difference).

among studies placing interpersonal and task orientation on two ends of a single dimension. In contrast, unique measures predominated in studies of democratic versus autocratic style.

Table 3 describes the settings of the organizational studies and the subject populations of the assessment and laboratory studies. Among the organizational studies, educational settings predominated; the greatest number of these studies examined elementary school principals or university administrators. College undergraduates predominated in both the assessment and the laboratory studies.

Overall Sex Differences in Leadership Style

The summary given in Table 4 allows one to determine if men and women differed in leadership style. An overall sex difference is shown by a mean effect size that differed significantly from the 0.00 value that indicates exactly no difference (i.e., by a confidence interval that did not include 0.00). The sign of these means is positive for stereotypic differences and negative for counterstereotypic differences. These means and confidence intervals are given both aggregated over all types of style and computed separately for each style.

In general, leadership styles were slightly gender stereotypic: The weighted mean computed across all types of style was slightly but significantly stereotypic (see Table 4).[15] However, computed within each type, these means indicated *no sex difference* for (a) the task comparisons and (b) the interpersonal versus task comparisons. These means indicated *stereotypic differences* for (a) the interpersonal comparisons (women were more interpersonally oriented) and (b) the democratic versus autocratic comparisons (women were more democratic). Yet the mean effect size for interpersonal style was quite small. The largest overall sex difference was obtained for the democratic versus autocratic comparisons: Sex comparisons for this type of style were significantly more stereotypic than those for each of the other three types of style (as shown by appropriate contrasts; see description of contrast procedure in next subsection). This pattern was similar for the unweighted means, although the task style difference became significant in the counterstereotypic direction (i.e., women were more task oriented). The medians of the effect sizes were similar to the weighted and unweighted means.

As shown by the homogeneity statistics given in Table 4, the sex comparisons were not homogeneous (i.e., consistent) across the studies. As also indicated in Table 4, the removal of various numbers of outliers allowed homogeneity to be attained. Suggesting relatively stable findings, the procedure eliminated small proportions of effect sizes for all of the types of style except the democratic versus autocratic style, which required eliminating 22% to attain homogeneity. The confidence intervals associated with the weighted means after outlier removal showed that the overall tendencies for women to be more interpersonally oriented, more task oriented, and more democratic than men were all significant.

There is no completely satisfactory method to compute a mean effect size that takes into account the nonsignificant comparisons that could not be represented as effect sizes because of a lack of sufficient information. Nevertheless, one possible solution is to give these comparisons the value of 0.00 (indicating

exactly no sex difference).[16] When this step was taken, the mean unweighted effect sizes (see means reported in Table 4 under "All reports") became slightly smaller than the unweighted means (before outlier removal) that omitted these 0.00 values, but the pattern was the same (i.e., women were more interpersonally oriented, more task oriented, and more democratic).

Table 4 also reports the proportion of sex comparisons that were stereotypic in direction. These proportions differed significantly from .50, the proportion expected under the null hypothesis, for the interpersonal, task, and democratic versus autocratic comparisons ($ps < .01$ or smaller). Consistent with the pattern we have already described, these differences were counterstereotypic for the task style and stereotypic for the interpersonal and the democratic versus autocratic styles.

Accounting for Variability in the Effect Sizes

Categorical and continuous models were fitted to the effect sizes following Hedges and Olkin's (1985) statistical procedures (see *Method*).

Test of our major hypothesis. To test our hypothesis that sex differences in leadership style are less stereotypic in organizational settings than in other settings, we classified the effect sizes into the three types of studies: organizational, assessment, and laboratory. Consistent with the significant between-classes effects for type of study shown in Table 5, the expected pattern was obtained for interpersonal style and task style. For interpersonal style, a priori comparisons among the mean weighted effect sizes for the three classes of studies (see Hedges & Becker, 1986; Hedges & Olkin, 1985) showed that the sex difference for the organizational studies was significantly less stereotypic than that for the assessment studies ($p < .01$) or the laboratory studies ($p < .001$). For task style, these comparisons also showed that the sex difference for the organizational studies was significantly less stereotypic than that for the assessment studies ($p < .05$) or the laboratory studies ($p < .025$). For measures of interpersonal versus task style as well as democratic versus autocratic style, type of study had no significant effect. The significant effect that type of study produced when all the effect sizes were analyzed thus reflects primarily the trends observed for the interpersonal and task styles.

Table 5 also reports categorical models that were based on classifying the effect sizes into the four types of style and were computed within each type of study (i.e., organizational, assessment, laboratory). The significant between-styles effect for the organizational studies primarily reflects the relatively large mean for the democratic versus autocratic style, and the significant effect for the assessment studies primarily reflects the relatively large means for the interpersonal and the democratic versus autocratic styles. The nonsignificance of the between-styles effect for the laboratory studies suggests that leadership

---

[15] The weighted means were computed by weighting each known effect size by the reciprocal of its variance (Hedges & Olkin, 1985), a procedure that gives more weight to effect sizes that are more reliably estimated.

[16] Because these 0.00 values do not ordinarily provide accurate estimates of the true effect sizes, they were omitted from further analyses.

Table 2
Summary of Leadership Style Measures Used in Studies

Measure	Reference[a]	All comparisons (n = 370)	Interpersonal style comparisons (n = 153)	Task style comparisons (n = 154)	Interpersonal vs. task style comparisons (n = 35)	Democratic vs. autocratic style comparisons (n = 28)
Leader Behavior Description Questionnaire (Form XII)[b]	Stogdill (1963), Stogdill, Goode, & Day (1962)	93	47	46	—	—
Leader Behavior Description Questionnaire (early form)	Halpin (1957), Halpin & Winer (1957), Hemphill & Coons (1957)	42	21	21	—	—
Leadership Effectiveness and Adaptability Description	Hersey & Blanchard (1977, 1982)	46	23	23	—	—
Leadership Opinion Questionnaire	Fleishman (1953, 1957, 1960)	28	14	14	—	—
Organizational Climate Description Questionnaire[c]	Halpin (1966)	12	6	6	—	—
Interaction Process Analysis and variants	Bales (1950)	9	4	5	—	—
Supervisory Behavior Description Questionnaire	Fleishman (1970)	6	3	3	—	—
Styles of Management Inventory	Blake & Mouton (1964, 1978)	6	3	3	—	—
Educational Administrative Style Diagnosis Test	Reddin & Reddin (1979)	4	2	2	—	—
Organizational Climate Survey	Coleman (1979)	4	2	2	—	—
Measures of McGregor's Theory X, Theory Y	Barone (1982), Jacoby & Terborg (1975), Marnani (1982), Myers (1970), Tanner (1982)[d]	8	3	3	2	—
Least Preferred Co-Worker	Fiedler (1967)	29	—	—	29	—
Vroom and Yetton Problem Set	Vroom & Yetton (1973)	6	—	—	—	6
Principal Behavior Checklist	Alpren (1954), Grobman & Hines (1956), Van Aken (1954)	4	—	—	—	4
Sargent and Miller Leadership Questionnaire	Sargent & Miller (1971)	2	—	—	—	2
Unique measure or measure constructed by authors from components given in document		71	25	26	4	16

[a] References listed provide information regarding the development of each measure of style. [b] Used consideration and initiation of structure scales. [c] Used consideration and production emphasis scales. [d] Scales developed by authors listed to assess McGregor's (1960) Theory X and Theory Y concepts.

styles were stereotypic in laboratory studies regardless of the type of style assessed. Although the number of laboratory studies on leadership style is unfortunately quite small, the relative consistency of this stereotypic trend across the types of style lends confidence to our generalization that leaders' behavior is somewhat gender stereotypic in experimental settings.

Models involving characteristics of research report. The sex of the authors of the research reports also related to the effect sizes; female authors obtained more stereotypic findings on the whole ($p < .001$ for categorical model). Yet when the effect sizes were examined within the four types of style, this overall trend

was intact only for the interpersonal and the democratic versus autocratic styles ($ps < .001$ for categorical models). To the extent that women especially value interpersonally oriented and democratic styles, this finding suggests a tendency for authors to portray their own sex favorably. Eagly and Carli (1981) and Wood (1987) reported this tendency in earlier meta-analyses.

As shown by one of the models given in Table 6, date of publication related significantly to all of the sets of effect sizes. On an overall basis, sex differences were more stereotypic in the more recent studies, and this trend was also obtained for the interpersonal and the task styles, which predominated among

244   ALICE H. EAGLY AND BLAIR T. JOHNSON

Table 3
Summary of Setting or Subject Population for Organizational, Assessment, and Laboratory Studies

Type of study/setting or subject population	All comparisons (n = 370)	Interpersonal style comparisons (n = 153)	Task style comparisons (n = 154)	Interpersonal vs. task style comparisons (n = 35)	Democratic vs. autocratic style comparisons (n = 28)
Organizational studies					
Educational	210	94	93	11	12
Elementary school	93	41	41	5	6
Middle or junior high school	4	2	2	0	0
High school	13	6	6	1	0
University or college	47	22	21	2	2
Student organizations	6	2	2	0	2
Athletic teams	3	1	1	1	0
Other, mixed, or unknown	44	20	20	2	2
Business	26	11	11	3	1
Governmental	19	9	8	2	0
Miscellaneous[a]	34	17	16	1	0
Assessment studies					
College undergraduates	29	6	6	10	7
Business graduate students	2	0	0	1	1
Other graduate students	4	2	2	0	0
Other or mixed subjects[b]	21	7	7	5	2
Laboratory studies					
College undergraduates	21	6	10	2	3
Other or mixed subjects[c]	4	1	1	0	2

[a] Includes military, religious, hospital, and other settings.   [b] Includes candidates for managerial positions, participants in management training programs, and nonmanagerial employees of business firms.   [c] Includes graduate students and mixed samples of undergraduate and graduate students.

our effect sizes. However, sex differences became less stereotypic over time in our two smaller samples of effect sizes, namely interpersonal versus task style and democratic versus autocratic style. This lack of consistency over the four types of style and the confounding of publication date with various study attributes clouds interpretation of these secular trends.[17]

Among the characteristics of the research reports that did not relate to the magnitude of the sex differences is whether the report was published (i.e., journal article or other published document) or unpublished (i.e., dissertation or other unpublished document). Although it is common in meta-analyses that effects are larger in published than unpublished studies (see Glass, McGaw, & Smith, 1981), this relation is often absent in meta-analyses of sex differences in social behavior, presumably because these reports are often incidental to studies' main hypotheses and therefore have little impact on publishability (see Eagly, 1987).

Models involving characteristics of studies' methods. Most aspects of the studies' methods that we coded either did not relate to the effect sizes or related relatively weakly. Furthermore, interpretation of those few relations that did prove significant was often hampered by skewed distributions of many of these features (see Table 1) as well as by (a) confounding between these features and (b) relatively small numbers of effect sizes for two of the styles (i.e., interpersonal vs. task and democratic vs. autocratic). Nonetheless, we note some of the many analyses we performed.

We were particularly interested, for example, in whether studies in which sex was known to be confounded with personal attributes such as age and job seniority (or was likely to have

been so confounded) would produce more stereotypic sex comparisons. We did not obtain such tendencies. Nor did sex comparisons appear to be more stereotypic in self-selected samples or in samples for which random selection was seriously compromised. Furthermore, sex comparisons did not become less stereotypic when the rating underlying the style measure was more directly linked to behavior and therefore presumably less vulnerable to biases based on gender stereotypes. The impact of the specific measuring instrument used to assess style (see Table 2) was difficult to evaluate because of small sample sizes for most measures and the confounding of measures with characteristics of the instruments such as the identity of the raters.

The identity of the raters who provided the data for the style measure did have some impact on sex differences in both interpersonal and task orientation. Most of the measures of these two styles were based on self ratings or subordinate ratings (see Table 1), and self ratings were significantly more stereotypic than subordinate ratings for interpersonal style ($p < .01$) and task style ($p < .001$). For the two other types of style, skewed

---

[17] Neither on an overall basis nor for interpersonal and task styles do these findings support the idea that social change or similar factors have caused leaders to become less stereotypic in their styles. Yet a variant of the social change interpretation suggests that in earlier years when women typically faced more formidable barriers to attaining leadership roles, the women in these roles may have been even more highly selected for similarity to their male counterparts. This interpretation is consistent with an increase in the tendency for leaders to use stereotypic styles.

Table 4
Summary of Sex Differences in Leadership Style

Criterion	All comparisons	Interpersonal style comparisons	Task style comparisons	Interpersonal vs. task style comparisons	Democratic vs. autocratic style comparisons
			Known effect sizes		
Sample size (n)	329	136	139	31	23
Mean weighted d (d_+)[a]	0.03	0.04	0.00	−0.03	0.22
95% CI for d_+	0.01/0.05	0.01/0.07	−0.03/0.03	−0.10/0.03	0.15/0.29
Homogeneity (Q) of ds comprising d_+[b]	1234.44*	373.87*	501.46*	70.40*	252.63*
Mean unweighted d	0.02	0.08	−0.10	−0.03	0.42
95% CI for mean unweighted d	−0.03/0.07	0.01/0.14	−0.17/−0.02	−0.17/0.10	0.17/0.66
Median d	0.02	0.07	−0.07	0.00	0.25
		Known effect sizes excluding outliers			
Sample size (n)	275	118	125	27	18
n removed outliers	54 (16%)	18 (13%)	14 (10%)	4 (13%)	5 (22%)
Mean weighted d (d_+)	0.02	0.13	−0.06	0.02	0.27
95% CI for d_+	−0.00/0.05	0.10/0.17	−0.10/−0.03	−0.06/0.09	0.19/0.35
Homogeneity (Q) of ds comprising d_+	311.19	140.12	142.76	32.97	27.40
			All reports		
Sample size (n)	370	153	154	35	28
Mean unweighted d	0.02	0.07	−0.09	−0.03	0.34
95% CI for mean unweighted d	−0.03/0.06	0.01/0.13	−0.16/−0.02	−0.15/0.09	0.13/0.55
Stereotypic differences[c]	175/341 (.51)	87/141 (.62)	52/144 (.36)	14/32 (.44)	22/24 (.92)

Note. When all reports were included, a value of 0.00 (exactly no difference) was assigned to sex differences that could not be calculated and were reported as nonsignificant. Effect sizes were calculated for all significant differences. Effect sizes are positive for differences that are stereotypic and negative for differences that are counterstereotypic. CI = confidence interval; d = effect size; d_+ = mean weighted effect size; Q = homogeneity of effect sizes.
[a] Effect sizes were weighted by the reciprocal of the variance. [b] Significance indicates rejection of the hypothesis of homogeneity. [c] Frequencies are number of differences in the stereotypic direction divided by the number of differences of known direction. The proportion appears in parentheses.
* $p < .001$.

distributions of the raters' identity precluded meaningful analyses. In addition, sex of the raters showed no relation to the effect sizes.

As shown in one of the models given in Table 6, the level of aggregation of the style measure related significantly to the total set of effect sizes as well as to the effect sizes for the task, interpersonal versus task, and autocratic versus democratic styles. Specifically, as the number of judgments underlying each data point increased, women became relatively more task oriented than men and relatively more democratic. Thus, in the case of the task and the democratic versus autocratic styles, the overall tendencies for women to be more task oriented and more democratic than men (see Table 4) were more pronounced in studies using measures that can be presumed to be more reliable by virtue of their higher level of aggregation.

Models involving characteristics of social settings and leadership roles. Organizational size had little effect on the sex differences, but information necessary to code this variable was often missing from the reports. The organizational level of leaders had little impact on the effect sizes except for task style: A tendency for men to be more task oriented than women

obtained for first-level (i.e., line) managers reversed slightly for the midlevel managers ($p < .001$ for contrast). The basis by which leaders were selected in laboratory studies also related to the effect sizes: Leaders who were appointed on a random basis or on the basis of their own qualifications behaved more stereotypically than leaders who emerged on their own ($p < .025$ for categorical model).

The percentage of men among the people whose style was assessed related significantly to sex differences in both the interpersonal and the democratic versus autocratic styles (see Table 6). To the extent that men predominated, the tendencies weakened for women (vs. men) to show more concern about interpersonal relations and to be more democratic.

Two additional variables—the percentage of men among leaders' subordinates and the age of the people whose style was assessed—related significantly to the effect sizes for some of the styles within the organizational sample, which maintained moderate numbers of effect sizes for these analyses. Specifically, larger proportions of male subordinates were associated with male leaders being more task-oriented than female leaders ($p < .001$), but more interpersonally oriented on interpersonal ver-

Table 5
Categorical Models for Predicting Sex Differences in Leadership Style From Type of Study and Type of Style

Type of study	All effect sizes			Interpersonal style effect sizes			Task style effect sizes			Interpersonal vs. task style effect sizes			Democratic vs. autocratic style effect sizes			Between types of style effect
	n	d_{i+}	Q_{wi}^a	n	d_{i+}	Q_{wi}	n	d_{i+}	Q_{wi}	n	d_{i+}	Q_{wi}	n	d_{i+}	Q_{wi}	Q_B
Organizational	269	−0.00	1009.37***	120	−0.01	284.54***	120	−0.02	439.90***	16	−0.03	38.73***	13	0.21†	224.58***	21.62***
Assessment	43	0.12†	138.77***	12	0.25†	28.64**	12	0.08	31.48***	13	−0.04	28.08**	6	0.29†	18.51**	32.06***
Laboratory	17	0.22†	50.43***	4	0.37†	16.34***	7	0.19	20.96**	2	0.12	3.27	4	0.20†	8.52*	1.34
Q_B (Between types of study effect)		35.87***			44.35***			9.12**			0.32			1.03		

Note. Effect sizes are positive for differences that are stereotypic and negative for differences that are counterstereotypic. d_{i+} = weighted mean of effect sizes for the ith class; Q_{wi} = homogeneity of effect sizes within the ith class; Q_B = between-classes goodness-of-fit statistic.
^{a} Significance indicates rejection of the hypothesis of homogeneity.
* $p < .05$. ** $p < .01$. *** $p < .001$.
† Differs significantly ($p < .05$ or smaller) from 0.00 (exactly no difference).

sus task measures ($p < .05$) and less democratic ($p < .01$).[18] Also within the organizational studies, age was a significant predictor of sex differences in task and interpersonal styles: Older leaders were more stereotypic in their interpersonal style but less stereotypic in their task style ($ps < .001$). However, interpretation of these relations involving age and the sex distribution of subordinates was limited by relatively large amounts of missing data as well as by confounding of these variables with types of studies (i.e., organizational, assessment, laboratory).

Models involving gender congeniality of leadership roles. As shown by the analyses using our gender congeniality measures as predictors (see Table 6), questionnaire respondents' judgments of the leadership roles related significantly to sex differences in task style. In general, leaders of each sex were especially task oriented when their role was viewed as congenial to their gender. Specifically, these effect sizes were larger (i.e., positive, indicating men were more task oriented than women) to the extent that (a) male (compared with female) respondents rated themselves as more competent in the role, (b) male respondents rated themselves as more interested in occupying the role, (c) respondents of both sexes judged the average man more interested in occupying the role than the average woman, and (d) respondents of both sexes judged the role required relatively little interpersonal ability. Similarly, these effect sizes were smaller (i.e., negative, indicating women were more task oriented than men) to the extent that the roles were more congenial to women on these indexes. Because respondents' judgments of the leadership roles were significantly related only to sex differences in task style, the significant relations obtained when all the effect sizes were analyzed reflected primarily the task style findings.[19]

Discussion

Interpersonal and Task Styles

Our major hypothesis was that stereotypic sex differences would be less pronounced in organizational studies than in assessment or laboratory studies. Indeed, this hypothesis was confirmed for both interpersonal and task styles. These findings support our arguments that the criteria organizations use for selecting managers and the forces they maintain for socializing managers into their roles minimize tendencies for the sexes to lead or manage in a stereotypic manner. Yet these data also suggest that people not selected or trained for leadership roles do manifest stereotypic leadership behavior when placed in these roles, as shown by the data from the assessment and the

---

[18] The sex of subordinates may affect the behavior of leaders of both sexes more than it affects sex differences in leaders' styles. Consistent with this suggestion, Carli (1989) found in a laboratory experiment that subjects used more aggressive and direct styles of influence when dealing with men than with women.

[19] Numerous categorical and continuous models thus yielded significant prediction of the effect sizes. However, homogeneity was rarely attained within the classes of the categorical models nor were correctly specified models achieved for the continuous models.

Table 6
Continuous Models for Sex Differences in Leadership Style

Predictor	All effect sizes		Interpersonal style effect sizes		Task style effect sizes		Interpersonal vs. task style effect sizes		Democratic vs. autocratic style effect sizes	
	b	b^*	b	b^*	b	b^*	b	b^*	b	b^*
Date of publication	0.01***	.14	0.01***	.19	0.03***	.37	−0.02*	−.25	−0.02**	−.20
n of observations aggregated into each data point	−0.00****ᵃ	−.13	−0.00	−.06	−0.00***ᵇ	−.26	−0.03***	−.53	0.02***	.42
Percentage of men among people whose style was assessed	−0.00***ᶜ	−.13	−0.00***ᵈ	−.21	−0.00	−.03	−0.00	−.12	−0.01***	−.32
Respondent judgments of roles										
Competence sex differenceᵉ	0.18***	.16	−0.01	−.01	0.46***	.40	−0.04	−.06	−0.02	−.01
Interest sex difference	0.22***	.15	0.09	.07	0.48***	.32	−0.13	−.11	−0.14	−.05
Stereotypic interest difference	0.11***	.16	0.01	.01	0.28***	.40	−0.09	−.17	0.01	.01
Interpersonal ability ratingᶠ	−0.05***	−.12	−0.01	−.02	−0.10***	−.20	−0.07	−.26	−0.04	−.07
Task ability rating	−0.01	−.02	0.01	.02	0.04	.08	−0.05	−.26	−0.05	−.08
Minimum n^g	288		124		127		20		17	

Note. Models are weighted least squares simple linear regressions calculated with weights equal to the reciprocal of the variance for each effect size. Effect sizes are positive for differences that are stereotypic and negative for differences that are counterstereotypic. b = unstandardized regression coefficient. b^* = standardized regression coefficient.
ᵃ $b = -0.0092$, $SE(b) = .000016$. ᵇ $b = -0.0017$, $SE(b) = .000029$. ᶜ $b = -0.0028$, $SE(b) = .000052$. ᵈ $b = -0.0040$, $SE(b) = .000099$. ᵉ For the first three variables constructed from judgments of the leadership roles, values are positive for differences in the masculine direction (greater male estimates of competence and of interest; ascription of greater interest to average men). ᶠ For the last two variables constructed from judgments of the leadership roles, values are larger to the extent that a role was judged to require more interpersonal or task ability. ᵍ n varied across the analyses because of missing data (e.g., the absence of judgments of the leadership roles for the assessment studies).
* $p < .05$. ** $p < .01$. *** $p < .001$.

laboratory studies. Moreover, our claim that selection criteria lessen sex differences is strengthened by the finding that those few laboratory leaders who gained their positions through emergence did not manifest the stereotypic styles of laboratory leaders who were appointed. Evidently sex differences were leveled even by the implicit leader selection criteria of initially leaderless groups.

When we ignored whether the sex comparisons were from organizational, assessment, or laboratory studies (see Table 4), sex differences in interpersonal and task styles were quite small, with overall trends toward women being more concerned about both maintenance of interpersonal relationships and task accomplishment. In view of these trends, it is not surprising that measures placing interpersonal and task orientation on the ends of a single dimension produced no sex difference in any of the overall summaries. On such bipolar measures, the stereotypic interpersonal sex difference and the counterstereotypic task difference would cancel one another, resulting in no difference.

Given the variety of settings, roles, and measures encountered in this research, the sex comparisons for the task and interpersonal styles were expected to be inconsistent across the studies. Yet the removal of relatively small numbers of the effect sizes (10% to 13%) produced homogeneous sets of effect sizes consistent with description in terms of single means. This aspect of the findings lends some confidence to our statements that if we take the entire research literature into account, women's leadership styles emphasize both interpersonal relations and task accomplishment to a slightly greater extent than men's styles.

Democratic Versus Autocratic Style

The strongest evidence we obtained for a sex difference in leadership style occurred on the tendency for women to adopt a more democratic or participative style and for men to adopt a more autocratic or directive style. Moreover, this sex difference did *not* become smaller in the organizational studies, as did the differences in the interpersonal and task styles. Although the overall mean weighted effect size ($d_+ = 0.22$) was not large, the mean became larger once outliers were removed ($d_+ = 0.27$), and 92% of the available comparisons went in the direction of more democratic behavior from women than men. Despite this impressive consistency in the direction of the sex difference, the effect sizes themselves were quite heterogeneous, requiring the removal of 22% to obtain a set that did not reject the hypothesis of homogeneity. Yet substantial inconsistency across the studies is not unexpected for this type of style in view of the tendency for investigators to construct unique measures and not to rely on standard instruments, as did most investigators of the other types of leadership style that we reviewed (see Table 2).

Our interpretation of the sex difference in the extent to which leaders behave democratically versus autocratically is necessarily speculative, but follows from some of the considerations that we presented early in this article (see *Reasons to Expect the Presence of Sex Differences in Leadership Style*). We thus argued that women and men recruited into leadership roles in organizations may not be equivalent in personality and behavioral tendencies, even though they satisfy the same selection criteria. In particular, we noted that women's social skills might enable them to perform managerial roles differently than men. Interpersonal behavior that is skillful (e.g., in terms of understanding others' feelings and intentions) should facilitate a managerial style that is democratic and participative. Making decisions in a collaborative style requires not only the soliciting of suggestions from one's peers and subordinates, but also the preservation of good relationships with them when evaluating and perhaps rejecting their ideas. The give-and-take of collaborative decision making introduces interpersonal complexity not encountered by leaders who behave in an autocratic or directive manner. This interpretation is supported by research showing that teachers who lacked social skills, as indexed by their relative inability to decode nonverbal cues, had more autocratic attitudes and were generally more dogmatic (Rosenthal, Hall, DiMatteo, Rogers, & Archer, 1979).

Another perspective on the democratic–autocratic sex difference acknowledges the attitudinal bias against female leaders that we considered in the beginning of the article. The skepticism that many people have expressed concerning women's capabilities in managerial and leadership roles may be exacerbated by any tendency for women in these roles to take charge in an especially authoritative manner. Placating subordinates and peers so that they accept a woman's leadership may to some extent require that she give them input into her decisions and allow some degree of control over these decisions. Moreover, to the extent that women leaders have internalized to some degree the culture's reservations about their capability for leadership, they may gain confidence as leaders by making collaborative decisions that they can determine are in line with their associates' expectations. Thus, proceeding in a participative and collaborative mode may enable many female leaders to win acceptance from others, gain self-confidence, and thereby be effective. Because men are not so constrained by attitudinal bias, they are freer to lead in an autocratic and nonparticipative manner should they so desire.[20]

The Impact of Gender Congeniality of Leadership Roles and Sex Distribution of Role Occupants

Our findings suggested that leaders of each sex emphasized task accomplishment when they were in a leadership role regarded as congruent with their gender. Thus, only the sex differences in task style were significantly correlated with the tendency for the leadership roles to be regarded as more congenial for men or women, as indexed by our questionnaire respondents' judgments (see Table 6). Male leaders tended to be more task oriented than female leaders to the extent that a leadership role was more congenial to men; female leaders tended to be more task oriented than male leaders to the extent that a leadership role was more congenial to women. Furthermore, women tended to be more task oriented than men in leadership roles that are feminine in the sense that our respondents judged they require considerable interpersonal ability.[21]

These findings suggest that being out of role in gender-relevant terms has its costs for leaders in terms of some decline in their tendency to organize activities to accomplish relevant tasks. Because our meta-analytic data are not informative concerning the mediation of these effects, these provocative findings should be explored in primary research. Perhaps people

who are out of role lack (or are perceived to lack) the skills necessary to organize the task-relevant aspects of their environment. Out-of-role leaders may be somewhat deficient in the knowledge and authority required to organize people and resources to accomplish task-relevant goals.

The extent to which leadership roles were male dominated numerically also related to sex differences in leadership style. Specifically, the tendencies for female leaders to be more interpersonally oriented and more democratic than male leaders weakened to the extent that a role was male dominated. Thus, when women were quite rare in leadership roles and therefore tended to have the status of token in organizations or groups, they abandoned stereotypically feminine styles characterized by concern for the morale and welfare of people in the work setting and consideration of these people's views when making decisions. These findings suggest that women may tend to lose authority if they adopt distinctively feminine styles of leadership in extremely male-dominated roles. Women who survive in such roles probably have to adopt the styles typical of male role occupants.

Conclusion

The view, widely accepted by social scientists expert on leadership, that women and men lead in the same way should be very substantially revised. Similarly, the view, proclaimed in some popular books on management, that female and male leaders have distinctive, gender-stereotypic styles also requires

---

[20] A subsequent meta-analysis by Eagly, Makhijani, and Klonsky (1990) showed that subjects evaluate autocratic behavior by female leaders more negatively than they evaluate the equivalent behavior by male leaders. An additional consideration in interpreting the democratic–autocratic sex difference is that measures of this type were based primarily on leaders' self-reports (see Table 1), and, at least for task and interpersonal styles, leaders' self-reports were more stereotypic than subordinates' reports on leaders (see *Results*). Thus, it is possible that the tendency for women to be more democratic than men was exaggerated somewhat by the reliance on leaders' self-reports in these studies. Yet, because the sex comparisons for the democratic versus autocratic style were more stereotypic than the subset of sex comparisons for the interpersonal and task styles that were based on self-reports, it is very unlikely that this methodological feature of the democratic–autocratic studies fully accounts for the sex difference in this type of style.

[21] We explored whether a tendency for laboratory leadership roles to be more congenial for men might have contributed to the more stereotypic task styles found in laboratory (vs. organizational) studies (see Table 4). Indeed, our questionnaire respondents judged the laboratory (vs. organizational) roles as somewhat more congenial to men on the measures of sex differences in competence and interest and on the measure of stereotypic sex differences in interest (ps < .05 or smaller). In addition, the laboratory roles were judged to require less interpersonal ability than organizational roles but, contrary to the idea that the laboratory roles were relatively masculine, they were also judged to require less task ability (ps < .001). Thus, there was some degree of confounding between the type of study and the gender congeniality of the roles. Nonetheless, the significant relations between the congeniality measures and sex differences in task style reported in Table 6 remained significant when examined within the set of organizational studies.

revision. Our quantitative review has established a more complex set of findings. Although these findings require further scrutiny before they should be taken as definitive, the agreement of these findings with our role theory framework substantiates our interpretation of them. Thus, consistent with research on sex differences in numerous social behaviors (Eagly, 1987; Hall, 1984), we have established that leadership style findings generated in experimental settings tend to be gender stereotypic. Indeed, these findings concur with the generalizations of those narrative reviewers who noted that male and female leaders often differ in laboratory experiments (Brown, 1979; Hollander, 1985). In such settings, people interact as strangers without the constraints of long-term role relationships. Gender roles are moderately important influences on behavior in such contexts and tend to produce gender-stereotypic behavior (see Eagly, 1987). In addition, somewhat smaller stereotypic sex differences were obtained in assessment studies, in which people not selected for leadership responded to instruments assessing their leadership styles. Because respondents not under the constraints of managerial roles completed questionnaires in these studies, some tendency for leadership styles to appear stereotypic was expected from the perspective of our social role framework.

When social behavior is regulated by other, less diffuse social roles, as it is in organizational settings, behavior should primarily reflect the influence of these other roles and therefore lose much of its gender-stereotypic character. Indeed, the findings of this meta-analysis for interpersonal and task styles support this logic. Nonetheless, women's leadership styles were more democratic than men's even in organizational settings. This sex difference may reflect underlying differences in female and male personality or skills (e.g., women's superior social skills) or subtle differences in the status of women and men who occupy the same organizational role. Deciding among the various causes that we have discussed would require primary research targeted to this issue.

The magnitude of the aggregate effect sizes we obtained in this meta-analysis deserves comment. When interpreting effect sizes, reviewers should take the methods of the studies into account, and, as Glass, McGaw, and Smith (1981) argued, they should avoid applying numerical guidelines to identify effect sizes as small or large. One feature of research on leadership style that is especially relevant to interpreting the magnitude of our aggregate effect sizes is that investigators face many barriers to achieving well-controlled studies. In organizational studies, the environments in which managers carry out their roles are quite diverse, even within a single organization. Because managers' leadership styles are evaluated either by themselves or by their associates, the various managers in a study are not necessarily evaluated by the same standard. Although more control of environmental influences can be achieved in laboratory studies of leadership (e.g., all leaders can be observed in a similar social setting), even these studies are relatively uncontrolled because each leader interacts with a unique group of followers. Counterbalancing the greater control of environmental factors in laboratory than organizational studies is the less rigorous selection of research participants for laboratory research and the resulting greater variability of leadership style within each sex. In general, uncontrolled variability in both organizational and laboratory studies of leadership would inflate the standard deviations that are the denominators of the effect sizes and thereby decrease the magnitude of these effect sizes. As a consequence, neither sex nor other variables would ordinarily produce large effect sizes in studies of leadership style. Therefore, we believe that effect sizes we obtained are considerably more consequential than effect sizes of the same magnitude obtained in more controlled forms of research.

Our review has not considered the extent to which the sex differences in leadership style that we have documented might produce differences in the effectiveness of leaders. Whether men or women are more effective leaders as a consequence of their differing styles is a complex question that could be addressed meta-analytically only by taking measures of group and organizational outcomes into account along with measures of leadership style. Because experts on leader effectiveness ordinarily maintain that the effectiveness of leadership styles is contingent on features of the group or organizational environment (e.g., Fiedler, 1967; Vroom & Yetton, 1973), we are unwilling to argue that women's relatively democratic and participative style is either an advantage or disadvantage. No doubt a relatively democratic style enhances a leader's effectiveness under some circumstances, and a relatively autocratic style enhances it under other circumstances.[22] Nonetheless, we note that in recent years many management and organizational consultants have criticized traditional management practices for what they believe are overly hierarchical and rigidly bureaucratic forms (Foy, 1980; Heller & Van Til, 1986; Kanter, 1983; Naisbett, 1982; Ouchi, 1981; Peters & Waterman, 1982). Moreover, it is consistent with many feminist theorists' descriptions of hierarchy and domination (e.g., Elshtain, 1981; Miller, 1976) to argue that employment would be less alienating if forms of interaction in the workplace were less hierarchical and instead characterized by cooperation and collaboration between collegial groups of co-workers. Indeed, both consultants and feminists have advocated organizational change toward the more democratic and participative leadership styles that our meta-analysis suggests are more prevalent among women than men.

---

[22] Consistent with the position that effectiveness of leadership styles depends on a group's task and other considerations, Wood (1987) argued, based on her meta-analysis of sex differences in group performance, that women's distinctive style of social interaction facilitated group performance at tasks requiring positive social activities such as cooperation but lacked this facilitative effect for other types of tasks.

References

Alpren, M. (1954). The development and validation of an instrument used to ascertain a school principal's pattern of behavior (Doctoral dissertation, University of Florida). *Dissertation Abstracts International, 33,* 1579A.

Arcy, J. A. B. (1980). Self-perceptions of leader behavior of male and female elementary school principals in selected school districts in the midwest United States (Doctoral dissertation, Iowa State University, 1979). *Dissertation Abstracts International, 40,* 3638A.

Ashmore, R. D., Del Boca, F. K., & Wohlers, A. J. (1986). Gender stereotypes. In R. D. Ashmore & F. K. Del Boca (Eds.), *The social psychology of female-male relations: A critical analysis of central concepts* (pp. 69–119). Orlando, FL: Academic Press.

Bales. R. F. (1950). *Interaction process analysis: A method for the study of small groups.* Reading, MA: Addison-Wesley.

Barone. F. J. (1982). A comparative study of Theory X–Theory Y attitudes among managers and OD agents. *Dissertation Abstracts International, 42,* 4260A. (University Microfilms No. 82-07,156)

Bartol, K. M., & Martin, D. C. (1986). Women and men in task groups. In R. D. Ashmore & F. K. Del Boca (Eds), *The social psychology of female-male relations: A critical analyses of central concepts* (pp. 259–310). Orlando. FL: Academic Press.

Bass. B. M. (1981). *Stogdill's handbook of leadership: A survey of theory and research* (rev. ed.). New York: Free Press.

Baugher. S. L. (1983). Sex-typed characteristics and leadership dimensions of vocational education administrators in a midwest region of the United States (Doctoral dissertation. University of Missouri–Columbia, 1982). *Dissertation Abstracts International, 44,* 22A.

Bayes. M., & Newton, P. M. (1978). Women in authority: A sociopsychological analysis. *Journal of Applied Behavioral Science, 14,* 7–20.

Birdsall. P. (1980). A comparative analysis of male and female managerial communication style in two organizations. *Journal of Vocational Behavior, 16,* 183–196.

Blake, R. R., & Mouton, J. S. (1964). *The managerial grid.* Houston, TX: Gulf.

Blake. R. R., & Mouton, J. S. (1978). *The new managerial grid.* Houston, TX: Gulf.

Brown. S. M. (1979). Male versus female leaders: A comparison of empirical studies. *Sex Roles, 5,* 595–611.

Butterfield, D. A., & Powell, G. N. (1981). Effect of group performance, leader sex, and rater sex on ratings of leader behavior. *Organizational Behavior and Human Performance, 28,* 129–141.

Carli. L. L. (1989). Gender differences in interaction style and influence. *Journal of Personality and Social Psychology, 56,* 565–576.

Coleman. D. G. (1979). *Barnard's effectiveness and efficiency applied to a leader style model.* Unpublished manuscript, Northeast Missouri State University, Kirksville, MO.

Crocker. J., & McGraw, K. M. (1984). What's good for the goose is not good for the gander: Solo status as an obstacle to occupational achievement for males and females. *American Behavioral Scientist, 27,* 357–369.

Crudge. J. (1983). The effect of leadership styles on the rehabilitation training of student-workers (Doctoral dissertation, United States International University, 1982). *Dissertation Abstracts International, 43,* 3300A.

Dobbins. G. H. (1986). Equity vs equality: Sex differences in leadership. *Sex Roles, 15,* 513–525.

Dobbins. G. H., Pence, E. C., Orban, J. A., & Sgro, J. A. (1983). The effects of sex of the leader and sex of the subordinate on the use of organizational control policy. *Organizational Behavior and Human Performance, 32,* 325–343.

Dobbins. G. H., & Platz, S. J. (1986). Sex differences in leadership: How real are they? *Academy of Management Review, 11,* 118–127.

Eagly, A. H. (1987). *Sex differences in social behavior: A social-role interpretation.* Hillsdale, NJ: Erlbaum.

Eagly, A. H., & Carli, L. L. (1981). Sex of researchers and sex-typed communications as determinants of sex differences in influenceability: A meta-analysis of social influence studies. *Psychological Bulletin, 90,* 1–20.

Eagly, A. H., Makhijani, M. G., & Klonsky, B. G. (1990). *Gender and the evaluation of leaders: A meta-analysis.* Manuscript submitted for publication.

Eagly, A. H., & Steffen, V. J. (1984). Gender stereotypes stem from the distribution of women and men into social roles. *Journal of Personality and Social Psychology, 46,* 735–754.

Eagly, A. H., & Wood, W. (in press). Explaining sex differences in social behavior: A meta-analytic perspective. *Personality and Social Psychology Bulletin.*

Elshtain, J. (1981). *Public man, private woman: Women in social and political thought.* Princeton, NJ: Princeton University Press.

Feldman, D. C. (1976). A contingency theory of socialization. *Administrative Science Quarterly, 21,* 433–452.

Fiedler, F. E. (1967). *A theory of leadership effectiveness.* New York: McGraw-Hill.

Fleishman, E. A. (1953). The management of leadership attitudes in industry. *Journal of Applied Psychology, 36,* 153–158.

Fleishman, E. A. (1957). The Leadership Opinion Questionnaire. In R. M. Stogdill & A. E. Coons (Eds), *Leader behavior: Its description and measurement* (pp. 120–133). Columbus, OH: Bureau of Business Research, Ohio State University.

Fleishman, E. A. (1960). *Manual for the Leadership Opinion Questionnaire.* Chicago: Science Research Associates.

Fleishman, E. A. (1970). *Manual for the Supervisory Behavior Description Questionnaire.* Washington, DC: American Institutes for Research.

Foy, N. (1980). *The yin and yang of organizations.* New York: Morrow.

Ghiselli, E. E. (1964). *Theory of psychological measurement.* New York: McGraw-Hill.

Glass, G. V., McGaw, B., & Smith, M. L. (1981). *Meta-analysis in social research.* Beverly Hills, CA: Sage.

Graen. G. (1976). Role-making processes within complex organizations. In M. D. Dunnette (Ed.), *Handbook of industrial and organizational psychology* (pp. 1201–1245). Chicago: Rand McNally.

Grobman, H., & Hines, V. A. (1956). What makes a good principal? *National Association of Secondary School Principals Bulletin, 40,* 5–16.

Gupta, N., Jenkins, G. D., Jr., & Beehr, T. A. (1983). Employee gender, gender similarity, and supervisor-subordinate cross-evaluations. *Psychology of Women Quarterly, 8,* 174–184.

Gustafson, L. C. (1982). The leadership role of the public elementary school media librarian as perceived by the principal and its relationship to the factors of the sex, educational background, and the work experience of the media librarian (Doctoral dissertation, University of Maryland). *Dissertation Abstracts International, 43,* 2206A.

Gutek, B. A., & Morasch, B. (1982). Sex-ratios, sex-role spillover, and sexual harassment of women at work. *Journal of Social Issues, 38,* 55–74.

Hall, A. H. (1983). The influence of a personal planning workshop on attitudes toward managerial style (Doctoral dissertation, University of Maryland, 1983). *Dissertation Abstracts International, 44,* 2953A.

Hall, J. A. (1984). *Nonverbal sex differences: Communication accuracy and expressive style.* Baltimore, MD: Johns Hopkins University Press.

Halpin, A. W. (1957). *Manual for the Leader Behavior Description Questionnaire.* Columbus, OH: Bureau of Business Research, Ohio State University.

Halpin, A. W. (1966). *Theory and research in administration.* New York: Macmillan.

Halpin, A. W., & Winer, B. J. (1957). A factorial study of the leader behavior descriptions. In R. M. Stogdill & A. E. Coons (Eds.), *Leader behavior: Its description and measurement* (pp. 39–51). Columbus, OH: Bureau of Business Research, Ohio State University.

Hedges, L. V. (1981). Distribution theory for Glass's estimator of effect size and related estimators. *Journal of Educational Statistics, 6,* 107–128.

Hedges, L. V. (1982a). Fitting categorical models to effect sizes from a series of experiments. *Journal of Educational Statistics, 7,* 119–137.

Hedges, L. V. (1982b). Fitting continuous models to effect size data. *Journal of Educational Statistics, 7,* 245–270.

Hedges, L. V. (1987). How hard is hard science, how soft is soft science? The empirical cumulativeness of research. *American Psychologist, 42,* 443–455.

Hedges, L. V., & Becker, B. J. (1986). Statistical methods in the meta-analysis of research on gender differences. In J. S. Hyde & M. C. Linn (Eds.), *The psychology of gender: Advances through meta-analysis* (pp. 14–50). Baltimore, MD: Johns Hopkins University Press.

Hedges, L. V., & Olkin, I. (1985). *Statistical methods for meta-analysis.* Orlando, FL: Academic Press.

Heft, M., & Deni, R. (1984). Altering preferences for leadership style of men and women undergraduate residence advisors through leadership training. *Psychological Reports, 54,* 463–466.

Heller, T., & Van Til, J. (1986). Leadership and followership: Some summary propositions. In T. Heller, J. Van Til, & L. A. Zurcher (Eds.), *Contemporary studies in applied behavioral science: Vol. 4. Leaders and followers: Challenges for the future* (pp. 251–263). Greenwich, CT: JAI Press.

Hemphill, J. K., & Coons, A. E. (1957). Development of the Leader Behavior Description Questionnaire. In R. M. Stogdill & A. E. Coons (Eds.), *Leader behavior: Its description and measurement* (pp. 6–38). Columbus, OH: Bureau of Business Research, Ohio State University.

Hennig, M., & Jardin, A. (1977). *The managerial woman.* New York: Anchor Press.

Hersey, P., & Blanchard, K. H. (1977). *Management of organizational behavior: Utilizing human resources* (3rd ed.). Englewood Cliffs, NJ: Prentice-Hall.

Hersey, P., & Blanchard, K. H. (1982). *Management of organizational behavior: Utilizing human resources* (4th ed.). Englewood Cliffs, NJ: Prentice-Hall.

Hollander, E. P. (1985). Leadership and power. In G. Lindzey & E. Aronson (Eds.), *Handbook of social psychology* (3rd ed., Vol. 2, pp. 485–537). New York: Random House.

Hughes, H., Jr., Copeland, D. R., Ford, L. H., & Heidt, E. A. (1983). *Leadership and management education and training (LMET) course requirements for recruit company and "A" school instructors* (Tech. Rep. No. 154, Report No. AD-A137306). Orlando, FL: Department of the Navy.

Hurst, A. G., Stein, K. B., Korchin, S. J., & Soskin, W. F. (1978). Leadership style determinants of cohesiveness in adolescent groups. *International Journal of Group Psychotherapy, 28,* 263–277.

Jacoby, J., & Terborg, J. R. (1975). *Managerial Philosophies Scale.* Conroe, TX: Teleometrics International.

Kanter, R. M. (1977a). *Men and women of the corporation.* New York: Basic Books.

Kanter, R. M. (1977b). Some effects of proportions on group life: Skewed sex ratios and responses to token women. *American Journal of Sociology, 82,* 965–990.

Kanter, R. M. (1983). *The change masters: Innovations for productivity in the American corporation.* New York: Simon and Schuster.

Koberg, C. S. (1985). Sex and situational influences on the use of power: A follow-up study. *Sex Roles, 13,* 625–639.

Kruse, L., & Wintermantel, M. (1986). Leadership Ms.-qualified: I. The gender bias in everyday and scientific thinking. In C. F. Graumann & S. Moscovici (Eds.), *Changing conceptions of leadership* (pp. 171–197). New York: Springer-Verlag.

Lanning, G. E., Jr. (1982). A study of relationships and differences between management styles and staff morale as perceived by personnel in the colleges of the Ventura County community district. *Dissertation Abstracts International, 43,* 996A. (University Microfilms No. 82-20, 739)

Lee, D. M., & Alvares, K. M. (1977). Effects of sex on descriptions and evaluations of supervisory behavior in a simulated industrial setting. *Journal of Applied Psychology, 62,* 405–410.

Lewin, K., & Lippitt, R. (1938). An experimental approach to the study of autocracy and democracy: A preliminary note. *Sociometry, 1,* 292–300.

Likert, R. (1961). *New patterns of management.* New York: McGraw-Hill.

Loden, M. (1985). *Feminine leadership or how to succeed in business without being one of the boys.* New York: Times Books.

Maccoby, E. E. (1988). Gender as a social category. *Developmental Psychology, 24,* 755–765.

Marnani, E. B. (1982). Comparison of preferred leadership styles, potential leadership effectiveness, and managerial attitudes among black and white, female and male management students (Doctoral dissertation, United States International University, 1981). *Dissertation Abstracts International, 43,* 1271A.

Martinez, M. R. (1982). A comparative study on the relationship of self-perceptions of leadership styles between Chicano and Anglo teachers (Doctoral dissertation, Bowling Green State University). *Dissertation Abstracts International, 43,* 766A.

McGregor, D. (1960). *The human side of enterprise.* New York: McGraw-Hill.

McNemar, Q. (1962). *Psychological statistics* (3rd ed.). New York: Wiley.

Miller, J. B. (1976). *Toward a new psychology of women.* Boston: Beacon Press.

Money, J., & Ehrhardt, A. A. (1972). *Man & woman, boy & girl.* Baltimore, MD: Johns Hopkins University Press.

Moore, S. F., Shaffer, L., Goodsell, D. A., & Baringoldz, G. (1983). Gender or situationally determined spoken language differences? The case of the leadership situation. *International Journal of Women's Studies, 6,* 44–53.

Myers, M. S. (1970). *Every employee a manager.* New York: McGraw-Hill.

Naisbitt, J. (1982). *Megatrends: Ten new directions transforming our lives.* New York: Warner Books.

Nieva, V. F., & Gutek, B. A. (1981). *Women and work: A psychological perspective.* New York: Praeger.

O'Leary, V. E. (1974). Some attitudinal barriers to occupational aspirations in women. *Psychological Bulletin, 81,* 809–826.

Ott, E. M. (1989). Effects of the male-female ratio at work: Policewomen and male nurses. *Psychology of Women Quarterly, 13,* 41–57.

Ouchi, W. G. (1981). *Theory Z: How American business can meet the Japanese challenge.* Reading, MA: Addison-Wesley.

Peters, T. J., & Waterman, R. H., Jr. (1982). *In search of excellence: Lessons from America's best-run companies.* New York: Harper & Row.

Powell, G. N. (1988). *Women & men in management.* Newbury Park, CA: Sage.

Reddin, W. J., & Reddin, M. K. (1979). *Educational Administrative Style Diagnosis Test (EASDT).* Fredericton, New Brunswick, Canada: Organizational Tests.

Renwick, P. A. (1977). The effects of sex differences on the perception and management of superior-subordinate conflict: An exploratory study. *Organizational Behavior and Human Performance, 19,* 403–415.

Rice, R. W. (1978). Construct validity of the Least Preferred Co-Worker score. *Psychological Bulletin, 85,* 1199–1237.

Rice, R. W., Instone, D., & Adams, J. (1984). Leader sex, leader success, and leadership process: Two field studies. *Journal of Applied Psychology, 69,* 12–31.

Riger, S., & Galligan, P. (1980). Women in management: An exploration of competing paradigms. *American Psychologist, 35,* 902–910.

Rosenthal, R., Hall, J. A., DiMatteo, M. R., Rogers, P. L., & Archer, D. (1979). *Sensitivity to nonverbal communication: The PONS test.* Baltimore, MD: Johns Hopkins University Press.

Rosenthal, R., & Rubin, D. B. (1986). Meta-analytic procedures for combining studies with multiple effect sizes. *Psychological Bulletin, 99,* 400–406.

Russell, J. E. A., Rush, M. C., & Herd, A. M. (1988). An exploration of women's expectations of effective male and female leadership. *Sex Roles, 18,* 279–287.

Sargent, A. G. (1981). *The androgynous manager.* New York: Amacom.

Sargent, J. F., & Miller, G. R. (1971). Some differences in certain communication behaviors of autocratic and democratic group leaders. *Journal of Communication, 21,* 233–252.

Shakeshaft, C. (1987). *Women in educational administration.* Newbury Park, CA: Sage.

Sirianni-Brantley, K. (1985). The effect of sex role orientation and training on leadership style (Doctoral dissertation, University of Florida, 1984). *Dissertation Abstracts International, 45,* 3106B.

Stake, J. E. (1981). Promoting leadership behaviors in low performance-self-esteem women in task-oriented mixed-sex dyads. *Journal of Personality, 49,* 401–414.

Stogdill, R. M. (1963). *Manual for the Leader Behavior Description Questionnaire–Form XII.* Columbus, OH: Bureau of Business Research, Ohio State University.

Stogdill, R. M., Goode, O. S., & Day, D. R. (1962). New leader behavior description subscales. *Journal of Psychology, 54,* 259–269.

Tanner, J. R. (1982). Effects of leadership, climate and demographic factors on school effectiveness: An action research project in leadership development (Doctoral dissertation, Case Western Reserve University, 1981). *Dissertation Abstracts International, 43,* 333A.

Taylor, S. E., Fiske, S. T., Etcoff, N., & Ruderman, A. (1978). The categorical and contextual bases of person memory and stereotyping. *Journal of Personality and Social Psychology, 36,* 778–793.

Terborg, J. R. (1977). Women in management: A research review. *Journal of Applied Psychology, 62,* 647–664.

Van Aken, E. W. (1954). An analysis of the methods of operation of principals to determine working patterns (Doctoral dissertation, University of Florida). *Dissertation Abstracts International, 14,* 1983.

Vroom, V. H., & Yetton, P. W. (1973). *Leadership and decision-making.* Pittsburgh, PA: University of Pittsburgh Press.

Wanous, J. P. (1977). Organizational entry: Newcomers moving from outside to inside. *Psychological Bulletin, 84,* 601–618.

Wood, W. (1987). Meta-analytic review of sex differences in group performance. *Psychological Bulletin, 102,* 53–71.

Yoder, J. D., & Sinnett, L. M. (1985). Is it all in the numbers? A case study of tokenism. *Psychology of Women Quarterly, 9,* 413–418.

Appendix

Studies Used in the Meta-Analysis

Adamitis. J. A. (1982). Self-perceived leadership styles of baccalaureate crime-study administrators in the United States (Doctoral dissertation, Miami University, 1981). *Dissertation Abstracts International, 42,* 3815A.

Adams. E. F. (1978). A multivariate study of subordinate perceptions of and attitudes toward minority and majority managers. *Journal of Applied Psychology, 63,* 277–288.

Adams, J., & Hicks, J. M. (1980). Leader sex, leader descriptions of own behavior, and subordinates description of leader behavior (Project Athena: West Point). *International Journal of Women's Studies, 3,* 321–326.

Andwood, D. (1984). A comparison of perceptions and expectations for a central administrative leadership role of library media director as an indicator of his/her role behavior (Doctoral dissertation, St. John's University, 1983). *Dissertation Abstracts International, 45,* 693A.

Arkoff, A., & Shears, L. M. (1961). Conceptions of "ideal" leadership in accepted and rejected principal training candidates. *Journal of Educational Research, 55,* 71–74.

Arnett, M. D., Higgins, R. B., & Priem, A. P. (1980). Sex and Least Preferred Co-Worker score effects in leadership behavior. *Sex Roles, 6,* 139–152.

Arons, E. L. (1980). Male and female administrative potential—is there a difference? *National Association of Secondary School Principals Bulletin, 64,* 5–8.

Baber, C. R. (1985). Organizational perspective and selected characteristics of public school principals (Doctoral dissertation, Purdue University, 1984). *Dissertation Abstracts International, 45,* 1927A.

Baird, J. E., Jr., & Bradley, P. H. (1979). Styles of management and communication: A comparative study of men and women. *Communication Monographs, 46,* 101–111.

Barbieri, E. A. (1984). Trait patterns for effective marketing performance (Doctoral dissertation, Claremont Graduate School, 1983). *Dissertation Abstracts International, 44,* 3790A.

Barone, F. J. (1982). A comparative study of Theory X–Theory Y attitudes among managers and OD agents. *Dissertation Abstracts International, 42,* 4260A. (University Microfilms No. 82-07, 156)

Bartol, K. M. (1973). *Male and female leaders in small work groups.* East Lansing, MI: MSU Business Studies.

Bartol, K. M., & Wortman, M. S., Jr. (1975). Male versus female leaders: Effects on perceived leader behavior and satisfaction in a hospital. *Personnel Psychology, 28,* 533–547.

Bartol, K. M., & Wortman, M. S., Jr. (1976). Sex effects in leader behavior self-descriptions and job satisfaction. *Journal of Psychology, 94,* 177–183.

Bass, W. D. (1985). A comparison of leader behavior of elementary principals in the municipal separate, county, and consolidated school districts in Mississippi (Doctoral dissertation, University of Southern Mississippi, 1984). *Dissertation Abstracts International, 46,* 1449A.

Baugher, S. L. (1983). Sex-typed characteristics and leadership dimensions of vocational education administrators in a midwest region of the United States (Doctoral dissertation, University of Missouri-Columbia, 1982). *Dissertation Abstracts International, 44,* 22A.

Begin, F. C. (1981). An analysis of the leadership style and motivational concerns of experienced government managers (Doctoral dissertation, University of Iowa). *Dissertation Abstracts International, 42,* 1862A.

Birdsall, P. (1980). A comparative analysis of male and female managerial communication style in two organizations. *Journal of Vocational Behavior, 16,* 183–196.

Boonon, S. (1980). Leadership styles as related to self-concept of public school principals (Doctoral dissertation, University of Alabama, 1979). *Dissertation Abstracts International, 40,* 4480–4481A.

Bredo, A. E. (1983). Principal-teacher influence relations in elementary schools. *Dissertation Abstracts International, 44,* 332A. (University Microfilms No. 83-14, 438)

Brenner, O. C., & Bromer, J. A. (1981). Sex stereotypes and leaders' behavior as measured by the agreement scale for leadership behavior. *Psychological Reports, 48,* 960–962.

Brown, E. D., Jr. (1986). A study of the leadership styles of principals in the exemplary secondary schools of the United States (Doctoral dissertation, University of Alabama, 1985). *Dissertation Abstracts International, 47,* 722A.

Buckenmaier, C. S. (1982). Relationships among leadership dimensions and field dependence/independence of elementary school administrators (Doctoral dissertation, Vanderbilt University, 1981). *Dissertation Abstracts International, 42,* 4983A.

Buckiewicz, D. R. (1975). An analysis of leader behavior in the physical education departments of the community colleges of California, Oregon and Washington (Doctoral dissertation, University of Oregon, 1974). *Dissertation Abstracts International, 35,* 5087A.

Butters, M. A., & Gade, E. M. (1982). Job satisfaction and leadership behavior of residence hall assistants. *Journal of College Student Personnel, 23,* 320–324.

Cain, R. A. (1980). Collective negotiation attitudes and principal leadership style (Doctoral dissertation, United States International University, 1979). *Dissertation Abstracts International, 41,* 862A.

Camden, C., & Witt, J. (1983). Manager communicative style and productivity: A study of female and male managers. *International Journal of Women's Studies, 6,* 258–269.

Carpeno, L. (1976). Expectations of male/female leadership styles in an educational setting. *Dissertation Abstracts International, 37,* 1482B. (University Microfilms No. 76-21, 223)

Chapman, J. B. (1974). A comparative analysis of male and female leadership styles in similar work environments (Doctoral dissertation, University of Nebraska). *Dissertation Abstracts International, 35,* 2456A.

Charters, W. W., Jr., & Jovick, T. D. (1981). The gender of principals and principal-teacher relations in elementary schools. In P. A. Schmuck, W. W. Charters, Jr., & R. O. Carlson (Eds.), *Educational policy and management: Sex differentials* (pp. 307–331). New York: Academic Press.

Christensen, C. E., Milner, K., & Christensen, J. E. (1978). An analysis of faculty perceptions of leadership qualities of male and female physical education departments. *Research Quarterly, 49,* 269–277.

Cimperman, R. M. (1986). A comparison of perceived primary leadership style, style range, and leadership style adaptability of female and male administrators in the Wisconsin vocational, technical, and adult education system. *Dissertation Abstracts International, 46,* 2141A. (University Microfilms No. 85-24, 461)

Cole, K. W. (1977). The perceptions of leader behavior of male and female administrators in the Archdiocese of Washington, D. C., secondary schools (Doctoral dissertation, Catholic University of America). *Dissertation Abstracts International, 38,* 1769A.

Cormell, M. S. (1979). *Leadership styles of effective school principals.* Unpublished doctoral dissertation, United States International University.

Dansby, M. R. (1979). Leader effectiveness as a function of leader's sex and leadership style (Doctoral dissertation, University of Florida). *Dissertation Abstracts International, 40,* 1951B.

Davenport, I. W. (1977). Analysis of the perceived leader behavior of male and female elementary school principals (Doctoral dissertation, University of Missouri–Columbia, 1976). *Dissertation Abstracts International, 37,* 5476A.

Davis, M., & Songer-Nocks, E. (1978, March). *Comparing leader-group relations in male and female groups.* Paper presented at the meeting of the Southeastern Psychological Association, Atlanta, GA.

Day, D. R., & Stogdill, R. M. (1972). Leader behavior of male and female supervisors: A comparative study. *Personnel Psychology, 25,* 353–360.

Denmark, F. L., & Diggory, J. C. (1966). Sex differences in attitudes toward leaders' display of authoritarian behavior. *Psychological Reports, 18,* 863–872.

De Rosa, C. A. (1981). A study of the relationship between selected variables and a teacher's perception of an elementary school principal's administrative behavior (Doctoral dissertation, University of Michigan). *Dissertation Abstracts International, 42,* 2389A.

Dollinger, L. D. (1980). Leadership styles of male and female elemen-tary principals in the states of Iowa and Missouri. *Masters Abstracts International, 18,* 274. (University Microfilms No. 13-14, 888)

Donnell, S. M., & Hall, J. (1980). Men and women as managers: A significant case of no significant difference. *Organizational Dynamics, 8,* 60–77.

Douglas, L. D., & Simonson, S. V. (1982). A comparison of life experiences and leader behaviors between male and female superintendents. *Dissertation Abstracts International, 43,* 602A. (University Microfilms No. 82-18, 109)

Dragon, A. C. (1977). Self-descriptions and subordinate descriptions of the leader behavior of library administrators (Doctoral dissertation, University of Minnesota, 1976). *Dissertation Abstracts International, 37,* 7380.

Duhon, M. D. (1986). Androgyny and LPC as factors in leadership style: A study of effectiveness and interactional processes. *Dissertation Abstracts International, 47,* 2209B. (University Microfilms No. 86-17, 891)

Dumas, A. P. (1981). An investigation of the relationship between leadership style and philosophical orientation of elementary and secondary school principals. *Dissertation Abstracts International, 42,* 1872A. (University Microfilms No. 81-23, 012)

East, E. (1981). A comparative study of male and female perceptions of leadership styles of selected elementary school principals in Florida. *Dissertation Abstracts International, 42,* 2391A. (University Microfilms No. 81-25, 820)

Eblen, A. (1984). Communication, gender, leadership, and commitment in the organization (Doctoral dissertation, University of Oregon, 1983). *Dissertation Abstracts International, 44,* 2291A.

Eskilson, A. (1975). Sex composition and leadership in small groups (Doctoral dissertation, University of Illinois, 1974). *Dissertation Abstracts International, 35,* 7027B.

Espy, A. M. (1976). The principal's leadership style and the job satisfaction of teachers in a selected urban school district (Doctoral dissertation, University of Florida, 1975). *Dissertation Abstracts International, 36,* 7770A.

Farber, B. E. (1969). Organizational climate of public elementary schools as related to dogmatism and selected biographical characteristics of principals and teachers, and selected school and school community characteristics (Doctoral dissertation, Wayne State University, 1968). *Dissertation Abstracts International, 29,* 3368A.

Feldman, J. R. (1986). Leadership emergence in adult students (Doctoral dissertation, Georgia State University, 1985). *Dissertation Abstracts International, 46,* 2580A.

Fitzpatrick, R., & Cole, M. E. (1977). *Some characteristics of female and male managers.* Pittsburgh, PA: Psychological Service of Pittsburgh.

Francke, C. A. (1975). Perceived performance differences between women and men supervisors and implications for training (Doctoral dissertation, Michigan State University). *Dissertation Abstracts International, 36,* 1349A.

Friedman, M. J. (1981). Differences in assessment center performance as a function of the race and sex of ratees and the race of assessors (Doctoral dissertation, University of Tennessee at Knoxville, 1980). *Dissertation Abstracts International, 41,* 3924B.

Gaudreau, P. A. (1975). Investigation of sex differences across job levels. *Dissertation Abstracts International, 36,* 1957B. (University Microfilms No. 75-22, 019)

Gilligan, T. P. (1982). An analysis of the leader style of elementary public school principals as perceived by their faculty (Doctoral dissertation, George Washington University). *Dissertation Abstracts International, 43,* 604A.

Gorman, H. T. (1980). The relationship between gender, sex-role description, attitudes toward women, and the perceived leadership behavior of male and female elementary school principals. *Disserta-*

tion Abstracts International, 41, 476A. (University Microfilms No. 80-17, 538)

Grimes, E. S. (1983). Leadership styles of female and male elementary principals (Doctoral dissertation, University of Northern Illinois, 1982). *Dissertation Abstracts International, 44,* 28A.

Grimsley, L. G. C. (1980). Sex effects in leader problem-solving: A bilateral model of leadership behavior. *Dissertation Abstracts International, 41,* 1090B. (University Microfilms No. 80-20, 531)

Grobman, H., & Hines, V. A. (1956). What makes a good principal? *National Association of Secondary School Principals Bulletin, 40,* 5–16.

Gupta, N., Jenkins, G. D., Jr., & Beehr, T. A. (1983). Employee gender, gender similarity, and supervisor-subordinate cross-evaluations. *Psychology of Women Quarterly, 8,* 174–184.

Hamilton, E. E. (1983). Androgyny and leadership: An empirical field study of effective influence in decision-making groups. *Dissertation Abstracts International, 43,* 2379B. (University Microfilms No. 82-23, 210)

Heischmidt, K. A. (1985). Developmental task resolution as a predictor of leadership style (Doctoral dissertation, University of Southern Illinois, 1984). *Dissertation Abstracts International, 46,* 1562A.

Helmich, D. L. (1974). Male and female presidents: Some implications of leadership style. *Human Resource Management, 12,* 25–26.

Hemphill, J. K., Griffiths, D. E., & Frederiksen, N. (1962). *Administrative performance and personality: A study of the principal in a simulated elementary school.* New York: Teachers College, Columbia University.

Jago, A. G., & Vroom, V. H. (1982). Sex differences in the incidence and evaluation of participative leader behavior. *Journal of Applied Psychology, 67,* 776–783.

Jocelyn, J. (1985). The sex variable of participative decision making (Doctoral dissertation, University of Oregon, 1984). *Dissertation Abstracts International, 46,* 82A.

Joerger, J. H. (1985). A field study of fear of success, internal-external locus of control and performance ratings among professional men and women (Doctoral dissertation, University of Northern Colorado, 1984). *Dissertation Abstracts International, 45,* 3371B.

Johnson, F. D. H. (1977a). *The relationship between rule administration and the leadership behavior of black male and female urban elementary school principals* (Report No. EA-010-524). Norfolk, VA: Annual National Conference on Urban Education. (ERIC Document Reproduction Service No. ED 153 338)

Johnson, F. D. H. (1977b). The relationship between rule administration, leadership behavior and the sex of elementary school principals (Doctoral dissertation, Pennsylvania State University). *Dissertation Abstracts International, 38,* 571A.

Johnson, K. A. (1983). The perceived real and ideal leader behavior of selected male and female department heads of physical education in colleges and universities (Doctoral dissertation, University of Georgia, 1982). *Dissertation Abstracts International, 43,* 2274A.

Kappelman, S. K. (1981). Teachers' perceptions of principals' bases of power in relation to principals' styles of leadership. *Dissertation Abstracts International, 42,* 2405A. (University Microfilms No. 81-25, 884)

Keener, B. J. (1977). An analysis of the perceptions of the leadership behavior of male and female University of Florida administrators (Doctoral dissertation, University of Florida, 1976). *Dissertation Abstracts International, 37,* 4023A.

King, P. J. (1978). An analysis of teachers' perceptions of the leadership styles and effectiveness of male and female elementary school principals (Doctoral dissertation, University of Southern California). *Dissertation Abstracts International, 39,* 2658A.

King, W. C. (1981). Relationship between stress and leadership style of school managers (Doctoral dissertation, University of La Verne, 1979). *Dissertation Abstracts International, 41,* 4237A.

Kobayashi, K. J. (1974). A comparison of organizational climate of schools administered by female and male elementary school principals (Doctoral dissertation, University of the Pacific). *Dissertation Abstracts International, 35,* 129A.

Konitsney, D. A. (1982). Self-efficacy of perceived performance of leader behaviors under varied group sex compositions: Towards an understanding of sex differences in leadership. *Dissertation Abstracts International, 42,* 4260A. (University Microfilms No. 82-07, 156)

Korabik, K. (1982). Sex-role orientation and leadership style. *International Journal of Women's Studies, 5,* 329–337.

Lampos, J. A. (1985). The role of counseling training in the leadership style of secondary school principals as perceived by themselves and their subordinates. *Dissertation Abstracts International, 45,* 3499A. (University Microfilms No. 85-03, 176)

Lanning, G. E., Jr. (1982). A study of relationships and differences between management styles and staff morale as perceived by personnel in the colleges of the Ventura County community district. *Dissertation Abstracts International, 43,* 996A. (University Microfilms No. 82-20, 739)

Latta, J. A., & Emener, W. G. (1983). State vocational rehabilitation agency leadership behavior styles. *Journal of Rehabilitation Administration, 7,* 141–148.

Lemon, D. K., Hovel, L., Lindquist, J., & Porter, A. (1982). *The elementary school principalship in North Dakota* (Report No. EA-015-599). Grand Forks, ND: Bureau of Educational Research and Services. (ERIC Document Reproduction Service No. ED 228 746)

Lewis, J. P. (1987). The relationship between supervisors' attributions for the causes of employee performance and supervisors' structuring and consideration behavior. *Dissertation Abstracts International, 47,* 4331B. (University Microfilms No. 87-01, 756)

Linimon, D., Barron, W. L., III, & Falbo, T. (1984). Gender differences in perceptions of leadership. *Sex Roles, 11,* 1075–1089.

Longstreth, C. A. (1973). An analysis of the perceptions of the leadership behavior of male and female secondary school principals in Florida (Doctoral dissertation, University of Miami). *Dissertation Abstracts International, 34,* 2224A.

Malone, P. F. (1984). Cognitive style and leader adaptability of managers (Doctoral dissertation, University of Oklahoma). *Dissertation Abstracts International, 45,* 1268A.

Marnani, E. B. (1982). Comparison of preferred leadership styles, potential leadership effectiveness, and managerial attitudes among black and white, female and male management students (Doctoral dissertation, United States International University, 1981). *Dissertation Abstracts International, 43,* 1271A.

McDonnell, J. F. (1974). An analysis of participative management as a choice of leadership style (Doctoral dissertation, Claremont Graduate School). *Dissertation Abstracts International, 35,* 1339A.

McGrath, W. M. (1982). Leadership style of selected Arizona community college administrators. *Dissertation Abstracts International, 43,* 1776A. (University Microfilms No. 82-24, 793)

McMahon-Dumas, C. E. (1981). An investigation of the leadership styles and effectiveness dimensions of principals, and their relationship with reading gain scores of students in the Washington, D. C., public schools. *Dissertation Abstracts International, 42,* 1881A. (University Microfilms No. 81-21, 448)

Meyer, E. J. (1983). An analysis of self-perceived leadership of Air Force communications-electronics junior grade officers employing the Leader Effectiveness and Adaptability Description (Doctoral dissertation, University of Southern Mississippi). *Dissertation Abstracts International, 44,* 1277A.

Millard, R. J., & Smith, K. H. (1985). Moderating effects of leader sex on the relation between leadership style and perceived behavior patterns. *Genetic, Social and General Psychology Monographs, 111,* 305–316.

Miller, N. S. (1979). Male and female leadership style and self-perceived behavior compared (Doctoral dissertation, State University of New York at Buffalo). *Dissertation Abstracts International, 40*, 1794A.

Milner, E. K., King, H. A., & Pizzini, E. L. (1979). Relationship between sex and leadership behavior of department heads in physical education. *Research in Higher Education, 10*, 113–121.

Mitchell, T. R. (1969). Leader complexity, leadership style and group performance (Doctoral dissertation, University of Illinois at Urbana). *Dissertation Abstracts International, 30*, 3375B.

Modiste, C. J. (1984). An investigation of management styles of selected black public school administrators as affected by sex, age, and geographical location. *Dissertation Abstracts International, 45*, 41A. (University Microfilms No. 84-07, 303)

Monie, W. D., Jr. (1981). The relationship between seventh and ninth grade teachers' leadership style preferences and administrator perceptions of their effectiveness. *Dissertation Abstracts International, 42*, 2413A. (University Microfilms No. 81-21, 098)

Morrison, A. M., White, R. P., & Van Velsor, E. (1987). *Breaking the glass ceiling: Can women reach the top of America's largest corporations?* Reading, MA: Addison-Wesley.

Morsink, H. M. (1970). Leader behavior of men and women principals. *National Association of Secondary School Principals Bulletin, 54*, 80–87.

Moye, J. W. (1980). The relationship between personal and experience variables of Dade County secondary school principals and subordinates' perceptions of leader behavior (Doctoral dissertation, Mississippi State University). *Dissertation Abstracts International, 41*, 1323A.

Mulkerne, S. M. (1980). A comparative study of perceived leadership behavior in male and female exceptional student education directors in the state of Florida. *Dissertation Abstracts International, 41*, 3988A. (University Microfilms No. 81-05, 598)

Nimry, F. F. (1986). The association of leadership style with job satisfaction in consulting businesses (Doctoral dissertation, American University). *Dissertation Abstracts International, 47*, 978A.

Oddou, G. R. (1984). The emergence of leaders in natural work groups: A test of self-monitoring theory (Doctoral dissertation, Brigham Young University, 1983). *Dissertation Abstracts International, 44*, 2284B.

Orr, W. L. (1980). An investigation of leadership styles of middle school principals in Delaware, New Jersey and Pennsylvania (Doctoral dissertation, Temple University). *Dissertation Abstracts International, 41*, 1878A.

Osborn, R. N., & Vicars, W. M. (1976). Sex stereotypes: An artifact in leader behavior and subordinate satisfaction analysis? *Academy of Management Journal, 19*, 439–449.

Parke, J. E. P. (1986). Comparisons of decision-making styles of Florida community and junior college department chairpersons and division directors (Doctoral dissertation, University of North Carolina at Greensboro, 1985). *Dissertation Abstracts International, 46*, 1802A.

Parks, D. J. (1970). A study of relationships between interpersonal relations orientations and leader behaviors of elementary principals. *Dissertation Abstracts International, 31*, 2657A. (University Microfilms No. 70-24, 104)

Pate, T. M., Jr. (1979). The relationship of the elementary principal's leadership style to his self-concept of his ability to communicate and his knowledge of his job (Doctoral dissertation, George Peabody College for Teachers, 1978). *Dissertation Abstracts International, 39*, 6445A.

Perea, R. D. (1981). *The relationship of initiating structure, consideration and locus of control on leader behavior of women and men in educational leadership roles.* Unpublished doctoral dissertation, University of New Mexico.

Peregrine, P. E. (1983). The robustness of managerial life in schools: A test of contingency theory. *Dissertation Abstracts International, 43*, 2849A. (University Microfilms No. 83-00, 320)

Perritt, L. J. C. (1983). Job satisfaction as a function of worker and supervisor characteristics (Doctoral dissertation, University of Kentucky). *Dissertation Abstracts International, 44*, 2002B.

Petty, M. L. (1986). A profile of college student leaders relating personality types, learning styles, and leadership approaches (Doctoral dissertation, Florida State University, 1985). *Dissertation Abstracts International, 46*, 3621A.

Petty, M. M., & Bruning, N. S. (1980). A comparison of the relationships between subordinates' perceptions of supervisory behavior and measures of subordinates' job satisfaction for male and female leaders. *Academy of Management Journal, 23*, 717–725.

Petty, M. M., & Lee, G. K., Jr. (1975). Moderating effects of sex of supervisor and subordinate on relationships between supervisory behavior and subordinate satisfaction. *Journal of Applied Psychology, 60*, 624–628.

Powell, G. N., Butterfield, D. A., & Mainiero, L. A. (1981). Sex-role identity and sex as predictors of leadership style. *Psychological Reports, 49*, 829–830.

Pruitt, P. J. (1977). Perceived leader behavior of male and female intercollegiate athletic directors in the United States (Doctoral dissertation, University of Kentucky, 1976). *Dissertation Abstracts International, 37*, 6199A.

Quinn, K. I. (1977). Self-perceptions of leadership behaviors and decision-making orientations of men and women elementary school principals in Chicago public schools (Doctoral dissertation, University of Illinois at Urbana-Champaign, 1976). *Dissertation Abstracts International, 37*, 6199A.

Rice, R. W., Bender, L. R., & Vitters, A. G. (1980). Leader sex, follower attitudes toward women, and leadership effectiveness: A laboratory experiment. *Organizational Behavior and Human Performance, 25*, 46–78.

Richardson, D. K. (1981). A study of the leadership styles of the chief student affairs administrators in Southern Baptist colleges and universities. *Dissertation Abstracts International, 41*, 2963A. (University Microfilms No. 80-29, 015)

Robertson, D. R. (1981). A study of leadership style: A comparison of secular and biblical settings (Masters thesis, Oral Roberts University, 1980). *Masters Abstracts International, 19*, 274.

Robson, G. N. (1985). A comparison of leadership styles of male and female elementary school administrators in Prince George's County, Maryland. *Dissertation Abstracts International, 46*, 1152A. (University Microfilms No. 85-15, 767)

Rogers, D. R. H. (1980). A comparison of teachers' perceptions of female versus male principals' leader behavior and organizational climate in elementary schools (Doctoral dissertation, East Tennessee State University). *Dissertation Abstracts International, 41*, 1881A.

Rogers, M. (1977). A descriptive study of leadership effectiveness of male and female elementary school principals based upon self perception and the perception of their teachers (Doctoral dissertation, United States International University). *Dissertation Abstracts International, 41*, 1880A.

Rosenfeld, L. B., & Fowler, G. D. (1976). Personality, sex, and leadership style. *Communication Monographs, 43*, 320–324.

Roussell, C. (1974). Relationship of sex of department head to department climate. *Administrative Science Quarterly, 19*, 211–220.

Ruch, L. O., & Newton, R. R. (1977). Sex characteristics, task clarity, and authority. *Sex Roles, 3*, 479–494.

Sabermahani, M. A. (1984). The relationship between leadership styles and graduate academic majors. *Dissertation Abstracts International, 45*, 1262A. (University Microfilms No. 84-18, 591)

Samuelson, J. L. (1984). The relationship between gender and the interpersonal communication skills of midlevel managers in California community colleges (Doctoral dissertation, University of San Francisco, 1983). *Dissertation Abstracts International, 45,* 1008A.

Scafidel, R. J. (1983). An analysis of the relationship between teachers' perceived leadership style of the principal and the implementation of continuous progress. *Dissertation Abstracts International, 43,* 2850A. (University Microfilms No. 82-23, 268)

Schneier, C. E. (1978). The contingency model of leadership: An extension to emergent leadership and leader's sex. *Organizational Behavior and Human Performance, 21,* 220–239.

Schneier, C. E., & Bartol, K. M. (1980). Sex effects in emergent leadership. *Journal of Applied Psychology, 65,* 341–345.

Shareatpanahi, M. (1982). The relationship between gender and perceived leader behavior of male and female elementary school principals (Doctoral dissertation, University of San Francisco). *Dissertation Abstracts International, 43,* 618A.

Sheffield, A. C. (1983). A study of the relationship between the leadership dimensions of initiating structure and consideration of school principals and their attitudes toward conflict management (Doctoral dissertation, Vanderbilt University). *Dissertation Abstracts International, 44,* 1656A.

Sims, A. L. (1982). Effects of sex differences on leadership styles and probable effectiveness of elementary principals: As perceived by themselves and their teachers using the Hersey-Blanchard instrument in four medium-sized California school districts (Doctoral dissertation, Brigham Young University, 1981). *Dissertation Abstracts International, 42,* 3378A.

Sirotti, S. B. (1986). The effect of task responsibilities on assistant principals' roles (Doctoral dissertation, Western Michigan University, 1985). *Dissertation Abstracts International, 47,* 746A.

Smith, A. C., Jr. (1982). Correlates of first-line supervisory effectiveness (Doctoral dissertation, Virginia Polytechnic Institute and State University, 1981). *Dissertation Abstracts International, 42,* 4429A.

Smith, B. B. (1976). The relationship between leadership behavior and need-press measures of male and female supervisors in masculine and feminine sex-typed work settings. *Dissertation Abstracts International, 36,* 4710B. (University Microfilms No. 75-29, 753)

Smith, M. D. (1983). Differences in leadership behaviors of male and female elementary school principals in West Virginia as perceived by the superintendent, the male elementary principal, and the female elementary principal (Doctoral dissertation, West Virginia University, 1982). *Dissertation Abstracts International, 43,* 3481A.

Snell, S. J. A. (1981). A tripartite comparative analysis by sex of the perceptions of public school superintendents and their school board presidents relating to selected dimensions of administrative behavior (Doctoral dissertation, Ohio University, 1980). *Dissertation Abstracts International, 42,* 2427A.

Snodgrass, S. E., & Rosenthal, R. (1984). Females in charge: Effects of sex of subordinate and romantic attachment status upon self-ratings of dominance. *Journal of Personality, 52,* 355–371.

Spence, B. A. (1971). Sex of teachers as a factor in their perception of selected leadership characteristics of male and female elementary school principals (Doctoral dissertation, Purdue University). *Dissertation Abstracts International, 32,* 2985A.

Spillman, B., Spillman, R., & Reinking, K. (1980). *A dynamic analysis of the effects of sex and androgyny on leadership emergence* (Report No. CS-502855). Davis, CA: University of California. (ERIC Document Reproduction Service No. ED 184 175)

Steers, R. M. (1977). Individual differences in participative decision-making. *Human Relations, 30,* 837–847.

Stemler, J. G. (1981). Fiedler's LPC scale: Behavioral and attitudinal correlates (Doctoral dissertation, University of Cincinnati, 1980). *Dissertation Abstracts International, 41,* 3938B.

Sunderland, J. D. (1982). A comparison of the leadership attitudes of male and female athletic directors (Doctoral dissertation, University of Oregon, 1981). *Dissertation Abstracts International, 42,* 3502A.

Tanner, J. R. (1982). Effects of leadership, climate and demographic factors on school effectiveness: An action research project in leadership development (Doctoral dissertation, Case Western Reserve University, 1981). *Dissertation Abstracts International, 43,* 333A.

Thomas, V. G., & Littig, L. W. (1985). A typology of leadership style: Examining gender and race effects. *Bulletin of the Psychonomic Society, 23,* 132–134.

Van Aken, E. W. (1954). An analysis of the methods of operation of principals to determine working patterns (Doctoral dissertation, University of Florida). *Dissertation Abstracts International, 14,* 1983.

Van Meir, E. J., Jr. (1973). Leadership behavior of male and female elementary principals: A comparison by sex. *Marquette University Education Review, 4,* 8–11.

Vaughans, K. C. (1985). The efficacy of student leadership training (Doctoral dissertation, Adelphi University). *Dissertation Abstracts International, 46,* 2107B.

Wall, J. K. (1982). The relationship of gender and perceived sex role identity to the leadership style, range, and adaptability of selected graduate students. *Dissertation Abstracts International, 43,* 2046B. (University Microfilms No. 82-26, 272)

Ward, J. M., Jr. (1977). Normative determinants of leadership. *Dissertation Abstracts International, 37,* 47108B. (University Microfilms No. 77-5, 206)

Webb, J. G. (1981). The communication behavior of leaders in small group discussion (Doctoral dissertation, University of Michigan). *Dissertation Abstracts International, 42,* 456A.

Wexley, K. N., & Hunt, P. J. (1974). Male and female leaders: Comparison of performance and behavior patterns. *Psychological Reports, 35,* 867–872.

Williams, L. C. (1982). Relationship of sex of coach, level of school, and type of sport on measures of actual and ideal leadership behavior (Doctoral dissertation, University of Southern California). *Dissertation Abstracts International, 43,* 109A.

Winther, D. A., & Green, S. B. (1987). Another look at gender-related differences in leadership behavior. *Sex Roles, 16,* 41–56.

Wood, J. T. (1981). Sex differences in group communication: Directions for research in speech communications and sociometry. *Journal of Group Psychotherapy, Psychodrama and Sociometry, 34,* 24–31.

Yoder, J. D., Adams, J., & Hicks, J. M. (1986). *When sex-roles and work roles conflict: A critical look at standards of evaluation.* Unpublished manuscript, Webster University.

Young, E. M. W. (1981). A study of the self-perception and subordinate perception of the leadership behavior of black library directors (Doctoral dissertation, Vanderbilt University, 1980). *Dissertation Abstracts International, 42,* 499A.

Young, J. C. (1981). *Comparisons of leader style, behaviors and effectiveness of male and female coaches* (Report No. SP-022744). College Park, MD: University of Maryland. (ERIC Document Reproduction No. ED 231 830)

Received November 14, 1988
Revision received October 25, 1989
Accepted November 16, 1989 ∎

Name Index